EARLE SCRIVEN

SAINTS

A COMPLETE RECORD OF
SOUTHAMPTON FOOTBALL CLUB
1885-1987

SAINTS

A COMPLETE RECORD OF SOUTHAMPTON FOOTBALL CLUB 1885-1987

GARY CHALK
and
DUNCAN HOLLEY

Breedon Books Sport

First published in Great Britain by
The Breedon Books Publishing Company Limited
45 Friar Gate, Derby DE1 1DA
1987

ISBN 0 907969 22 4

Printed by Butler and Tanner Limited, Frome
Jacket designed by Graham Hales

Contents

Acknowledgements

P.Ashton, S.Ballantyne (both *Southern Evening Echo*), J.Rollin, A.Harris, K.Warsop, T.Marshall, A.Chalk, R.Harris, M.Davage, R.Spiller (Association of Football Statisticians), Southampton City Library, A.Murray, M.Cooper, B.Tubbs, J.Tubbs, L.Westwick, D.R.M.Holley, H.Miles, F.Grayer, A.Holt, T.Paine, I.Belbin, M.Channon, R.Payne.

Photographic Credits

Photographs have been supplied by the *Southern Evening Echo*, All-Sport, BBC Hulton Picture Library and Colorsport.

Foreword
by Mick Channon

HAVING been associated with Southampton Football Club, a great and caring club, for 16 years, I feel privileged to be asked to write a foreword to this book. During my time at The Dell, I not only served under two magnificent managers, but played with some equally magnificent players whose careers this history bring back to life. To me, the Saints have traditionally been synonymous with attacking and enjoyable football and I look forward to their continued success as well as wishing this publication the very best.

Thanks for the memories.

Introduction

THE year 1966 will be remembered by Southampton football fans, not only for England winning the World Cup, but for the Saints eventually reaching the First Division after many years of trying. Apart from a brief spell in Division Two — and even then they won the FA Cup — Saints have since been one of the major teams in the country, qualifying for Europe on no less than seven occasions and finishing First Division runners-up to Liverpool in 1983-4.

Whilst recent club history has justifiably been well-documented, it was regrettable that the early days of the Saints had never been thoroughly explored. How many fans knew, for instance, that Saints were the first Southern League side to reach an F.A.Cup Final, in 1900; or for that matter, how in the previous decade the club had dominated football in the south of England — London included. The 1920s, too, was an exciting period in Southampton FC's history, with two FA Cup semi-final appearances and the emergence of some excellent local players such as Tom Parker, Mike Keeping and Bill Rawlings, all to play for their country.

Hopefully this book will finally and comprehensively put into perspective the whole 102-year history of Southampton Football Club as well as reviving many memories and settling many disputes.

Whilst every possible effort has been made to establish the facts, the authors appreciate that no history can be one hundred per cent accurate and will gladly accept any new information offered from knowledgeable sources.

Gary Chalk
Duncan Holley

May 1987

The Saints Story
Season-by-Season

HISTORY records that Southampton Football Club was founded in November 1885. However, its conception goes back perhaps another seven years to 1878, when soccer was virtually unknown to a Southampton public whose main leisure pursuits in those Victorian days were rowing, yachting, Rugby Union and boxing.

The men who introduced the 'new' game to the area were amongst the large number of northerners who had come down to work for the shipbuilding firm of Oswald & Mordaunt (now Vosper Thorneycrofts). They formed a team called Southampton Rangers and played regularly on the Common. The team make-up was constantly changing, due to the transient nature of shipyard work, but one man, a schoolteacher named Mr A.Wood, eventually became the permanent secretary of the Rangers club.

In 1880, Mr Wood, along with fellow teachers, G.McIvor, A.Fry and F.Montgomery, formed the Deanery Football Club. And as these four men were present five years later when the Southampton St Mary's FC was formed, it can be argued, perhaps, that the Deanery club was the forerunner of today's Saints. Certainly there was a direct thread running back as far as that original Rangers team.

In the late 1930s, Mr Montgomery wrote an article stating that when the St Mary's club was formed in November 1885, so many members of the Deanery club were present that an amalgamation took place. Montgomery's claim further substantiates the view that the origins of the modern Southampton FC go beyond the date accepted as the club's official foundation.

The Rev Sole was the club's first president and it was he who chaired the meeeting in Grove Street which led to St Mary's foundation. The Rev Sole soon moved to Winchester and his place was taken by Dr Bencraft. Mr C.Abbott was the first secretary and Mr A.A.Fry became the first captain.

1885-86

ON 21 November 1885, Southampton St Mary's first kicked a ball in earnest. Their opponents were a team called Freemantle, who were known locally as the 'Magpies'. Southampton St Mary's were kitted out in white 'tunics' with a diagonal red sash, and the venue was a pitch upon which now stands the Hampshire Bowling Club in Northlands Road.

Saints fielded the following team for their first-ever match, a 5-1 victory over Freemantle: Ruffell; Muir, McDonald, A.G.Fry, Deacon, A.Gandy, A.A.Fry, C.Bromley, G.Gandy, McIvor, Varley. Scorers for Saints were Charles Bromley (3) and Arthur Fry (2), Bromley thus scoring the first-ever hat-trick for the club.

Freemantle, who were St Mary's main rivals in the early battle to become Southampton's top club, were beaten 5-1 and the *Hampshire Independent* commented that Saints had 'the material to form a fairly strong club'. It is interesting to look at some of the men who represented St Mary's that day: Ralph Ruffell, the goalkeeper, was an engineer working at Southampton docks; A.A.Fry, the captain, was a teacher who later became headmaster of Foundry Lane School; George Muir was also a teacher and a

George Muir played in Saints' first-ever match and devoted his life to soccer. After retiring as a player he became a referee when the Southern League was formed. Muir refereed an Amateur Cup Final and served the Hampshire FA for many years, twice being elected its president. In 1915 he renewed his association with Saints when he was elected to the board. He saw the club well established in the Football League before resigning in 1936. Muir was also captain and secretary of the Deanery Cricket Club and secretary of Hampshire CCC.

future headmaster of Mount Pleasant School and director of Southampton FC; the third teacher in the team was G.McIvor, and he, too, became a headmaster, at Eastern District School.

For the duration of this, their first season, St Mary's confined themselves to building up experience through playing friendly matches. They arranged five such games, winning four and drawing one and thus ending their inaugural season undefeated.

1886-87

THERE were few changes in the Saints' squad for their

second season. Arthur Fry was succeeded as team captain by Charles Bromley and new players included Mullens and Sommerville. Of the 13 friendly games played, nine were won and two drawn, showing that the club was progressing satisfactorily.

Saints' biggest victory came on 16 February when goals from Hickman (2), Deacon, Sommerville and C.Bromley saw them defeat Handel College 5-1 on the Common. The result completed a 'double' for St Mary's, for they had put four goals past the College without reply at the begining of December.

Southampton Harriers, however, proved much more difficult opposition and they defeated Saints 2-0 on the Common, and drew the other two meetings between the clubs that season.

1887-88

IN 1887 the Hampshire Football Association was founded and with it, the Hampshire Senior and Junior Cup competitions. Thus, St Mary's had the opportunity to broaden their sphere from friendly matches and on 26 November 1887, the Saints played Totton in their first-ever cup tie, on a field at the rear of the Anchor Hotel at Redbridge.

Hampshire Junior Cup

Round 1
Nov 26 v Totton (a) 1-0
C.Bromley
Ruffell; Carter, Muir, Deacon, Varley, A.G.Fry, A.A.Fry, Crossley, Warn, Gandy, C.Bromley.
Round 2
Dec 17 v Petersfield (at Antelope Ground) 10-0
Deacon, A.A.Fry 5, Bromley 4
Ruffell; Carter. Muir, Deacon, Varley, A.G.Fry, Gandy, Sommerville, A.A.Fry, Warn, C.Bromley.
Round 3
Jan 21 v Lymington (at Redbridge) 4-0
F.Bromley, Gandy, McDonald 2
Ruffell; Carter, Muir, Deacon, F.Bromley, Gandy, A.A.Fry, Crossley, McDonald, Warn, C.Bromley.
Semi-final
Feb 18 v Bournemouth Arabs (at County Ground) 2-1
McDonald, C.Bromley
Ruffell; Carter, Muir, Deacon, Varley, Gandy, Sommerville, A.A.Fry, Warn, McDonald, C.Bromley.
Final
Mar 10 v Southampton Harriers (at County Ground) 2-2
C.Bromley, Warn
Ruffell; Carter, Muir, Gandy, Varley, Crossley, A.A.Fry, Sommerville, C.Bromley, McDonald, Warn.
Replay
Mar 24 v Southampton Harriers (at County Ground) 2-1
McDonald, Warn
Ruffell; Carter, Muir, Deacon, Varley, Gandy, A.A.Fry, McDonald, Sommerville, Warn, C.Bromley.

The old players' dressing-room at the Antelope, Saints' first regular home.

A crowd of between 3,000 and 4,000 people saw the Saints emerge victorious by 1-0. Petersfield were their second-round opponents at the Antelope, and the Saints underlined their growing supremacy with a 10-0 win. In the third round, Lymington were beaten 4-0 in a match played at Redbridge, on a field loaned to the Saints by a Mr Steadfast. Some Saints supporters misbehaved to the extent that Mr Steadfast demanded all 'gate' money be donated to the South Hampshire Hospital, and the club quickly sent officials to apologise. Mr Steadfast is reported to have reluctantly accepted them.

Victory over Bournemouth Arabs gave the Saints a cup final place and they met Southampton Harriers at the County Ground. The score after 90 minutes was 2-2 but Harriers skipper, George Noble, refused to play extra-time as two of his players were injured. A replay was arranged at the County Ground and this time Saints won 2-1. Thus, Southampton St Mary's had won their first trophy but the Harriers were so devastated that they immediately disbanded and several of their players joined Freemantle.

The first known photograph of Southampton St Mary's. This picture shows the side with the club's first trophy, the Hampshire Junior Cup which they won in 1888. Back row (left to right): F.J.Montgomery, G.Carter, M.Warn, J.L.Sommerville, A.A.Fry, G.C.Gandy. Middle: A.Varley, C.E.Bromley (captain), G.Muir, A.Gandy. Front: C.Deacon, F.J.Crossley, R.Ruffell. Charlie Deacon was a powerful half.back who was employed as a clerk in Southampton Telegraph Office until his untimely death, from a brain tumour, in 1893.

1888-89

Charles Bromley, the Saints' captain, moved to London to study dentistry and therefore relinquished the captaincy, although he remained 'attached' to St Mary's for cup matches, making special journeys to Southampton for such important games. The captaincy fell upon the shoulders of George Carter, whose job with the Ordnance Office had brought him to Southampton from Hereford in 1887.

Carter, a fine full-back who also excelled at cricket and water polo, was to remain captain for eight years and he was actively connected with the club, as reserve-team manager, until he retired at the outbreak of World War One.

Three new players joined the club this season. 'Banquo' Stride, who had previously played for the now defunct Harriers, George Varley and F.A.Delamotte. A later recruit was J.T.Arter — which meant that Saints now had Carter and Arter at full-back. George Muir, club secretary the previous year, moved to a teacher-training job at Winchester and his duties were taken over by Delamotte.

Southampton St Mary's 1888-89. Standing (left to right): M.Warn, R.Ruffell, G.C.Gandy, W.Pickford, F.J.Montgomery, C.S.Deacon, F.A.Delamotte. Middle: W.F.Stride, E.C.Bromley, G.Carter (captain), A.A.Fry. Front: G.H.Muir, G.W.Verney, A.G.Farwell. William Stride played for Freemantle and Harriers before the latter club disbanded. Nicknamed 'Banquo', Stride represented Hampshire and was also a fine runner, winning several prizes at AAA meetings.

St Mary's continued to play friendlies but, naturally, it was the Hampshire Junior Cup which aroused most interest. Saints, the holders, trounced Havant in the first round at the County Ground with Frank Bromley scoring four goals. A bye saw Saints through to a third-round tie against Fordingbridge Turks, but here St Mary's foresaw problems, for the game coincided with a Hampshire county game against Berks & Bucks — and Ruffell, Carter, Stride and Bromley had been selected for Hampshire.

Saints officials tried to have the game moved to another date but their New Forest opponents refused. The St Mary's club then withdrew their four stars from the Hampshire team but now a new problem beset them. Because of doubts over when the game would be played, Saints had no ground organised and it was not until the morning of the match that the Woolston Works team came to their rescue and offered them the Antelope ground. Saints responded by beating Fordingbridge 3-2 in a close-fought encounter.

The semi-final meeting with Isle of Wight club, Cowes, was the talk of the local football fraternity for weeks before the game — and what a tie it turned out to be, with four meetings before the issue was settled.

The first match took place at Northwood Park, Cowes, where the islanders scored after 20 minutes. There were only three minutes to play when Arthur Farwell equalised for Saints. Cowes wanted to play 30 minutes' extra-time, but the wily Carter declined, saying that his team had to catch the boat home. When the sides drew 1-1 at the County Ground two weeks later, the Cowes skipper offered the same reason for not wanting extra-time. Carter was hardly in a position to object but the Hants FA ordered the second replay to be staged at the County Ground again, the following Wednesday.

By this time, interest in the game was at fever pitch and a large crowd saw Charles Bromley's goal just before half-time equalise an early Cowes effort. In the second half, when Cowes' goalkeeper, Lieverman, fisted out a shot from Warn,

Saints players protested that the ball had crossed the line and after some deliberation, the goal was given.

It proved to be Saints' winner but more drama was to unfold when Cowes lodged a protest with the Football Association. The FA initially rejected the appeal but when Cowes produced a new 'witness', the Hants FA performed a *volte face* and ordered the match to be replayed. A coin was tossed to decide the venue and the County Ground was again chosen.

Interest was now so great that cheap railway tickets were issued for spectators travelling from the New Forest, and boats from the island were packed. Interestingly, this was the last time that ladies were admitted free for a match of such importance and there were about 1,000 of them in the estimated 3,000 crowd. This time St Mary's left nothing to chance and won handsomely, 4-1.

For the Final, against Christchurch, St Mary's recalled George Muir from Winchester College to replace the injured Arter at full-back. The game, played at Bar End, Winchester, was something of an anti-climax after the excitement and controversy of the semi-final. Christchurch were also hampered by injuries and goals from Delamotte, Charles Bromley and Warn gave St Mary's an easy 3-0 victory.

> It was during the 1888-89 season that the nickname 'Saints' was coined, thanks to an enterprising soul at the Ordnance Office. He designed a white shield with a red stripe across it. Printed on the shield were the words, 'Play Up Saints'. Hundreds of the shields were distributed throughout the town and worn in the hat-bands of club supporters.

Hampshire Junior Cup

Round 1
Nov 24 v Havant (h) 5-0
Delamotte, F.Bromley 4
Ruffell; Carter, A.A.Fry, Deacon, Stride, Crossley, Mate, Delamotte, Warn, Farwell, F.Bromley.
Round 2
Southampton St Mary's awarded a bye
Round 3
Jan 12 v Fordingbridge Turks (h) 4-2
Arter, Deacon, C.Bromley, Warn
Ruffell; Arter, Carter, Deacon, Stride, Verney, A.A.Fry, Delamotte, C.Bromley, Warn, Farwell.
Semi-final
Feb 24 v Cowes (a) 1-1
Farwell
Ruffell; Carter, Arter, Deacon, Stride, Verney, Warn, Farwell, C.Bromley, Delamotte, A.A.Fry.
Replay
Mar 9 v Cowes (h) 1-1
A.A.Fry
Ruffell; Arter, Carter, Deacon, Stride, Verney, Delamotte, A.A.Fry, C.Bromley, Farwell, Warn.
Second replay
Mar 13 v Cowes (h) 2-1*
C.Bromley, Warn
Ruffell; Carter, Arter, Deacon, Stride, Verney, Delamotte, A.A.Fry, C.Bromley, Farwell, Warn.
**Cowes protested and the game was ordered to be replayed.*
Third replay
Mar 16 v Cowes (h) 4-1
Verney, Delamotte 2, A.A.Fry
Ruffell; Carter, Arter, Deacon, Williams, Verney, Delamotte, A.A.Fry, C.Bromley, Farwell, Warn.
Final
Apr 6 v Christchurch (at Bar End, Winchester) 3-0
Delamotte, C.Bromley, Warn
Ruffell; Muir, Carter, Stride, Deacon, Verney, A.A.Fry, Delamotte, Bromley, Farwell, Warn.

1889-90

THIS was a period of strong local rivalry in Southampton,

11

with St Mary's justly claiming to be the premier club in the area. Freemantle stubbornly contested this claim although they could not match Saints outstanding record in the Hampshire Junior Cup.

For the 1889-90 season, the team 'uniform' was improved and whereas before, each player had simply sewn a red sash across his white shirt, now specially manufactured shirts of cherry and white squares were worn. Changes in the playing staff included Duff, a member of the Military Staff Corps, who replaced Arter at full-back. Arthur (A.A) Fry retired to be replaced by Bob Kiddle, and F.C.Bromley, scorer of four goals against Havant in the previous season's Junior Cup, became a permanent replacement for his brother, C.E., who had received a serious injury in a six-a-side tournament a few weeks after the 1889 Final.

The season was quite spectacular as the Saints, or the 'Cherry Squares' as they were sometimes known, went through the campaign undefeated. They were drawn against their arch rivals, Cowes, in the third round of the Junior Cup. In a gale-force wind at the Antelope, St Mary's this time managed to dispose of the island team at the first attempt.

Southampton St Mary's 1889-90. Back row (left to right): C.Gidden, H.B.Johns, F.J.Montgomery, W.Warn, C.Deacon, R.Ruffell, W.Duff, A.C.Gandy, A.Farwell. Front: W.Stride, G.Carter, G.W.Verney, F.A.Delamotte, R.S.Kiddle. Delamotte was particularly noted for charging opponents' goalkeepers and the crowd would often call: 'Go for him, Delly'. He left the club for good in 1893 and was later Borough Engineer and Surveyor at Conway, North Wales.

The semi-final, against Winchester Rovers, was played in a snowstorm and Saints were considered fortunate to sneak home 1-0. The Final was against Lymington, who had beaten Freemantle in the semi-final, and the biggest attendance ever to watch a soccer match in Hampshire assembled at the County Ground. They paid receipts of just over £51 — a sum which Mr Pickford, the Hampshire FA secretary, considered 'a fortune'. St Mary's duly won 2-0 to win the Junior Cup for the third consecutive time and so retain that particular trophy permanently.

> Ten St Mary's players were selected for the Hampshire team which met Dorset in 1889-90. This caused an uproar in places like Lymington and Cowes and those clubs voiced their protests in local newspapers. St Mary's officials, sensitive to the criticism, withdrew all ten from the team. Thereafter, a different selection method was employed, although Saints always provided more players than any other Hampshire club.

Hampshire Junior Cup

> **Round 1**
> **Southampton St Mary's received a bye**
> **Round 2**
> **Dec 7 v Bournemouth (a) 2-0**
> *Warn, Farwell*
> Ruffell; Carter, A.A.Fry, Stride, Brown, Verney, Warn, Farwell, Kiddle, Bromley, Delamotte.
> **Round 3**
> **Jan 25 v Cowes (h) 2-1**
> *Bromley, Farwell*
> Ruffell; Carter, Denning, Measures, Verney, Deacon, Bromley, Kiddle, Delamotte, Warn, Farwell.
> **Semi-final**
> **Mar 1 v Winchester Rovers (at County Ground) 1-0**
> *Kiddle*
> Ruffell; Carter, Duff, Stride, Deacon, Verney, Warn, Farwell, Kiddle, Bromley, Delamotte.
> **Final**
> **Mar 29 v Lymington (at County Ground) 2-0**
> *Farwell, opp.og*
> Ruffell; Carter, Duff, Verney, Deacon, Stride, Kiddle, Bromley, Delamotte, Warn, Farwell.

1890-91

THIS season saw the Saints continue to supplement their cup fixtures by playing friendly games, although the quality of the opposition improved and St Mary's had to suffer several defeats at the hands of such sides as Reading and Swindon. There were only two new faces amongst the regular playing staff, those of George Marshall and Ernie Nicholls. F.A.Delamotte retired as secretary and his place was taken by John Hendin. Harry Johns was treasurer and Dr Bencraft was president.

Having made the Hampshire Junior Cup their own, Saints now turned their attentions to the Senior Cup. After receiving a bye in the first round they met Geneva Cross (Netley) and won 5-0. Bannister Court were beaten 3-1 in their semi-final. The score was apparently kept down by the Court goalkeeper, W.P.Cole, who, according to one newspaper report, 'threw the ball out like an expert labourer, with pints of beer in him, excavating a trench'.

Saints opponents in the Final were the Aldershot-based Royal Engineers who had won the Senior Cup for the previous two years and who were firm favourites to make the trophy theirs. Excitement was high and, for the first time, a match-programme was produced, in the form of a card. A crowd numbering between three thousand and four thousand paid £63 to see Saints win 3-1.

It was a superb victory. Nicholls gave the Saints a 20th-minute lead and although the Engineers equalised before half-time, Bromley and Kiddle scored the goals which ensured Saints victory. The RE's had intended to celebrate their victory in Aldershot; instead they remained in Southampton as guests of the St Mary's club. The Engineers' left-back, 'Taffy' Hamer, later became a Saints player.

By now, membership of the St Mary's club stood at a record 400 and the bank balance was a healthy £100. Southampton St Mary's officials decided that new challenges were needed and an application was made to compete in the FA Cup in 1891-92.

> At the season's end, Saints offered the Junior Cup as the prize in a competition to decide the best team in Hampshire. In a repeat of the Senior Cup Final, they met the Royal Engineers and beat them to hold on to the trophy.

Hampshire Senior Cup

Round 1
Southampton St Mary's received a bye
Round 2
Jan 24 v Geneva Court (h) 5-0
F.Bromley, Farwell, Kiddle, Nicholls, Verney
Ruffell; Carter, G.Marshall, Stride, Verney, Deacon, Delamotte, Farwell, Kiddle, F.Bromley, Nicholls.
Semi-final
Feb 24 v Bannister Court (at County Ground) 3-0
F.Bromley, Farwell, Nicholls
A.A.Fry; Carter, G.Marshall, Stride, Deacon, Verney, Kiddle, F.Bromley, Nicholls, Farwell, Delamotte.
Final
Mar 14 v Royal Engineers (at County Ground) 3-1
Delamotte, Kiddle, Stride
Ruffell; Carter, G.Marshall, Verney, Deacon, Stride, Kiddle, F.Bromley, Nicholls, Delamotte, Farwell.

Hampshire County Cricket Club Charity Cup

Semi-final
Apr 18 v Bournemouth (at County Ground) 2-2
Farwell, Nicholls
Ruffell; Carter, G.Marshall, Stride, Deacon, Verney, Kiddle, F.Bromley, Nicholls, Farwell, Delamotte.
Bournemouth scratched and no replay took place.
Final
Apr 24 v Royal Engineers (at County Ground) 1-0
Nicholls
Ruffell; Carter, G.Marshall, Stride, Deacon, Verney, Kiddle, F.Bromley, Nicholls, Farwell, Delamotte.

1891-92

THIS season saw Saints make their first foray into the FA Cup, then still known as the English Cup. Unlike the Hampshire competitions, in which the club was immediately successful, it was to be 85 years before the Saints lifted the FA Cup, although they came desperately close to doing so only eight years after first entering.

Southampton St Mary's 1891-92. Back row (left to right): F.J.Montgomery, E.J.Nicholls, F.A.Delamotte, J.Henden (secretary). Middle: T.Price, W.Stride, G.Carter, R.Ruffell, R.S.Kiddle. Front: G.Marshall, G.W.Verney. Ernie Nicholls had the honour of scoring the club's first-ever FA Cup goal. He left Saints before they entered the Southern League but remained in the town and played cricket for the Deanery club between 1901 and 1922.

In those days, as a smaller club outside the Football League, which itself was still a lusty infant, Saints had to play in a qualifying competition. In the first round of that qualifying competition Saints were drawn away to Warmley, a Bristol club whose team was comprised mainly of bootmakers.

Although the Saints were entering into the humbler stage of the Cup, the fact that it was a truly national competition meant that the event aroused great interest and special arrangements and preparations were needed. The journey west began on the Friday before the match and although only a few supporters actually made the trip, two of them cycled there and back.

They found the Warmley ground to be rather rough, with a reserved enclosure roped off for VIPs. The local public house provided the dressing-rooms. The poor state of the pitch meant that entertaining football was at a premium but, undaunted, Saints took the lead after only 15 minutes, through Nicholls. Delamotte increased it just before half-time and although Warmley managed a goal early in the second half, further goals from Carter and Nicholls ensured progress to round two.

Reading were the visitors for the first FA Cup match ever to be played in Southampton and two weeks before the tie at the Antelope Ground, Saints arranged an exhibition match against the 93rd Highlanders. By the time the Reading game came around, two of the Highlanders, Jock Fleming and Sandy McMillan found themselves in the Saints team.

Fleming was outstanding at centre-forward, with a hat-trick in Saints' 7-0 victory. After the game, the Reading secretary, Mr H.Walker, asked his Southampton counterpart, Mr Hendin, for an advance on the 'gate' money. Using the advance for the deposit which had to be lodged, Mr Walker then appealed to the FA about the ineligibility of the two Highlanders.

St Mary's sent Mr Hendin to argue their case but he was to telegraph back, 'Poor old Saints. Disqualified. Hendin'. Reading thus progressed to the next round (where they were thrashed 18-0 by mighty Preston) and Fleming and McMillan had starkly contrasting fortunes. Fleming left the army to play for Aston Villa; poor McMillan died in India a few months later, of enteric fever.

Disappointment at their disqualification from the FA Cup was tempered somewhat when Saints retained the Hampshire Senior Cup, a success which extended their unbeaten run in Hampshire Cup matches to five seasons.

In 1891 it was agreed that players boots and knickers be provided by the club. Dr Bencraft pointed out, however, that this would breach FA rules. The answer was to 'loan' the players the cost of the equipment. The club allowed 12s (60p) for a pair of boots, 7s (35p) for a shirt, and 4s 2d (21p) for a pair of knickers. The players were still responsible for washing and mending.

FA Cup

1st Qualifying Round
Oct 3 v Warmley (a) 4-1
Carter, Delamotte, Nicholls 2
Ruffell; G.Marshall, Carter, Stride, Measures, Verney, Delamotte, Farwell, Nicholls, Mulford, Kiddle.
2nd Qualifying Round
Oct 24 v Reading (h) 7-0*
Fleming 3, Verney, Nicholls, Delamotte, opp.og
Ruffell; G.Marshall, Carter, Stride, McMillan, Verney, Kiddle, Nicholls, Fleming, Delamotte, Farwell.
**Southampton St Mary's expelled after Reading protested over ineligibility of Fleming and McMillan.*

Hampshire Senior Cup

Hampshire County Cricket Club Charity Cup

1892-93

ST MARY'S had seen only a gradual turnover of players in the seven years of their existence, yet by the start of the 1892-3 season only one of the original 1885 team remained — Ralph Ruffell, the stalwart goalkeeper.

In 1892, many players decided to leave and St Mary's faced a lean autumn. Delamotte and Nicholls were two of the more prominent members to leave the club, although both had returned by the end of the season. Another change was the appointment of Cecil Knight as secretary.

In the FA Cup, Maidenhead caused a sensation by winning 4-0 at the Antelope when a player called Janes hit three goals. It was the first cup match the club had ever lost — discounting the Hampshire CCC Charity Cup Final defeat by Royal Engineers the previous season — and the membership, which now numbered 600, was shocked.

After Christmas, however, with the return of Delamotte and Nicholls, Saints' fortunes improved and they again reached the Hampshire Senior Cup Final. Never had a game been so eagerly awaited in Southampton, for their opponents were their old rivals, Freemantle.

Estimates of a 6,000 crowd were perhaps modest, for the County Ground was fairly bursting at the seams and the receipts were over £122. It was a gloriously sunny day and all roads to the ground were jammed long before kick-off.

Vic Barton, the veteran Hampshire cricketer, had now replaced Ruffell, but he was injured and so Ruffell was recalled for the Final. Officials faced an uphill battle to keep the fans from spilling on to the pitch and at half-time Freemantle led 1-0. Early in the second half, Dollin equalised for Saints and the crowd were anticipating a replay when Stride, Saints' half-back, tripped Horton, a Freemantle forward.

Saints' players protested that the foul was outside the penalty area but referee Mr Royston Bourke was adamant and the resultant kick was duly converted. After the game, St Mary's skipper, Carter, told Mr Bourke that he could point out the exact spot — outside the penalty area — where the offence took place. "Are you sure?" asked the referee. "Absolutely," replied Carter. "In that case," said Mr Bourke, "I suggest you have a tombstone erected over it." And with those words, St Mary's relinquished their hold on the Senior Cup.

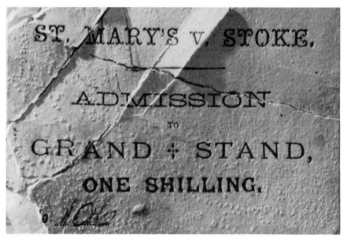

Ticket for the visit of Stoke in 1892-3. This was a 'plum' fixture for Saints because Stoke finished seventh in Division One that season. The Potteries club underlined their status, however, with an 8-0 drubbing of the Southampton club.

On 26 April, a few weeks after that disappointment, Saints met Stoke, then one of the leading First Division sides, in a prestigious friendly match at the County Ground. The Potteries side gave the Saints a harsh reminder of the gulf between non-League football and the top flight clubs, hammering St Mary's 8-0. Ironically, several of this Stoke side were to join Saints in controversial circumstances a few years later.

FA Cup

Hampshire Senior Cup

Hampshire County Cricket Club Charity Cup

Semi-final
Apr 15 v Cowes (at County Ground) 0-0
Ruffell; Carter, Taylor, Verney, G.Marshall, Stride, Dollin, Nineham, Dorkin, Kiddle, Nicholls.
Replay
Apr 22 v Cowes (at County Ground) 3-1
G.Marshall, Dorkin, Nicholls
Ruffell; Carter, Taylor, Verney, G.Marshall, Stride, Miller, Farwell, Dorkin, Nineham, Nicholls.
•*Note: The 1892-3 Final of the above competition was never played.*

1893-94

THE advent of professionalism the previous season meant that Saints now began to cast their scouting net far and wide in an attempt to compete with the best teams. Angus was signed from Ardwick, and Offer from Woolwich Arsenal. Another acquisition was Ernest Taylor who had been on Everton's books but whose work for an American shipping company had taken him south.

The season began promisingly, with the newcomers settling well, but after Christmas, a crop of injuries, notably to full-backs Carter and Price, saw a slump in form. The Senior Cup semi-final saw Saints gain revenge over Freemantle with victory after a drawn first game which attracted another big attendance. In the replay, Saints could count themselves fortunate after Freemantle had hit the crossbar and Angus had been sent off.

There was to be no such deliverance in the Final where the Royal Engineers won 1-0 and Saints suffered severe injury problems. Inside the first five minutes, Rowthorn sustained such serious internal injuries that he was in a critical condition for days after the game. Midway through the second half, Ruffell dislocated a knee-cap and Saints fought bravely with only nine men. It was argued that they were as unlucky to lose the Final as they had been lucky to win through the semi-final.

> *During 1893-4, Saints arranged a match under Well Patent lights but it was called off due to bad weather and it was not until the 1950s that Southampton made their debut under floodlights.*

The balance sheet at the end of the season showed a 'profit' of almost £86. Membership subscriptions totalled over £156; gate receipts were £612. Expenditure included wages (£221), rent for the Antelope ground (£42), home match expenses (£181), and away expenses (£56).

FA Cup

1st Qualifying Round
Nov 4 v Uxbridge (h) 3-1
Taylor, Ward, Nicholls
Ruffell; Carter, Offer, Verney, G.Marshall, Taylor, Ward, Angus, Dorkin, Nineham, Nicholls.
2nd Qualifying Round
Nov 25 v Reading (a) 1-2
opp.og
Ruffell; Carter, Offer, Verney, G.Marshall, Price, Nicholls, Kiddle, Dorkin, Angus, Ward.

> *Saints played 23 friendlies in 1893-4, winning 13 and drawing four. There were big victories over Christchurch (9-2), Royal Engineers (7-0) and Cameronians (6-1), whilst Second Division Woolwich Arsenal were beaten 4-2.*

Hampshire Senior Cup

Round 1
Dec 9 v Cowes (h) 2-0
Dorkin, Nicholls
Ruffell; Carter, Price, Taylor, G.Marshall, Verney, Nicholls, Nineham, Dorkin, Angus, Ward.
Semi-final
Feb 3 v Freemantle (at County Ground) 1-1
Dorkin
Ruffell; G.Marshall, Rowthorn, Taylor, Stride, Verney, Offer, Nineham, Dorkin, Angus, Ward.
Replay
Feb 24 v Freemantle (at County Ground) 2-1
Dorkin, Ward
Ruffell; G.Marshall, Rowthorn, Taylor, Stride, Verney, Nineham, Offer, Dorkin, Angus, Ward.
Final
Mar 10 v Royal Engineers (at County Ground) 0-1
Ruffell; G.Marshall, Rowthorn, Taylor, Stride, Verney, Nicholls, Nineham, Dorkin, Offer, Ward.

Hampshire County Cricket Club Charity Cup

Semi-final
Apr 18 v Lancaster Regiment (at County Ground) 2-2
Dorkin, Offer
Barratt; G.Marshall, Thomson, Taylor, Furby, Verney, Dorkin, Nineham, Offer, Angus, Miller.
Replay
Apr 21 v Lancaster Regiment (at County Ground) 3-0
Angus, Dorkin, Offer
Barratt; G.Marshall, Thomson, Taylor, Furby, Verney, Dorking, Nineham, Offer, Angus, Miller.
Final
Apr 23 v 15 Coy, Royal Artillery (at County Ground) 5-0
Offer 2, Dorkin, Furby, Angus
Barratt; G.Marshall, Thomson, Taylor, Furby, Verney, Dorkin, Nineham, Offer, Angus, Miller.

Portsmouth & District Cup

Semi-final
Dec 23 v 15 Coy, Royal Artillery (h) 3-2
Angus 2, Offer
Ruffell; Carter, Price, Taylor, Dorkin, Verney, Nineham, R.Kiddle, Offer, Angus, Ward.
Final
Mar 17 v Freemantle (at United Services Ground, Portsmouth) 0-2
Barratt; Nicholls, G.Marshall, M.Marshall, Stride, Verney, Dorkin, Nineham, Offer, Ward, R.Kiddle.

Southampton St Mary's 1893-94. Back row (left to right): V.Barton, Dr Bencroft, R.Ruffell, E.J.Taylor, G.Carter, G.Price, J.Dorkin, C.Knight (secretary), H.Johns (treasurer). Front: C.Miller, G.Nineham, E.J.Nicholls, W.Stride, G.W.Verney, J.Dollin, G.Marshall.

1894-95

WHEN the Southern League was formed in 1894, Southampton St Mary's application to join was originally turned down. Fortunately for the Saints, the 2nd Scots Guards had to withdraw from the new competition before a ball was kicked and St Mary's were duly offered their place.

The decision to join the Southern League was a bold move on the part of the Southampton committee, but one which they had to make if they were not to remain just another local town side. Such ambition would, of course, mean additional financial burdens, but by increasing membership subscriptions, the committee were confident that the club would progress favourably.

On the playing side, most of the previous season's players were re-engaged, with the exception of George Carter who had been forced into retirement by injury. Goalkeeper Ralph Ruffell had also finally decided to call it a day, thus severing the final link with the original 1885 team.

Baker, Thomson and Littlehales had been signed from Stoke, whilst Hollands arrived from Millwall. For its inaugural season the Southern League comprised nine teams and Saints' first-ever game in the competition took place on 6 October 1894, against Chatham, and Southampton St Mary's won 3-1 with goals from Offer, Angus and Hollands. It was Harry Offer, the former Swindon and Woolwich Arsenal player, who had the honour of scoring Saints' first goal in the Southern League.

Saints maintained steady progress and their supporters were satisfied with third place. The most resounding win of the season came on 30 March when Swindon were trounced 7-0 at the Antelope.

Saints supplemented their fixtures with several friendlies, including matches against Football League clubs, Stoke and Bolton Wanderers. Bolton, in particular, were impressed by their Southern League opponents as Saints ran out 5-2 winners.

In another friendly, St Mary's met the Wiltshire Regiment at the Antelope and won 13-0. Right-back Joe Rogers played centre-forward that day and responded with ten goals.

Local cup-ties were still regarded with some importance and Saints won the Hampshire Senior Cup for the third time, beating the Royal Artillery in the Final.

FA Cup

NEWBURY, the Berkshire club, were unfortunate to meet St Mary's in particularly rampant mood in the 1894-95 FA Cup competition. They visited the Antelope in October that season and were subjected to a humiliating 14-0 defeat. The goals were evenly spread around the Saints team and the result is still Southampton's biggest victory in a competitive match.

Reading were beaten 5-2 in the next round — this time there was no protest after the final whistle — and a Saints team growing visibly in confidence had easy wins in the next two qualifying matches, against Marlow and Warmley.

The prize for reaching the first round proper of the FA Cup was a visit from First Division club, Nottingham Forest. The status of their opponents did nothing to diminish the confidence of Saints' supporters — had their side not already scored 31 goals in the competition? — but although they showed a great deal of pluck and determination, St Mary's were no match for the skill, subtlety and cohesion of one of the country's top teams.

Like the weather, the Saints players 'froze' at the big occasion and Forest, adapting themselves well, had little difficulty in winning 4-1 on a hard, snow-covered Antelope pitch.

Jack Dorkin was one of Saints' first professionals. He played only three games and scored three goals. Dorkin was born at sea aboard the SS Tamar.

Southampton St Mary's advert covering the first-ever Southern League game at the Antelope and the English Cup match against Newbury which Saints were to win 14-0.

1894-95
Southern League

		Result	Scorers	Angus J	Baker C	Barratt H	Dorkin J	Furby W	Hamer D	Hollands F	Jeffery J	Littlehales A	Marshall G	Nineham G	Offer H	Rogers J	Taylor EJ	Thomson WJG	Ward A	Ward H	Williamson H
Oct 6	(h) Chatham	W 3-1	Angus, Hollands, Offer	10	9	1				6	11	4	2	7	8		3	5			
20	(h) Royal Ordn'ce	W 3-1	H.Ward 2, Offer	10	7	1				3	11	5	2		8		4	6		9	
27	(a) Luton T	L 1-4	Angus	10	8	1		6		3	11	5	2	7	9		4				
Nov 17	(h) Millwall	D 2-2	Baker, Thomson	10	7					11	3	5	2		8		4	6		9	1
Dec 8	(a) Reading	W 1-0	H.Ward	10	7					11	3	5	2		8		4	6		9	1
22	(a) Luton T	L 1-2	Baker	10	7					11	3	5	2		8		4	6		9	1
29	(a) Ilford	W 2-1	Hollands, Nineham		7			4		11	3	5	2	10	8			6		9	1
Jan 5	(h) Reading	L 1-3	Offer		10			4		11	3	5	2	8	7	9		6			1
12	(a) Clapton	W 3-1	Baker, Offer, Rogers	8	9	1		6		11	3	4	2		7	10		5			
Feb 23	(a) Swindon T	W 3-2	Baker, Nineham, H.Ward		9			4		11	3	5	2	10	7			6		8	1
Mar 9	(a) Chatham	D 1-1	Baker	10	9					11	3	5	2		7	8	4	6			1
14	(a) Royal Ordn'ce	L 0-2		10	9					11	3	5	2		7	8	4	6			1
23	(a) Millwall	L 0-4		10	9					11	3	5	2				4	6	8	7	1
30	(h) Swindon T	W 7-1	Angus 2, H.Ward 2, Baker, Dorkin, Hollands	10	9		8			11	3	5				2	4	6		7	1
Apr 12	(h) Clapton	W 3-0	Nineham 2, Dorkin	10			9			11	3	5		8	7	2	4	6			1
13	(h) Ilford	W 3-0	Angus 2, Dorkin	10	7		9				3	5	6	8		2	4			11	1
			App	13	15	4	3	5	3	15	13	16	14	7	13	7	11	15	1	9	12
			Goals	6	6		3			3				4	4	1		1		6	

	P	W	D	L	F	A	Pts
Millwall	16	12	4	0	68	19	28
Luton T	16	9	4	3	36	22	22
Southampton	16	9	2	5	34	25	20
Ilford	16	6	3	7	40		15
Reading	16	6	2	8	33	38	14
Chatham	16	4	5	7	22	25	13
Royal Ordnance	16	3	6	7	20	30	12
Clapton	16	5	1	10	22	38	11
Swindon T	16	4	1	11	24	48	9

Back row (left to right): W.Wheeler (trainer) G.Marshall, H.Johns (hon treasurer), H.F.Ward, H.Barrett, Dr Bencraft (President), D.Hamer, C.Knight (hon secretary), G.H.Muir. Middle row: E.J.Taylor, A.Littlehales, J.Angus, W.J.G..Thompson, F.Hollands. Front row: G.Nineham, H.Offer.

ST. MARY'S V. WILTSHIRE REGIMENT, ALDERSHOT.

In the presence of a fair sprinkling of spectators, and on a swampy surface, the local pros. antagonised a selection from the Wiltshire Regiment in an exhibition match at the Antelope Ground, Southampton, on Saturday afternoon. The visitors mustered minus the services of five of their Cup combination, though substantial substitutes were obtainable. Lowering clouds hung overhead, and a drizzling rain had commenced to fall when the combatants took up their respective stations as appended:—

```
                    ST. MARY'S.
                    Williamson
         Marshall                  Jeffery
    Furby        Littlehales       Thomson
 Offer                                  Nineham
   Baker      Rogers              Hollands
                    O
  Pte. Baby      Corpl. Bateman      Band. Regan
  Corpl. Watts                       Band. Warner
  Band. Hatrill  Drum. Bettridge     Pte. Hatton
      Sergt. Barnes        Drum. Hobson
               Pte. Sheppard
                WILTSHIRE REGIMENT.
```

Referee, Mr. G. Muir.
Linesmen, Mr. E. C. Jarvis (St. Mary's), and Drummer Sheppard (Wiltshire Regiment).

The soldiers started with the odds of a light breeze against them, and the homesters advanced. Rogers struck the horizontal with an express effort when in close quarters, and Offer landed the leather to the rear of the net. Barnes relieved, but Furby returned the Saints to the attack. Offer then skirted the mouth of the goal, which gave Nineham an opening. That player failed to convert, and the military beat up on the left. Marshall repelled, and succeeding an ineffective shot by Baker, Littlehales received from the opposing custodian and penetrated Sheppard's stronghold with a long-reaching drop. Re-starting, the home brigade again assumed the aggressive, Offer being a frequent offender. A corner accrued in favour of the Saintly ones, and from a timely centre by Furby, Rogers further augmented the home account. Resuming, the Regimentals gained turf, and forced a fruitless minor. The invasion was merely temporary, however the "cherry squares" retaliating through the instrumentality of Thomson. Offer initiated a combined movement, and as the issue of a series of deserving endeavours Rogers was responsible for another addition. The ground was now a perfect mire, being saturated by the now steady prevailing shower, the contestants skidding about like ninepins. The visitors were penalised for an infringement of the rules. A thrice of corners resulted, ...

TO-MORROW (SATURDAY)

ANTELOPE GROUND.

GRAND MATCH.

FIRST ROUND OF ENGLISH CUP
(PROPER.)

NOTTS FOREST v. ST. MARY'S.

GROUND CLEARED FOR SPECTATORS.

KICK OFF 2.30.

ADMISSION, 6D.
GRAND STAND, 1s. EXTRA.
ALL PAY.

Left: Newspaper advertisement for the Saints' FA Cup game against Forest. Right: Report of the friendly game in which Joe Rogers scored ten goals.

1895-96

BEFORE their second season in the Southern League could get underway, Southampton St Mary's became involved in an incident that had many repercussions both on and off the pitch. It became quite a celebrated affair and for many years afterwards, Southampton football supporters spoke of the 'Stoke Invasion'.

Southern League clubs, unrestricted by the maximum wages rule of the Football League, were able to 'poach' League club players simply by paying them more money. Southampton were not slow to employ such tactics and Mr Robson, the Saints' new secretary, and Mr McMinn proved they were good judges of football talent when buying Jack Farrell, 'Chippy' Naughton and Sam Meston from Stoke, Watty Keay from Derby, Joe Turner from Dresden United and A.E. Wood from Burslem Port Vale.

Alas, Saints were in such haste to secure the League club players that they signed them before the League season was over. An emergency FA meeting was held at Sheffield and the St Mary's club was severely censured for negligence, if not wilful, violation of the rules. Saints were ordered to pay their own costs plus £4 6s 3d to Stoke and £1 13s to Port Vale. St Mary's official Mr McMinn was suspended for a year. Dawson, who had been Stoke's trainer for many years before accompanying the Potters' players to Southampton, received a month's suspension; and Wood had his registration cancelled and, ironically, moved to Stoke from Vale. That particular decision robbed Saints of a fine footballer.

Saints began the season badly and the new players' inability to settle in the area was blamed. Under Dawson's guidance, however, the team eventually began to string together some fine victories and again they finished third in a league now extended from 16 to 18 clubs.

Highlight of the season was the visit to the Antelope of Millwall, the reigning champions and at that stage unbeaten in the Southern League. A crowd, reported in some newspapers to be as much as 8,000 strong, saw Millwall's fine record fall with goals from Baker and Turner giving Saints victory.

The Saints committee decided to enter the reserve team in the Hampshire Senior Cup and they performed well before losing to Royal Artillery in the Final.

FA Cup

SAINTS again won through from the qualifying rounds of the FA Cup before going down at home to a First Division club. This time it was Sheffield Wednesday — in those days known simply as 'The Wednesday' — who brought the fans flocking to the Antelope.

For the first time in the history of the club, Saints' players were given 'special training' and they spent a week on Shawford Downs under the experienced eye of trainer Dawson. Twelve thousand supporters packed the Antelope and they saw a thrilling game.

Excitement grew when Watty Keay scored for the home side, but the cheers had scarcely subsided when Wednesday equalised through Brady, the same player putting the Yorkshire club into the lead before half-time. Soon after the restart, Davis increased Wednesday's lead and the Saints' chances seemed doomed, but Turner headed them back into contention and set the scene for a rousing finalé. Southampton could not find another goal, but it was no disgrace to lose so narrowly to the team that was to win the Cup that season.

1st Qualifying Round
Oct 12 v Freemantle (a) 5-1
Farrell 2, Littlehales, Naughton, Turner
Cox; Thomson, Meston, Dale, Littlehales, Marshall, Baker, Naughton, Farrell, Keay, Turner.
Att: 5,354
2nd Qualifying Round
Nov 2 v Marlow (h) 5-0
Turner 2, Farrell 2, Meston
Cox; Thomson, Meston, Dale, Littlehales, Marshall, Baker, Keay, Farrell, Angus, Turner.
Att: 4,000
3rd Qualifying Round
Nov 23 v Reading (h) 3-0
Taylor, Naughton, Keay
Cox; Thomson, Meston, Taylor, Littlehales, Rogers, Naughton, Baker, Farrell, Keay, Turner.
Att: 5,000
4th Qualifying Round
Dec 14 v Uxbridge (h) 3-0
Naughton, Keay, Turner
Cox; Meston, Hamer, Thomson, Littlehales, Marshall, Naughton, Baker, Farrell, Keay, Turner.
Att: 4,000
Round 1
Feb 1 v Sheffield Wednesday (h) 2-3
Keay, Turner
Cox; Meston, Thomson, Taylor, Littlehales, Hodgkinson, Baker, Naughton, Farrell, Keay, Turner.
Att: 12,000

During 1895-6 season, it was proposed to alter the club's name from Southampton St Mary's to plain 'Southampton FC'. Sentimentalists objected, claiming that club could no longer be called 'the Saints' if the official name was changed. A proposal to change the arrangement of club colours met with more approval and it was agreed that the jerseys would now be red and white halves.

Saints did not draw a single Southern League game during 1895-6, the only season this has ever happened.

1895-96
Southern League

Date		Opponent	Result	Scorers	Angus J	Baker C	Barratt H	Cain T	Cox W	Dale J	Farrell J	Hamer D	Hodgkinson J	Inglis	Keay W	Kiddle R	Littlehales A	McMillan J	Marshall G	Meston S	Naughton W	Phillips Gunner	Reilly M	Rogers J	Smith V	Taylor EJ	Thomson WJG	Turner J
Sep 14	(a)	Millwall	L 0-1			7	1				9				10		5			3	8			2		4	6	11
21	(a)	Chatham	L 1-3	Naughton		7	1				9				10		5			3	8			2		4	6	11
28	(a)	Reading	L 2-3	Naughton, Turner		7	1				9				10		5			3	8			2		4	6	11
Oct 5	(a)	Royal Ordn'nce	W 2-1	Farrell 2		7			1		9				10		5			3	8			2		4	6	11
19	(a)	Clapton	L 3-7	Angus, Baker, Farrell	10	7		1		4	9				11	5			6	3	8			2				
26	(h)	Luton T	W 2-1	Naughton, Turner	10	7		1		4	9						5		6	2	8						3	11
Nov 16	(a)	Ilford	W 1-0	Rogers	10	7		1		4							5		6	2	8			9			3	11
30	(a)	New Brompton	L 0-1			7		1			9				10		5		6	2	8			4			3	11
Dec 7	(h)	Swindon T	W 4-2	Littlehales, Naughton, Taylor, J Turner		7		1			9				10		5		6	2	8					4	3	11
21	(h)	Reading	W 5-0	Keay 3, Farrell, Littlehales		7					9				10		5		6	2	8				1	4	3	11
Jan 18	(h)	Chatham	W 4-0	Farrell 2, Naughton 2		7		1			9	3	6		10		5			2	8					4		11
25	(h)	Royal Ordn'nce	W 5-0	Baker, Keay, Littlehales, Naughton, Turner		7					9	3	6		10		5			2	8	1				4		11
Feb 15	(a)	Swindon T	W 2-0	Baker, Littlehales		7		1			10	3	6				5			2	8		9			4		11
Mar 7	(a)	Luton T	L 0-3			7		1			9	3	6		10		5			2	8					4		11
21	(h)	Millwall	W 2-0	Baker, Turner		7			1		9		6		10		5	4		2	8						3	11
28	(h)	New Brompton	W 5-0	Hodgkinson 2, Baker, Farrell, Naughton		7			1		9		6		10		5	4		2	8						3	11
Apr 3	(h)	Clapton	W 2-0	Farrell, Keay		7		1			9		6		10		5	4		2	8						3	11
4	(h)	Ilford	W 4-0	Farrell 2, Keay, Turner		7		1			9	3	6		10		5	4		2	8							11
App					3	18	3	10	3	3	17	4	7	1	15	1	17	4	8	18	17	1	2	8	1	8	12	17
Goals					1	5					10		2		6		4				8			1		1		6

Standing (left to right): E.C.Jarvis, S.Meston, G.Marshall, H.Barratt, A.Littlehales, W.Cox, A.Wood, W.Dawson (trainer). Sitting: C.Baker, W.Naughton, J.Rogers, J.Farrell, W.J.G.Thomson, W.Keay, J.Turner.

	P	W	D	L	F	A	Pts
Millwall	18	16	1	1	75	16	33
Luton T	18	13	1	4	68	14	27
Southampton	18	12	0	6	44	23	24
Reading	18	11	1	6	45	38	23
Chatham	18	9	2	7	43	45	20
New Brompton	18	7	7	4	30	37	18
Swindon T	18	6	4	8	38	41	16
Clapton	18	4	2	12	30	67	10
Royal Ordnance	18	3	3	12	23	44	9
Ilford	18	0	0	18	10	81	0

'Taffy' Hamer (left) was in his second spell with Saints in 1895-6 and later returned for a third period of duty, as assistant first-team trainer. Charles Robson (right) who served Hampshire as a batsman-wicketkeeper, was appointed Saints' secretary in 1895.

R.S.Kiddle was past his best by the time Saints entered the Southern League but he had the satisfaction of making an appearance in the competition against Clapton on October 1895, although he finished on the losing side.

1896-97

WITH the conclusion of the 1895-96 season, the Saints vacated the Antelope ground and took up temporary residence at the Hampshire County Cricket Ground in Northlands Road. In the close season the committee had also been busy, again signing several Football League players eager to earn more money in the Southern League.

Amongst the new recruits were Bob Buchanan from Woolwich Arsenal, and Harry Haynes (Small Heath). Goalkeeper George Clawley was signed from Tottenham Hotspur and began a long and illustrious career with Saints. Mr Robson resigned as secretary and was replaced by Mr McMinn, whilst Mr E.Arnfield became assistant secretary.

As if to celebrate their move to the County Ground, St Mary's surpassed all their previous achievements by winning the Southern League title without losing a match. Millwall, champions in the Southern League's first two seasons, were runners-up and they provided the opposition for Saints' last game of the season.

Although Saints had already ensured their title, they were anxious to maintain their unbeaten record — and Millwall, having gone through 1894-95 unbeaten, were equally keen to prevent Saints emulating that feat. Millwall scored first in the opening minutes, but St Mary's fought back and Joe Turner went on one of his mesmerising dashes down the wing before cutting in to equalise with a brilliant shot.

The Southern League Championship shield was presented at a 'smoker' held at the Artillery Drill Hall, and it was Dr Bencraft, president of both the club and the league, who handed the trophy to St Mary's captain, Jack Farrell. Each player received a gold medal, with trainer Dawson and linesman Joyce also being awarded mementoes.

During the season Saints continued to look for a ground they could call their permanent home and there was talk of amalgamating with Freemantle in order to obtain their Shirley Road ground beside the Western School. Despite detailed discussions, however, the proposal came to nothing.

FA Cup

SAINTS were drawn against their great rivals, Cowes, in the first qualifying round. Five thousand people saw the Saints comprehensively outplay Cowes to the tune of 6-0. St Mary's had to travel again in the next round, this time to Reading where they arrived to find the Elm Park pitch waterlogged. Mr McMinn lodged an appeal with the referee but the tie went ahead and, perhaps to McMinn's embarrassment, Saints won 4-1.

In true tradition of Saints-Reading cup ties, Reading then protested and an FA hearing was needed before Saints proceeded to the next round. Although Swindon scored first in the fourth qualifying round at the County Ground, Southampton, Saints then ran riot with eight goals, Farrell scoring three of them.

Derbyshire club Heanor Town scrambled a draw at Southampton in the first round proper, but in the following Wednesday's replay they had the misfortune to lose winger Hardy who broke a leg. The Saints went through with a goal from Farrell and the *Southern Evening Echo* set up a fund which raised £40 for the luckless Hardy.

A crowd of 8,000 saw the Saints draw their second round tie against Newton Heath — later Manchester United — at the County Ground, but in the replay Southampton badly missed the injured Naughton and went out to goals from Bryant (2) and Cassidy.

2nd Qualifying Round
Nov 21 v Cowes (a) 6-0
Buchanan 2, Farrell 2, Turner 2
Clawley; Meston, McKie, McMillan, Littlehales, Hodgkinson, Naughton, Buchanan, Farrell, Keay, Turner.
Att: 5,000

3rd Qualifying Round
Dec 12 v Reading (a) 4-1
Buchanan 2, Farrell, Turner
Clawley; Meston, McKie, McMillan, Littlehales, Hodgkinson, Naughton, Buchanan, Farrell, Keay, Turner.
Att: 5,000

4th Qualifying Round
Jan 2 v Swindon Town (h) 8-2
Farrell 3, Littlehales, Hodgkinson, Keay, Turner, Buchanan
Clawley; Meston, Haynes, McMillan, Littlehales, Hodgkinson, Naughton, Buchanan, Farrell, Keay, Turner.
Att: 5,000

Round 1
Jan 30 v Heanor Town (h) 1-1
Turner
Clawley; Meston, McKie, McMillan, Littlehales, Hodgkinson, Naughton, Buchanan, Farrell, Keay, Turner.
Att: 8,500

Replay
Feb 3 v Heanor Town (a) 1-0
Farrell
Clawley; Meston, McKie, McMillan, Littlehales, Hodgkinson, Naughton, Buchanan, Farrell, Keay, Turner.
Att: 3,000

Round 2
Feb 13 v Newton Heath (h) 1-1
Turner
Clawley; Meston, McKie, McMillan, Littlehales, Hodgkinson, Naughton, Buchanan, Farrell, Keay, Turner.
Att: 4,000

Replay
Feb 13 v Newton Heath (a) 1-3
Buchanan
Clawley; Meston, McKie, McMillan, Littlehales, Hodgkinson, Buchanan, Spellacy, Farrell, Keay, Turner.
Att: 7,000

George Clawley joined Saints in 1896 and did not miss a game for two seasons as Southampton won successive Southern League titles.

> For 1896-97, Saints strip was again changed, this time to red and white striped shirts and blue shorts. It was to be the last change for 80 years.

> Players' wages for this season amounted to £1,529 6s 3d.

1896-97
Southern League

Date	Venue	Opponent	Result	Scorers	Buchanan R	Clawley G	Farrell J	Hamer D	Haynes H	Hayter F	Hodgkinson J	Keay W	Littlehales A	McKay	McKie J	McMillan J	Meston S	Naughton W	Ponting W	Seeley G	Shenton	Turner J
Sep 19	(h)	Chatham	W 4-1	Farrell 2, Buchanan, Turner	8	1	9		6			10	5	2	3	4	7					11
26	(h)	Sheppy U	W 6-1	Buchanan 3, Meston 2, Turner	8	1	9		5		6	10		2	3	4	7					11
Oct 18	(h)	Wolverton	W 5-2	Buchanan, Farrell, Haynes, Meston, Turner	8	1	9		5		6	10		2	3	4	7					11
24	(a)	Northfleet	W 2-1	Farrell, McMillan	8	1	9		5		6	10		2		4	3	7				11
Nov 7	(h)	New Brompton	W 8-3	Naughton 3, Buchanan 2, Littlehales 2, Farrell	8	1	11		5		6		9	2		4	3	7				10
14	(h)	Reading	W 6-0	Turner 2, Hodgkinson, Keay, Naughton, opp own goal	8	1	9				6	10	5	2		4	3	7				11
28	(a)	Sheppy U	W 1-0	opp own goal	8	1	9				6	10	5	2		4	3	7				11
Dec 5	(a)	Swindon T	W 2-0	Farrell, Naughton	8	1	10		5		6		9	2		4	3	7				11
19	(a)	Chatham	W 1-0	Turner	8	1	9				6	10	5		3	4	2	7				11
Jan 16	(a)	Gravesend	D 1-1	Meston	8	1	9		6			10	5		3	4	2	7				11
Feb 6	(a)	New Brompton	W 3-1	Farrell, Shenton, Turner	8	1	9				6	10	5		3	4	2				7	11
27	(h)	Swindon T	W 2-0	Farrell, Turner	8	1	9		3	10	6		5			4	2	7				11
Mar 6	(a)	Millwall	D 0-0		8	1	9		3	10	6		5			4	2	7				11
13	(h)	Northfleet	W 6-2	Farrell 2, Keay 2, Buchanan, Turner	8	1	9	2	3		6	10	5			4		7				11
29	(h)	Tottenham H	D 1-1	Littlehales	8	1	9		3		6	10	5			4	2	7		11		
31	(a)	Reading	W 5-1	Buchanan, Farrell, Haynes, Littlehales, Turner	8	1	9		3			10	5			4	2	7	6			11
Apr 8	(a)	Tottenham H	D 2-2	Farrell, Keay	8	1	9		3			10	5			4	2	7	6			11
10	(h)	Gravesend	W 5-0	Buchanan 2, Farrell, Naughton, Turner	8	1	9		3			10	5			4	2	7	6			11
14	(a)	Wolverton	W 2-1	Keay, Littlehales	8	1	9		3			10	5			4	2	7	6			11
26	(h)	Millwall	D 1-1	Turner	8	1	9		3			10	5			4	2	7	6			11
App					20	20	20	1	16	2	13	16	17	8	6	20	19	16	5	1	1	19
Goals					11		13		2		1	5	5			1	4	6			1	12

2 own-goals

Back row (left to right): Meston, Clawley, McKie. Middle row: Shenton, McMillan, Littlehales, Hodgkinson, Haynes, Dawson (trainer). Front row: Naughton, Buchanan, Farrell, Keay, Turner.

	P	W	D	L	F	A	Pts
Southampton	20	15	5	0	63	18	35
Millwall	20	13	5	2	63	24	31
Chatham	20	13	1	6	54	29	27
Tottenham H	20	9	4	7	43	29	22
Gravesend	20	9	4	7	35	35	22
Swindon T	20	8	3	9	31	37	19
Reading	20	8	3	9	31	49	19
New Brompton	20	7	2	11	32	42	16
Northfleet	20	5	4	11	24	46	14
Sheppey U	20	5	1	14	34	47	11
Wolverton	20	2	0	18	17	74	4

Sammy Meston in grand form.

A goal-kick for Lincoln.

The Referee gets one in the eye.

A contemporary artist's somewhat whimsical view of Saints' friendly game against Lincoln City in 1896.

Donald McKay's favourite attitude.

1897-98

SOUTHAMPTON continued their policy of signing experienced Football League players and for the opening of the 1897-8 season they had new men Nicol, Yates, Petrie and Chadwick to strengthen an already formidable line-up. Although Bristol City, then Tottenham Hotspur, dominated the early part of the season, it was Saints who finished top of the table for the second successive season.

Medal struck by the club to commemorate the winning of the Southern League title in 1897-98, for the second consecutive season.

> *In the 1897 close season it was decided to form a limited liability company and change the club's name to 'Southampton Football and Athletic Company Limited'. A share issue of £5,000 was put towards acquiring a new ground.*

FA Cup

ALTHOUGH Saints' success in the Southern League naturally stirred great excitement in Southampton, it was their FA Cup run which captured the national interest.

Saints' opening tie was against Bristol City, newly admitted to the Southern League and on the crest of a wave. Buchanan scored after only ten seconds and from that moment Saints were in absolute control, Yates adding a second. At Swindon in the next round, Saints had the game won by half-time, and Eastville Rovers (later Bristol Rovers) proved no match in the final qualifying round when Southampton won 8-1.

In the first round proper, Saints scored a fine win over Leicester Fosse, then lying seventh in Division One. Another League giant, Newcastle United, then put up a great fight at the County Ground before Saints squeezed through with a goal from Buchanan. Credit for this splendid victory over the Tynesiders went to Saints' defence who absorbed everything that Newcastle threw at them.

St Mary's were now in the third round, further than they had ever progressed before. When they drew Bolton Wanderers, however, few people gave Saints a chance of reaching the semi-final. One local critic wrote: '.....although they need not altogether abandon hope when they enter the gates of Lancashire, they will be lucky indeed if they escape defeat'.

Saints, however, confounded every doubter by drawing 0-0 at Burnden Park, and 15,000 people crammed into the County Ground for the replay. They paid a county record of £530 to witness an outstanding display from the home team who inflicted a 4-0 defeat on one of the leading clubs in English football.

Bolton were undoubtedly overawed by the hugely partisan crowd which at one stage spilled on to the pitch and put the immediate future of the match in doubt.

Reaching the semi-final was rightly regarded as a fine achievement for a club from the provincial south and the game against Nottingham Forest at Sheffield was eagerly awaited.

Forest took the lead after only five minutes and then Saints' centre-forward Farrell collided with the Forest goalkeeper and was reduced to a passenger for the rest of the game. Despite this handicap, Southampton equalised through Haynes to earn a replay at the Crystal Palace.

Saints exerted much pressure, even without the injured Farrell, and just before half-time they missed a penalty. In the second half, snow began to fall and play was halted for a while. The match restarted but the snow returned and Saints found themselves kicking into a blizzard. In the last minute, with Clawley blinded by the driving snow, Forest scored twice but no amount of protests to the FA would change the result and it was Forest who went through to the Final, although Saints had now acquired a much wider following.

3rd Qualifying Round
Oct 30 v Bristol City (h) 2-0
Yates, Buchanan
Clawley; Nicol, Haynes, Meston, A.Chadwick, Petrie, Yates, Naughton, Farrell, Buchanan, Turner.
Att: 11,000

4th Qualifying Round
Nov 20 v Swindon Town (a) 3-0
Farrell 2, Buchanan
Clawley; Nicol, Haynes, Meston, A.Chadwick, Petrie, Yates, Buchanan, Farrell, Keay, Turner.
Att: 5,000

5th Qualifying Round
Dec 11 v Eastville Rovers (h) 8-1
Yates 2, Buchanan 2, Keay 2, Turner 2
Clawley; Nicol, Haynes, Meston, A.Chadwick, Petrie, Yates, Buchanan, Farrell, Keay, Turner.
Att: 8,000

Round 1
Jan 29 v Leicester Fosse (h) 2-1
Meston, Buchanan
Clawley; Nicol, Haynes, Meston, A.Chadwick, Petrie, Yates, Buchanan, Farrell, Keay, Turner.
Att: 10,000

Round 2
Feb 12 v Newcastle United (h) 1-0
Buchanan
Clawley; Nicol, Haynes, Meston, A.Chadwick, Petrie, Yates, Buchanan, Farrell, Keay, Turner.
Att: 12,000

Round 3
Feb 26 v Bolton Wanderers (a) 0-0
Clawley; Nicol, Haynes, Meston, A.Chadwick, Petrie, Yates, Buchanan, Farrell, Keay, Turner.
Att: 15,000

Replay
Mar 2 v Bolton Wanderers (h) 4-0
Turner 2, Yates, Farrell
Clawley; Nicol, Haynes, Meston, A.Chadwick, Petrie, Yates, Buchanan, Farrell, Keay, Turner.
Att: 15,000

Semi-final
Mar 19 v Nottingham Forest (at Bramall Lane) 1-1
Haynes
Clawley; Nicol, Haynes, Meston, A.Chadwick, Petrie, Stevens, Buchanan, Farrell, Keay, Turner.
Att: 20,000

Replay
Mar 23 v Nottingham Forest (at Crystal Palace) 0-2
Clawley; Nicol, Haynes, Meston, A.Chadwick, Petrie, Brown, Stevens, Buchanan, Keay, Turner.
Att: 12,000

Team page from the match programme for Saints' FA Cup semi-final meeting with Nottingham Forest at Bramall Lane.

1897-98
Southern League

Date		Result	Scorers	Brown R	Buchanan R	Chadwick A	Clawley G	Farrell J	Haynes H	Keay W	Littlehales A	McMillan J	Meston S	Naughton W	Nicol TH	Petrie R	Reynolds J	Stevens D	Turner J	Yates J
Sep 18	(a) Tottenham H	L 0-2		8			1	9	3	10	5	4	2			6			11	7
Oct 2	(a) Sheppy U	W 1-0	Keay	8	9	5	1		3	10			4		2	6			11	7
9	(a) Millwall	W 3-2	Buchanan 2, Yates		9	5	1		3	10			4	8	2	6			11	7
16	(a) Reading	W 2-0	Naughton, Turner		9	5	1	10	3				4	8	2	6			11	7
23	(h) Tottenham H	W 4-1	Yates 2, Farrell, Turner			5	1	9	3	10			4	8	2	6			11	7
Nov 6	(h) Swindon T	W 4-1	Buchanan 3, Keay		8	5	1	9	3	10		4	2			6			11	7
13	(a) New Brompton	W 1-0	Farrell		8	5	1	9	3	10			4		2	6			11	7
27	(a) Wolverton	W 2-0	Petrie, Yates		8	5	1	9	3	10			4		2	6			11	7
Jan 1	(h) Bristol C	W 4-0	Keay 2, Chadwick, Petrie		8	5	1	9	3	10			4		2	6			11	7
8	(h) Sheppy U	W 4-0	Buchanan 2, Farrell, Meston	7	8	5	1	9	3	10			4		2	6			11	
15	(a) Bristol C	L 2-5	Yates		8	5	1	9	3	10			4		2	6			11	7
22	(h) New Brompton	W 4-1	Turner 3, Buchanan	7	8	5	1	9	3				4		2	6			11	10
Feb 5	(a) Chatham	D 1-1	Buchanan	7	8	5	1	11	3	10			9		2	6	4			
19	(h) Reading	W 2-1	Chadwick, Keay		9	5	1	11	3	10		6	4		2			8		7
Mar 5	(a) Swindon T	W 2-0	Petrie, Yates		8	5	1	9	3	10			4		2	6			11	7
12	(h) Wolverton	W 3-0	Turner 2, Farrell	9	8	5	1	10	3				6	2			4	7	11	
26	(a) Gravesend	W 3-1	Petrie, Stevens, Turner	7	9	5	1		3	10		4	2			6		8	11	
Apr 4	(h) Gravesend	W 5-1	Stevens 2, Brown, Buchanan, Turner	7	9	5	1		3	10			4		2	6		8	11	
11	(h) Northfleet	W 3-1	McMillan 2, Brown	7	9	5	1		3			10	4		2	6		8	11	
16	(a) Northfleet	W 2-0	Meston, Stevens	7	9	5	1		3	10			4		2	6		8	11	
20	(h) Millwall	W 1-0	Turner	7		5	1	9	3	10			4		2	6		8	11	
May 1	(h) Chatham	L 0-1		7	9	5	1		3	10		4	2			6		8	11	
			App	12	19	21	22	15	22	18	1	7	22	3	17	20	2	8	20	13
			Goals	2	10	2		5		5		2	2	1		4		4	10	6

Standing (left to right): Dawson (trainer), McMillan, Meston, Clawley (captain), Haynes, Chadwick, Petrie, Joyce (linesman). Seated: Nicol, Brown, Stevens, Buchanan, Keay, Turner.

	P	W	D	L	F	A	Pts
Southampton	22	18	1	3	53	18	37
Bristol C	22	13	7	2	67	33	33
Tottenham H	22	12	4	6	52	31	28
Chatham	22	12	4	6	50	34	28
Reading	22	8	7	7	39	31	23
New Brompton	22	9	4	9	37	37	22
Sheppey U	22	10	1	11	40	49	21
Gravesend	22	7	6	9	28	39	20
Millwall	22	8	2	12	48	45	18
Swindon T	22	7	2	13	36	48	16
Northfleet	22	4	3	15	29	60	11
Wolverton	22	3	1	18	28	82	7

Former Burnley and Blackburn player Tom Nichol joined Saints in 1897 and missed only five games in the Southern League title-winning side.

Saints finished sixth in the nine-team United League in 1897-8, losing twice to Luton, the eventual champions. In consecutive games in March Saints conceded a total of 12 goals, losing 5-0 at Millwall and then 7-0 at Tottenham. There were 17 first-team friendlies played, of which Southampton won 11 and lost only two.

23

1898-99

ONE year after becoming a limited company, the Saints became tenants of a new stadium which was nicknamed 'The Dell'. Mr George Thomas, a director, was the instigator of the club's move to an area not 200 yards from the County Ground. He saw the potential of a wooded hollow surrounding a lake and after a great deal of work in draining and filling in the area, a pitch was levelled out — all at a total cost of £10,000.

The pitch was actually 'built' over the lake and that has caused its fair share of problems over the years. In 1898, however, The Dell was considered to be the most compact ground in the country and the players got their first taste of its atmosphere when they took part in a sports meeting there on 27 August 1898. The following week the ground was officially opened and Saints celebrated with a Southern League victory over Brighton United. Saints won 4-1 and the popular Watty Keay had the honour of scoring the first goal at The Dell.

Not content to rest on the successes of the previous season, Saints were again on the look-out for fresh faces and of their 23 professionals, four — Wood, Robinson, Robertson and Meehan — were internationals. Saints again forged ahead but Bristol City chased them hard and when the last day of the season arrived, there was the mouth-watering prospect of Saints visiting City — with both teams having the same number of points.

The Bristol club were unbeaten at home and led 2-0 at half-time. Saints looked finished, especially when goalkeeper Robinson injured a hand and continued in great pain. The stage was set for an epic finish and Saints responded magnificently. They fought back to score a sensational 4-3 victory and retain the title.

A band met them at the Docks station and thousands of fans were in the streets outside to greet Saints, whose third successive Southern League title was marked by the presentation of a silk flag to the club.

FA Cup

HAVING reached the semi-final the previous year, Southampton were excused the qualifying competition and in the first round proper they met New Brompton (now Gillingham). Abe Hartley, playing at centre-forward, scored Saints' winner 20 minutes from time. Hartley was again on target when Saints beat Notts County in the next round, dribbling through a bewildered defence before scoring with a glorious shot.

Nicol became the first Saints player to score an FA Cup goal at The Dell when Derby County, the previous seasons beaten Finalists played in the first FA Cup game staged at the new ground. But Bloomer and MacDonald eased Derby through 2-1 and on their way to another Final. One man who was especially frustrated at the result was the Saints former Derby goalkeeper, Jack Robinson, who had earlier been reported to the FA for allegedly trying to lure Bloomer, the great Derby star, to Southampton.

> **Round 1**
> **Jan 28 v New Brompton (a) 1-0**
> *Hartley*
> Robinson; Meehan, Durber, Meston, Haynes, Petrie, Nicol, Wood, Hartley, Keay, Robertson.
> *Att: 5,000*
> **Round 2**
> **Feb 11 v Notts County (a) 1-0**
> *Hartley*
> Robinson; Meehan, Durber, Meston, Haynes, Petrie, Nicol, Wood, Hartley, Keay, Robertson.
> *Att: 18,000*
> **Round 3**
> **Feb 25 v Derby County (h) 1-2**
> *Nicol*
> Robinson; Meehan, Durber, Meston, Haynes, Petrie, Nicol, Wood, Hartley, Keay, Robertson.
> *Att: 14,000*

> *In November 1898, referee Mr Saywell mistakenly ended the Millwall-Saints Southern League match ten minutes early with Saints leading 4-1. Realising his error he tried to bring the team back but the crowd had invaded the pitch and refused to disperse. Millwall were fined £5 — later rescinded on appeal — and the match was completed some five months later, before a Western League game at The Dell, with no further score.*

> *Arthur Chadwick was the first Saints player to be sent off in a League match, when he was dismissed at Sheppey in January 1899.*

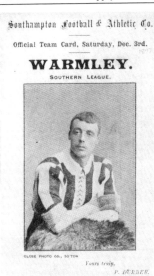

Official team card for the visit of Warmley on 3 December 1898. Saints won 6-0 and Warmley withdrew from the Southern League later that season.

Tom Nicol scores the first-ever FA Cup goal at The Dell, against Derby County on 25 February 1899.

1898-99
Southern League

	Date		Opponent	Result	Scorers	Buchanan R	Chadwick A	Dewar G	Durber P	Fairgrave W	Hartley A	Haynes H	Keay W	McKenzie J	McLean D	McLeod R	Meehan P	Meston S	Nicol TH	Petrie R	Robertson JT	Robinson JW	Seeley G	Smith T	Stevens D	Wood H	Yates J
Sep	3	(h)	Brighton U	W 4-1	Keay, Hartley, McKenzie, Smith		5				9	3	10	11					4	2	6	1		7		8	
	17	(h)	New Brompton	L 0-2			5			7	9	3	10						4	2	6	1	11			8	
	24	(a)	Gravesend	W 2-1	Hartley, Petrie	9			2		10	11						6	4	3	5	1		7		8	
Oct	1	(h)	Millwall	W 2-0	Wood 2						9	3		11				6	4	2	5	1		7	8	10	
	8	(h)	Royal Artillery	W 4-1	Hartley, McKenzie, Meston, Wood						9			11			6	3	4	2	5	1		7	8	10	
	15	(h)	Reading	D 0-0			5				9	3		11					4	2	6	1		7	8	10	
	22	(a)	Swindon T	D 1-1	Hartley	8	5		2		9	3		11					4		6	1		7		10	
Nov	5	(h)	Gravesend	W 4-1	Hartley, Keay, McKenzie, Wood		5		2		9	3	10	11					4		6	1		7		8	
	12	(h)	Sheppy U	W 6-0	Wood 3, Hartley 2, Keay		5	2			9	3	10	11					4		6	1		7		8	
	26	(a)	Millwall *	W 4-1	Hartley 2, Chadwick, Keay		5	6	2		9	3	10						4		1	7	11			8	
Dec	17	(a)	Royal Artillery	D 1-1	Keay		5	4			9	3	10					2			6	1	11	7		8	
	24	(h)	Swindon T	W 4-1	Wood 2, Hartley, Keay		5				9	3	10					2	4		6	1	11	7		8	
	26	(h)	Tottenham H	D 1-1	Wood		5	4			9	3	10					2			6	1	11	7		8	
	31	(h)	Bedminster	W 1-0	Wood		5		6		9	3						2	4		1	1	11	7	8	10	
Jan	7	(a)	Sheppy U	L 1-2	Seeley		5		6		9	3						2	4		1	1	11	7	10	8	
Feb	18	(a)	Reading	L 0-2				3			9	5						2	4	7	6	11	1		8	10	
Mar	11	(h)	Bristol C	W 4-1	Hartley 3, Nicol			3			9	5				8		2	4	7	6	1	11			10	
	18	(h)	Chatham	W 4-1	Hartley, McLean, Wood, opp own goal			3			9	5		10	11			2	4		6	1			8		7
	27	(a)	Brighton U	W 2-0	Stevens 2		5	3			9	6			11			2	4			1			8	10	7
	31	(a)	Tottenham H	W 1-0	Wood		5	3			9				11			2	4		6	1			8	10	7
Apr	4	(a)	Bedminster	L 1-2	Haynes		5	3			9	11			4			2			6	1			8	10	7
	22	(a)	Chatham	W 2-1	McLean, Wood		5	3				11		9	8			2	4		6	1				10	7
	24	(a)	New Brompton	D 1-1	Haynes		5	3				11		9	8			2	4		6	1				10	7
	29	(a)	Bristol C	W 4-3	Wood 2, Chadwick, McLean		5	3				6		9	8			2	4		11	1				10	7
				App		2	17	4	16	1	21	21	10	6	8	3	15	18	8	9	19	24	8	14	9	24	7
				Goals			2				14	2	6	3	3			1	1	1	1		1	1	2	16	

*Played ten minutes short. Match completed on 12 April 1899.

1 own-goal

Standing (left to right): Hamer (trainer), G.Payne (director), S.Meston, H.Ashton (director), P.Meehan, Dr Stancomb (chairman), J.W.Robinson, P.Durber, A.A.Wood (director), A.Chadwick, H.Haynes, W.Dawson. Sitting: E.Arnfield (secretary), J.Yates, R.McLeod, H.Wood, D.McLean, J.T.Robertson, W.Joyce.

	P	W	D	L	F	A	Pts
Southampton	24	15	5	4	54	24	35
Bristol C	24	15	3	6	55	33	33
Millwall	24	12	6	6	59	35	30
Chatham	24	10	8	6	32	23	28
Reading	24	9	8	7	31	24	26
New Brompton	24	10	5	9	38	30	25
Tottenham H	24	10	4	10	40	36	24
Bedminster	24	10	4	10	35	39	24
Swindon T	24	9	5	10	43	49	23
Brighton U	24	9	2	13	37	48	20
Gravesend	24	7	5	12	42	52	19
Sheppey U	24	5	3	16	23	53	13
RA Portsmouth	24	4	4	16	17	69	12

On 1 April 1899, Saints played a friendly against the Corinthians with C.B.Fry turning out for the Corinthians. Fry needlessly charged Robinson, the Southampton goalkeeper, late in the first half and broke his own cheekbone. After receiving treatment from the Saints' Dr Bencraft, he had to be helped from the pitch. Fry's over-zealousness meant the Corinthians were down to ten men, but despite this they still managed to score in the second half to win 2-1.

In 1898-9 Southampton finished runners-up in the United League, six points behind Millwall from whom they took three points during the season. Saints' biggest win was over the previous seasons champions, Luton, who they beat 8-0 at The Dell. Twelve days after hammering Luton, Saints were themselves hit for eight without reply by Rushden.

Jack Robertson joined Saints in the close season of 1898, shortly after winning his first cap for Scotland.

1899-1900

SOUTHERN League Champions for three consecutive seasons, Saints began the 1899-1900 season in confident mood. Jack Farrell had returned from New Brighton, Arthur Turner, the only Hampshire-born player in the team, signed from Camberley St Michael's, and Alf Milward was recruited from Everton.

With the defence unchanged, Saints started well and by February they were top of the table. Then they became embroiled in a hugely successful FA Cup run and their League form suffered. The title was relinquished and Southampton finished third behind Tottenham and Portsmouth.

FA Cup

THE disappointment of losing their 1898 FA Cup semi-final to Nottingham Forest still rankled the Saints but now, two years later, they at last made it to the Cup Final.

Their march began with a splendid 3-0 victory over Everton, when the former Goodison Park player, Alf Milward, scored two goals against his old club. Newcastle, who already had memories of FA Cup defeat at Southampton, were the next visitors to The Dell but they must have felt confident when Saints' centre-forward, Farrell, dislocated his collarbone and left the pitch. Yet the gods were on the side of the Saints when Derby referee, Alf Kingscott, abandoned the game after 50 minutes due to a heavy snowstorm.

When the game was staged again the following Saturday, Saints could bring in Roddy McLeod to replace the injured Farrell. McLeod seized upon the opportunity and scored twice in Saints' easy 4-1 win. The Scot was on target again seven days later, with a goal in the 2-1 third-round defeat of West Brom.

Southampton now faced Southern League rivals, Millwall, in the semi-final at the Crystal Palace, but a 30,000 crowd saw a disappointing goalless draw. When the sides met again the following Wednesday at Reading's Elm Park, Milward returned to his electrifying best and his two goals helped Saints to their first appearance in an FA Cup Final.

Thus, only 15 years after their formation, Southampton had reached the showpiece of the English game. It was testimony to the positive support of the club's directors in Saints' early days. Some 4,000 fans made the trip to the Crystal Palace on 21 April 1900, hoping to see an end to the monopoly which the northern clubs had held on the FA Cup in recent times.

Saints support came not only from Southampton, for they were the first Southern League club to reach the Cup Final and as such they carried the hopes of all southern professional clubs. But they failed to produce anything like their best form, conceding three goals in the first 20 minutes to eventually lose 4-0.

Now the recriminations began. Rumours swept the town and one particular story gained credence — that there had been internal bickering between the English and Scottish players in the Southampton side. It was said to revolve around the centre-forward position — the English had wanted Farrell to play; the Scots favoured McLeod who did play. Whatever the reasons for such an inept performance, it was a sad end to what should have been Saints' finest day.

Round 1
Jan 27 v Everton (h) 3-0
Milward 2, Turner
Robinson; Meehan, Durber, Meston, A.Chadwick, Petrie, Turner, Yates, Farrell, Wood, Milward.
Att: 10,000
Round 2
Feb 17 v Newcastle United (h) 4-1
McLeod 2, Yates, Turner
Robinson; Meehan, Durber, Meston, A.Chadwick, Petrie, Turner, Yates, McLeod, Wood, Milward.
Att: 8,000
Round 3
Feb 24 v West Bromwich Albion (h) 2-1
Turner, McLeod
Robinson; Meehan, Durber, Meston, A.Chadwick, Petrie, Turner, Yates, McLeod, Wood, Milward.
Att: 9,000
Semi-final
Mar 24 v Millwall (at Crystal Palace) 0-0
Robinson; Meehan, Durber, Meston, A.Chadwick, Petrie, Turner, Yates, Farrell, Wood, Milward.
Att: 30,000
Replay
Mar 28 v Millwall (at Elm Park) 3-0
Milward 2, Yates
Robinson; Meehan, Durber, Meston, A.Chadwick, Petrie, Turner, Yates, Farrell, Wood, Milward.
Att: 10,000
Final
Apr 21 v Bury (at Crystal Palace) 0-4
Robinson; Meehan, Durber, Meston, A.Chadwick, Petrie, Turner, Yates, Farrell, Wood, Milward.
Att: 75,000

Saints' FA Cup run in 1899-1900 helped turn a £1,000 deficit into a profit of £31.

Saints' outside-left Alf Milward makes a fine run at the Bury defence during the 1900 FA Cup Final.

A Bury throw-in at the Crystal Palace.

1899-1900
Southern League

Date	Opponent	Result	Scorers	Cavendish S	Chadwick A	Crabbe W	Durber P	Englefield F	Farrell J	French J	Gill	Greenless D	Haynes H	Joyce J	Keay W	McLeod R	Meehan P	Meston S	Milward A	Petrie R	Robinson J	Scott	Smith V	Turner A	Wood H	Yates J
Sep 2	(h) New Brompton	W 6-2	Milward 2, Yates 2, Farrell, Wood		5		3		9							8	2	4	11	6	1				10	7
9	(a) Gravesend	D 2-2	Farrell, Milward		5		3		9							8	2	4	11	6	1				10	7
16	(h) Swindon T	L 0-1			5		3		9							8	2	4	11	6	1				10	7
23	(a) Bristol C	W 3-1	Milward 2, Farrell		5		3		9							8	2	4	11	6	1				10	7
Oct 14	(a) Millwall	W 2-0	Milward, Turner		5		3		9								2	4	11	6	1			7	10	8
21	(h) Queen's Park R	W 5-1	Milward 2, Yates 2, Turner		5		3		9			4	1				2		11	6				7	10	8
Nov 4	(h) Reading	L 0-2			5		3		9				1				2	4	11	6				7	10	8
11	(a) Sheppey U	W 2-0	Meston 2		5		3		9				1	10		8	2	4	11	6				7		
25	(a) Bedminster	W 2-0	Farrell, Milward		5		3	6	9			4					2		11		1			7	10	8
Dec 2	(h) Bristol R	W 4-0	Milward 2, Farrell, McLeod		5		3		10							9	2	4	11	6	1			7		8
16	(h) Thames Iron	W 3-1	Milward 2, Turner		5		3		9			4					2		11	6	1			7	10	8
20	(h) Chatham	W 9-0	Turner 4, Farrell, Milward, Petrie, Wood, Yates		5		3		9								2	4	11	6	1			7	10	8
26	(h) Tottenham H	W 3-1	Farrell 2, Milward		5		3		9			2						4	11	6	1			7	10	8
30	(a) New Brompton	W 2-1	Farrell, Milward		5		3		9			2						4	11	6	1			7	10	8
Jan 6	(h) Gravesend	W 8-0	Farrell 2, Milward 2, Cavendish, Chadwick, Meehan, Yates	10	5		3		9								2	4	11	6	1			7		8
13	(a) Swindon T *	L 1-2	Meston	9		2	3						6	5	1	10		4	11				8	7		
Mar 3	(a) Chatham	L 0-1		5			3					2				9		4	11	6	1			7	10	8
10	(a) Reading	L 0-2			5		3									9	2	4	11	6	1			7	10	8
17	(h) Sheppey U	W 5-0	Milward 2, Wood 2, Farrell		5		3		9	2			1			8		4	11	6					10	7
31	(h) Bedminster	W 3-2	Milward 2, McLeod				3		9	5		6				8	2	4	11		1			7	10	
Apr 7	(a) Bristol R	W 3-1	McLeod, Wood, Yates				3			5		6	1			9	2	4	11					7	10	8
9	(a) Thames Iron	L 1-4	McLeod		5		3	4								9	2	6	11		1			7	10	8
13	(a) Tottenham H	L 0-2			5		3									9	2	4	11	6	1			7	10	8
14	(h) Portsmouth	L 0-2			5		3		9								2	4	11	6	1			7	10	8
16	(a) Portsmouth	L 0-2			5		3		9								2	4	11	6	1			7	10	8
23	(h) Bristol C	W 4-1	Milward 2, McLeod, Wood		5		3		9							8	2	4	11	6	1				10	7
25	(h) Millwall	W 2-1	McLeod, Yates		5							6				9	2	4	11		1	7	3		10	8
28	(a) Queen's Park R	L 0-1			5		3		9			6	1			8	2	4	11						10	7
App				3	24	1	27	1	21	3	1	8	4	7	1	17	21	27	28	21	21	1	2	20	24	25
Goals				1	1				12							6	1	3	24	1				7	6	8

*Played at Reading due to the closure of Swindon's ground.

1899 team with silk banner presented to the club in 1898 by the Southern League for winning the Championship in three successive seasons. Back row (left to right): E.Arnfield (secretary), W.Dawson (trainer), S.Meston, H.Haynes, A.Chadwick, J.Robinson, D.Greenless, P.Meehan, P.Durber, E.C.Jarvis (director). Bottom: A.Turner, R.McLeod, J.Yates, J.Farrell, H.Wood, R.Petrie, A.Milward.

	P	W	D	L	F	A	Pts
Tottenham H	28	20	4	4	67	26	44
Portsmouth	28	20	1	7	58	28	41
Southampton	28	17	1	10	70	33	35
Reading	28	15	2	11	41	28	32
Swindon T	28	15	2	11	50	42	32
Bedminster	28	13	2	13	44	35	28
Millwall	28	12	3	13	36	37	27
Queen's Park R	28	12	2	14	49	57	26
Bristol C	28	9	7	12	43	47	25
Bristol R	28	11	3	14	46	55	25
New Brompton	28	9	6	13	39	49	24
Gravesend	28	10	4	14	38	58	24
Chatham	28	10	3	15	38	58	23
Thames Ironworks	28	8	5	15	30	45	21
Sheppey U	28	3	7	18	24	66	13

Saints competed in the Southern District Combination in 1899-1900, finishing sixth out of nine clubs. They had a particularly bad end to the season, losing five of their last six games and conceding 13 goals and scoring only three.

Robinson is left helpless as Bury score again.

27

1900-01

IRONICALLY, Jack Farrell and Roddy McLeod, the two men alleged to be at the heart of the row which turned Saints' 1900 FA Cup Final appearance into such a catastrophe for the club, had both left Southampton by the start of the following season.

Harry Wood became the makeshift centre-forward early in the campaign, with W.Toman taking over later in the season as Saints fought hard to redeem themselves in the eyes of their supporters. Edgar Chadwick took over from Wood at inside-left and resumed a partnership with Alf Milward that had been described as 'the best in the League' when the two were starring for Everton.

Two new defenders came into the side, men who were both to catch the eye. Right-back C.B.Fry, who played five times,

was already a distinguished cricketer and long-jumper, and he was to establish an uncanny understanding with Molyneux; the other newcomer was half-back Bert Lee who came as a triallist from Poole Town. It was a shame that Saints could not have a man of Fry's stature in their side regularly, but even to have him on their books was an immense boost. Lee, on the other hand, was able to devote all his energies to the club and he went on to give Saints years of valuable service.

With such a talented side, Saints naturally led the way, fighting off a challenge from Bristol City to become Southern League Champions for the fourth time in five years. Edgar Chadwick (14 goals) and Milward (12) led the scorers and although the season ended with a 3-0 defeat at Kettering, by then the title was already in Southampton's grasp.

FA Cup

FOR the second consecutive year, Everton were drawn as Southampton's first-round opponents in the FA Cup. This time, however, they proved much tougher opposition.

The game was originally due to take place on 26 January but all football was postponed that day following the death of Queen Victoria. By the time the game was staged, a fortnight later, both Harry Wood and Arthur Chadwick were unable to play because of injury.

Saints struggled and although Edgar Chadwick gave them a half-time lead, they conceded three goals in the second half. The scorer of Everton's final goal was Joe Turner, the former Saints player who had joined the Merseysiders from Stoke. The following year, Turner was back with Saints and playing for them in another FA Cup Final.

> **Round 1**
> **Feb 9 v Everton (h) 1-3**
> *E.Chadwick*
> Robinson; Fry, Molyneux, Meston, Killean, Lee, Turner, Yates, Toman, E.Chadwick, Milward.
> *Att: 12,000*

> The 1900-01 season saw the first and so far only full international played at The Dell when England met Ireland in March. Southampton provided three players — Robinson, Fry and Arthur Turner, for the England team.

> At the conclusion of the season the Saints embarked on their first foreign tour, taking in Belgium, Austria and Hungary. The standard of the teams in Europe was not good in those days and Saints won all six matches, scoring 44 goals and conceding three.

> A decline in attendances meant Saints made a loss of £740 on the season and the dwindling crowds were partially blamed on the imposition of the 'shilling gate' for certain matches, felt to be unreasonable by the Southampton public.

The great athlete C.B.Fry made his Southern League debut for Southampton in 1900-01 and also played for England at The Dell.

Alf Milward was already an experienced First Division player and an England international when he joined Saints, resuming his lethal partnership with Edgar Chadwick (right).

1900-01
Southern League

Date	Opponent	Result	Scorers	Blackburn A	Cavendish S	Chadwick A	Chadwick E	French J	Fry CB	Harrison F	Killean F	Lee EA	Meston S	Milward A	Molyneux G	Moger HH	Paddington A	Robinson JW	Sharp B	Toman W	Turner A	Waller WH	Wood H	Yates J
Sep 1	(a) Luton T	W 4-3	Turner 2, E.Chadwick, Yates	2		5	10						4	11	3				6		7	1	9	8
15	(a) West Ham U	L 0-2		2		5	10						4	11	3			1	6		7		9	8
22	(a) Portsmouth	D 0-0		2			10	5					4	11	3			1	6	9	7			8
29	(a) New Brompton	W 1-0	E.Chadwick	2			10	5					4	11	3			1	6	9	7			8
Oct 6	(h) Bristol R	W 5-3	E.Chadwick 2, Milward, Toman, Wood	2			10	5					4	11	3			1	6	9	7			8
13	(h) Reading	W 1-0	Toman	2			10					5	4	11	3		6	1		9	7			8
20	(h) Kettering T	W 4-3	Lee, Meston, Milward, E.Chadwick	2			10					5	4	11	3		6	1		9	7			8
27	(h) Gravesend	W 6-0	Turner 2, Wood 2, A.Chadwick, E.Chadwick			5	10					2	4	11	3			1	6		7		9	8
Nov 3	(h) Millwall	W 2-1	E.Chadwick, Wood	2		5	10						4	11	3			1	6	9	7			8
10	(a) Queen's Park R	W 1-0	Turner	2		5	10					6	4	11	3			1			7		8	9
24	(h) Bristol C	W 2-1	E.Chadwick, Lee			5	10					6	4	11	3	1			2		7		9	8
Dec 1	(a) Swindon T	L 1-2	E.Chadwick			5	10					6	4	11	3	1			2		7		9	8
8	(h) Watford	W 1-0	Wood			5	10					6	4	11	3	1			2		7		9	8
17	(h) Luton T	W 5-0	Milward 3, E.Chadwick, Turner			5	10					6	4	11	3				2		7	1	9	8
26	(h) Tottenham H	W 3-1	E.Chadwick, Toman, Wood			5	10				2	6	4	11	3			1		9	7			8
30	(a) West Ham U	W 3-2	Meston, Milward, Wood			5	10				2	6	4	11	3			1			7		9	8
Jan 12	(h) New Brompton	W 5-0	Wood 2, E.Chadwick, Milward, Toman			5	10					6	4	11	3	1			2	9	7			8
19	(a) Bristol R	D 0-0			2	5	10					6	4	11	3			1		9	7			8
Feb 16	(a) Gravesend	W 4-0	Toman 2, E.Chadwick, Turner				10					5	4	11	3		6	1	2	9	7			8
23	(a) Millwall	L 0-1				5	10					6	4	11	3			1	2	9	7			8
Mar 2	(h) Queen's Park R	W 5-1	Milward 3, E.Chadwick, Toman				10		5			6	4	11	3			1	2	9			8	7
16	(a) Bristol C	D 1-1	Sharp				10		5	2			4	11	3			1	6	9			8	7
23	(a) Swindon T	L 0-1				5	10					6	4	11	3			1	2	9			8	7
30	(a) Watford	D 1-1	Wood			5	10					6	4	11	3			1	2	9			8	7
Apr 5	(a) Tottenham H	L 0-1				10			5		2		4	11	3			1	6	9			8	7
6	(h) Portsmouth	W 2-0	Milward 2			5	10					6	4	11	3			1	2	9			8	7
8	(h) Reading	D 0-0				5	10				7	6	4	11	3			1	2	9			8	
10	(a) Kettering T	L 0-3				5	10					6	4	11	3			1	2	9			8	7
App				9	1	19	27	3	5	1	2	21	28	28	28	4	3	22	22	19	20	2	27	17
Goals						1	14					2	2	12					1	7	7		10	1

Standing (left to right): Unknown, E.Arnfield (secretary), S.Meston, A.Lee, A.Blackburn, J.W.Robinson, A.Chadwick, G.Molyneux, B.Sharp, W.Dawson (trainer). Sitting: A.Turner, J.Yates, H.Wood, W.Toman, E.Chadwick, J.French, A.Milward.

	P	W	D	L	F	A	Pts
Southampton	28	18	5	5	58	26	41
Bristol C	28	17	5	6	54	27	39
Portsmouth	28	17	4	7	56	32	38
Millwall	28	17	2	9	55	32	36
Tottenham H	28	16	4	8	55	33	36
West Ham U	28	14	5	9	40	28	33
Bristol R	28	14	4	10	46	35	32
Queen's Park R	28	11	4	13	43	48	26
Luton T	28	11	2	15	43	49	24
Reading	28	8	8	12	24	25	24
Kettering T	28	7	9	12	33	46	23
New Brompton	28	7	5	16	34	51	19
Gravesend	28	6	7	13	22	85	19
Watford	28	6	4	18	24	52	16
Swindon T	28	3	8	17	19	47	14

Southampton finished seventh in the Western League in 1900-01. Portsmouth won the title of the nine-team league and Saints lost both of their games to them.

Goalkeeper Jack Robinson won five England caps during his stay at The Dell.

1901-02

SAINTS found themselves without some key players for the new season when Milward joined New Brompton, Arthur Chadwick signed for Portsmouth, and Toman returned to Everton. Lesser performers like Blackburn and Sharp also decided to seek new pastures and, despite the arrival of Bowman, Brown and Henderson, and the return of Joe Turner from Everton, Saints were left with their smallest-ever professional squad.

Yet, despite all this, Southampton embarked upon another fine season although it was the FA Cup, not the Southern League, which brought rewards. Yet again, a successful Cup run saw Saints release their hold on the Championship, which this time went to Portsmouth, but there was the highlight of Saints' record League win in the very last match of 1901 when they thrashed Northampton Town 11-0. Albert Brown, who had arrived at The Dell that very year, scored seven times, a feat which is still Saints' record individual score in a League game.

FA Cup

SOUTHAMPTON Football Club confirmed their growing reputation with a series of quite brilliant performances in the FA Cup. The run began with a superb victory over Spurs, the Cup holders, and ended in the Final when only last-ditch defending by Sheffield United denied Saints their first Cup triumph.

It took Saints three games to overcome Tottenham, the second replay at Reading's snow-covered Elm Park bringing Southampton victory when they capitalised on two errors by the Spurs' defence.

Five days later, Saints met Liverpool in the second round. Any reservations that the Southampton players would be jaded were soon pushed aside and one newspaper report said that 'Saints stepped on to the Anfield arena, lively as kittens'. They gave a superb performance to win by the astonishing scoreline of 4-1, overcoming a First Division club on its own ground.

The third round tie against Bury was a real thriller. Injuries to Wood and Joe Turner meant that the Saints were down to nine men and defending desperately with the score at 2-2. Indeed, Bury forced seven successive corners and the Saints' best hopes were for a replay when Brown collected a rebound and sprinted towards the Bury goal with almost all the Shakers' players in Saints' half.

In full flight Brown unleashed a shot of such power that, after hitting the woodwork, it rebounded over his own head. Luckily, Edgar Chadwick had decided to follow up and he trapped the ball, feinted to shoot one way, then coolly planted the ball in the other corner.

A revenge victory over Bury was sweet, and a semi-final win over Nottingham Forest was sweeter still. Forest had knocked Saints out of an earlier semi-final and at the end of 90 minutes in this one the score's were level. Brown put Saints ahead from the penalty spot in extra-time, then added a third, seconds from time, 'a wonderful goal with a screw shot from an oblique angle'.

Into their second Final in three years, Saints met Sheffield United at the Crystal Palace. United had lost the previous season's Final to Spurs and Saints sent Harry Woods to 'spy' on them in their semi-final against Derby. Southampton overcame a scare when Fry became ill — he recovered in time to play — and after falling behind, equalised through Wood, although the Blades protested fiercely that he was offside.

The day of the replay was bitterly cold and after only two minutes, Robinson slipped to allow Hedley in for United's first goal. Brown equalised in the second half, after some clever footwork from Joe Turner, but although they pressed hard, Southampton could not find the winner and six minutes from time, Robinson made another costly error and Barnes gratefully walked the ball into an empty net.

Round 1
Jan 25 v Tottenham Hotspur (a) 1-1
Bowman
Robinson; Fry, Molyneux, Meston, Bowman, Lee, A.Turner, Wood, Brown, E.Chadwick, J.Turner.
Att: 20,000
Replay
Feb 1 v Tottenham Hotspur (h) 2-2
E.Chadwick, J.Turner
Robinson; Fry, Molyneux, Meston, Bowman, Lee, A.Turner, Wood, Brown, E.Chadwick, J.Turner.
Att: 10,000
Second Replay
Feb 3 v Tottenham Hotspur (at Elm Park, Reading) 2-1
A.Turner, Brown
Robinson; Fry, Molyneux, Meston, Bowman, Paddington, A.Turner, Wood, Brown, E.Chadwick, J.Turner.
Att: 6,000
Round 2
Feb 8 v Liverpool (a) 4-1
E.Turner 2, J.Turner, Lee
Robinson; Fry, Molyneux, Meston, Bowman, Lee, A.Turner, Wood, Brown, E.Chadwick, J.Turner.
Att: 20,000
Round 3
Feb 22 v Bury (a) 3-2
Wood, E.Chadwick, J.Turner
Robinson; Fry, Molyneux, Meston, Bowman, Lee, A.Turner, Wood, Brown, E.Chadwick, J.Turner.
Att: 25,000
Semi-final
Mar 15 v Nottingham Forest (at White Hart Lane) 3-1
Brown 2, E.Chadwick
Robinson; Fry, Molyneux, Meston, Bowman, Lee, A.Turner, Brown, E.Chadwick, J.Turner.
Att: 30,000
Final
Apr 19 v Sheffield United (at the Crystal Palace) 1-1
Wood
Robinson; Fry, Molyneux, Meston, Bowman, Lee, A.Turner, Wood, Brown, E.Chadwick, J.Turner.
Att: 74,479
Replay
Apr 28 v Sheffield United (at the Crystal Palace) 1-2
Brown
Robinson; Fry, Molyneux, Meston, Bowman, Lee, A.Turner, Wood, Brown, E.Chadwick, J.Turner.
Att: 40,000

Sheffield United's winning goal in the Final. Robinson had made a hash of Needham's shot and Barnes walked the ball home.

30

1901-02
Southern League

Date	Venue/Opponent	Res	Score	Scorers	Bowman T	Brown A	Cavendish S	Chadwick E	Fry CB	George	Harrison F	Henderson W	Howland CAS	Lee EA	McDonald A	Meston S	Moger HH	Molyneux G	Northey G	Paddington A	Robinson JW	Small H	Smith V	Triggs W	Turner A	Turner J	Whiting R	Wilson GP	Wood H
Sep 7	(h) New Brompton	D	1-1	A.Turner	6	9		10				2		5	8	4		3			1				7	11			
14	(a) Northampton T	W	2-1	Chadwick, McDonald	6	9		10				2		5	8	4		3			1				7	11			
21	(h) Watford	W	5-0	McDonald 4, J.Turner	6			10				2		5	8	4		3			1				7	11			9
Oct 12	(a) Portsmouth A	D	2-2	Brown, Harrison	5	9		10	2		11			6		4		3			1				7				8
19	(h) Swindon T	W	6-1	Wood 2, Chadwick, Harrison, Meston, A.Turner	5			10	2		11			6		4	1	3							7			9	8
26	(h) Brentford	W	1-0	J.Turner	5			10	2					6		4	1	3							7	11		9	8
Nov 2	(h) Portsmouth	L	3-4	Chadwick 2, J.Turner	5			10	2					6		4	1	3							7	11		9	8
9	(a) Luton T	W	2-0	Brown, Meston	5	9		10	2					6		4		3			1				7	11			8
16	(h) Millwall	W	3-0	Brown 2, J.Turner	5	9			2					6	10	4		3			1				7	11			8
23	(a) Queen's Park R	W	1-0	Brown	5	9			2		11			6	8	4		3			1				7	10			
30	(h) Reading	W	2-0	J.Turner, Wood	5	9		10	2					6		4		3			1				7	11			8
Dec 12	(h) West Ham U	W	4-0	J.Turner 2, Brown, Wood	5	9		10	2					6		4		3			1				7	11			8
14	(a) Brentford	D	1-1	Brown	5	9		10			7	2		6		4		3			1					11			8
21	(a) New Brompton	L	0-3		5	9		10				2		6		4		3			1				7	11			8
26	(h) Tottenham H	W	1-0	Wood	5	9		10	2					6		4		3			1				7	11			8
28	(h) Northampton T	W	11-0	Brown 7, Meston 2, Harrison, A.Turner	5	9		10			11	2		6		4		3			1				7				8
Jan 4	(a) Watford	W	2-1	Brown, Wood	5	9		10			7	2		6		4		3			1					11			8
18	(h) Wellingborough T	W	3-0	A.Turner 2, Brown	5	9		10				2		6		4		3			1				7	11			8
Feb 1	(a) Swindon T	D	0-0			9		10			11	2				4		3		6	1			5	7				8
15	(h) Kettering T	W	3-1	A.Turner, Wood	5		9	10				2						3		6	1				7	11	4		8
Mar 1	(a) Millwall	D	1-1	Brown	5	9		8			11	2		6				3			1	4		10	7				
5	(a) Bristol R	L	0-1			9		10			11	2	3	6							1	4	8	5	7				
8	(h) Queen's Park R	W	4-2	Brown 2, Harrison, A.Turner	5	9		8			11	2		6		4		3			1			10	7				
19	(a) Reading	L	0-2		5	9		10		7		2		6		4		3			1					11			8
22	(a) West Ham U	L	1-2	Brown		9					11	2		6	5	4		3			1			10	7				8
28	(a) Tottenham H	D	2-2	A.Turner, J.Turner	5	9	8	10				2		6		4		3			1				7	11			
29	(h) Bristol R	W	6-0	Brown 3, Cavendish, Harrison, J.Turner	5	9	8	10			7	2		6		4		3								11	1		
Apr 2	(a) Kettering T	L	1-2	Wood	5	9		10			7	2			4			3		6	1					11			8
5	(a) Wellingborough T	W	2-1	Brown, Wood	5	9		10			11	2			4			3		6	1				7				8
9	(h) Luton T	W	1-0	Brown	5	9		10			11	2		6		4		3			1				7				
App					27	25	5	25	9	1	15	21	1	27	5	26	3	27	1	7	26	4	2	2	25	20	1	3	22
Goals						25	1	4			5				5	4									9	9			9

Back row (left to right): C.B.Fry, H.H.Moger, G.Molyneux. Middle: S.Meston, H.Wood, T.Bowman, A.Chadwick, E.A.Lee, Dawson (trainer). Seated: J.Turner, A.Brown, F.Harrison.

	P	W	D	L	F	A	Pts
Portsmouth	30	20	7	3	67	24	47
Tottenham H	30	18	6	6	61	22	42
Southampton	30	18	6	6	71	28	42
West Ham U	30	17	6	7	45	28	40
Reading	30	16	7	7	57	29	39
Millwall	30	13	6	11	48	31	32
Luton T	30	11	10	9	31	36	32
Kettering T	30	12	5	13	44	39	29
Bristol R	30	12	5	13	43	39	29
New Brompton	30	10	7	13	39	38	27
Northampton T	30	11	5	14	51	62	27
Queen's Park R	30	8	7	15	34	56	23
Watford	30	9	4	17	36	60	22
Wellingborough T	30	9	4	17	34	72	22
Brentford	30	7	6	17	34	61	20
Swindon T	30	2	3	25	17	92	7

Action from the FA Cup semi-final against Nottingham Forest at White Hart Lane.

1902-03

SOUTHAMPTON'S directors made every effort to retain the complete 11 that figured in the previous season's great FA Cup run, but they were unsuccessful. Arthur Turner signed for Derby County where he teamed up with the legendary Steve Bloomer. Henderson also moved, to Everton, because he wanted regular first-team football and Fry's intermittent availability was frustrating his ambitions — although, as it turned out, Fry was to make only two appearances in 1902-03, both of them at centre-forward.

Edgar Chadwick and Brown also left the Saints, the latter joining Queen's Park Rangers, but new players included Tom Robertson, Jack Fitchett, Mark Bell, Dick Evans, Jack Fraser and Tommy Barlow.

Saints began the Southern League season in style, beating Brentford 6-0 with new man Feaser grabbing a hat-trick. From that moment on, Saints gave the other clubs hardly a backward glance as they stormed to yet another Championship. Only two games were lost (both to Tottenham) and the Saints scored 83 goals and conceded only 20. Although he played in only 13 games, Fred Harrison finished leading scorer with 17 goals, hotly pursued by Fraser (15), Joe Turner (14) and Wood (12).

In one game, against Watford just before Christmas, the Saints equalled their record League victory of 11-0, set against Northampton. In the New Year, Harrison soon proved to be a prolific goalscorer. In March he scored five at home to Wellingborough and in the home match against Northampton, a fortnight later, scored another five.

FA Cup

AFTER the previous season's exploits, anything short of winning the FA Cup was going to be an anticlimax but Saints disappointed their expectant fans by going out at the first hurdle, to Notts County, although it took the Midlanders three games before they proceeded to the next round.

In Nottingham, Saints created enough chances to win the game there and then but had to settle for a replay. "Wait 'till we get them back to the mousetrap — then we'll whack 'em," Meston was heard to comment after the game. The 'mousetrap' was the players nickname for The Dell but his optimism of catching Notts there was misplaced. Sixteen thousand fans saw County go in at half-time with a 2-0 lead under their belts.

That stunned Saints fans into silence but they were soon cheering again when Bell and Turner scored in the second half. Thereafter, Notts' goal underwent some fierce pressure but they held on and the teams went to St Andrew's, Birmingham, five days later for a second replay.

Early in the second half, Humphreys scored for the Nottingham club, then Barlow equalised after a scrimmage in the Notts' goalmouth. Extra-time was again needed but this time Notts found the goal that put them through to the next round.

Round 1
Feb 7 v Notts County (a) 0-0
Robinson; Robertson, Molyneux, Meston, Bowman, Lee, Turner, Wood, Fraser, Barlow, Bell.
Att: 15,000
Replay
Feb 11 v Notts County (h) 2-2
Turner, Bell
Robinson; Robertson, Molyneux, Lee, Bowman, Paddington, Turner, Wood, Fraser, Barlow, Bell.
Att: 16,734
Second Replay
Feb 16 v Notts County (at St Andrew's) 1-2
Barlow
Robinson; Robertson, Molyneux, Fitchett, Bowman, Lee, Turner, Wood, Fraser, Barlow, Bell.
Att: 20,000

Saints embarked on another foreign tour in 1902, this time taking in Denmark as well as Belgium, Austria and Hungary. All the games were won, two of them by scorelines of 15-0.

Fred Harrison had made his debut the previous season, but it was not until 1902-03 that he burst on the scene with 17 goals in only 13 Southern League games.

Saints skipper Harry Wood missed only two League games and finished with 12 goals.

Full-back Henderson left Saints in the 1902 close season. Frustrated at not enjoying a regular first-team place, he moved to Everton.

1902-03
Southern League

Date	Match	Result	Scorers	Barlow T	Bell M	Bowman T	Brown A	Bunday A	Evans R	Fitchett J	Fraser J	Fry CB	Harrison F	Hoare JH	Lee EA	Meston S	Moger HH	Molyneux G	Paddington A	Pike E	Robertson T	Robinson JW	Turner J	Wood H	Whiting R
Sep 6	(h) Brentford	W 6-0	Fraser 3, Barlow 2, Wood	10		5			7	4	9				6			3			2	1	11	8	
27	(h) Portsmouth	D 1-1	Fraser	10		5			7	4	9				6			3			2	1	11	8	
Oct 4	(a) New Brompton	W 2-1	Turner, Wood	10		5			7	4	9				6			3			2	1	11	8	
11	(h) Swindon T	W 1-0	Wood	10		5	9		7	4					6			3			2	1	11	8	
18	(a) Kettering T	D 1-1	Evans	8	7	5			11		9			4	6			3			2	1		10	
25	(h) Luton T	W 2-0	Bowman, Turner	10		5			7	4	9				6	2		3				1	11	8	
Nov 1	(a) Reading	W 1-1	Turner	10		5			7		9				6	4	1	3			2		11	8	
8	(h) Queen's Park R	W 2-0	Barlow, Evans	10	11	5			7		9				6	4	1	3			2			8	
15	(a) Millwall	W 3-1	Wood 2, Fraser	10		5			7		9				6	4	1	3			2		11	8	
22	(a) Wellingborough T	D 1-1	Evans	10		5			7		9				6	4	1	3			2		11	8	
29	(h) Bristol R	W 3-1	Barlow, Fraser, opp own goal	10		5			7		9				6	4	1	3			2		11	8	
Dec 6	(a) Northampton T	W 4-1	Wood 2, Barlow, Turner	10		5			7		9				6	4		3			2	1	11	8	
13	(h) Watford	W 11-0	Fraser 4, Bell 2, Turner 2, Wood 2, Robertson	10	7	5					9				6	4		3			2	1	11	8	
20	(a) Brentford	W 4-0	Evans, Fraser, Meston, Wood	10		5			7		9				6	4		3			2	1	11	8	
25	(a) West Ham U	W 2-1	Lee, Turner	10		5			7		9				6	4		3			2	1	11	8	
26	(h) Tottenham H	L 0-1		10		5			7		9				6	4		3			2	1	11	8	
Jan 10	(a) Portsmouth	W 3-0	Bell, Fraser, Wood	10	7	5					9				6	4		3			2	1	11	8	
17	(h) New Brompton	W 1-0	Fraser	10	7	5					9				6	4		3			2	1	11	8	
24	(a) Swindon T	D 1-1	Bell	10	11	5				4	9				6			3			2	1	7	8	
31	(h) Kettering T	D 3-3	Barlow, Harrison, Turner	10	8	5				4	9		11		6			3			2	1	7		
Feb 14	(h) Reading	W 4-1	Bell 2, Bunday, Fraser		11	5		9		8	10	7			6	4			2	3		1			
21	(a) Queens Park R	D 0-0			11	5					10		9		6		1	3	2				7	8	4
28	(h) Millwall	W 1-0	Harrison			5			7		10		9		6	4		3			2	1	11	8	
Mar 7	(h) Wellingborough T	W 5-0	Harrison 5			5			7		10		9		6	4		3			2	1	11	8	
14	(a) Bristol R	D 1-1				5			7		10		9		6	4		3			2	1	11	8	
21	(h) Northampton T	W 7-0	Harrison 5, Turner 2						7		10		9		6	4	1	3			2		11	8	5
28	(a) Watford	W 3-1	Harrison 2, Wood	6		5			7		10		9			4		3			2	1	11	8	
Apr 4	(a) Luton T	W 3-1	Evans 2, Turner			5			7		10		9	3	6	4					2	1	11	8	
10	(a) Tottenham H	L 1-2	Fraser			5			7		10		9		6	4		3			2	1	11	8	
13	(h) West Ham U	W 6-0	Harrison 2, Turner 3, Evans	6					7		10		9		2	5	4	3				1	11	8	
App				22	9	28	1	1	23	8	26	2	13	4	29	24	7	25	2	1	26	23	26	28	2
Goals				6	6	1		1	7		15		17		1	1					1		14	12	

1 own goal

	P	W	D	L	F	A	Pts
Southampton	30	20	8	2	83	20	48
Reading	30	19	7	4	72	30	45
Portsmouth	30	17	7	6	69	32	41
Tottenham H	30	14	7	9	47	31	35
Bristol R	30	13	8	9	46	34	34
New Brompton	30	11	11	8	37	35	33
Millwall	30	14	3	13	52	37	31
Northampton T	30	12	6	12	39	48	30
Queen's Park R	30	11	6	13	34	42	28
West Ham U	30	9	10	11	35	49	28
Luton T	30	10	7	13	43	44	27
Swindon T	30	10	7	13	38	46	27
Kettering T	30	8	11	11	33	40	27
Wellingborough T	30	11	3	16	36	56	25
Watford	30	6	4	20	35	87	16
Brentford	30	2	1	27	16	84	5

Back row (left to right): T.Robertson, J.W.Robinson, G.Molyneux. Middle row: W.Dawson (trainer), A.Brown, J.Fitchett, T.Bowman, A.Lee, M.Bell. Front: R.Evans, H.Wood (captain), J.Fraser, T.Barlow, J.Turner.

George Carter returned to develop the club's younger players.

> *Southampton finished 1902-03 in third place in the Western League with 20 points from 16 games.*

33

1903-04

SOUTHAMPTON won the Southern League title for the sixth time in ten seasons and, although their record was slightly inferior to the previous season's, the success was made that much more satisfying by the fact that Saints had become the side that everyone wanted to beat. In those circumstances, the team's ability to retain the shield was convincing proof of its excellence.

Clawley had returned from Tottenham Hotspur to replace Jack Robinson in goal — Robinson moved to Plymouth Argyle — whilst half-back Bert Houlker signed from Portsmouth. At first Houlker had difficulty settling into the Southampton team and he had particular problems in linking up with Molyneux, the full-back who played behind him, although both men had represented England the previous season.

Full-back Robertson met with a severe injury in the opening game of the season, at home to Luton, and he was sidelined for a couple of months, after which he struggled to recapture his old form.

With the Saints attack having its problems it was as well that the forward line, led by the admirable Fred Harrison, had lost none of their bite. Harrison learned much from playing alongside George Hedley and he had his best season to date. Harry Wood, too, although nearing the end of his distinguished career, was worth his place simply for his leadership and the advice he dispensed so freely to the younger players.

Saints' main challengers for the title were Pompey and Bristol Rovers but in March, Southampton beat both these clubs (Bristol by 6-1, incidentally) and so the title remained at The Dell. The one disappointing — and potentially disastrous — factor was that, out of nine penalties awarded, Saints managed to convert only three.

FA Cup

AFTER comfortably disposing of Burslem Port Vale in the FA Cup first round, Saints were drawn away to Bolton and found themselves battling on a Burnden Park pitch waterlogged by heavy rain that continued throughout the match.

Saints, without the injured Fraser and Evans, were a goal down after only 12 minutes but a few minutes later, Mouncher, who had been brought in to replace Fraser, scored with a left-foot shot. Saints were then awarded a penalty when Harrison was fouled, but Meston made a hash of the kick and the miss had a demoralising effect on the Saints' players.

From having a golden opportunity to take the lead in difficult conditions on an opponent's ground, Saints collapsed and conceded a further three goals. Bolton went on to reach the Final where they lost 1-0 to Manchester City.

> **Round 1**
> **Feb 6 v Burslem Port Vale (h) 3-0**
> J.Turner, Wood, Fraser
> Clawley; Roberston, Molyneux, Lee, Bowman, Meston, J.Turner, Hedley, Harrison, Wood, Fraser.
> Att: 9,000
> **Feb 20 v Bolton Wanderers (a) 1-4**
> Mouncher
> Clawley; Roberston, Molyneux, Lee, Bowman, Meston, J.Turner, Hedley, Harrison, Wood, Mouncher.
> Att: 15,000

> *Southampton's success in the Southern League meant that Sammy Meston picked up his sixth Southern League Championship medal. No other player in the game could boast such a feat.*

> *On a train to London, for a match against Tottenham Hotspur, Meston and Harry Wood were joined in their crowded compartment by two Spurs supporters who proceeded to discuss Wood in not particularly complimentary terms. They were unaware that the subject of their conversation was sitting with them. Meston, it was reported, was convulsed with laughter although Wood's reaction was not recorded.*

> *For the end of season tour, Saints became the first English team to tour Argentina. Southampton won many friends and so impressed the Argentinians that their government ordered that soccer be taught to all army regiments.*

Dick Evans

Joe Turner

Jack Fraser

1903-04
Southern League

Date		Opponent	Result	Scorers	Bowman T	Byrne M	Clawley G	Evans R	Fraser J	Harrison F	Hedley GA	Houlker AE	Lee EA	Meston S	Molyneux G	Mouncher F	Robertson T	Smoker	Spence G	Turner H	Turner J	Wood H
Sep 5	(h)	Luton T	D 1-1	Harrison	5		1	7	10	9			6	4	3		2				11	8
12	(a)	New Brompton	W 3-0	Evans, Lee, Wood	5		1	7	10	9			6	4	2		3				11	8
19	(h)	Kettering T	W 4-1	Evans 2, Harrison 2	5		1	7	10	9			6	4	2		3				11	8
21	(a)	Millwall	L 1-2	Harrison	5		1	7	10	9			6	4	2		3				11	8
26	(a)	Swindon T	D 1-1	Evans	5		1	7	10	9			6	4	2		3				11	8
Oct 3	(a)	Fulham	D 2-2	Harrison, Fraser	5		1	7	10	9			6	4	2		3				11	8
10	(h)	Millwall	W 3-1	Harrison 2, Evans	5		1	7	10	9	8	6		4	2		3				11	
17	(a)	Queen's Park R	W 3-0	Evans, Harrison, Hedley	5		1	7	10	9	8	6		4	2		3				11	
24	(h)	Plymouth A	L 3-5	Bowman, J.Turner 2	5		1	7	10	9	8	6		4	2		3				11	
31	(a)	Reading	W 2-1	Harrison, Hedley	5		1	7	10	9	8	6		4	2		3				11	
Nov 7	(h)	Wellingborough T	L 0-1		5		1		10	11	9	6		4	2		3	7				8
14	(a)	Bristol R	D 1-1	Evans	5		1	7	10	9			6	4	2		3		11			8
21	(h)	Brighton & HA	W 5-1	Hedley 2, Wood 2, Evans	5		1	7	11		9		6	4	3		2		10			8
28	(a)	Portsmouth	W 1-0	opp own goal	5		1	7	10	9	8		6	4	3		2		11			
Dec 7	(h)	Northampton T	W 5-1	Harrison 3, Fraser, J.Turner	5		1	7	10	9	8		6	4	3		2				11	
12	(a)	Northampton T	W 2-0	Hedley 2	5		1	7	10	9	8		6	4	3		2				11	
25	(a)	West Ham U	L 1-2	Meston	5		1	7		9	8		6	4	3		2				11	10
26	(h)	Tottenham H	W 1-0	Harrison	5		1		11	9	8		4	6	3		2		7			10
Jan 2	(a)	Luton T	L 0-1		5		1		10	9			4	6	3		2	7	8		11	
9	(h)	New Brompton	W 4-0	Hedley 2, Harrison, Spence	5		1			9	8		4	6	3		2		7		11	10
23	(h)	Swindon T	W 2-0	Hedley, Wood	5	1			11	9	8		4	6	3		2		7			10
30	(h)	Fulham	W 2-0	J.Turner, Wood	5	1			11	9	8			4	2		3		6		7	10
Feb 13	(h)	Queen's Park R	W 2-1	Hedley 2	5		1		11	9	8		4	6	3		2		7			10
27	(h)	Reading	D 1-1	Harrison	5		1			9	8		4	6	3	11	2		7			10
Mar 5	(a)	Wellingborough T	W 4-2	Harrison 2, J.Turner, Wood	5		1			9	8		4		3	11	2		6		7	10
9	(a)	Plymouth A	W 2-0	Harrison, Hedley	5		1			9	8		4		3		2		6	7	11	10
12	(h)	Bristol R	W 6-1	Harrison 3, H.Turner 2, Hedley	5		1			9	8		4		3	11	2		6	7		10
19	(a)	Brighton & HA	W 3-1	Harrison, Hedley, Wood	5		1			9	8		4		3	11	2		6	7		10
26	(h)	Portsmouth	W 2-0	Harrison 2	5		1			9	8		4		3	11	2		6	7		10
Apr 1	(a)	Tottenham H	L 1-2	Mouncher	5		1			9			6		3	7	2		4	8	11	10
2	(a)	Brentford	W 1-0		5		1			9			6		3	7	2		4	8	11	10
4	(h)	West Ham U	D 1-1	Harrison	5		1	7		9		6		4	2	11	3		10			8
6	(a)	Kettering T	W 4-0	Spence 2, Evans, Harrison	5		1	7		9		6		4	2	11	3		10			8
9	(h)	Brentford	W 1-0	Hedley	5	1		7		9	8		6	4	2		3				11	10
App					34	3	31	18	22	32	24	17	33	24	34	10	19	2	14	10	22	25
Goals					1			9	2	27	15		1	1			1		3	2	5	7

1 own-goal

Saints' 1903-04 line-up which retained the Southern League championship. Pictured with the shield, back row (left to right): Robertson, Byrne, Clawley, Molyneux. Middle row: Lee, Bowman, Hedley, Harrison, Houlker, Meston. Front row: W.Dawson (trainer), Evans, Spence, Wood (captain), Fraser, Turner.

	P	W	D	L	F	A	Pts
Southampton	34	22	6	6	75	30	50
Tottenham H	34	17	10	7	52	34	42
Bristol R	34	17	8	9	66	42	42
Portsmouth	34	17	7	9	40	37	41
Reading	34	14	13	7	48	35	41
Millwall	34	16	8	9	63	40	40
Luton T	34	14	12	8	38	33	40
Queen's Park R	34	14	11	8	51	36	39
Plymouth A	34	13	10	11	44	34	36
Fulham	34	9	12	13	34	35	30
Swindon T	34	9	11	14	29	42	29
West Ham U	34	10	7	17	39	43	27
Brentford	34	9	9	16	34	48	27
Wellingborough T	34	11	4	19	41	60	26
Northampton T	34	10	6	18	35	60	26
New Brompton	34	6	13	15	26	43	25
Brighton & HA	34	6	12	16	45	69	24
Kettering T	34	6	7	21	39	78	19

During the 1903-04 season, the Saints' stalwart, Harry Wood, received a benefit cheque from the club amounting to £250 5s. A friendly match against Aston Villa had realised 'gate' money of £106 5s 6d, whilst the rest was made up of donations from the Southampton public and his fellow professionals throughout the football world.

35

1904-05

SOUTHAMPTON's team failed to settle into any kind of rhythm in 1904-05 as there were many comings and goings. Arthur Turner returned from his travels and competed with the newly-signed Webb for the right-wing position, but neither man showed any consistency.

Harry Wood, who everyone thought of as an evergreen character, was now too old and his influence, especially on the younger members of the team, was sorely missed. On the left flank, Hedley and Fraser dovetailed well but Harrison, despite being top-scorer again, suffered from illness and struggled to find the form which had made him such a devastating opponent the previous season.

With the Saints' attack in such disorder, it was fortunate that Lee and Dainty gave such sterling service at the heart of the Southampton defence. Dainty, in particular, had a very good season and proved such a dependable performer that when he moved to Dundee at the season's end, Saints supporters were extremely upset.

Because of their inconsistency, Saints were always going to struggle in their bid to retain the Championship. In the end they finished third, five points behind Bristol Rovers, who took the title, and level on points with runners-up, Reading. Almost incredibly, Saints lost their last four home matches — although they managed to win at Tottenham — and that dreadful form at The Dell ensured that the title went to the Bristol club.

FA Cup

AFTER only a quarter of an hour of their first round FA Cup match against Millwall at The Dell, Saints had scored three goals, although one of these was an own-goal from Benson. Bluff edged Saints two goals in front again, with his second of the match, and that was how the scoreline remained to give Southampton an away tie against Wolves.

Benson was having one of those unlucky periods which can dog the career of any footballer and at Molineux he handled the ball in his own penalty area. Fortunately, Wolves missed the resultant spot kick and Saints went on to overturn the form book and beat the First Division side 3-2.

Such a fighting display gave Saints supporters every hope of a similar victory at Goodison Park in the third round. It was Everton, however, who took the initiative early in the game and never let it go. Despite some heroics by Clawley in the Southampton goal, they coasted through to the semi-final with a hat-trick from England international, Jimmy Settle, and a goal from their former Celtic player, Tom McDermott.

> **Round 1**
> **Feb 4 v Millwall (h) 3-1**
> *Bluff 2, Harrison*
> Clawley; Benson, Molyneux, Lee, Dainty, Houlker, Webb, Bluff, Harrison, Hedley, Fraser.
> *Att: 14,000*
> **Round 2**
> **Feb 18 v Wolverhampton Wanderers (a) 3-2**
> *Harrison 2, Bluff*
> Clawley; Benson, Molyneux, Lee, Dainty, Houlker, Webb, Bluff, Harrison, Hedley, Fraser.
> *Att: 27,000*
> **Round 3**
> **Mar 4 v Everton (a) 0-4**
> Clawley; Benson, Molyneux, Lee, Dainty, Houlker, Webb, Bluff, Harrison, Hedley, Fraser.
> *Att: 30,000*

> *Herbert Dainty played so well in 1904-05 that when it was announced that he was moving to Dundee at the end of that season, there were vociferous complaints from Saints' supporters.*

Saints' Bert Lee watches as Everton prepare to take a throw-in at Goodison during Southampton's FA Cup defeat.

1904-05
Southern League

Date		Opponent	Result	Scorers	Benson RW	Bluff E	Burrows T	Byrne M	Clawley G	Dainty HC	Fraser J	Gordon D	Harrison F	Haxton F	Hedley GA	Hoare JH	Houlker AE	Lee EA	Meston S	Molyneux G	Mouncher F	Shand H	Turner A	Turner H	Webb C	Whiting R	Wood H	Yates J
Sep 3	(a)	Luton T	W 2-1	Fraser 2					1	5	10		9		8		6	4	2	3	11			7				
10	(h)	Swindon T	W 4-3	H.Turner 2, Harrison, A.Turner					1	5		2	9		8		6	4		3	11		7	10				
17	(a)	New Brompton	D 1-1	Fraser					1	5	10	3	9		8	2	6	4			11			7				
24	(h)	Wellingborough T	W 1-0	H.Turner		8			1	5		3	9			2	6	4			11		10	7				
Oct 1	(h)	Brighton & HA	D 1-1	Webb	2	10			1	5			9		8		6	4		3	11				7			
8	(a)	Fulham	D 0-0		2	9			1	5	10				8		6	4		3	11				7			
15	(h)	Watford	W 2-1	Hedley, Fraser	2	9			1	5	10				8		6	4		3	11		7					
22	(a)	Plymouth A	L 0-1		2				1	5	10	8	9				6	4		3	11		7					
29	(h)	West Ham U	D 2-2	Bluff, H.Turner	2	8			1	5			9				6	4		3	11		7	10				
Nov 5	(a)	Reading	L 0-2		2	8			1	5	10		9				6	4		3	11		7					
12	(h)	Bristol R	W 4-2	Bluff, Fraser, Hedley, Webb	2	8			1	5	11		9		10		6	4		3					7			
19	(a)	Northampton T	W 3-0	Hedley 2, Houlker		8			1	5	11		9		10		6	4	2	3			7					
26	(h)	Portsmouth	W 1-0	Dainty		8			1	5	11		9		10		6	4	2	3			7					
Dec 3	(a)	Brentford	W 1-0	Hedley		8			1	5	11		9		10		6	4	2	3			7					
17	(a)	Millwall	W 2-1	Bluff, Harrison		8			1	5			9		10		6	4	2	3	11		7					
26	(h)	Tottenham H	D 1-1	Webb	2	8			1	5			9		10		6	4		3	11				7			
31	(h)	Luton T	W 4-1	Bluff 2, Hedley, Houlker	2	8	1			5			9		10		6	4		3	11		7					
Jan 7	(a)	Swindon T	W 2-0	Bluff, Hedley	2	8			1	5	11		9		10		6	4		3			7					
14	(h)	New Brompton	W 2-1	Bluff, Houlker	2	8			1		11		9		10		6	4	5	3			7					
21	(a)	Wellingborough T	W 3-1	Webb 2, Bluff	2	8			1				9		10		6	4	5	3	11				7			
28	(a)	Brighton & HA	L 0-1		2	8			1				9		10		6	4	5	3	11		7					
Feb 11	(a)	Watford	W 4-0	Harrison 2, Bluff, Fraser	2	8			1	5	11		9		10		6	4		3			7					
25	(a)	West Ham A	L 1-2	Harrison	2				1	5	11		9		10		6	4		3			7		8			
Mar 11	(a)	Bristol R	L 1-6	Harrison	2	8			1	5	11		9		10		6	4		3			7					
18	(h)	Northampton T	D 1-1	Wood					1	5	11	3	9		10		6	4	2				7				8	
25	(h)	Portsmouth	W 2-1	Harrison, Fraser					1	5	11		9	6	10			4	2	3			7		8			
Apr 1	(h)	Brentford	W 2-0	Fraser, Wood					1	5	11		9		10		6	4	2	3			7				8	
3	(h)	Reading	W 3-0	Bluff, Hedley, Lee		8		1		5	11		9		10		6	4	2	3			7					
8	(a)	Queen's Park R	D 1-1	Hedley		8			1	5	11		9		10		6	4	2	3			7					
10	(h)	Plymouth A	L 0-3			8			1	5	11		9		10			4	2	3		6	7					
15	(h)	Millwall	L 1-3	Harrison		8			1	5			9		10		6	4	2	3	11		7					
21	(a)	Tottenham H	W 2-1	Harrison, Hedley	2	8			1	5			9		10		4	6			11		7					
24	(a)	Fulham	L 0-1		2	8			1	5	10	3	9				4	6			11			7				
29	(h)	Queen's Park R	L 0-1		2	8	1			5		3	9		10		6	4			11			7				
App					19	26	1	2	31	31	25	6	25	2	30	3	29	33	18	28	20	1	13	5	16	1	8	1
Goals						10				1	8		9		10		3	1					1	4	5		2	

Back row (left to right): Hoare, Clawley, Byrne, Molyneux. Second row: Meston, Houlker, Dainty, Hedley, Lee, Gordon. Third row: Dawson (trainer), Webb, Wood, Harrison, Fraser, Mouncher. Seated: E.Arnfield, W.Bulpitt, H.Ashton, W.Hammock, E.C.Jarvis.

	P	W	D	L	F	A	Pts
Bristol R	34	20	8	6	74	36	48
Reading	34	18	7	9	57	38	43
Southampton	34	18	7	9	54	40	43
Plymouth A	34	18	5	11	57	39	41
Tottenham H	34	15	8	11	53	34	38
Fulham	34	14	10	10	46	34	38
Queen's Park R	34	14	8	12	51	47	36
Portsmouth	34	16	4	14	61	56	36
Watford	34	15	3	16	44	44	33
New Brompton	34	11	11	12	40	41	32
West Ham U	34	12	8	14	48	42	32
Brighton & HA	34	13	6	15	44	45	32
Northampton T	34	12	8	14	43	54	29
Brentford	34	10	9	15	33	38	29
Millwall	34	11	7	16	38	47	29
Swindon T	34	12	5	17	41	59	29
Luton T	34	12	3	19	45	45	27
Wellingborough T	34	5	3	26	25	107	13

George Hedley in action against Queen's Park Rangers in April 1905. Hedley scored the goal which earned Saints a point.

1905-06

THE introduction of a wage limit by the Southern League was largely responsible for a partial decline in Saints' fortunes, although the effect was not properly felt until the following season.

Players who left the club included Fraser, Dainty, Webb, Benson and Molyneux, whilst Wood joined Portsmouth in the capacity of trainer. Wood had been Southampton's club captain, and even though he had only played eight times the previous season, he was still an influential figure. Upon his departure, the club made the astonishing statement that the captain would be announced before each game.

Lee acted as skipper most of the time but, like the fans, he thought that the arrangement was absurd and the fiasco was not repeated after this season.

Despite losing so many players, Saints still had a useful squad and they managed to finish runners-up, five points behind Fulham. Midway through the season they paid £300 for the signature of Sid Johnston, Belfast Distillery's Irish international centre-half. Saints had high hopes of the Irishman but after only 12 minutes of his debut, in a Western League game at Tottenham, he was injured and never kicked another ball for Saints. The directors sent him to London for an operation but he refused to have anaesthetic and returned to Belfast, leaving Saints left to rue an expensive 12 minutes.

FA Cup

SAINTS again reached the Cup quarter-finals and again were denied a place in the last four by a Merseyside team. This time it was Liverpool who barred their way with a 3-0 win at Anfield.

Local rivals Portsmouth were easily beaten in the first round when, for this match, Harrison switched positions with Hedley, combining with Tomlinson on the right wing with great effect. Both Tomlinson and Harrison were very fast, and Molyneux, the Portsmouth full-back who used to play for Saints, was given a torrid time. Saints were forced to field a third-choice goalkeeper for this match as both Clawley and Burrows were injured, allowing Stead to make his FA Cup debut.

Southampton earned a replay in a dour and colourless game at New Brompton. The second game went much the same way as both defences dominated. The penalty problem still dogged Saints and Houlker missed from the spot — one of six Saints' failures out of seven awarded — before Harrison centred in the closing moments for Hedley to score 'amid deafening enthusiasm'.

When Middlesbrough arrived for the third round tie at The Dell they found that the name of their outside-left, Thackery, had been omitted from the list of players sent overnight to Southampton as required by the competition rules. The Saints directors did not, however, object to him playing but the Southampton forwards were in less charitable mood as they rattled in six goals.

A Middlesbrough critic who watched the game wrote that,

on this form, Saints would beat any team in the country. Thus, Southampton travelled to Liverpool full of confidence. They did not, however, carry it on to the pitch and when Houlker was injured and left a passenger on the wing, Saints surrendered and allowed themselves to be eliminated from the Cup.

Round 1
Jan 13 v Portsmouth (h) 5-1
Brown 2, Tomlinson, Harrison, Hedley
Stead; Warner, Hartshorne, Hogg, Houlker, Lee, Tomlinson, Harrison, Hedley, Brown, Mouncher.
Att: 14,000
Round 2
Feb 3 v New Brompton (a) 0-0
Clawley; Clarke, Hartshorne, Hogg, Lee, Houlker, Tomlinson, Harrison, Hedley, Brown, Mouncher.
Att: 4,289
Replay
Feb 7 v New Brompton (h) 1-0
Hedley
Clawley; Clarke, Hartshorne, Hogg, Lee, Houlker, Tomlinson, Harrison, Hedley, Brown, Mouncher.
Att: 7,500
Round 3
Feb 24 v Middlesbrough (h) 6-1
Hedley 2, Brown 2, Tomlinson, Harrison
Clawley; Clarke, Hartshorne, Hogg, Lee, Houlker, Tomlinson, Harrison, Hedley, Brown, Mouncher.
Att: 10,000
Round 4
Mar 10 v Liverpool (a) 0-3
Clawley; Clarke, Hartshorne, Hogg, Lee, Houlker, Tomlinson, Harrison, Hedley, Brown, Mouncher.
Att: 20,000

Former Northampton Town defender W. Clarke was a regular in this, his first season with Saints. But his health deteriorated and he never reproduced the form which had induced Southampton to sign him.

George Hedley, the former Sheffield United and England player, already had two FA Cup medals to his name and although he did not add a third with Southampton — he did manage another with Wolves after leaving The Dell — he scored some vital Cup goals for the Saints.

1905-06
Southern League

	Date	V	Opponent	Res	Score	Scorers	Bluff E	Brown H	Burrows T	Clawley G	Clarke W	Edmonds T	Harris G	Harrison F	Hartshorne A	Haxton F	Hedley GA	Hogg J	Houlker AE	Jefferis F	Lee EA	Liddell E	Meston S	Metcalf T	Mouncher F	Soye J	Stead I	Tomlinson I	Warner J
Sep	2	(h)	Brentford	L	0-1		8		1	2	5	10	9							6	4				11			7	3
	9	(a)	Norwich C	D	1-1	Harrison		1		2	5	10	9								4	6			11	8		7	3
	23	(a)	Northampton T	W	2-1	Harrison 2	10	1		2	5		9	3									4	6	11	8		7	
	30	(a)	Reading	W	2-0	Harrison, Tomlinson		1		2	5	10	9	3							6	4			11	8		7	
Oct	7	(h)	Watford	W	2-1	Brown, Lee	10	1		2	5	11	9	3			4				6					8		7	
	14	(a)	Brighton & HA	W	3-1	Tomlinson 2, Brown	10	1		2				9	3	8	4	6			5				11			7	
	21	(h)	West Ham U	W	1-0	Brown	10	1		2				9	3	8	4	6			5				11			7	
	28	(a)	Fulham	D	1-1	Mouncher	10	1		2				9	3		4				5	6			11	8		7	
Nov	4	(h)	Queen's Park R	W	2-1	Soye 2	9	1				10		3			4				5	6			11	8		7	2
	11	(a)	Bristol R	L	1-5	Mouncher	8	1		2		10		3	6		5				4				11	9		7	
	18	(h)	New Brompton	D	1-1	Harris			1	2		10		3			5		8	4	6				11	9		7	
	25	(a)	Portsmouth	L	0-1		10	1		2				3		9	5				4	6			11	8		7	
Dec	2	(h)	Swindon T	W	2-0	Brown, Hedley	8	1				10		3		9	5				4	6			11			7	2
	9	(a)	Millwall	D	3-3	Hedley 3		1	2	6				3		9	5		10	4					11	8		7	
	16	(h)	Luton T	W	2-1	Brown, Harrison	10	1	2					9	3		8	5			4	6			11			7	
	25	(a)	Plymouth A	D	0-0			1				10		3		9	5				4	6			11	8		7	2
	26	(h)	Tottenham H	W	1-0	Soye	10	1	2				9				5				4	6			11	8		7	3
	30	(a)	Brentford	L	1-2	Soye			2			10	9	3			8	5			4	6			11	7	1		
Jan	6	(h)	Norwich C	W	2-1	Harris, Tomlinson	10		2			11		3			9	4	6		5				8	1		7	
	27	(h)	Northampton T	W	9-1	Brown 3, Harrison 2, Mouncher 2, Hedley, Tomlinson	10	1						8	3		9	4	6	5					11			7	2
Feb	10	(a)	Watford	L	1-4	Harris		1	2			10						4	6	8	5				11	9		7	3
	17	(h)	Brighton & HA	W	1-0	Hogg		1	2			10	8	3			9	4			5				11			7	
	26	(a)	West Ham U	L	0-3		9	1	2			10					6	7	5		4				11	8			3
Mar	3	(h)	Fulham	W	2-1	Brown, Harrison	10	1	2				8	3			9	4	6		5				11			7	
	14	(a)	Queen's Park R	W	3-0	Harrison 2, Jefferis		1	2			10	9	3			4		8	5	6				11			7	
	17	(h)	Bristol R	W	3-0	Harris, Jefferis, Tomlinson		1				10	9	3			4		8	5	6				11			7	2
	24	(a)	New Brompton	W	4-0	Harrison, Lee, Mouncher, Tomlinson		1				10	9	3			4	6	8	5					11			7	2
	31	(h)	Portsmouth	L	1-2	opp own goal	10	1					9	3			4	6	8	5					11			7	2
Apr	7	(a)	Swindon T	W	3-0	Harrison, Lee, Soye	10	1		2	4		9	3					8	5	6				11	7			
	13	(a)	Tottenham H	D	1-1	Mouncher		1		2	4	10	9						8	5	6				11	7			3
	14	(h)	Millwall	D	0-0			1		2	10	8					9		6		5	4			11			7	3
	16	(h)	Plymouth A	W	1-0	Tomlinson		1		2	5		9				10		6	8		4			11			7	3
	21	(a)	Luton T	L	0-5			1		2		10					9		6	8	5		4		11			7	3
	28	(h)	Reading	W	2-1	Brown, Jefferis	10	1					7	3			9	4		8	5		6		1				2
			App				1	18	10	22	26	9	20	23	25	1	16	24	13	13	31	1	22	1	32	18	2	29	17
			Goals					10					4	12			5	1		3	3				6	5		8	

1 own-goal

Back row: (left to right): J.Warner, W.Clarke, G.Clawley, T.Burrows, A.Hartshorne. Third row: A.Lee, S.Meston, T.Edmonds, G.Hedley, A.Houlker. Second row: W.Dawson (trainer), I.Tomlinson, F.Jefferis, J.Soye, H.M.Ashton, F.Harrison, Sir G.A.E.Hussey, H.Brown, G.Harris, F.Mouncher. Seated: E.Arnfield, G.Payne, W.Bulpitt, Dr E.H.Stancomb (chairman), A.A.Wood, C.Robson, E.C.Jarvis.

	P	W	D	L	F	A	Pts
Fulham	34	19	12	3	44	15	50
Southampton	34	19	7	8	58	39	45
Portsmouth	34	17	9	8	61	35	42
Luton T	34	17	7	10	64	40	41
Plymouth A	34	16	7	11	52	33	39
Tottenham H	34	16	7	11	46	29	39
Norwich C	34	13	10	11	46	38	36
Bristol R	34	15	5	14	56	66	35
Brentford	34	14	7	13	43	52	35
Reading	34	12	9	13	53	46	33
West Ham U	34	14	5	15	42	39	33
Millwall	34	11	11	12	38	41	33
Queen's Park R	34	12	7	15	58	44	31
Watford	34	8	10	16	38	57	26
Swindon T	34	8	9	17	31	52	25
Brighton & HA	34	9	7	18	30	55	25
New Brompton	34	7	8	19	20	62	22
Northampton T	34	8	5	21	32	79	21

> When the Saints were drawn away to New Brompton, in the English Cup, the directors tried hard to persuade their New Brompton counterparts to switch the game to The Dell. This was strictly for financial reasons as the Kent club's followers were not as numerous as Southampton's and the Saints directors were concerned about the lack of 'gate' money. Predictably, New Brompton turned down Saints' request and Mr Arnfield, the Southampton secretary, secured 50 seat tickets, price 2s 6d(12½p) each, for the Saints' travelling fans.

1906-07

SAINTS finished 11th in this, their 13th season of Southern League football — and as they had never before finished lower than third, this was viewed with some alarm.

The wage limit which now applied to the Southern League had meant that many players, hitherto better off in the Southern, opted to return to the Football League. It had been felt that all the southern clubs would be 'in the same boat', but Saints, who had one of the best sides, suffered more than most by comparison.

After a poor start to the season, and with the directors apparently quite unprepared to spend money on bringing fresh talent to The Dell, attendances began to fall.

Saints goalkeeper George Clawley fists out a Portsmouth shot during the Western League match between the two South Coast rivals in September 1906. Fred Harrison scored twice for Saints but Pompey won 3-2.

FA Cup

SOUTHAMPTON badly needed a Cup run to tempt the absent supporters back to The Dell, but when Watford were drawn at home in the first round, the Saints directors increased the admission to one shilling. As Watford were a fellow Southern League club, and therefore not a special attraction, the fans stayed away in even greater numbers and less than 4,000 turned up to watch Hoskins (in the first minute) and Mouncher (in the last seconds) give Saints victory. Receipts of £236 were less than for an average Southern League game.

When Sheffield Wednesday visited The Dell in the second round, 15,000 people showed that they did not object to paying increased prices if quality opposition was on show. Hoskins scored against First Division Wednesday in the second half and Saints held that lead until just before the end when Wilson, with his back to goal and chancing his luck, hooked the ball over his head. It flew past Clawley and earned Wednesday a replay.

Saints' replay chances suffered a severe setback when Eastham sustained a serious injury and missed the game. His replacement at full-back was Hogg, normally a wing-half, and he was so overawed by the occasion that he repeatedly fluffed his clearances. His performance hardly inspired confidence and with Harrison feeling unwell during the game, Saints went down 3-1.

Round 1
Jan 12 v Watford (h) 2-1
Hoskins, Mouncher
Clawley; Eastham, Glover, Hogg, Robertson, Gray, Jefferis, Hoskins, Harrison, Glen, Mouncher.
Att: 3,886
Round 4
Round 2
Feb 2 v Sheffield Wednesday (h) 1-1
Hoskins
Clawley; Eastham, Glover, Robertson, Bowden, Gray, Jefferis, Hoskins, Harrison, Glen, Mouncher.
Att: 15,000
Replay
Feb 7 v Sheffield Wednesday (a) 1-3
Hoskins
Clawley; Hogg, Glover, Roberston, Bowden, Gray, Jefferis, Hoskins, Harrison, Glen, Mouncher.
Att: 30,000

The average age of Saints' team during the 1906-07 season was proudly revealed by the Sports Echo as being a mere 23 years.

During a tour of Germany by Southampton, player Glenn revealed an unlikely talent of speaking fluent German and became the club's official interpreter.

1906-07
Southern League

Date		Opponent	Result	Scorers	Angel JN	Beare G	Bell E	Blake J	Bowden T	Burrows T	Clarke W	Clawley G	Dyer AE	Eastham JR	Everist F	Glen A	Glover HV	Gray W	Harris G	Harris JW	Harrison F	Hoare JH	Hogg J	Hoskins AH	Jefferis F	Jepp SR	McLean R	Mouncher F	Norbury V	Patten J	Radford I	Robertson JN	Thorpe F	Toomer WE
Sep 1	(a)	Swindon T	L 0-1						5		2	1				10	3	6			7		4		8			11			9			
8	(h)	Norwich C	D 2-2	Harris, Mouncher					5		2	1				8	3		10		7		4					11			9	6		
15	(a)	Luton T	L 1-2	Harris					5		2	1	3			8			10		7		4				6	11			9			
22	(h)	Crystal P	D 1-1	Glen					5		2	1				8	3	6	10		9							11			7	4		
29	(a)	Brentford	L 1-2	Harrison	4				5		2	1			7	10					9				8		6	11				3		
Oct 6	(h)	Millwall	W 5-1	Glen 2, Blake, Harrison, opp own goal	4			7	5		2	1				8		6	10		9							11				3		
13	(a)	Clapton O	L 2-3	Jefferis, Mouncher	4						2	1			3	8		6	10		9		5		7			11						
20	(h)	Portsmouth	W 2-0	Harrison, Mouncher					5		2	1				8	3	6	10		9		4		7			11						
27	(a)	New Brompton	W 2-0	Glen, Harrison					5		2	1				8	3	6	10		9		4		7			11						
Nov 3	(h)	Plymouth A	W 3-1	Harrison 2, Glen					5		2	1				8	3	6	10		9		4		7			11						
10	(a)	Brighton & HA	L 0-2						5		2	1				8	3	6	10		9		4		7			11						
17	(h)	Reading	W 2-0	Harrison, Jefferis					5		2	1				8	3	6	10		9		4		7			11						
24	(a)	Watford	D 1-1	Jefferis					5		2	1				8	3	6	10		9		4		7			11						
Dec 1	(h)	Northampton T	W 1-0	Harrison					5		2	1				8	3	6	10		9		4		7			11						
8	(a)	Queen's Park R	W 2-1	Glen, Mouncher							2	1				8	3	6	10		9		4		7			11				5		
15	(h)	Fulham	L 1-2	Mouncher							2	1				8	3	6	10		9		4		7			11				5		
22	(a)	Bristol R	L 0-5								2	1				8	3	6	10		9		4		7			11				5		
25	(a)	West Ham U	L 0-1									1		2			3	6	10		9		4	8	7			11				5		
26	(h)	Tottenham H	W 2-1	Glen, Harrison								1		2		8	3	6	10		9		4		7			11				5		
29	(h)	Swindon T	D 1-1	Harrison								1		2	11	8	3	6	10		9		4		7							5		
Jan 5	(a)	Norwich C	D 1-1	Everist								1		2	11	10	3	6			9		4	8								5		7
19	(h)	Luton T	W 1-0	Glen								1		2		10	3	6			9		4	8	7			11				5		
26	(a)	Crystal P	D 1-1	Harrison					5			1		2		10	3	6			9			8	7			11				4		
Feb 9	(a)	Millwall	L 0-4						5			1				9	3	6	10					8	7			11	2			4		
16	(h)	Clapton O	D 0-0						5		2	1				10	3	6			9			8	7			11				4		
23	(a)	Portsmouth	W 2-1	Glen, Harrison					5		2	1				8	3	6	10		9				7			11				4		
Mar 2	(h)	New Brompton	D 1-1	Everist					5		2	1			7	8	3	6	10		9							11				4		
9	(a)	Plymouth A	L 0-1						5		2	1			7	8	3	6	10		9							11				4		
16	(a)	Brighton & HA	L 0-1						5		2	1			7	8	3	6	10		9							11				4		
18	(h)	Brentford	W 5-0	Harris 2, Glen, Jepp, Mouncher					5		2	1				8	3	6	10						7	9	4	11						
25	(a)	Reading	L 1-5	Harris					5		2	1		3		8		6	10		9				7	4		11						
29	(a)	Tottenham H	L 0-1						5		2	1		4	10		3				9			8				11			6			7
30	(h)	Watford	D 0-0						5			1		2			3	6		11	9			8	7					10	4			
Apr 1	(h)	West Ham U	L 2-3	Jefferis, Patten					5			1		2			3	6		8	9				7			11		10	4			
6	(a)	Northampton T	W 4-2	Radford 2, Mouncher, Patten			6					1	8	2			3		10									11	7	9	4	5		
13	(h)	Queen's Park R	L 0-3			7	6					1		2			3		10	4				8	9			11				5		
20	(a)	Fulham	L 0-3			7	6					1		2			3							8	10			11		9	4	5		
27	(h)	Bristol R	W 2-1	Eastham, Jefferis		6	8					1		2			3		10						7			11		9	4	5		
App					3	1	2	1	29	1	25	37	1	16	8	29	32	28	28	3	31	1	19	10	26	4	4	34	3	4	9	23	4	2
Goals								1						1	2	10			5		12				5	1		7		2	2			

1 own-goal

Top row (left to right): E.Arnfield, E.C.Jarvis, H.M.Ashton, Dr.E.Stancomb, A.A.Wood, W.Bulpitt, W.A.Hammock. Second row: W.Dawson, W.Clark, J.Blacktin, G.Clawley, T.Burrows, H.V.Glover, J.Eastham. Third row: I.Radford, A.Hoskins, J.Hogg, W.Gray, A.Glen, J.N.Robertson, R.McLean, T.Bowden, F.Everist. Bottom row: McConnachie, F.Jefferis, F.Harrison, G.Harris, F.Mouncher.

	P	W	D	L	F	A	Pts
Fulham	38	20	13	5	58	32	53
Portsmouth	38	22	7	9	64	36	51
Brighton & HA	38	18	9	11	53	43	45
Luton T	38	18	9	11	52	52	45
West Ham U	38	15	14	9	60	41	44
Tottenham H	38	17	9	12	63	45	43
Millwall	38	18	6	14	71	50	42
Norwich C	38	15	12	11	57	48	42
Watford	38	13	16	9	46	43	42
Brentford	38	17	8	13	57	56	42
Southampton	38	13	9	16	49	56	35
Reading	38	14	6	18	58	47	34
Leyton	38	11	12	15	38	60	34
Bristol R	38	12	9	17	55	54	33
Plymouth A	38	10	13	15	43	50	33
Swindon T	38	11	11	16	44	55	33
New Brompton	38	12	9	17	47	59	33
Queen's Park R	38	11	10	17	47	55	32
Crystal P	38	8	9	21	46	66	25
Northampton T	38	5	9	24	30	88	19

1907-08

SAINTS against finished 11th in the Southern League table, which still compared unfavourably with their earlier days in the competition.

One of the few Southampton players to emerge from the League season with any credit was the Welsh international forward, Lewis, who had started his League career just down the road at Portsmouth in 1900. Lewis found his way to Saints via Burton United, Bristol Rovers and Brighton and his first season with Southampton saw him develop a useful partnership with Harrison.

Indeed, Lewis finished top scorer, albeit it with only ten goals, but although Saints finished the season with a flourish — scoring eight goals in two games, against Queen's Park Rangers and Bradford — the story of the 1907-08 campaign really belongs to another exciting FA Cup run.

FA Cup

ANOTHER new face, the Seaham-born Bainbridge, scored both goals in Saints' creditable 2-1 victory over Second Division Burnley at Turf Moor in the first round of the Cup. Tom Robertson's goal against West Brom at The Dell ensured a safe passage to the third round where 16,000 saw Bristol Rovers go down 2-0 at Southampton to ease Saints into the quarter-finals.

When the draw paired Saints with First Division Everton, the previous season's losing Finalists, at Goodison Park, few people expected them to proceed further. Yet Southampton fought hard to earn a creditable 0-0 draw and set up a potentially thrilling encounter at The Dell.

Excitement in the south was so intense that people travelled from as far as London to see the big match. Locally, all workshops were closed for the afternoon and it soon became obvious that not everyone who wanted to see the replay would be able to squeeze into The Dell. The turnstiles were closed 15 minutes before kick-off and those people who could not gain admission resorted to clambering up surrounding telegraph poles and trees. Many more perched precariously on the grandstand roof.

All in all, The Dell was quite a sight that March afternoon and the atmosphere charged with excitement. The game itself quite lived up to the occasion and with less than five minutes played, the Everton and Scotland forward, Sandy Young, opened the scoring. Undeterred, Saints pushed forward and were soon level through Costello, who hooked a Johnston cross past Scott in the Everton goal. On the half-hour, Saints took the lead when Bainbridge deflected a Johnston shot into the net.

Saints increased that lead in the second half when Bainbridge beat two men before sending over a cross which Costello seemed to have overrun, but with an incredible contortion he managed to somehow reach back and head the ball into the net from a seemingly impossible angle. It was one of the greatest individual goals in the Saints' history.

Everton penned Saints in their own half for long periods and Bolton pulled a goal back to cause Southampton fans some agonizing last minutes before the final whistle sounded. The crowd, who had paid a total of £1,067, streamed out of The Dell and Saints now looked ahead to the semi-final clash with Wolves at Stamford Bridge.

Wolves were then a Second Division club and Saints now felt they could go to the Final. But the match at Chelsea's ground was an anti-climax and Saints really lost it in the first half through a series of missed chances. Wolves went through 2-0, and to add insult to injury, one of their goals was scored by ex-Saints star, George Hedley, who went on to win his third Cup-winners' medal.

Round 1
Jan 11 v Burnley (a) 2-1
Bainbridge 2
Lock; Eastham, Glover, Johnston, Thorpe, Hedley, Bainbridge, Jefferis, G.Smith, Costello, Hodgkinson.
Att: 14,000

Round 2
Feb 1 v West Bromwich Albion (h) 1-0
Robertson
Lock; Eastham, Glover, G.Smith, Thorpe, Robertson, Bainbridge, Jefferis, Costello, Lewis, Hodgkinson.
Att: 19,000

Round 3
Feb 22 v Bristol Rovers (h) 2-0
Bainbridge, Costello
Lock; Eastham, Glover, Johnston, Thorpe, Robertson, Bainbridge, Jefferis, Costello, Hodgkinson, G.Smith.
Att: 16,000

Round 4
Mar 7 v Everton (a) 0-0
Lock; Eastham, Glover, Johnston, Thorpe, Robertson, Bainbridge, Jefferis, G.Smith, Costello, Hodgkinson.
Att: 40,000

Replay
Mar 11 v Everton (h) 3-2
Costello 2, Bainbridge
Lock; Eastham, Glover, Johnston, Thorpe, Robertson, Bainbridge, Jefferis, G.Smith, Costello, Hodgkinson.
Att: 21,690

Semi-final
Mar 28 v Wolverhampton Wanderers (at Stamford Bridge) 0-2
Burrows; Eastham, Glover, Johnston, Thorpe, Robertson, Bainbridge, Jefferis, G.Smith, Costello, Hodgkinson.
Att: 45,000

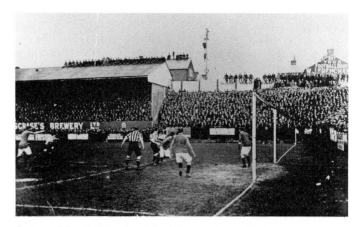

A view of The Dell for the visit of Everton in the FA Cup. Note the fans sitting on the roof of the stand and clambering up the telegraph pole outside the ground.

1907-08
Southern League

Date		Opponent	Result	Scorers	Bainbridge JH	Bell EI	Bird	Blake JJ	Burrows T	Costello FG	Eastham JR	Glover HV	Hadley H	Harrison F	Hodgkinson AV	Hoskins AH	Jacques	Jefferis F	Jepp SR	Johnston JS	Lewis J	Lock H	Mead P	Mouncher F	Robertson JN	Smith G	Smith WG	Thorpe F
Sep 2	(h)	Luton T	W 2-1	Jefferis, Lewis	7				1	2		3	6	9				10		4	8			11				5
7	(h)	Crystal P	L 2-3	Hodgkinson, Lewis	7				1	2		3	6	9	11			10		4	8							5
9	(a)	New Brompton	L 1-2	Glover					1	2		3	6	9	11	7		10		4	8							5
14	(a)	Luton T	W 2-0	Bainbridge, Costello	7					10	2	3	6	9	11			8		4		1						5
21	(h)	Brighton & HA	W 3-2	Glover, Hodgkinson, Jefferis	7					10	2	3	6	9	11			8		4		1						5
28	(a)	Portsmouth	L 0-3		7					10	2	3	6	9	11			8		4		1						5
Oct 5	(h)	Bradford	W 2-1	Harrison, Hodgkinson	7					2		3	6	9	11			10		8		1				4		5
12	(a)	Millwall	L 1-2	opp own goal	7					2		3	6	9	11			10		4	8	1						5
19	(h)	Brentford	W 3-0	Hodgkinson, Jefferis, Johnston	7					2		3	6	9	11			10		4	8	1						5
26	(a)	Bristol R	L 2-4	Costello, Lewis		7				10	2		6	9	11					4	8	1			3			5
Nov 2	(h)	Leyton	W 1-0	Lewis	7					10		3	6	9						4	8	1		11	2			5
9	(a)	Reading	L 1-2	Smith	7							3		9				10		6	8	1		11	2	4		5
16	(a)	Watford	D 1-1	Jefferis	7							3	6	9	11	8		10		4		1			2			5
23	(a)	Norwich C	W 1-0	Smith	7					10		3	6		11					4	9	1			2	8		5
30	(h)	Northampton T	W 2-0	Costello, Lewis						10		3	6		11			7		4	9	1			2	8		5
Dec 14	(a)	Plymouth A	L 0-2							10		3	6		11		9	7		4		1			2	8		5
21	(h)	West Ham U	D 0-0		7					10		3	6		11			9		4		1			2	8		5
25	(a)	Swindon T	W 2-0	Bainbridge 2	7					10		3	6		11			9		4		1			2	8		5
26	(h)	Tottenham H	D 1-1	Lewis						10		3	6		11			7		4	9	1			2	8		5
30	(a)	Queen's Park R	L 0-3							10		3	6		11			7		4	9	1			2	8		5
Jan 4	(a)	Crystal P	L 0-1		7				1	9	2	3	6		11			8				10			4			5
25	(h)	Portsmouth	W 1-0	Hodgkinson	7					10	2	3	6		11			8		4		1			9			5
Feb 8	(h)	Millwall	W 3-2	Bainbridge, Lewis, Smith	7					10	2	3			11			8			9	1			6	4		5
15	(a)	Brentford	L 0-4		7						2				11			8	6	4	10	1			3	9		5
29	(a)	Leyton	D 1-1	Robertson	7						2	3	6		11			8		4		1		10	9			5
Mar 14	(a)	Watford	W 1-0	Smith						10	2	3	6	7	11			8		4		1			9			5
18	(a)	Brighton & HA	L 2-3	Hodgkinson 2	9	6		1		10	2	3	4		11			7							8			5
21	(h)	Norwich C	L 0-3				11		1	10	2		6	7						4		8			9	3		5
30	(h)	Reading	L 1-3	Smith						10	2	3	6	7	11			8		4		1				9		5
Apr 4	(h)	New Brompton	W 2-0	Costello, Glover	7				1	10	2	3			11			8		4					6	9		5
6	(a)	Bristol R	W 1-0	Costello	7				1	10	2	3			11			8		4					6	9		5
9	(a)	Northampton T	L 0-4		7				1	10	2				11				6	4	8				3	9		5
11	(h)	Plymouth A	D 1-1	Lewis	7			11	1			3						9		6	8				2	4		5
17	(a)	Tottenham H	L 0-3		7				1	10		3			11			9		4		8			2	6		5
18	(a)	West Ham U	L 2-4	Bainbridge, Costello	7			11	1	10		3	6		8			9		4					2			5
20	(h)	Swindon T	D 1-1	Jefferis	7					10		3	6		11	8		9		4		1			2			5
28	(h)	Queen's Park R	W 5-2	Lewis 2, Bainbridge, Costello, Jefferis	7					10		3	6		11			8		4	9	1			2			5
30	(a)	Bradford	W 3-1	Costello 2, Bainbridge	7				1	10		3			11			8		4	9				2	6		5
				App	28	2	1	3	14	28	22	33	29	13	29	11	1	31	5	33	24	23	1	3	25	21	3	35
				Goals	7					9		3		1	7			6		1	10				1	5		

1 own-goal

	P	W	D	L	F	A	Pts
Queen's Park R	38	21	9	8	82	57	51
Plymouth A	38	19	11	8	50	31	49
Millwall	38	19	8	11	49	32	46
Crystal P	38	17	10	11	54	51	44
Swindon T	38	16	10	12	55	40	42
Bristol R	38	16	10	12	59	56	42
Tottenham H	38	17	7	14	59	49	41
Northampton T	38	15	11	12	50	41	41
Portsmouth	38	17	6	15	64	52	40
West Ham U	38	15	10	13	47	48	40
Southampton	38	16	6	16	51	60	38
Bradford	38	12	12	14	53	54	36
Reading	38	15	6	17	56	50	36
Watford	38	12	10	16	47	59	34
Brentford	38	14	5	19	49	52	33
Norwich C	38	12	9	17	46	49	33
Brighton & HA	38	12	8	18	46	59	32
Luton T	38	12	6	20	33	56	30
Leyton	38	8	11	19	51	74	27
New Brompton	38	9	7	22	44	75	25

Back row (left to right): W.Hammock, E.Arnfield, J.S.Johnston, A.A.Wood, H.V.Glover, G.Payne, H.Hadley, E.C.Jarvis, G.Smith, Sir G.A.E.Hussey, W.Bulpitt. Middle row: Dawson (trainer), F.Jefferis, W.Clarke, A.E.Dyer, T.Burrows, Seare, S.R.Jepp, A.V.Hodgkinson, J.N.Robertson, A.H.Hoskins, F.Thorpe, J.R.Eastham. Front row: J.H.Bainbridge, J.Lewis, E.I.Bell, F.Harrison, F.G.Costello, F.W.Mouncher.

43

1908-09

WITH the previous year's disappointing Cup defeat put firmly behind them, Saints opened up the new League season in style by reeling off seven consecutive victories. This fine start was even more surprising because before the season began, officials, players and supporters were shocked by the untimely death of George Smith.

Smith was a seasoned professional who had played for several League clubs before becoming a vital member of the Saints forward line in 1907. Yet the gap left by his sudden death was immediately filled by Arthur Hughes, the former Bolton Wanderers player. Hughes settled well and by mid-October had scored ten goals. Then a bad leg injury sidelined him and, as so often happens when a key player is injured, further mishaps irritatingly deprived Saints of the services of vital players like Jefferis, Thorpe, Johnston and Robertson.

All this happened at a crucial period and it was not until later in the season that the Saints were again able to field their best team. Considering the Saints' fine start, and the fact that they lost only one of their last six games after harmony had been restored, it can be seen what an effect those injuries had on Southampton's title aspirations.

Saints ended the season in third place, still quite an improvement on the previous two seasons. Besides Hughes, who made the best impression up to his injury, other young players to appear this season were Jepp, Shearer and Jordan. Shearer, a young Scot, showed considerable promise but he lacked the experience to make best use of his undoubted natural ability. He eventually gave way to Jordan who, although less skilful that Shearer, was a more thrustful player.

Jepp was a loyal servant who, although never one of those eye-catching footballers, nevertheless gave many useful performances in Saints' colours.

The forward line's strength lay in the right-wing pairing of Bainbridge and Jefferis whilst in goal, Lock had a good season until he was injured at Watford. As he had been injured at Watford the previous season, Lock vowed never to play at Cassio Road again. He moved to Glasgow Rangers at the end of the season, so the resolution was never put to the test.

FA Cup

FOR the first time in six seasons, the Saints were eliminated from the FA Cup in the first round. At the time the club was in the middle of the injury crisis which arguably cost them the Southern League title, and it was no surprise when Bristol City triumphed after a replay.

The first game was played at Ashton Gate where Southampton did well to draw 1-1. Lock was the real hero, for after Jordan had scored for the Saints with a speculative long shot, the goalkeeper made a superb save from a penalty kick in the dying minutes.

Over 19,000 spectators were at The Dell for the replay the following Wednesday afternoon, and Saints' directors erred when they recalled Hughes to play despite his obvious lack of fitness. To start the game with only ten fit men was too big an obstacle for Saints to overcome and City went through 2-0 and on towards an eventual Cup Final appearance against Manchester United.

> **Round 1**
> **Jan 16 v Bristol City (a) 1-1**
> *Jordan*
> Lock; Eastham, Glover, Johnston, Trueman, Jepp, Bainbridge, Jefferis, Costello, Jordan, Blake.
> *Att: 14,000*
> **Replay**
> **Jan 20 v Bristol City (h) 0-2**
> Lock; Eastham, Glover, Johnston, Trueman, Jepp, Bainbridge, Jefferis, Hughes, Jordan, Blake.
> *Att: 19,000*

Pictured below are three men who made varying impacts on the season. Sam Jepp made 18 appearances and proved a versatile footballer. Bob Carter signed from Fulham in March and hit three goals in seven games. Frank Jordan returned from South Africa and soon became a first-team regular.

Sam Jepp

Bob Carter

Frank Jordan

1908-09
Southern League

Date	Opponent	Result	Scorers	Bainbridge JH	Bamford W	Blake JJ	Burrows T	Campbell AK	Carter R	Costello FG	Eastham JR	Foster J	Glover HV	Hodgkinson AV	Hughes A	Jefferis F	Jepp SR	Johnston JS	Jordan F	Lock H	McGhee GD	Prince P	Robertson JN	Shearer S	Smith S	Smith WG	Thorpe F	Toomer WE	Trueman AH	Ward R
Sep 2	(a) Brighton & HA	W 3-1	Bainbridge, Jefferis, Thorpe	7							2		3	11	9	8			4	1			6	10			5			
Sep 5	(a) Brentford	W 3-2	Hodgkinson, Hughes, Thorpe	7							2		3	11	9	8			4	1			6	10			5			
Sep 7	(h) Brighton & HA	W 4-1	Jefferis 3, Bainbridge	7						11	2				9	8			4	1			3	10			5		6	
Sep 12	(h) Luton T	W 6-0	Hughes 3, Blake, Johnston, Thorpe	7	11						2				9	8			4	1			3	10			5		6	
Sep 16	(a) Crystal P	W 3-2	Hodgkinson, Hughes, Jefferis	7							2			11	9	8		10	4	1			3				5		6	
Sep 19	(a) Swindon T	W 2-0	Hughes, Jordan	7							2			11	9	8		10	4	1			3				5		6	
Sep 26	(h) Portsmouth	W 2-0	Bainbridge, Hughes	7	11						2				9	8			4	1			3	10			5		6	
Oct 5	(h) Crystal P	D 4-4	Hodgkinson 2, Bainbridge, Hughes	7	10						2		3	11	9	8	6			1							5		4	
Oct 10	(h) Northampton T	L 2-3	Hodgkinson, Hughes	7	10						2		3	11	9	8	6			1							5		4	
Oct 14	(a) Exeter C	W 2-1	Hughes, Jefferis	7									3	11	9	8	6			1	10				2		5		4	
Oct 17	(a) New Brompton	D 1-1	Jefferis	7							2		3	11		8	6			1	9	10					5		4	
Oct 24	(h) Millwall	W 4-1	Hodgkinson, Jordan, Prince, Thorpe	7									3	11		8	6		10	1		9	2				5		4	
Oct 31	(a) Southend U	L 0-2		7		1							3	11	9	8	6	10							2		5	4		
Nov 7	(h) Coventry C	W 2-1	Bainbridge, Hughes	7	11					10	2		3		9	8			4	1							5		6	
Nov 14	(a) Bristol R	L 1-4	Jefferis	7						10	2			11	9	8			4	1			3				5		6	
Nov 21	(h) Watford	W 1-0	Hughes	7						10	2			11	9	8			4	1			3				5		6	
Nov 28	(h) Norwich C	D 2-2	Hodgkinson, Jefferis	7						10	2			11		8	4	9		1			3				5		6	
Dec 5	(h) Reading	D 1-1	Blake	7	11					10	2					8	4		1	9			3				5		6	
Dec 12	(h) Plymouth A	W 4-2	Bainbridge, Costello, Jefferis, Thorpe	7	11					9	2					8		10	4	1			3				5		6	
Dec 25	(a) West Ham U	L 0-1			11					9	2	3				8		10	4	1						7	5		6	
Dec 26	(h) Queen's Park R	L 1-4	Jordan		11					9	2	3				8		10	4	1						7	5		6	
Jan 2	(h) Brentford	W 1-0	Ward							9	2		3	11					4	1	10	6				7	5			8
Jan 9	(a) Luton T	L 0-1		7	6						2		3	11	9	8		10	4	1							5			
Jan 23	(a) Swindon T	L 0-6		7	6					9	2			11		8		10		1						3	5		4	
Jan 30	(a) Portsmouth	L 0-3			6	7				9	2		3	11		8		10	4	1							5			
Feb 6	(a) Leyton	D 2-2	Hodgkinson 2	7							2		3	11	9	8	6	10		1							5		4	
Feb 13	(a) Northampton T	D 1-1	Hodgkinson							9	2		3	11			6	10		1					8		5		4	7
Feb 20	(h) New Brompton	W 2-0	Hodgkinson, Hughes				7				2		3	11	9		6	10		1					8		5		4	
Feb 27	(a) Millwall	L 1-3	Ward	7	6		4				2		3					10		1		8	11				5			9
Mar 6	(h) Southend U	D 1-1	Bainbridge	7	6	11	4				2	9	3			8				1			10				5			
Mar 13	(a) Coventry C	L 0-2		7							2	9	3	11				10	4	1			8				5		6	
Mar 20	(h) Bristol R	W 1-0	Bainbridge	7			11				2	9	3			8		10		1			4				5		6	
Mar 27	(a) Watford	L 0-3		7			4	11			2	9	3			8		10		1			6				5			
Apr 3	(h) Norwich C	W 1-0	Jefferis	7					1	9	2		3	11		8		10					4				5		6	
Apr 9	(a) Queen's Park R	W 2-1	Foster, Jordan						1	7	2	9	3	11		8		10	4								5		6	
Apr 10	(a) Reading	D 0-0		7					1		2	9	3	11	8			10					4				5		6	
Apr 12	(h) West Ham U	D 2-2	Hughes 2	7					1		2		3	11	9	8		10	4				6				5			
Apr 13	(h) Exeter C	W 2-0	Carter, Jefferis	7	11	1			9	2		3				8		10	4				6				5		6	
Apr 17	(a) Plymouth A	D 0-0		7					1	9	2			11		8		10	4							3	5		6	
Apr 24	(h) Leyton	W 3-0	Carter 2, Jefferis	7					1	9	2		3	11		8		10	4								5		6	
App				33	5	12	8	3	7	13	37	6	28	28	21	33	18	25	25	32	2	3	20	11	3	5	26	1	31	4
Goals				8		2			3	1		1		11	15	13		1	4			1					5		2	

	P	W	D	L	F	A	Pts
Northampton T	40	25	5	10	90	45	55
Swindon T	40	22	5	13	96	55	49
Southampton	40	19	10	11	67	58	48
Portsmouth	40	18	10	12	68	60	46
Bristol R	40	17	9	14	60	63	43
Exeter C	40	18	6	16	56	65	42
New Brompton	40	17	7	16	48	59	41
Reading	40	11	18	11	60	57	40
Luton T	40	17	6	17	59	60	40
Plymouth A	40	15	10	15	46	47	40
Millwall	40	16	6	18	59	61	38
Southend U	40	14	10	16	52	54	38
Leyton	40	15	8	17	52	55	38
Watford	40	14	9	17	51	64	37
Queen's Park R	40	12	12	16	52	50	36
Crystal P	40	12	12	16	62	62	36
West Ham U	40	16	4	20	56	60	36
Brighton & HA	40	14	7	19	60	61	35
Norwich C	40	12	11	17	59	75	34
Coventry C	40	15	4	21	64	91	34
Brentford	40	13	7	20	59	74	33

Back row (left to right): H.V.Glover, J.N.Robertson, T.Burrows, J.S.Johnston, J.Dawson, A.H.Trueman, H.Lock, S.R.Jepp, J.R.Eastham. Middle row: W.Dawson (trainer), J.H.Bainbridge, F.Jefferis, A.Webb, F.Thorpe, A.Hughes, F.G.Costello, A.V.Hodgkinson. Front row: A.A.Wood, W.Bulpitt, H.M.Ashton, E.C.Jarvis, E.Arnfield.

1909-10

SAINTS began the season well. Indeed, they lost only one Southern League match during the first four months. Yet from that Championship-winning form they deteriorated to such an extent that, from New Year's Day they won only four out of 20 matches and finished fifth.

The forwards missed some easy chances, particular McGibbon despite being the possessor of a powerful shot. Defensively, Eastham. Glover, Johnston, Trueman and Robertson still figured soundly, but goalkeeper Burrows, who had taken over from Lock, lacked experience. At centre-half, Davidson started the season but did not command the directors' confidence and it was left to the faithful Jepp to fill the berth, despite lacking the necessary speed and skill.

FA Cup

SAINTS were eliminated in the second round after an excellent win at the Goldstone Ground in the first round. Manchester City won conclusively at The Dell when poor Burrows conceded five goals and Saints' forwards, despite playing some attractive football, could not reply.

The effect of the defeat seriously affected gate receipts and the season's gross results were £3,302 15s 11d — a drop of nearly £1,000 on the previous season. Rigid economy measures and the genrerosity of directors and friends averted a crisis.

Round 1
Jan 15 v Brighton & HA (a) 1-0
McGibbon
Burrows; Eastham, Glover, Johnston, Robertson, Trueman, Bainbridge, Jefferis, McGibbon, Carter, Blake.
Att: 11,000
Round 2
Feb 5 v Manchester City (h) 0-5
Burrows; Eastham, Glover, Johnston, Robertson, Trueman, Bainbridge, Jefferis, McGibbon, Carter, Blake.
Att: 15,695

Pre-World War One crowd at The Dell for a match against Brentford, showing that ground advertising was a source of revenue, even in those days.

1909-10
Southern League

Date	Opponent	Result	Scorers	Bainbridge JH	Bamford HW	Blake JJ	Brittleton S	Brown GS	Buckenham WE	Burrows T	Carter R	Clark T	Davidson AC	Davies TO	Eastham JR	Glover HW	Goodchild AJ	Jefferis F	Jepp SR	Johnston JS	Jordan F	McGibbon CE	McKeer WC	Moon CH	Prince P	Robertson JN	Shearer S	Smith WG	Toomer WE	Trueman AH
Sep 1	(h) Plymouth A	W 1-0	Jefferis							1	11		5	7	2	3		8			4	10					9			6
4	(h) Millwall	W 1-0	McGibbon							1	11		5	7	2	3		8			4	10				6	9			
8	(a) Plymouth A	D 1-1	Carter							1	9		5	7	2	3		8			4	10	11			6				
11	(a) New Brompton	L 0-2			11					1	9		5	7	2	3		8			4	10				6				
13	(h) Exeter C	W 3-2	Jefferis, Jordan, McGibbon							1	11			7	2	3		8			4	10				5	9			6
18	(h) Northampton T	L 2-3	Davies, Jefferis							1	11		5	7	2	3		8			4	10					9			6
25	(a) Queen's Park R	D 1-1	McGibbon			10				1	7				2	3		8	5		11	9				4				6
Oct 2	(h) Luton T	W 3-2	McGibbon 3			10	11			1	7				2	3		8	5	4		9				6				
9	(a) Swindon T	D 1-1	Blake			10	11			1	7				2	3		8	5	4		9				6				
16	(h) Crystal P	L 0-3				11	9			1						7		8	5	4		10				2				6
23	(a) Brighton & HA	D 2-2	McGibbon 2	7		10				1						3		8	5	4	11	9				2				6
25	(h) Croydon Com	W 3-0	Jefferis 2, Brittleton	7		10	11			1						3		8	5	4		9				2				6
30	(h) West Ham U	D 2-2	Bainbridge, Jepp	7		10	11			1						3		8	5	4		9				2				6
Nov 6	(a) Portsmouth	D 1-1	Blake	7		10	11			1						3		8	5	4		9				2				6
13	(h) Bristol R	W 3-0	McGibbon 2, Jefferis	7		10	11			1						3		8	5	4		9				2				6
20	(a) Norwich C	W 3-0	McGibbon 2, Carter	7			11			1	10					3		8	5	4		9				2				6
27	(h) Brentford	W 1-0	Jefferis	7			11			1	10					3		8	5	4		9				2				6
Dec 8	(a) Croydon Com	W 2-1	Trueman 2	7			11			1	10					3		8	5	4		9				2				6
11	(h) Watford	D 2-2	Jefferis, opp own goal	7			11			1	10					3		8	5	4		9				2				6
18	(a) Reading	W 2-1	Carter, McGibbon	7			11			1	10					3		8	5	4		9				2				6
25	(a) Leyton	W 2-1	Blake, McGibbon	7			11			1	10					3		8	5	4		9				6				
27	(h) Southend U	W 6-2	McGibbon 3, Carter 2, Clark				11			1	10	7			2	3		8	5	4		9				6				
Jan 1	(a) Exeter C	L 0-2				10	11			1	9	8		7	2	3			5	4						6				
8	(a) Millwall	D 1-1	Jefferis	7			11			1	10				2	3		8	5	4		9								6
22	(a) New Brompton	D 1-1	Bainbridge	7			11			1	10				2	3		8		4		9				5				6
29	(a) Northampton T	L 0-2					11			1	10				2	3		8	5	4		9						7		6
Feb 12	(a) Luton T	W 4-3	McGibbon 2, Bainbridge, Carter	7			11			1	10				2	3		8	5	4		9								6
26	(a) Crystal P	L 0-2		7						1	10				2	3		8	5	4		9				11				6
Mar 5	(h) Brighton & HA	W 2-1	Carter 2	7			11			1	10				2			8	5	4		9				3				6
12	(a) West Ham U	D 1-1	Brittleton			10	11			1	7				2		9	8	5	4						3				6
14	(a) Coventry C	D 2-2	Carter, Glover			10	11			1	7				2	3		8	5	4		9								6
19	(a) Portsmouth	L 1-2	Brittleton			10	11			1	7				2			8	5	4		9				3				6
25	(a) Southend U	L 0-2				10	11			1	7				2	3		8	5	4		9								6
26	(a) Bristol R	L 0-1				10	11	3		1	7				2			8		4		9				6	5			
28	(h) Leyton	D 0-0		7		10	11			1	9				2	3		8	5	4						6				
Apr 2	(h) Norwich C	D 0-0		6		11		3		1	7				2			8	5	4		9				10				
4	(h) Swindon T	D 1-1	Bainbridge	7						1					2	3		8	5		11	9				6	10	4		
9	(a) Brentford	L 0-1		7						1	11				2	3		8	5			9				6	10	4		
13	(h) Queen's Park R	D 1-1	Prince	7						1	11				2	3		8	5	4					9	6	10			
16	(h) Coventry C	W 3-2	Jefferis 2, Prince	7						1	11				2	3		8	5	4					9	6	10			
23	(a) Watford	D 2-2	Bainbridge, Jefferis	7		10	11			1	9							8	5	4						3	2			6
30	(h) Reading	W 3-1	Buckenham, Eastham, Jefferis	7			11		9	1					2			8	5	4				10		3				6
App				23	1	23	17	2	1	41	34	2	5	8	30	38	1	41	34	37	17	28	1	1	2	36	6	4	2	27
Goals				5		3	3		1		9	1		1	1	1		13		1	1	19			2					2

1 own-goal

Top row (left to right): McGibbon, Burrows, Harris, Jordan, Doon. Second row: Davies, Smith, Eastham, Glover, Hodgson, Grayer, Wright. Third row: W.Bulpitt, H.M.Ashton, Jepp, Davidson, Robertson, Johnston, Trueman, Bamford, Prince, W.Dawson (trainer), G.Rainsley (assistant trainer). Bottom row: A.A.Wood, Bainbridge, Jefferis, Brittleton, Carter, Blake, E.Arnfield (secretary).

	P	W	D	L	F	A	Pts
Brighton & HA	42	23	13	6	69	28	59
Swindon T	42	22	10	10	92	46	54
Queen's Park R	42	19	13	10	56	47	51
Northampton T	42	22	4	16	90	44	48
Southampton	42	16	16	10	64	55	48
Portsmouth	42	20	7	15	70	63	47
Crystal P	42	20	6	16	69	50	46
Coventry C	42	19	8	15	71	60	46
West Ham U	42	15	15	12	69	56	45
Leyton	42	16	11	15	60	46	43
Plymouth A	42	16	11	15	61	54	43
New Brompton	42	19	5	18	76	74	43
Bristol R	42	16	10	16	37	48	42
Brentford	42	16	9	17	50	58	41
Luton T	42	15	11	16	72	92	41
Millwall	42	15	7	20	45	59	37
Norwich C	42	13	9	20	59	78	35
Exeter C	42	14	6	22	60	69	34
Watford	42	10	13	19	52	76	33
Southend U	42	12	9	21	51	90	33
Croydon Common	42	13	5	24	52	96	31
Reading	42	7	10	25	38	73	24

1910-11

POOR showings in recent seasons enforced the realisation amongst Saints fans that their club was not the force of old. The 1910-11 season simply increased their dismay as Saints plunged to their worst position since joining the Southern League in 1894.

After keeping an unchanged team for the first three games, Saints thereafter never fielded the same team twice in succession, with goalkeeper and centre-half proving especially troublesome. Playing William Beaumont at centre-half proved particularly catastrophic.

The forward line also gave directors some sleepless nights. McGibbon returned to Arsenal, leaving Jefferis as the only proven goalscorer at The Dell and when he moved to Everton in March it effectively left the team without an experienced forward. Saints failed to win another game and were fortunate to avoid relegation.

A loss on the season of £108 4s 4d seems small but taking into account the fee received for Jefferis and the fact that amateurs Monk, Price and Brown received no wages, it had an ominious appearance.

FA Cup

HARRY Brown, in his second spell with Southampton, netted Saints' only goal of the 1910-11 FA Cup competition as they went out to Leicester Fosse.

Since their 1908 semi-final against Wolves, Saints had failed to get past the second round.

> **Round 1**
> **Jan 14 v Leicester Fosse (a) 1-3**
> *H.Brown*
> A.Brown; Eastham, Glover, Beaumont, Monk, Trueman, Jefferis, Dunne, Kimpton, H.Brown, Blake.
> *Att: 12,000*

Another view of The Dell crowd for a match before World War One. Military uniforms are making an appearance.

1910-11
Southern League

Date		Opponent	Result & Scorers	Bamford HW	Beaumont WE	Blake JJ	Brown AC	Brown H	Buckenham WE	Burrows T	Clark T	Coham WH	Dunne M	Eastham JR	Glover HW	Goodchild AJ	Grayer F	Jefferis F	Jepp SR	Johnston JS	Kimpton GS	McKeer WC	Monk FV	Penton B	Prince P	Robertson JN	Slade D	Smith S	Smith WG	Southern A	Toomer W	Trueman AH	Wheeler F
Sep 3	(a)	Luton T	L 2-3 Buckenham, Dunne		11				7	1			10	2	3			8	5						9	4							6	
10	(h)	Portsmouth	W 3-0 Dunne, Jefferis, Prince		11				7	1			10	2	3			8	5						9	4							6	
17	(a)	Northampton T	L 0-3		11				7	1			10	2	3			8	5						9	4							6	
24	(h)	Brighton & HA	L 1-2 Dunne		11	1			7				10	2	3			8	5						9	4							6	
Oct 1	(a)	Exeter C	D 0-0		11	1				9	7		10	2	3			8		4													6	5
8	(h)	Swindon T	L 0-4		11	1					7		10	2				8	5	4					9	3							6	
15	(a)	Bristol R	D 0-0		11	1				9	7		10	2	3			8	5							4							6	
22	(h)	Crystal P	L 0-3		11	1		10					8	2	3			7			9		5			4						6	
29	(a)	Brentford	L 2-3 Dunne, Kimpton	4	11	1		10					8	2				7			9	6	5			3							
Nov 5	(h)	Leyton	W 2-1 H.Brown 2	4	11	1		10					8	2				7			9		5			3						6	
12	(a)	Watford	D 1-1 Dunne	4	11	1		10					8	2				7			9		5			3						6	
19	(h)	Plymouth A	W 5-0 H.Brown 3, Jefferis, Trueman	4	11	1		10					8	2	3			7			9		5									6	
26	(h)	Norwich C	W 2-1 Jefferis, Trueman	4	11	1		10					8	2	3			7			9		5									6	
Dec 7	(a)	Southend U	W 1-0 Kimpton	4	11	1							8	2				7	5		9					3						6	10
10	(h)	Coventry C	W 2-1 H.Brown, Jefferis	4	11	1		10					8	2				7			9		5			3						6	
17	(a)	New Brompton	W 3-0 Jefferis 2, Dunne	4	11			10					8	2		1		7			9		5			3						6	
24	(h)	Millwall	L 0-1	4	11	1		10					8	2				7			9		5			3						6	
26	(h)	Queen's Park R	W 1-0 Kimpton	4	11	1		10					8	2	3			7			9		5									6	
27	(a)	Queen's Park R	L 1-3 Jefferis	4	11	1							8	2	3			7	5		9											6	10
31	(h)	Luton T	D 0-0		11									2	3	1		8		4	9		5		7							6	10
Jan 7	(a)	Portsmouth	W 1-0 Dunne		11	1		10					8	2	3					4	9		5		7							6	
21	(h)	Northampton T	W 1-0 Kimpton	4	11	1		10						2	3			8			9		5		7							6	
28	(a)	Brighton & HA	L 0-2	5	11	1								2	3			8		4	9	10			7							6	
Feb 4	(h)	Exeter C	L 1-3 opp own goal	4	10	1						11		2	3			8			9		5		7							6	
11	(a)	Swindon T	L 1-5 Jefferis	5			11	10							3	1	2	8		4					7							6	9
18	(a)	Bristol R	L 1-5 Kimpton	5	11			10						2	3	1		8			9				7						4	6	
25	(a)	Crystal P	D 2-2 H.Brown, Dunne	4		1		10				11	8	2	3			7	5		9											6	
Mar 4	(h)	Brentford	W 2-0 Kimpton, Penton	5	11	1		10						2	3			7		4	9			8								6	
11	(a)	Leyton	L 0-4	4	11	1		10						2	3			8			9		5	7								6	
18	(h)	Watford	D 2-2 H.Brown, Dunne	5	11	1		10					8	2	3			7		4	9											6	
25	(a)	Plymouth A	D 1-1 Penton	5		1	11	10				3		2				7		4	9			8								6	
Apr 1	(a)	Norwich C	L 1-2 Penton	5		1	11							2	3			7		4	9			8								6	10
8	(h)	Southend U	L 2-4 Eastham, Kimpton	5	11			10						2	3	1		7			9							6		8	4		
14	(a)	West Ham U	L 1-4 Southern	5	11	1								2	3			7		4				8		10		6		9			
15	(a)	Coventry C	L 0-2	6	11	1								2	3			7		4			5	8		10				9			
17	(h)	West Ham U	L 0-1	5	11	1		10					8	2	3			7		4	9											6	
22	(h)	New Brompton	D 0-0	6	11	1		10					8		3			7		4	9		5			2							
29	(a)	Millwall	L 0-4	5	11	1		10						2				7		4	9					3		6		8			
App				1	27	33	25	19	5	9	3	6	30	34	29	4	3	26	9	15	29	3	19	12	9	21	2	6	1	3	3	29	3
Goals								8	1				9	1				8			7			3	1					1		2	

1 own-goal

Back row (left to right): W.Bulpitt, W.Hammock, Glover, Eastham, Brown, Goodchild, Burrows, Grayer, W.Smith, S.Smith, E.Arnfield (secretary). Standing: H.M.Ashton, Mabbett, Passmore, Jepp, Trueman, Robertson, Monk, Bamford, Christmas, G.Rainsley (asst trainer), W.Dawson (trainer). Seated: A.A.Wood, Buckenham, Jefferis, Prince, Dunne, Blake, Carter. On ground: Hargreaves, Clark, McKeer Wheeler, Coham.

	P	W	D	L	F	A	Pts
Swindon T	38	24	5	9	80	31	53
Northampton T	38	18	12	8	54	27	48
Brighton & HA	38	20	8	10	58	36	48
Crystal P	38	17	13	8	55	48	47
West Ham U	38	17	11	10	63	46	45
Queen's Park R	38	13	14	17	52	41	40
Leyton	38	16	8	14	57	52	40
Plymouth A	38	15	9	14	54	55	39
Luton T	38	15	8	15	67	63	38
Norwich C	38	15	8	15	46	48	38
Coventry C	38	16	6	16	65	68	38
Brentford	38	14	9	15	41	42	37
Exeter C	38	14	9	15	51	53	37
Watford	38	13	9	16	49	65	35
Millwall	38	11	8	18	42	54	31
Bristol R	38	10	10	18	42	55	30
Southampton	38	11	8	19	42	67	30
New Brompton	38	11	8	19	34	65	30
Southend U	38	10	9	19	47	64	29
Portsmouth	38	8	11	19	34	53	27

1911-12

NEW secretary-manager George Swift — the first appointment in the club's history — spent £820 on 11 new players in six weeks as he set about rebuilding the team.

Swift's arrival saw the departure of Dawson, who had been trainer for 17 years, whilst Mr Arnfield moved from general secretary to financial secretary. Swift had been selected from 140 applicants as the Southampton directors made a concerted effort to end the club's dreadful run of form.

Two of the new recruits were old friends — Dan Gordon, who returned to Saints from Hull City via St Mirren, Middlesbrough and Bradford, and Bert Lee, who had left Southampton in 1906 and now returned after having captained Dundee to victory in the Scottish Cup Final.

Other new men were players of some reputation and with the new broom to sweep clean, Saints supporters looked forward with relish to a new season and a fresh start. It was quite a shock, then, when the 1911-12 season turned out to be even worse than the previous campaign when, at least, expectations had not been particularly high.

By the New Year, Southampton had won only five League games and locals were close to despair as the 'big-name' players failed to make any impression. Of the new men only Knight (a goalkeeper from Aston Villa's nursery club, Stourbridge), Denby (a half-back who had followed his manager from Chesterfield), McAlpine (another half-back, from Strathclyde) and the ever-dependable Lee (who eventually settled into the troublesome centre-half spot) acquitted themselves to the fans' satisfaction.

The forward line was again at sixes and sevens and it was only when Kimpton, Small, Prince, Dawe and Blake were plucked from the reserves and plunged into Southern League action that the front line began to recapture some of its old cohesion. Eventually, a few respectable results were strung together and Saints avoided relegation by three points.

The former Sheffield Wednesday forward, Hamilton, finished the season as leading scorer with ten goals, despite the fact that he moved to Belfast Celtic before the campaign was finished.

FA Cup

FOR the first time in their history, Southampton were eliminated from the FA Cup by a fellow Southern League side when Coventry City won 2-0 at Highfield Road. It was an uninspiring Cup match and at the time Saints were in the middle of a dreadful run which, this Cup defeat included, brought six consecutive defeats with 14 goals conceded and only three scored.

> **Round 1**
> **Jan 13 v Coventry City (a) 0-2**
> A.Brown; Eastham, Robertson, Kimpton, Lee, McAlpine, Wilcox, H.Brown, Hamilton, Prince, Handley.
> *Att: 12,649*

> *Another poor season led to Southampton announcing a working loss of £1,792. The directors made efforts to launch a public appeal for funds but met with little success. First, the appeal was deferred because of a coal miners' strike — and in keeping with that year's general disappointments, the second attempt coincided with the sinking of the Titanic and was duly forgotten by the end of the season.*

W.Dawson, Saints trainer for 17 years, left the club upon the appointment of their first secretary-manager, George Swift.

General secretary Mr E.Arnfield moved to the post of financial secretary when Swift was appointed.

1911-12
Southern League

Date	Opponent	Res	Score	Scorers	Blake JJ	Brown A	Brown H	Christmas ECR	Curry J	Dawe LS	Denby J	Eastham JR	Gibson A	Gordon D	Grayer F	Hamilton HG	Handley GA	Ireland S	Kimpton GS	Knight W	Lee EA	McAlpine J	Monk FV	Nihan M	Penton B	Prince P	Robertson JN	Sheeran CF	Slade D	Small AR	Wilcox J
Sep 2 (h)	Millwall	D	1-1	Wilcox		1	8	6		5	2	10				9	11				4					3					7
9 (a)	West Ham U	D	2-2	H.Brown, Small		1	10	6		5	2					9	11				4					3				8	7
16 (h)	Bristol R	L	0-1			1	10	6		5	2					9	11				4				8	3					7
23 (a)	Swindon T	L	1-2	Handley		1				5	2	10				9	11				4	6				3				8	7
30 (h)	Northampton T	W	2-1	Handley, Wilcox		1				5	2	10				9	11				4	6				3				8	7
Oct 7 (a)	Brighton & HA	L	0-5			1				5	2	10				9	11				4	6				3				8	7
14 (h)	Stoke C	W	1-0	Hamilton		1				5	2	10				9	11				4	6				3				8	7
21 (a)	Coventry C	L	1-2	Wilcox		1	10			5	2					9	11				4	6				3				8	7
28 (h)	Leyton	W	3-2	Gibson 2, H.Brown		1	8			5	2	10	9				11				4	6				3					7
Nov 4 (a)	Norwich C	D	0-0			1	8			5	2	10	9				11				4	6				3					7
11 (h)	Crystal P	L	2-4	Kimpton, Wilcox	11	1	8				2	10	9						5		4	6				3					7
18 (a)	Luton T	D	1-1	Hamilton			8			5	2	10				9	11			1	4	6				3					7
25 (a)	Plymouth A	L	0-2				8			5	2	10				9	11			1	4	6				3					7
Dec 2 (h)	Coventry C	L	1-2	Hamilton		1	8			5	2	10				9	11				4	6					3				7
9 (a)	Watford	D	0-0				8				2	10				9	11		5	1	4	6					3				7
16 (h)	New Brompton	W	3-0	Hamilton 2, Prince			8				2					9	11		5	1	4	6				10	3				7
23 (a)	Exeter C	D	2-2	H.Brown, Eastham			8				2	11				9			5	1	4	6				10	3				7
25 (h)	Brentford	L	0-4		11		8				2					9			5	1	4	6				10	3				7
26 (h)	Brentford	W	3-2	Blake, H.Brown, Wilcox	11	1	8				2					9			5		4	6				10	3				7
30 (a)	Millwall	D	3-3	Hamilton 2, H.Brown	11		8				2					9			5	1	4	6				10	3				7
Jan 1 (h)	Reading	L	0-2		11		8				2					9			5	1	4	6				10	3				7
6 (h)	West Ham U	L	1-2	Prince		1	8	6			2					9	11		5		4					10	3				7
20 (a)	Bristol R	L	0-2				8	6			2		9				11		5	1	4	10					3				7
27 (h)	Swindon T	L	1-3	Gibson			8	6			2	10	9				11		5	1	4						3				7
Feb 10 (a)	Brighton & HA	L	1-3	Gibson			8				2	10	9				11		5	1	4	6					3				7
17 (a)	Stoke C	W	3-0	Hamilton 2, Denby			8				2	10				9	11	7	5	1	4	6					3				
Mar 2 (a)	Leyton	L	0-1				8				2	10				9	11		5	1	4	6					3				7
9 (h)	Norwich C	D	1-1	Lee			8				2	10				9	11		5	1	4	6					3				7
16 (a)	Crystal P	L	1-3	H.Brown		10	9				2						11		5	1	4	6					3			8	7
23 (h)	Luton T	W	3-2	Prince 2, Blake	11						2		9	3				7	5	1	4	6				10				8	
30 (h)	Plymouth A	W	1-0	Prince	11						2		9	3				7	5	1	4	6				10				8	
Apr 5 (a)	Queen's Park R	D	1-1	Prince	11	10					2			3				7	5	1	4	6				9				8	
6 (a)	Reading	D	2-2	H.Brown, Small		10	5				2			3			11	7		1	4	6				9				8	
8 (h)	Queen's Park R	D	0-0		11	10					2			3				7	5	1	4	6				9				8	
13 (h)	Watford	W	2-1	Dawe 2	11					5	2		9	3				7		1	4	6				10				8	
20 (a)	New Brompton	L	0-1		11	10					2			3				7	5	1	4	6				9				8	
25 (a)	Northampton T	L	0-4		11	10					2			3				7	5	1	4	6				9				8	
27 (h)	Exeter C	W	3-0	Blake, Dawe, Small	11					5	2		9	3						1	4	6				10				8	7
App					13	14	29	2	7	3	33	22	18	12	3	23	24	11	27	24	25	33	1	2	1	18	28	2	1	15	27
Goals					3		7			3	1	1	4			9	2		1		1					6				3	5

Back row (left to right): W.A.Hammock (director), I.Turner (trainer), J.Robertson, J.McAlpine, W.Knight, A.C.Brown, D.Gordon, E.Salway, D.Slade, G.Swift (secretary). Second row: G.Rainsley (asst trainer), E.Arnfield (financial secretary), A.Small, B.Penton, J.R.Eastham, S.Ireland, A.Lee, J.Curry, G.Smith, F.Grayer, H.M.Ashton (director), W.Bulpitt (director). Sitting: C.Sheeran, A.Gibson, H.Hamilton, G.S.Kimpton, H.Brown, J.Denby, G.Handley. On ground: J.Wilcox, S.Chalcraft.

	P	W	D	L	F	A	Pts
Queen's Park R	38	21	11	6	59	35	53
Plymouth A	38	23	6	9	63	31	52
Northampton T	38	22	7	9	82	41	51
Swindon T	38	21	6	11	82	50	48
Brighton & HA	38	19	9	10	73	35	47
Coventry C	38	17	8	13	66	54	42
Crystal P	38	15	10	13	70	46	40
Millwall	38	15	10	13	60	57	40
Stoke C	38	13	10	15	51	63	36
Watford	38	13	10	15	55	68	36
Reading	38	11	14	13	43	58	36
Norwich C	38	10	14	14	40	60	34
West Ham U	38	13	7	18	64	69	33
Brentford	38	12	9	17	60	65	33
Exeter C	38	11	11	16	48	62	33
Southampton	38	10	11	17	46	63	31
Bristol R	38	9	13	16	41	62	31
New Brompton	38	11	9	18	35	72	31
Luton T	38	9	10	19	49	61	28
Leyton	38	7	11	20	27	62	25

51

1912-13

AFTER the previous season's near disaster, it was hardly surprising that Southampton began the new campaign with a different manager.

The new face was Jimmy McIntyre, a man with a growing reputation who had spent the previous seven seasons as trainer at Coventry, the team which had dumped Saints out of the FA Cup earlier that year.

Unfortunately for McIntyre, he found the club's purse practically empty as Swift had spent relatively heavily. McIntyre was able to bring in only three new players — Coates, Taylor and Andrews.

The transfer of Len Andrews from Reading was one of the best moves of McIntyre's managerial career, for Andrews soon proved to be a goalscoring outside-left and something of a penalty expert — a role that Saints had badly needed to fill in years gone by. Andrews gave Saints valuable service, seeing them into the Football League and then through to the Second Division before he left for Watford in 1924.

Apart from these three signings the Southampton team was very similar to the previous year's, so it was hardly surprising that they achieved similar results. The forward line was particularly inexperienced and an amateur player, Percy Prince, finished leading scorer with Andrews close behind.

In the first half of the season Saints' front line struggled to discover any semblance of rhythm and by the end of October they had won only one match. In desperation, McIntyre made two more signings in the shape of Kitchen, a goalkeeper from West Ham, and Turnbull, a forward from McIntyre's former club, Coventry.

These experienced players were expected to add some stability to the Saints team, but Turnbull, who had spent several years in Newcastle's reserves, was past his best, and Kitchen had also seen better days. On 16 November 1912, he was the luckless goalkeeper directly on the receiving end of Saints' worst-ever defeat in a competitive match. They went down 8-0 on a foggy afternoon at Crystal Palace.

Yet this crushing defeat was followed by something of a revival — four wins and a draw — to underline the erratic nature of the Southampton team. The New Year brought more defeats, however, and Saints ended the season fourth from bottom.

Despite all this, there were some encouraging signs in the fact that the younger players were finding their feet under McIntyre's guidance. Indeed, some of the youngsters in the reserve team were pushing hard for a Southern League place. One player in particular emerged from the second team at the end of the season — a figure who was to become one of the great names for Saints in the inter-war period. Arthur Dominy made his debut at Stoke, and in the last home game of the season, against Gillingham, he scored two goals to give The Dell fans some early indication of what was to come.

A common joke that was doing the rounds amongst Southampton fans during this season, went as follows: Q. Why do the Southampton directors smoke Woodbines? A. Because they can't afford Players!

On 16 November it was decided to give Percy Prince a rest from first team duties, but as the reserves were struggling to field a full team he played for them as a last-minute stop-gap. During the match he received a severe kick which prevented him from being available for first-team selection the following week.

Part of the crowd who saw Saints draw with Reading at The Dell on 12 April 1913. The newspaper seller's placard (extreme left of picture) announces the release from prison of Mrs Pankhurst, the suffragette leader.

FA Cup

ELIMINATION from the first round of the FA Cup was becoming something of a tradition for Southampton and they maintained that by losing to Bury.

Their real chance went when they failed to take advantage of a home draw against Bury and after failing to make the most of the advantages afforded by playing at The Dell, it surprised nobody when Bury won the replay at Gigg Lane.

With advent of new laws for shops, many people now had to work on Saturday afternoons and with this in mind, Saints' directors decided to enter the Southern Alliance League which played in midweek, thus still giving Saturday workers the opportunity to watch first-class football.

Round 1
Jan 11 v Bury (h) 1-1
Andrews
Kitchen; Lee, Ireland, Denby, Tyson, McAlpine, Blackmore, Turnbull, Kimpton, Brown, Andrews.
Att: 9,000
Replay
Jan 15 v Bury (a) 1-2
Turnbull
Kitchen; Lee, Ireland, Denby, Tyson, McAlpine, Blackmore, Taylor, Turnbull, Brown, Andrews.
Att: 8,000

1912-13
Southern League

The table below records each match with the shirt numbers worn by each player. Player columns (left to right): Andrews LTA, Bennett R, Binder T, Blackmore W, Blake JJ, Bradley JW, Brooks R, Brown H, Browning RE, Cunningham CA, Coates A, Dawe LS, Denby J, Diaper A, Dominy A, Hardy GD, Ireland S, Kimpton GS, Kitchen GW, Knight W, Lee EA, McAlpine J, Penton B, Prince P, Richards L, Salway EE, Sanders W, Selstone SC, Small AR, Taylor F, Toomer WE, Turnbull F, Tyson CF.

Date		Opponent	Res	Scorers	And	Ben	Bin	Blm	Blk	Bra	Bks	Brn	Brg	Cun	Coa	Daw	Den	Dia	Dom	Har	Ire	Kim	Kit	Kni	Lee	McA	Pen	Pri	Ric	Sal	San	Sel	Sml	Tay	Too	Tur	Tys
Sep 4	(h)	Northampton T	D 2-2	Blake, Kimpton	10				11					2		9	4				3	7		1	5	6								8			
7	(a)	Millwall	L 0-4		10				11					2		9	4				3	7		1	5	6								8			
12	(a)	Northampton T	W 2-1	Andrews, Taylor	11		7							2			4				3		9	1	5	6		10						8			
14	(h)	Bristol R	D 2-2	Andrews, Kimpton	11		7							2			4				3	9		1	5	6		10						8			
21	(a)	Swindon T	L 0-5		11			7						2			4				3		9	1	5	6		10						8			
28	(h)	Portsmouth	L 2-3	Andrews, Denby	11			7						2			4				3		9	1		6		10						8			5
Oct 5	(a)	Exeter C	L 0-1		11			7						2			4				3		9	1	5			10		6				8			
12	(h)	West Ham U	L 1-3	Prince	11												4				3	7		1	2	5	9	10		6				8			
19	(a)	Brighton & HA	L 2-5	Kimpton, Turnbull						10				2			4				3	7		1		6								8		9	5
26	(h)	Coventry C	D 0-0		11					10							4				3	7	1		2	6								8		9	5
Nov 2	(a)	Watford	L 0-2		11					10											3			1	2	6						7	4	8		9	5
9	(h)	Merthyr T	W 3-0	Andrews 2, Brown	11							10					4				3	7		1	2	6		9						8			5
16	(a)	Crystal P	L 0-8		11							10					4				3	7		1	2	6		9						8			5
23	(h)	Plymouth A	W 2-0	Andrews, Prince	11							10					4				3	7		1	2	6		9						8			5
30	(h)	Stoke C	W 2-1	Lee, Taylor	11												4				3	7		1	2	6		9					10	8			5
Dec 7	(a)	Reading	D 1-1	Prince	11								10				4				3	7		1	2	6		9						8			5
14	(h)	Norwich C	W 1-0	Andrews	11								10	2			4				3	7		1		6		9						8			5
21	(a)	Gillingham	W 1-0	Andrews	11									2			4				3	7		1		6		10	5		9			8			
25	(a)	Queen's Park R	L 0-1		11	7								2			4				3			1		6		9	5					8	10		
26	(h)	Queen's Park R	L 0-1		11	7								2			4		10		3			1		6		9	5					8			
28	(h)	Millwall	L 0-4		11						7		10	2			4				3			1		6		9	5					8			
Jan 4	(a)	Bristol R	L 0-2		11	7								2		8	4				3		9	1		6			5						10		
18	(h)	Swindon T	W 2-0	Prince 2			7	11						2			4				3			1	5	6		9						8	10		
25	(a)	Portsmouth	L 0-2				7	11						2		8	4				3			1	5	6		9							10		
Feb 3	(h)	Exeter C	D 2-2	Blake, Prince	10				11					2			4				3	7	1		5	6		9	8								
15	(a)	West Ham U	D 1-1	Kimpton	11							10		2			4				3	7	1		5	6		9		8							
22	(h)	Brighton & HA	D 1-1	Prince	11							10		2			4				3		1		5	6		9			7	8					
Mar 1	(a)	Coventry C	D 1-1	Turnbull	11							10		2			4				3			1	5	6		9			7			8			
8	(h)	Watford	L 0-1		11							10		2			4				3			1	5	6		9			7			8			
15	(a)	Merthyr T	D 0-0		11							10					4				3	7		1	2	6		9						8			5
21	(a)	Brentford	W 2-1	Lee, Prince	7			11			2	10					4				3			1	5	6		9						8			
22	(h)	Crystal P	W 1-0	Prince	10			11			2						4				3			1		6		9				7		8			5
24	(a)	Brentford	W 3-1	Andrews, Lee, Prince	7			11			2							4			3			1	5	6		9		10				8			
29	(a)	Plymouth A	L 1-6	Denby	7			11			2						4				3			1	5	6		9		10				8			
Apr 5	(a)	Stoke C	L 1-3	Prince	7			11			2						4		8		3			1	5	6		9		10							
12	(h)	Reading	D 1-1	Blake	7			11	9								4				3			1	2	6				10				8			5
19	(a)	Norwich C	L 0-3		10	2	7	11	9								4		8		3			1	5	6											
26	(h)	Gillingham	D 3-3	Dominy 2, Bradley			7	11	9								4		8	10	3			1	2	6											5
App					32	1	2	7	19	3	5	6	6	21	1	8	31	1	3	1	38	23	24	14	30	36	1	30	1	10	2	4	5	13	2	23	14
Goals					9				3	1		1					2		2			4			3			11						2		2	

FW Williams played number 11 against Brighton & HA (a) on 19 October 1912

	P	W	D	L	F	A	Pts
Plymouth A	38	22	6	10	77	36	50
Swindon T	38	20	8	10	66	41	48
West Ham U	38	18	12	8	66	46	48
Queen's Park R	38	18	10	10	46	36	46
Crystal P	38	17	11	10	55	36	45
Millwall	38	19	7	12	62	43	45
Exeter C	38	18	8	12	48	44	44
Reading	38	17	8	13	59	55	42
Brighton & HA	38	13	12	13	48	47	38
Northampton T	38	12	12	14	61	48	36
Portsmouth	38	14	8	16	41	49	36
Merthyr T	38	12	12	14	43	60	36
Coventry C	38	13	8	17	53	59	34
Watford	38	12	10	16	43	50	34
Gillingham	38	12	10	16	36	53	34
Bristol R	38	12	9	17	55	64	33
Southampton	38	10	11	17	40	72	31
Norwich C	38	10	9	19	39	50	29
Brentford	38	11	5	22	42	55	27
Stoke C	38	10	4	24	39	75	24

Standing (left to right): A.A.Wood, E.Arnfield, W.Bulpitt, A.Coates, W.Knight, A.Lee, J.McAlpine, S.Ireland, H.Ashton, J.McIntyre (trainer), C.Payne. Sitting: G.Kimpton, F.Taylor, L.Dawe, L.Andrews, J.Blake.

1913-14

THERE had been encouraging signs towards the end of the previous season and, indeed, the 1913-14 campaign saw a considerable improvement in performance and results.

Despite no major 'star' signing, Southampton scored more goals than the previous season and conceded less. The club decided to ignore the big-name players who might have been available and, instead, they concentrated on acquiring promising young players in the shape of Steventon, a goalkeeper who had been spotted playing local football in the Black Country, and Hadley. a Scottish junior international half-back from Wellinghall Swifts.

Other new arrivals included Bill Smith (from Brentford), Small (Sunderland) and Curtin (Norwich). The highlight of the season came on Boxing Day when Pompey visited The Dell. A record League attendance of 19,291 saw Saints win 4-3 in a splendid game.

Arthur Dominy carried on where he had left off the previous season, netting 13 League goals to finish top scorer. Andrews showed his worth with 12 goals and he missed only one League game. Both he and Dominy were inside-forwards who looked to have a good future in the game.

FA Cup

In the FA Cup, Saints had the misfortune to be drawn away to Wolves in the first round but, despite their recent poor showing in the Cup, there was such a huge demand from Southampton supporters who wanted to travel to the game that an extra train was needed and 600 fans gladly parted with the 5s 9d return fare. Their support was not enough to prevent Southampton going down 3-0, however.

> **Round 1**
> **Jan 10 v Wolverhampton Wanderers (a) 0-3**
> Steventon; F.Smith, Ireland, Hadley, Denby, McAlpine, Kimpton, Dominy, Prince, Andrews, Blake.
> *Att: 18,000*

> *Saints continued to field a team in the midweek Southern Alliance League. Len Andrews was top scorer with eight goals.*

SAINTS V NORTHAMPTON Nº 1

Everyone seems to be wearing a hat in this section of the crowd which saw Saints lose 2-1 to Northampton Town at The Dell in April 1914.

Bill Smith, from Brentford, had a rather inconsistent time with Saints and although the club had high hopes of him, he left the area in 1914 after only one season with the club.

1913-14
Southern League

Date		Opponent	Result	Scorers	Andrews LTA	Binder T	Blake JJ	Brooks R	Buckley A	Curtin C	Denby J	Dominy A	Eke H	Green G	Hadley G	Hollins A	Ireland S	Kimpton GS	Kitchen GW	Lee EA	McAlpine J	Prince P	Small J	Smith F	Smith W	Steventon E
Sep 3	(a)	Brighton & HA	L 0-1		11	7					5	8					3	1	2	6	10	4			9	
Sep 6	(h)	Exeter C	W 2-0	Small, W.Smith	11	7					5	8					3	1	2	6	10	4			9	
Sep 10	(h)	Brighton & HA	D 0-0		11	7	2				5	8					3	1		6	10	4			9	
Sep 13	(a)	Cardiff C	W 2-1	Andrews, Prince	11	7	2				5	8					3	1		6	10	4			9	
Sep 20	(h)	Swindon T	L 1-2	W.Smith	11	7	2				5	8					3	1		6	10	4			9	
Sep 27	(a)	Bristol R	W 3-1	Andrews, Binder, Prince	11	7	2				5	8					3	1		6	9	4			10	
Oct 4	(h)	Merthyr T	W 3-0	Dominy, McAlpine, Prince	11	7	2				5	8					3	1		6	9	4			10	
Oct 11	(a)	West Ham U	L 1-5	Dominy	11	7	3				5	8						1	2	6	9	4			10	
Oct 18	(h)	Plymouth A	L 1-2	Prince	11	7					5	8					3	1	2	6	9	4			10	
Oct 25	(a)	Queen's Park R	L 1-3	W.Smith	11	7					5		8				3	1	2	6	9	4			10	
Nov 1	(a)	Reading	L 0-2		10	7	11					8			6		3	1		5		4	2		9	
Nov 8	(h)	Crystal P	D 2-2	Andrews, Dominy	10		11				5	8			6		3	7				4	2	9		1
Nov 15	(a)	Coventry C	D 2-2	Dominy 2	10		11				4	8			6		3	7	5				2	9		1
Nov 22	(h)	Watford	L 1-3	W.Smith	10		11				4	8			6		3	7	1	5			2	9		
Dec 6	(h)	Gillingham	W 3-1	Dominy 2, Hadley	10		11				5	8			4		3	7			6	9	2			1
Dec 13	(a)	Northampton T	D 0-0		10		11				5	8			4		3	7			6	9	2			1
Dec 20	(h)	Southend U	W 4-2	Andrews, Denby, Dominy, Kimpton	10		11				5	8			4		3	7			6	9	2			1
Dec 25	(a)	Portsmouth	L 0-2		10		11				5	8			4		3	7			6	9	2			1
Dec 26	(h)	Portsmouth	W 4-3	Kimpton 2, Andrews, Dominy	10		11					8			4		3	7	5	6	9		2			1
Dec 27	(a)	Exeter C	L 0-2				11					8			4		3	7	5	6	9		2	10		1
Jan 3	(h)	Cardiff C	W 2-0	Andrews 2	10		11				5	8			4		3	7		6	9		2			1
Jan 17	(a)	Swindon T	L 0-3		10		11	3			5	8			4			7	2	6				9		1
Jan 24	(h)	Bristol R	W 2-0	Andrews, Dominy	10		11	2	9		5	8			4		3	7		6					1	
Jan 31	(a)	Norwich C	L 1-2	Andrews	10		11	2			5	8			4		3	7	1	6				9		
Feb 7	(a)	Merthyr T	W 2-1	Dominy 2	10		11	2			5	8			4		3	7		6				9		1
Feb 14	(h)	West Ham U	L 2-3	Andrews, Blake	10		11	2			5	8			4		3	7		6				9		1
Feb 21	(a)	Plymouth A	D 1-1	Kimpton	10	7	11	2			5	8				9	3			6		4				1
Feb 28	(h)	Queen's Park R	L 0-2		10		11	2				8			9	3	7		5	6		4				1
Mar 7	(h)	Reading	W 2-1	Andrews, Hollins	10		11					8			9	3	7		5	6		4	2			1
Mar 14	(a)	Crystal P	D 0-0		10		11					8			6	9	3	7		5			4	2		1
Mar 21	(h)	Coventry C	W 3-0	Hollins, Kimpton, Lee	10		11					8			6	9	3	7		5			4	2		1
Mar 28	(a)	Watford	L 1-2	Dominy	10		11					8			6	9	3	7		5			4	2		1
Apr 4	(h)	Norwich C	W 2-0	Hollins 2	10		11					8			4	9	3	7		2	6		5			1
Apr 10	(a)	Millwall	W 4-0	Hollins 3, Hadley	10		11		5			8			8	9	3	7		2	6		4			1
Apr 11	(a)	Gillingham	L 1-3	Andrews	10		11	2	5			8			8	9	3	7			6		4			1
Apr 13	(h)	Millwall	W 1-0	Small	10		11		5			8			8	9	3	7		2	6		4			1
Apr 18	(h)	Northampton T	L 1-2	Hadley	10		11		7	5			2	8	9	3					6		4			1
Apr 25	(a)	Southend U	D 0-0		11				7	5					9	3	8			6			4	2	10	1
App					37	8	31	14	1	2	30	31	1	1	24	11	36	26	13	19	31	17	24	16	20	25
Goals					12	1	1				1	13			3	7		5		1	1	4	2		4	

Back row (left to right): Arnfield, F.Smith, Denby, Steventon, McAlpine, Brookes, Small, McIntyre.
Middle row: Carter, Ashton, Diaper, Kimpton, Lee, Ireland, Hadley, Butt, Wood, Bulpitt. Sitting: Binder, Dominy, W.Smith, Prince, Andrews.

	P	W	D	L	F	A	Pts
Swindon T	38	21	8	9	81	41	50
Crystal P	38	17	16	5	60	32	50
Northampton T	38	14	19	5	50	37	47
Reading	38	17	10	11	43	36	44
Plymouth A	38	15	13	10	46	42	43
West Ham U	38	15	12	11	61	60	42
Brighton & HA	38	15	11	12	43	45	42
Queen's Park R	38	16	9	13	45	43	41
Portsmouth	38	14	12	12	57	48	40
Cardiff C	38	13	12	13	46	42	38
Southampton	38	15	7	16	55	54	37
Exeter C	38	10	16	12	39	38	36
Gillingham	38	13	9	16	48	49	35
Norwich C	38	9	17	12	49	51	35
Millwall	38	11	12	15	51	56	34
Southend U	38	10	12	16	41	66	32
Bristol R	38	10	11	17	46	67	31
Watford	38	10	9	19	50	56	29
Merthyr T	38	9	10	19	38	61	28
Coventry C	38	6	14	18	43	68	26

1914-15

DESPITE the outbreak of war on 4 August 1914, the Southern League programme kicked-off as usual one month later. Saints continued their improvement and were happy with fifth place at the end of a difficult season.

The forwards had a fine campaign, scoring more goals (78) than any other team in the division. Alas, at the same time the defence was almost equally busy, conceding 74, a figure 'beaten' only by Gillingham and Bristol Rovers.

As the war was still in its early stages Saints lost only three players to the services and, although a further 20 signed up as reservists, Southampton were able to field their first-choice team in most matches.

Attendances grew as Southampton was particularly busy in its capacity as a port. The regular Saturday afternoon crowds now included soldiers and sailors from all parts of the United Kingdom who found themselves stationed in the area.

To Arthur Dominy fell the honour of being the leading scorer in the Southern League with 30 goals. Andrews, meanwhile, proved himself a reliable penalty-taker, converting eight out of nine spot kicks.

FA Cup

LUTON proved disappointing opponents in the first round of the FA Cup. They spent the whole of the match on the defensive — although whether this was in search of a replay or simply that they were overwhelmed is not clear — and Saints went through 3-0.

Andrews opened the scoring with a penalty after 15 minutes, and in the second half he made it 2-0 with a superb goal. With his back to goal and surrounded by defenders, he cleverly back-heeled the ball, ran around the outside of the attendant posse of Hatters' players and struck a fine shot past the startled Luton 'keeper. A Kimpton header completed Luton's misery.

In these days, extra-time was played if the first game ended in a draw after 90 minutes, so Saints sensibly went on the attack at Craven Cottage in the second round. They fell behind to a first-half goal and with five minutes remaining were trailing 2-1 when Andrews equalised with a controversial penalty after a Fulham defender accidently handled. Saints continued to attack and six minutes from the end of extra-time, Kimpton hit the winner.

Hull City were the next Cup visitors to The Dell and after Saints won the toss they set the Tigers to face the sun which shone from a bright winter's sky. Despite that potential handicap, Hull scored first, following a 25th-minute corner, and although Saints fought back relentlessly, it was three minutes from the end before Andrews levelled the scores. In extra-time, Jones put Saints ahead for the first time in the match but the plucky Yorkshiremen themselves equalised five minutes from the end.

In the replay at Anlaby Road a week later, Saints were outclassed as Hull went into the fourth round for the first time in their history.

Round 1
Jan 9 v Luton Town (h) 3-0
Andrews 2 (1 pen), Kimpton
Wood; Small, Ireland, Hadley, Denby, McAlpine, Curtin, Dominy, Kimpton, Jones, Andrews.
Att: 11,000
Round 2
Jan 21 v Fulham (a) 3-2
Jones, Andrews (pen), Kimpton
Wood; Small, Ircland, Hadley, Denby, McAlpine, Curtin, Dominy, Kimpton, Jones, Andrews.
Att: 8,898
Round 3
Feb 20 v Hull City (h) 2-2
Andrews, Jones
Wood; Small, Ireland, Hadley, Denby, McAlpine, Curtin, Dominy, Kimpton, Jones, Andrews.
Att: 15,607
Replay
Feb 27 v Hull City (a) 0-4
Wood; Small, Ireland, Hadley, Denby, McAlpine, Curtin, Dominy, Kimpton, Jones, Andrews.
Att: 11,000

Saints made a loss of £1,911 15s 8d during the season, pushing their total debt to £3,942 5s 6d.
At the annual meeting, Mr George Muir, secretary of the club in the early amateur days at St Mary's, was elected to the board in place of the late Mr H.M.Ashton.

SAINTS' SUPPORTERS.

Leaflet exhorting Saints fans to turn out in numbers for the visit of Portsmouth on Boxing Day.

At this juncture the Directors of the Club wish to return their thanks for the support which has been accorded them this season. It is not, of course, up to average proportions—but then we did not expect it to be, in view of the war; for thousands of our regular supporters are now away serving their King and Country, some at the Front, others on the sea, others again in India, and hundreds of them in Kitchener's Army. Our Players, too, are doing their little bit towards protecting our hearths and homes. Over 20 are in military service, and those who are entertaining you this afternoon, as well as the Reserves, are devoting several hours daily to drill. We are all, Players and Supporters, taking some part, it may be only a small part, in that greater game on the military field.

But we must keep things going at home as usual. There are many thousands in this town and port who, in various capacities, are doing the Empire's work; and the only entertainment the majority of them get is their Saturday's match at The Dell. It is the duty of this Club to provide that entertainment, but it cannot do so without sufficient funds.

If normal conditions were prevailing, there would be no need to appeal for additional support, but, owing to the war, everything is abnormal, and there has been a tremendous slump in our gates. Notwithstanding the most rigid economy on the part of the Directorate, and a monetary sacrifice, cheerfully borne, by the Players, the financial position is steadily getting worse.

The only immediate prospect of arresting this decline is for a bumper gate to be secured on Boxing Day, when we play Portsmouth.

In previous years this match has invariably yielded our best League gate, because of the keen rivalry between the teams, and the excellence of their football. It is certain that the forthcoming fixture will also maintain the best traditions of the two Clubs.

The Directors therefore make a special appeal to their Supporters for a big rally on this occasion, in order to keep the old ship afloat in this time of stress and trouble.

It will require a strong, united effort on the part of everyone who has the interest of the Club at heart. So come yourself on Boxing Day, and bring every friend you can influence with you.

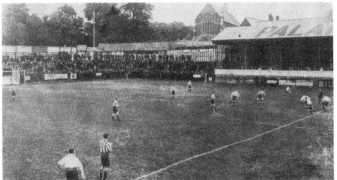

General view of The Dell in 1914. The teams appear to have just kicked-off.

Jock McAlpine, signed from Strathclyde, was a regular right up to the outbreak of war.

1914-15
Southern League

Date		Opponent	Res	Score	Scorers	Andrews LTA	Blake JJ	Crick GW	Curtin C	Denby J	Dominy A	Green G	Hadley G	Hall H	Hinton J	Hollins A	Ireland S	Jones F	Kimpton GS	Lee EA	Loasby FT	McAlpine J	Mounsey F	Slade R	Small J	Steventon E	Wheeler LC	Wood A
Sep 2	(h)	Luton T	D	3-3	Dominy, Hollins, Jones	11				5	8	2				9	3	10	7			6			4	1		
5	(a)	Southend U	L	0-4		11				5	8	2				9	3	10	7			6			4	1		
9	(a)	Luton T	L	2-3	Dominy, Hollins	11				5	8	2	6			9	3	10	7						4	1		
12	(h)	Queen's Park R	W	3-0	Andrews, Dominy, Jones	9	11		7	5	8	2	6				3	10							4	1		
19	(a)	Millwall	W	2-1	Dominy, Jones	9	11		7	5	8	2	6				3	10							4	1		
26	(h)	Bristol R	W	3-1	Dominy, Jones, Kimpton	9	11			5	8	2	6				3	10	7						4	1		
Oct 3	(a)	Croydon Com	L	0-2		9	11			5	8	2	6				3	10	7						4	1		
10	(h)	Reading	L	2-4	Dominy, Jones	9	11				8	2	6				3	10	7	5					4	1		
17	(h)	Crystal P	L	2-3	Dominy 2	10	11				8	2				9	3		7			6	5		4	1		
24	(a)	Northampton T	L	0-2		11					8	2	4				3	10	7			6		5	1	9		
31	(h)	Watford	W	3-1	Dominy 2, Jones	11			7		8	2	4				3	10	9			6		5	1			
Nov 7	(a)	Plymouth A	L	2-6	Dominy, McAlpine	11			7	5	8	2	4				3	10	9			6				1		
14	(h)	West Ham U	W	3-1	Curtain, Dominy, Andrews	11			7	5	8		4				3	10	9	2		6				1		
21	(a)	Norwich C	D	0-0		11			7	5	8		4				3	10	9			6			2	1		
28	(h)	Gillingham	W	2-1	Denby, Kimpton	11			7	5	8		4				3	10	9			6			2	1		
Dec 6	(a)	Brighton & HA	L	0-4		11			7	5	8		4				3	10	9			6			2	1		
12	(h)	Cardiff C	D	1-1	Dominy		11		7	5	8		4				3	10	9			6			2	1		
19	(a)	Exeter C	W	2-1	Denby, Jones	11			7	5	8		4				3	10	9			6			2	1		
25	(a)	Portsmouth	W	1-0	Andrews	11			7	5	8		4				3	10	9			6			2	1		
26	(h)	Portsmouth	W	4-3	Andrews, Curtain, Dominy, Kimpton	11			7	5	8		4				3	10	9			6			2			1
Jan 2	(h)	Southend U	W	2-0	Jones, Kimpton	11			7	5	8		4				3	10	9			6			2			1
16	(a)	Queen's Park R	L	3-4	Andrews, Curtain, Kimpton	11			7	5			4		10	8			9			6		3	2			1
23	(h)	Millwall	W	4-2	Dominy 2, Andrews, Curtain	11	4		7	5	8						3	10	9			6			2			1
Feb 6	(h)	Croydon Com	W	4-0	Andrews, Dominy, Jones, Kimpton	11			7	5	8		4				3	10	9			6			2			1
13	(h)	Reading	W	1-0	Dominy	11			7	5	8		4				3	10	9			6			2			1
Mar 3	(a)	Crystal P	W	2-1	Jones, Kimpton		4		7	5	8	2		11			3	10	9			6						1
6	(a)	Watford	L	2-5	Dominy 2	11	4		7	5	8	2					3	10	9			6						1
13	(h)	Plymouth A	W	2-1	Denby, Jones	11			7	5	8	2	4				3	10	9			6						1
17	(a)	Bristol R	L	1-3	Hollins	11	5		7			2	4	8	10	9						6		3				1
20	(a)	West Ham U	L	0-3		11			7	5	8	2	4			9		10				6		3				1
27	(h)	Norwich C	D	2-2	Dominy, Jones	11		7		5	8		4				3	10	9			6						1
Apr 2	(a)	Swindon T	L	0-2		10	11	2	7	5	8		4				3		9			6						1
3	(a)	Gillingham	L	3-4	Dominy 3	11	4		7	5	8						3	10	9			6			2			1
5	(h)	Swindon T	W	4-1	Curtain, Dominy, Hadley, Kimpton	10	11		7	5	8	2	4				3		9			6						1
10	(h)	Brighton & HA	W	4-2	Andrews 3, Dominy	10	11		7	5	8	2	4				3		9			6						1
17	(a)	Cardiff C	D	1-1	Jones	11			7	5	8	2	4				3	10	9			6						1
21	(h)	Northampton T	W	5-2	Dominy 2, Kimpton 2, Denby	11	2		7	5	8		4				3	10	9			6						1
24	(h)	Exeter C	W	3-0	Dominy 2, Andrews	11		7		5	8	2	4				3	10	9			6						1
App						36	12	8	27	33	37	20	33	1	2	7	35	31	34	3	1	32	1	3	23	19	1	19
Goals						11			5	4	30		1			3		13	10			1						

Back row (left to right): T.Dominy, Salway, Wood, Steventon, Slade, Hinton. Second back row: Diaper, Mounsey, Crick, Denby, Small, Ireland, McAlpine, Loasby, Green. Middle row: A.Lee, Curtin, Hall, Jones, Wheeler, Young, Hadley, J.McIntyre. Seated: Mr Geo Carter, Mr W.A.Hammock, Mr A.A.Wood, Mr W.Bulpitt, Mr E.Arnfield. Front row: Kimpton, A.Dominy, Hollins, Andrews, Blake.

	P	W	D	L	F	A	Pts
Watford	38	22	8	8	68	46	52
Reading	38	21	7	10	68	43	49
Cardiff C	38	22	4	12	72	38	48
West Ham U	38	18	9	11	58	47	45
Northampton T	38	16	11	11	56	51	43
Southampton	38	19	5	14	78	74	43
Portsmouth	38	16	10	12	54	42	42
Millwall	38	16	10	12	50	51	42
Swindon T	38	15	11	12	77	59	41
Brighton & HA	38	16	7	15	46	47	39
Exeter C	38	15	8	15	50	41	38
Queen's Park R	38	13	12	13	55	56	38
Norwich C	38	11	14	13	53	56	36
Luton T	38	13	8	17	61	73	34
Crystal P	38	13	8	17	47	61	34
Bristol R	38	14	3	21	53	75	31
Plymouth A	38	8	14	16	51	61	30
Southend U	38	10	8	20	44	64	28
Croydon Common	38	9	9	20	47	63	27
Gillingham	38	6	8	24	43	83	20

Saints during World War One
1915-16

WITH the war not 'over by Christmas' as many people had predicted, the abandonment of League football seemed likely. In July 1915, representatives of all the major competitions decided, at a meeting in Blackpool, that although strictly competitive football should be suspended, it was in the interests of public morale that the game should be kept going in some form.

Friendly matches were therefore allowed and professional players were allowed to continue playing as amateurs for the duration of the war. In Southampton at this time there were a considerable number of repair shops and shipyards, all engaged on essential war work — Harland & Wolf and Thorneycrofts being but two — and most of the Saints players found employment in these.

The club was thus able to embark on a number of friendly games with their regular players, whilst at the same time being able to call upon a number of guest players. There was little semblance of order in the arrangement and in that first wartime season, Saints used no less than 56 players.

Many of the friendlies were against other Southern League clubs and it was in company with these clubs that Saints helped form the South Western Combination for the second half of the season.

Saints did well in this new, temporary competition, finishing runners-up to Portsmouth. Blake, Dominy and Wheeler were the mainstays of the forward line, whilst Lee, now a veteran, was a tower of strength at centre-half. A.K.Campbell was a reliable partner for Lee and another player introduced at this turbulent time was W.Ellerington, father of Bill Ellerington who was to play for Saints in the post-World War Two years.

South Western Combination

Jan	8	(h)	Bristol C	W	2-1
	15	(a)	Bristol C	L	0-4
	22	(h)	Newport C	W	8-1
Feb	12	(h)	Cardiff C	W	6-3
	19	(a)	Bristol R	W	4-2
Mar	4	(a)	Cardiff C	L	0-2
	18	(a)	Swindon T	L	1-3
	25	(h)	Swindon T	W	5-3
Apr	1	(a)	Newport C	D	0-0
	21	(a)	Portsmouth	W	2-0
	24	(h)	Portsmouth	W	3-0
	29	(h)	Bristol R	W	7-0

Hampshire FA Fund

Apr	8	(h)	Portsmouth	L	2-3
	8	(a)	Portsmouth	L	0-7

Friendlies

Sep	4	(h)	Newport C	W	7-0
	11	(a)	Portsmouth	D	2-2
	18	(h)	Bristol R	W	4-3
	25	(a)	Newport C	W	2-0
Oct	2	(h)	Portsmouth	L	1-2
	9	(h)	Bristol C	L	2-3
	23	(a)	Bristol R	L	2-4
	30	(h)	1st Battalion Footballers (17th Msx)	W	4-3
Nov	6	(a)	Reading	L	1-2
	13	(h)	Cardiff C	D	2-2
	27	(a)	Bristol C	L	1-2
Dec	4	(h)	RAMC (Aldershot)	W	6-2
	11	(h)	Reading	W	4-2
	18	(h)	Swindon T	W	3-1
	26	(a)	Portsmouth	D	1-1
	27	(h)	Portsmouth	W	2-1
Jan	1	(a)	Cardiff C	L	0-1
Feb	5	(a)	Portsmouth	W	6-3
Mar	11	(h)	Portsmouth	W	4-2
Apr	1	(h)	England XI	W	4-2
	15	(h)	Royal Flying Corps	W	10-1
	22	(h)	Royal Flying Corps	L	1-2
May	6	(h)	Royal Flying Corps*	W	5-2 (Charity)

*Not included in players' totals

	P	W	D	L	F	A	Pts
Portsmouth	12	9	0	3	29	11	18
Southampton	12	8	1	3	38	19	17
Cardiff C	12	7	0	5	21	18	14
Bristol R	12	5	3	4	17	20	13
Bristol C	12	5	1	6	13	16	11
Swindon T	11	2	2	7	12	17	6
Newport C	11	1	1	9	8	32	3

Alec Campbell joined up on the outbreak of war but still managed to play some football for the Saints.

Goalkeeper Arthur Wood joined the army but still managed to make many wartime appearances for Saints.

APPEARANCES	SWC	Fr	Gls
Wheeler L	9	21	28
Dominy A	8	19	37
Blake J	8	18	5
Lee A	8	14	
Slade R	5	16	
Campbell A	8	13	2
Kingston G	9	11	7
Wood A	6	12	
Small J	6	12	
Ellerington W	9	9	2
Wilcox J	9	8	2
Passmore	4	12	1
Andrews L	2	14	8
Denham W	1	12	
Gibbon L	3	8	
Salway E	3	8	1
Eglin J	8	1	
Blackmore W	2	7	1
Webb J	3	3	
Milne J	3	3	2
Porter R	1	4	
Hood W	3	2	
Tomkins E	3	5	
Youtman B	1	3	1
Pearson R	1	3	3
Kenny O		3	
Evans R	2	1	
Chambers D		3	2
Wright C	1	2	
Hartnell S	2		3
Denyer A		1	1
Frisby W	2		
Thompson R		2	
Page P		2	1
McAlpine J		2	
Blanchard P		2	
Jones T		2	
Orbell G		2	
Hadley G	1	1	

One appearance in SWC: Hayward, Bourne W, Morris.
One appearance in Friendlies: O'Neil H, Lovell E, Clay, Henderson, Hinton G, Cooper H, Hallworth A, Gubbins W, Read H, Bone W, Quin J, Bradley JW, Lawson B, Ronna.

> Saints's defeat of the Footballers' Battalion (17th Middlesex) was a fine achievement. Under England player Frank Buckley the Battalion had many stars to call upon.

1916-17

FOR this season, Saints joined the London Combination, formed the previous season and still running today, incidentally, as the Football Combination.

Saints began well and remained unbeaten until the last Saturday of 1916 when Arsenal snatched a 1-0 victory. From February, however, Saints slumped to ten successive defeats. The standards of the London clubs were high and Southampton found the going tough. Again Dominy headed the scorers, although this time his total was a modest 15.

Saints used over 60 players in the season — including no less than 11 different goalkeepers, enough to form their own team. They were Wood, Webb, Pickup, Steventon, Johnson, Cooper, Skiller, Bourne, Jobbins, Atkinson and Rose.

Men were still being called up for military service or munitions work and often the team was not finalised until a few minutes before kick-off. Nevertheless, football was still being played and, interestingly, the Saints announced their first profit — £228 1s 1d — for many years.

London Combination

Sep	2	(h) Watford	W	5-0
	9	(a) Brentford	D	1-1
	16	(h) Clapton O	D	1-1
	23	(a) Chelsea	L	0-3
	30	(h) Fulham	W	4-3
Oct	7	(a) Arsenal	D	2-2
	14	(h) Queen's Park R	W	2-0
	21	(a) Luton T	L	1-3
	28	(h) West Ham U	W	3-0
Nov	4	(a) Portsmouth	W	1-0
	11	(h) Tottenham H	W	1-0
	25	(a) Watford	D	0-0
Dec	2	(h) Brentford	W	3-1
	9	(a) Clapton O	W	2-1
	16	(h) Chelsea	W	2-0
	23	(a) Fulham	L	1-8
	25	(a) Crystal P	D	2-2
	26	(h) Crystal P	D	2-2
	30	(h) Arsenal	L	0-1
Jan	6	(a) Queen's Park R	L	0-4
	13	(h) Luton T	W	3-1
	20	(a) West Ham U	D	0-0
	27	(h) Portsmouth	W	1-0
Feb	3	(a) Tottenham H	L	1-3
	10	(h) Millwall	L	1-3
	17	(a) West Ham U	L	2-5
	24	(h) Arsenal	L	0-2
Mar	3	(a) Portsmouth	L	0-1
	10	(h) Tottenham H	L	2-4
	17	(a) Fulham	L	1-3
	23	(a) Crystal P	L	2-4
	31	(h) West Ham U	L	1-2
Apr	6	(a) Clapton O	L	0-4
	7	(a) Arsenal	D	2-2
	9	(h) Clapton O	W	2-1
	14	(h) Portsmouth	W	2-1
	21	(a) Tottenham H	L	0-4
	23	(h) Fulham	D	2-2

	P	W	D	L	F	A	Pts
West Ham U	40	30	5	5	110	45	65
Millwall	40	26	6	8	85	48	58
Chelsea	40	24	5	11	93	48	53
Tottenham H	40	24	5	11	112	64	53
Arsenal	40	19	10	11	62	47	48
Fulham	40	21	3	16	102	63	45
Luton T	39	20	3	16	101	82	43
Crystal P	38	14	7	17	68	72	35
Southampton	39	13	8	18	57	80	34
Queen's Park R	39	10	9	20	48	86	29
Watford	40	8	9	22	69	115	25
Brentford	40	9	7	24	56	99	25
Portsmouth	40	9	4	27	58	117	22
Clapton O	40	6	7	27	49	104	19

APPEARANCES
27 Milne J, 26 Campbell A, 25 Dominy A, 24 Blake J, Tomkins E, 20 Quin J, 19 Blackmore W, 18 Ellerington W, 17 Henry W, Hunter G, Ireland S, Kimpton S, 16 Giles C, Pearson R, 13 Lee A, 11 Wood A, 9 Wheeler L, 7 Brodrick M, Burt J, Donaldson S, Gowers W, 6 Atkinson H, Jobbins P, 5 Orbell G, Pearce J, Slade D, 4 Cooper H, Skiller L, Wright C, 3 Boynton J, Duxbury P, Frisby W, Johnson B, Moore J, 2 Elliot C, Kiddle R, Lewis L, Mitton J, Willis E, 1 Bourne J, Brown J, Craig R, Dawson H, Duncan G, Farwell J, Greer A, Hughes T, Jones T, Lovell E, Page P, Pickup F, Price A, Rose F, Steventon E, Swift H, Taylor A, Thwaites A, Walker J, Webb J, White H.

GOALS
15 Dominy, 11 Quin, 7 Milne, 6 Wheeler, 4 Blackmore, 3 Kimpton, 2 Pearce, 1 Burt, Brown, Donaldson, Lee, Lovell, Slade.

The Dell in 1916 when American football was played there between US Army teams. Wearing the top hat is the late Alderman Sir Sidney Kimber, Freeman of the City and Mayor in 1918 and 1919.

Saints in 1916-17, just a handful of the 60-odd players used. Back row (left to right): Mr G.H.Muir (director), Mr A.A.Wood (director), Gr J.Mitton, RGA., Ellerington, Airman Frisby, RFC., Gr A.Wood, RGA., A.K.Campbell, Mr W.Hammock (director), Airman A.Tompkins, RFC, Mr W.Bulpitt JP (director), A.Lee (trainer). Front: G.Kimpton, A.Dominy, D.Slade, Sgt Milne, AOC., J.Blake.

1917-18

AT a meeting of the London Combination in July 1917, the London clubs proposed to expel Southampton, Portsmouth, Luton and Watford on the grounds that railway travel to such places was becoming more difficult as the war ground on.

Mr Bulpitt, a Saints director, made an impassioned speech and even offered to pay the train fares of 12 players from each club, but the non-London clubs were eventually voted out by nine votes to four with Brentford abstaining.

Without a fixture list, Saints tried to form a United Services League with teams comprised of servicemen, but that proved impractical and Saints fell back on friendly games although many of their old adversaries had suspended operations for the duration.

In November some form of salvation came with the formation of the South Hants War League with clubs such as Portsmouth, Cowes, Thorneycrofts and Harland & Wolf also taking part. It was something of a disaster for Southampton who fielded 80 different players — men like Dominy, Blake, Kimpton, Ellerington and Slade were often found in the ranks of other sides — and at centre-forward alone, Southampton called up 13 different players. A measure of the farce can be gauged by the fact that one Sgt W.J.Davies finished leading Saints scorer with 18 goals — and he played in only four games.

A loss of £557 1s 9d was blamed on the lack of a quality league competition.

South Hants War League

Jan	19	(a) Harland & Wolf	L	2-3
	26	(h) Harland & Wolf	D	1-1
Feb	2	(h) Cowes	W	4-1
	9	(h) Thorneycrofts	L	1-2
	16	(a) Cowes	W	1-0
	23	(h) RN Torpedo Depot	W	6-2
Mar	2	(a) RN Torpedo Depot	L	0-1
	9	(h) RFC School	D	1-1
	16	(a) Thorneycrofts	L	1-2
	29	(a) Portsmouth	L	2-4
Apr	1	(h) Portsmouth	L	0-4
	27	(a) RFC School	D	0-0

Friendlies

Sep	1	(h) Portsmouth	W	3-2
	8	(a) Portsmouth	D	4-4
	15	(h) Swindon T	D	1-1
	22	(a) Luton T	L	0-4
	29	(h) Luton T	W	3-2
Oct	6	(a) Royal Aircraft	W	4-0
	13	(h) Royal Aircraft	W	6-0
	20	(h) CW Wright XI	L	1-4
	27	(h) London Scottish	D	1-1
Nov	3	(a) Portsmouth	L	0-3
	10	(h) RGA Siege Battalion	W	6-2
	24	(h) Swindon T	D	2-2
Dec	1	(h) RFC North Raven	W	5-0
	8	(h) Bristol C	W	2-1
	15	(h) County of London	W	10-2
	21	(a) Gervais	W	8-2
	21	(a) Bournemouth League	W	8-2
	25	(a) Portsmouth	D	1-1
	26	(h) Portsmouth	L	2-3
	29	(h) United Services	W	6-3
Jan	12	(h) RGA	W	5-1
Mar	23	(h) RGA Hilsea	W	10-1
	30	(h) Remount Depot	W	10-3
Apr	6	(a) Harland & Wolf	W	3-1
	13	(h) Tank Corps Regiment	L	1-4
	20	(h) Portsmouth	L	2-3
May	11	(h) Thorneycrofts, Harland & Wolf Combined	W	3-0

	P	W	D	L	F	A	Pts
Portsmouth	12	11	0	1	53	5	22
Thorneycrofts	12	9	1	2	37	12	19
Harland & Wolf	12	8	2	2	32	11	18
Southampton	12	3	3	6	19	21	9
RFC School	12	2	3	7	8	11	7
Cowes	12	2	2	8	12	33	6
RN Torp Depot	12	1	1	10	7	45	3

Arthur Dominy (top) was often to be found playing against Southampton. Tom Parker (bottom) made his Saints debut to begin a fine career.

APPEARANCES	SHWL	Fr	Gls
Blackmore W	11	24	9
Milne J	10	19	17
Pearce J	5	18	4
Piggin L	9	12	
Lee J	4	16	12
McClure A	5	13	1
Wright C	3	15	4
Hadfield P	8	10	
Roots P	7	10	2
Hall H	2	12	
Moore J	1	12	12
Bradley JW	10	3	7
Tomkins J		9	
McAlpine J		8	3
E.Blight	5	3	
F.Simmonds	5	3	5
J.Rutherford		7	1
D.Andrews	2	5	3
Porter P	6	1	
Parker T	2	5	
Smethurst E	2	5	4
Dominy A		6	3
Rose L	2	3	
Townsend W	3	1	
Campbell A		4	
Davies W		4	18
Worcester D	1	3	
Bown A	3		2
Slade D	2	1	1
Johnson B	2	1	
Bailey A	1	2	1
Dunford E	2	1	
Prince P	2	1	2
Pepper H	2	1	2
Giles C		2	
Blake J	2	1	1
Butt J	2	1	1
Foster A		2	
Dalton E		2	
Ottaway J		2	
Simms F		2	
Smith F		2	

One appearance in SHWL: Ryder J, Millar J, Youtman B, Heath A, White A, Buchan A. One appearance in Friendlies: McFayden C, Priestley H, Walker J, Croel A, Heathcote R, Stoker A, Massey E, Quinton A, Tiller A, Ramson A, Newman A, Franklin J, Lyons A, Jones T, Amos A, Jollins B, Harman H, Weeks H, Fletcher A, Bradburn G, Raybould W, Gray T, Claxton A, Duncan H, Wheeler L, Taylor E, Duffy A, Butt J, Dines J, Scott W. One appearance and one goal in Friendlies: Goodwin A, Jefferson A, Pearson R. There were two own-goals.

Ten of the eighty players used by Southampton in 1917-18. Left to right: Blackmore, Roots, Parker, Dominy, Slade, Hadfield, Asher, Milne, Prince, Blake.

1918-19

THANKFULLY this was to be the last season of wartime football, for some 20 years at least, and Saints again had to content themselves with the South Hants War League supplemented by a series of friendlies.

With most of the Southampton regulars again appearing for the opposition, Saints struggled and finished second from bottom of the table. But things were stirring and Mr McIntyre was re-appointed secretary-manager. He set about assembling a nucleus of good young players. Rawlings and Parker were two such players, whilst the names of Barratt, Bradburn and Foxall also appeared. Wood, Dominy and Campbell were the only players remaining from before the war but with hostilities at an end, local fans once again looked forward to regular competitive League football at The Dell.

South Hants War League

Sep	21	(h) Cowes	W	7-0
Oct	5	(h) Thorneycrofts	D	3-3
	19	(a) Harland & Wolf	D	1-1
	28	(h) Harland & Wolf	D	2-2
Nov	30	(a) Cowes	L	2-4
Dec	14	(a) Thorneycrofts	L	1-2
	25	(a) Portsmouth	L	1-5
	26	(h) Portsmouth	L	3-6
Jan	11	(h) Cowes	W	6-1
	18	(a) Cowes	D	3-3
	25	(h) Thorneycrofts	W	1-0
Feb	15	(a) Harland & Wolf	L	0-1
	22	(h) Harland & Wolf	L	0-1
Mar	1	(a) Thorneycrofts	W	3-1
Apr	18	(a) Portsmouth	D	1-1
	21	(h) Portsmouth	W	9-1

	P	W	D	L	F	A	Pts
Harland & Wolf	16	10	2	4	37	26	22
Portsmouth	16	8	3	5	55	40	19
Thorneycrofts	16	7	4	5	37	39	18
Southampton	16	5	5	6	43	32	15
Cowes	16	2	2	12	22	57	6

Friendlies

Sep	7	(a) Portsmouth	L	2-5
	14	(h) Portsmouth	D	1-1
	23	(h) RN Depot	L	0-2
Oct	12	(h) Swindon T	W	14-3
Nov	2	(h) RE Bordon	W	9-2
	9	(a) Reading	D	1-1
	16	(h) RAF Farnborough	L	2-5
	23	(h) 5th Res Cavalry Reg, Tidworth	L	2-3
Dec	7	(a) Aldershot Comm	L	3-4
	21	(a) Harland & Wolf	W	5-1
	28	(h) RE Amesbury	W	2-0
Jan	4	(h) Thorneycrofts	L	3-5
Feb	1	(h) 5th Res Cavalry Reg, Tidworth	W	3-1
Mar	8	(a) Anti Aircraft Res Brigade, Newport	W	7-3
	13	(h) RAF Blandford	W	6-1
	22	(h) Harland & Wolf	W	3-2
	29	(a) Reading	L	1-2
Apr	5	(h) Aldershot Comm	W	2-1
	12	(a) Boscombe	D	1-1
	19	(h) Anti Aircraft Res Brigade, Newport	W	6-1
	26	(h) RASC Bulford	W	5-1
	30	(h) Thorneycrofts	W	2-1
May	1	(a) Boscombe	L	1-2
Jly	26	(a) Portsmouth	L	3-5

Victory Cup

Feb	8	(a) Boscombe	L	0-1

A youthful Bill Rawlings who began his fine career in the last season of wartime football.

APPEARANCES	SHWL	VC	Fr	Gls
Parker T	16	1	22	12
Jewett A	14	1	16	
Blackmore W	12		16	4
Roots P	9	1	18	
Prince P	10	1	14	5
Wright C	7	1	9	8
Hadfield P	5		9	
Rawlings W	6		9	16
Smethurst E	5		6	6
Phillips H	6		5	7
Youtman B	3	1	9	3
Diaper A	8		3	1
Blight E	6		3	
Moore J	2		6	10
Lacy A	4		4	5
Cooper	4	1	5	
Andrews A	5	2		
Wood	2		5	
Simmonds F	2		4	4
Page E	4	1	1	5
Goode B	4		2	2
Campbell A	2		4	2
Gilboy B	3	1	2	1
Burt S	1		4	5
Edgar J			6	1
Betteridge A	3		1	
Girling F			4	7
Windhurst A			6	1
Worcester D	2		1	
Lazenby A	1		2	
Stemp F	2		1	
Dunford E	2		1	2
Figgins W	3			1
Colar C	2		1	
Green G	1		2	
Hackett L	2		1	
Johnstone D	2		1	
Pritchard F	2		1	5
Foxall F	2		1	3
Webb W	2			
Bosbury C	2			
Whitrow F	2			
Titmuss F			2	
Piggin L			2	
Edey G	1		1	2

One Victory Cup appearance: Ireland S. One SHWL appearance: Roots H, Payne A, Pepper H, Williams J, Johnson B, Butt J. One Friendly appearance: Blake J, Chalk G, McLean W, Burrows T, Brooks A, Slade A, Stride N, Kneller T, Mitchell J, Barrett J, Seddon H, Gibbings A, Bourne R, Crisp A, Forsyth J, Rutherford J, Lomas J, Wiseman A, Asher R, Bradley JW, Bradley J, Fenwick H, Leigh C. One Friendly appearance plus one goal: Ewart J, Goldsmith J, Tempest W, Wilson C, Elliott D.

The Friendly matches played on 1st May and 26th July are not included in the above.

Saints in 1918-19 as the club looked forward to the resumption of League football. Left to right: Smethurst, Blackmore, Roots, Parker, Tempest, Hadfield, Moore, Wright, Milnes, Jewett, Asher.

1919-20

ON 30th August 1919, Saints played their first Southern League match for over four years. After all the horrors of the war — and like every other town and city in Britain, Southampton had hardly a family untouched by tragedy in some way — it was understandable that League football signalled a return to normality. Consequently attendances at The Dell were good and the crowd's enthusiasm seemingly unbounded.

Yet that enthusiasm did not appear to convey itself to the Saints team on the opening day of the season and they managed only a 1-1 draw against Exeter before losing their next two games, against Swansea and Cardiff.

Saints fans knew, however, that Mr McIntyre had built up a fine squad of talented young players and the only one to have cost a transfer fee was Jimmy Moore, who came from Barnsley. The only players now left from 1914-15 were Dominy and Wood and around these experienced three, the new recruits improved as the 1919-20 season progressed.

In defence Tom Parker and Fred Titmuss developed into 'the best pair of backs in the South', whilst Bill Rawlings' emerging partnership with the ever-reliable Dominy was to be a feature of the Saints forward line for several seasons.

Indeed, Dominy was Saints' top scorer and was selected to play for the Southern League against the Irish League whilst also attracting bids from several First Division clubs like Manchester United and Everton, and West Ham who had just been elected to the Second Division.

Another success in McIntyre's team-building programme was the discovery of Albert Shelley. In the Cup defeat by West Ham, the Saints' right-half, Andrews, broke his leg. Saints' directors wanted to buy an immediate replacement but Bert Lee, who was still on the training staff, insisted that a young Romsey man by the name of Shelley was the ideal replacement. Romsey were playing in the Hampshire League but Lee's judgement was utterly vindicated.

Shelley made the most of his unexpected opportunity and began a career which saw him make more appearances (410 in League games alone) that any other Saints player at the time. In that first season Shelley played in Southampton's last 18 League games of the season and was on the losing side only five times as the team consolidated itself and went on to finish in eighth position. Only Portsmouth, the Champions, scored more goals than Southampton in what was to prove the Saints' last season in the Southern League.

FA Cup

SAINTS drew West Ham United at The Dell in the first round of the FA Cup and on a muddy pitch both sides showed plenty of spirit but little skill. Southampton had slightly the better of the play but poor finishing, combined with some fine goalkeeping from Hufton, prevented them from finding the back of the net.

Saints were hindered by an injury to Andrews only 12 minutes into the replay and Dominy had to drop back into the half-back line. The game became more physical and only goalkeeper Wilcock could look back on the game with any personal satisfaction.

He could not be blamed for any of the goals as the Saints fell apart. Sid Puddefoot scored twice and the Hammers coasted home before a 26,000 crowd.

Round 1
Jan 10 v West Ham United (h) 0-0
Wilcock; Parker, Titmuss, Andrews, Bradburn, Hackett, Barratt, Dominy, Rawlings, Moore, Foxall.
Att: 12,142
Replay
Jan 15 v West Ham United (a) 1-3
Barratt
Wilcock; Parker, Titmuss, Andrews, Bradburn, Hackett, Barratt, Dominy, Rawlings, Moore, Foxall.
Att: 26,000

Southampton's gate receipts totalled £15,111 in 1919-20 and the club showed a profit of £3,360 on the season.

Three Saints stalwarts whose fine careers spanned the move from Southern League football into the Football League. From left: Bill Rawlings, Arthur Dominy and Fred Titmuss. The forward partnership between Rawlings and Dominy began to emerge during Saints' last season in the Southern League. Titmuss was also developing a flourishing partnership, with Tom Parker.

1919-20
Southern League

Back row (left to right): Couldery, Cooper, Parker, Wood, Titmuss. Middle row: Arnfield, Mr Wood, Kiddle, Prince, Fenwick, Campbell, Bradburn, Andrews, Boyes, McIntyre, Hackett, Bulpitt, H.Lewis. Front row: Barratt, Pritchard, Dominy, Jones, Moore, Foxall.

Results

Date		Opponent	Result	Scorers
Aug 30	(h)	Exeter C	D 1-1	Moore
Sep 1	(h)	Swansea T	L 1-2	Rawlings
6	(a)	Cardiff C	L 0-3	
8	(a)	Swansea T	W 2-1	Barratt, Dominy
13	(h)	Queen's Park R	W 2-1	Foxall, Moore
15	(h)	Reading	L 0-2	
20	(a)	Swindon T	W 2-1	Barratt, Foxall
27	(h)	Millwall	W 4-1	Rawlings 2, Barratt, Dominy
Oct 4	(a)	Brighton & HA	L 0-1	
11	(h)	Newport C	W 2-0	Moore, Rawlings
18	(a)	Portsmouth	L 1-5	Dominy
22	(a)	Reading	L 1-2	Dominy
25	(h)	Northampton T	L 2-6	Foxall, Moore
Nov 1	(a)	Crystal P	L 0-3	
8	(h)	Southend U	W 4-0	Rawlings 3, Dominy
15	(a)	Norwich C	L 1-2	Rawlings
22	(h)	Brentford	L 0-1	
29	(a)	Merthyr T	D 1-1	Foxall
Dec 6	(h)	Plymouth A	D 2-2	Rawlings 2
13	(a)	Bristol R	D 1-1	Dominy
25	(a)	Luton T	W 1-0	Rawlings
26	(h)	Luton T	W 2-1	Dominy, Rawlings
27	(h)	Watford	W 5-1	Rawlings 3, Dominy, Moore
Jan 3	(a)	Exeter C	l 1-4	Rawlings
17	(h)	Cardiff C	D 2-2	Moore, Parker
24	(a)	Queen's Park R	L 1-2	Boyes
Feb 7	(a)	Millwall	D 2-2	Barratt, Rawlings
14	(h)	Brighton & HA	W 3-0	Dominy 2, Parker
21	(a)	Newport	D 1-1	Dominy
28	(h)	Portsmouth	D 0-0	
Mar 6	(a)	Northampton T	L 1-3	Moore
8	(h)	Swindon T	W 1-0	Moore
13	(h)	Crystal P	W 5-1	Dominy 3, Rawlings 2
20	(a)	Southend U	L 1-2	Moore
27	(h)	Norwich C	W 3-0	Barratt, Jones, Parker
Apr 2	(a)	Gillingham	L 0-2	
3	(a)	Brentford	W 3-2	Dominy 2, Jones
5	(h)	Gillingham	W 2-0	Jones, Moore
10	(h)	Merthyr T	W 8-1	Campbell 2, Dominy 2, Jones 2, Foxall, Parker
17	(a)	Plymouth A	W 1-0	Dominy
24	(h)	Bristol R	W 2-0	Dominy, Shelley
May 1	(a)	Watford	L 0-3	

Appearances and Goals

	Andrews A	Barratt J	Blake JJ	Boyes K	Bradburn G	Brown C	Campbell A	Dominy A	Donelly A	Fenwick H	Foxall F	Grumbley A	Hackett LR	Jones GE	Kimpton GS	Moore J	Parker T	Prince P	Rawlings W	Shelley A	Titmuss F	Turner W	Wilcock GH	Wood A
App	10	41	1	4	28	3	16	41	1	11	38	1	31	7	2	41	40	4	33	18	22	27	20	22
Goals		5		1		2		20			5			5		10	4		19	1				

League Table

	P	W	D	L	F	A	Pts
Portsmouth	42	23	12	7	73	27	58
Watford	42	26	6	10	69	42	58
Crystal P	42	22	12	8	69	43	56
Cardiff C	42	18	17	7	70	43	53
Plymouth A	42	20	10	12	57	29	50
Queen's Park R	42	18	10	14	62	50	46
Reading	42	16	13	13	51	43	45
Southampton	42	18	8	16	72	63	44
Swansea T	42	16	11	15	53	45	43
Exeter C	42	17	9	16	57	52	43
Southend U	42	13	17	12	46	48	43
Norwich C	42	15	11	16	64	57	41
Swindon T	42	17	7	18	65	68	41
Millwall	42	14	12	16	52	55	40
Brentford	42	15	10	17	52	59	40
Brighton & HA	42	14	8	20	61	72	36
Bristol R	42	11	13	18	62	78	35
Newport C	42	13	7	22	45	70	33
Northampton T	42	12	9	21	64	103	33
Luton T	42	10	10	22	51	76	30
Merthyr T	42	9	11	22	47	78	29
Gillingham	42	10	7	25	34	74	27

1920-21

AT the end of the 1919-20 season, the Southern League sides applied *en masse* to join the Football League and the result was the creation of the Third Division (later to become the Third Division South when a similar section for northern clubs was formed).

Thus, on 28 August 1920, Southampton FC played their first game in the Football League, vying with 21 other clubs for the one promotion place to the Second Division. Arthur Dominy scored Saints' first-ever goal in the competition, in a 1-1 draw at Gillingham, the historic effort being the result of a shot from an oblique angle.

That first away point set the scene for Saints' early days in the Football League and by 9 October, victory over Swansea at The Dell put them top of the table. Their home form was particularly impressive and it was 4 December before they were beaten at The Dell, Grimsby inflicting a 1-0 defeat on them.

That game against the Mariners was a particularly wretched affair for the Saints. Tom Parker missed a penalty, then Jimmy Moore was sent off although he was later to escape with only a caution.

During the close season, Southampton had signed Tommy Allen from Sunderland on a free-transfer, and his goalkeeping was a major factor in Saints' consistency. By Easter they were comfortably placed behind Crystal Palace, the Third Division leaders, and were scheduled to play Palace twice over the holiday period.

It was almost certain that a win and a draw from the two games would ensure the sole promotion place available. On 28 March, at The Dell, Palace grabbed an equaliser in the very last seconds of the game and the goal caused such excitement that several barriers at the Milton Road end collapsed, injuring several spectators. The following day, at The Nest, another 1-1 draw kept the Londoners above Saints.

Southampton's final charge disappeared with that result. From their last nine games they picked up ten points — two wins and six draws — and Crystal Palace became the first club to be promoted to Division Two, five points ahead of Saints who were left to rue those dropped points.

FA Cup

NORTHAMPTON Town ran Saints hard in a gruelling first round match at the County Ground, but as the goalless affair drew to its close, Southampton were well on top and when the sides met again, at The Dell, Saints picked up where they had left off to coast home 4-1.

The Dell pitch was slippery but Saints adapted well with Barratt, playing on the right wing, having a particularly fine match despite the conditions. Barratt caused havoc in the Cobblers' defence, and the Saints' goalkeeper, Allen, had little to do. Interestingly, both matches generated record ground receipts of £1,017 and £1,118 respectively.

Grimsby Town were the next opponents and Saints gained ample revenge for the puncturing of their unbeaten home record the previous October. Rawlings (2) and Dominy gave them victory and afterwards Dominy said that he thought the Saints had won because they were 'the faster team and altogether more together as a side than Grimsby'. Rawlings, in particular, had enjoyed a splendid game.

In the third round, Cardiff won a game of missed chances by the only goal of the match. It came after 20 minutes at The Dell and followed a rare defensive mistake. Rawlings, Parker and Shelley were Saints' best players that day, but their endeavours went unrewarded. Some small consolation was that for the second time that season The Dell receipts record was broken when over 21,000 people paid £1,708.

Fred Foxall rejoined Aston Villa at the end of the season but Saints had not given their permission and he was ordered to re-sign for Southampton.

Tommy Allen joined Saints on a free-transfer from Sunderland and missed only two games in the club's first Football League season.

Round 1
Jan 7 v Northampton Town (a) 0-0
Allen; Parker, Titmuss, Shelley, Moorhead, Turner, Barratt, Dominy, Rawlings, Moore, Foxall.
Att: 15,542
Replay
Jan 11 v Northampton Town (h) 4-1
Dominy 2, Rawlings 2
Allen; Parker, Titmuss, Shelley, Moorhead, Turner, Barratt, Dominy, Rawlings, Moore, Foxall.
Att: 16,000
Round 2
Jan 28 v Grimsby Town (a) 3-1
Dominy, Rawlings 2
Allen; Parker, Titmuss, Shelley, Moorhead, Turner, Barratt, Dominy, Rawlings, Moore, Foxall.
Att: 14,000
Round 4
Feb 19 v Cardiff City (h) 0-1
Allen; Parker, Titmuss, Shelley, Moorhead, Turner, Barratt, Dominy, Rawlings, Moore, Foxall.
Att: 21,363

Saints players relaxing in the New Forest before the FA Cup match against Cardiff. Standing (left to right): Butt, Allen, Lee, Moorhead, Parker, Titmuss, Moore, Mr Wood, Turner. Sitting: Rawlings, Dominy, Barratt, Shelley, Foxall.

1920-21

Division 3

Date		Opponent	Result		Scorers	Att	Allen T	Barratt J	Bradburn G	Brown C	Butt L	Campbell A	Dominy A	Foxall F	Moore J	Moorhead G	Parker T	Rawlings W	Reader G	Shelley A	Titmuss F	Turner W	Williams G	Wood A	Wright F
Aug 28	(a)	Gillingham	D	1-1	Dominy	11,500	1	7				5	8	11	10		2	9		4	3	6			
30	(h)	Swindon T	W	4-0	Dominy 2, Barratt, Rawlings	11,500	1	7				5	8	11	10		2	9		4	3	6			
Sep 4	(h)	Gillingham	W	3-0	Brown, Rawlings, Foxall	14,000	1	7		8		5		11	10		2	9		4	3	6			
6	(a)	Swindon T	L	2-3	Williams, Rawlings	9,000	1	7				5		11	10		2	9		4	3	6	8		
11	(h)	Portsmouth	W	2-0	Parker, Moore	18,300	1	7	5					11	10		2	9		4	3	6	8		
18	(a)	Portsmouth	W	1-0	Rawlings	20,585	1	7				5	8	11	10		2	9		4	3	6			
25	(a)	Norwich C	W	1-0	Rawlings	9,000	1	7				5	8	11	10		2	9		4	3	6			
Oct 2	(h)	Norwich C	W	1-0	Dominy	15,000	1	7				5	8	11	10		2	9		4	3	6			
9	(h)	Swansea T	W	3-0	Parker, Shelley, Moore	15,000	1	7		8		5		11	10		2	9		4	3	6			
16	(a)	Swansea T	D	1-1	Barratt	12,000	1	7				5	8	11	10		2	9		4	3	6			
23	(h)	Brentford	W	3-0	Shelley, Rawlings, Foxall	13,000	1	7				5	8	11	10		2	9		4	3	6			
30	(a)	Brentford	D	1-1	Moore	12,000		7			6	5	8	11	10			9		4	3	2		1	
Nov 6	(h)	Queen's Park R	D	2-2	Campbell, Moore	15,000		7				5	8	11	10		2	9		4	3	6		1	
13	(a)	Queen's Park R	D	0-0		15,000	1	7				5	8	11	10		2		9	4	3	6			
20	(h)	Bristol R	W	4-0	Barratt, Brown, Rawlings, Foxall	17,000	1	7		8		5		11	10		2	9		4	3	6			
27	(a)	Bristol R	W	2-1	Rawlings, Moore	17,000	1	7		8		5		11	10		2	9		4	3	6			
Dec 4	(h)	Grimsby T	L	0-1		11,000	1	7		4		5		11	10		2	9	8		3	6			
11	(a)	Grimsby T	L	0-3		9,000	1			8		5	9	11	10		2			4	3	6			7
18	(a)	Reading	W	4-0	Dominy 2, Rawlings, Moore	9,000	1	7					8	11	10	5	2	9		4	3	6			
25	(a)	Luton T	D	1-1	Moore	14,000	1	7					8	11	10	5	2	9		4	3	6			
26	(h)	Luton T	D	1-1	Moore	19,793	1	7					8	11	10	5	2	9		4	3	6			
Jan 1	(h)	Reading	L	1-2	Moore	7,000	1	7					8	11	10	5	2		9	4	3	6			
14	(a)	Watford	D	0-0		9,000	1	7					8	11	10	5	2	9		4	3	6			
21	(h)	Watford	W	4-1	Dominy 3, Rawlings	14,000	1	7					8	11	10	5	2	9		4	3	6			
Feb 5	(a)	Brighton & HA	D	1-1	Rawlings	8,000	1	7					8	11	10	5	2	9		4	3	6			
11	(a)	Northampton T	L	0-2		6,000	1	7	4				8	11	10	5	2	9			3	6			
23	(h)	Brighton & HA	W	1-0	Rawlings	8,000	1	7					8	11	10	5	2	9		4	3	6			
26	(a)	Southend U	L	0-1		7,000	1	7	5				8	11	10		2	9		4	3	6			
Mar 5	(h)	Southend U	W	3-0	Moore 2, Rawlings	10,000	1	7				5	8	11	10		2	9		4	3	6			
9	(h)	Northampton T	W	3-1	Foxall 2, Campbell	7,000	1	7				5	8	11	10		2	9		4	3	6			
12	(a)	Merthyr T	D	1-1	Dominy	12,000	1			7		5	8	11	10		2	9		4	3	6			
19	(h)	Merthyr T	W	5-0	Rawlings 4, Brown	8,000	1			7	6	5	8	11	10			9		4	3	2			
26	(h)	Plymouth A	W	1-0	Campbell	14,000	1			7	6	5	8	11	10			9		4	3	2			
28	(h)	Crystal P	D	1-1	Moore	20,000	1			7	6	5	8	11	10			9		4	3	2			
29	(a)	Crystal P	D	1-1	opp own goal	15,000	1		3	7	6	5	8	11	10			9		4		2			
Apr 2	(a)	Plymouth A	D	0-0		10,000	1			7	6	5	8	11	10			9		4	3	2			
9	(h)	Exeter C	W	3-0	Shelley, Dominy, Rawlings	10,000	1	7			6	5	8	11	10			9		4	3	2			
16	(a)	Exeter C	L	0-1		7,000	1			7	6	5	8	11	10			9		4	3	2			
23	(h)	Millwall	D	1-1	Brown	10,000	1			7	6	5	8	11	10			9		4	3	2			
30	(a)	Millwall	W	1-0	Dominy	18,000	1			7	6	5	8	11	10			9		4	3	2			
May 2	(h)	Newport C	D	0-0		7,000	1			7	6	5	8	11	10			9		4	3	2			
7	(a)	Newport C	D	0-0		8,000	1		4	7	6	5	8	11	10			9			3	2			
App							40	30	5	16	13	31	35	42	42	9	30	39	3	39	41	42	2	2	1
Goals								3		4		3	12	5	12		2	18		3			1		

1 own-goal

Back row (left to right): Parker, Allen, Titmuss. Middle: Arnfield (secretary), Lee (trainer), Shelley, Moorhead, Turner, Mr Wood, McIntyre (manager). Front: Barratt, Dominy, Rawlings, Moore, Foxall.

	P	W	D	L	F	A	Pts
Crystal P	42	24	11	7	70	34	59
Southampton	42	19	16	7	64	28	54
Queen's Park R	42	22	9	11	61	32	53
Swindon T	42	21	10	11	73	49	52
Swansea T	42	18	15	9	56	45	51
Watford	42	20	8	14	59	44	48
Millwall	42	18	11	13	42	30	47
Merthyr T	42	15	15	12	60	49	45
Luton T	42	16	12	14	61	56	44
Bristol R	42	18	7	17	68	57	43
Plymouth A	42	11	21	10	35	34	43
Portsmouth	42	12	15	15	46	48	39
Grimsby T	42	15	9	18	49	59	39
Northampton T	42	15	8	19	59	75	38
Newport C	42	14	9	19	43	64	37
Norwich C	42	10	16	16	44	53	36
Southend U	42	14	8	20	44	61	36
Brighton & HA	42	14	8	20	42	61	36
Exeter C	42	10	15	17	39	54	35
Reading	42	12	7	23	42	59	31
Brentford	42	9	12	21	42	67	30
Gillingham	42	8	12	22	34	74	28

1921-22

SOUTHAMPTON began this season in much the same way as they had finished the previous campaign. The defence was as consistent as ever, and with the attack in such impressive form, the Saints, along with Plymouth, forged their way to the top of the division. Rawlings, in particular, was enjoying a purple patch and in one month he twice scored four goals in a match.

In February, just when the fans were confidently predicting promotion, the directors shocked them by announcing the double transfer of wingers Foxall and Barratt who both moved to Birmingham, with the Blues' Elkes (a forward) and Getgood (half-back) moving in the other direction.

Selling the club's regular first-team wingers was seen as a terrible mistake by the mystified Southampton supporters, yet they had to admit that the arrival of the new men did not unduly upset the team's balance. Indeed, both men enjoyed good debuts, against Southend, and Elkes even obliged with two goals in Saints' 5-0 win.

Unfortunately, Elkes suffered a broken collar bone in the next match and missed the rest of the season which was now building up into an exciting finish. Plymouth enjoyed a good Easter by beating Saints at Home Park and drawing at The Dell, and they surged ahead in the title race.

With Saints having two games remaining, and Plymouth only one, the Devon club led the table by four points and seemed certain of promotion. On 1 May, Saints picked up two vital points with a 1-0 win at Merthyr, a result which left the positions tantalisingly poised as the last Saturday of the season arrived.

The odds were still on Plymouth, for even if Southampton won their match against Newport County at The Dell, they still had to hope that Plymouth would obligingly lose to Queen's Park Rangers at Loftus Road.

Two members of the Saints' board, Messrs Hammock and Muir, were despatched to West London to keep The Dell in touch by telephone. The Saints did all that was asked of them, winning 5-0 with a splendid attacking performance. Normally that would have been enough to send the crowd happily on their way. But this time, no-one left The Dell.

Eventually the telephone rang in the secretary's office and Saints knew their fate. Plymouth had been unable to prevent defeat and Southampton would be playing Second Division football the following season. The fans, according to one report, 'went wild with excitement, storming the ground, demanding to see the players'.

FA Cup

COMPARED to the excitement generated by the promotion race, the FA Cup offered little for Saints fans in 1921-22, despite a convincing first-round defeat of South Shields at The Dell.

In the next round Saints were again favoured with a home tie, this time against Cardiff City. Excitement was so intense during the eventual 1-1 draw that the surging crowd flattened railings at the Archers Road end of The Dell.

Saints had to travel to Ninian Park without Parker, Campbell, Turner and Barratt, who all had influenza, and although the makeshift team put up a plucky fight, they went down 2-0.

Round 1
Jan 7 v South Shields (h) 3-1
Johnson, Rawlings, Dominy
Allen; Parker, Titmuss, Shelley, Campbell, Turner, Barratt, Dominy, Rawlings, Johnson, Foxall.
Att: 14,497
Round 2
Jan 28 v Cardiff City (h) 1-1
Rawlings
Allen; Parker, Titmuss, Shelley, Campbell, Turner, Barratt, Dominy, Rawlings, Johnson, Foxall.
Att: 19,291
Replay
Feb 1 v Cardiff City (a) 0-2
Allen; Hooper, Titmuss, Shelley, Bradburn, Butt, Brown, Dominy, Rawlings, Andrews, Foxall.
Att: 40,000

In 1922 Saints set two club records, one overlapping the other. After conceding a 35th-minute goal at Plymouth on 15 April, they did not concede another goal in League football until Leeds United netted on 28 August the following season — a total of 845 minutes of successful defending.
Saints' fifth goal against Newport on the final day of the season was their last for some 500 minutes of League football. The famine was finally ended when Albert Shelley scored against Barnsley in the 25th minute of the game at The Dell on 16 September.

Arthur Dominy was awarded a benefit match in 1921-2, against Preston. Both teams were guests of the Saints directors for the show at The Palace and on the Sunday they enjoyed a charabanc trip to the New Forest with lunch at Lymington. On Monday the northerners 'did the town' before the match (won 3-1 by Saints) and afterwards they dined at the South African Hotel before another show, this time at The Hippodrome.

Saints' players were paid bonuses of £2 for a win and £1 a draw throughout the 1921-2 season.

Saints skipper Alec Campbell leads the team out at The Dell.

Division 3 (South)

Date		Opponent	Res	Scorers	Att	Allen T	Andrews L	Barratt J	Boyes K	Bradburn G	Brown C	Butt L	Campbell A	Cooper J	Dominy A	Elkes J	Foxall F	Getgood G	Hooper H	Horton J	Hough E	Johnson H	Meston S	Parker T	Rawlings W	Shelley A	Titmuss F	Turner W
Aug 27	(h)	Gillingham	W 2-0	Dominy, Rawlings	11,000	1	10				7		5		8		11							2	9	4	3	6
29	(a)	Luton T	D 0-0		10,000	1	10				7		5		8		11							2	9	4	3	6
Sep 3	(a)	Gillingham	L 0-2		6,000	1	10				7		5		8		11							2	9	4	3	6
5	(h)	Luton T	W 2-1	Rawlings, Foxall	11,000	1	10	7					5		8		11							2	9	4	3	6
10	(h)	Swindon T	W 3-1	Campbell, Barratt, Rawlings	12,000	1	10	7					5		8		11							2	9	4	3	6
17	(a)	Swindon T	W 3-2	Rawlings 2, Andrews	9,000	1	10	7					5		8		11							2	9	4	3	6
24	(h)	Brighton & HA	W 3-0	Turner, Rawlings, Foxall	13,000	1	10	7					5		8		11							2	9	4	3	6
Oct 1	(a)	Brighton & HA	W 1-0	Rawlings	10,000	1	10	7					5		8		11							2	9	4	3	6
8	(a)	Norwich C	D 2-2	Rawlings, Andrews	9,000	1	10	7					5		8		11							2	9	4	3	6
15	(h)	Norwich C	W 2-0	Rawlings 2	12,000	1	10	7	11				5		8									2	9	4	3	6
22	(a)	Watford	D 1-1	Campbell	6,000	1	10	7				6	5		8		11		2						9	4	3	
29	(h)	Watford	W 2-0	Campbell, Andrews	11,000	1	10	7					5		8		11			9				2		4	3	6
Nov 5	(a)	Reading	W 1-0	Dominy	12,000	1	10	7					5		8		11							2	9	4	3	6
12	(h)	Reading	D 0-0		11,000	1	10	7					5		8		11							2	9	4	3	6
19	(h)	Charlton A	W 6-0	Rawlings 3, Dominy 2, Barratt	10,000	1	10	7					5		8		11							2	9	4	3	6
28	(a)	Charlton A	W 2-1	Dominy, Rawlings	9,000	1	10	7					5		8		11							2	9	4	3	6
Dec 3	(a)	Millwall	W 1-0	Rawlings	10,000	1	10	7					5		8		11							2	9	4	3	6
10	(h)	Bristol R	W 1-0	Foxall	14,000	1					7		5		8		11					10		2	9	4	3	6
24	(h)	Northampton T	W 8-0	Rawlings 4, Dominy 2, Johnson 2	10,000	1		7					5		8		11					10		2	9	4	3	6
26	(a)	Queen's Park R	D 2-2	Campbell, Rawlings	12,000	1		7					5		8		11					10		2	9	4	3	6
27	(h)	Queen's Park R	D 1-1	Rawlings	20,940	1		7					5		8		11					10		2	9	4	3	6
31	(h)	Brentford	D 0-0		10,000	1		7				6	5	8			11					10		2	9	4	3	
Jan 14	(a)	Brentford	L 0-1		11,000	1		7					5		8		11					10		2	9	4	3	6
21	(h)	Millwall	W 4-2	Rawlings 4	5,000	1		7					5		8		11					10		2	9	4	3	6
Feb 4	(h)	Exeter C	W 2-0	Dominy 2	7,000	1	11			5	7	6			8				2			10			9	4	3	
11	(a)	Exeter C	D 0-0		6,000	1	11				7		5		8				2			10			9	4	3	6
20	(h)	Swansea T	D 1-1	Rawlings	5,000	1	10	7					5		8		11							2	9	4	3	6
25	(a)	Swansea T	L 0-1		14,000	1	10	7					5		8		11							2	9	4	3	6
Mar 4	(h)	Southend U	W 5-0	Dominy 2, Elkes 2, Campbell	11,000	1	11				7		5		8	10		6						2	9	4	3	
11	(a)	Southend U	D 0-0		6,000	1	11				7		5		8	10		6						2	9	4	3	
18	(a)	Portsmouth	W 2-0	Rawlings 2	26,382	1	11				7		5		8			6				10		2	9	4	3	
25	(h)	Portsmouth	D 1-1	Rawlings	17,000	1	10				7	6			8			5					11	2	9	4	3	
Apr 8	(h)	Merthyr T	D 1-1	Brown	9,000	1	10		11		7		5		8			6						2	9	4	3	
14	(a)	Bristol R	D 0-0		25,000	1	10		11		7				8			5						2	9	4	3	6
15	(a)	Plymouth A	L 0-1		24,000	1	10		11		7				8			5						2	9	4	3	6
17	(h)	Aberdare	W 1-0	Johnson	13,000	1	11				7				8			6			5	10		2	9	4	3	
18	(a)	Aberdare	W 1-0	Campbell	17,000	1	11				7		5		8							10		2	9	4	3	6
22	(h)	Plymouth A	D 0-0		12,000	1	11				7		5		8							10		2	9	4	3	6
24	(a)	Northampton T	D 0-0		7,000	1	11				7		5		8							10		2	9	4	3	6
29	(a)	Newport C	W 1-0	Campbell	4,000	1	11				7		5	9	8			6				10		2		4	3	
May 1	(a)	Merthyr T	W 1-0	Brown	8,000	1					7		5	9	8		11					10		2		4	3	6
6	(h)	Newport C	W 5-0	Dominy 2, Campbell, Rawlings, Johnson	9,000	1	11				7		5		8			6	2			10			9	4	3	
App						42	34	22	4	1	20	4	37	3	41	2	25	11	4	1	1	18	1	38	38	42	42	31
Goals							3	2			2		8		13	2	3					4			30			1

Back row (left to right): Abraham, Reader, Hooper, Parker, Allen, Titmuss, Shelley, Swinnerton, Keeping, Turner, J.Butt (asst trainer). Middle: G.Muir (director), W.Bulpitt (director), Johnson, Dawson, Bradburn, Horton, Cooper, Brown, Butt, Campbell, A.Lee (trainer), J.McIntyre (manager). Front: W.Hammock (director), Barratt, Dominy, Rawlings, Andrews, Foxall, Boyes, E.Arnfield (secretary).

	P	W	D	L	F	A	Pts
Southampton	42	23	15	4	68	21	61
Plymouth A	42	25	11	6	63	24	61
Portsmouth	42	18	17	7	62	39	53
Luton T	42	22	8	12	64	35	52
Queen's Park R	42	18	13	11	53	44	49
Swindon T	42	16	13	13	72	60	45
Aberdare A	42	17	10	15	57	51	44
Watford	42	13	18	11	54	48	44
Brentford	42	16	11	15	52	43	43
Swansea T	42	13	15	14	50	47	41
Merthyr T	42	17	6	19	45	56	40
Millwall	42	10	18	14	38	42	38
Reading	42	14	18	10	40	47	38
Bristol R	42	14	10	18	52	67	38
Norwich C	42	12	13	17	50	62	37
Charlton A	42	13	11	18	43	56	37
Northampton T	42	13	11	18	47	71	37
Gillingham	42	14	8	20	47	60	36
Brighton & HA	42	13	9	20	45	51	35
Newport C	42	11	12	19	44	61	34
Exeter C	42	11	12	19	38	59	34
Southend U	42	8	11	23	34	74	27

Saints conceded a mere 21 goals in 42 games in 1921-2 season, a Football League record until Liverpool's defence let in 16 in 1978-9, 57 years later.

1922-23

THE problems of playing in a truly national League for the first time soon became evident when the Saints were scheduled to play at South Shields in their opening game. The team's train journey to the North-East took 20 hours, and in that first season they travelled over 8,000 miles for League games. Initially, life in Division Two proved tough, with goals especially hard to come by. Indeed, Rawlings was replaced by Johnson for the third game, at home to South Shields, and it was not until the sixth game, against Barnsley, that Southampton eventually found the net. During this tentative opening period, the Saints also lost their 18-month unbeaten home record. Manager McIntyre, however, kept faith with his players and they repaid his loyalty by rallying to finish a creditable 11th with the amazing record of: Played 42, Won 14, Lost 14, Drawn 14, Goals for 40, Goals against 40, points 42.

Southampton goalkeeper Allen makes a fine save against Bury.

Centre-forward Rawlings was dropped early in the season, as Saints struggled to come to terms with Second Division football, but he was soon reinstated and was one of the heroes of the FA Cup run that year, scoring in the fine win over Newcastle and in the drawn replay with West Ham.

FA Cup

Round 1
Jan 13 v Newcastle U (a) 0-0
Allen; Parker, Titmuss, Shelley, Campbell, Turner, Blyth, Dominy, Rawlings, Elkes, Andrews.
Att: 35,000

Replay
Jan 17 v Newcastle U (h) 3-1
Dominy 2, Rawlings
Allen; Parker, Titmuss, Shelley, Campbell, Turner, Brown, Dominy, Rawlings, Elkes, Andrews.
Att: 18,000

Round 2
Feb 3 v Chelsea (a) 0-0
Allen; Parker, Titmuss, Shelley, Campbell, Turner, Brown, Dominy, Rawlings, Elkes, Andrews.
Att: 67,105

Replay
Feb 7 v Chelsea (h) 1-0
Dominy
Allen; Parker, Titmuss, Shelley, Campbell, Turner, Brown, Dominy, Rawlings, Elkes, Andrews.
Att: 25,000

Round 3
Feb 24 v Bury (a) 0-0
Allen; Parker, Titmuss, Shelley, Campbell, Turner, Brown, Dominy, Rawlings, Elkes, Andrews.
Att: 25,000

Replay
Feb 28 v Bury (h) 1-0
Dominy
Allen; Parker, Titmuss, Shelley, Campbell, Turner, Brown, Dominy, Rawlings, Elkes, Andrews.
Att: 16,000

Round 4
Mar 4 v West Ham U (h) 1-1
Elkes
Allen; Parker, Titmuss, Shelley, Campbell, Turner, Brown, Dominy, Rawlings, Elkes, Andrews.
Att: 21,690

Replay
Mar 14 v West Ham U (a) 1-1
Rawlings
Lock; Parker, Titmuss, Shelley, Campbell, Turner, Brown, Dominy, Rawlings, Elkes, Andrews.
Att: 20,000

Second Replay
Mar 19 v West Ham U (at Villa Park) 0-1
Lock; Parker, Titmuss, Shelley, Campbell, Turner, Brown, Dominy, Rawlings, Elkes, Clarke.
Att: 22,184

ALTHOUGH the League produced only an average return for Saints, the FA Cup more than made up for it. Few people gave Southampton a chance at St James's Park in the first round. The Geordies were a formidable First Division force but the Saints, with goalkeeper Allen having a particularly fine game, fought the muddy battle well to earn a draw. In the replay, despite conceding a soft goal in the opening minute, Saints recovered well to win 3-1 with 'some of the best football ever seen at The Dell'. Dominy and Campbell were outstanding.

A visit to Stamford Bridge was scant reward for such a famous victory but again the Saints showed character to force a replay and win at The Dell. In the third round the pattern was repeated when Bury were beaten in a replay at Southampton. This time, however, the Saints' name emerged first when the fourth-round draw was made and West Ham found themselves scheduled to visit The Dell. Vic Watson opened the scoring for the Hammers early on, but Elkes equalised with a 'clever header'. The Upton Park replay produced another tough game and another 1-1 draw before the now weary teams travelled to Villa Park.

In a scrappy match, West Ham scraped home by the only goal, going on to contest the first FA Cup Final ever to be staged at Wembley. Southampton's disappointment at being eliminated was tempered somewhat by their £28,482 in Cup receipts and some £4,000 of that was spent in improving facilities at The Dell.

> *Goalkeeper Lock's re-introduction for the West Ham replay meant that there were six Hampshire-born players in the Southampton side: Dominy, Lock, Campbell, Parker, Rawlings and Shelley.*

1922-23

Division 2

Date	Opponent	Result	Scorers	Att.	Allen T	Andrews L	Blyth R	Brown C	Campbell A	Christie A	Clarke J	Cooper J	Dominy A	Elkes J	Getgood G	Hooper H	Hough E	Johnson H	Lock H	McCall W	Meston S	Parker T	Rawlings W	Shelley A	Titmuss F	Turner W
Aug 26	(a) South Shields	D 0-0		13,000	1			7	5		11		8	10	6							2	9	4	3	
28	(h) Leeds U	L 0-1		16,000	1			7	5		11		8	10	6							2	9	4	3	
Sep 2	(h) South Shields	L 0-2		18,000	1	11		7	5				8	10	6			9				2		4	3	
4	(a) Leeds U	L 0-1		6,000	1	11		7					8	10	5		3					2	9	4		6
9	(a) Barnsley	L 0-3		10,000	1			7			11		8	10	5		3					2	9	4		6
16	(h) Barnsley	D 2-2	Shelley, Rawlings	15,000	1			7			11		8	10	5		3					2	9	4		6
23	(a) Blackpool	W 2-1	Dominy, Rawlings	14,000	1			7			11		8	10	5		3					2	9	4		6
30	(h) Blackpool	D 1-1	Elkes	16,000	1			7			11		8	10	5		3					2	9	4		6
Oct 7	(a) West Ham U	D 1-1	Elkes	20,000	1			7			11		8	10	5							2	9	4	3	6
14	(h) West Ham U	W 2-0	Dominy, Rawlings	17,000	1			7			11		8	10	5							2	9	4	3	6
21	(a) Wolves	D 0-0		15,000	1			7			11		8	10	5							2	9	4	3	6
28	(h) Wolves	W 3-0	Getgood, Dominy, Rawlings	13,000	1			7			11		8	10	5							2	9	4	3	6
Nov 4	(h) Bradford C	W 2-0	Dominy, Elkes	14,000	1			7			11		8	10	5							2	9	4	3	6
11	(a) Bradford C	D 0-0		15,000	1			7			11		8	10	5							2	9	4	3	6
18	(a) Leicester C	L 1-2	Dominy	18,000	1			7			11		8	10	5							2	9	4	3	6
25	(h) Leicester C	D 0-0		17,000	1			7			11		8	10	5							2	9	4	3	6
Dec 2	(a) Derby C	W 2-0	Dominy, Elkes	10,000	1			7			11		8	10	5							2	9	4	3	6
9	(h) Derby C	L 0-4		15,000	1			7			11		8	10	5							2	9	4	3	6
16	(a) Notts C	L 0-1		9,000	1			7	5		11		8	10				9				2		4	3	6
23	(h) Notts C	L 0-1		9,000	1			7	5		11		8	10				9				2		4	3	6
25	(a) Hull C	W 3-1	Dominy 2, Elkes	14,000	1			7	5		11		8	10				9				2		4	3	6
26	(h) Hull C	W 2-1	Campbell, opp own goal	16,000	1			7	5		11		8	10				9				2		4	3	6
30	(h) Fulham	W 2-0	Dominy, Rawlings	7,000	1	11		7	5				8	10								2	9	4	3	6
Jan 1	(a) Sheffield W	D 0-0		30,000	1	11		7					8	10	5							2	9	4	3	6
6	(a) Fulham	D 1-1	Dominy	25,000	1	11		7					8	10	5							2	9	4	3	6
20	(h) Crystal P	L 0-2		13,000	1	11		7	5				8	10								2	9	4	3	6
27	(a) Crystal P	L 0-1		9,000	1	11		7					8	10	5							2	9	4	3	6
Feb 10	(h) Coventry C	W 3-0	Brown, McCall, opp own goal	7,000	1	10		7	5				8							11		2	9	4	3	6
17	(a) Port Vale	D 0-0		14,000	1			7	5				8	10						11		2	9	4	3	6
Mar 3	(a) Manchester U	W 2-1	Brown, Rawlings	20,000	1			7		4			8	10				3		11		2	9	5		6
5	(h) Port Vale	W 3-1	Johnson, Rawlings, McCall	5,000	1	10		7		4			8					3		11		2	9	5		6
17	(h) Bury	L 0-3		12,000				7		4			8	10					1	11		2	9	5	3	6
24	(a) Bury	D 0-0		9,000		10		7					8		5				1	11		2	9	4	3	6
31	(h) Rotherham C	W 4-2	Rawlings 3, Dominy	10,000		11		7	5				8	10					1			2	9	4	3	6
Apr 2	(h) Sheffield W	D 1-1	Rawlings	16,000		11		7					8	10	5				1			2	9	4	3	6
7	(a) Rotherham C	D 0-0		11,000		11		7					8	10	5				1			2	9	4	3	6
11	(h) Manchester U	D 0-0		5,500				7	5				8	10					1	11		2	9	4	3	6
14	(h) Clapton O	W 2-0	Dominy, Rawlings	9,000		11		7	5				8			10			1			2	9	4	3	6
21	(h) Clapton O	L 0-1		15,000		11		7		4			8			10			1			2	9	5	3	6
28	(h) Stockport C	W 1-0	Dominy	7,000		11		7		4			8			10			1		9	2		5	3	6
30	(a) Coventry C	L 0-2		12,000		11		7					8		5	10			1			2	9	4	3	6
May 5	(a) Stockport C	L 0-3		15,000		10		7					8		5			9	1	11		2		4	3	6
App					31	18	8	32	15	5	20	2	40	31	24	11	7	9	11	8	1	38	35	42	35	39
Goals								2	1				13	5	1			1		2			12	1		

2 own-goals

	P	W	D	L	F	A	Pts
Notts C	42	23	7	12	46	34	53
West Ham U	42	20	11	11	63	38	51
Leicester C	42	21	9	12	65	44	51
Manchester U	42	17	14	11	51	36	48
Blackpool	42	18	11	13	60	43	47
Bury	42	18	11	13	55	46	47
Leeds U	42	18	11	13	43	36	47
Sheffield W	42	17	12	13	54	47	46
Barnsley	42	17	11	14	62	51	45
Fulham	42	16	12	14	43	32	44
Southampton	42	14	14	14	40	40	42
Hull C	42	14	14	14	43	45	42
South Shields	42	15	10	17	35	44	40
Derby C	42	14	11	17	46	50	39
Bradford C	42	12	13	17	41	45	37
Crystal P	42	13	11	18	54	62	37
Port Vale	42	14	9	19	51	49	37
Coventry C	42	15	7	20	46	63	37
Clapton O	42	12	12	18	40	50	36
Stockport C	42	14	8	20	43	58	36
Rotherham C	42	13	9	20	44	63	35
Wolves	42	9	9	24	42	77	27

Standing (left to right): Christie, Parker, Lock, Allen, Titmuss, Hooper. Sitting: Brown, Dominy, Rawlings, Elkes, Andrews, Campbell. On ground: Shelley, Turner.

1923-24

SAINTS missed promotion to Division One by only three points and it was generally believed, had they not been involved in an FA Cup run which included two replays, they would have achieved First Division football at the second attempt.

Outside-left Jimmy Carr was the only new signing when Saints kicked off the new season. Carr came from Reading and resumed the successful partnership he had forged with Len Andrews at Elm Park. There was a newcomer on the other wing, but Sammy Meston had not cost a fee. The son of Saints' great servant of the Southern League days, Meston had joined the club from local football. Alas, after a promising start Meston was injured and then returned only to break a leg in the match against Bristol City at The Dell.

Saints wasted no time and propelled into the transfer market, signing Henderson from Luton and Price from Halifax. Henderson cost the Saints £500 and he missed only three out of the next 26 League games.

By Christmas, Saints were handily placed in the promotion racc but when the Cup programme began they found themelves having to sandwich vital League matches between gruelling Cup games. In particular, two defeats by Leeds United, the leaders, came when Saints were without the services of Parker, Campbell, Titmuss and Carr, and the first-team squad was just not big enough to sustain a run in the Cup and a promotion chase.

FA Cup

SAINTS were drawn at Stamford Bridge in the first round of the FA Cup and found themselves facing a centre-forward who had just cost Chelsea a record British fee. Andrew Wilson had joined the Londoners from Middlesbrough for £6,000 and how tight a rein Campbell could keep on the Londoners' new star was seen as a major factor in the outcome of the game.

Although Wilson scored a brilliant individual goal, Saints managed to hold Chelsea to a draw and in the replay, with Wilson now well-shackled by Campbell, Southampton went through with goals from Dominy, who netted following Turner's free-kick, and Rawlings, who converted Henderson's centre.

In the next round Southampton made home advantage count to beat Blackpool 3-1, and that left them with an attractive home tie with Liverpool, the League Champions, who had beaten Cup-holders, Bolton, in the previous round.

The Merseysiders, with six internationals in their side, gave the determined Saints a hard game and no-one was surpised at the goalless outcome.

Southampton were always going to find the Anfield replay difficult but their task was made even more onerous by a freak injury to Titmuss which left them with only ten men. The lace on the ball became loose and when the full-back stopped a shot full in the face, the lace gashed his eyeball, bursting a blood vessel. For some time afterwards it was feared that Titmuss would suffer permanent damage.

A near 50,000 crowd spurred the home side on and Chambers had put them ahead just after the interval. Even then, Saints did not give up and it was six minutes from the end before Forshaw made it 2-0.

Round 1
Jan 12 v Chelsea (a) 1-1
Dominy
Allen; Parker, Titmuss, Shelley, Campbell, Turner, Brown, Dominy, Rawlings, Price, Carr.
Att: 34,586
Replay
Jan 16 v Chelsea (h) 2-0
Dominy, Rawlings
Allen; Parker, Titmuss, Shelley, Campbell, Turner, Henderson, Dominy, Rawlings, Price, Carr.
Att: 17,000
Round 2
Feb 2 v Blackpool (h) 3-1
Rawlings, Dominy, Price
Allen; Parker, Titmuss, Shelley, Campbell, Turner, Henderson, Dominy, Rawlings, Price, Carr.
Att: 18,000
Round 3
Feb 23 v Liverpool (h) 0-0
Allen; Parker, Titmuss, Shelley, Campbell, Turner, Henderson, Dominy, Rawlings, Price, Carr.
Att: 18,671
Replay
Feb 27 v Liverpool (a) 0-2
Allen; Parker, Titmuss, Shelley, Campbell, Turner, Henderson, Dominy, Rawlings, Price, Carr.
Att: 49,569

Mr E. Arnfield handed over the post of secretary to Mr Goss in August 1923 after 30 years service. Arnfield was later given a place on the board.

Team page from the Saints v Sheffield Wednesday match at The Dell on 15 September 1923. Note that the Yorkshire club were then known simply as 'The Wednesday'.

Harrow, the Chelsea skipper, greets Saints' captain Arthur Dominy before the FA Cup match between the two sides.

1923-24
Division 2

Date	Opponent	Result	Scorers	Att	Allen T	Andrews L	Bradford A	Brown C	Bruton L	Campbell A	Carr J	Dominy A	Harkus G	Henderson W	Hooper H	Hough E	Johnson H	MacDonald E	Meston S	Parker T	Pearson H	Price C	Rawlings W	Salter J	Shelley A	Titmuss F	Turner W
Aug 25	(a) Bury	L 0-1		14,000	1	10				5	11	8							7	2			9		4	3	6
27	(a) Manchester U	L 0-1		35,000	1	10				5	11	8							7	2			9		4	3	6
Sep 1	(h) Bury	W 3-0	Meston 2, Carr	15,000	1	10				5	11	8							7	2			9		4	3	6
3	(h) Manchester U	D 0-0		20,000	1	10				5	11	8							7	2			9		4	3	6
8	(a) Sheffield W	D 1-1	opp own goal	20,000	1					5	11	8						10	7	2			9		4	3	6
11	(a) Nelson	D 0-0		8,000	1					5	11	8						10	7	2			9		4	3	6
15	(h) Sheffield W	W 3-0	Pearson 2, Dominy	10,000	1					5	11	8		3				10		2	7		9		4		6
22	(a) Coventry C	D 0-0		10,000	1					5	11	8						10		2	7		9		4	3	6
24	(a) Stoke C	D 1-1	Pearson	11,000	1					5	11	8						10		2	7		9		4	3	6
29	(h) Coventry C	L 1-3	Carr	12,000	1					5	11	8						10		2	7		9		4	3	6
Oct 6	(h) Bristol C	W 1-0	Rawlings	12,000	1				8	5	11							10	7	2			9		4	3	6
13	(a) Bristol C	D 1-1	Rawlings	12,000	1			7	8	5	11							10		2			9		4	3	6
15	(h) Stoke C	L 0-1		10,000	1	10		7	8	5	11									2			9		4	3	6
20	(h) Derby C	D 0-0		11,000	1			7	10	5	11	8								2			9		4	3	6
27	(a) Derby C	L 0-1		13,000	1			7	10	5	11	8								2	9				4	3	6
Nov 3	(h) Fulham	W 1-0	opp own goal	10,000	1			7		5	11	8						10		2	9				4	3	6
10	(a) Fulham	L 2-3	Rawlings 2	15,000	1					5	11	8		7						2			9	10	4	3	6
17	(h) Blackpool	W 3-2	Dominy, Rawlings, Carr	9,000	1	10				5	11	8		7						2			9		4	3	6
24	(a) Blackpool	L 0-2		8,000	1	10				5	11	8		7						2			9		4	3	6
Dec 8	(h) Nelson	W 3-0	Dominy, Rawlings, Pearson	11,000	1						11	8		7		5				2	10		9		4	3	6
15	(h) South Shields	D 0-0		11,000	1						11	8		7		5				2	10		9		4	3	6
22	(a) South Shields	W 2-1	Dominy, Rawlings	4,000	1			7		5	11	8								2	10		9		4	3	6
29	(h) Hull C	W 2-0	Dominy, Carr	11,000	1			7		5	11	8								2	10		9		4	3	6
Jan 5	(a) Hull C	D 0-0		9,000	1			7		5	11	8								2	10		9		4	3	6
19	(h) Barnsley	W 6-0	Rawlings 3, Johnson 2, Dominy	7,000	1						8	4	7				10	11		2			9		5	3	6
26	(a) Barnsley	D 1-1	Johnson	7,000	1				5		8		7				10	11		2			9		4	3	6
Feb 9	(a) Bradford C	L 1-2	Price	10,000	1				5		8		7					11		2		10	9		4	3	6
11	(h) Bradford C	W 2-0	Henderson, Price	8,000	1				5		8		7					11		2		10	9		4	3	6
16	(h) Port Vale	D 1-1	Dominy	9,000	1				5		8		7					11		2		10	9		4	3	6
Mar 1	(h) Leeds U	L 0-1		8,000	1						8	4	7	3				11		2		10	9		5		6
8	(a) Leeds U	L 0-3		18,000	1						8	4	7	3				11		2		10	9		5		6
15	(a) Leicester C	W 1-0	Dominy	20,000	1						8	4	7	3				11		2		10	9		5		6
17	(a) Port Vale	L 0-1		9,000	1						8	4	7					11		2		10	9		5	3	6
22	(h) Leicester C	W 1-0	Parker	9,000	1						8	4	7					11		2		10	9		5	3	6
29	(a) Clapton O	D 0-0		18,000	1						8	4	7					11		2		10	9		5	3	6
Apr 5	(h) Clapton O	W 5-0	Rawlings 3, Dominy, Parker	7,000	1						8	4	7					11		2		10	9		5	3	6
12	(a) Stockport C	W 3-2	Shelley, Dominy, Rawlings	11,000	1						8	4	7	3				11		2		10	9		5		6
18	(a) Crystal P	D 0-0		8,000	1		5				8	6	7					11		2		10	9		4	3	
19	(h) Stockport C	D 0-0		10,000	1		5				8	6	7					11		2		10	9		4	3	
21	(h) Crystal P	W 1-0	Rawlings	10,000	1				5		8	6	7					11		2		10	9		4	3	
26	(a) Oldham A	W 3-1	Rawlings 3	6,000	1				5		8	6	7					11		2		10	9		4	3	
May 3	(h) Oldham A	W 3-1	Dominy, Rawlings, Price	8,000	1				5		8	6	7					11		2		10	9		4	3	
App					42	7	2	12	5	29	24	39	14	23	4	4	11	18	7	41	8	19	36	1	42	37	37
Goals											4	11		1			3		2	2	4	3	19		1		

2 own-goals

Back row (left to right, players only): Shelley, Parker, Allen, Titmuss, Hough, Turner. Front: Brown, Dominy, Rawlings, Keeping, Andrews.

	P	W	D	L	F	A	Pts
Leeds U	42	21	12	9	61	35	54
Bury	42	21	9	12	63	35	51
Derby C	42	21	9	12	75	42	51
Blackpool	42	18	13	11	72	47	49
Southampton	42	17	14	11	52	31	48
Stoke C	42	14	18	10	44	42	46
Oldham A	42	14	17	11	45	52	45
Sheffield W	42	16	12	14	54	51	44
South Shields	42	17	10	15	49	50	44
Clapton O	42	14	15	13	40	36	43
Barnsley	42	16	11	15	57	61	43
Leicester C	42	17	8	17	64	54	42
Stockport C	42	13	16	13	44	52	42
Manchester U	42	13	14	15	52	44	40
Crystal P	42	13	13	16	53	65	39
Port Vale	42	13	12	17	50	66	38
Hull C	42	10	17	15	46	51	37
Bradford C	42	11	15	16	35	48	37
Coventry C	42	11	13	18	52	68	35
Fulham	42	10	14	18	45	56	34
Nelson	42	10	13	19	40	74	33
Bristol C	42	7	15	20	32	65	29

1924-25

YET again an average performance in the Second Division was eclipsed by a fine run in the FA Cup. Saints finished seventh in the table, a position that, it could be argued, was slightly better than average. Yet the supporters were frustrated that the Saints had not shown the same fighting spirit in the League as they had in the Cup.

Manager Jimmy McIntyre probably also felt that frustration,

for in December 1924, he resigned. His departure took the directors' by surprise and they announced that the board would take over the manager's job, with help from secretary Goss. Being managerless did not seem to bother the players unduly and within one month they had embarked on the Cup run that was to take them to within 90 minutes of Wembley.

FA Cup

SOUTHAMPTON'S great Cup run of 1925 had a false start when they were leading 5-0 at home to Exeter, only to be robbed of outright victory when fog descended and the game was abandoned with only ten minutes to play.

Some Saints fans went on to the pitch 'in an effort to let the game go on', but the referee was adamant and Southampton had to wait four days before going through, this time 3-1. A fourth-minute penalty by Parker was enough to beat Brighton in the next round before Badford City came to The Dell and were defeated 2-0 to put Southampton in the quarter-finals.

The luck of the draw certainly favoured Saints this season and yet again they were drawn at home, this time to Liverpool, the team who had won an Anfield replay between the two sides the previous season. This time Southampton made sure at the first attempt and they had a fine opportunist goal from Rawlings to thank for their passage into the semi-final.

Sheffield United at Stamford Bridge stood between Saints and their first Wembley appearance. Alas, the day was one of unmitigated disaster for the Southampton fans who made the journey. Fate struck even before the kick-off when Titmuss reported ill and Ted Hough took over at left-back.

Yet despite this upset to their defensive balance, Southampton began well even though they had to kick into a strong wind. But as the game progressed, Saints forwards began to lose their cohesion and with the ball in the air for long periods, United began to pin their opponents back.

Harkus had the best chance for Saints in the first half, but he shot wide with only the goalkeeper to beat. The Saints suffered another cruel blow when Tom Parker, attempting to put the ball away for a corner, sliced it past Allen to put United ahead.

Parker's dreadful afternoon was not over. In the second half Rawlings was tripped in the penalty area but the Saints right-back drove the spot-kick straight at the Blades' goalkeeper. To compound Saints' misery, a mix-up between Allen and the luckless Parker gave Sheffield their second goal. It was not to be Southampton's or Tom Parker's day.

Round 1
Jan 14 v Exeter City (h) 3-1*
Dominy, Rawlings, Price
Allen; Parker, Titmuss, Shelley, Campbell, Harkus, Henderson, Dominy, Rawlings, Price, Carr
Att: 15,000
. First game abandoned (fog) after 80 mins with Saints leading 5-0 (Dominy 2, Price 2, Parker). Att: 15,902
Round 2
Jan 31 v Brighton & HA (h) 1-0
Parker (pen)
Allen; Parker, Titmuss, Shelley, Campbell, Harkus, Henderson, Dominy, Rawlings, Woodhouse, Cribb.
Att: 17,795
Round 3
Feb 21 v Bradford City (h) 2-0
Dominy, Harkus
Allen; Parker, Titmuss, Shelley, Campbell, Bradford, Henderson, Dominy, Rawlings, Harkus, Cribb.
Att: 19,098
Round 4
Mar 7 v Liverpool (h) 1-0
Rawlings
Allen; Parker, Titmuss, Shelley, Campbell, Bradford, Henderson, Dominy, Rawlings, Harkus, Carr.
Att: 21,501
Semi-final
Mar 28 v Sheffield United (at Stamford Bridge) 0-2
Allen; Parker, Hough, Shelley, Campbell, Bradford, Henderson, Dominy, Rawlings, Harkus, Carr.
Att: 65,754

Tom Parker drives the ball past his own goalkeeper and Saints fall behind in the semi-final at Stamford Bridge.

Parker's afternoon of misery is almost complete as he drives a penalty kick straight at the Sheffield goalkeeper who is able to parry it away.

1924-25

Division 2

Date		Opponent	Res	Score	Scorers	Att	Allen T	Barrett A	Bradford A	Broad T	Bullock J	Campbell A	Carr J	Cribb S	Dominy A	Gallagher J	Harkus G	Henderson W	Hough E	Jones D	Keeping A	Parker T	Price C	Price F	Rawlings W	Shelley A	Titmuss F	Woodhouse S	Yeomans H
Aug 30	(h)	Oldham A	D	0-0		11,000	1				5	11		8			6	7	3			2			9	4		10	
Sep 1	(a)	Stoke C	L	0-2		12,000	1					11		8		5	6	7	3			2			9	4		10	
6	(a)	Sheffield W	L	0-1		25,000	1					11		8	10		6	7	3	4		2			9	5			
8	(h)	Stoke C	W	3-0	Dominy 2, Rawlings	8,867	1					11		8	10		6	7	3	4		2			9	5			
13	(h)	Clapton O	W	2-0	Dominy 2	6,000	1					11		8	10		6	7	3	4		2			9	5			
15	(a)	Coventry C	L	0-1		9,000	1							8	10		6	7	3	4		2		11	9	5			
20	(a)	Crystal P	L	1-3	Rawlings	10,000	1					5		8	10		6	7				2		11	9	4	3		
27	(h)	Portsmouth	D	0-0		19,366	1					5	11	8	10		6	7				2			9	4	3		
Oct 4	(h)	Chelsea	D	0-0		12,000	1					5		8	10		6	7				2		11	9	4	3		
11	(a)	Stockport C	D	1-1	Rawlings	12,000	1		7	9		5					6					2		11	8	4	3	10	
13	(a)	Port Vale	D	1-1	Woodhouse	9,000	1		7			5					6					2		11	9	4	3	10	
18	(h)	Manchester U	L	0-2		14,000	1		7			5					6					2	10	11	9	4	3		
25	(a)	Hull C	D	1-1	C.Price	10,000	1					5					6	7			3	2	10	11	9	4			
Nov 1	(h)	Blackpool	W	2-1	Rawlings, C.Price	4,000	1					5					6	7			3	2	10	11	9	4			
8	(a)	Derby C	L	0-3		14,000	1					5					6	7			3	2	10	11	9	4			
15	(h)	South Shields	D	1-1	Parker	8,000	1					5		11			6	7	3	4		2	10		9			8	
22	(a)	Bradford C	W	2-1	Dominy, Rawlings	10,000	1					5		11	10		6	7	3			2			9	4			
29	(a)	Portsmouth	D	1-1	Dominy	25,000	1					5		11	10		6	7	3			2			9	4			
Dec 6	(a)	Middlesbrough	D	0-0		12,000	1					5		11	10		6	7	3			2			9	4			
13	(h)	Barnsley	W	3-1	Parker, Rawlings, C.Price	7,000	1					5		11	10		6	7				2			9	4	3		
20	(a)	Wolves	L	0-3		13,000	1					5		11	10		6	7				2			9	4	3		
26	(h)	Fulham	W	1-0	C.Price	17,000	1					5		11	10		6	7				2			9	4	3		
27	(a)	Oldham A	D	1-1	Dominy	6,000	1					5		11	10		6	7				2			9	4	3		
Jan 3	(h)	Sheffield W	W	1-0	Rawlings	7,000	1					5		11	10		6	7				2			9	4	3		
17	(a)	Clapton O	L	0-1		12,000	1							11	10		6	7	5			2			9	4	3		
24	(h)	Crystal P	W	2-0	Rawlings, Carr	9,000	1						10	11	8		6	7	5			2			9	4	3		
Feb 7	(a)	Chelsea	L	0-1		30,000	1					5			11	8	6	7		10		2			9	4	3		
14	(h)	Stockport C	W	2-1	Rawlings 2	8,000	1			6		5			11	8	10	7	3			2			9	4			
28	(h)	Hull C	D	2-2	Harkus, Cribb	7,000	1			6		5			11	8	10	7				2			9	4	3		
Mar 14	(h)	Derby C	W	2-0	Rawlings, Carr	12,000	1	6				5			11	8	10	7	2						9	4	3		
21	(a)	South Shields	D	1-1	Dominy	8,000	1			6					11	8	10	7	2	4	3				9	5			
Apr 1	(a)	Blackpool	L	0-1		9,000	1			6		5			11	8	10	7	3			2			9	4			
4	(h)	Port Vale	W	1-0	Dominy	5,000	1			6		5			11	8	10	7	3			2			9	4			
10	(a)	Fulham	L	0-1		12,000	1			6		5			11	8	10	7							9	4	3		
11	(h)	Middlesbrough	D	1-1	C.Price	10,000	1		5	7					11	8			9	2			10			4	3	6	
13	(h)	Leicester C	D	0-0		6,000	1		5	7					11	8				2			10		9	4	3	6	
14	(a)	Leicester C	D	0-0		25,000				7					11	8	4		2		3		10		9	5		6	1
18	(a)	Barnsley	D	1-1	Rawlings	8,000			5	7					11	8	6			2			10		9	4	3		1
22	(a)	Manchester U	D	1-1	Dominy	40,000			5	7					11	8	6			2	3		10		9	4			1
25	(h)	Wolves	D	1-1	C.Price	6,000			5	7					11	8	6			2	3		10		9	4			1
30	(h)	Bradford C	W	2-0	Rawlings 2	5,500	1		5						11	8	6	7	2						9	4	3	10	
May 2	(h)	Coventry C	W	3-0	Dominy 3	5,000	1		5						11	8	6	7	2				10		9	4	3		
App							38	1	13	9	1	26	28	6	40	1	40	34	27	7	7	30	24	9	41	41	22	13	4
Goals													2	1	13		1					2	6		14			1	

Back row (left to right): J.McIntyre (manager), W.Rayner (asst trainer), Jones, Shelley, Parker, Allen, Titmuss, Harkus, Meston, J.Sarjantson (director), E.Arnfield (director). Middle: H.Lewis (director), G.Goss (secretary), A.Lee (trainer), Keeping, Hough, Campbell, Yeomans, Bradford, Bruton, Bullock, A.A.Wood (director), H.Hammock (director), W.Bulpitt (director), G.Muir (director). Front: Broad, Henderson, Dominy, Rawlings, C.Price, Carr, F.Price, Woodhouse.

	P	W	D	L	F	A	Pts
Leicester C	42	24	7	11	90	32	59
Manchester U	42	23	8	11	57	23	57
Derby C	42	22	9	11	71	36	55
Portsmouth	42	15	9	18	58	50	48
Chelsea	42	16	11	15	51	37	47
Wolves	42	20	16	6	55	51	46
Southampton	42	13	11	18	40	36	44
Port Vale	42	17	17	8	48	56	42
Gateshead	42	12	13	17	42	38	41
Hull C	42	15	16	11	50	49	41
Clapton O	42	14	16	12	42	42	40
Fulham	42	15	17	10	41	56	40
Middlesbrough	42	10	13	19	36	44	39
Sheffield W	42	15	19	8	50	56	38
Barnsley	42	13	17	12	46	59	38
Bradford C	42	13	17	12	37	50	38
Blackpool	42	14	19	9	65	61	37
Oldham A	42	13	18	11	35	51	37
Stockport C	42	13	18	11	37	57	37
Stoke C	42	12	19	11	34	46	35
Crystal P	42	12	20	10	38	54	34
Coventry C	42	11	22	9	45	84	31

73

1925-26

THE 1925-26 season began with players having to come to terms with the new offside law. Now only two opponents were needed to play an attacker onside and as footballers struggled with the new rule, so the goals rained in.

Southampton seemed particularly troubled by the change and they lost their first four games, conceding 11 goals and scoring only two. One particularly bitter blow was a home defeat by Portsmouth. But the root of Saints' troubles lay far deeper than the change in the law and the team lacked any direction. Eventually, a struggle against relegation soon developed.

The directors responded by appointing a new manager in the form of Arthur Chadwick, the old Saints player who had begun the season in charge of Reading. Chadwick's arrival made only a moderate impact but at the season's end Saints had risen to 14th place and safety.

Two highlights of the season were the emergence of Mike Keeping, a young full-back of immense promise, and a shock 5-0 victory over Bradford City at Valley Parade, a result which gave Saints their biggest away win in Division Two.

In the spring, Saints' directors surprised the fans by selling both full-backs. Titmuss went to Plymouth for £1,750 — perhaps understandable with the emergence of Keeping — and Parker moved to Arsenal for £3,250. Parker's departure caused uproar amongst supporters but the board explained that they needed the money to buy the freehold of The Dell.

Indeed, the purchase of the ground was completed in the following close season but the fans were still unconvinced and far from happy that a player of Parker's calibre should be released. Thus, a disappointing season ended with rumblings off the field.

FA Cup

REORGANISATION of the Cup meant that all First and Second Division clubs were exempted until the third round. One thing that did not change was that, for the third year running, Liverpool were drawn to play at The Dell.

Saints lined up without the injured Shelley and Price, but they did win the toss and set Liverpool to face a bright sun, low in the sky, in the first half. The match began at a fast pace and Saints were quite impressive until goalkeeper Allen collided with his fellow defender, Keeping. Allen had to leave the field with bruised ribs and with Bradford in goal and down to ten men, Southampton could be thankful for the goalless draw.

Allen was still missing when Saints took the field for the replay at Anfield where Hill, the former QPR goalkeeper, took over. Saints struggled manfully but Liverpool, with a near 42,000 crowd urging them on, won by the only goal of the match, scored by Dick Forshaw, in the 65th minute.

> **Round 3**
> **Jan 9 v Liverpool (h) 0-0**
> Allen; Parker, Keeping, Bradford, Campbell, Woodhouse, Henderson, Dominy, Rawlings, Harkus, Carr.
> *Att: 18,391*
> **Replay**
> **Jan 13 v Liverpool (a) 0-1**
> Hill; Parker, Keeping, Bradford, Campbell, Woodhouse, Henderson, Dominy, Rawlings, Harkus, Carr.
> *Att: 41,902*

> *In the close season, Rawlings, Harkus and Keeping were selected to tour Canada with the FA party.*

> *On 11 February 1926, the Saints supporters club was formed, with Mr Grant elected its first secretary.*

Saints, led by Arthur Dominy, take the field at The Dell for the Cup match against Liverpool. Note the official with his loud-hailer.

1925-26

Division 2

Date		Opponent	Result	Scorers	Att.	Allen T	Bradford A	Bruton L	Bullock J	Campbell A	Carr J	Coundon C	Cribb S	Dominy A	Harkus G	Henderson W	Hill L	Hough E	Keeping A	King E	Matthews F	Meston S	Parker T	Price C	Rawlings W	Shelley A	Titmuss F	Turner E	Woodhouse S	Yeomans H
Aug 29	(a)	Blackpool	L 1-2	Dominy	18,000				5	11				8	6	7	1						2	10	9	4	3			
31	(h)	Hull C	L 0-2		9,433				5				11	8	6	7	1						2		9	4	3	10		
Sep 5	(h)	Portsmouth	L 1-3	Price	18,000				5	11				8	6	7	1						2	10	9	4	3			
7	(a)	Hull C	L 0-4		10,000	5							11	8	6	7	1						2	10	9	4	3			
12	(h)	Nottingham F	W 2-0	Price 2	9,304				8	5			11			7							2	10	9	4	3		6	1
19	(a)	Derby C	D 2-2	Rawlings 2	4,000				5				11			7							2	10	9	4	3	8	6	1
26	(h)	Bradford C	L 1-2	Price	9,000		6		5				11			7							2	10	9	4	3	8		1
30	(a)	Darlington	L 1-3	Rawlings	4,838				5				11			7							2	10	9	4	3	8	6	1
Oct 3	(a)	Port Vale	D 1-1	Rawlings	10,000					5	11					7			3				2	10	9	4		8	6	1
5	(h)	Darlington	W 4-1	Campbell, Turner, Rawlings, Price	8,205					5	11					7			3				2	10	9	4		8	6	1
10	(h)	Barnsley	D 0-0		12,000					5	11					7			3				2	10	9	4		8	6	1
17	(a)	Wolves	L 1-4	opp own goal	20,000					5	11					7			3				2	10	9	4		8	6	1
24	(h)	Swansea T	W 4-1	Rawlings, Coundon, Price	13,000	1				5	11	7		8					3				2	10	9	4			6	
31	(a)	Preston NE	D 2-2	Turner, Price	12,000	1	5				11	7							3				2	10	9	4		8	6	
Nov 7	(h)	Middlesbrough	W 3-1	Coundon, Dominy, Carr	10,000	1	5				11	7		8					3				2	10	9	4			6	
14	(a)	Oldham A	L 0-1		12,000	1	5				11	7		8					3				2	10	9	4			6	
21	(h)	Stockport C	W 3-0	Coundon, Dominy, Rawlings	9,000	1	5				11	7		8	10				3				2		9	4			6	
28	(a)	Fulham	D 1-1	Rawlings	25,000	1	5				11	7		8					3				2	10	9	4			6	
Dec 5	(h)	South Shields	L 0-1		9,000	1	5				11	7		8					3				2		9	4		10	6	
12	(a)	Sheffield W	L 1-2	Rawlings	20,000	1				11				8	5	7				4	10		2		9		3		6	
19	(h)	Stoke C	L 1-2	Matthews	8,000	1	5			11				8	4	7					10		2		9		3		6	
25	(a)	Clapton O	L 1-2	Turner	14,000	1	5			11				8	4	7			3				2		9			10	6	
26	(h)	Clapton O	W 2-0	Dominy, Rawlings	16,000	1	5			11				8	4	7			3				2		9			10	6	
Jan 2	(h)	Blackpool	D 2-2	Woodhouse, Rawlings	6,000	1	4		5	11				8	10	7			3				2		9				6	
16	(a)	Portsmouth	W 2-1	Rawlings, Matthews	12,000		5			11				8	4	7	1		3		10		2		9				6	
23	(a)	Nottingham F	W 2-1	Dominy, Matthews	8,000		5			11				8	4	7	1		3		10		2		9				6	
Feb 6	(a)	Bradford C	W 5-0	Rawlings 2, Henderson, Bullock, Carr	14,000		5		8		11				4	7	1		3		10		2		9				6	
10	(h)	Derby C	W 2-1	Bullock 2	6,000		5		8		11				4	7	1	2			10				9	3			6	
13	(h)	Port Vale	L 2-3	Rawlings	11,000		5				11				4	7	1		3		10		2		9			8	6	
20	(a)	Barnsley	L 0-2		8,000		5				11			8	4	7	1		3		10		2		9				6	
27	(h)	Wolves	W 4-2	Parker, Henderson, Rawlings, Matthews	8,000	1	5				11			8	4	7			3		10		2		9				6	
Mar 6	(a)	South Shields	L 0-2		4,000	1	5				11			8	4	7		2	3		10				9				6	
13	(h)	Preston NE	W 2-0	Rawlings, Matthews	6,000	1	5				11			8	4	7		2	3		10				9				6	
20	(a)	Middlesbrough	L 0-3		10,000	1	5	8			11				4	7		2	3		10				9				6	
27	(h)	Oldham A	W 3-1	Keeping, Dominy, Carr	5,000	1	5				11			8	4	7		2	3						9			10	6	
29	(a)	Swansea T	L 1-3	Bullock	10,581	1	5	10	9		11			8	4	7		2	3										6	
Apr 2	(a)	Chelsea	D 0-0		40,000	1	5		9		11			8	4	7		2	3		10								6	
3	(a)	Stockport C	W 2-1	Woodhouse, Henderson	7,000	1	5		9		11			8	4	7		2	3		10								6	
5	(h)	Chelsea	L 0-1		17,000	1	5				11			8	4	7		2	3		10	9							6	
10	(h)	Fulham	W 2-0	Bradford, Rawlings	8,000	1	5				11			8	4	7		2	3		10				9				6	
24	(h)	Sheffield W	L 1-2	Keeping	8,000	1					10		11	8	4	7		2	3						9	5			6	
May 1	(a)	Stoke C	D 1-1	Carr	8,000	1			10		11			8	4	7		2	3						9	5			6	
App						24	22	2	10	19	34	8	9	27	28	34	10	13	31	1	16	1	29	16	35	21	11	16	37	8
Goals							1		4	1	4	3		6		3				2	5		1	7	20			3	2	

1 own-goal

Back row (left to right): A.Lee (trainer), Matthews, Hough, Parker, Allen, Yeomans, Hill, Titmuss, Keeping, Woodhouse, W.Rayner (asst trainer). Middle row: Meston, Bruton, King, Wilkinson, Shelley, Campbell, Bradford, Harkus, Turner, H.Hammock (director). Front row: Bullock, Henderson, Dominy, Rawlings, Price, Carr.

	P	W	D	L	F	A	Pts
Sheffield W	42	27	6	9	88	48	60
Derby C	42	25	7	10	77	42	57
Chelsea	42	19	14	9	76	49	52
Wolves	42	21	7	14	84	60	49
Swansea T	42	19	11	12	77	57	49
Blackpool	42	17	11	14	76	69	45
Oldham A	42	18	8	16	74	62	44
Middlesbrough	42	21	2	19	77	68	44
South Shields	42	18	8	16	74	65	44
Port Vale	42	19	6	17	79	69	44
Portsmouth	42	17	10	15	79	74	44
Preston NE	42	18	7	17	71	84	43
Hull C	42	16	9	17	63	61	41
Southampton	42	15	8	19	63	63	38
Darlington	42	14	10	18	72	77	38
Barnsley	42	12	12	18	58	84	36
Nottingham F	42	14	8	20	51	73	36
Bradford	42	13	10	19	47	66	36
Fulham	42	11	12	19	46	77	34
Clapton O	42	12	9	21	50	65	33
Stoke C	42	12	8	22	54	77	32
Stockport C	42	8	9	25	51	97	25

75

1926-27

ARTHUR Chadwick embarked on a massive team rebuilding programme in the close season of 1926. Over recent years, many of the players who had helped Saints gain promotion to Division Two had left The Dell. Now Arthur Dominy had gone, to Everton, George Harkus was appointed club captain and under his strong leadership, Saints started well. Indeed, by Christmas, they were only two points behind the leaders with promotion prospects to looking bright.

The New Year began badly, however, with defeat at Reading where Rawlings, by his own admission, had his worst-ever game for Saints. That reverse at Elm Park signalled a slump in Southampton's League fortunes and they eventually finished 13th.

Yet again, Saints enjoyed a good run in the FA Cup, but although these Cup campaigns were proving more than useful to the club's finances, supporters would have exchanged them for a more consistent time in the League and, therefore, promotion at last to the First Division.

FA Cup

SAINTS showed they were on song in the Cup, right from the third round when they beat Norwich City 3-0 at The Dell with goals from Rowley (2) and Keeping (penalty).

The luck of the draw still remained and Birmingham were the next visitors. They came to Southampton with four internationals in their team but they could not prevent Saints winning 4-1 with two goals from Rowley and one each from Rawlings and Harkus. Indeed, Southampton adapted much better to the slippery conditions as a rainstorm swept the ground. Allen distinguished himself by saving a penalty from Joe Bradford, Blues' England centre-forward.

In the fifth round Southampton were drawn at home for the tenth consecutive time. Their visitors were Newcastle United, who were to win the League Championship that season and who were led by the great Scottish international, Hughie Gallacher.

Another classic Cup match was in prospect and the teams did not disappoint. Despite a setback when Keeping handled and Tom McDonald scored from the penalty spot, Saints achieved a famous victory thanks to two goals from Rowley — his second 'double' in three Cup ties — and some resolute defending. Rowley, incidentally, was now inevitably attracting the attentions of the bigger clubs.

At last luck deserted Southampton when the draw was made and in the quarter-finals they met Millwall at The Den. A goalless draw, however, ensured that fans at The Dell would not miss their Cup treat and this time it was Rawlings' turn to score two goals for the second time in that season's competition. Saints had a scare earlier when Millwall were awarded a penalty, but Phillips, their inside-left, missed it.

In the semi-final, Southampton came up against their former star full-back, Tom Parker, who was now an Arsenal player. Parker's previous appearance in a semi-final had proved a disaster for both the player and the club. This time Parker was to be on the winning side, although not before some controversy.

In the traditions of Southampton semi-finals, Hough obligingly put Arsenal into the lead at Stamford Bridge with an own-goal. Charlie Buchan increased that lead but five minutes from time, Rawlings pulled back a goal for Saints. In the meantime, according to Saints — particularly director Mr A.A. Wood — Saints should have been awarded three penalties. All the complaining in the world did not alter the fact that Southampton would have to wait a good while longer for their first Wembley appearance.

Round 3
Jan 8 v Norwich City (h) 3-0
Keeping, Rowley 2
Allen; Hough, Keeping, Shelley, Harkus, Woodhouse, Henderson, Rowley, Rawlings, Taylor, Murphy.
Att: 15,587
Round 4
Jan 29 v Birmingham (h) 4-1
Rowley, Rawlings 2, Harkus
Allen; Hough, Keeping, Shelley, Harkus, Woodhouse, Henderson, Rowley, Rawlings, Taylor, Murphy.
Att: 15,804
Round 5
Feb 19 v Newcastle United (h) 2-1
Rowley 2
Allen; Hough, Keeping, Shelley, Harkus, Woodhouse, Henderson, Rowley, Rawlings, Taylor, Murphy.
Att: 21,408
Round 6
Mar 5 v Millwall (a) 0-0
Allen; Hough, Keeping, Shelley, Harkus, Woodhouse, Coundon, Rowley, Rawlings, Taylor, Murphy.
Att: 40,000
Replay
Mar 9 v Millwall (h) 2-0
Rawlings 2
Allen; Hough, Keeping, Shelley, Harkus, Woodhouse, Henderson, Rowley, Rawlings, Taylor, Murphy.
Att: 21,315
Semi-final
Mar 26 v Arsenal (at Stamford Bridge) 1-2
Rawlings
Allen; Hough, Keeping, Shelley, Harkus, Woodhouse, Henderson, Rowley, Rawlings, Taylor, Murphy.
Att: 52,133

Saints made a profit of £3,648 and decided to reconstruct The Dell, building the West Stand. For this purpose, the club borrowed £20,000 from the Norwich Union.

For the home League match against Portsmouth, record receipts of £1,296 16s 0d were taken. For the first time at The Dell, community singing was arranged.

Mike Keeping was now Southampton's regular left-back and he missed only one League and Cup game in 1926-27, having toured Canada with an FA XI in the close season.

1926-27
Division 2

Date	Opponent	Result	Scorers	Att.	Allen T	Bishop A	Bradford A	Bullock J	Coundon C	Cribb S	Harkus G	Henderson W	Hough E	Keeping A	King E	Matthews F	Murphy W	Rawlings W	Rowley R	Shelley A	Swinden J	Taylor S	Woodhouse S
Aug 28	(a) Portsmouth	L 1-3	Taylor	29,896	1		5				4	7	2	3			11	9	10			8	6
30	(h) Middlesbrough	W 2-1	Henderson 2	10,000	1		5				4	7	2	3			11	9	10			8	6
Sep 4	(h) Bradford C	D 0-0		10,000	1	10	5				4	7	2	3			11	9				8	6
11	(a) Chelsea	W 3-2	Rawlings 3	30,000	1	10				7	5		2	3			11	9		4		8	6
13	(h) Port Vale	D 2-2	Keeping, Shelley	9,000	1	10		7			5		2	3			11	9		4		8	6
18	(h) Preston NE	D 1-1	Rawlings	9,000	1	10					5	7	2	3			11	9		4		8	6
25	(a) South Shields	W 2-1	Matthews, Murphy	4,000	1	8					5	7	2	3		10	11	9		4			6
27	(a) Port Vale	L 1-3	Rawlings	9,594	1	8					5	7	2	3		10	11	9		4			6
Oct 2	(h) Hull C	L 0-1		9,000	1	8					5	7	2	3		10	11	9		4			6
9	(a) Wolves	D 2-2	Henderson, Taylor	11,705	1						5	7	2	3			11	9	8	4		10	6
16	(a) Manchester C	W 4-3	Rawlings 2, Rowley, Taylor	30,000	1						5	7	2	3			11	9	8	4		10	6
23	(h) Darlington	W 3-1	Rowley, Rawlings, Taylor	9,000	1						5	7	2	3			11	9	8	4		10	6
30	(a) Oldham A	D 1-1	Harkus	18,000	1						5	7	2	3			11	9	8	4		10	6
Nov 6	(h) Fulham	W 4-1	Rawlings 3, Rowley	7,000	1						5	7	2	3			11	9	8	4		10	6
13	(a) Grimsby T	W 1-0	Rawlings	8,000	1						5	7	2	3			11	9	8	4		10	6
20	(h) Blackpool	W 5-3	Rawlings 3, Murphy 2	10,000	1						5	7	2	3			11	9	8	4		10	6
27	(a) Middlesbrough	L 1-3	Rowley	15,000	1						5	7	2	3			11	9	8	4		10	6
Dec 4	(h) Swansea T	D 1-1	Rawlings	16,759	1						5	7	2	3			11	9	8	4		10	6
11	(a) Nottingham F	L 1-3	Murphy	10,000	1						5	7	2	3			11	9	8	4		10	6
18	(h) Barnsley	W 3-1	Henderson, Rowley, opp own goal	6,000	1						5	7		3	2		11	9	8	4		10	6
25	(a) Notts C	W 1-0	Rawlings	12,000	1						5	7	2	3			11	9	8	4		10	6
27	(h) Notts C	W 2-0	Shelley, Rawlings	19,120	1						5	7	2	3			11	9	8	4		10	6
Jan 1	(a) Reading	L 0-1		20,000	1				11		5	7	2	3				9	8	4		10	6
15	(a) Portsmouth	L 0-2		19,058	1						5	7	2	3			11	9	8	4		10	6
22	(a) Bradford C	L 0-2		10,000	1						5	7	2	3			11	9	8	4		10	6
Feb 5	(a) Preston NE	L 0-1		14,000	1						5	7	2	3			11	9	8	4		10	6
12	(h) South Shields	W 6-2	Rowley 2, Rawlings 2, Henderson, Taylor	8,000	1						5	7	2	3			11	9	8	4		10	6
26	(h) Wolves	W 1-0	Rowley	6,000	1		6				5	7	2	3			11	9	8	4		10	
Mar 12	(a) Darlington	W 2-1	Rowley, Taylor	9,000	1					7	5		2	3			11	9	8	4		10	6
14	(a) Hull C	D 0-0		6,000	1					7	5		2	3			11	9	8	4		10	6
19	(a) Oldham A	L 0-1		10,000	1						5	7	2	3			11	9	8	4		10	6
28	(a) Fulham	L 0-3		7,792	1		6				5	7	2	3			11	9	8	4		10	
Apr 2	(h) Grimsby T	D 0-0		6,000	1		5					7	2	3			11	9	8	4		10	6
4	(h) Chelsea	D 1-1	Rowley	5,368	1		5		11			7	2	3				9	8	4		10	6
9	(a) Blackpool	L 2-3	Rowley, Rawlings	7,000	1						5	7	2	3			11	9	8	4		10	6
15	(a) Clapton O	L 0-1		13,848	1			9			5	7	2	3			11		8	4		10	6
16	(h) Reading	D 1-1	Bullock	12,000	1			9			5	7	2	3			11		8	4		10	6
18	(h) Clapton O	L 1-2	Rowley	8,000	1			9			5	7	2	3			11		8	4		10	6
23	(a) Swansea T	D 2-2	Henderson, Taylor	6,000	1				11		5	7	2	3				9		4	8	10	6
25	(h) Manchester C	D 1-1	Rawlings	8,000	1						5	7	2	3			11	9	8	4		10	6
30	(h) Nottingham F	W 1-0	Rowley	7,000	1						5	7	2	3			11	9	8	4		10	6
May 7	(a) Barnsley	L 1-5	Rawlings	8,000	1						5	7	2	3			11	9	8	4		10	6
			App		42	7	7	4	3	3	40	38	41	42	1	3	39	38	35	39	1	39	40
			Goals					1			1	6		1		1	4	23	13	2		7	

1 own-goal

Back row (left to right): W.Rayner (asst trainer), Shelley, Wilkinson, Adams, Allen, Hough, Thitchener, Robson, Keeping, A.Chadwick (manager). Middle row: A.Lee (trainer), Swinden, King, Bullock, Harkus, Bradford. Woodhouse, Cooper, Matthews, Bishop, Findley, G.Goss (secretary). Front row: Coundon, Henderson, Taylor, Rawlings, Rowley, Murphy, Cribb.

	P	W	D	L	F	A	Pts
Middlesbrough	42	27	8	7	122	60	62
Portsmouth	42	23	8	11	87	49	54
Manchester C	42	22	10	10	108	61	54
Chelsea	42	20	12	10	62	52	52
Nottingham F	42	18	14	10	80	55	50
Preston NE	42	20	9	13	74	72	49
Hull C	42	20	7	15	63	52	47
Port Vale	42	16	13	13	88	78	45
Blackpool	42	18	8	16	95	80	44
Oldham A	42	19	6	17	74	84	44
Barnsley	42	17	9	16	88	87	43
Swansea T	42	16	11	15	68	72	43
Southampton	42	15	12	15	60	62	42
Reading	42	16	8	18	64	72	40
Wolves	42	14	7	21	73	75	35
Notts C	42	15	5	22	70	96	35
Grimsby T	42	11	12	19	74	91	34
Fulham	42	13	8	21	58	92	34
South Shields	42	11	11	20	71	96	33
Clapton O	42	12	7	23	60	96	31
Darlington	42	12	6	24	79	98	30
Bradford C	42	7	9	26	50	88	23

1927-28

WITH Portsmouth winning promotion to Division One in 1927, pressure now built up on Southampton to do likewise. Money, however, was in short supply due to ground improvements — indeed, had not one of the Saints' best players, Parker, been sold to finance such work?

Under such circumstances it was inevitable that Saints' promotion bid stuttered from the very start. Keeping, a vital member of the team, missed the kick-off to the new season, due to illness, and Henderson broke an arm in only the fourth game. These two players were especially missed and instead of promotion, Saints found that relegation was occupying their thoughts.

A further blow, particularly as far as the fans was concerned, came in March when Saints sold Bill Rawlings to Manchester United for £3,860 — and after Parker's departure this was seen as almost a betrayal of the club's interests by the directors. To compound the fans' dismay, Rawlings then went on to score 10 goals in 12 games for United that season,

helping the Old Trafford club avoid relegation from Division One.

To replace the ace goalscorer, Saints immediately signed Jerry Mackie, Portsmouth's Scottish inside-forward. Mackie's prospects looked bright when he scored a hat-trick against Barnsley on his home debut, but after seven appearances (and six goals) he was injured to ensure a gloomy end to the season. Saints finished 17th and First Division football seemed a million miles away.

There was a light note, however, when Saints met West Brom at The Dell on Easter Monday. Albion's goalkeeper, George Ashmore, was injured and went on the wing with a defender deputising in goal. In the second half, with the game delicately poised at 2-2, Ashmore found himself back helping out in defence. Forgetting that he was now an outfield player, Ashmore caught the ball in the penalty area and Cribb duly scored from the spot to give Saints victory.

FA Cup

SAINTS' good fortune in FA Cup draws came to an end when they were pulled out of the hat second for their game against Cardiff City. Cardiff were the Cup-holders, having beaten Arsenal at Wembley the previous year, and although Southampton put up a good show at Ninian Park, they went down by the odd goal in three. Rawlings scored for Saints in what proved to be his last Cup tie appearance for the club.

> **Round 1**
> Jan 14 v Cardiff City (a) 1-2
> *Rawlings*
> Allen; Bradford, Keeping, Shelley, Harkus, Woodhouse, Luckett, Rawlings, Bullock, Taylor, Murphy.
> *Att: 20,000*

> The newly-built West Stand was officially opened on 7 January 1928 and was regarded as one of the best in the country.

> Saints made a profit of £646 on the season's workings and the recently-formed supporters club began to help in the purchase of new players by lending the club the money to buy goalkeeper Willy White from Hearts.

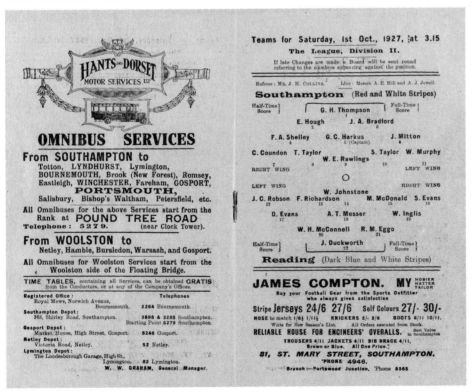

New-signing Luckett scored twice on his debut, against Notts County.

Programme for the visit of Reading on 1 October 1927. Ten thousand fans saw a goalless draw.

1927-28
Division 2

Date		Opponent	Res	Scorers	Att	Adams W	Allen T	Bradford A	Bullock J	Coundon C	Cribb S	Ellison J	Harkus G	Henderson W	Hough E	Keeping A	Luckett W	Mackie J	Mitton J	Murphy W	Petrie C	Rawlings W	Robinson E	Rowley R	Shelley A	Swinden J	Taylor S	Taylor T	Thompson G	Woodhouse S
Aug 27	(h)	Stoke C	L 3-6	Rawlings 2, Taylor	12,000	3	1						5	7	2					11		9		8	4		10			6
29	(a)	Clapton O	L 0-2		13,711		1	3					5	7	2					11		9		8	4		10			6
Sep 3	(a)	Leeds U	L 0-2		20,000		1	3			11		5	7	2			6			10	9		8	4					
5	(h)	Clapton O	L 1-3	Petrie	7,982		1	3			11		5	7	2			6			10	9		8	4					
10	(a)	Notts C	D 0-0		10,000			3	7		11		5		2			6			10	9		8	4			1		
17	(h)	Oldham A	W 5-2	Rawlings 2, Taylor 2, Murphy	10,000			3	7				5		2					11		9		8	4		10	1		6
24	(a)	Grimsby T	D 2-2	Taylor 2	10,000			3	7				5		2					11		9			4		10 8	1		6
Oct 1	(h)	Reading	D 0-0		10,000			3	7				5		2		6			11		9			4		10 8	1		
8	(a)	Blackpool	L 0-1		12,000			3	7				5		2		6			11		9		8	4		10	1		
15	(h)	Chelsea	L 2-4	Petrie 2	14,000			3	7				5		2		6			11	10	9		8	4		10	1		
22	(h)	Wolves	W 4-1	Rowley 2, Rawlings 2	8,000			5	7				4			2	3			11		9		8			10	1		6
29	(a)	Port Vale	L 0-4		9,000			5	7				4			2	3			11		9		8			10	1		6
Nov 5	(h)	South Shields	L 3-5	Rawlings 2, Taylor	8,000		1	5					4			2	3			11	8	9		7			10			6
12	(a)	Barnsley	W 1-0	Rowley	8,000		1	5	7				4			2	3			11		9		8			10			6
19	(h)	Fulham	W 5-2	Rawlings 2, Bradford, Rowley, Murphy	4,619		1	5	7				4			2	3			11		9		8			10			6
26	(a)	Hull C	L 0-1		10,000		1	5	7				4			2	3			11		9		8			10			6
Dec 3	(h)	Preston NE	D 0-0		10,000		1	5	7				4			2	3			11		9		8			10			6
10	(a)	Swansea T	L 0-2		13,000		1	5	7				4			2	3			11	8	9					10			6
17	(h)	Manchester C	D 1-1	Taylor	12,000		1	2	7				5				3			11	8	9			4		10			6
24	(a)	Nottingham F	D 1-1	Rawlings	4,000		1	2					5	7			3			11	8	9			4		10			6
26	(a)	Bristol C	L 0-3		17,072		1	3					5	7	2					11	8	9			4		10			6
27	(h)	Bristol C	W 3-2	Rawlings 2, Bullock	10,132		1		9					7	2	3		5		11		8			4		10			6
31	(a)	Stoke C	L 1-2	opp own goal	6,000		1		9				5	7		3				11		8	2		4		10			6
Jan 7	(a)	Leeds U	L 1-4	Murphy	14,000		1		5	9			4	7	2	3				11		8					10			6
21	(h)	Notts C	W 5-1	Luckett 2, Rawlings 2, Bullock	10,000		1	2	9				5			3	7			11		8			4		10			6
31	(a)	Oldham A	L 1-3	Bullock	6,365		1	2	9				5			3	7			11		8			4		10			6
Feb 4	(h)	Grimsby T	W 5-0	Taylor 2, Rawlings, Bullock, Murphy	8,000		1	2	9				5			3	7			11		8			4		10			6
11	(h)	Reading	D 0-0		8,000		1		9				5	7	2	3				11		8			4		10			6
18	(h)	Blackpool	W 2-0	Rawlings, Bullock	12,000		1	2	9				5	7		3				11		8			4		10			6
25	(a)	Chelsea	W 2-0	Rawlings 2	40,000		1	2	9				5	7		3				11		8			4		10			6
Mar 3	(a)	Wolves	L 1-2	Rawlings	13,000		1	2	9				5	7		3				11		8			4		10			6
10	(h)	Port Vale	L 1-2	Taylor	10,000		1		9	2			5	7		3	11					8			4		10			6
17	(a)	South Shields	L 1-2	Bullock	3,000		1	2	9	7	11		5			3		8							4		10			6
24	(h)	Barnsley	W 6-1	Mackie 3, Woodhouse, Petrie, Cribb	11,000		1	2			11		5	7		3		8			10			9	4					6
31	(a)	Fulham	L 0-1		7,000		1	2			11		5	7		3		8			10			9	4					6
Apr 7	(h)	Hull C	W 2-0	Mackie, Cribb	11,000		1	2	9		11		5	7		3		8			10				4					6
9	(h)	West Brom A	W 3-2	Mackie, Bullock, Cribb	15,763		1	3	9		11		5	7	2			8			10				4					6
10	(a)	West Brom A	L 1-2	Bullock	10,000		1		9		11		5	7	2		8	4			10				3					6
14	(a)	Preston NE	W 2-1	Mackie, Petrie	10,000		1	2	9				5	7	3		11	8			10				4					6
21	(h)	Swansea T	L 0-2		8,000			2	9				5	7		3				11		8			4		10		1	6
28	(a)	Manchester C	L 1-6	T.Taylor	40,000			2			11		5	7		3		9				4		8				10	1	6
May 5	(h)	Nottingham F	W 2-1	Rowley, T.Taylor	10,000			2					5	7		3	11					9		4	8			10	1	6
App						1	32	36	17	15	10	1	41	23	25	28	6	7	8	29	15	32	1	20	33	2	30	4	10	36
Goals								1	8		3						2	6		4	5	20		5			10	2		1

1 own-goal

Back row (left to right): Shelley, Mr Wood (director), Lee (trainer), Hough, Allen, Keeping, A.Chadwick (manager), Petrie, Woodhouse. Front row: Henderson, Rowley, Rawlings, Taylor, Murphy, Harkus.

	P	W	D	L	F	A	Pts
Manchester C	42	25	9	8	100	59	59
Leeds U	42	25	7	10	98	49	57
Chelsea	42	23	8	11	75	45	54
Preston NE	42	22	9	11	100	66	53
Stoke C	42	22	8	12	78	59	52
Swansea T	42	18	12	12	75	63	48
Oldham A	42	19	8	15	75	51	46
West Brom A	42	17	12	13	90	70	46
Port Vale	42	18	8	16	68	57	44
Nottingham F	42	15	10	17	83	84	40
Grimsby T	42	14	12	16	69	83	40
Bristol C	42	15	9	18	76	79	39
Barnsley	42	14	11	17	65	85	39
Hull C	42	12	15	15	41	54	39
Notts C	42	13	12	17	68	74	38
Wolves	42	13	10	19	63	91	36
Southampton	42	14	7	21	68	77	35
Reading	42	11	13	18	53	75	35
Blackpool	42	13	8	21	83	101	34
Clapton O	42	11	12	19	55	85	34
Fulham	42	13	7	22	68	89	33
South Shields	42	7	9	26	56	111	23

1928-29

RATHER surprisingly, considering the disappointment of the 1927-28 campaign, Saints finished higher in the League than ever before.

The close season had witnessed plenty of comings and goings, although the directors had wisely resisted big offers for Hough, Bradford, Cribb and Rowley. The major signing was the Portsmouth forward, Willie Haines. 'The Farmer's Boy', as he was known, was an immediate success and his goals were a major factor in Saints finishing fourth in the League. His four against Blackpool was the first such haul by a Southampton player in one Second Division match.

Unusually, Saints' away record was particularly good and they were the last side in the four divisions to suffer defeat on an opponent's ground. Had the team avoided injuries, then they would surely have won promotion, but after Christmas they were never able to field the same line-up two games in succession. Haines, Hough and Harkus were all sidelined and so the necessary consistency was lacking.

FA Cup

SAINTS met Clapton Orient in the third round of the FA Cup and although they were again favoured with home advantage, they failed to play to their full potential at The Dell.

The most exciting moment came when Rowley's shot hit a post. Harkus was clearly unfit, whilst Haines had a poor game at centre-forward.

In the replay, however, things went Saints' way for a while and Bradford opened the scoring with Cribb almost making it 2-0. But on a frozen, snow-covered pitch, Orient slowly got on top and equalised before half-time.

In the second half, with Waterston having a nightmare of a game at centre-forward, Saints rarely looked dangerous. Thompson, deputising in goal for 'flu victim White, had a busy time. Inevitably, it seemed, Orient would get the winner and they did, leaving Saints to concentrate on trying to win promotion.

Round 1
Jan 12 v Clapton Orient (h) 0-0
White; Hough, Keeping, Shelley, Harkus, Woodhouse, Weale, Mackie, Haines, Rowley, Cribb.
Att: 15,000
Replay
Jan 17 v Clapton Orient (a) 1-2
Bradford
Thompson; Hough, Keeping, Shelley, Bradford, Woodhouse, Weale, Mackie, Waterston, Rowley, Cribb.
Att: 10,000

Hours after the season ended on 4 May, the East Stand burned to the ground. At one stage, a strong wind fanned the flames and put nearby St Mark's School and houses in Milton Road at risk. A spectator's cigarette was blamed and Saints were forced to borrow a further £10,000 from the Norwich Union to start rebuilding. The fire meant that the schoolboys final against Northumberland Boys had to be transferred to Bannister Stadium.

The home attendance of 24,247 against Chelsea was a new record for a League game at The Dell.

The scene during the fire which destroyed the East Stand on 4 May 1929. The *Southern Evening Echo* reported, 'East Stand goes West'.

Division 2

Date		Opponent	Result	Scorers	Att.	Arnold J	Bradford A	Coates H	Cribb S	Haines W	Harkus G	Hough E	Jepson A	Keeping A	Luckett W	Mackie J	Murphy W	Petrie C	Rowley R	Shelley A	Sloan T	Stoddart W	Taylor T	Thompson G	Vernon D	Waterston D	Weale R	White W	Woodhouse S
Aug 25	(a)	Hull C	D 2-2	Keeping, Petrie	9,000				9	5	2	7	3	8			11	10		4								1	6
27	(h)	Port Vale	L 1-2	Taylor	12,000		5		11	9	2		3	8						4		7	10	1					6
Sep 1	(h)	Tottenham H	D 1-1	Taylor	22,961				11	9	5	2	3	8				7		4			10					1	6
8	(a)	Reading	W 1-0	Cribb	19,000				11	9	5	2	7	3		8		10		4								1	6
15	(h)	Preston NE	W 4-0	Shelley, Haines 2, Petrie	17,011				11	9	5	2	7	3		8		10		4								1	6
22	(a)	Middlesbrough	W 2-1	Haines, Cribb	12,000				11	9	5	2	7	3		8		10		4								1	6
24	(h)	Port Vale	W 2-1	Mackie 2	7,344				11		5	2	7	3		8	9	10		4								1	6
29	(h)	Oldham A	W 2-1	Cribb 2	16,945				11	9	5	2	7	3		8		10		4								1	6
Oct 6	(a)	Bristol C	D 1-1	Haines	15,000				11	9	5	2	7	3		8		10		4								1	6
13	(a)	Wolves	D 1-1	Haines	15,000				11	9	2	7	3	8				10		4		5						1	6
20	(h)	Barnsley	L 1-2	Haines	15,847				11	9	2	7	3	8				10		4		5						1	6
27	(a)	Chelsea	D 1-1	Cribb	35,000			10	11	9	5	2	3	8				7		4								1	6
Nov 3	(h)	Blackpool	W 8-2	Haines 4, Mackie 2, Cribb 2	15,146		2	10	11	9	5		3	8				7		4								1	6
10	(a)	Nottingham F	D 1-1	Rowley	5,000		2	10	11	9	5		3	8					7	4								1	6
17	(h)	Bradford	D 2-2	Jepson, Rowley	14,657		2	10	11		5	7	3	8					9	4								1	6
24	(a)	Grimsby T	L 1-2	Rowley	7,000		2		11		5	7	3	8					9	4			10					1	6
Dec 1	(h)	Stoke C	D 0-0		14,218		2	10	11		5	7	3	8					9	4								1	6
8	(a)	Clapton O	D 1-1	Murphy	11,000		2	10		5			3	8			11			4					9	7		1	6
15	(h)	West Brom A	D 1-1	Rowley	13,509		2			5			3	8			11		10	4					9	7		1	6
22	(a)	Swansea T	D 1-1	Mackie	5,000		2			9	5		3	8		11			10	4						7		1	6
25	(a)	Notts C	D 1-1	Haines	21,865		2			9	5		3	8		11			10	4						7		1	6
26	(h)	Notts C	W 4-0	Weale 3, Rowley	20,441		5		11	9			2	3					10	4						8	7	1	6
29	(h)	Hull C	W 3-2	Weale, Waterston, Rowley	18,765		5		11				2	3		8			10	4						9	7	1	6
Jan 5	(a)	Tottenham H	L 2-3	Weale, Bradford	25,000		5		11	9			2	3		8			10	4							7	1	6
19	(h)	Reading	D 2-2	Coates, Cribb	15,775		5	10	11		6		2	3		8			9	4	1						7		
26	(a)	Preston NE	W 1-0	Cribb	11,000		5		11	9	6		2	3		8			10	4							7	1	
Feb 2	(h)	Middlesbrough	D 1-1	Cribb	13,608		5		11	9			2	3	10					4		8					7	1	6
9	(a)	Oldham A	L 1-3	Weale	14,000		5		11				2	3		8			10	4					9		7	1	6
16	(h)	Bristol C	W 2-1	Mackie, Cribb	10,095		3		11		5	2		8					10	4					9		7	1	6
23	(h)	Wolves	W 2-1	Mackie, Coates	12,478		5	10			2		3	8		11				4					9		7	1	6
Mar 2	(a)	Barnsley	L 1-4	Rowley	4,000			3	11		5	2		8					10	4					9		7	1	6
9	(h)	Chelsea	L 1-2	Mackie	24,247		5		11				2	3		8			10	4					9		7	1	6
16	(h)	Blackpool	L 0-3		10,000		5		11				2	3		8			10	4						9	7	1	6
23	(h)	Nottingham F	W 2-1	Mackie, Cribb	10,292		3	10	11			2		8					9	4	5						7	1	6
29	(a)	Millwall	W 4-2	Rowley 2, Jepson, Mackie	21,817		5		11	9	2	7	3	8					10	4								1	6
30	(a)	Bradford	L 1-4	Haines	11,000		3		11	9	2	7		8						4	5					10		1	6
Apr 1	(h)	Millwall	W 3-0	Jepson, Haines, Coates	17,368	11	5	10		9	2	7	3	6	8					4								1	
6	(h)	Grimsby T	W 3-1	Haines, Coates, Cribb	17,700		5	10	11	9	2	7	3	6	8					4								1	
13	(a)	Stoke C	L 0-3		11,000	11	5			9	2	7	3	8					10	4								1	6
20	(h)	Clapton O	W 2-0	Haines, Coates	8,890	11		10		9	5	2	3	8				7		4								1	6
27	(a)	West Brom A	L 1-3	Coates	10,024	11		10		9	5	2	3	8						4						7		1	6
May 4	(h)	Swansea T	W 3-0	Jepson, Haines, Coates	6,510	11	3	10		9	5	2	7			4	8											1	6
		App				5	29	14	31	27	25	33	18	37	5	40	6	9	24	41	1	4	4	2	5	6	18	40	38
		Goals					1	7	13	16			4	1		10	1	2	9	1			2			1	6		

Back row (left to right): A.Lee (trainer), E.Hough, A.Shelley, G.Harkus, W.White, S.Woodhouse, A.M.Keeping, Mr A.Chadwick. Front: A.E.Jepson, J.Mackie, W.Haines, C.Petrie, W.Murphy.

	P	W	D	L	F	A	Pts
Middlesbrough	42	22	11	9	92	57	55
Grimsby T	42	24	5	13	82	61	53
Bradford	42	22	4	16	88	70	48
Southampton	42	17	14	11	74	60	48
Notts C	42	19	9	14	78	65	47
Stoke C	42	17	12	13	74	51	46
West Brom A	42	19	8	15	80	79	46
Blackpool	42	19	7	16	92	76	45
Chelsea	42	17	10	15	64	65	44
Tottenham H	42	17	9	16	75	81	43
Nottingham F	42	15	12	15	71	70	42
Hull C	42	13	14	15	58	63	40
Preston NE	42	15	9	18	78	79	39
Millwall	42	16	7	19	71	86	39
Reading	42	15	9	18	63	86	39
Barnsley	42	16	6	20	69	66	38
Wolves	42	15	7	20	77	81	37
Oldham A	42	16	5	21	54	75	37
Swansea T	42	13	10	19	62	75	36
Bristol C	42	13	10	19	58	72	36
Port Vale	42	15	4	23	71	86	34
Clapton O	42	12	8	22	45	72	32

1929-30

THE 1929-30 season opened with defeat at Oakwell where Jerry Mackie became the first Saints player for eight years to be ordered off the field. That Mackie's dismissal should come against Barnsley was ironic, since it was against the same Yorkshire club that he had scored a hat-trick on his home debut for Southampton.

Despite this early set-back, Saints recovered and quickly moved into the top half of the Second Division. Yet their poor away record — in contrast to the previous season — ensured that Saints never posed a serious threat to Blackpool and Chelsea for the promotion places.

Indeed, their form away from The Dell was so bad that on 14 December, manager Arthur Chadwick dropped seven players for the match at Reading where Saints went on to scrape a draw. Throughout the season the forward line was very unsettled and a total of 18 different players were tried as Chadwick looked for the right blend.

One rare away success came in November when Rowley became the first Southampton player to score four goals in an away League game, at Bradford City. Such scoring feats inevitably attracted the bigger clubs and in January, Saints transferred Rowley to Tottenham for £3,750. At the time of his departure, Rowley had scored 25 goals in 25 games and with him went Saints' last hopes of promotion.

The departure of Rowley was seen by the public as another significant blow to the club's fortunes, but they had to fully consider the club's financial problems after spending so much money on improving facilities at The Dell.

At the end of the season some 15 players refused to re-sign and Saints were forced to field weakened teams in two charity matches against Portsmouth. Old favourites Rawlings, Dominy, Harkus and Butt came out of retirement to assist the young reserves thrust into the first-team.

FA Cup

BRADFORD City were given an early opportunity to avenge their humiliation by Southampton when the Saints were drawn to visit Valley Parade in the first round of the FA Cup.

On a bitterly cold January afternoon, Mike Keeping won the toss and set Bradford to kick into the teeth of a biting wind that chilled the bone of every spectator. Yet that decision was about the only selfish act that Saints committed all afternoon. Thereafter, the defence proved in particularly generous mood and after an awful defensive mix-up, Thompson allowed a shot to crawl under his body and into the net.

Rowley managed an equaliser soon afterwards but further defensive generosity was responsible for two of City's next three goals. The game ended in a snowstorm and for Saints the final whistle could not come a moment too soon.

> Round 3
> **Jan 11 v Bradford City (a) 1-4**
> *Rowley*
> Thompson; Bradford, Keeping, Wilson, Stoddart, Luckett. Weale, Mackie, Rowley, Coates, Cribb.
> *Att: 25,000*

> *The home attendance against Tottenham was a new Saints record League 'gate' of 25,934.*

> *Saints made a close season tour of Denmark in 1930, winning three matches and losing one.*

> *Southampton had kept a side in the Southern League but now they resigned, thus ending a 36-year association with that competition.*

Pages from the Saints' 1929-30 handbook.

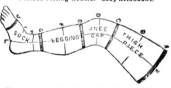

SOUTHAMPTON
Red and White Striped Shirts, Dark Knickers.

THE FOOTBALL LEAGUE—DIV. II.

Au. 31—Barnsley a	Dec.26—Tottenham H. h
Sept. 2—Hull City h	„ 28—Barnsley h
„ 7—Blackpool h	Jan. 4—Blackpool a
„ 9—West Brom. A. h	„ 18—Bury h
„ 14—Bury a	„ 25—Chelsea a
„ 16—Hull City a	Feb. 1—Nottingham F. h
„ 21—Chelsea h	„ 8—Oldham Athletic a
„ 28—Nottingham F. a	„ 15—Millwall h
Oct. 5—Oldham Athletic h	„ 22—Stoke City h
„ 12—Millwall a	Mar. 1—Wolverham'n W. a
„ 19—Stoke City a	„ 8—Bradford City h
„ 26—Wolverham'n W. h	„ 15—Swansea Town a
Nov. 2—Bradford City a	„ 22—Cardiff City h
„ 9—Swansea Town h	„ 29—Preston N.E. a
„ 16—Preston N.E. h	Apr. 5—Bristol City h
„ 23—Bristol City a	„ 12—Notts County a
„ 30—Bristol City h	„ 19—Reading h
Dec. 7—Notts County h	„ 21—Bradford h
„ 14—Reading a	„ 22—Bradford a
„ 21—Charlton Ath. h	„ 26—Charlton Ath. a
„ 25—Tottenham H. a	May 3—West Brom. A. a

FRIENDLY.—Wed., 25th Sept.—Aldershot a

Johnny Arnold scored seven goals in 18 League games to underline his potential as a scoring winger.

1929-30

Division 2

Date	Opponent	Result	Scorers	Att	Arnold J	Bradford A	Coates H	Cribb S	Dougal P	Fraser W	Haines W	Harkus G	Hough E	Jepson A	Keeping A	Littler O	Luckett W	Mackie J	Rowley R	Sharp A	Shelley A	Stoddart W	Thompson G	Warren E	Watson R	Weale R	White W	Wilson A	Woodhouse S
Aug 31	(a) Barnsley	L 1-3	Haines	5,000							9	5	2		3			8	10		4				11	7	1		6
Sep 2	(h) Hull C	D 2-2	Weale, Haines	11,419			10				9	5	2		3			8			4				11	7	1		6
7	(h) Blackpool	W 4-2	Watson 2, Coates, Rowley	9,838	4		10					5	2		3			8	9						11	7	1		6
9	(h) West Brom A	W 3-2	Rowley 2, Weale	20,035	4		8					5	2		3	10			9						11	7	1		6
14	(a) Bury	L 2-4	Rowley, Watson	14,000	5		10					4	2		3			8	9						11	7	1		6
16	(a) Hull C	L 0-2		7,115	4						9	5	2		3	10		8							11	7	1		6
21	(h) Chelsea	W 4-2	Rowley 3, Cribb	16,569	4		10	11				5	2		3			8	9							7	1		6
28	(a) Nottingham F	W 5-0	Rowley 3, Littler 2	7,000	4		10	11				5	2		3	8	6		9							7	1		
Oct 5	(a) Oldham A	W 2-0	Rowley, Coates	17,600	4		10	11				5	2		3	8	6		9							7	1		
12	(a) Millwall	D 1-1	Harkus	20,000	4		10	11				5	2		3	8	6		9							7	1		
19	(a) Stoke C	L 0-4		12,000			10					5	2		3			8	9		4				11	7	1		6
26	(h) Wolves	L 3-1	Rowley 2, Arnold	13,308	11		10					5	2		3			8	9		4					7	1		6
Nov 2	(a) Bradford C	W 5-2	Rowley 4, Coates	14,000	11		10					5	2		3			8	9		4					7	1		6
9	(h) Swansea T	W 2-1	Rowley, Arnold	16,600	11		10					5	2		3			8	9		4					7	1		6
16	(a) Cardiff C	L 2-5	Rowley, Littler	12,000	11							5	2		3	8		10	9		4					7	1		6
23	(h) Preston NE	L 1-2	Rowley	10,110	11		10					5	2		3			8	9		4		1			7			6
30	(a) Bristol C	L 1-3	Watson	9,000	5		10					4	2		3			8	9						11	7	1		6
Dec 7	(h) Notts C	D 2-2	Rowley, Coates	9,235			10					5	2		3			8	9		4				11	7	1		6
14	(a) Reading	D 1-1	Cribb	10,000		2	10	11	8		7				3	6			9		5						1	4	
21	(h) Charlton A	W 2-0	Jepson, Cribb	10,161		2	10	11		8				7	3	6			9		5						1	4	
25	(a) Tottenham H	L 2-3	Cribb 2	26,564		2	10	11						7	3	6		8	9		5						1	4	
26	(h) Tottenham H	W 1-0	Rowley	25,934		2	10	11						7	3	6		8	9		5						1	4	
28	(h) Barnsley	W 4-0	Rowley 2, Keeping, Weale	8,168		2	10	11	8						3	6			9		5					7	1	4	
Jan 4	(a) Blackpool	L 1-5	Rowley	10,000		2	10	11		8					3	6			9		5		1			7		4	
18	(h) Bury	D 0-0		12,293		2	10	11	8			5			3				9							7	1	4	6
25	(a) Chelsea	L 0-2		25,000	11	2	10			8		5			3				9							7	1	4	6
Feb 1	(h) Nottingham F	W 2-0	Weale, Haines	9,921	11	2	10		8		9	5			3											7	1	4	6
8	(a) Oldham A	L 2-3	Haines 2	15,000		2	10				9	5			3			8							11	7	1	4	6
22	(h) Stoke C	W 2-1	Haines 2	10,924		2	10		8		9	5			3										11	7	1	4	6
Mar 1	(a) Wolves	L 0-2		12,000		2	10			8	9	5			3										11	7	1	4	6
3	(h) Millwall	D 0-0		4,881		2	10				9				3			8			4				11	7	1	5	6
8	(h) Bradford C	W 2-1	Mackie, Arnold	11,091	11	2	10				9			7	3			8			4						1	5	6
15	(a) Swansea T	D 2-2	Mackie, Arnold	7,000	11	2	10				9			7	3			8			5						1	4	6
22	(h) Cardiff C	D 1-1	Haines	14,000	11	2	10				9	5			3			8						7			1	4	6
29	(a) Preston NE	D 1-1	Haines	6,000	11	2	10				9	5		7	3			8									1	4	6
Apr 5	(h) Bristol C	W 3-0	Jepson, Haines, Dougal	9,788	11	2			10		9	5		7	3			8									1	4	6
12	(a) Notts C	W 2-1	Jepson, Haines	10,500	11	2	10				9	5		7	3			8									1	4	6
19	(a) Reading	W 4-3	Haines 2, Jepson, Arnold	11,346	11	2	10				9	5		7	3			8									1	4	6
21	(h) Bradford	D 2-2	Mackie, Arnold	15,302	11	2	10				9	5		7	3			8									1	4	6
22	(a) Bradford	D 1-1	Haines	10,038	11	3	10				9		2	7				8			5						1	4	6
26	(a) Charlton A	L 1-4	Haines	8,000	11	3	10				9		2	7				8			5						1	4	6
May 3	(a) West Brom A	L 1-5	Arnold	10,000	11	3					9		2	7				8			5	10					1	4	6
App					18	32	25	11	12	10	19	30	21	14	39	12	12	20	25	1	11	8	2	1	14	27	40	24	33
Goals					7		4	5	1		15	1		4	1	3		3	25						4	4			

Back row: (left to right): Mackie, Thompson, Luckett, Rowley, Stoddart, Keeping, Bradford, Wilson.
Front row: Weale, Cribb, mascot, H.L.Coates.

	P	W	D	L	F	A	Pts
Blackpool	42	27	4	11	98	67	58
Chelsea	42	22	11	9	74	46	55
Oldham A	42	21	11	10	90	51	53
Bradford	42	19	12	11	91	70	50
Bury	42	22	5	15	78	67	49
West Brom A	42	21	5	16	105	73	47
Southampton	42	17	11	14	77	76	45
Cardiff C	42	18	8	16	61	59	44
Wolves	42	16	9	17	77	79	41
Nottingham F	42	13	15	14	55	69	41
Stoke C	42	16	8	18	74	72	40
Tottenham H	42	15	9	18	59	61	39
Charlton A	42	14	11	17	59	63	39
Millwall	42	12	15	15	57	73	39
Swansea T	42	14	9	19	57	61	37
Preston NE	42	13	11	18	65	80	37
Barnsley	42	14	8	20	56	71	36
Bradford C	42	12	12	18	60	77	36
Reading	42	12	11	19	54	67	35
Bristol C	42	13	9	20	61	83	35
Hull C	42	14	7	21	51	78	35
Notts C	42	9	15	18	54	70	33

1930-31

SAINTS entered the 1930s having been a Football League side for a decade during which time they had secured rapid promotion to Division Two as well as making two appearances in the FA Cup semi-finals.

Yet during the more recent seasons, many of the star players had been sold and most of the supporters were convinced that Southampton Football Club's directors lacked ambition. Perhaps some of those doubts were eased when Saints paid a club record fee of £2,650 for the services of Johnny McIlwane, the Portsmouth captain.

McIlwane had a mixed season, both in terms of form and with injuries, and altogether the team struggled to find its rhythm. Unusually, Saints' home form let them down although they did manage to beat Everton, the Champions, in their last home match of the season. Dixie Dean, almost inevitably, scored for the Merseysiders with a header but Wilson, playing on the left wing, hit two for Saints.

On 16 April, with relegation avoided and the season grinding towards an obscure end, Arthur Chadwick resigned, having been in management since 1908.

During the season the supporters club had again shown their worth by financing the building of a new gymnasium and recreation room.

FA Cup

WHEN Saints were drawn away to Sunderland in the first round of the FA Cup it was the first time that the two sides had met in any sort of competitive match. The weather had put the match in doubt and the Wearside club had to use burning braziers to thaw the pitch on another bitterly cold day.

Saints, playing in white shirts, won the toss and Sunderland were left to kick into a strong wind, but after only nine minutes Southampton found themselves a goal down. Sunderland made it 2-0 just after the restart and they were generally by far the better side.

McIlwane had a poor game at centre-forward and Shelley — who had been awarded a second testimonial in this, his 12th season — was the worst offender in an off-form Southampton defence. There was no doubt that the Saints missed centre-forward Haines, a last-minute absentee due to illness.

Round 3
Jan 10 v Sunderland (a) 0-2
White; Bradford, Keeping, Adams, Shelley, Woodhouse, Jepson, Cumming, McIlwane, Coates, Arnold.
Att: 28,931

Before the FA Cup match at Sunderland, the Saints party spent the whole week in special training at Saltburn-by-the-Sea, and before the game received a good luck telegram from Tom Parker, their former full-back, who was then playing for Arsenal.

After 12 games the Saints had accumulated more points than goals. Their record read: P12, W5, D6, L2, Goals for 14, Goals against 14, Points 15.

Whites centre-forward, Willie Haines, tries a shot at the Stripes' goal during a pre-season public practice match at The Dell on 23 August 1930 A large attendance was again attracted by this first opportunity to see the players on the eve of a new season.

1930-31

Division 2

Date		Opponent	Result	Scorers	Att.	Adams W	Arnold J	Bradford A	Coates H	Cowper P	Cumming L	Dougal P	Fraser W	Haddleton A	Haines W	Hough E	Jepson A	Keeping A	Luckett W	McIlwane J	Mackie J	Roberts A	Scriven H	Shelley A	Stage W	Watson R	White W	Wilson A	Woodhouse S
Aug 30	(a)	Preston NE	L 0-5		10,000			2				10		9			7	3		5	8					11	1	4	6
Sep 1	(h)	Nottingham F	D 0-0		12,000			2				10	9				7	3	11	5	8						1	4	6
6	(h)	Burnley	D 1-1	Jepson	13,485	11		2				10	9				7	3	4	5	8						1		6
8	(a)	Oldham A	L 1-2	Cumming	13,689	11		2			8	10	9				7	3					1	5				4	6
13	(a)	Plymouth A	W 3-2	Cumming 2, Wilson	25,000	4	11	2			8		9				7	3					1	5				10	6
15	(h)	Oldham A	W 1-0	Wilson	9,858	4	11	2			8		9				7	3					1	5				10	6
20	(a)	Reading	D 1-1	Jepson	8,000	4		2			8		9				7	3	11				1	5				10	6
27	(h)	Wolves	W 2-0	Fraser 2	13,552	4	11	2	10		8		9				7	3					1	5					6
Oct 4	(a)	Bradford	D 1-1	Coates	10,000	4	11	2	10		8		9				7	3					1	5					6
11	(h)	Stoke C	W 2-1	Cumming, Coates	14,772	4	11	2	10		8		9				7	3					1	5					6
18	(h)	West Brom A	D 1-1	Fraser	16,931	4	11	2	10		8		9				7	3					1	5					6
25	(a)	Swansea T	W 1-0	Fraser	10,000	4	11	2	10		8		9				7	3					1	5					6
Nov 1	(h)	Cardiff C	L 0-1		12,202	4	11	2	10		8		9				7	3					1	5					6
8	(a)	Bristol C	L 1-2	Jepson	15,000	4	11	2	10		8		9				7	3					1	5					6
15	(h)	Bradford C	W 4-1	Fraser 2, Arnold 2	10,356	4	11	2	10				9				7	3			8		1	5					6
22	(a)	Charlton A	L 1-3	Stage	5,000	4	11	2	10				9				7	3					1	5	8				6
29	(h)	Barnsley	W 4-0	McIlwane 2, Jepson, Coates	11,751	4	11	2	10								7	3		9			1	5	8				6
Dec 6	(a)	Port Vale	L 0-1		8,000	4	11	2	10								7	3		9			1	5	8				6
13	(h)	Bury	W 5-0	Coates 2, Arnold 2, McIlwane	12,889	4	11	2	10								7	3		9			1	5	8				6
20	(a)	Everton	L 1-2	Wilson	20,000	4	11	2									7	3		9	8		1	5				10	6
25	(h)	Tottenham H	W 3-1	McIlwane 2, Coates	37,000	4		2	10								7	3		9	8		1	5		11			6
26	(h)	Tottenham H	L 0-3		23,156	4	11	2	10								7	3		9	8		1	5					6
27	(h)	Preston NE	W 2-1	McIlwane, Haines	11,707	4	11	2	10						9		7	3		8			1	5					6
Jan 3	(a)	Burnley	L 2-3	Haines 2	10,000	4	11	2	10						9		7	3		8			1	5					6
17	(h)	Plymouth A	D 3-3	Haines 2, Coates	14,013		11	2	10						9		7	3		8		4	1	5					6
24	(h)	Reading	W 3-2	Haines 2, Arnold	10,446	4	11	2	10						9		7	3		8			1	5					6
31	(a)	Wolves	L 2-3	Mackie, Arnold	9,000	4	11	2							9		7	3			8		1	5				10	6
Feb 7	(h)	Bradford	L 2-3	Haines	11,212	4	11	2	10						9		7	3			8		1	5					6
14	(a)	Stoke C	W 3-1	Haines 2, Mackie	10,000	4	11	2	10						9		7	3			8		1	5					6
21	(a)	West Brom A	W 2-1	Dougal, opp own goal	18,000	4	11	2				10			9		7	3			8		1	5					6
28	(h)	Swansea T	L 1-2	Arnold	11,041	4	11	3	10						9		7	2			8		1	5					6
Mar 7	(a)	Cardiff C	W 1-0	Jepson	5,000	4	11	3	10						9		7	2			8		1	5					6
14	(h)	Bristol C	W 5-1	Mackie 2, Haines 2, Jepson	10,473	4	11	2	10						9		7	3			8		1	5					6
21	(a)	Bradford C	L 3-4	Mackie 2, Arnold	12,000	4	11	2	10						9		7	3			8		1	5					6
28	(h)	Charlton A	W 3-0	Haines, Watson, opp own goal	8,785	4		2	10						9		7	3		8			1	5		11			6
Apr 3	(a)	Millwall	L 0-1		18,000	4		2	10						9		7	3	11	8				5			1		6
4	(a)	Barnsley	L 1-3	Jepson	7,000	4		2	10						9		7	3	11	8				5			1		6
6	(h)	Millwall	W 3-1	Keeping, McIlwane, Fraser	12,137	4	11	2	10				9				7	3		8			1	5					6
11	(h)	Port Vale	W 2-0	Haines, Dougal	9,487	4		2		7		10			9			3		8			1	5				11	6
18	(a)	Bury	L 0-1		15,000	4		2		7		10			9			3		8			1	5				11	6
25	(h)	Everton	W 2-1	Wilson 2	9,553	4		2	10						9		7	3		8			1	5				11	6
May 2	(a)	Nottingham F	L 1-3	Haines	6,000	4		2	10						9		7	3		8			1	5				11	6
App						37	30	39	16	4	20	14	22	1	21	3	39	38	21	26	14	4	29	23	4	5	13	13	26
Goals							8		7		4	4	7		15		7	1		7	5				1	1		5	

2 own-goals

Back row (left to right): Adams, Luckett, Bradford, Scriven, Keeping, Mr Chadwick (manager), Woodhouse. Front row: Cowper, Osborne, Haines, Wilson, Arnold, McIlwaine.

	P	W	D	L	F	A	Pts
Everton	42	28	5	9	121	66	61
West Brom A	42	22	10	10	83	49	54
Tottenham H	42	22	7	13	88	55	51
Wolves	42	21	5	16	84	67	47
Port Vale	42	21	5	16	67	61	47
Bradford	42	18	10	14	97	66	46
Preston NE	42	17	11	14	83	64	45
Burnley	42	17	11	14	81	77	45
Southampton	42	19	6	17	74	62	44
Bradford C	42	17	10	15	61	63	44
Stoke C	42	17	10	15	64	71	44
Oldham A	42	16	10	16	61	72	42
Bury	42	19	3	20	75	82	41
Millwall	42	16	7	19	71	80	39
Charlton A	42	15	9	18	59	86	39
Bristol C	42	15	8	19	54	82	38
Nottingham F	42	14	9	19	80	85	37
Plymouth A	42	14	8	20	76	84	36
Barnsley	42	13	9	20	59	79	35
Swansea T	42	12	10	20	51	74	34
Reading	42	12	6	24	72	96	30
Cardiff C	42	8	9	25	47	87	25

1931-32

GEORGE Kay, the former West Ham captain, was named the new Southampton manager for the start of 1931-32 and under his guidance, the side began with a victory for the first time in ten years.

A win over Bury on 12 September sent Southampton to the top of the Second Division for the first time in the club's history. Saints, however, failed to maintain that promotion-winning form and again illness and injury upset their plans.

A settled side became an impossible dream and during the season Kay was forced to field 30 different players. There were two different goalkeepers, three right-backs, five left-backs, five right-halves, five centre-halves, nine right wingers, nine inside-rights, six centre-forwards, seven inside-lefts, and four left wingers.

There were some bright spots including the emergence of players like Ted Drake and Charlie Sillett. Arnold, too, had an excellent season, becoming top scorer with 20 goals, particularly good figures for a man who had played all his games at outside-left.

Mike Keeping's part in that good start to the season won him representative honours when he played for the Football League against the Irish League at Blackpool in September. A full cap seemed imminent but he went down with appendicitis in January and missed the rest of the season.

Centre-forward Haddleton set a record which lasted until the 1960s, when he scored in eight consecutive games at the beginning of the season. As often happens with such feats, Haddleton then managed only one goal for the remainder of the season, although it should be added that he played in only eight more games.

FA Cup

AFTER meeting Sunderland for the first time in 45 years the previous season, it was odd that Saints should again draw them in the FA Cup. Once again Saints did not relish a long journey to Roker Park to face such formidable opponents.

The game was played at a very fast pace and Scriven, Adams and Bradford all had outstanding games for Saints. Had Sillett made the most of his opportunities then there would have been no need for a replay.

At The Dell, Sunderland rattled in three first-half goals against a sluggish Southampton side, but in the second half Saints rallied to such an extent that they found themselves looking for an equaliser.

Indeed, Arnold might have made it 3-3 but missed a glorious opportunity and Saints' then conceded a penalty. Sunderland scored with their second attempt — the referee claimed that he was not ready the first time — and Southampton were left to examine how they had managed to lose at home after playing so well at Roker Park.

> **Round 3**
> **Jan 9 v Sunderland (a) 0-0**
> Scriven; Adams, Keeping, Shelley, Bradford, Luckett, Jepson, Osborne, Sillett, Wilson, Arnold.
> *Att: 28,931*
> **Replay**
> **Jan 13 v Sunderland (h) 2-4**
> *Sillett, Keeping*
> Scriven; Adams, Keeping, Shelley, Bradford, Luckett, Jepson, Osborne, Sillett, Wilson, Arnold.
> *Att: 22,927*

> *On 5 December 1931, Saints slumped to their biggest home defeat in the League when Plymouth won 6-0 at The Dell. Yet Southampton also managed to win seven away games, a club record for the Second Division.*

Johnny McIlwane, the former Pompey skipper, had another indifferent season although great things had been expected of him when he signed the previous season.

Arthur Bradford, Saints' versatile half-back, had an outstanding game against Sunderland in the FA Cup.

1931-32

Division 2

Date	V	Opponent	Result	Scorers	Att	Adams W	Arnold J	Bradford A	Brewis J	Campbell F	Charlton W	Coates H	Cowper P	Dougal P	Drake E	Fraser W	Haddleton A	Haines W	Harkus G	Jepson A	Keeping A	Luckett W	Matson F	McIlwane J	Neal R	O'Grady H	Osborne F	Roberts A	Scriven H	Shelley A	Sillett C	Thomas H	White W	Wilson A	Woodhouse S
Aug 29	(h)	Burnley	W 3-0	Jepson, O'Grady, Haines	14,516	4	11	2										9		7	3	6			5	8							1	10	
Sep 2	(a)	Manchester U	W 3-2	Fraser, Haddleton, Arnold	30,000	4	11	2								8	9			7	3	6			5								1	10	
Sep 6	(a)	Preston NE	L 1-2	Haddleton	16,000	3	11	2								8	9			7		6			5	10							1	4	
Sep 7	(h)	Tottenham H	W 2-1	Keeping, Haddleton	13,800	2	11			4						8	9			7	3	6			5								1	10	
Sep 12	(h)	Bury	W 2-1	Haddleton, Arnold	15,011	2	11			4						8	9			7	3	6			5								1	10	
Sep 14	(a)	Tottenham H	L 2-5	Haddleton 2	25,000	2	11			4			10			8	9			7	3	6			5								1		
Sep 19	(h)	Stoke C	L 1-2	Haddleton	14,671	4	11	2								8	9			7	3	6			5								1	10	
Sep 26	(a)	Charlton A	W 3-2	Fraser, Haddleton, Arnold	12,000	4	11	2				10				8	9			7	3	6							1	5					
Oct 3	(h)	Wolves	L 1-3	Haddleton	16,622	4	11	2				10				8	9			7	3	6							1	5					
Oct 10	(a)	Bradford	L 1-2	Arnold	14,000	2	11			4		10				8	9			7	3	6							1	5					
Oct 17	(a)	Port Vale	D 0-0		5,000	2	11			4		10				8	9				3	6						7	1	5					
Oct 24	(h)	Millwall	W 3-1	Arnold 2, Jepson	11,141	2	11			4		10				8	9			7	3	6							1	5					
Oct 31	(a)	Bradford C	L 2-5	Haddleton, Arnold	15,000	2	11			4		10				8	9			7	3	6							1	5					
Nov 7	(h)	Oldham A	D 1-1	Arnold	10,784	2	11			4		10				8	9			7	3	6							1	5					
Nov 14	(a)	Swansea T	W 4-3	Wilson 2, Fraser, Arnold	3,000	2	11			4						9	8			7	3	6							1	5				10	
Nov 21	(h)	Barnsley	W 2-0	Campbell, Arnold	11,991	2	11	3		4						9	8			7		6			5				1					10	
Nov 28	(a)	Notts C	L 0-5		11,000	2	11	3		4						9	8			7					5		10		1						6
Dec 5	(h)	Plymouth A	L 0-6		12,723	2	11	3		4							7		9						5		10		1			8			6
Dec 12	(a)	Bristol C	W 1-0	Wilson	5,000	2		5		4	11					8	9				3	6						7	1					10	
Dec 19	(h)	Leeds U	W 2-1	Keeping, Luckett	11,923	2		5													3	11	7	9		8			1	4				10	6
Dec 25	(a)	Chesterfield	L 0-1		14,508	2		5								8						11	7	9				3	1	4				10	6
Dec 26	(h)	Chesterfield	L 1-2	Arnold	22,353	2	11	5								8			9					7				3	1	4				10	6
Jan 2	(a)	Burnley	W 3-1	Sillett 2, Arnold	2,000	2	11	5												8	3	6				7			1	4	9			10	
Jan 16	(h)	Preston NE	D 3-3	Jepson, O'Grady, Arnold	8,050	2	11	5		4					9					7	3	6				8			1					10	
Jan 30	(a)	Stoke C	L 0-2		11,000	2	11	5												7		6				8		3	1	4	9			10	
Feb 3	(a)	Bury	L 0-3		4,000	2	11	3							10					7		6			5	8			1		9			4	
Feb 6	(h)	Charlton A	D 1-1	Fraser	6,439	2	11	3			7	10				8	9					6			5				1					4	
Feb 13	(a)	Wolves	L 1-5	Charlton	15,000	3	11	2		4	9	7										6			5				1	8				10	
Feb 20	(a)	Bradford	L 0-3		8,013	2	11	3														6			5	7	8		1		9			10	4
Feb 27	(h)	Port Vale	W 5-1	McIlwane 2, Arnold 2, Sillett	7,113	2	11	5														6		8		9	7	3	1		10				4
Mar 5	(a)	Millwall	W 1-0	Sillett	18,000	2	11	5														6		8		9	7	3	1		10				4
Mar 12	(h)	Bradford C	L 0-1		8,361	3	11	5														6		8		9	7		1		10	2			4
Mar 19	(a)	Oldham A	L 0-2		5,000	3	11	5	10													6		8		7			1		9	2			4
Mar 25	(a)	Nottingham F	L 0-2		11,639	3	11	5	8													6				9	7		1		10	2			4
Mar 26	(h)	Swansea T	W 3-0	Wilson 2, Arnold	6,375	3	11			5					9							6				7	8		1		4	2		10	
Mar 28	(h)	Nottingham F	W 4-0	Wilson 2, Drake, Arnold	11,409	3	11			5					9							6				7	8		1		4	2		10	
Apr 2	(a)	Barnsley	D 3-3	Neal, Drake, Arnold	5,000	3	11			5					9							6				7	8		1		4	2		10	
Apr 9	(h)	Notts C	W 3-1	Drake 2, Arnold	7,332	3	11			5					9							6				7	8		1		4	2		10	
Apr 16	(a)	Plymouth A	W 2-1	Neal, Arnold	12,000	3	11		10						9							6			5	7	8		1		4	2			
Apr 23	(h)	Bristol C	D 1-1	Drake	6,322	2	11		10	5					9											7	8		1		3			4	6
Apr 30	(a)	Leeds U	L 0-1		15,000	2			10	4					9					7					5	11	8		1		3				6
May 7	(h)	Manchester U	D 1-1	Neal	6,128	2			10	4					9	8						11			5	7			1		3				6
App						42	37	25	6	23	2	10	1	3	11	24	16	3	2	21	17	38	2	20	14	7	12	5	34	18	14	8	8	25	14
Goals							20			1	1				5	4	10	1		3	2	1		2	3	2					4			7	

Back row (left to right): Campbell, Adams, Scriven, Bradford, Luckett, O'Grady. Front row: Cowper, Sillett, W.Charlton, Wilson, Arnold, Harkus.

	P	W	D	L	F	A	Pts
Wolves	42	24	8	10	115	49	56
Leeds U	42	22	10	10	78	54	54
Stoke C	42	19	14	9	69	48	52
Plymouth A	42	20	9	13	100	66	49
Bury	42	21	7	14	70	58	49
Bradford	42	21	7	14	72	63	49
Bradford C	42	16	13	13	80	61	45
Tottenham H	42	16	11	15	87	78	43
Millwall	42	17	9	16	61	61	43
Charlton A	42	17	9	16	61	66	43
Nottingham F	42	16	10	16	77	72	42
Manchester U	42	17	8	17	71	72	42
Preston NE	42	16	10	16	75	77	42
Southampton	42	17	7	18	66	77	41
Swansea T	42	16	7	19	73	75	39
Notts C	42	13	12	17	75	75	38
Chesterfield	42	13	11	18	64	86	37
Oldham A	42	13	10	19	62	84	36
Burnley	42	13	9	20	59	87	35
Port Vale	42	13	7	22	58	89	33
Barnsley	42	12	9	21	55	91	33
Bristol C	42	6	11	25	39	78	23

1932-33

THERE had been an exodus of players from The Dell in the close season of 1932, the most significant departure being that of Johnny McIlwane who could not agree terms with the club and was consequently placed on the transfer list. Saints rated him at £2,500 but when no League club showed interest, and as was common in those days, McIlwane left the Football League and 'guested' for Llanelli in the Welsh League.

Despite all the departures, Saints' team had a much more settled look about it and, led by Ted Drake, they improved on the previous season, especially at home where they won 15 matches out of 21 — a club record.

The situation looked happy enough until February, when the directors sold Keeping and Arnold to Fulham for £5,000. Both men were in their prime and, not for the first time, the Southampton fans were in uproar. Jimmy McIntyre, the Fulham manager and former Saints boss, later claimed it was the best deal he had ever made. And, as if to emphasize McIntyre's words, Arnold won his first England cap within a couple of months.

The directors, meanwhile, responding to the fans' criticism, said that the club needed regular attendances of at least 14,000 to break even — but for the first home match after the double-transfer, only 2,949 turned up to see Bradford City, the lowest attendance for a League match at The Dell since the war. The poor turnout spoke volumes to the directors: if star players were not retained, then the fans would stay away.

Even when the supporters club announced that it would pay the entrance fee of any unemployed supporter, 'gates' still did not rise significantly.

This dilemma — whether to hold on to the players to please the fans, or whether to sell them to balance the books — was to be a perpetual headache for the directors throughout the 1930s. Indeed, the club's financial situation was such that the board asked the players if they could wait for their summer wages until the season started. Every player agreed, incidentally.

Ironically, amid all the hubbub, the team's form was not unduly affected in the wake of Keeping and Arnold's transfer, and a mid-table position was achieved without difficulty.

That said it all, really. Every team in Division Two when Saints were promoted had either gone up or down at least once. Saints, however, were to remain a Second Division side for another 20 years.

FA Cup

SAINTS desperately need a good Cup run and they were disappointed to be drawn at Stoke in the first round. Southampton took the field without Woodhouse and Brewis who were both suffering from 'flu, but the 200 fans who had made the journey north saw the Saints, playing in blue shirts, put up a spirited performance.

In the first half, Ted Drake saw his header cleared off the line, but in the second period Stoke took only three minutes to take the lead with what proved to be the only goal of the game.

Had Southampton managed an equaliser, then perhaps victory at The Dell would have signalled a Cup run that would have made the selling of Arnold and Keeping unnecessary.

> Round 1
> **Jan 14 v Stoke City (a) 0-1**
> Scriven; Adams, Keeping, Campbell, Bradford, Luckett, Neal, Osborne, Drake, Coates, Arnold.
> *Att: 18,526*

> *During the season, Saints played at home on a Good Friday for the first time, having reached an understanding with nearby St Mark's church never to play at home when there was a church service.*

> *At Bradford City's Valley Parade, Coates, an amateur who played in the forward line, had to deputise for Scriven when he was injured. According to the* Football Echo, *'Coates was tucking his jersey into his shorts when Bradford scored immediately following the restart and before the amateur was ready'. It was the only goal and it cost Saints the game.*

> *For the first time Saints formed an 'A' team. Under the guidance of Arthur Shelley it won promotion from the Hampshire League, Second Division, in its first season.*

Saints players Keeping, Bradford and Luckett under pressure at White Hart Lane in October 1932. Spurs won 5-0 on their way to promotion that season.

Division 2

Date	Venue	Opponent	Result	Scorers	Att	Adams W	Arnold J	Bradford A	Brewis J	Campbell F	Coates H	Drake E	Dunmore F	Foster R	Harris J	Holt A	Keeping A	Luckett W	Neal R	Osborne F	Roberts A	Ruddy T	Scriven H	Sillett C	Tilford A	Woodhouse S
Aug 27	(a)	Millwall	L 0-3		20,000	2			8	5	10	9			11		3	6	7				1			4
29	(h)	Port Vale	D 2-2	Drake 2	8,151	2			8	5	10	9		1	11		3	6	7							4
Sep 3	(h)	Manchester U	W 4-2	Brewis 3, Arnold	7,997		11	2	8	5	10	9					3	6	7				1			4
5	(a)	Port Vale	W 2-0	Drake, Coates	8,843		11	2	8	5	10	9					3	6	7				1			4
10	(h)	Bury	W 1-0	Arnold	11,769	4	11	2	8	5	10	9					3	6	7				1			
17	(a)	Lincoln C	L 0-1		12,000	2	11	3	8	5	10	9						6	7				1	4		
24	(h)	West Ham U	W 4-3	Arnold 3, Drake	11,668	4	11	2	8	5	10	9	7				3	6					1			
Oct 1	(a)	Fulham	L 2-4	Brewis, Coates	15,000	4	11	2	8	5	10	9						6	7		3		1			
8	(h)	Chesterfield	W 2-1	Drake 2	9,447	2	11	5	8		10	9					3	6	7				1			4
15	(a)	Bradford C	L 0-1		17,133	2	11	5	8		10	9					3	6	7				1			4
22	(a)	Tottenham H	L 0-5		25,704	2	11	5	8		10	9					3	6	7				1			4
29	(h)	Grimsby T	W 3-0	Drake 3	10,081	2	11	5	8		10	9					3	6	7				1			4
Nov 5	(a)	Oldham A	L 0-2		8,000	2	11	5	8		10	9					3	6	7				1			4
12	(h)	Stoke C	W 1-0	Campbell	11,862	2	11	5	8	9	10						3	6	7				1			4
19	(a)	Plymouth A	D 1-1	Arnold	20,000	2	11	5		9	10						3	6	7	8			1			4
26	(h)	Bradford	W 2-0	Arnold 2	11,693	2	11	5			10	9					3	6	7	8			1			4
Dec 3	(a)	Burnley	L 0-2		7,000	2	11	5			10	9					3	6	7	8			1			4
10	(h)	Nottingham F	L 0-2		7,753	2	11	5			10	9					3	6	7	8			1			4
17	(a)	Charlton A	L 0-2		12,000	2	11		8	5	10	9					3	6	7				1			4
24	(h)	Preston NE	W 1-0	Drake	9,569	2	11		8	5		9					3	6	7			10	1			4
26	(a)	Swansea T	L 1-2	Drake	17,791		11	2	8	5	10	9					3	6	7				1			4
27	(h)	Swansea T	W 2-0	Neal, Brewis	11,862	2	11	5	8	9	10						3	6	7				1			4
31	(h)	Millwall	L 2-3	Keeping, Drake	9,071		11	2	8	5	10	9					3	6	7				1			4
Jan 7	(a)	Manchester U	W 2-1	Brewis, Arnold	22,000	2	11	5	8							9	3	6	7	10			1			4
21	(a)	Bury	L 0-1		9,000	2	11	5	10	4		9				8	3	6	7				1			
28	(h)	Lincoln C	W 4-0	Arnold 2, Holt, Coates	7,225	2	11	5		8	10					9	3	6	7				1			4
Feb 4	(a)	West Ham U	L 1-3	Holt	20,000	2	11	5		8	10					9	3	6	7				1			4
11	(h)	Fulham	D 2-2	Keeping, Brewis	8,586	2	11	5	8							9	3	6	7			10	1			4
22	(a)	Chesterfield	L 0-1		5,134	2		5	8	4		9						11	7			10	1	3		6
25	(h)	Bradford C	W 3-1	Drake 2, Luckett	2,949	2		5		4	10	9						11	7			8	1		3	6
Mar 4	(h)	Tottenham H	D 1-1	Adams	11,806	2		5		4	10	9						11	7			8	1		3	6
11	(a)	Grimsby T	D 2-2	Drake, Luckett	5,000	2		5		4	10	9						11	7		3	8	1			6
18	(h)	Oldham A	L 0-2		6,815			5		4	10	9						11	7		3	8	1	2		6
25	(a)	Stoke C	L 1-3	Drake	18,900			5	8	4		9				10		11	7		3		1	2		6
Apr 1	(h)	Plymouth A	W 2-0	Neal, Coates	6,649	2		5		4	10	9						11	7			8	1		3	6
8	(a)	Bradford	L 1-2	opp own goal	8,000	2		5	10	4		9						11	7			8	1		3	6
14	(h)	Notts C	W 6-2	Brewis 2, Neal, Ruddy, Bradford, Luckett	8,108	2		5	8	4		9						11	7			10	1		3	6
15	(h)	Burnley	W 3-1	Luckett 2, Drake	7,302	2		5	8	4		9						11	7			10	1		3	6
17	(a)	Notts C	W 2-1	Drake 2	8,000	2		5	8	4		9						11	7			10	1		3	6
22	(a)	Nottingham F	L 2-4	Brewis, Holt	7,000			5	8	2	11					9		6	7			10	1	3		4
29	(h)	Charlton A	W 3-0	Neal, Drake, Bradford	4,000	2		5	8			9						11	7			10	1	4	3	6
May 6	(a)	Preston N.E	L 1-3	Ruddy	5,199			5		8		9						11	7			10	1	4	3	6
App						35	26	38	31	30	30	33	1	1	2	8	26	42	41	5	4	15	41	6	10	37
Goals						1	11	2	10	1	4	20				3	2	5	4			2				

1 own-goal

Back row (left to right): Ruddy, Woodhouse, Bradford, Scriven, Keeping, Luckett. Front row: Neale, Brewis, Drake, Coates, Arnold, Campbell.

	P	W	D	L	F	A	Pts
Stoke C	42	25	6	11	78	39	56
Tottenham H	42	20	15	7	96	51	55
Fulham	42	20	10	12	78	65	50
Bury	42	20	9	13	84	59	49
Nottingham F	42	17	15	10	67	59	49
Manchester U	42	15	13	14	71	68	43
Millwall	42	16	11	15	59	57	43
Bradford	42	17	8	17	77	71	42
Preston NE	42	16	10	16	74	70	42
Swansea T	42	19	4	19	50	54	42
Bradford C	42	14	13	15	65	61	41
Southampton	42	18	5	19	66	66	41
Grimsby T	42	14	13	15	79	84	41
Plymouth A	42	16	9	17	63	67	41
Notts C	42	15	10	17	67	78	40
Oldham A	42	15	8	19	67	80	38
Port Vale	42	14	10	18	66	79	38
Lincoln C	42	12	13	17	72	87	37
Burnley	42	11	14	17	67	79	36
West Ham U	42	13	9	20	75	93	35
Chesterfield	42	12	10	20	61	84	34
Charlton A	42	12	7	23	60	91	31

1933-34

TED Drake stole most of the headlines during the 1933-34 season. He scored a hat-trick in the opening match against Bury, led the Second Division goalscoring list at the end of the season, was sent-off against Grimsby (and suspended for two weeks), and finally, transferred to Arsenal for a record fee of £6,000.

Indeed, this was far from a dull season for Saints who equalled the previous season's record of 15 home wins to maintain their fine form at The Dell. It was a shame that their away form was quite abysmal and they failed to win a single game on opponents' grounds.

McIlwane returned from his sojourn in the Welsh League and although he had helped Llanelli win the title, his time out of League football had not sharpened his game.

Drake's departure was inevitable and again it was a case of selling a star player in order to balance the books. To be fair to the Southampton directors it must be recorded that they withstood several offers for Drake before Arsenal made them one they could not refuse.

With falling attendances and rising debts, their hands were forced and, in hindsight, it was fortunate that the club could produce outstanding young players in order to survive. Sadly, it meant that Saints could never seriously contemplate First Division football while they had to sell their best footballers.

FA Cup

SAINTS were drawn at home for the first time in five years and it was Northampton Town who provided the opposition. The Cobblers opened the scoring after 25 minutes and held on to their lead until half-time. Four minutes into the second half, Drake scored following a superb cross from Neal and the game ended all-square.

In the replay, Northampton showed themselves to be much the better team on the day. They were more composed and played much more as a team than Saints, winning by the only goal of the game.

The Cobblers' goalkeeper, who had played so well in both games, was none other than the former Southampton player, Tommy Allen, who was still enjoying his football in the Third Division South, despite being well into his 30s.

> **Round 3**
> **Jan 13 v Northampton Town (h) 1-1**
> *Drake*
> Scriven; Adams, Roberts, Campbell, Bradford, Woodhouse, Neal, Sillett, Drake, Holt, Tully.
> *Att: 21,847*
> **Replay**
> **Jan 17 v Northampton Town (a) 0-1**
> Scriven; Adams, Roberts, Campbell, Bradford, Woodhouse, Neal, Holt, Drake, Ruddy, Luckett.
> *Att: 16,161*

> *At Easter, Southampton were scheduled to play at Blackburn on Good Friday and at Plymouth the following day. This meant overnight coach travel after a 4-2 defeat at Ewood Park, yet the Saints players overcame that setback, and a lost night's sleep, to earn a creditable goalless draw at Home Park.*

Ted Drake had the most eventful season, culminating in a record transfer to Arsenal.

Sid Woodhouse was one of Saints' most loyal servants. In 1933-34 he missed only three League games.

1933-34
Division 2

Date		Opponent	Result	Scorers	Att.	Adams W	Bradford A	Brewis J	Burley B	Campbell F	Coates H	Cole N	Cummings J	Drake E	Gibbins V	Holt A	Light W	Luckett W	McIlwane J	Neal R	Roberts A	Ruddy T	Scriven H	Sillett C	Tully F	Ward F	Woodhouse S
Aug 26	(h)	Bradford C	W 4-1	Drake 3, Brewis	10,474	2	5	8		4				9						7		10	1		11	3	6
28	(a)	Oldham A	D 1-1	Drake	7,000	2		8		4				9						7	3	10	1		11	5	6
Sep 2	(a)	Port Vale	L 1-2	Drake	10,000	2		8		4				9						7	3	10	1		11	5	6
4	(h)	Oldham A	W 1-0	Drake	8,280	2		8		4				9						7	3	10	1		11	5	6
9	(h)	Notts C	W 3-2	Drake 2, Ruddy	12,237	2		8		4				9					11	7	3	10	1			5	6
16	(a)	Swansea T	L 0-1		10,000	2		8		4				9					11	7			1			5	6
23	(h)	Millwall	L 2-3	Neal 2	8,314	2	5	8		4	10			9					11	7			1			3	6
30	(a)	Lincoln C	D 1-1	Drake	9,000	2	5			4	10			9		8			11	7	3		1				6
Oct 7	(h)	Bury	W 1-0	Campbell	11,961	2	5	8		4	10			9					11	7	3		1				6
14	(a)	Hull C	L 0-1		12,000		3	8		6	10					9		5	11	7	2		1				4
21	(h)	Burnley	W 2-1	Drake 2	10,160	2	5	8		4				9		10			11	7	3		1				6
28	(a)	Brentford	L 0-2		16,000	2	5	10		4				9		8			11	7	3		1				6
Nov 4	(h)	Bolton W	W 1-0	Drake	15,084	2	5			4				9		8			11	7	3	10	1				6
11	(a)	Manchester U	L 0-1		15,000	2	5			4				9	8				11	7	3	10	1				6
18	(h)	Plymouth A	L 0-1		12,333	2	5			4				9	8				11	7	3	10	1				6
25	(a)	West Ham U	D 0-0		23,000	2	5	10		4				9		8			11		3		1		7		6
Dec 2	(h)	Nottingham F	W 2-0	Holt, Luckett	8,247	2	5	8		4				9		10			11	7	3		1				6
9	(a)	Grimsby T	L 1-3	Bradford	12,000	2	5			4				9		10			11	7	3		1	8			6
16	(h)	Bradford	W 5-0	Sillett 2, Drake 2, Holt	8,482	2	5			4				9		10			11	7	3		1	8			6
23	(a)	Preston NE	L 1-3		7,000	2	5			4				9		10			11	7	3		1	8			6
25	(a)	Fulham	L 0-1		21,788	2	5			4						10			9	7	3		1	8	11		
26	(h)	Fulham	W 2-0	Drake 2	24,797	2	5	8		4				9		10				7	3		1		11		6
30	(a)	Bradford C	D 2-2	Campbell, Holt	10,000	2	5	8		4		9				10				7	3		1		11		6
Jan 6	(h)	Port Vale	L 1-4	Campbell	9,800	2	5	8		4		9				10				7	3		1		11		6
20	(a)	Notts C	D 2-2	Neal, Drake	8,000	2		8						9		10	6	5		7	3		1		11		4
Feb 5	(h)	Swansea T	W 1-0	Holt	3,396	2		8		4				9		10	1	5		7	3				11		6
10	(h)	Lincoln C	W 3-1	Drake 2, Tully	8,044	2		8		4				9		10	1	5		7	3				11		6
17	(a)	Bury	L 0-1		9,263	2		8		4				9		10	1	5		7	3				11		6
24	(h)	Hull C	D 1-1	Drake	8,000	2		8		4				9		10	1	5		7	3				11		6
Mar 3	(a)	Burnley	L 1-2	Drake	7,000	2		8		4				9		10		5		7	3		1		11		6
10	(h)	Brentford	D 0-0		10,439	2		8		4				9		10	6	5		7	3		1		11		
17	(a)	Bolton W	L 0-2		10,000	2	5	8						9		10	6			7	3		1		11		
24	(h)	Manchester U	W 1-0	Cole	4,900	2	5	8				9				10	6			7	3		1		11		4
30	(a)	Blackpool	L 2-4	Holt, Tully	20,966	2	5	8				9				10	6			7	3		1		11		4
31	(a)	Plymouth A	D 0-0		10,000	2				4		9				10	6			7	3		1	8	11	5	
Apr 2	(h)	Blackpool	W 3-2	Adams, Brewis, Cole	10,221	2	3	8				9				10	6			7			1		11	5	4
7	(h)	West Ham U	W 3-2	Coles 3	7,000	2	5	8				9				10	6			7	3		1		11		4
9	(a)	Millwall	L 0-1		8,000	2				4		9	8			10	6			7	3		1		11	5	
14	(a)	Nottingham F	L 1-4	Tully	8,000	2	5	8				9				10	6			7	3		1		11		4
21	(h)	Grimsby T	W 4-2	Adams, Brewis, McIlwane, Holt	9,000	2	5	8								10	6		9	7	3		1		11		4
28	(a)	Bradford	L 1-3	Tully	6,000	2	5	8	11							9	6			7	3		1		10		4
May 5	(h)	Preston NE	L 0-1		9,000	2	5	8	11							10	6		9	7	3		1				4
App						39	30	32	2	32	4	10	1	27	2	32	4	29	11	41	39	9	38	5	26	10	39
Goals						2	1	3		3		5		22		6		1	1	3		1		2	4		

J. A. SHELLEY   S. SCRIVEN   J. BRADFORD   A. CAMPBELL   E. DRAKE   F. TULLY
J. BREWIS   T. RUDDY
S. WOODHOUSE   WARD   W. ADAMS   R. NEAL

SOUTHAMPTON FOOTBALL CLUB

	P	W	D	L	F	A	Pts
Grimsby T	42	27	5	10	103	59	59
Preston NE	42	23	6	13	71	52	52
Bolton W	42	21	9	12	79	55	51
Brentford	42	22	7	13	85	60	51
Bradford	42	23	3	16	86	67	49
Bradford C	42	20	6	16	73	67	46
West Ham U	42	17	11	14	78	70	45
Port Vale	42	19	7	16	60	55	45
Oldham A	42	17	10	15	72	60	44
Plymouth A	42	15	13	14	69	70	43
Blackpool	42	15	13	14	62	64	43
Bury	42	17	9	16	70	73	43
Burnley	42	18	6	18	60	72	42
Southampton	42	15	8	19	54	58	38
Hull C	42	13	12	17	52	68	38
Fulham	42	15	7	20	48	67	37
Nottingham F	42	13	9	20	73	74	35
Notts C	42	12	11	19	53	62	35
Swansea T	42	10	15	17	51	60	35
Manchester U	42	14	6	22	59	85	34
Millwall	42	11	11	20	39	68	33
Lincoln C	42	9	8	25	44	75	26

1934-35

SAINTS began the season badly — only one point from their first five games — and although there was some cheer in the arrival of winger Laurie Fishlock from Millwall, it was obvious that this was going to be a difficult season.

One of their problems the previous season had been the lack of fire-power from the wingers and Fishlock, an England amateur international and also a fine cricketer, did manage to score on his debut, although Saints still went down 4-1 at Port Vale.

Indeed, their depressing away run lasted until their 34th match on opponents' grounds. On Christmas Day 1934, Fishlock's goal gave Saints an away win, at Swansea, thus ending a sequence that went back to April 1932.

Victory at the Vetch Field was followed by the defeat of Swansea at The Dell, a dropped point at home to Burnley, and an emphatic 3-0 defeat at Old Trafford to bring Southampton back to earth with a jolt. Then came another rare away performance — a fine win at Oldham — but that was Saint's last such success of the season and they became serious candidates for relegation.

Ted Drake's departure the previous year had left a big gap in the Saints' forward line and manager George Kay scoured the country in search of a replacement, at one time being quoted a quite ridiculous fee of £3,000 for a First Division club's reserve.

Adding to Kay's problems was a large number of injuries suffered by key players such as Neal (appendicitis), Campbell (cartilage), Holt (thigh) and Adams and Fishlock (who both suffered pulled muscles).

Despite his injury, Fishlock did, at least, appear a promising signing and Saints eventually struggled to 19th position. Indeed, it was probably Fishlock who kept them in the Second Division. He scored seven goals, although three came in games which Saints lost, and, more importantly, laid off several for his colleagues.

Overall, however, Southampton's future looked bleak and with the jubilee season approaching, the club was now so hard-up that the supporters club had to lend them £200 to help finance summer wages.

FA Cup

In the FA Cup, Saints were drawn away to giantkillers Walsall, recent conquerors of mighty Arsenal, and the party travelled to Fellows Park amidst a severe snowstorm. The outlook was even bleaker when Walsall's prolific scorer, Alsop, put them ahead.

But there was rescue in sight, in the form of Fishlock. The winger's two goals nosed Saints ahead for what was their first FA Cup win for eight years. More incredibly, it was their last Cup success until 1947.

For the visit of Birmingham in the fourth round, Saints found themselves without their hero, Fishlock. Into his place came a young amateur, Reid, who was, alas, overawed by the experience. Birmingham proved themselves classy opponents and they had the match sewn up by half-time.

Two goals in front at the interval, Birmingham went further ahead, although not before Saints had pushed forward and Scriven in the Southampton goal, had made some outstanding saves. But it was Birmingham who had created most of the chances and they were well worth their win.

The record crowd of over 28,000 paid £2,676 9s 6d to show that there was plenty of potential support in Southampton for a successful team.

> Saints switched to wearing striped stockings during the season in an effort to help the players spot each other more easily.

Round 3
Jan 12 v Walsall (a) 2-1
Fishlock 2
Scriven; Adams, Sillett, King, McIlwane, Luckett, Neal, Tully, Cole, Holt, Fishlock.
Att: 14,475
Round 4
Jan 26 v Birmingham (h) 0-3
Scriven; Adams, Sillett, King, McIlwane, Luckett, Neal, Tully, Horton, Holt, R.Reid.
Att: 28,291

Bert Scriven made some outstanding saves against Birmingham but could not deny the Blues victory in the FA Cup.

1934-35
Division 2

Date	Opp	Result	Scorers	Att	Adams W	Bradford A	Brewis J	Campbell F	Cole N	Fishlock L	Holt A	Horton J	King C	Light W	Luckett W	McIlwane J	Neal R	Pollard W	Roberts A	Rowe D	Scriven H	Sillett C	Tully F	Ward F	Wheeler A	Woodhouse S
Aug 25	(a) Burnley	L 0-3		12,000	2	5	8	4	9						6				11		1	3	7	10		
27	(h) Port Vale	D 0-0		7,000	2	5	8		9						11						1	3	7	4	10	6
Sep 1	(h) Oldham A	D 2-2	Rowe, Cole	7,042	2	5	8		9						6			3	11	1			7	10		4
3	(h) Port Vale	L 1-4	Fishlock	7,746	2	3	8		9	11	10	7			6	5					1			4		
8	(a) Bolton W	L 0-4		17,000	2	3	8		9	11	10				6	5					1		7	4		
15	(h) Hull C	W 3-0	Adams, Brewis, Fishlock	6,500	2		8		9	11	10				6	5					1	3	7	4		
22	(h) Notts C	D 1-1	Brewis	4,800	2		8		9	11	10				6	5					1	3	7	4		
29	(a) Bradford C	D 1-1	Wheeler	9,000	2		8		9	11					6	5					1	3	7	4	10	
Oct 6	(h) Sheffield U	D 1-1	Tully	9,913	2	3	8			11					6	5					1	9	7	4	10	
13	(a) Barnsley	D 1-1	Cole	8,000	2		8		9	11	10				6	5					1	3	7	4		
20	(a) Nottingham F	L 1-3	Cole	10,000	2		8		9	11	10				6	5					1	3	7	4		
27	(h) Brentford	W 1-0	Tully	10,415	2		8			11	10	9			6	5					1	3	7	4		
Nov 3	(a) Fulham	D 3-3	McIlwane, Luckett, Horton	20,000	2		8			11	10	9			6	5					1	3	7	4		
10	(h) Bradford	W 4-1	Wheeler 3, Fishlock	10,000	2		8			11	10				6	5					1	3	7		9	4
17	(a) Plymouth A	L 0-4		17,501		2	8			11	10				6	5					1	3	7		9	4
24	(h) Norwich C	L 1-4	Wheeler	11,400	2		8			11					6	5	7				1	3	10		9	4
Dec 1	(a) Newcastle U	L 0-1		13,000	2				10	11	9		4		6	5	7				1	3	8			
8	(h) West Ham U	D 2-2	Cole, Fishlock	8,500	2				9	11			4		6	5	7				1	3	8	10		
15	(a) Blackpool	L 1-4	Fishlock	10,000	2	10			9	11					6	5	7				1	3	8	4		
22	(h) Bury	W 2-1	Cole 2	7,300	2	10			9	11					6	5	7				1	3	8	4		
25	(a) Swansea T	W 1-0	Fishlock	2,000	2				9	11			4			5	7				1	3	8		10	6
26	(h) Swansea T	W 1-0	Wheeler	18,351	2				9	11			4			5	7				1	3	8		10	6
29	(h) Burnley	D 0-0		11,257					9	11	10		4		6	5	7	3			1	2	8			
Jan 1	(a) Manchester U	L 0-3		15,174	2	5			9	11	10				6		7				1	3	8	4		
5	(a) Oldham A	W 2-0	Cole 2	7,000	2				9	11	10		4		6	5	7				1	3	8			
19	(h) Bolton W	L 1-2	Neal	16,575	2				9	11	10		4		6	5	7				1	3	8			
31	(a) Hull C	D 0-0		5,130					9				4		11	5	7	3			1	2	8		10	6
Feb 2	(a) Notts C	L 1-3	Tully	11,000					9		10		4		11	5	7	3			1	2	8			6
9	(h) Bradford C	D 1-1	Holt	6,472					9		11				6	5	7	10	3		1	2	8	4		
16	(h) Sheffield U	L 1-6	Pollard	5,000	3		8		9				4		6	5	11	10			1	2	7			
23	(h) Barnsley	L 0-1		5,625	2		8		9				4		6	5	11	10			1	3	7			
Mar 2	(h) Nottingham F	L 1-2	McIlwane	5,790	5		8								11	9			3		1	2	7	4	10	6
9	(a) Brentford	L 2-3	Neal, Brewis	13,111	5		8		10	11					6	9	7		3		1	2		4		
16	(h) Fulham	D 1-1	McIlwane	8,946	5		8		10				4	1		9	11		3			2	7			6
23	(a) Bradford	L 1-3	Neal	5,000	5		8		10				4	1		9	11		3			2	7			6
30	(h) Plymouth A	W 1-0	McIlwane	7,271	5				10					1	6	9	11	8	3			2	7			4
Apr 6	(a) Norwich C	L 0-4		8,000	5		8		9					1	6		11	10	3			2	7			4
13	(h) Newcastle U	W 2-0	Tully, McIlwane	9,125	5				11	10				1	6	9		8	3			2	7			4
20	(a) West Ham U	L 1-2	Fishlock	31,000	5		8		9	11				1	6			10	3			2	7			4
22	(h) Manchester U	W 1-0	McIlwane	12,458	5				11	10				1	6	9		8	3			2	7			4
27	(h) Blackpool	W 2-0	Woodhouse, McIlwane	6,758	5		8		11					1	6	9		10	3			2	7			4
May 4	(a) Bury	L 1-4	Holt	5,000	5		8				9			1	6		11	10	3			2	7			4
App					25	20	27	1	24	28	27	4	13	9	38	24	22	10	16	2	33	39	40	17	11	22
Goals					1		3		8	7	2	1			1	7	3	1		1			4		6	1

Back row (left to right): Cummins, McIlwane, Adams, Scriven, Bradford, Light, Roberts, Woodhouse, Heslop. Middle row: Kay, Lee, Ward, Sillett, Campbell, Luckett, King, Keleher, Wheeler, Butt (asst trainer) Shelley. Front row: Bloomfield, Tully, Brewis, Cole, Holt, Rowe.

	P	W	D	L	F	A	Pts
Brentford	42	26	9	7	93	48	61
Bolton W	42	26	4	12	96	48	56
West Ham U	42	26	4	12	80	63	56
Blackpool	42	21	11	10	79	57	53
Manchester U	42	23	4	15	76	55	50
Newcastle U	42	22	4	16	89	68	48
Fulham	42	17	12	13	76	56	46
Plymouth A	42	19	8	15	75	64	46
Nottingham F	42	17	8	17	76	70	42
Bury	42	19	4	19	62	73	42
Sheffield U	42	16	9	17	79	70	41
Burnley	42	16	9	17	63	73	41
Hull C	42	16	8	18	63	74	40
Norwich C	42	14	11	17	71	61	39
Bradford	42	11	16	15	55	63	38
Barnsley	42	13	12	17	60	83	38
Swansea T	42	14	8	20	56	67	36
Port Vale	42	11	12	19	55	74	34
Southampton	42	11	12	19	46	75	34
Bradford C	42	12	8	22	50	68	32
Oldham A	42	10	6	26	56	95	26
Notts C	42	9	7	26	46	97	25

1935-36

AFTER their dismal showing in the League the previous season, Saints approached their jubilee season with a pronounced air of pessimism. The struggle against relegation and the lack of funds had not helped confidence and there seemed little to celebrate.

Fortified, however, by two close-season signings, Watson and Gurry, the Saints made a good start with four wins and two draws in their first six games. Watson in particular, with 300 League goals for West Ham to his name, was vastly experienced and he achieved some success as Saints' new centre-forward.

On 21 September, Southampton sat on top of the Second Division, but this early form was built on rather insecure foundations and in the period up to Christmas, only two further games were won. One of those victories came on 23 November, in a League game against Spurs which was also designated as a match to mark the club's jubilee. A crowd of over 21,000 saw Tully and Holt score the vital goals.

Alas, with the arrival of the New Year, Saints' form went from bad to worse and after 29 games the team had won only 25 points, exactly the same number they had at the same stage of the previous season.

The slump reached its lowest point in two games at the end of March when Saints suffered their heaviest-ever League defeat by losing 8-0 at Tottenham, and then had their lowest-ever League attendance at The Dell when only 1,875 turned up to watch Port Vale two days later.

Admittedly, the Port Vale match was played in heavy rain but the paltry attendance showed that Saints' fans' loyalties were wearing thin. At Highbury, Ted Drake was leading Arsenal to success in the FA Cup but that did not make the Southampton directors think twice about the wisdom of selling the club's most promising players. They transferred goalkeeper Bill Light to West Brom for £2,000.

That decision naturally displeased the fans and it could be said that the jubilee season of Southampton Football Club was hardly the most auspicious in the club's history.

FA Cup

AFTER their lone FA Cup victory of the previous season, Saints reverted to their more traditional Cup form of the 1930s and were knocked out in the first round, this time 1-0 at Middlesbrough.

Southampton were unfortunate to have McIlwane injured in the second half and, whilst the team was reorganising, Cunliffe, the 'Boro international, netted the only goal.

> Round 3
> **Jan 11 v Middlesbrough (a) 0-1**
> Light; Adams, Roberts, Brewis, McIlwane, Sillett, Neal, Holt, Watson, Tully, Fishlock.
> *Att: 29,950*

> To celebrate the club's 50th anniversary, a dinner was held at the South Western Hotel. There were 180 guests including many former players. Three of the Saints' original 1885 line-up were there, A.A.Fry, G.Muir and R.Ruffell, as well as the famous sportsman, C.B.Fry.

> In November, water flowing under The Dell built up so much pressure that the pitch erupted, making a deep hole in the Milton Road goalmouth. Fortunately, no match was in progress at the time.

> The 7-2 home win over Nottingham Forest was the first time that two Saints players had scored hat-tricks in the same match. Watson (3), Holt (3) and Neal scored in Saints' first seven-goal haul in a Division Two match.

> At the beginning of the season Bert Lee, Saints' long-serving trainer, retired and was replaced by another former player, Albert Shelley.

Lawrie Fishlock missed only one game in 1935-36.

Cover from the special programme published for the golden jubilee game against Tottenham Hotspur on 23 November 1935.

1935-36

Division 2

Date	Venue	Opponent	Result	Scorers	Att	Adams W	Bradford A	Brewis J	Catlin N	Fishlock L	Gurry J	Henderson D	Holt A	King C	Light W	Luckett W	McIlwane J	Neal R	Pollard W	Roberts A	Scriven H	Sillett C	Tully F	Watson V	Woodhouse S
Aug 31	(h)	Swansea T	W 4-3	McIlwane, Pollard, Watson, Fishlock	12,528					11	4		10	1	5		7	8		3		2		9	6
Sep 2	(a)	Doncaster R	W 1-0	Fishlock	14,227					11			10	1	5	6	7	8		3		2		9	4
Sep 7	(a)	Leicester C	D 1-1	Neal	18,000					11			10	1	5	6	7	8		3		2		9	4
Sep 9	(h)	Doncaster R	W 1-0	Watson	10,126		4			11			10	1	5	6	7			3		2	8	9	
Sep 14	(h)	Bradford	W 3-0	Brewis, Pollard, Fishlock	15,315			8		11				1	5	6	7		10	3		2		9	4
Sep 16	(h)	Bury	D 0-0		10,320			8		11				1	5	6	7		10	3		2		9	4
Sep 21	(a)	Sheffield U	L 1-2	Watson	13,000			8		11			10	1	5	6	7			3		2		9	4
Sep 28	(h)	Manchester U	W 2-1	Holt, Fishlock	17,678			8		11			10	1	5	6	7			3		2		9	4
Oct 5	(h)	Norwich C	D 1-1	Watson	15,073			8		11			10	1	5	6	7			3		2		9	4
Oct 12	(a)	Nottingham F	L 0-2		10,000	4				11	8			1	5	6	7		10	3		2		9	
Oct 19	(a)	Port Vale	W 2-0	Watson 2	5,000	4				11			10	1	5	6	7			3		2	8	9	
Oct 26	(h)	Fulham	L 1-2	Holt	14,999	4		8		11			10	1	5	6	7			3		2		9	
Nov 2	(a)	Burnley	L 0-2		8,524	4				11			10	1	5	6	7	8		3		2		9	
Nov 9	(h)	Charlton A	L 2-5	Sillett, Watson	11,050					11		4	10	1	5	6	7	8		3		2		9	
Nov 16	(a)	Hull C	D 2-2	Holt, Watson	8,000					11			8	1	5	6	10	4		3		2	7	9	
Nov 23	(h)	Tottenham H	W 2-0	Tully, Holt	21,333					11			8	1	5	6	10	4		3		2	7	9	
Nov 30	(a)	Plymouth A	D 0-0		14,356					11			8	1	5	6	10	4		3		2	7	9	
Dec 7	(h)	Bradford C	D 0-0		9,525			10		11			8	1	5	6		4		3		2	7	9	
Dec 14	(a)	Newcastle U	L 1-4	Brewis	15,000			10		11			8	1	5	6		4		3		2	7	9	
Dec 21	(h)	Barnsley	L 0-1		6,622					11			8	1	5		10	4		3		2	7	9	6
Dec 25	(a)	West Ham U	D 0-0		27,609		6			11			8	1	5		10	4		3		2	7	9	
Dec 26	(h)	West Ham U	L 2-4	Holt, Watson	18,967					11			8	1	5		10	4		3		2	7	9	6
Dec 28	(a)	Swansea T	D 0-0		8,076	2	5		7	11		4		1			10			3		6	8	9	
Jan 1	(a)	Bury	D 0-0		3,000	5			7	11		4		1			10			3		2	8	9	6
Jan 4	(h)	Leicester C	W 1-0	Neal	11,848	2	3	10		11			8	1	5			4				6	7	9	
Jan 18	(a)	Bradford	L 1-2	Fishlock	8,548	2				11			8	1	5		10	4		3		6	7	9	
Feb 1	(a)	Manchester U	L 0-4		20,000	2	8		4	11				1	5		10			3		6	7	9	
Feb 5	(h)	Sheffield U	L 0-1		5,053	5	4			11			8	1			10			3		2	7	9	6
Feb 8	(a)	Norwich C	L 1-5	Holt	12,000	5	4		7	11			10	1						3		2	8	9	6
Feb 15	(h)	Nottingham F	W 7-2	Watson 3, Holt 3, Neal	5,253					11			10	1	5		8	4		3		2	7	9	6
Feb 29	(a)	Bradford C	L 1-2	Neal	5,000					11			10	1	5	6	8	4		3		2	7	9	
Mar 7	(h)	Hull C	W 1-0	Fishlock	5,476					11			10	1	5		8	4		3		2	7	9	6
Mar 14	(a)	Charlton A	L 0-2		25,000					11			10	1	5	6	8	4		3		2	7	9	
Mar 21	(h)	Burnley	W 1-0	Holt	5,095	5				11			10	1			8	4		3		2	7	9	6
Mar 28	(a)	Tottenham H	L 0-8		28,907	5				11			10	1			8	4		3		2	7	9	6
Mar 30	(h)	Port Vale	L 0-1		1,875	5				11			10	1			8	4		3		2	7	9	6
Apr 4	(h)	Plymouth A	W 2-0	Sillett, Holt	5,882				8	11			10	1	5	6		4		3		2	7	9	
Apr 10	(a)	Blackpool	L 1-2	King	18,447				8	11			10	1	5	6		4		3		2	7	9	
Apr 11	(a)	Fulham	W 2-0	Watson, Fishlock	15,000				7	11			10	1	5	6		4		3		2	8	9	
Apr 13	(h)	Blackpool	W 1-0	Holt	11,911					11			10	1	5	6	8	4		3		2	7	9	
Apr 18	(h)	Newcastle U	L 1-3	Holt	6,670					11			10	1	5	6	8	4		3		2	7	9	
Apr 25	(a)	Barnsley	L 1-3	Watson	5,202					11			10	1	5	6	8	4		3		2	7	9	
App						17	12	19	5	41	9	8	37	21	32	19	33	32	13	32	10	42	28	36	16
Goals								2		7			13	1			1	4	2			2	1	14	

	P	W	D	L	F	A	Pts
Manchester U	42	22	12	8	85	43	56
Charlton A	42	22	11	9	85	58	55
Sheffield U	42	20	12	10	79	50	52
West Ham U	42	22	8	12	90	68	52
Tottenham H	42	18	13	11	91	55	49
Leicester C	42	19	10	13	79	57	48
Plymouth A	42	20	8	14	71	57	48
Newcastle U	42	20	6	16	88	79	46
Fulham	42	15	14	13	76	52	44
Blackpool	42	18	7	17	93	72	43
Norwich C	42	17	9	16	72	65	43
Bradford C	42	15	13	14	55	65	43
Swansea T	42	15	9	18	67	76	39
Bury	42	13	12	17	66	84	38
Burnley	42	12	13	17	50	59	37
Bradford	42	14	9	19	62	84	37
Southampton	42	14	9	19	47	65	37
Doncaster R	42	14	9	19	51	71	37
Nottingham F	42	12	11	19	69	76	35
Barnsley	42	12	9	21	54	80	33
Port Vale	42	12	9	22	56	106	32
Hull C	42	5	10	27	47	111	20

Back row (left to right): A.Shelley (trainer), V.Watson, A.Bradford, W.Light, W.Luckett, L.Fishlock, J.Brewis. Front: R.Neal, F.Tully, J.McIlwane, C.Sillett, A.Holt, A.Roberts.

1936-37

DURING the close season of 1936 the club was involved in its biggest upheaval so far regarding personnel comings and goings. Nine members of the board resigned (two were later re-elected) and manager George Kay left for Liverpool, taking with him Albert Shelley. George Goss became secretary-manager, with Johnny McIlwane his assistant and club coach.

The main reason for this massive reorganisation was the club's worsening financial situation. Mr Penn-Barrow the chairman, had decided that a fresh approach to raising money was needed and his remedy was to issue new shares. This had precipitated the mass resignations of directors.

The newly-elected board, comprising Messrs Penn-Barrow, Blagrave, Corbett, Cosgrove, Hoskins, Jukes, Ransom, Sarjantson, and Major Sloane-Stanley, thus decided on a 'forward policy' of buying rather than selling players, and Saints' supporters were pleased to see several additions to the playing staff.

One of the new faces was the Republic of Ireland forward, Jimmy Dunne, who had once cost Arsenal £8,000. Dunne joined the Saints for £1,000, and although he was perhaps past his best, it was a sign that the Saints' directorate were now thinking more positively.

Later in the season McIlwane, feeling the pressures of being assistant manager, coach, player and captain, decided to leave. When Mr Goss also resigned, the club advertised for a new manager.

The man they selected was Tom Parker, their former player who had been in charge of Norwich. Parker was selected from 120 applicants and was immediately faced with the daunting task of settling the playing staff and building the foundations of a new era for the club.

With so many comings and goings at boardroom level, it was not suprising that the team should come close to relegation. The drop was narrowly avoided and, impressed by the directors' apparent willingness to build rather than dismantle, and attracted by an improved brand of football, the fans came to The Dell in increasing numbers, so much so that the aggregate attendance figure was 50,000 up on 1935-36.

FA Cup

FOR the FA Cup third-round tie against League Champions, Sunderland, both sides adopted a change strip — Saints playing in blue and Sunderland in white. Kennedy, the Southampton half-back, was injured so Henderson took his place in the Saints line-up.

The fans were flooding into The Dell long before the start and eventually a record attendance of 30,380 had paid a total of £2,741 19s 6d. The crush was so great that most of the young boys in the ground were passed down to the front of the terraces and sat on the running track for safety.

The afternoon was gloriously sunny and although the pitch was soft and covered in sand, it did not daunt the Wearsiders who stormed into a 2-0 half-time lead. Twenty minutes into the second-half, Sunderland scored a third and it appeared that they were home and dry.

Saints, however, were not giving up quite so easily and within five minutes Holt had pulled back a goal with a hard shot. With 11 minutes remaining, Summers grabbed a second for Southampton following a pass by Neal and now the Saints really were back in the hunt.

There was a nail-biting finalé as Saints, urged on by their biggest-ever crowd, searched for the equaliser. Sunderland were too experienced a side to release their hold on the game, although they were no doubt relieved to hear the final whistle.

> **Round 1**
> **Jan 16 v Sunderland (h) 2-3**
> *Holt, Summers*
> Scriven; Sillett, Roberts, King, Henderson, Kingdon, Summers, Neal, Dunne, Holt, Smallwood.
> *Att: 30,380*

> *When Saints visited newly-relegated Aston Villa on 5 September 1936, it was the first time that a Second Division match had been played at Villa Park.*

> *Saints regular forward line in 1936-37 consisted of players from four different countries: Summers and Holt (England), Boyd (Scotland), Smallwood (Wales) and Dunne (Ireland).*

> *Mr J.Corbett's election to the board began a remarkable period of service to Southampton FC. By 1987, Mr Corbett had completed 51 years as a director, a club record. When he joined in 1936 he was instrumental in having the summer wage bill paid by Cooper's Brewery of which he was then joint managing director.*

Saints' programme for the 1936-7 season.

Full-back Bowen (far left), signed from Crystal Palace two years earlier, played only two games for Saints, at the end of 1936-7.
Henry Long (left), a product of local football, played twice in the half-back line this season.

96

1936-37
Division 2

Date	Opponent	Result	Scorers	Att	Bernard E	Bowen L	Boyd W	Brewis J	Browning D	Catlin N	Charles A	Dunne J	Gueran S	Henderson D	Holt A	Kennedy W	King W	Kingdon W	Long H	Luckett W	McIlwane J	Mayer W	Neal R	Roberts A	Scriven H	Sillett C	Smallwood F	Summers J	Tully F	Whitelaw E	Withers E
Aug 29 (h)	Chesterfield	W 3-2	Holt, Dunne, Smallwood	15,938	1		10					9			8		5	4		6			7	3		2	11				
31 (a)	Doncaster R	L 0-2		12,258	1		9	8							10		4	6				5	7	3		2	11				
Sep 5 (a)	Aston Villa	L 0-4		45,000			10					9			8		5	6					7	3	1	2	11	4			
7 (h)	Doncaster R	W 1-0	Holt	9,306			10					9			8		5		6				7	3	1	2	11	4			
12 (h)	Bradford C	W 2-0	Holt, Smallwood	9,652			10					9			8	5		6					7	3	1	2	11	4			
16 (a)	Nottingham F	D 1-1	Smallwood	14,300			10					9			8	5		6					7	3	1	2	11	4			
19 (a)	Swansea T	L 1-5	Smallwood	10,000			10					9			8	5		6						3	1	2	11	4			7
26 (h)	Sheffield U	W 4-0	Dunne 2, Boyd 2	15,104			10					9			8	5		6						3	1	2	11	7		4	
Oct 3 (h)	Burnley	D 1-1	Boyd	16,066			10					9			8	5		6						3	1	2	11	7		4	
10 (a)	Fulham	L 0-2		18,000			10					9			8	5		6						3	1	2	11	7		4	
17 (a)	Tottenham H	L 0-4		25,000			10					9			8	5		6						3	1	2	11	7		4	
24 (h)	Blackpool	W 5-2	Summers 2, Dunne 2, Smallwood	16,779								9			10	5		6						3	1	2	11	7		4	
31 (a)	Blackburn R	L 0-1		13,000								9			10	5		6						3	1	2	11	7		4	8
Nov 7 (h)	Bury	W 4-1	Boyd 2, Summers, Smallwood	14,471		8						9			10	5		6						3	1	2	11	7		4	
14 (a)	Leicester C	D 2-2	Dunne 2	10,000		8						9			10	5		6						3	1	2	11	7		4	
21 (h)	West Ham U	L 0-2		17,587				8				9			10	5		6						3	1	2	11	7		4	
28 (a)	Norwich C	L 2-4	Dunne, Holt	11,250				8				9			10			6				5		3	1	2	11	7		4	
Dec 5 (h)	Newcastle U	W 2-0	Whitelaw, Boyd	16,038			10					9			8	5		6						3	1	2	11	7		4	
12 (a)	Bradford	L 1-3	Boyd	8,000			10					9			8	5		6						3	1	2	11	7		4	
19 (h)	Barnsley	L 1-3	Holt	10,674			10					9			8	5		6						3	1	2	11	7		4	
25 (a)	Coventry C	L 0-2		32,042								9			10	8	5	6			11			3	1	2		7		4	
26 (a)	Chesterfield	L 0-3		12,000								9			10	8	5	6						3	1	2	11	7		4	
28 (h)	Coventry C	D 1-1	Summers	9,016					2			9			10	8	4	6				5			1	3	11	7			
Jan 2 (h)	Aston Villa	D 2-2	Smallwood 2	20,853								9			10	5	4	6				8		3	1	2	11	7			
9 (a)	Bradford C	D 2-2	Summers, Dunne	7,000					10	9					8	5	4	6						3	1	2	11	7			
23 (a)	Swansea T	W 2-1	Holt, Smallwood	7,123					2			9			10	5	4	6				8		3	1		11	7			
Feb 6 (a)	Burnley	W 3-1	Dunne, Holt, opp own goal	11,000								9			10	5	4	6				8		3	1	2	11	7			
11 (a)	Sheffield U	D 0-0		10,327								9			10	5	4	6				8		3	1	2	11	7			
13 (h)	Fulham	D 3-3	Dunne 2, Summers	14,317								9			10	5	4	6				8		3	1	2	11	7			
24 (h)	Tottenham H	W 1-0	Summers	5,226					2			9			10	5	4	6				8			1	3	11	7			
27 (a)	Blackpool	L 0-2		11,000					2			9			10	5	4	6				8			1	3	11	7			
Mar 6 (h)	Blackburn R	D 2-2	Kingdon, Holt	14,402					2			9			10	5	4	6				8			1	3	11	7			
13 (a)	Bury	L 1-2	Dunne	8,000					2			9			10	5	4	6				8			1	3	11	7			
20 (h)	Leicester C	D 1-1	Dunne	13,601					2			9			10	5	4	6				8			1	3	11	7			
26 (a)	Plymouth A	L 1-3	Holt	24,000				10	2			9			8	5	4	6							1	3	11	7			
27 (a)	West Ham U	L 0-4		26,000				2	7							5	4	6				8	10		1	3	11			9	
29 (h)	Plymouth A	D 0-0		20,007					2			9			10	5	4	6				8	7		1	3	11				
Apr 3 (h)	Norwich C	W 3-1	King, Holt, Smallwood	12,597					2			9			10	5	4	6				8	7		1	3	11				
10 (a)	Newcastle U	L 0-3		20,000			10					9			8	5		6						3	1	2	11	7		4	
17 (h)	Bradford	D 0-0		9,384					2			9			10	5	4	6				8			1	3	11	7			
24 (a)	Barnsley	L 1-2	Holt	7,000	3							9			8	5	4	6							1	2	11	7		10	
May 1 (h)	Nottingham F	L 0-3		4,529	3						8		5	9			4	6					7		1	2	11			10	
App					2	2	19	3	12	1	1	36	1	1	40	33	28	41	2	1	3	9	20	29	40	41	40	28	3	20	6
Goals							7					14			11		1	1									10	7		1	

1 own-goal

Back row (left to right): Sillett, Browning, Kingdon, Stansbridge, Scriven, Bowen, Whitelaw, Roberts, Summers, Neal. Middle: Butt, Broadhead, Brewis, Kennedy, Henderson, McIlwane, King, Long, Luckett, Moor, Shelley, G.W.S.Goss (secretary-manager). Front: Catlin, Withers, Holt, Dunne, Miller, Boyd, Tully, Smallwood.

	P	W	D	L	F	A	Pts
Leicester C	42	24	8	10	89	57	56
Blackpool	42	24	7	11	88	53	55
Bury	42	22	8	12	74	55	52
Newcastle U	42	22	5	15	80	56	49
Plymouth A	42	18	13	11	71	53	49
West Ham U	42	19	11	12	73	55	49
Sheffield U	42	18	10	14	66	54	46
Coventry C	42	17	11	14	66	54	45
Aston Villa	42	16	12	14	82	70	44
Tottenham H	42	17	9	16	88	66	43
Fulham	42	15	13	14	71	61	43
Blackburn R	42	16	10	16	70	62	42
Burnley	42	16	10	16	57	61	42
Barnsley	42	16	9	17	50	64	41
Chesterfield	42	16	8	18	84	89	40
Swansea T	42	15	7	20	50	65	37
Norwich C	42	14	8	20	63	71	36
Nottingham F	42	12	10	20	68	90	34
Southampton	42	11	12	19	53	77	34
Bradford	42	12	9	21	52	88	33
Bradford C	42	9	12	21	54	94	30
Doncaster R	42	7	10	25	30	84	24

1937-38

DURING the 1937 close season Tom Parker busied himself with an assessment of the playing staff and quickly showed that he had an eye for talent by signing Harry Osman from Plymouth, as well as a whole host of youngsters from his former club, Norwich. One of those youngsters was Ted Bates and during the coming season Bates was to make 15 League appearances.

With all the disruptions of the previous campaign, the team was still far from settled and this was reflected by yet another dismal start. In September, Parkin was signed from Middlesbrough, for £1,500, and when he scored on his debut it was Saints' first League goal for 524 minutes.

On the positive side, Osman quickly proved himself as a fine forward and his tally of 22 goals, scored from the left wing, created a club record and, inevitably, attracted the attentions of the 'glamour' clubs.

The board had kept their promise to make money available for signings and overall Parker spent a total of £9,000 in an effort to rebuild the team. Hill had arrived from Blackpool, for a record fee of £2,200, and despite Saints again managing only 15th position, it was evident that the team was improving. Thoughts of promotion were beginning to edge their way into peoples' minds.

FA Cup

SAINTS dominated much of their third round FA Cup game at the City Ground but found the Nottingham Forest defence in an uncompromising mood. Forest had scored first, after 20 minutes, but fine work by Bates enabled Dunn to equalise just before half-time.

Although Forest went ahead within a minute of the restart, it was Saints who still continued to do most of the attacking. Arthur Holt saw a tremendous 30-yard shot fly inches over the crossbar, but it was the home side who finally settled the issue with a breakaway goal six minutes from the end.

> Round 3
> **Jan 8 v Nottingham Forest (a) 1-3**
> *Dunn*
> Warhurst; Sillett, Roberts, King, Affleck, Hill, Bevis, Bates, Dunn, Holt, Osman.
> *Att: 24,096*

> *To help Saints' improve their financial position, the Mayor of Southampton started a 'shilling fund' and over £500 was subscribed by the public.*

> *Various changes were made to The Dell during the season, including a unique half-time scoreboard that gave the scores from all four divisions of the Football League.*

By 1937-38 the Saints' programme cover design had changed again.

1937-38

Division 2

Date		Opponent	Res	Score	Scorers	Att	Affleck D	Bates E	Bevis W	Browning D	Chalk N	Day A	Dunn W	Gaughran B	Gueran S	Henderson D	Hill F	Holt A	Kelly G	Kennedy W	King C	Kingdon W	Long H	Mayer W	Osman H	Parkin R	Roberts A	Scott J	Sillett C	Smallwood F	Stansbridge L	Summers J	Warhurst S	Woodford G	Woolf L
Aug 28	(a)	Norwich C	L	3-4	Dunn, Holt, Osman	23,172			2				9	8				10		5	4	6			11				3				7	1	
Sep 1	(h)	Chesterfield	L	0-1		13,478			2				9	8				10		5	4	6			11				3				7	1	
4	(h)	Aston Villa	D	0-0		25,561			2			4	9					8		5		6	10		11				3				7	1	
6	(a)	Chesterfield	L	0-5		14,489			2			4	9					8		5		6	10		11				3				7	1	
11	(a)	Bradford	L	0-2		10,845	5		2			4	9					10				6			11	8			3				7	1	
15	(h)	Plymouth A	D	0-0		11,845	5		2			4	9					8				6	10		11				3				7	1	
18	(h)	West Ham U	D	3-3	Sillett, Parkin, Osman	19,478	5		2			4	9					10				6			11	8			3				7	1	
25	(a)	Manchester U	W	2-1	Bevis, Holt	20,000	5		2			4	9				6	10							11	8			3				7	1	
Oct 2	(a)	Blackburn R	L	0-4		14,000	5		2			4	9				6	10							11	8			3				7	1	
9	(h)	Sheffield W	W	5-2	Holt 2, Osman 2, Gaughran	19,542	5		2			4		9			6	8							11				3	10			7	1	
16	(h)	Stockport C	W	4-1	Gaughran 2, Parkin, Osman	20,039	5		2			4		9			6							11	10	8			3				7	1	
23	(a)	Barnsley	W	2-0	Osman 2	10,000	5		2			4		9			6							11	10	8			3				7	1	
30	(h)	Luton T	L	3-6	Osman 3	20,544	5		2			4		9			6							11	10	8			3				7	1	
Nov 6	(a)	Newcastle U	L	0-3		30,000	5		2			4		9			6							11	10	8			3				7	1	
13	(h)	Nottingham F	W	2-0	Bevis 2	16,253	5		2			4	9				6	10							11	8			3				7	1	
20	(a)	Burnley	L	0-4		10,000	5		2			4	9				6	10		7					11	8			3					1	
27	(h)	Bury	W	4-1	Parkin, Gaughran, Holt, Osman	13,023	5		2			4		9			6	10							11	8			3				7	1	
Dec 11	(h)	Tottenham H	W	2-1	Parkin 2	17,718	5		2			4					6	10							11	9			3				7	1	8
18	(a)	Sheffield U	L	0-5		20,000	5		2			4	9				6	10							11	8			3				7	1	
25	(h)	Swansea T	D	1-1	Osman	13,583	5		2			4					6	8						11	10	9			3				7	1	
27	(a)	Swansea T	D	0-0		20,685	5	8	7								6				4			11	10	9			3			2		1	
Jan 1	(h)	Norwich C	W	3-1	Osman 2, Dunn	14,217	5	8	7				9				6				4			11	10		1		3			2			
15	(a)	Aston Villa	L	0-3		20,000	5	8	7									10	4		6			11	9		1		3			2			
22	(a)	Coventry C	L	0-2		20,000	5	8	7								6		4						9		1		3	10	11	2			
29	(a)	West Ham U	L	1-3	Kelly	21,200	5	8	7								6	10	4					11	9		1		3			2			
Feb 2	(h)	Bradford	W	2-1	Bevis, Osman	7,870	5	8	7	2						3	6	10	4					11	9		1								
5	(h)	Manchester U	D	3-3	Osman 2, Holt	20,654	5	8	7	2						3	6	10	4					11	9		1								
12	(h)	Blackburn R	W	1-0	opp own goal	16,293	5		7	2						3	6	10	4					11	9	8	1								
19	(a)	Sheffield W	D	0-0		15,000	5	8	7	2						3		10	4		6			11	9		1								
26	(a)	Stockport C	D	0-0		12,000	5	8		2						3	6	10	4	7				11	9		1								
Mar 5	(h)	Barnsley	W	2-0	Kelly, Osman	14,769			7	2						3	6	10	4	5				11	9	8	1								
12	(a)	Luton T	W	3-1	Osman 2, Parkin	14,428	5	8	7	2						3	6	10	4					11	9		1								
19	(h)	Newcastle U	W	1-0	Parkin	20,204	5	8	7	2						3	6	10	4					11	9		1								
26	(a)	Nottingham F	L	1-2	Holt	8,000	5	8	7	2						3	6	10	4					11	9		1								
Apr 2	(h)	Burnley	D	0-0		15,113	5	8	7	2						3	6	10	4					11	9		1								
9	(a)	Bury	L	1-2	Bevis	8,000	5		7			6				3		11	9		4				10	8	1					2			
15	(a)	Fulham	L	0-1		13,141	5		7			6						11		7	4				9	8	1			10		2			
16	(h)	Coventry C	L	0-4		20,760	5	10	7			6				3		11			4				9	8	1					2			
18	(h)	Fulham	W	4-0	Osman 2, Hill, Dunn	14,884	5		7							3	6	10	4					11	9	8	1					2			
23	(a)	Tottenham H	L	0-5		15,000	5					6	9			3		10	4				7	11		8	1					2			
30	(h)	Sheffield U	W	2-1	Bates, Parkin	12,611	5	8	7							3	6	10	4					11		9	1					2			
May 7	(a)	Plymouth A	L	0-4		15,575	5				6		9			3		8	4					11	10		1					2	7		
App							36	15	31	14	1	22	14	7	2	9	32	33	14	10	24	7	3	5	40	27	27	1	28	8	1	3	41	6	1
Goals								1	5				3	4			1	7	2						22	8			1						

1 own-goal

	P	W	D	L	F	A	Pts
Aston Villa	42	25	7	10	73	35	57
Manchester U	42	22	9	11	82	50	53
Sheffield U	42	22	9	11	73	56	53
Coventry C	42	20	12	10	66	45	52
Tottenham H	42	19	6	17	76	54	44
Burnley	42	17	10	15	54	54	44
Bradford	42	17	9	16	69	56	43
Fulham	42	16	11	15	61	57	43
West Ham U	42	14	14	14	53	52	42
Bury	42	18	5	19	63	60	41
Chesterfield	42	16	9	17	63	63	41
Luton T	42	15	10	17	89	86	40
Plymouth A	42	14	12	16	57	65	40
Norwich C	42	14	11	17	56	75	39
Southampton	42	15	9	18	55	77	39
Blackburn R	42	14	10	18	71	80	38
Sheffield W	42	14	10	18	49	56	38
Swansea T	42	13	12	17	45	73	38
Newcastle U	42	14	8	20	51	58	36
Nottingham F	42	14	8	20	47	60	36
Barnsley	42	11	14	17	50	64	36
Stockport C	42	11	9	22	43	70	31

Back row (left to right): King, Sillett, Warhurst, Affleck, Woodford. Front: Kingdon, Bevis, Bates, Hill (captain), Holt, Osman.

1938-39

THE last season before the outbreak of war turned out to be one of great disappointment for Southampton fans who had expected better things. Many players had come and gone over the previous 18 months and the public had hoped that the club would now be showing greater signs of progress.

Four consecutive defeats at the start of the season set the tone for the rest of the campaign, and with the international situation and the future uncertain, the directors were naturally unwilling to spend money on new players.

The growing turmoil had an unsettling effect on the team and Osman in particular struggled to find the exciting form he had shown the previous season. In March, Saints sold him to Millwall for £2,000 which, in hindsight, turned out to be one of the best pieces of business conducted by the club.

Two months earlier, Southampton had suffered the humiliation of being knocked out of the Cup by a non-League side, convincing Parker than another signing was essential. Frank Perfect, from Tranmere, was purchased and Parker was well acquainted with Perfect's talents, having managed him at Norwich.

Coinciding with the shock Cup defeat was the rumour that Chelsea wanted Parker as their manager but, whether or not the stories were true, Parker remained at The Dell. Progress was minimal to say the least, but Parker's apparent decision to remain loyal to the club gave supporters hope. They reasoned that he must have thought better times were near.

Before those hopes could be tested, however, war was declared and the curtain rang down on a relatively dismal decade for Southampton Football Club.

FA Cup

TO underline the terrible FA Cup record that Saints had endured since 1927, the team hit rock bottom with a 4-1 away defeat at the hands of Chelmsford City.

Having recently acquired professional status, the Essex club were anxious to gain entry to the Football League and they deserved their win on an admittedly difficult pitch where the icy conditions made football a lottery.

After Briggs missed an early chance for the Saints, Chelmsford took hold of the game and only in the latter stages of the match did Southampton begin to play like a Second Division side. The only Saints player to emerge from the afternoon with any credit was goalkeeper Warhurst, whose daring saved Saints from an even bigger defeat. Chelmsford were beaten 6-0 in the next round to underline Saints' appalling performance.

> **Round 3**
> **Jan 7 v Chelmsford City (a) 1-4**
> *Tomlinson*
> Warhurst; Henderson, Emanuel, Parkin, Carnaby, Brophy, Bevis, Holt, Tomlinson, Briggs, Hill.
> *Att: 10,741*

> When war was declared in September 1939, Saints had a bank overdraft of £20,000, plus £2,000 still outstanding on the mortgage at The Dell.

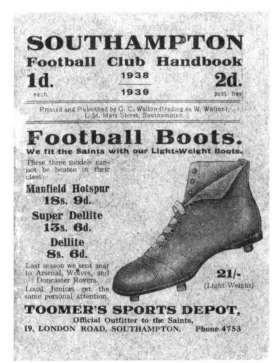

Southampton Football Club handbook for 1938-39. The 84-page annual gave a host of information together with individual portraits of all the first-team players.

1938-39
Division 2

Date		Opponent	Result	Scorers	Att	Affleck D	Bates E	Bevis W	Bowden O	Briggs F	Brophy H	Carnaby T	Chalk N	Clark W	Cutting S	Emanuel T	Griggs P	Henderson D	Hill F	Holt A	Kelly G	King C	McGibbon D	Osman H	Parkin R	Perfect F	Smith G	Stansbridge L	Tomlinson R	Wallace L	Warhurst S	Webber E	Wilkinson C	Williams F	Woodford G
Aug 27	(h)	Tottenham H	L 1-2	Brophy	22,653	5	8	7		10	9								6			4		11				1						3	2
30	(a)	Burnley	L 1-2	Brophy	13,334	5		7			9								6	10		4		11	8			1						3	2
Sep 3	(a)	Bury	L 2-5	Brophy, Osman	9,000	5	8	7			9								3	10		6		11	4			1							2
10	(a)	Coventry C	L 0-3		20,326	5		7											6	10		4		11	8				9	1				2	3
14	(h)	Plymouth A	W 2-1	Osman 2	12,406	5	10	7										3	6			4		11	8				9	1				2	
17	(h)	Nottingham F	D 2-2	Brophy, Hill	15,196	5		7			6							3	11			4		10	8				9					2	
24	(a)	Newcastle U	L 0-1		35,000	5		7		10	6					3				8				11	4				9					2	
Oct 1	(h)	West Brom A	W 2-1	Holt, Osman	16,423	5		7		10	6					3				8		4		11				1	9					2	
8	(a)	Norwich C	L 1-2	Parkin	12,000	5		7		10	6					3			11	8					4				9					2	
15	(h)	Sheffield W	W 4-3	Tomlinson 2, Briggs, Osman	17,123	5		7		10	6					3				8				11	4				9					2	
22	(a)	Fulham	D 1-1	Tomlinson	20,000	5		7		10	6					3				8				11	4				9					2	
29	(h)	Tranmere R	W 3-1	Holt, Tomlinson, Briggs	16,341	5		7		10	6					3				8				11	4				9					2	
Nov 5	(a)	Millwall	W 1-0	Briggs	35,000	5		7		10	6					3				8				11	4				9					2	
12	(h)	Manchester C	L 1-2	Briggs	23,104	5		7		10	6					3				8				11	4				9					2	
19	(a)	Bradford	L 1-2	Osman	10,000	5		7	10	9	6					3				8				11	4									1	
26	(h)	Swansea T	W 4-1	Briggs 3, Holt	14,178	5		7		10						3			6	8				11	4				9					1	
Dec 3	(a)	Chesterfield	L 1-6		10,000	5		7		10						3			6	8				11	4				9					1	
10	(h)	Blackburn R	L 1-3	Tomlinson	15,649	5	8	7		10						3		2	6					11	4				9					1	
17	(a)	West Ham U	W 2-1	Briggs, Tomlinson	16,500	5		7		8	6					3				10				11	4				9					1	
24	(a)	Tottenham H	D 1-1	Tomlinson	7,428			7		8	6	5				3				10				11	4				9					1	
26	(a)	Sheffield U	L 1-5	Briggs	31,303					8	6	5				3			11	10				7	4				9					1	
27	(h)	Sheffield U	D 2-2	Holt, Hill	19,489					9	6	5				3			11	8	7			10	4									1	
31	(h)	Bury	D 0-0		13,844			7		10	6	5				3		2	11	8					4				9					1	
Jan 14	(h)	Coventry C	L 0-2		11,578		8			7	6	5							4	10				11					9					3	2
28	(h)	Newcastle U	D 0-0		15,802	5		7		8	3								6	10				11	4	2			9					1	
Feb 4	(a)	West Brom A	L 0-2		20,000	5		7		8	3	4								10				11		2	6		9					1	
8	(a)	Nottingham F	W 2-0	Bevis, Tomlinson	3,000	5		7		8	3	4				2				10				11			6		9					1	
11	(h)	Norwich C	W 3-1	Osman 2, Tomlinson	11,880	5		7		8	3	4				2				10				11			6		9					1	
18	(a)	Sheffield W	L 0-2		25,000	5				8	3	4								10	7			11			6		9					1	
25	(h)	Fulham	W 2-1	Tomlinson, Briggs	12,512	5	8	7		10	4					3								11			2	6	9					1	
Mar 4	(a)	Tranmere R	D 1-1	Osman	7,000		8	7		10	4	5				3								11			2	6	9					1	
11	(h)	Millwall	D 1-1	Bevis	14,411		8	7		10	5					3								11	4		2	6	9					1	
18	(a)	Manchester C	L 1-2	Bates	18,000		8	7		10	5					3									4		2	6	9		11	1		
25	(h)	Bradford	W 3-2	Parkin, Bates, Briggs	9,679		8	7		10	5					3			11						4		2	6	9			1			
Apr 1	(a)	Swansea T	W 3-1	Bevis 3	8,000		8	7		10	6		5			3			11						4		2		9			1			
7	(a)	Luton T	L 2-6	Bevis, Tomlinson	15,946		8	7		10	6		5			3			11						4		2		9			1			
8	(h)	Chesterfield	D 2-2	Brophy, Briggs	14,904		8	7		10	6		5	4	3				11								2		9			1			
10	(h)	Luton T	L 0-4		15,114		8	7		11	6		5	4	3					10							2		9			1			
15	(a)	Blackburn R	L 0-3		12,000			7		10	6	5		11	3				8								2		9			1	4		
22	(h)	West Ham U	L 0-2		9,931			7		8	6	5				3			10	11					4		2		9			1			
29	(h)	Burnley	W 2-1	Briggs, Tomlinson	4,196			7		8	6	5				3			10	11					4		2		9			1			
May 6	(a)	Plymouth A	L 0-2		6,000					10	6	5		11	4	3	8								7		9				2	1		
		App				25	14	37	2	36	37	14	4	2	3	33	1	4	19	29	5	7	1	30	29	15	9	5	36	1	37	1	3	22	1
		Goals					2	6		14	5								2	4				9	2				12						

Back row (left to right): F.Perfect, T.Carnaby, S.Warhurst, D.Affleck, R.Tomlinson. Front row: H.Brophy, F.Briggs, W.Bevis, A.Holt, G.Smith, H.Osman.

	P	W	D	L	F	A	Pts
Blackburn R	42	25	5	12	94	60	55
Sheffield U	42	20	14	8	69	41	54
Sheffield W	42	21	11	10	88	59	53
Coventry C	42	21	8	13	62	45	50
Manchester C	42	21	7	14	96	72	49
Chesterfield	42	20	9	13	69	52	49
Luton T	42	22	5	15	82	66	49
Tottenham H	42	19	9	14	67	62	47
Newcastle U	42	18	10	14	61	48	46
West Brom A	42	18	9	15	89	72	45
West Ham U	42	17	10	15	70	52	44
Fulham	42	17	10	15	61	55	44
Millwall	42	14	14	14	64	53	42
Burnley	42	15	9	18	50	56	39
Plymouth A	42	15	8	19	49	55	38
Bury	42	12	13	17	65	74	37
Bradford	42	12	11	19	61	82	35
Southampton	42	13	9	20	56	82	35
Swansea T	42	11	12	19	50	83	34
Nottingham F	42	10	11	21	49	82	31
Norwich C	42	13	5	24	50	91	31
Tranmere R	42	6	5	31	39	99	17

Southampton 1939-40, back row (left to right): J.R.Scott (coach), F.Briggs, G.Kelly, E.T.Bates, J.Bradley, W.Dodgin, A.G.Holt, T.Emanuel, F.T.Perfect, N.Higham, F.A.Williams, B.C.Bush (asst secretary). Standing: J.E.Broadhead (asst trainer and masseur), R.M.Gates (groundsman), R.Parkin, R.W.Tomlinson, D.R.Affleck, T.E.Carnaby, L.E.C.Stansbridge, H.F.Brophy, S.L.Warhurst, E.V.Webber, D.McGibbon, A.J.Cummins, C.E.Wilkinson, H.W.Cope (trainer and coach). Seated: Mr C.J.Cosgrove, Councillor G.E.H.Prince OBE, Mr A.E.Jukes, Mr J.R.Sarjantson (chairman), Major R.C.H.Sloane-Stanley (president), Messrs B.H.Ransom, C.F.Hoskins, W.Penn-Barrow, T.R.Parker (secretary-manager). On ground: G.Smith, W.E.Bevis, C.G.Dean, R.Veck, E.H.Pearce, J.Cocker, L.A.White, R.Perrett.

Southampton 1940-41, back row (left to right): J.Eckford, A.Creecy, C.White, D.Angell, H.Lanham. Standing: T.Keleher, S.Hooper, D.Roper, K.Fisher, T.Parker, W.Ellerington, P.Barry, W.Stroud, Mr J.Angell. Sitting: J.Harris, Mr Wright, Mr Sarjantson, Mr Jukes, L.Laney. On ground: G.Fox, T.Hassell, R.Noss.

Southampton 1941-42, back row (left to right): Creecy, Hankey, Roles, Harris, Affleck, Ellerington. Front: V.Smith, Tait, Roper, Stroud, Laney.

Saints during World War Two
1939-40

NO sooner had the 1939-40 season started than it was abandoned upon the outbreak of war. Saints had played three League games when the competition was suspended and no further matches were seen at The Dell for almost two months because Southampton had been designated an 'unsafe area' due to the production of armaments.

That did not prevent Saints from playing, however, and they travelled to meet clubs in neighbouring but safer areas for friendly games. Organised football returned in late October when clubs were divided into regional groups, Saints were placed in South 'B'.

The immediate effect of the war was not too drastic as far as the club's playing staff was concerned. Only about half the full-time professionals had left Southampton and, like football in World War One, there were plenty of guest players stationed in the area and only too willing to take their places. Young Saints reserves also found themselves with unexpected first-team opportunities.

Saints were to struggle throughout the season, gaining only four victories in their sectional matches and suffering their heaviest defeat — 9-4 — at the hands of Brighton. If entertainment value can be measured only in the number of goals scored, then Saints fans were certainly entertained. They saw no fewer than 104 goals scored in 18 games. Unfortunately, 63 of them were scored against the Saints who finished bottom of the table.

With the South 'B' fixtures completed, an additional competition was started, giving Saints a further 18 matches, but against different opposition. Spurs, Arsenal and West Ham were amongst the teams who Southampton met in Group 'C' and Saints improved slightly. The highlight was a 3-2 victory over mighty Arsenal at The Dell.

Because of the bad winter, the season was extended into June and it was in that month, at Fulham, that Southampton fielded five guest players from Arsenal. Compton, Hapgood, Collett, Joy and Jones helped a number of Saints youngsters win the game 2-1. In goal for Saints that day was 16-year-old Raymond Perez.

A Basque refugee, Perez had arrived in England in 1938, together with another Basque, Sabin Boragra, and these two played a major part in Southampton's nursery team before the war. At the end of the season, both returned to their native Spain and joined top clubs with whom they were to gain international honours.

Football League South B
Oct 21 v Bournemouth (h) 1-2
Bradley
Oct 28 v Chelsea (a) 2-6
Holt, McGibbon
Nov 3 v Brentford (a) 1-3
Perrett
Nov 11 v Brighton & HA (h) 3-2
Briggs, Bates, McGibbon
Nov 18 v Reading (a) 3-5
Briggs 2, McGibbon
Nov 25 v Fulham (h) 5-2
Briggs 2, Dodgin, Bevis, Bradley
Dec 2 v Portsmouth (a) 1-4
Bradley
Dec 9 v Queen's Park R (h) 1-2
Briggs
Dec 16 v Aldershot (a) 0-3
Dec 23 v Bournemouth (a) 2-3
Bradley 2
Dec 25 v Chelsea (h) 5-2
Bates 2, Roy 2, Bradley
Dec 26 v Brentford (h) 2-3
Bates, McGibbon
Dec 30 v Brighton & HA (a) 4-9
Bradley 2, Bates, McGibbon
Jan 6 v Reading (h) 5-6
Bradley 2, Bates, Briggs, Hassell
Jan 13 v Fulham (a) 1-4
Bates
Jan 20 v Portsmouth (h) 2-0
Briggs, opp own goal
Feb 8 v Queen's Park R (a) 1-4
Bates
Mar 13 v Aldershot (h) 2-3
Bradley 2

Football League South C

Feb 10 v Millwall (h) 2-2
Briggs, Osman
Feb 17 v Chelsea (a) 1-5
McGibbon
Feb 24 v Fulham (h) 0-4
Mar 2 v Tottenham H (a) 1-4
Bates
Mar 9 v Arsenal (h) 3-2
Bates, Hassell, Osman
Mar 16 v Brentford (a) 0-5

Mar 22 v West Ham U (h) 1-6
Hassell
Mar 23 v Portsmouth (a) 1-3
Bates
Mar 25 v West Ham U (a) 2-2
Bates, Bradley
Mar 30 v Charlton A (a) 1-4
Osman
Apr 6 v Millwall (a) 2-5
Logie, Gilmour
Apr 10 v Brentford (h) 4-1
Bradley 2, McGibbon, Perrett
Apr 13 v Chelsea (h) 3-0
Bradley 2, Perrett
Apr 24 v Portsmouth (h) 1-0
Bradley
May 18 v Tottenham H (h) 3-3
Bradley 2, Bates
Jun 1 v Arsenal (a) 0-5
Jun 6 v Fulham (a) 2-1
Webber 2
Jun 8 v Charlton A (h) 1-3
Bradley

War Cup South (Division B)

Apr 19 v Bristol R (h) 1-1
Bates
Apr 27 v Bristol R (a) 1-3
Osman

Friendlies

Sep 9 v Bournemouth (a) 2-2
Tomlinson 2
Sep 16 v Portsmouth (a) 3-2
Tomlinson 3
Sep 30 v Brighton & HA (a) 4-1
Bradley 2, Bates, Perrett
Oct 7 v Swindon T (a) 0-2
Oct 14 v Bournemouth (a) 2-3
Perrett, Dean
May 4 v Chelmsford (a) 1-5
Gilmour
May 11 v Guildford (a) 1-4
Bradley

Division Two
(abandoned after three games)
APPEARANCES
3 Affleck D, Briggs F, Emanuel T, Perrett R, Warhurst F, 2 Bevis W, Dodgin W, Higham N, Parkin R, Perfect F, Tomlinson R, 1 Bates E, Brophey H, Holt A, Kelly G, Smith G, Williams F.

GOALSCORERS
2 Higham, Holt, 1 Briggs.

Football League South 'B'
APPEARANCES
18 Bradley J, Webber E, 17 Harris J, Smith G, 16 Holt A, Warhurst S, 15 Bates E, Briggs F, 11 McGibbon D, 8 Dodgin W, Perrett R, 7 Roles A, 5 Bevis W, Laney L, 4 Hassell T, Wilkinson C, 2 Bernard E, Buckley J, Hooper L, Roy J, Barry P, Dean C, Hayhurst A, Noyce L, Osman H, Pitts H.

GOALSCORERS
12 Bradley, 8 Briggs, Bates, 5 McGibbon, 2 Roy, 1 Holt, Perrett, Dodgin, Bevis, Hassell, Opp own goal 1.

Football League South 'C'
APPEARANCES
18 Webber E, 16 Harris J, 15 Hassell T, 14 Bates E, Bradley J, Holt A, Warhurst S, 12 Briggs F, 9 Osman H, 7 Mordey H, 5 Allen J, Buckley J, McGibbon D, Perrett R, 4 Smith G, Targett A, 3 Gilmour G, Perez R, 2 Creecy A, Hapgood E, Jones L, West H, 1 Barry P, Bewley D, Burgess H, Collett E, Compton L, Dean C, Joy B, Kiernan T, Laney L, Logie J, Roles A, Roper D, Salter J, Sanders J, Scott J, Smyth C, Spence R, Stroud W, Sykes J, Tennant A, Vaux E, Walsh W, Weaver S.

GOALSCORERS
9 Bradley, 5 Bates, 2 Briggs, Hassell, McGibbon, Osman, Perrett, Webber, 1 Gilmour, Logie.

War Cup South 'B' Division
APPEARANCES
2 Allen J, Bates E, Bradley J, Harris J, Holt A, Mordey H, Warhurst S, Webber E, 1 Briggs F, Hassell T, McGibbon D, Osman H, Perrett R, Walsh W.

GOALSCORERS
1 Bates, Osman.

South 'B'

	P	W	D	L	F	A	Pts
Queen's Park R	18	12	2	4	49	26	26
Bournemouth	18	11	2	5	52	37	24
Chelsea	18	9	5	4	43	37	23
Reading	18	10	2	6	47	42	22
Brentford	18	8	2	8	42	41	18
Fulham	18	7	4	7	50	51	18
Portsmouth	18	7	2	9	37	42	16
Aldershot	18	5	4	9	38	49	14
Brighton & HA	18	5	1	12	42	53	11
Southampton	18	4	0	14	41	63	8

South 'C'

	P	W	D	L	F	A	Pts
Tottenham H	18	11	4	3	43	30	26
West Ham U	18	10	4	4	53	28	24
Arsenal	18	9	5	4	41	26	23
Brentford	18	8	4	6	42	34	20
Millwall	18	7	5	6	36	30	19
Charlton A	18	7	4	7	39	56	18
Fulham	18	8	1	9	38	42	17
Southampton	18	5	3	10	28	55	13
Chelsea	18	4	3	11	33	53	11
Portsmouth	18	3	3	12	26	45	9

1940-41

IN the first full season of wartime football, Saints found themselves faced with problems. First, they were again refused matches against London clubs due to travelling difficulties; then, when their fixtures did get underway, enemy air-raids interfered with them.

Throughout September, matches were either interrupted, abandoned or delayed. Indeed, one match lasted only five minutes before German bombers were sighted. To add still further to Saints' misery, The Dell was bombed in November, one bomb leaving an 18-feet wide crater in the Milton Road end penalty area, smashing a culvert carrying a stream under the pitch and flooding the ground to a depth of more than 3ft for around a month.

Of course, Saints were forced to play all their remaining matches away from home — with the exception of a 'home' cup game against Brentford at Fratton Park — and the rest of the season developed into a saga of tedious journeys in the blackout.

It was on one such trip, returning from Cardiff, that the players not only got lost but endured a night in the open after their coach first hit a brick wall, then suffered a puncture. It was noon on Sunday before they arrived back in Southampton.

Saints team that season included many of the nursery side which had appeared in local leagues before the war. Manager Tom Parker, together with his assistant, Toby Keleher, had the difficult task of putting together a side from a raw and inexperienced squad. The team's average age was only 19 and John Harris, the only non-Hampshire man and the most experienced player, led the side.

Although the young team did not achieve many encouraging results, there was no lack of enthusiasm. This was noted by the great Arsenal player, Alec James, who commented that he thought the set of Southampton youngsters "a very fine bunch."

Aug 31 v Brighton & HA (h) 3-1
Roper 2, Laney
Sep 7 v Aldershot (a) 1-4
Roper
Sep 14 v Bournemouth (h) 6-1
C.Smith 2, Messom, Hassell, Roper, Laney
Sep 28 v Watford (h) 2-5
Roper 2
Oct 5 v Aldershot (h) 2-3
Roper, Laney
Oct 12 v Brighton & HA (a) 0-0
Oct 19 v Watford (a) 2-3
Bates, Hassell
Oct 26 v Crystal P (h) 1-4
Hassell
Nov 2 v Watford (h) 0-4
Nov 9 v Cardiff C (h) 1-3
Roper
Nov 16 v Cardiff C (a) 1-1
Stroud
Nov 23 v Reading (h) 2-3
Bates 2
Nov 30 v Bournemouth (a) 1-1
Roper
Dec 7 v Bristol C (a) 2-6
Roper, Laney
Dec 14 v Reading (a) 0-8
Dec 21 v Watford (a) 2-4
A.Harris, Laney
Dec 25 v Portsmouth (a) 2-1
Hassell, Roper
Dec 28 v Bristol C (a) 0-5
Jan 11 v Bournemouth (a) 3-5
Roper, Stroud, opp own goal
Jan 25 v Watford (a) 1-7
Hassell

Feb 1 v Southend U (a) 4-6
Stroud 2, Fox, Mee
Feb 8 v Portsmouth (a) 2-5
J.Harris, Hassell
Mar 1 v Bournemouth (a) 3-3
Hassell, Stroud, Laney
Mar 8 v Brighton & HA (a) 1-3
Stroud
Mar 15 v Portsmouth (a) 0-6
Mar 22 v Watford (a) 0-2
Mar 29 v Luton T (a) 1-3
Roper
Apr 12 v Bournemouth (a) 2-4
Dean 2
Apr 14 v Brighton & HA (a) 3-6
Hassell, Stroud, Mee
Apr 19 v Brighton & HA (a) 1-3
Hassell
Apr 26 v Southend U (a) 4-1
Stroud 2, L.A.White, Hassell

Southern Regional League
(including War Cup)
APPEARANCES
32 Hassell T, 31 Harris J, 30 Barry P, 28 Creecy A, Roper D, 23 White C, 22 Stroud W, 19 Laney L, Roles A, 16 Mee B, 14 Messom G, 11 Bates E, 10 Ellerington W, 9 Fisher K, Fox G, Permain A, Smith C, 6 House A, 5 Lanham H, 4 Angell R, McSweeny T, 3 Eckford J, Harris N, Higham N, Noss R, 2 Cummins A, Hooper S, Perrett R, Salter R, 1 Brophy H, Dean C, Lewis J, Southern L, White L.

GOALSCORERS
League: 12 Roper, 10 Hassell, 9 Stroud, 6 Laney, 3 Bates, Harris J, 2 Dean, Mee, Smith, 1 Fox, Messom, White L, Opp own goal 1.
War Cup: 2 Stroud, 1 Harris J, Harris N.

Southern Regional League

	P	W	D	L	F	A	Ave
Crystal P	27	16	4	7	86	44	1.954
West Ham U	25	14	6	5	70	39	1.794
Coventry C	10	5	3	2	28	16	1.750
Arsenal	19	10	5	4	66	38	1.736
Cardiff C	24	12	5	7	75	50	1.500
Reading	26	14	5	7	73	51	1.431
Norwich C	19	9	2	8	73	55	1.327
Watford	35	15	6	14	96	73	1.315
Portsmouth	31	16	2	13	92	71	1.296
Tottenham H	23	9	5	9	53	41	1.292
Millwall	31	16	5	10	73	57	1.280
West Brom A	28	13	5	10	83	69	1.202
Leicester C	33	17	5	11	87	73	1.191
Northampton T	30	14	3	13	84	71	1.183
Bristol C	20	10	2	8	55	48	1.145
Mansfield T	29	12	6	11	77	68	1.132
Charlton A	19	7	4	8	37	34	1.088
Aldershot	24	14	2	8	73	68	1.073
Brentford	23	9	3	11	51	51	1.000
Chelsea	23	10	4	9	57	58	0.981
Birmingham	16	7	1	8	38	43	0.883
Fulham	30	10	7	13	62	73	0.849
Luton T	35	11	7	17	82	100	0.820
Stoke C	36	9	9	18	76	96	0.791
Queen's Park R	23	8	3	12	47	60	0.783
Brighton & HA	25	8	7	10	51	75	0.680
Nottingham F	25	7	3	15	50	77	0.649
Bournemouth	27	9	3	15	59	92	0.641
Notts C	21	8	3	10	42	66	0.636
Southend U	29	12	4	13	64	101	0.633
Southampton	31	4	4	23	53	111	0.477
Swansea T	10	2	1	7	12	33	0.363
Clapton O	15	1	3	11	19	66	0.287

League table calculated on goal average

1941-42

THIS was a curious season, for without the London clubs and Portsmouth, who had joined the London competition, Southampton had to make fixtures as and when they could. With only five other professional clubs as opponents in the League South competition, Southampton had to include army, navy and police teams to supplement their season.

The return to The Dell was briefly delayed due to fire partly destroying the West Stand at the end of September. Southampton's opening home League game was staged at the Pirelli sports ground in Dew Lane, Eastleigh, when Cardiff City were the visitors on 4 October 1941. A crowd of 1,850 saw Saints lose 3-1 to a strong Cardiff team.

Just one week later, Saints celebrated their return to The Dell when they defeated local rivals, Bournemouth, in an exciting game by the odd goal in seven.

The most unusual incident during the season was the final League South match at The Dell on Christmas Day when Bristol City were the opponents. City set out in three cars, the last carrying two players and the kit. This vehicle arrived first and although the referee delayed the kick-off, there was no sign of the other two cars.

Eventually the referee insisted that the game must start and with that, Saints manager Tom Parker, offered City five reserves plus trainer Gallagher. City were still only up to eight men and so three spectators stripped to make up the side. The game eventually kicked off one hour later and after 20 minutes the other nine City players arrived, crammed into one car. The other had broken down and the occupants of the second had stopped to help.

The latecomers saw Gallagher score against his own club but Saints eventually won 5-2, Howard netting four times. What most of the spectators did not know, however, was the drama which had unfolded at half-time. With City three goals down and one of their spectator reserves injured, the Bristol club planned to replace the injured man with one of their own latecomers.

Ernie Brinton changed into the muddy kit, applied further mud to his knees, face and hair, and took the field as though he had been playing all match. Almost immediately, he was called upon to take a throw-in, whereupon an eagle-eyed

linesman spotted the 'ringer' and the embarrassed Brinton was sent back to the dressing-room.

The second part of the season was much like the first half with games against the same opponents. This time, however, the results also counted towards the League War Cup qualifying competition and several guest players had now arrived to strengthen the Saints' young side.

Houldsworth, Tait and Bidwell, all with League experience, assisted the club together with another up and coming youngster from Portsmouth called Wally Barnes who was to find fame with Arsenal and Wales. Although Saints qualified for the first round of the War Cup, they suffered a quick exit at the hands of a strong Cardiff side who beat them 4-2 on aggregate.

Sep 27 v Cardiff C (a) 3-5
Roper 3
Oct 4 v Cardiff C (h) 1-3
Laney
Oct 11 v Bournemouth (a) 1-6
opp own goal
Oct 18 v Bournemouth (h) 4-3
Roper 3, Tait
Oct 25 v Luton T (a) 1-2
Tait
Nov 1 v Luton T (h) 5-0
Higham 2, Tait, Roper, Stroud
Nov 22 v Bournemouth (h) 5-2
Laney 2, J.Harris, Tait, Stroud
Nov 29 v Bournemouth (a) 0-5
Dec 20 v Bristol C (a) 2-4
Roper 2
Dec 25 v Bristol C (h) 5-2
Howard 4, Roper

War Cup Qualifying competition

Dec 27 v Cardiff C (h) 2-5
Hassell, Roper
Jan 3 v Cardiff C (a) 1-9
Higham
Jan 31 v Bournemouth (a) 4-3
Higham 2, Roper 2
Feb 7 v Luton T (h) 3-0
Roper 2, Ellerington
Feb 14 v Luton T (a) 6-1
Roper 3, Hassell, Fisher, Bidewell

Feb 21 v Bournemouth (h) 2-2
Creecy, J.Harris
Feb 28 v Bournemouth (a) 0-2
Mar 7 v Bournemouth (h) 1-0
Hassell
Mar 21 v Bristol C (a) 1-5
Roper
Mar 28 v Bristol C (h) 5-1
Roper 2, Tait 2, Ellerington

War Cup

Round 1 (1st leg)
Apr 4 v Cardiff C (a) 1-3
Laney

Round 1 (2nd leg)
Apr 6 v Cardiff C (h) 1-1 (agg 2-4)
J.Harris

Hampshire Combination Cup

May 2 v Aldershot (a) 1-3
Laney

Friendlies

Sep 13 v Army XI (a) 2-5
V.Smith, Stroud
Nov 8 v Southampton Police (h) 5-2
Stroud 2, Laney, Roper, Tait

Nov 15 v Army XI (a) 3-3
Messom, Higham, Roper
Dec 6 v Royal Navy XI (a) 4-5
Laney 2, Hassell, Higham
Dec 13 v Army XI (h) 3-2
Roper, Higham, Laney
Jan 10 v Army XI (h) 1-3
Roper
Mar 14 v Royal Navy XI (h) 6-1
Roper 5, Laney
Apr 28 v Army XI (a) 6-2
Roper 2, Wood 2, Laney, Willis
May 9 v Army XI (h) 3-2
Hassell, Laney, N.Harris

League South

	P	W	D	L	F	A	Pts	Ave
Leicester C	17	11	3	3	40	17	25	26.40
West Brom A	13	9	1	3	62	26	19	26.30
Cardiff C	15	9	1	5	43	28	19	22.80
Norwich C	8	4	2	2	13	10	10	22.50
Bournemouth	10	6	0	4	26	18	12	21.60
Bristol C	15	9	0	6	46	45	18	21.60
Walsall	18	9	1	8	49	45	19	19.00
Northampton T	16	7	2	7	39	38	16	18.00
Wolves	16	6	2	8	27	36	14	15.75
Southampton	10	4	0	6	27	32	8	14.40
Luton T	18	5	1	12	34	73	11	11.00
Nottingham F	13	2	1	10	18	39	5	6.90
Swansea T	9	1	0	8	18	39	2	4.00

Average points calculated on 18 matches

League South
(including War Cup)
APPEARANCES
22 Roper D, 21, Ellerington W, Harris J, Laney L, Stroud W, 19 Roles A, 15 Hassell T, 14 Creecy A, 10 Tait T, 9 Bernard E, Houldsworth F, 8 Fisher K, Higham N, 7 Bidewell S, 6 Messom G, 4 Affleck D, 3 Barnes W, Hankey C, Smith V, 2 Harris N, Howard B, Lanham H, Parrett R, 1 Abbott D, Bryant S, Ellis E, Fox G, House A, McGibbon D, Middleton A, Rolfe, Smith F, Young R.

GOALSCORERS
League: 10 Roper, 4 Howard, Tait, 3 Laney, 2 Higham, Stroud, 1 Harris J, Opp own goal 1.
War Cup: 11 Roper, 3 Hassell, Higham, 2 Ellerington, Harris J, Tait, 1 Bidewell, Creecy, Fisher, Laney.

1942-43

THIS season saw the return of the London club's after a two-season absence and the more glamourous fixture list was a welcome sight. There was a less than glamorous start, however, when a star-studded Aldershot side beat Saints 5-1 at the Recreation Ground.

The following week, Saints made their first trip to London for two years and their only reward was a 6-1 thrashing by Arsenal. It was after these two defeats that Saints, bolstered by several new guest players, turned the corner, as Watford discovered when they were beaten 4-1 at The Dell.

Growing in confidence they went on to record wins of 4-0 and 5-2, against Clapton Orient and Charlton respectively. Then Arsenal visited The Dell for the return fixture. The status of the opposition and Southampton's improved form swelled the attendance to 11,666 and they saw an exciting match.

The clever Tom Finney was drafted into the side and he struck up quite an understanding with Ted Bates. Although Arsenal won the match 3-1, it was the opinion of Saints'

followers that their team had been unlucky. Indeed, had Saints not been reduced to ten men when Bill Stroud sustained an eye injury early in the game.

Three weeks later, an even bigger crowd — 15,363 — paid £1,174 6s 6d to watch the Boxing Day 'derby' against Portsmouth. It was, though, a disappointing game and Saints failed to reproduce anything like their best form.

The most amazing result of the season came on 16 January when Luton were hammered 11-0 at The Dell. This equalled Saints' best score in League football, although the vagaries of wartime soccer should be taken into consideration for this particular goal glut. Against Luton, Alf Whittingham, a guest player from Bradford City, set up a club record by scoring eight goals for Saints that day, thus beating by one goal Albert Brown's feat against Northampton Town some 33 years earlier.

Whittingham was ably supported throughout the season by Bates and Stamps. These three between them netted 72 goals for Southampton in 1942-43.

Derby County centre-forward Jack Stamps had been out of football for 18 months through a knee injury when he met Charlie Mitten on London's Waterloo station late in 1942.

Stamps recalls: "I was fit again and Charlie asked me if I'd turn out for Southampton at Reading that weekend.

"We won 7-2 and I got a goal. Tom Parker asked me if I could play regularly and I stayed with them until the end of the season.

"They were some of the happiest times of my football career. Southampton was a good club and the atmosphere was marvellous. Great days."

Aug 29 v Aldershot (a) 1-5
Barnes
Sep 5 v Arsenal (a) 1-6
Bates
Sep 12 v Watford (h) 4-1
Whittingham 2, Hassell, Stroud
Sep 19 v Reading (a) 2-2
Whittingham 2
Sep 26 v Tottenham H (a) 1-1
Bates
Oct 3 v Clapton O (h) 5-2
Barnes 3, Hassell, Whittingham
Oct 10 v Luton T (a) 0-0
Oct 17 v Chelsea (h) 1-2
J.Harris
Oct 24 v Fulham (h) 4-2
Barnes 2, Whittingham 2
Oct 31 v Queen's Park R (a) 1-3
N.Harris
Nov 7 v Charlton A (h) 4-0
Barnes, J.Harris, Stroud, Whittingham
Nov 14 v Brighton & HA (h) 2-2
J.Harris 2
Nov 22 v Crystal P (a) 1-2
Bates
Nov 28 v Aldershot (h) 2-1
Bates, Stroud
Dec 5 v Arsenal (h) 1-3
Whittingham
Dec 12 v Watford (a) 4-3
Buchanan 2, Barnes, Mitten
Dec 19 v Reading (a) 7-2
Whittingham 4, J.Harris, Stamps, Laney
Dec 25 v Portsmouth (a) 3-2
Whittingham 2, Bates
Dec 26 v Portsmouth (h) 0-2
Jan 2 v Tottenham H (h) 2-1
Bates, Barnes

Jan 9 v Clapton O (a) 2-2
Whittingham, Bates
Jan 16 v Luton T (h) 11-0
Whittingham 8, Stamps 2, Pond
Jan 23 v Chelsea (a) 1-3
J.Harris
Jan 30 v Fulham (a) 8-2
Stamps 2, Whittingham, J.Harris
Feb 6 v Queen's Park R (h) 4-2
Whittingham 2, Barnes, Bates
Feb 13 v Charlton A (a) 3-4
Bates 2, Mitten
Feb 20 v Brighton & HA (a) 6-2
Stamps 3, Mitten 2, Wardle
Feb 27 v Crystal P (h) 5-1
Bates 2, Barnes, J.Harris, Whittingham

South Cup (Group Two)

Mar 6 v Clapton O (h) 1-0
Whittingham
Mar 13 v Queen's Park R (a) 1-2
Whittingham
Mar 20 v Brentford (a) 6-1
Stamps 3, Bates, Griffiths, Whittingham
Mar 27 v Clapton O (a) 0-1
Apr 3 v Queen's Park R (h) 4-1
Davie 2, Barnes, J.Harris
Apr 10 v Brentford (h) 2-1
Barnes, J.Harris

Friendlies

Apr 17 v Millwall (h) 9-3
Bates 3, Stamps 3, Whittingham 3
Apr 24 v Portsmouth (a) 0-0
Apr 26 v West Ham U (a) 0-6
May 1 v West Ham U (h) 5-1
Whittingham 3, Stamps 2

League South

	P	W	D	L	F	A	Pts
Arsenal	28	21	1	6	102	40	43
Tottenham H	28	16	6	6	68	28	38
Queen's Park R	28	18	2	8	64	49	38
Portsmouth	28	16	3	9	66	52	35
Southampton	28	14	5	9	86	58	33
West Ham U	28	14	5	9	80	66	33
Chelsea	28	14	4	10	52	45	32
Aldershot	28	14	2	12	87	77	30
Brentford	28	12	5	11	64	63	29
Charlton A	28	13	3	12	68	75	29
Clapton O	28	11	5	12	54	72	27
Brighton & HA	28	10	5	13	65	73	25
Reading	28	9	6	13	67	74	24
Fulham	28	10	2	16	69	78	22
Crystal P	28	7	5	16	49	75	19
Millwall	28	6	5	17	66	88	17
Watford	28	7	2	19	51	88	16
Luton T	28	4	6	18	43	100	14

South Cup (Group Two)

	P	W	D	L	F	A	Pts
Queen's Park R	6	4	1	1	16	8	9
Southampton	6	4	0	2	14	6	8
Clapton O	6	1	2	3	6	14	4
Brentford	6	1	1	4	7	15	3

League South
(including South Cup)

APPEARANCES
34 Harris J, 31, Roles A, Stroud W, 30 Bates E, 29, Tann B, Whittingham A, 28 Barnes W, 21 Mitten C, 18 Pond N, 14 Stamps, 13 Light W, 11 Rothery H, 10 Buchanan P, Hassell T, 8 Lancy L, Tweedy G, 7 Creecy A, 6 Jones J, 4 Messom G, Roper D, 3 Houldsworth F, Rudkin T, Wardle W, Wright R, 2 Cruckshank J, Davie J, Ferrier R, Griffiths M, Rigg T, Tomlinson R, Bevis W, Bushby T, Finney T, Harris N.

GOALSCORERS
League: 28 Whittingham, 13 Bates, 12 Barnes, 8 Harris J, Stamps, 5 Mitten, 3 Stroud, 2 Buchanan, Hassell, 1 Harris N, Laney, Pond, Wardle, 1 Opp own goal.
South Cup: 3 Stamps, Whittingham, 2 Barnes, Davie, Harris J, 1 Bates, Griffiths.

1943-44

MANY new players were introduced in 1943-44, with 53 taking part in the main programmme compared to 37 used during the previous campaign. It was also a season when several old faces were missing. Gone were the likes of Barnes, Harris (who had been with Saints since the outbreak of war) and Mitten who had all moved to London clubs.

The most signficant absentee, however, was the club's secretary-manager, Tom Parker, who resigned in June to take up employment outside the town. Southampton chairman Mr Sarjantson, a director since 1914, stood down to take over as secretary-manager, with former player, Arthur Dominy, assuming the role of team manager. Not surprisingly, in view of all the changes, Saints had a disappointing season and won only 12 League and Cup games. Less goals were scored, and more conceded than the previous season. Saints worst-ever reverse was recorded when Aldershot, packed with international guest players, hammered Southampton 10-1 at the Recreation Ground in December.

Whittingham, still 'on loan' from Bradford City, topped the scorers with 28 goals from 29 games, followed by Roper (20) and Bates (18). Of the new men introduced during the season, mainly guest players with League experience, was a young serviceman called Alf Ramsey. Although he made only six appearances, Ramsey quickly caught the eye.

Aug 28 v Aldershot (h) 2-2
Davie, Seddon
Sep 4 v Arsenal (a) 1-4
Bates
Sep 11 v Watford (a) 1-6
Bates
Sep 18 v Charlton A (h) 1-2
Davie
Sep 25 v Tottenham H (a) 2-2
Davie, Wardle
Oct 2 v Millwall (h) 1-0
Davie
Oct 9 v Luton T (a) 3-2
Roper, Bates, Evans
Oct 16 v West Ham U (h) 2-4
Bates, Whittingham

Oct 23 v Fulham (h) 2-3
Whittingham 2
Oct 30 v Queen's Park R (a) 0-7
Nov 6 v Reading (a) 5-3
Roper 3, Bates, Whittingham
Nov 13 v Brighton & HA (a) 4-2
Stroud, Roper, Whittingham, Evans
Nov 20 v Crystal P (h) 2-2
Whittingham 2
Nov 27 v Aldershot (a) 1-10
Wardle
Dec 4 v Arsenal (h) 1-2
Stroud
Dec 11 v Watford (h) 4-1
Stroud, Roper, Whittingham, Wardle

Dec 18 v Brentford (a) 2-7
Roper, Stroud
Dec 25 v Portsmouth (h) 6-3
Whittingham 2, Dodgin, Bates, opp own goal 2
Dec 27 v Portsmouth (a) 2-4
Whittingham, Sheppard
Jan 1 v Charlton A (a) 2-2
Whittingham, Roper
Jan 8 v Reading (a) 3-2
Roper 2, Whittingham
Jan 15 v Tottenham H (a) 2-3
Roper, Staton
Jan 22 v Millwall (a) 5-1
Roper 2, Roles, Whittingham, Wardle
Jan 29 v Luton T (h) 3-0
Roper 2, Whittingham

1943-44

Feb 5 v West Ham U (a) 1-4
Roper
Feb 12 v Fulham (a) 2-6
Whittingham 2
Apr 4 v Queen's Park R (h) 2-2
Bates, Grant
Apr 22 v Brentford (h) 2-2
Roper, Whittingham
Apr 29 v Brighton & HA (h) 3-0
Roper, Bates, Whittingham
May 6 v Crystal P (a) 0-0

League South Cup

Feb 19 v Chelsea (a) 2-3
Whittingham 2
Feb 26 v West Ham U (h) 1-2
Whittingham
Mar 4 v Watford (h) 3-1
Whittingham 3
Mar 11 v Chelsea (h) 1-5
Grant
Mar 18 v West Ham U (a) 1-5
Whittingham
Mar 25 v Watford (a) 4-1
Whittingham, Roper, Bates, Grant

Hampshire Combination Cup

Apr 10 v Army XI (h) 4-2
Dawes 2, Bates, Roper

Friendlies

Aug 21 v Army XI (h) 10-3
Davie 4, Bates 2, Roper 2, Halton, Golden
Apr 8 v Portsmouth (a) 1-2
Hodges
Apr 15 v Portsmouth (h) 3-0
Barnes 2, Whittingham

League South
(including South Cup)
APPEARANCES
36 Roles A, Roper D, 35 Bates E, 28 Dodgin W, Stroud W, Whittingham A, 21 Drinkwater J, 20 Jones J, 17 Evans H, 15 Pond H, Shimwell E, 13 Wardle W, 10 Hamilton D, 9 Houldsworth F, 7 Davie J, Grant W, 6 Halton R, Warhurst S, 5 Ramsey A, Staton N, Tann B, 4 Corbett N, 3 Anderson J, Bonass A, Coupland J, Seddon E, Sneddon T, 2 Almond K, Eggleston T, Sheppard D, Webber E, 1 Affleck D, Allen J, Arnold J, Carter V, Clements S, Corbett W, Crossland B, Fisher F, Freeman A, Laney L, Lewis D, Miles A, Mitten C, Ramsbottom E, Smith J, Thomas R, Whitworth J.

GOALSCORERS
League: 19 Whittingham, 18 Roper, 7 Bates, 4 Davie, Stroud, Wardle, 2 Evans, 1 Dodgin, Grant, Roles, Seddon, Sheppard, Smith, Staton, Opp own goal 2.
South Cup: 8 Whittingham, 2 Grant, 1 Bates, Roper.

League South

	P	W	D	L	F	A	Pts
Tottenham H	30	19	8	3	71	36	46
West Ham U	30	17	7	6	74	39	41
Queen's Park R	30	14	12	4	69	54	40
Arsenal	30	14	10	6	72	42	38
Crystal P	30	16	5	9	75	53	37
Portsmouth	30	16	5	9	68	59	37
Brentford	30	14	7	9	71	51	35
Chelsea	30	16	2	12	79	55	34
Fulham	30	11	9	10	80	73	31
Millwall	30	13	4	13	70	66	30
Aldershot	30	12	6	12	64	73	30
Reading	30	12	3	15	73	62	27
Southampton	30	10	7	13	67	88	27
Charlton A	30	9	7	14	57	73	25
Watford	30	6	8	16	58	80	20
Brighton & HA	30	9	2	19	55	82	20
Luton T	30	3	5	22	42	104	11
Clapton O	30	4	3	23	32	87	11

League South Cup

	P	W	D	L	F	A	Pts
Chelsea	6	4	1	1	17	10	9
West Ham U	6	3	0	3	15	11	6
Watford	6	2	1	3	7	13	5
Southampton	6	2	0	4	12	17	4

1944-45

SAINTS played 41 matches, 30 in the League and six in the Cup, with four friendlies and a Hampshire Combination Cup match against Chelsea making up the rest.

Saints did well in the League, winning 17 matches, and missed leadership of their Cup group by only one point, behind Chelsea, the eventual winners of the trophy. Goals came freely — 153 in 41 matches giving an average of 3.75 per game. It was in the Cup that Saints found the net most consistently, scoring 29 in six games, an average of almost five per match.

In one game Saints fans saw 15 goals scored when Luton crashed 12-3 at The Dell. It was Southampton's highest score in wartime soccer, beating their 11-0 scoreline over the same opponents two seasons earlier.

In the League, Saints got off to a fine start, beating Watford 9-0 at The Dell and quickly following up that with away wins at Queen's Park Rangers and Millwall. During the season they enjoyed unbeaten runs of eight and seven matches respectively and they completed their programme with three wins and 14 goals.

Don Roper proved to be Saints' chief League marksman, with 20 goals, and he added three in the Cup and 12 in other games. Whittingham (27) and Dorsett (25) were hard on his heels.

Saints called up 43 players and only 16 played in ten or more matches. Most of the team were on Saints' books and only 14 guests appeared throughout the season.

League South

	P	W	D	L	F	A	Pts
Tottenham H	30	23	6	1	81	30	52
West Ham U	30	22	3	5	96	47	47
Brentford	30	17	4	9	87	57	38
Chelsea	30	16	5	9	100	55	37
Southampton	30	17	3	10	96	69	37
Crystal P	30	15	5	10	74	70	35
Reading	30	14	6	10	78	68	34
Arsenal	30	14	3	13	77	67	31
Queen's Park R	30	10	10	10	70	61	30
Watford	30	11	6	13	66	84	28
Fulham	30	11	4	15	79	83	26
Portsmouth	30	11	4	15	56	61	26
Charlton A	30	12	2	16	72	81	26
Brighton & HA	30	10	2	18	66	95	22
Luton T	30	6	7	17	56	104	19
Aldershot	30	7	4	19	44	85	18
Millwall	30	5	7	18	50	84	17
Clapton O	30	5	7	18	39	86	17

League South Cup (Group Four)

	P	W	D	L	F	A	Pts
Chelsea	6	5	1	0	13	3	11
Southampton	6	4	2	0	29	11	10
Charlton A	6	4	1	1	16	5	9
Luton T	6	1	1	4	8	25	3
Crystal P	6	0	2	4	5	13	2
Watford	6	0	1	5	6	20	1

Aug 26 v Watford (h) 9-0
Whittingham 4, Roper 3, Bates, Walker
Sep 2 v Queen's Park R (a) 5-4
Roper 2, Walker 2, Whittingham
Sep 9 v Millwall (a) 4-1
Grant 2, Roper, Whittingham
Sep 16 v Arsenal (h) 0-2
Sep 23 v Tottenham H (h) 1-3
Bates
Sep 30 v Portsmouth (a) 1-3
Whittingham
Oct 7 v Fulham (a) 3-4
Roper 2, Bates
Oct 14 v Charlton A (h) 3-3
Grant 2, Walker
Oct 21 v Clapton O (h) 6-2
Roper 5, Hassell
Oct 28 v Reading (a) 5-1
Dorsett 2, H.Evans, Mills, Grant
Nov 4 v Chelsea (h) 3-3
Dorsett 3
Nov 11 v Brentford (a) 1-0
Grant
Nov 18 v West Ham U (h) 2-1
Bates, Roper
Nov 25 v Aldershot (h) 7-2
Dorsett 3, Stroud, Roper, Bates, Walker
Dec 2 v Watford (a) 1-2
Walker

Dec 9 v Queen's Park R (h) 4-5
Hassell, Bates, Dorsett, Mills
Dec 16 v Millwall (h) 5-3
Whittingham 3, Dorsett, Hassell
Dec 23 v Brighton & HA (h) 3-2
Whittingham 2, Walker
Dec 26 v Brighton & HA (a) 0-2
Dec 30 v Arsenal (a) 4-2
Roper, Bates, Whittingham, Hassell
Jan 6 v Tottenham H (a) 0-4
Jan 13 v Portsmouth (h) 2-4
Roper, Whittingham
Jan 20 v Fulham (h) 3-0
Dorsett 2, Whittingham
Jan 27 v Charlton A (a) 5-3
Whittingham 3, Dorsett, Hassell
Mar 17 v Clapton O (a) 0-1
Mar 24 v Reading (h) 1-1
Dorsett
Mar 31 v Chelsea (a) 4-3
Dorsett 2, Mills 2
Apr 14 v Brentford (h) 4-2
Bradley 3, Hassell
Apr 21 v West Ham U (a) 5-3
Bradley 2, Roper 2, Bates
Apr 28 v Aldershot (a) 5-3
Bradley 2, Roper, Bates, Mills

107

League South Cup

Feb 3 v Crystal P (h) 4-1
Dorsett 2, Roper, Whittingham
Feb 10 v Luton T (a) 2-2
Bates, Roper
Feb 17 v Watford (a) 6-1
Dorsett 3, Bates, Roper, Whittingham
Feb 24 v Crystal P (a) 3-3
Dorsett 2, Whittingham
Mar 3 v Luton T (h) 12-3
Whittingham 4, Ramsey 4, Hassell 2, Bates, Stroud
Mar 10 v Watford (h) 2-1
Bates, Whittingham

Hampshire Combination Cup

May 21 v Chelsea (h) 4-6
Roper 4

Friendlies

Apr 2 v Brighton & HA (h) 2-2
Dorsett 2
Apr 7 v Portsmouth (a) 4-7
Hassell 2, N.Corbett, Roper
May 9 v Army XI (h) 9-2
Osgood 3, Roper 2, Veck 2, Dodgin, De Lisle
May 12 v RAF XI (a) 9-3
Roper 5, Osgood 2, Higgins, Stroud

League South
(including South Cup)

APPEARANCES
36 Bates E, Roles A, Stroud W, 33 Roper D, 30 Dodgin W,
24 Hassell T, 21 Warhurst S, 20 Evans H, Whittingham A,
16 Dorsett R, 15 Moss F, 14 Stansbridge L, 13 Walker S,
11 Evans R, Ramsey A, 10 Grant W, 9 Eggleston T,
7 Mills G, Stear J, 6 Roberts E, 4 Bradley J, 2 Clements S,
Tann B, Taylor R, 1 Corbett R, Dempsey A, Jones C,
Lonnon C, McDonald J, Miles G, Pond H, Rothery H,
Sheppard D, Summerbee G, Swindin G.

GOALSCORERS
League: 20 Roper, 18 Whittingham, 16 Dorsett, 9 Bates,
7 Bradley, Walker, 6 Grant, Hassell, 5 Mills, 1 Evans H,
Stroud.
South Cup 8 Whittingham, 7 Dorsett, 4 Bates, Ramsey,
3 Roper, 2 Hassell, 1 Stroud.

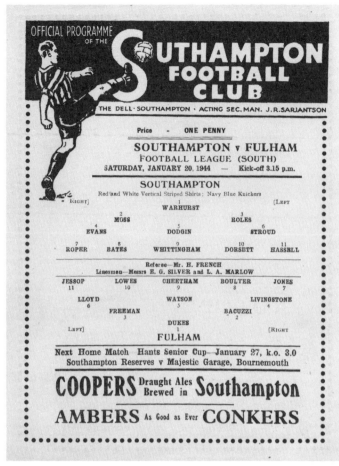

Match programme for Saints' League South game against Fulham on 20 January 1945. The printer, however, seems to have forgotten to change his calendar.

1945-46

ALTHOUGH the war in Europe was over, there was no quick return to the peacetime football set-up. The League South, however, was reinforced by Midlands clubs and the old 42-match programme reintroduced in preparation for the resumption of the Football League the following season.

Birmingham won the League title whilst Southampton, with a new side taking shape, finished with 37 points. It proved to be a season of ups and downs, with some exhilarating successes and some downright flops.

Saints' biggest win was their 7-0 success over Chelsea when Doug McGibbon set his personal record of six goals in a game. McGibbon also wrote his name in the record books with what is claimed as the fastest-ever goal from a kick-off.

The Saints man had the ball in the net within seconds of the second half starting. Some sources give the time as less than five seconds, although it is hard to imagine it would be possible to work the ball into the net from the centre-spot in such a time. Whatever the time, Chelsea were hammered

— and that after they had sportingly loaned Peter Buchanan to ten-man Saints.

Saints also scored impressive victories over Charlton and Derby, that season's FA Cup Finalists, although at the Baseball Ground, Derby beat Southampton 8-1 when hat-tricks from Angus Morrison and Jack Stamps inflicted upon Southampton their heaviest defeat of the season. Stamps was the man who had scored some useful goals as a Saints guest in 1942-43.

Don Roper played in every match with 15 players each making double-figure appearances. McGibbon easily topped the scoring list with 29 goals in 34 appearances. Bates, who was the most consistent of the forwards, and Bradley each scored 16 goals, with Roper finding the net 12 times.

The team had made good progress and, with a nicely balanced blend of youth and experience, was ready for the return of League football.

Southampton were presented with a complete set of kit by the Argentinian FA.

Admiral Louis Mountbatten became Saints' president in this, their diamond jubilee year.

Aug 25 v Plymouth A (h) 5-5
Ramsey 2, Bates, Bradley, Hassell
Sep 1 v Plymouth A (a) 3-0
Ramsey 2, Bradley
Sep 8 v Portsmouth (a) 2-3
Bradley 2
Sep 12 v Chelsea (a) 0-1
Sep 15 v Portsmouth (h) 3-1
Bradley, Bates, Roper
Sep 22 v Nottingham F (h) 5-2
Bradley, Bates, Roper, Veck, opp own goal
Sep 29 v Nottingham F (a) 0-4
Oct 6 v Newport C (a) 6-2
Ramsey 3, Bates, Evans, Roper
Oct 13 v Newport C (h) 0-0
Oct 20 v Wolves (h) 2-4
McGibbon 2
Oct 27 v Wolves (a) 2-3
Hassell, McGibbon
Nov 3 v West Ham U (a) 1-3
McGibbon
Nov 10 v West Ham U (h) 3-3
McGibbon 2, Bradley
Nov 17 v West Brom A (h) 1-2
Hassell
Nov 24 v West Brom A (a) 2-5
Roper, opp own goal
Dec 1 v Birmingham C (h) 1-1
Stroud
Dec 8 v Birmingham C (a) 1-4
Stroud
Dec 15 v Tottenham H (h) 3-2
McGibbon 2, Day
Dec 22 v Tottenham H (a) 3-4
Bates, McGibbon, Roper
Dec 25 v Brentford (a) 4-1
Bates, Bradley, Evans, McGibbon
Dec 26 v Brentford (h) 3-4
Bates, Bradley, McGibbon
Dec 29 v Chelsea (h) 7-0
McGibbon 6, Bates
Jan 12 v Swansea T (a) 1-4
Roper
Jan 19 v Swansea T (h) 5-2
McGibbon 2, Roper 2, Veck
Feb 2 v Derby C (a) 1-8
Bradley
Feb 9 v Leicester C (a) 2-1
Evans, Veck
Feb 16 v Leicester C (h) 3-1
Bradley, McGibbon, G.Smith
Feb 23 v Coventry C (h) 4-3
McGibbon 2, Bates, G.Smith
Mar 2 v Coventry C (a) 1-0
Evans
Mar 9 v Luton T (a) 2-4
McGibbon, G.Smith

Mar 16 v Luton T (h) 2-2
Bates, Bradley
Mar 23 v Aston Villa (h) 3-5
Bradley 2, Bates
Mar 30 v Aston Villa (a) 0-2
Apr 6 v Arsenal (a) 1-1
Bates
Apr 8 v Millwall (a) 3-5
Bates, Evans, Heathcote
Apr 13 v Arsenal (h) 1-1
Roper
Apr 19 v Charlton A (h) 3-1
McGibbon 2, Veck
Apr 20 v Fulham (a) 1-4
McGibbon
Apr 22 v Charlton A (a) 1-1
Roper
Apr 27 v Fulham (h) 1-1
Evans
Apr 29 v Derby C (h) 4-2
Bates, Bevis, Roper, Veck
May 4 v Millwall (h) 2-4
McGibbon, opp own goal

FA Cup

Round 3 (1st leg)
Jan 5 v Newport C (h) 4-3
Bates, Bradley, McGibbon, Roper
Stansbridge; Emanuel, Roles, Evans, Dodgin, Stroud, Bates, McGibbon, Roper, Veck, Bradley.

League South

	P	W	D	L	F	A	Pts
Birmingham C	42	28	5	9	96	45	61
Aston Villa	42	25	11	6	106	58	61
Charlton A	42	25	10	7	92	45	60
Derby C	42	24	7	11	101	62	55
West Brom A	42	22	8	12	104	69	52
Wolves	42	20	11	11	75	48	51
West Ham U	42	20	11	11	94	76	51
Fulham	42	20	10	12	93	73	50
Tottenham H	42	22	3	17	78	81	47
Chelsea	42	19	6	17	92	80	44
Arsenal	42	16	11	15	76	73	43
Millwall	42	17	8	17	79	105	42
Coventry C	42	15	10	17	70	69	40
Brentford	42	14	10	18	82	72	38
Nottingham F	42	12	13	17	72	73	37
Southampton	42	14	9	19	97	105	37
Swansea T	42	15	7	20	90	112	37
Luton T	42	13	7	22	60	92	33
Portsmouth	42	11	6	25	66	87	28
Leicester C	42	8	7	27	57	101	23
Newport C	42	9	2	31	52	125	20
Plymouth A	42	3	8	31	39	120	14

Round 3 (2nd leg)
Jan 10 v Newport C (a) 2-1 (agg 6-4)
McGibbon, Veck
Stansbridge; Emanuel, Roles, Evans, Dodgin, Stroud, Bates, McGibbon, Roper, Veck, Bradley.
Round 4 (1st leg)
Jan 26 v Queen's Park R (h) 0-1
Stansbridge; Ellerington, Roles, Evans, Dodgin, Stroud, Roper, Bates, McGibbon, Bradley, Veck.
Round 4 (2nd leg)
Jan 30 v Queen's Park R (a) 3-4 (agg 3-5)
Bradley, Bevis, Ellerington
Stansbridge; Ellerington, Roles, Evans, Dodgin, Stroud, Roper, Bates, McGibbon, Bradley, Bevis.

Hampshire Combination Cup

May 11 v Bournemouth (h) 3-4
Davies 2, Bates

Friendlies

May 2 v Bournemouth (a) 3-1
Sherratt 2, Veck
May 28 v Le Havre (a) 1-1
Roper

League South
APPEARANCES
42 Roper D, 40 Bates E, Roles A, 36 Stroud W, 34 Evans H, 30 McGibbon D, 28 Ellerington W, Veck R, 25 Bradley J, 19 Warhurst S, 18 Dodgin W, 15 Smith G, 14 Webber E, 13 Ramsey A, 12 Hassell T, 7 Bevis W, 6 Ephgrave G, Sibley E, 5 Black I, Egglestone T, Emanuel T, 4 Cruickshank J, Stansbridge L, 3 Gregory J, Jones J, Stear J, Wilkins L, 2 Davies M, Day E, 1 Brooks W, Clements S, Hancon W, Heathcote W, Kingston A, McDonald J, Mountford R, Powell S, Stout I, Whittingham A.

GOALSCORERS
27 McGibbon, 14 Bates, Bradley, 11 Roper, 7 Ramsey, 6 Evans, 5 Veck, 3 Hassell, Smith, 1 Bevis, Day, Heathcote, Stroud, Opp own goal 3.

FA Cup
APPEARANCES
4 Bates E, Bradley J, Dodgin W, Evans H, McGibbon D, Roles A, Roper D, Stansbridge L, Stroud, 3 Veck R, 2 Ellerington W, Emanuel T, 1 Bevis W.

GOALSCORERS
2 Bradley, McGibbon, 1 Bates, Bevis, Ellerington, Roper, Veck.

Back row (left to right): Dominy, Stroud, Ellerington, Warhurst, Jones, Roles, J.R.Sarjantson (director), G.Smith, Gallagher, L.Wilkins. Front: H.Evans, Bates, McGibbon, W.Dodgin (manager), Roper, B.Veck, E.Webber.

1946-47

ALTHOUGH the FA Cup had started in earnest in 1945-46, it was not until September 1946 that Southampton's League season began. Strangely, the much-awaited kick-off was delayed when their original opening match, against Newport County, was called off due to a waterlogged pitch.

When the season eventually got underway, Saints notched up a fine 4-0 win over another Welsh club, Swansea Town, with McGibbon scoring a hat-trick. The result was a credit to a side that contained no less than eight League debutants — although it has to be said that, after seven years of war, most teams included a similar number.

In the last few years of wartime football Mr Sarjantson had built a sound squad of players, including men like Webber, Bates, Bevis and Smith who had all been at The Dell in pre-war days. Although Saints were not serious promotion candidates, it was apparent that, with the emergence of players like Ellerington, Ramsey and Day, Southampton would be a force in future seasons.

FA Cup

THE Saints were fortunate to be drawn at home against Bury in the third round of the Cup. On a rainy day and with a muddy pitch to overcome, Southampton won the toss and attacked the Milton Road goal.

It took ten minutes for Saints to mount a serious attack, but when they did, it brought them a goal from Bradley. Lewis made it 2-0 from a free-kick and Bevis added a third by converting an Eric Day cross.

Although Saints had built up a handsome lead, Bury kept Ephgrave busy in the Southampton goal. After 32 minutes, Bury reduced the deficit with a penalty kick, but any hopes of a famous fightback were dashed when Lewis added two more goals in the second half to complete a well-deserved hat-trick.

In the next round the Saints were drawn against Newcastle at St James's Park. About 700 Southampton fans made the journey north and the gates were closed 15 minutes before kick-off with almost 56,000 in the ground.

Saints won the toss and soon found their rhythm. Roper gave them a surprise but deserved lead, a lead which Southampton held until half-time.

That was when things began to go badly wrong for the Hampshire club. The man who destroyed them was Charlie Wayman. Wayman equalised within five minutes of the restart, and nine minutes later a mistake by Ephgrave let him in for his second.

In the dying seconds, with Saints still pushing forward in search of an equaliser, Wayman confirmed that their Cup aspirations were over for another season.

The defeat at Newcastle was significant for two reasons. First, Bill Ellerington was missing because of pneumonia and Alf Ramsey took his place. It was the start of a long run in the first team for Ramsey and within 18 months Saints were to possess, unusually for a Second Division club, two England right-backs.

It was in this Cup match that manager Bill Dodgin first appreciated the goalscoring skills of Charlie Wayman, who was to become a great asset to Southampton.

> **Round 3**
> **Jan 11 v Bury (h) 5-1**
> *Lewis 3, Bradley, Bevis*
> Ephgrave; Ellerington, Rochford, Stroud, Webber, Smith, Bevis, Roper, Lewis, Bradley, Day.
> *Att: 19,707*
> **Round 4**
> **Jan 25 v Newcastle United (a) 1-3**
> *Roper*
> Ephgrave; Ramsey, Rochford, Stroud, Webber, Smith, Bevis, Roper, Lewis, Bradley, Day.
> *Att: 55,873*

> Saints aggregate home attendance was 336,823, giving an average of 16,039 per match. The 'gate' of 4,289 for the visit of Coventry is the lowest attendance at The Dell for a post-war League game.

> Saints' balance sheet for the first post-war season showed a total income of £41,032, from which £22,935 was spent on salaries and transfers. A further £1,986 went on home match expenses, whilst £7,952 was paid to the government as entertainment tax.

Tom Lewis scored a hat-trick against Bury in the FA Cup

Alf Ramsey continued his illustrious career after Ellerington was sidelined through illness.

110

1946-47
Division 2

Date		Opponent	Res	Score	Scorers	Att	Bates E	Bevis W	Bradley W	Bushby W	Clements S	Day E	Ellerington W	Ephgrave G	Evans H	Freeman G	Grant W	Gregory J	Horsfall G	Lewis T	McGibbon D	Mallett J	Ramsey A	Rochford W	Roper D	Smith G	Stansbridge L	Stroud W	Veck R	Webber E
Sep 4	(h)	Swansea T	W	4-0	McGibbon 3, Veck	8,000			10				2	1			8				9			3	7	6		4	11	5
7	(h)	Bury	D	1-1	Bradley	23,000	8		10				2	1							9			3	7	6		4	11	5
9	(a)	Tottenham H	L	1-2	McGibbon	22,153	8		10				2	1							9			3	7	6		4	11	5
14	(h)	Nottingham F	W	5-2	Freeman 2, McGibbon 2, Bradley	17,991			10				2	1		8					9			3	7	6		4	11	5
21	(a)	Coventry C	L	0-2		20,000			10				2	1		8					9			3	7	6		4	11	5
28	(h)	Birmingham C	W	1-0	Bradley	24,920	8		10				2	1							9			3	7	6		4	11	5
Oct 3	(a)	Swansea T	L	2-4	Bates, Bradley	21,523	8		10				2	1							9			3	7	6		4	11	5
5	(a)	West Brom A	L	0-2		28,000	8		10	4			2	1						11	9			3	7	6				5
12	(h)	Newcastle U	D	1-1	Bates	25,746	8	7					2	1			10			11	9			3		6		4		5
19	(a)	Luton T	D	2-2	Grant, Opp own goal	20,000	8	7					2	1			10			11	9			3		6		4		5
24	(a)	Newport C	W	2-1	Bevis, Lewis	11,149		8	10				2	1						11	9			3	7	6		4		5
26	(h)	Plymouth A	W	5-1	Bradley 2, Grant 2, McGibbon	18,252			10					1			8			11	9		2	3	7	6		4		5
Nov 2	(a)	Leicester C	L	0-2		20,000			10					1			8			11	9		2	3	7	6		4		5
9	(h)	Chesterfield	D	1-1	McGibbon	18,006			10				2	1			8			11	9			3	7	6		4		5
16	(a)	Millwall	L	1-3	Smith	24,413	8		10			11	2	1							9			3	7	6		4		5
23	(h)	Bradford	W	3-2	Stroud, Bevis, Roper	16,249		8	10			11	2	1	9									3	7	6		4		5
30	(a)	Manchester C	D	1-1	Bates	24,867	8		10			11	2	1							9			3	7	6		4		5
Dec 7	(h)	West Ham U	W	4-2	Ellerington, Bevis, Roper, McGibbon	17,305		8	10			11	2	1							9			3	7	6		4		5
14	(a)	Sheffield W	L	0-3		10,000		8	10			11	2	1							9			3	7	6		4		5
25	(a)	Barnsley	D	4-4	Lewis 2, Stroud, Bevis	16,200		8	10			11	2	1						9				3	7	6		4		5
26	(h)	Barnsley	D	1-1	Ramsey	21,556		8	10			11		1						9			2	3				4		5
28	(h)	Newport C	W	5-1	Bradley 2, Stroud, Bevis, Lewis	17,778		8	10			11		1						9			2	3	7			4		5
Jan 4	(a)	Bury	L	1-2	Lewis	16,000			10			11		1			7			9			2	3			4	8		5
18	(a)	Nottingham F	L	0-6		20,000	7					11	2	1			10			9				3		6		4		5
Feb 1	(a)	Birmingham C	L	1-3	Bradley	32,878			10	4		11					7			9			2	3	8	6	1			5
5	(h)	Coventry C	W	5-2	Lewis 2, Roper, Bradley, Day	4,289			10			11					7			9			2	3	8	4	1	6		5
8	(h)	West Brom A	L	0-1		8,000			10			11					7			9			2	3	8	4	1	6		5
15	(a)	Newcastle U	W	3-1	Stroud, Roper, Day	35,000			10			11					7			9			2	3	8	4	1	6		5
22	(h)	Luton T	L	1-3	Roper	11,700			10			11					7	3		9			2		8	4	1	6		5
Mar 1	(a)	Plymouth A	W	3-2	Lewis 2, Mallett	24,071			6			11					7			9		8	2	3	10	4	1			5
22	(h)	Millwall	L	1-2	Lewis	14,922			6			11					7			9		8	2	3	10	4	1			5
29	(a)	Bradford	W	3-2	Lewis 2, Roper	10,000			10			1					11			9		8	2	3	7	4				5
Apr 4	(a)	Burnley	L	0-1		31,713			6			10					1			11	9	8	2	3	7	4				5
4	(h)	Manchester C	L	0-1		24,197			6			10					1			11	9	8	2	3	7	4				5
7	(a)	Burnley	L	0-1		19,319			6			10					1			11	9	8	2	3	7	4				5
12	(a)	West Ham U	L	0-4		21,000			6			11					1			9		8	2	3	7	4		10		5
19	(h)	Sheffield W	W	3-1	Bradley 2, Roper	13,514			10								1			11	9	8	2	3	7	4	1	6		5
26	(h)	Fulham	D	0-0		14,087			10								1			11	9	8	2	3	7	4	1	6		5
May 3	(a)	Chesterfield	L	0-5		10,000			10			11						6	9			8	2	3	7	4	1			5
10	(a)	Tottenham H	W	1-0	Roper	12,436			10									6	9			8	2	3	7	4	1		11	5
24	(h)	Fulham	W	2-0	Bates, Bradley	9,738	8		10		5						9					6	2	3	7	4	1		11	
26	(h)	Leicester C	D	1-1	Bradley	9,905			10		5			8			9					6	2	3	7	4	1		11	
App							22	14	38	2	2	19	19	29	1	7	21	1	2	28	12	13	23	41	40	34	13	29	12	40
Goals							4	5	14			2	1			2	3			12	9	1	1		8	1		4	1	

Opp own goal 1

	P	W	D	L	F	A	Pts
Manchester C	42	26	10	6	78	35	62
Burnley	42	22	14	6	65	29	58
Birmingham C	42	25	5	12	74	33	55
Chesterfield	42	18	14	10	58	44	50
Newcastle U	42	19	10	13	95	62	48
Tottenham H	42	17	14	11	65	53	48
West Brom A	42	20	8	14	88	75	48
Coventry C	42	16	13	13	66	59	45
Leicester C	42	18	7	17	69	64	43
Barnsley	42	17	8	17	84	86	42
Nottingham F	42	15	10	17	69	74	40
West Ham U	42	16	8	18	70	76	40
Luton T	42	16	7	19	71	73	39
Southampton	42	15	9	18	69	76	39
Fulham	42	15	9	18	63	74	39
Bradford	42	14	11	17	65	77	39
Bury	42	12	12	18	80	78	36
Millwall	42	14	8	20	56	79	36
Plymouth A	42	14	5	23	79	96	33
Sheffield W	42	12	8	22	67	88	32
Swansea T	42	11	7	24	55	83	29
Newport C	42	10	3	29	61	133	23

Back row (left to right): Veck, Stroud, Bushby, Ellerington, Ephgrave, S.Warhurst (trainer), Rochford, Smith, J.R.Sarjantson (secretary), Wilkins. Front: Roper, Bates, Lewis, W.Dodgin (manager), Bradley, Grant, Webber.

1947-48

IN the close season Bill Dodgin replaced Sarjantson as Saints' manager and, after selling rising star and local favourite Don Roper to Arsenal (Curtis and Rudkin coming to The Dell in part-exchange), spent a fruitless summer trying to sign more new players.

The task proved immensely frustrating with either the fee too large or the players themselves reluctant to undergo the upheaval of moving perhaps hundreds of miles. In those days, of course, the maximum wage meant that there was no financial inducement — at least no legal one — that could tempt a player, and, many of the men Saints approached no doubt felt they would be no better off for uprooting their families.

Nevertheless, Dodgin was busy and, according to the *Football Echo*, he tried to sign Munro, Eastham and Blair (Blackpool), Wayman and Stobbart (Newcastle), Turnbull and Smith (Hibernian), Stamps (Derby), Mulraney (Birmingham), Carter (Bury) and Allen (Queen's Park Rangers).

Such an extensive search led to only one new player — but what an asset he turned out to be. Charlie Wayman, the man who scored a Cup hat-trick against Saints the previous year, made his debut, against Birmingham, in front of a packed crowd at The Dell. He quickly became a local hero and the spearhead of a rapidly improving side.

Promotion was a serious possibility and Saints ended the season with a flourish, collecting nine out of ten points to finish third and give supporters great hope for 1948-49.

FA Cup

SUNDERLAND, fielding three of their 1937 Cup-winning team in the shape of goalkeeper Mapson and wingers Duns and Burbanks, were the third round visitors to The Dell. The Wearsiders began as though they would take charge but Black, in the Saints' goal, held firm and then Wayman's shot was followed up by Day for the only goal of the game.

It was Day who settled the fourth round issue against Blackburn, also at The Dell. He and Curtis were particularly effective on a soft pitch and Day's winning goal, five minutes from time, was watched by a crowd of more than 24,000 who paid record receipts of £3,008.

Saints passage into the quarter-finals was relatively easy. Another home draw brought Swindon to The Dell and the Wiltshire club were down to ten men after only eight minutes when Kaye, their right-half, was injured. Wayman with a shot from a narrow angle, Curtis with a header, and an own-goal sent Saints safely through.

Yet again Southampton were drawn at home. Tottenham, then also a Second Division side, were such attractive visitors that the Saints' directors decided to make the game all-ticket. Demand was so intense that, according to one report, some 66,000 people applied for the 6,000 Milton Road tickets available.

Sadly, the game did not fulfil expectations and, although Saints were the better side, it was Spurs who scored the only goal of the game 20 minutes from time after an error by Webber. Saints were thus denied their first semi-final appearance for 21 years.

Round 3
Jan 10 v Sunderland (h) 1-0
Day
Black; Ellerington, Ramsey, Smith, Webber, Mallett, Day, Curtis, Wayman, Bates, Wrigglesworth.
Att: 24,288
Round 4
Jan 24 v Blackburn Rovers (h) 3-2
Day 2, Wayman
Black; Ramsey, Rochford, Smith, Webber, Mallett, Day, Curtis, Wayman, Bates, Wrigglesworth.
Att: 24,274
Round 5
Feb 7 v Swindon Town (h) 3-0
Wayman, Curtis, opp.og
Black; Ramsey, Rochford, Smith, Webber, Mallett, Day, Curtis, Wayman, Bates, Rudkin.
Att: 29,134
Feb 28 v Tottenham Hotspur (h) 0-1
Black; Ramsey, Rochford, Smith, Webber, Mallett, Day, Curtis, Wayman, Bates, Grant.
Att: 28,425

At the end of the season, Saints sailed aboard the Andes to Brazil where they became the first English League club to tour that country. Referee George Reader, later to become Saints' chairman, went with them.

During the season, the pitch at The Dell was widened by one yard.

For coaching purposes, a model football pitch, scale one-inch to one-yard, was installed in the home dressing-room at The Dell.

Total home attendance: 435,435. Average: 20,735.

Spurs goalkeeper, Ted Ditchburn, collects the ball during the FA Cup sixth round tie at The Dell in February 1948.

1947-48
Division 2

Date	V	Opponent	R	Score	Scorers	Att	Ballard E	Bates E	Beattie G	Black I	Bradley J	Clements S	Curtis G	Day E	Ellerington W	Ephgrave G	Grant W	Lewis T	Mallett J	Ramsey A	Rochford W	Rudkin T	Scott A	Smith G	Stansbridge L	Veck R	Wayman C	Webber E	Wrigglesworth W
Aug 23	(a)	Doncaster R	D	1-1	Bradley	30,000					10		8				7	9	6	2	3	11	4	1	5				
27	(h)	Sheffield W	W	3-1	Bradley 2, Ramsey	16,751					10		8				7	9	6	2	3	11	4	1	5				
30	(h)	Leeds U	L	1-2	Bradley	20,801					10		8				7	9	6	2	3	11	4	1	5				
Sep 1	(a)	Sheffield W	W	2-1	Bradley 2	23,077					10		8	7				9	6	2	3	11	4	1	5				
6	(h)	Bury	W	1-0	Bradley	17,617					10		8	7				9	6	2	3	11	4	1	5				
8	(a)	Cardiff C	L	1-5	Day	40,000					10		8	7				9	6	2	3	11	4	1	5				
13	(a)	West Ham U	L	0-2		20,709					10		8	7	1			9	6	2	3	11	4		5				
17	(h)	Cardiff C	D	2-2	Day, Bradley	17,000					10	5	8	7	1			9	6	2	3	11	4						
20	(h)	Chesterfield	W	3-0	Day 3	18,590					10	5	8	7				9	6	2	3	11	4	1					
27	(a)	Millwall	L	0-3		23,000					10	5	8	7				9	6	2	3	11	4	1					
Oct 4	(h)	Tottenham H	D	1-1	Day	23,840					10	5	8	7				9	6	2	3	11	4	1					
11	(a)	Fulham	W	2-0	Bates 2	24,437		10	9	5			8	7					6	2	3	11	4	1					
18	(h)	Coventry C	W	3-1	Wrigglesworth, Bates, Ramsey	21,767		10		5			8	7				9	6	2	3		4	1					11
25	(a)	Newcastle U	L	0-5		50,000		10		5			8	7				9	6	2	3	11	4	1					
Nov 1	(h)	Birmingham C	W	2-0	Ramsey, Curtis	27,000		10		5			8	7					6	2	3	11	4	1			9		
8	(a)	West Brom A	L	0-1		35,000		10		5			8	7					6	2	3	11	4	1			9		
15	(h)	Barnsley	W	4-1	Bates 2, Wayman, Wrigglesworth	21,563		10		5			8	7					6	2	3		4	1			9		11
22	(a)	Plymouth A	L	1-3	Wayman	21,561		10		5			8	7					6	2	3		4	1			9		11
29	(h)	Luton T	W	3-1	Ellerington, Curtis, Wayman	18,369	4			5			8		2			9	6	3			7	1			10		11
Dec 6	(a)	Brentford	D	2-2	Day, Wayman	18,660		10		5			8	7	4	1			6	2	3						9		11
13	(h)	Leicester C	W	3-1	Day, Wrigglesworth, Bates	18,441		10					8	7	4	1			6	2	3						9	5	11
20	(h)	Doncaster R	W	6-1	Wayman 2, Ramsey, Day, Curtis, Wrigglesworth	17,925		10					8	7	2	1			6		3		4				9	5	11
26	(a)	Bradford	W	3-1	Wayman 2, Ellerington	22,823		10					8	7	2	1			6		3		4				9	5	11
27	(h)	Bradford	L	1-2	Opp own goal	24,734		10					8	7	2	1			6		3		4				9	5	11
Jan 3	(a)	Leeds U	D	0-0		23,194		10		1			8	7	3				6	2			4				9	5	11
17	(a)	Bury	L	0-3		13,679		10		1			8		7				6	2	3		4				9	5	11
31	(h)	West Ham U	W	3-1	Bates 2, Wayman	20,178	6	10		1			8	7						2	3		4				9	5	11
Feb 14	(h)	Millwall	W	5-1	Bates 2, Day, Wayman, Grant	19,625	6	10		1			8	7			11			2	3		4				9	5	
21	(a)	Tottenham H	D	0-0		29,784	6	10		1			8				11			2	3		7	4			9	5	
Mar 6	(a)	Coventry C	W	1-0	Scott	23,687	6	10		1			8	7			11			2	3		4				9	5	
13	(h)	Newcastle U	W	4-2	Wayman 2, Scott, Grant	26,780	6	10		1			8	7			11			2	3		4				9	5	
20	(a)	Birmingham C	D	0-0		42,000	6	10		1			8	7			11			2	3		4				9	5	
26	(a)	Nottingham F	W	2-1	Scott, Wayman	22,788	6	10		1			8	7			11			2	3		4				9	5	
27	(h)	West Brom A	D	1-1	Scott	27,330	4	10		1			8	7	2		11				3		6				9	5	
29	(a)	Nottingham F	D	1-1	Ellerington	24,738	6	10		1			8	7	2		11	9			3		4					5	
Apr 3	(a)	Barnsley	L	1-2	Grant	20,000	6	10		1			8	7			11			2	3		4				9	5	
10	(h)	Plymouth A	L	2-3	Wayman 2	20,544		10					8	7			11		6	2	3		4	1			9	5	
14	(a)	Chesterfield	W	1-0	Wayman	13,378		10		1			8	7			11		6	2	3		4				9	5	
17	(a)	Luton T	W	2-0	Ramsey, Scott	17,202		10		1			8	7			11		6	2	3		4				9	5	
21	(a)	Fulham	W	1-0	Wayman	15,280		10		1			8	7			11		6	2	3		4				9	5	
24	(h)	Brentford	W	2-1	Grant 2	18,512		10		1			8	7			11		6	2	3		4				9	5	
28	(a)	Leicester C	D	0-0		17,874		10		1			8	7			11		6	2	3		4				9	5	
App							7	22	1	17	11	13	41	35	9	7	19	15	32	42	35	5	20	39	18	6	27	29	12
Goals								10			8		3	10	3		5			5			5				17		4

Opp own goal 1

Back row (left to right): G.Smith, J.Mallett, A.Ramsey, W.Rochford. Middle row: W.Dodgin (manager), E.Day, E.Webber, W.Ellerington, I.Black, E.Ballard, W.Grant, S.Warhurst (trainer). Front row: G.Curtis, C.Wayman, E.Bates, W.Wrigglesworth.

	P	W	D	L	F	A	Pts
Birmingham C	42	22	15	5	55	24	59
Newcastle U	42	24	8	10	72	41	56
Southampton	42	21	10	11	71	53	52
Sheffield W	42	20	11	11	66	53	51
Cardiff C	42	18	11	13	61	58	47
West Ham U	42	16	14	12	55	53	46
West Brom A	42	18	9	15	63	58	45
Tottenham H	42	15	14	13	56	43	44
Leicester C	42	16	11	15	60	57	43
Coventry C	42	14	13	15	59	52	41
Fulham	42	15	10	17	47	46	40
Barnsley	42	15	10	17	62	64	40
Luton T	42	14	12	16	56	59	40
Bradford	42	16	8	18	68	72	40
Brentford	42	13	14	15	44	61	40
Chesterfield	42	16	7	19	54	55	39
Plymouth A	42	9	20	13	40	58	38
Leeds U	42	14	8	20	62	72	36
Nottingham F	42	12	11	19	54	60	35
Bury	42	9	16	17	58	68	34
Doncaster R	42	9	11	22	40	66	29
Millwall	42	9	11	22	44	74	29

113

1948-49

OF all the post-war seasons, 1948-49 is arguably the one that senior Saints fans talk about most. At one stage it looked impossible for Saints to fail to achieve promotion. Only the identity of who would join them in Division One seemed to be in doubt.

The team, with everyone playing well, quickly swept to the top of the table and Wayman was again an inspiration. He finished the season with 32 goals including five against Leicester which remains a League record for Southampton to this day.

The Saints looked on course for Division One when they met fellow promotion seekers, Tottenham Hotspur, at White Hart Lane in late March. On that Saturday morning, Saints stood top of Division Two with 49 points. Fulham were second with 43 points, and then came West Brom (42) and Spurs (41).

A massive crowd of over 69,000 gathered to watch the 'four-pointer', and they saw Saints suffer a dreadful blow when Wayman tore a thigh muscle and had to go out on the wing where he became a virtual passenger.

Southampton continued to press forward, despite Wayman's injury, and Bates saw his shot hit the woodwork midway through the second half. With only eight minutes remaining,

the same player worked his way through the Spurs defence and, instinctively, the hobbling Wayman followed up.

Bates found his injured colleague and Wayman momentarily forgot his pain and got in a shot which Ditchburn could only parry. The ball rebounded to Wayman and, incredibly, he steadied himself and cracked in another shot with his injured right leg. This time Ditchburn stood no chance and Saints were in the lead.

At the final whistle Saints heard that Fulham had lost and West Brom drawn. With seven games remaining, Saints were eight points clear.

Wayman's injury, worsened by his brave effort in winning the game, was so serious that Bill Dodgin announced that he would not play again that season (he actually played twice more but was not fit). Without him Saints' confidence evaporated and of the last 14 points available they collected only four, allowing both Fulham and West Brom to overhaul them.

In retrospect it can be seen that the lack of decent cover for Wayman could be blamed for Saints' failure to win promotion. The Spurs programme for that fateful match said: 'Only a series of unlikely disasters will deprive Southampton of First Division football in 1949-50'. They were prophetic words.

FA Cup

DRAWN away against fellow Second Division side, Sheffield Wednesday, Saints were always going to find it difficult to progress to the fourth round.

Surprisingly, Grant had given the Saints the lead with a low 30-yard shot, but Wednesday soon equalised through Dailey. After 60 minutes Quigley fooled Rochford and ran through to shoot past the diving Black — and Saints were out of the Cup.

> **Round 3**
> **Jan 8 v Sheffield Wednesday (a) 1-2**
> *Grant*
> Black; Ramsey, Rochford, Wilkins, Webber, Mallett, Scott, Curtis, Wayman, Bates, Grant.
> *Att: 44,292*

> A Saints record League crowd of 30,586 saw the last home game of the season, against West Brom. The record lasted for over 20 years. The post-war boom saw crowds increase everywhere and 10,000 watched Saints Reserves play Arsenal Reserves at The Dell. Saints total home League attendance was 534,785, an average of 25,465 per game.

> In September 1948, The Dell celebrated its golden jubilee and even in those days there was talk of building a new stadium at Western Esplanade, at an estimated cost of £250,000.

Charlie Wayman scored five against Leicester.

Ted Bates scores the only goal of the game against Chesterfield at The Dell in December 1948.

1948-49

Division 2

Date		Opponent	Result	Scorers	Att.	Bates E	Black I	Curtis G	Day E	Ellerington W	Gallego J	Grant W	Heaton W	Mallett J	Ramsey A	Rochford W	Roles A	Rudkin T	Scott A	Smith G	Stansbridge L	Veck R	Wayman C	Webber E	Wheatley R	Wilkins L
Aug 21	(h)	Blackburn R	W 3-0	Wayman 2, Scott	26,018		1	10	7			11		6	2	3			8	4			9	5		
25	(a)	Plymouth A	W 2-1	Wayman, Day	29,443		1	8	7			11		6	2	3			10	4			9	5		
28	(a)	Cardiff C	L 1-2	Wayman	40,000		1	10	7			11		6	2	3			8	4			9	5		
Sep 1	(h)	Plymouth A	W 2-0	Wayman, Curtis	23,613		1	10	7			11		6	2	3			8	4			9	5		
4	(h)	Queen's Park R	W 3-0	Scott 2, Ramsey	27,600		1	10				11		6	2	3		7	8	4			9	5		
8	(a)	Fulham	L 0-1		24,700		1	10				11		6	2	3		7	8	4			9	5		
11	(a)	Luton T	D 1-1	Wayman	20,257		1	10	7					6	2	3		11	8	4			9	5		
15	(a)	Fulham	W 3-0	Wayman 2, Day	25,424	8	1	10	7	2				6		3		11		4			9	5		
18	(h)	Bradford	D 2-2	Wayman 2	26,659	11	1	10	7	2				6		3			8	4			9	5		
25	(a)	Sheffield W	L 0-2		38,347	6		10	7						2	3			8	4	1	11	9	5		
Oct 2	(a)	Barnsley	L 0-3		23,168	10	1	8	7		11			6	2	3				4			9	5		
9	(h)	Coventry C	W 5-2	Grant 2, Ramsey, Wayman, Bates	23,362	10	1	8	7			11		6	2	3				4			9	5		
16	(a)	Leeds U	D 1-1	Grant	34,300	10	1	8	7			11		6	2	3				4			9	5		
23	(h)	Leicester C	W 6-0	Wayman 5, Bates	23,907	10	1	8	7			11		6	2	3							9	5		4
30	(a)	Brentford	D 0-0		29,812	10	1	8	7					6	2	3						11	9	5		4
Nov 6	(h)	Tottenham H	W 3-1	Wayman, Bates, Day	29,000	10	1	8	7			11		6	2	3							9	5		4
13	(a)	West Ham U	D 1-1	Wayman	35,000	10	1	8				11		6	2	3	7						9	5		4
20	(h)	Bury	W 2-0	Grant, Bates	25,057	10	1	8	7			11		6	2	3							9	5		4
27	(a)	West Brom A	L 0-2		45,000	10	1	8	7			11		6	2	3							9	5		4
Dec 4	(h)	Chesterfield	W 1-0	Bates	22,697	10	1	8	7	3		11		6	2								9	5		4
11	(a)	Lincoln C	W 2-1	Wayman 2	14,207	10	1	8	7			11		6	2	3							9	5		4
18	(a)	Blackburn R	W 2-1	Bates 2	24,700	10	1	11	7					6	2	3			8				9	5		4
25	(a)	Nottingham F	L 1-2	Curtis	25,151	10	1	11	7					6	2	3			8				9	5		4
26	(h)	Nottingham F	W 2-1	Wayman, Curtis	24,330	10	1	8	7			11		6	2	3							9	5		4
Jan 1	(h)	Cardiff C	W 2-0	Wayman, Scott	20,937	10	1	8				11		6	2	3			7				9	5		4
22	(h)	Luton T	D 1-1	Wayman	24,815	10	1	8		2		11		6		3			7				9	5		4
29	(a)	Queen's Park R	W 3-1	Wayman, Ellerington, Curtis	20,000	10	1	8		2		11		6		3			7				9	5		4
Feb 12	(h)	Lincoln C	W 4-0	Wayman 2, Day, Bates	22,782	10	1	8	7	2			11	6		3							9	5		4
19	(h)	Sheffield W	W 1-0	Bates	29,445	10	1	8	7	2			11	6		3							9	5		4
26	(h)	Barnsley	W 3-0	Wayman, Day, Curtis	25,892	10	1	8	7	2			11	6		3							9	5		4
Mar 5	(a)	Coventry C	D 2-2	Ellerington	21,920	10	1	8	7	2			11	6		3							9	5		4
12	(h)	Leeds U	W 2-1	Wayman, Day	25,736	10	1	8	7	2			11	6		3							9	5		4
19	(a)	Leicester C	W 3-1	Wayman 2, Bates	32,700	10	1	8	7	2			11	6		3							9	5		4
26	(h)	Brentford	W 2-0	Mallett, Bates	25,217	10	1	8	7	2			11	6		3							9	5		4
Apr 2	(a)	Tottenham H	W 1-0	Wayman	69,265	10	1	8	7	2			11	6		3							9	5		4
4	(a)	Bradford	L 0-2		9,293	8	1		7	2			11	6		3							9	5	10	4
9	(h)	West Ham U	L 0-1		25,644		1	10	7	2			11	6		3			8				9	5		4
15	(a)	Grimsby T	W 1-0	Ellerington	25,931	9	1	10	7	2			11	6		3			8					5		4
16	(a)	Bury	L 0-1		20,355	9	1	10	7	2			11	6		3			8					5		4
18	(h)	Grimsby T	D 0-0		26,064	10	1		7	2			11	6		3			8				9	5		4
23	(h)	West Brom A	D 1-1	Day	30,586	9	1	10	7	2			11	6		3			8					5		4
30	(a)	Chesterfield	L 0-1		12,801	10	1	8		2			11	6		3			7				9	5		4
App						34	41	40	37	20	1	17	15	41	25	38	1	4	22	13	1	3	37	42	1	29
Goals						11		5	7	3		4		1	2				4				32			

Back row (left to right): Dodgin (manager) Day, Smith, Ramsey, Black, Rochford, Wilkins, Webber, Mallett, Ellerington, Warhurst. Front row: Scott, Curtis, Wayman, Bates, Grant.

	P	W	D	L	F	A	Pts
Fulham	42	24	9	9	77	37	57
West Brom A	42	24	8	10	69	39	56
Southampton	42	23	9	10	69	36	55
Cardiff C	42	19	13	10	62	47	51
Tottenham H	42	17	16	9	72	44	50
Chesterfield	42	15	17	10	51	45	47
West Ham U	42	18	10	14	56	58	46
Sheffield W	42	15	13	14	63	56	43
Barnsley	42	14	12	16	62	61	40
Luton T	42	14	12	16	55	57	40
Grimsby T	42	15	10	17	72	76	40
Bury	42	17	6	19	67	76	40
Queen's Park R	42	14	11	17	44	62	39
Blackburn R	42	15	8	19	53	63	38
Leeds U	42	12	13	17	55	63	37
Coventry C	42	15	7	20	55	64	37
Bradford	42	13	11	18	65	78	37
Brentford	42	11	14	17	42	53	36
Leicester C	42	10	16	16	62	79	36
Plymouth A	42	12	12	18	49	64	36
Nottingham F	42	14	7	21	50	54	35
Lincoln C	42	8	12	22	53	91	28

1949-50

SAINTS began the new season under new management as Sid Cann had replaced Bill Dodgin, now manager of Fulham. Mr Cann had been at The Dell since 1946 and was the directors' unanimous choice from amongst 20 applicants. Bill Rochford was to be player-coach, with Sam Warhurst continuing as trainer.

No-one envied Cann's position at the start of the season, with both players and supporters still demoralised after missing out on what had seemed like certain promotion. Instead of lining up against the likes of Arsenal, Manchester United and Newcastle, Saints still faced the prospect of trips to Chesterfield, Bradford and Plymouth.

Cann's problems were not eased when Southampton began 1949-50 in much the same way as they had ended the previous season, losing their first three games. Cann, however, knew that the team was basically sound and it was a question of building confidence and boosting morale.

Ramsey had left the club for Spurs in the close season and it was ironic that Ellerington, his obvious replacement, spent much of the season injured. Yet despite these early setbacks, Cann quietly set about the task of restoring the team's fortunes and Saints duly responded by climbing the table until they were once again in a challenging position.

Astonishingly, they again missed promotion — this time by an even narrower margin than the previous year. The two Sheffield clubs and Saints all finished on equal points, but it was Wednesday, with a goal-average of 1.398, who joined Spurs in Division One, whilst Sheffield United (1.387) and Saints (1.333) were left to look back on missed opportunities.

In the very last game of the season, Southampton needed to beat West Ham by 3-0 and were devastated when the Hammers scored twice midway through the first half, leaving Saints now needing seven. They found three of them to win the game, but such a magnificent effort was still insufficient.

Gregory, the West Ham goalkeeper, and the woodwork denied Saints on several occasions and left everyone at The Dell shattered at yet another near-miss. Some fans were so upset that they vowed never to watch the club again; others cruelly suggested that the directors simply did not want promotion and the extra responsibilities of running a First Division club. Cann, meanwhile, simply took stock of what was becoming an uphill struggle.

FA Cup

NORTHAMPTON Town set a record attendance in January 1950 when over 23,000 saw them hold Saints to a draw in the third round of the FA Cup.

It was a brave effort by Southampton who were down to only nine fit men when Jones and Webber were both injured in the first half. Scott put Saints ahead but Northampton soon equalised and would have won but for a brave display by Black and some poor finishing by the home forwards.

Saints must have fancied their chances against the Third Division side at The Dell but they were outplayed by a Cobblers team that included three Scots, McCulloch, Dixon and Murphy.

Northampton missed three easy chances before Dixon put them ahead only a minute into the second half. Against the run of play, Wayman scored twice, but the visitors responded through Hughes and Candlin. In the final minute Wayman proved that even he was fallible and missed an open goal.

Round 3
Jan 7 v Northampton Town (a) 1-1
Scott
Black; Wilkins, Ballard, Curtis, Webber, Wheatley, Day, Scott, Wayman, Bates, Jones.
Att: 23,209
Replay
Jan 11 v Northampton Town (h) 2-3
Wayman 2
Black; Wilkins, Ballard, Curtis, Clements, Wheatley, Grant, Bates, Wayman, Scott, Day.
Att: 24,806

During this season, Saints changed the colour of their shorts from navy-blue to black.

The 70,302 crowd at White Hart Lane was the biggest ever to watch Saints play in a League game.

In October 1950, Saints decided to install floodlights at The Dell, at a cost of £5,000, of which the supporters club contributed half. Originally the lights were to allow the training of young players on winter evenings.

Total home attendance: 501,789. Average: 23,894.

HUGHES HEADED NUMBER TWO

Northampton's second goal (above) against Southampton came after 17 minutes of the second half when Hughes headed the ball in from a corner.

1949-50

Division 2

Date		Opponent	Res	Scorers	Att	Anderson A	Ballard E	Bates E	Black I	Curtis G	Day E	Edwards J	Ellerington W	Elliott B	Grant W	Jones E	Lowder T	McGowan J	Mallett J	Molloy W	Rochford W	Scott A	Stansbridge L	Stevenson E	Veck R	Wayman C	Webber E	Wheatley R	Wilkins L
Aug 20	(h)	Grimsby T	L 1-2	Edwards	26,222				1	8	7	10	2		11				6		3					9	5		4
24	(a)	Barnsley	L 1-2	Wayman	17,762				1	8	7	10	2		11				6		3					9	5		4
27	(a)	Queen's Park R	L 0-1		23,040	2			1	8	7	10			11				6		3					9	5		4
31	(h)	Barnsley	D 0-0		22,319	2			1	8		10	7		11				6		3					9	5		4
Sep 3	(h)	Preston NE	W 1-0	Bates	26,317		3	10	1	4	8	7				11			6							9	5		2
5	(a)	West Ham U	W 2-1	Wayman, Bates	26,317		3	10	1	4	8	7				11			6							9	5		2
10	(a)	Swansea T	L 0-4		29,000		3	10	1	4	8	7				11			6							9	5		2
17	(h)	Leeds U	W 2-1	Wayman 2	23,214		3	10	1	4	7	8	2			11			6							9	5		
24	(a)	Bury	D 1-1	Bates	15,095		3	8	1	4	7	10	2			11			6							9	5		
Oct 1	(a)	Coventry C	W 2-1	Edwards, Day	22,549		3	8	1	4	7	10	2			11			6							9	5		
8	(h)	Tottenham H	D 1-1	Bates	30,240		3	8	1	4	7	10	2			11			6							9	5		
22	(h)	Blackburn R	W 3-1	Bates, Day, Wayman	21,406			8	1	4	7		2			11			6	10	3					9	5		
29	(a)	Brentford	W 1-0	Jones	21,860			10	1	4	7		2			11			6		3					9	5	8	
Nov 5	(h)	Hull C	W 5-0	Wayman 3, Bates, Edwards	23,275			8	1	4	7	10	2			11			6		3					9	5		
12	(a)	Sheffield W	D 2-2	Wayman, Edwards	32,146			8	1	4	7	10	2			11			6		3					9	5		
19	(h)	Plymouth A	D 3-3	Bates 2, Wayman	25,129	2		8	1	4	7	10				11			6		3					9	5		
26	(a)	Chesterfield	D 0-0		10,605			8	1	4	7	10	2			11					3					9	5	6	
Dec 3	(h)	Bradford	W 3-1	Day, Bates, Edwards	20,876			8	1	4	7	10				11			6		3					9	5		2
10	(a)	Leicester C	D 2-2	Wayman, Bates	22,167			8	1	4	7	10				11			6		3					9	5		2
17	(h)	Grimsby T	D 1-1	Wayman	14,000			8	1	4	7	10				11			6		3					9	5		2
24	(h)	Queen's Park R	L 1-2	Wayman	21,391		3		1	4	7	10				11			6				8			9	5		2
26	(a)	Luton T	D 1-1	Wayman	18,765		3	10	1	4	7					11							8			9	5	6	2
27	(h)	Luton T	W 2-1	Day, Bates	26,928		3	10	1	4	7					11									8	9	5	6	2
31	(a)	Preston NE	W 3-0	Wayman 2, Day	27,000		3	10	1	4	7					11							8			9	5	6	2
Jan 14	(h)	Swansea T	L 1-2	Wayman	24,674			8	1	4	7	10				11			6		3					9	5		2
21	(a)	Leeds U	L 0-1		38,500			8	1	4	7	10	3			11			6							9	5		2
Feb 4	(h)	Bury	W 4-1	Bates 2, Wayman 2	20,689			8	1	4	7		3			11			6							9	5	10	2
11	(a)	Sheffield U	W 1-0	Wheatley	30,000			8	1	4	7		3			11			6							9	5	10	2
18	(h)	Coventry C	D 1-1	Veck	23,412			8	1	4	7		3			11			6						9		5	10	2
25	(a)	Tottenham H	L 0-4		70,302			8	1	10	11				3	6		7	4							9	5		2
Mar 4	(h)	Cardiff C	W 3-1	McGowan, Bates, Day	23,375			9	1	8	7				11	3	4	10	6								5		2
11	(a)	Blackburn R	D 0-0		18,300			9	1	8	7				11	3	4	10	6								5		2
18	(a)	Brentford	L 2-3	Day 2	22,429	3			1	4	7				11	10			6				8			9	5		
25	(a)	Hull C	W 2-1	Stevenson 2	32,000			9	1	4	7	10	3			11			6					8			5		2
Apr 1	(h)	Chesterfield	W 1-0	Stevenson	21,964	2	9			4	7	10	3			11			6			1		8			5		
8	(a)	Bradford	D 0-0		16,363	2				4	7	10	3			11			6			1		8		9	5		
10	(h)	Sheffield U	W 1-0	Wayman	23,528	2	3			4	7	10				11			6			1		8		9	5		
15	(h)	Sheffield W	W 1-0	Wayman	28,529	2		8	1	4	7		3			11			6					10		9	5		
17	(h)	Cardiff C	D 1-1	Wayman	21,247	2		8	1	4	7		3			11			6					10		9	5		
22	(a)	Plymouth A	D 0-0		22,873	2			1	4	7	10	3			11			6					8		9	5		
29	(h)	Leicester C	W 5-3	Wayman 2, Bates 2, Stevenson	21,091	2	3	8	1	4	7					11			6					10		9	5		
May 6	(h)	West Ham U	W 3-2	Jones 2, Stevenson	24,778	2		8	1	4	7		3			11			6					10		9	5		
		App				8	17	33	39	42	38	28	25	2	4	30	10	3	38	1	14	3	3	12	2	36	42	8	24
		Goals						16			8	5				3		1						5	1	24		1	

Back row (left to right): W.Ellerington, G.Curtis, I.Black, E.Ballard, E.Webber, J.Mallett. Front row, left to right: E.Day, E.Bates, C.Wayman, J.Edwards, E.Jones.

	P	W	D	L	F	A	Pts
Tottenham H	42	27	7	8	81	35	61
Sheffield W	42	18	16	8	67	48	52
Sheffield U	42	19	14	9	68	49	52
Southampton	42	19	14	9	64	48	52
Leeds U	42	17	13	12	54	45	47
Preston NE	42	18	9	15	60	49	45
Hull C	42	17	11	14	64	72	45
Swansea T	42	17	9	16	53	49	43
Brentford	42	15	13	14	44	49	43
Cardiff C	42	16	10	16	41	44	42
Grimsby T	42	16	8	18	74	73	40
Coventry C	42	13	13	16	55	55	39
Barnsley	42	13	13	16	64	67	39
Chesterfield	42	15	9	18	43	47	39
Leicester C	42	12	15	15	55	65	39
Blackburn R	42	14	10	18	55	60	38
Luton T	42	10	18	14	41	51	38
Bury	42	14	9	19	60	65	37
West Ham U	42	12	12	18	53	61	36
Queen's Park R	42	11	12	19	40	57	34
Plymouth A	42	8	16	18	44	65	32
Bradford	42	10	11	21	51	77	31

1950-51

BEARING in mind the club's recent disappointments, it was perhaps surprising that Saints began the new season with a seven-match unbeaten run, and that by Christmas they were top of the Second Division following a 2-1 victory over Sheffield United.

Even more surprising was the fact that Southampton achieved all this without the services of Charlie Wayman, who had moved to Preston North End before the start of the season.

Wayman's replacement, however, was soon amongst the goals. Centre-forward Eddie Brown came from Deepdale and finished the season as Saints' highest scorer with 20 goals from 36 League games.

Saints, however, could not maintain their momentum and a bad slump in League form ensured that they did not see another Second Division victory until 17 March. The club eventually finished in a mid-table position and it cannot have escaped the supporters' notice that up in Lancashire Wayman was helping Preston win the Division Two Championship.

FA Cup

SAINTS must have been apprehensive when they were drawn away to Notts County in the third round of the FA Cup, but on the day they showed no signs of being overawed and deservedly won by the odd goal in seven.

All Southampton's goals were gems, in contrast to County's which all came from goalmouth scrambles. Eric Day, in particular, had a fine game, giving Corkhill, the veteran County left-back, a torrid time.

After the game, Eric Houghton, the Notts County manager, said, "Southampton are a fine side and they deserved to win.....they played football the easy way."

In the fourth round, Saints were drawn away to Sunderland and a crowd of more than 61,000 packed Roker Park to see the home side win 2-0. Yet Saints might have held the Wearsiders had their defence not had the jitters.

Mallett, Curtis and Elliott dominated the midfield, but they could not create any clear-cut chances, and with Irish international Hugh Kelly having an unhappy time in goal, Saints were again knocked out of the competition by Sunderland.

Round 3
Jan 6 v Notts County (a) 4-3
Brown 2, Day 2
Kelly; Ellerington, Kirkman, Elliott, Webber, Mallett, Day, Curtis, Brown, Bates, Edwards.
Att: 29,260
Round 4
Jan 27 v Sunderland (a) 0-2
Kelly; Ellerington, Kirkman, Elliott, Webber, Mallett, Day, Curtis, Brown, Bates, Edwards.
Att: 61,319

In the FA Cup match at Roker Park, Saints wore amber jerseys and black shorts for the first time. They borrowed the kit from the Hampshire Regiment. Sunderland, meanwhile, borrowed a set of black and white striped shirts from Newcastle United. And on the same day, Newcastle played in Sunderland's jerseys against Bolton Wanderers.

On 31 October 1950, Saints played a floodlit match against Bournemouth at The Dell, watched by a crowd of 10,000.

Southampton's president, Lord Mountbatten, saw the home defeat by Hull City.

Total home attendance: 457,179. Average: 21,770.

Eric Day had a fine game against Notts County and scored twice as Saints moved through to the fourth round of the FA Cup.

Division 2

Date		Opponent	Res	Score	Scorers	Att	Anderson A	Ballard E	Bates E	Brown E	Christie J	Clements S	Curtis G	Day E	Dudley F	Edwards J	Ellerington W	Elliott B	Gregory J	Jones E	Judd W	Kelly H	Kirkman N	Lowder T	Mallett J	Mitchell J	Stansbridge L	Stevenson E	Thomas E	Webber E	Wheatley R	Wilkins K	Wilkins L
Aug 19	(a)	Barnsley	W	2-1	Bates 2	19,835			9				4	7		10	2			11		1	3		6			8	5				
23	(h)	Doncaster R	D	1-1	Edwards	24,579			9				4	7		10	2			11		1	3		6			8	5				
26	(h)	Sheffield U	W	1-0	Ellerington	22,859		3	9				4	7		10	2			11		1			6			8	5				
30	(a)	Doncaster R	D	0-0		23,389		3	9				4	7		10	2			11		1			6			8	5				
Sep 2	(a)	Luton T	W	1-0	Bates	16,942		3	8				4	7		10	2			9		1			6	11			5				
6	(h)	Blackburn R	D	1-1	Day	22,561	2	3	8				4	7		10				9		1			6	11			5				
9	(h)	Leeds U	W	2-0	Bates, Edwards	25,806	2	3	8	9			4	7		10						1			6	11			5				
11	(a)	Blackburn R	L	0-1		17,515	2		8	9				7				3				1			6	11	10		5			4	
16	(a)	West Ham U	L	0-3		22,500	2		8	9				7		10		4		11		1			6				5			3	
23	(h)	Swansea T	W	2-1	Day, Brown	22,420	2		8	9				7		10		4	3			1			6	11			5				
30	(a)	Hull C	L	1-4	Brown	25,000		3	8	9			4	7		10	2					1			6	11			5				
Oct 7	(h)	Birmingham C	L	0-2		25,499		3	8	9			4	7		10	2					1			6	11		1	5				
14	(a)	Cardiff C	D	2-2	Stevenson 2	27,000		3		9			4	8			2		7			1	11		6			10	5				
21	(h)	Notts C	W	1-0	Brown	25,905		3		9			4	8			2		7			1	11		6			10	5				
28	(a)	Grimsby T	L	2-4	Bates, Brown	13,383		3	8	9			4				2		7			1	11		6			10	5				
Nov 4	(h)	Bury	W	1-0	Brown	20,335		3		9				8	7	11	2	4				1			6			10	5				
11	(a)	Preston NE	L	2-3	Day, Brown	32,000		3	10	9				8	7	11	2	4				1			6				5				
18	(h)	Coventry C	W	5-4	Day 2, Brown, Bates, Edwards	22,438		3	10	9				8	7	11	2	4				1			6				5				
25	(a)	Manchester C	W	3-2	Day, Bates, Edwards	38,972		3	10	9				8	7	11	2	4				1			6	1			5				
Dec 2	(h)	Leicester C	D	2-2	Brown, Bates	22,375		3	10	9				8	7		2	4				1			6			11	5				
9	(a)	Chesterfield	W	3-2	Day 2, Bates	12,200		3	10	9				8	7	11	2	4				1			6				5				
16	(h)	Barnsley	W	1-0	Brown	17,207		3	10	9				8	7	11	2	4				1			6	1			5				
23	(a)	Sheffield U	W	2-1	Brown, Edwards	27,013		3	10	9				8	7	11	2	4				1			6	1			5				
26	(a)	Brentford	L	0-4		22,435		3	10	9				8	7	11	2	4				1			6	1			5				
30	(h)	Luton T	D	1-1	Bates	21,094	2	3	10	9				8	7		11	4				1			6				5				
Jan 13	(a)	Leeds U	L	3-5	Day, Brown, Stevenson	29,253			10	9				8	7		2	4				1	3		6			11	5				
20	(h)	West Ham U	D	2-2	Ellerington, Brown	21,167			10	9				8	7		2	4				1	3		6			11	5				
Feb 3	(a)	Swansea T	L	1-2	Brown	17,451			8	9	1				7	10	11	2	4					3	6				5				
17	(h)	Hull C	L	2-3	Dudley 2	23,720	3			9	1	5	8	7	10	11	2	4							6								
28	(a)	Birmingham C	L	1-2	K.Wilkins	12,593			9			5	4		10	11	2			7		1	3		6					8			
Mar 3	(h)	Cardiff C	D	1-1	Edwards	23,493	2		9	1	5	4	7	10	11								3		6					8			
10	(a)	Notts C	D	2-2	Brown, Dudley	25,712			8	9	5	4	7	10	11	2							1	3	6								
17	(h)	Grimsby T	W	5-1	Brown 2, Dudley 2, Day	14,598			8	9	5	4	7	10	11	2							1	3	6								
23	(a)	Queen's Park R	L	0-2		19,711			8	9	5	4	7	10	11	2							1	3	6								
24	(a)	Bury	L	0-1		11,433	2		8	9	5	4	7	10	11								1	3	6								
26	(h)	Queen's Park R	D	2-2	Dudley 2	20,875	2			9	5		7	10	11			4					1	3	6					8			
31	(h)	Preston NE	D	3-3	Brown 2, Edwards	27,306				9	5	8	7	10	11	2		4					1	3	6								
Apr 7	(a)	Coventry C	D	2-2	Curtis, Edwards	20,156				9	5	10	7	8	11	2	4	3					1		6								
14	(h)	Manchester C	W	2-1	Day, Brown	24,579				9	5	10	7	8	11	2	4	3					1		6								
21	(a)	Leicester C	L	1-3	Dudley	16,000			7		5	10		8	11	2	4	3	9				1		6								
28	(h)	Chesterfield	D	1-1	Brown	13,922			9	1	5	10	7	8		2	4	3	11						6								
May 5	(h)	Brentford	W	2-1	Brown, Day	14,441			9	1	5	10	7	8	11	2	4	3							6								
App							9	21	29	36	5	14	37	37	15	36	34	23	6	12	1	28	13	3	42	7	4	12	5	28	1	2	2
Goals									10	20			1	12	8	8	2			1								3			1		

Back row (left to right): J.Eassom, Curtis, Kirkman, Webber, Kelly, Edwards, Ellerington, Warhurst. Front row: Wilkins, Day, Bates, Wayman, Elliott, Jones, Mallett.

	P	W	D	L	F	A	Pts
Preston NE	42	26	5	11	91	49	57
Manchester C	42	19	14	9	89	61	52
Cardiff C	42	17	16	9	53	45	50
Birmingham C	42	20	9	13	64	53	49
Leeds U	42	20	8	14	63	55	48
Blackburn R	42	19	8	15	65	66	46
Coventry C	42	19	7	16	75	59	45
Sheffield U	42	16	12	14	72	62	44
Brentford	42	18	8	16	75	74	44
Hull C	42	16	11	15	74	70	43
Doncaster R	42	15	13	14	64	68	43
Southampton	42	15	13	14	66	73	43
West Ham U	42	16	10	16	68	69	42
Leicester C	42	15	11	16	68	58	41
Barnsley	42	15	10	17	74	68	50
Queen's Park R	42	15	10	17	71	82	40
Notts C	42	13	13	16	61	60	39
Swansea T	42	16	4	22	54	77	36
Luton T	42	9	14	19	57	70	32
Bury	42	12	8	22	60	86	32
Chesterfield	42	9	12	21	44	69	30
Grimsby T	42	8	12	22	61	95	28

1951-52

OVER the previous two seasons Southampton had experienced massive disappointments when expected promotion did not materialise. One man who must have felt those disappointments more keenly than most was manager Sid Cann. It was no surprise then, when after an indifferent first three months of the season (including an 8-2 defeat at Bury), Cann resigned.

Now managerless, the club's team affairs were run by a committee formed by the directors and 'helped' by the training and coaching staff. It seemed an extremely democratic affair and three players — Mallett, Clements and Horton — were 'co-opted' to help with team selection.

This rather unorthodox approach did not seem to hinder the team unduly. Indeed, results actually improved and Saints crept away from the relegation zone, albeit unconvincingly.

In March, the club advertised the manager's position and received over 60 applications, including one from Frank Hill, a Saints player in the 1930s, and Mike Keeping, a star of the '20s. Many fans even called for the return of Tom Parker, but eventually the directors settled for George Roughton who had been in charge of Exeter City. Incidentally, Norman Kirkman, the Saints full-back, replaced Roughton at Exeter.

The new Southampton manager faced a largely uphill struggle as the side that had knitted together so well in the seasons immediately after the war was now virtually dismantled.

Quite simply, Roughton needed to build a new team. The attack had lost the services of experienced men such as Brown, Curtis and Edwards, and relied heavily on Bates and Day to keep the goals coming. The defence was particularly weak and needed immediate strengthening.

FA Cup

WHEN Saints were drawn away to Third Division South side, Southend United, they faced a difficult task, for although Southend were in a lower division, they had home advantage and were anxious to perform some kind of giant-killing act.

Southampton took the field on a fine but windy day, with Kiernan, Sillett and Judd making their first appearances in the FA Cup. Judd might have marked the occasion with an early goal, but in a rough and tumble first half it was Southend who opened the scoring.

After half-time, the bruising play continued and the referee had to stop the game and lecture both sets of players. Saints never settled in this atmosphere and were indeed knocked out of their stride. Southend took the fullest advantage, scoring twice more within the space of three minutes, and yet again, Southampton made an early exit from the Cup.

Round 3
Jan 12 v Southend United (a) 0-3
Kiernan; Ellerington, Sillett, Elliott, Horton, Mallett, Day, Bogan, Judd, Dudley, Edwards.
Att: 18,920

On 1 October 1951, Saints staged what is believed to be the first competitive match under floodlights in Britain. Spurs Reserves were the visitors for a Football Combination game and a crowd of 13,654 watched Spurs win 1-0.
Saints also arranged several floodlit friendlies and when they entertained Dundee, it was the first visit of a Scottish club to The Dell for 53 years.

During the season George Reader, who had refereed the 1950 World Cup Final, was made a director of Southampton Football Club.

Total home attendance: 400,932. Average: 19,092.

Although well into the veteran stage, Joe Mallett continued to give Saints sterling service in 1951-52 when he missed only seven matches.

England full-back Bill Ellerington, another fine servant to Saints, missed only three League games this season.

Division 2

Date		Opponent	Result	Scorers	Att.	Anderson A	Bates E	Bogan T	Brown E	Christie J	Clements S	Curtis G	Day E	Dudley F	Edwards J	Ellerington W	Elliott B	Gregory J	Horton H	Jones E	Judd W	Kiernan F	Kirkman N	Lowder T	McGowan J	Mallett J	Parker P	Purves C	Sillett P	Stansbridge L	Thomas E	Wilkins L
Aug 18	(h)	Everton	W 1-0	Day	25,929			9		5	10	7	8	11	2	4	3									6				1		
22	(a)	Nottingham F	L 0-3		32,320			9	1	5	10	7	8	11	2	4	3									6						
25	(a)	Barnsley	L 1-3	Brown	16,212			9	1	5	10	7	8	11	2	4	3	6														
29	(h)	Nottingham F	W 5-2	Brown 3, Curtis, Bates	19,632		10	9	1	5	8	7		11	2	4	3	6														
Sep 1	(a)	Sheffield W	L 1-3	Dudley	32,016		10	9	1	5	8	7		11		2			4							6		3				
3	(a)	Leicester C	L 0-3		21,183			9	1			8	7	10	11	2			6									3		5		4
8	(h)	Leeds U	D 0-0		19,667	3	8	9				4	7	11	10	2			6											1		5
12	(h)	Doncaster R	W 2-0	Brown, Dudley	16,649	3		9				4	7	11	10	2			6									8		1		5
15	(a)	Rotherham U	L 1-4	Day	17,000	3		9				4	7	11	10	2			6									8		1		5
22	(h)	Cardiff C	D 1-1	Horton	21,672			9				10	7	8	11	2			4							6			3	1		5
29	(a)	Birmingham C	D 1-1	Dudley	26,000							8	9	11	2				4	7						6		10	3	1		5
Oct 6	(h)	Hull C	D 1-1	Wilkins	22,823							8	9	11	2				4	7		1				6		10	3			5
13	(a)	Blackburn R	W 1-0	Brown	25,000			9					7	10	11	2			4			1				6		8	3			5
20	(h)	Queen's Park R	D 1-1	Day	19,200			9					7	10	11				4		1	2				6		8	3			5
27	(a)	Notts C	W 4-3	Brown 2, Edwards 2	31,540			9					7	10	11	2			4		1			8		6			3			5
Nov 3	(h)	Luton T	L 2-3	Brown, Dudley	20,002			9					7	10	11	2		3	4		1			8		6						5
10	(a)	Bury	L 2-8	Brown, Dudley	14,752			9					7	10	11	2		3	4		1			8		6						5
17	(h)	Swansea T	W 3-2	Day, Dudley, Edwards	15,724			9					7	10	11	2			4		1		3	8		6						5
24	(a)	Coventry C	L 1-3	Dudley	14,540			9					7	10	11	2			4		1		3	8		6						5
Dec 1	(h)	West Ham U	L 1-2	Brown	17,473			9					7	10	11	2			4		1		3	8		6						5
8	(a)	Sheffield U	D 2-2	Brown, Curtis	25,000			9				8	7	11		2	4		10		1					6			3			5
15	(a)	Everton	L 0-3		35,000			9				8	7	11		2	4		10		1					6			3			5
22	(h)	Barnsley	D 1-1	Judd	15,735		8					10	7			2	4		5		9	1		11		6			3			
25	(a)	Brentford	W 2-1	Judd, Dudley	25,841		8						7	10		2	4		5		9	1		11		6			3			
26	(h)	Brentford	W 2-1	Judd, Day	21,625		8						7	10		2	4		5		9	1		11		6			3			
29	(h)	Sheffield W	L 1-4	Dudley	21,535							8	7	10		2	4		5		9	1	3	11		6						
Jan 5	(a)	Leeds U	D 1-1	Bogan	25,319		8						7	10		2	4		5		9	1		11		6			3			
19	(h)	Rotherham U	W 3-1	Judd, Bates, Lowder	16,678	10							7			4	3	5			9	1		11	8	6			2			
26	(a)	Cardiff C	L 0-1		23,205	10		9					7			4	3	5				1		11	8	6			2			
Feb 9	(h)	Birmingham C	W 2-0	Judd, Day	18,688	10				5			7			2	4	3			9	1		11	8	6						
16	(h)	Hull C	D 0-0		26,000	10				5			7			2	4	3			9	1		11	8	6						
23	(h)	Leicester C	W 2-0	Judd, Day	19,121	10				5			7			2	4	3			9	1		11	8	6						
Mar 1	(h)	Blackburn R	W 2-1	McGowan, Judd	22,095	10				5			7			2	4	3			9	1		11	8	6						
8	(a)	Queen's Park R	L 1-2	Day	18,936	10				5			7			2	4	3			9	1		11	8	6						
15	(h)	Notts C	W 4-0	Day, McGowan, Judd, Lowder	20,604	10				5			7			2	4	3			9	1		11	8	6						
22	(a)	Luton T	L 1-2	McGowan	16,000	10				5			7			2	4				9	1		11	8	6			3			
29	(h)	Bury	W 4-2	Bates 3, Day	8,760	10				5			7			2	4				9	1		11	8	6			3			
Apr 5	(a)	Swansea T	D 1-1	Bates	20,000	10				5			7			2	4				9	1		11	8	6			3			
12	(h)	Coventry C	D 2-2	Judd, Bates	20,790	10				5			7			2	4				9	1		11	8	6			3			
14	(a)	Doncaster R	W 1-0	Bates	19,784	10				5			7			2	4				9	1		11	8	6			3			
19	(a)	West Ham U	L 0-4		18,500	10				5			7			2	4				9	1		11	8	6			3			
26	(h)	Sheffield U	L 0-1		16,530	10				5			7			2	4				9	1		11	8	6			3			
App						3	18	4	21	5	18	14	42	26	18	39	27	14	27	2	19	31	7	20	21	35	1	6	21	3	3	17
Goals							8	1	12			2	10	9	3				1		9			2	3							

Back row (left to right): W.Ellerington, F.Kiernan, P.Sillett, L.Wilkins, J.Mallett. Front row: E.Day, C.Purves, H.Horton, E.Brown, F.Dudley, J.Edwards.

	P	W	D	L	F	A	Pts
Sheffield W	42	21	11	10	100	66	53
Cardiff C	42	20	11	11	72	54	51
Birmingham C	42	21	9	12	67	56	51
Nottingham F	42	18	13	11	77	62	49
Leicester C	42	19	9	14	78	64	47
Leeds U	42	18	11	13	59	57	47
Everton	42	17	10	15	64	58	44
Luton T	42	16	12	14	77	78	44
Rotherham U	42	17	8	17	73	71	42
Brentford	42	15	12	15	54	55	42
Sheffield U	42	18	5	19	90	76	41
West Ham U	42	15	11	16	67	77	41
Southampton	42	15	11	16	61	73	41
Blackburn R	42	17	6	19	54	63	40
Notts C	42	16	7	19	71	68	39
Doncaster R	42	13	12	17	55	60	38
Bury	42	15	7	20	67	69	37
Hull C	42	13	11	18	60	70	37
Swansea T	42	12	12	18	72	76	36
Barnsley	42	11	14	17	59	72	36
Coventry C	42	14	6	22	59	82	34
Queen's Park R	42	11	12	19	52	81	34

1952-53

THERE was an air of optimism as Saints began the new season under a new manager, but 1952-53 ended in disaster when Saints were relegated for the first time in their 68-year history.

The build-up of a strong squad of players immediately after the war had not been capitalised upon, and the fans were critical of the way the transfer market had not been properly utilized.

Of course, as so often happens when a team is struggling against relegation, the Saints' injury list was huge and was a significant factor in the club's decline. To emphasise Saints' terrible luck with injuries and illness, no fewer than three players suffered appendicitis during 1952-53 — and Parker broke his leg for the second time.

Simpson also had the misfortune to break a leg, Horton broke his jaw, and the unfortunate McGowan missed virtually the whole season due to a lung condition.

Yet, even when all these unavoidable problems are taken into account, it still appears that the Saints did not play well, even when they had a full team. Home form was particularly poor and at the death, it was no surprise when Saints tumbled into Division Three South.

They had been in Division Two for 31 years and it was ironic that the only time Saints won two consecutive matches (one by a 6-1 scoreline) was right at the end of the season when their fate had already been sealed.

FA Cup

SAINTS' FA Cup form was a contrast to their League performances and they enjoyed something of a run in the competition before being eliminated in the fifth round, by a Blackpool team which went on to win the trophy in what became known as the 'Matthews Final'.

Their Cup success is even more surprising when one considers that their luck with the draw deserted them and they were pulled out of the hat second on all three occasions.

Dudley gave Saints a 41st-minute lead in the third round at a foggy Sincil Bank after Sillett had put him through and the Lincoln goalkeeper got a hand to Dudley's shot but could not prevent it going in. Lincoln equalised six minutes into the second half after Christie had mishandled.

The replay produced another close game and this time it was Lincoln who took the lead on a slippery pitch. Purves equalised for Saints following a scramble in the Imps' penalty area, and Day hit the winner with a left-foot drive 20 minutes from the end.

Saints were forced to kick into a gusting wind at Shrewsbury's Gay Meadow in the fourth round, but after surviving the first-half they pushed forward and Hoskins scored after 53 minutes. Against the run of play, Shrewsbury levelled matters within three minutes but Walker soon restored Saints' lead with a header and then Day and Hoskins again completed the rout.

Star-studded Blackpool provided the fifth round opposition and Saints played gallantly at Bloomfield Road. Blackpool took the lead after 64 minutes but Horton headed home a lobbed cross six minutes from time.

Over 29,000 packed into The Dell four days later and they saw Saints storm into a well-deserved lead through Walker. Sensing that they could put the tie beyond Blackpool's reach, Southampton continued to press forward and at one stage Saints' fans were treated to the rare sight of Stanley Matthews falling back to help his beleaguered colleagues.

In the second half, with Matthews now virtually a midfielder working valiantly to marshall his team, Blackpool broke away to score twice — against the run of play according to Southampton fans who were present — and dogged by some wretched luck and controversial refereeing, Saints could not find the equaliser.

Blackpool goalkeeper, George Farm, fists the ball away from Frank Dudley in the FA Cup fifth-round replay at The Dell.

Round 3
Jan 10 v Lincoln City (a) 1-1
Dudley
Christie; Ellerington, Sillett, Elliott, Horton, Simpson, Day, Purves, Dudley, Walker, Hoskins.
Att: 14,335
Replay
Jan 14 v Lincoln City (h) 2-1
Purves, Day
Christie; Ellerington, Traynor, Elliott, Horton, Simpson, Day, Purves, Dudley, Walker, Hoskins.
Att: 16,750
Round 4
Jan 31 v Shrewsbury Town (a) 4-1
Hoskins 2, Walker, Day
Christie; Ellerington, Sillett, Elliott, Clements, Simpson, Day, Purves, Dudley, Walker, Hoskins.
Att: 17,249
Round 5
Feb 14 v Blackpool (a) 1-1
Horton
Christie; Ellerington, Sillett, Elliott, Horton, Simpson, Day, Purves, Dudley, Walker, Hoskins.
Att: 27,543
Replay
Feb 18 v Blackpool (h) 1-2
Walker
Christie; Ellerington, Sillett, Elliott, Horton, Simpson, Day, Purves, Dudley, Walker, Hoskins.
Att: 29,223

Total home attendance: 339,712. Average: 16,176.

1952-53

Division 2

Date	Opponent	Result	Scorers	Att	Bates E	Bogan T	Christie J	Clements S	Day E	Dudley F	Ellerington W	Elliott B	Flood J	Gregory J	Horton H	Hoskins J	Judd W	Kiernan F	Lowder T	McDonald J	McGarrity T	McGowan J	Mallett J	Page J	Purves C	Sillett P	Simpson A	Traynor T	Walker J	Wilkins K	Wilkins L	Williams R
Aug 23	(a) West Ham U	L 0-1		26,000	10			5	7		2	4					9	1		11			8	6		3						
27	(h) Plymouth A	L 2-3	Judd, Bates	20,089	10			5	7		2	4		3			9	1		11			8	6								
30	(h) Leicester C	W 5-2	Day 2, Purves, Judd, McDonald	17,089	10			5	7		2	4					9	1		11			8		6	3						
Sep 3	(a) Plymouth A	L 1-3	Ellerington	26,440	10			5	7		2	4					9	1		11			8		6	3						
6	(a) Notts C	W 2-1	Judd, McDonald	25,160	10			5	7		2	4					9	1		11			8		6	3						
10	(h) Rotherham U	L 2-3	Judd, McDonald	14,413	10			5	7		2	4					9	1		11			8		6	3						
13	(h) Everton	D 1-1	Horton	18,041				5	7		2	4			10		9	1		11			8		6	3						
15	(a) Rotherham U	D 2-2	Purves, McDonald	16,032				5	7		2	4			10		9	1		11			8		6	3						
20	(h) Bury	L 1-2	Bates	14,543	10			5	7		2	4					9	1		11			8		6	3						
24	(a) Leeds U	D 1-1	Mallett	13,300	10			5	7	8	2	4					9	1		11			6			3						
27	(h) Birmingham C	L 0-2		22,000	10			5	7	8	2	4					9	1		11			6			3						
Oct 4	(h) Luton T	L 1-3	Walker	17,593				5	7	8	2	4					9	1		11			6			3			10			
11	(a) Brentford	L 0-3		18,000		8		5	7	9	2	4					11	1								3		10	6			
18	(h) Doncaster R	D 3-3	Dudley 3	14,759		8		5	7	9		4						1			11				2	3		10	6			
25	(a) Swansea T	W 2-1	Dudley, Walker	24,000	10			5	7	9		4						1			11				2	3		8	6			
Nov 1	(h) Huddersfield T	L 0-2		20,867				5	7	9		4			10			1			11				2	3		8	6			
8	(a) Sheffield U	L 3-5	Day, Dudley, Opp own goal	30,000	10			5	7	9		4						1			11	8			2	3			6			
15	(h) Barnsley	L 1-2	Walker	10,447				5	7	9		4						1			11	8			2	3		10	6			
22	(a) Lincoln C	D 2-2	Clements, Dudley	13,060	10		1	5	7	9	2	4									11				6	3			8			
29	(h) Hull C	W 5-1	Sillett, Elliott, McGarrity, Dudley, Bates	8,865	10		1	5	7	9	2	4									11	8			6	3						
Dec 6	(a) Blackburn R	L 0-3		19,100	8		1	5	7	9	2	4			11						10				6	3						
13	(h) Nottingham F	D 2-2	Sillett, Hoskins	14,216	8		1		7	9	2	4			5	11					10				6	3						
20	(h) West Ham U	L 1-2	Hoskins	12,274	8		1		7	9	2	4			5	11					10				6	3						
26	(a) Fulham	D 1-1	Dudley	15,000			1		7	9	2	4			5	11									6	3			10			8
27	(h) Fulham	W 5-3	Dudley 3, Williams, Walker	21,935			1		7	9	2	4			5	11									6	3			10			8
Jan 3	(a) Leicester C	L 1-4	Day	22,000			1		7	9	2	4			5	11									6	3			10			8
17	(h) Notts C	D 1-1	Dudley	16,262			1		7	9		4	2		5	11							8		6	3						10
24	(a) Everton	D 2-2	Day, Hoskins	25,278			1		7	9		4	2		5	11							8		6	3						10
Feb 7	(a) Bury	D 0-0		12,864			1		7		2	4			5	11							8		6	3			10	9		
21	(a) Luton T	W 2-1	Day, Walker	18,000			1		7	9	2	4			5	11							8		6	3			10			
28	(h) Brentford	L 0-2		20,327			1		7		2	4			5	11					9		8		6	3			10			
Mar 7	(a) Doncaster R	L 0-1		18,000			1		7		2	4			5	11					9				6	3			10			8
14	(h) Swansea T	L 1-4	Dudley	16,881			1		7	9	2	4			5				11						6	3			10			8
21	(a) Huddersfield T	L 0-5		21,797					11	9	2				5			1			10		6		7	3		8			4	
28	(h) Sheffield U	D 4-4	Hoskins 2, Day, Dudley	14,267				5	7	9	2	4			6	11		1							8	3						10
Apr 4	(a) Barnsley	W 1-0	Sillett	6,466				5	7		2	4			6	11		1			9				8	3						10
6	(h) Leeds U	D 2-2	Horton, Day	17,704				5	7		2	4			6	11		1			9				8	3						10
11	(h) Lincoln C	W 1-0	Walker	14,922				5	7		2	4			6	11		1			9				8	3			10			
15	(h) Birmingham C	D 1-1	Sillett	18,387				5	7		2	4			6	11		1							8	3	9		10			
18	(a) Hull C	L 0-1		25,312				5	7		2	4			6	11		1							8	3	9		10			
25	(h) Blackburn R	W 6-1	Day 3, Horton 2, Flood	15,831				5	9		2	4	7		10	11		1							6	3	8					
29	(a) Nottingham F	W 3-2	Horton, Day, Bogan	7,283		8		5	9		2	4	7		10	11		1							6	3						
App					15	4	15	29	42	23	35	41	2	3	27	20	14	27	6	16	16	2	14	2	21	38	13	10	20	1	7	10
Goals					3	1		1	12	14	1	1	1		5	5	4			4	1		1		2	4			6			1

Opp own goal 1

Back row (left to right, players only): Luckett, Bogan, Traynor, K.Wilkins, F.Kiernan, Stansbridge, Christie, Parker, Dudley, Elliott. Standing: Featherstone, McGowan, Purves, Porter, Judd, Clements, Oakley, Ellerington. On ground: Day, L.Wilkins, Bates, Flood, Gregory, Mulholland.

	P	W	D	L	F	A	Pts
Sheffield U	42	25	10	7	97	55	60
Huddersfield T	42	24	10	8	84	33	58
Luton T	42	22	8	12	84	49	52
Plymouth A	42	20	9	13	65	60	49
Leicester C	42	18	12	12	89	74	48
Birmingham C	42	19	10	13	71	66	48
Nottingham F	42	18	8	16	77	67	44
Fulham	42	17	10	15	81	71	44
Blackburn R	42	18	8	16	68	65	44
Leeds U	42	14	15	13	71	63	43
Swansea T	42	15	12	15	78	81	42
Rotherham U	42	16	9	17	75	74	41
Doncaster R	42	12	16	14	58	64	40
West Ham U	42	13	13	16	58	60	39
Lincoln C	42	11	17	14	64	71	39
Everton	42	12	14	16	71	75	38
Brentford	42	13	11	18	59	76	37
Hull C	42	14	8	20	57	69	36
Notts C	42	14	8	20	60	88	36
Bury	42	13	9	20	53	81	35
Southampton	42	10	13	19	68	85	33
Barnsley	42	5	8	29	47	108	18

1953-54

NOT unnaturally, most Southampton fans expected Saints to bounce straight back to the Second Division. Anything less would be considered a failure.

Before the season began, however, the directors sold Sillett to Chelsea and although the board blamed the move on the club's precarious financial position, Saints fans felt that the move had an ominous significance.

Older supporters, in particular, remembered the days when the club always seemed to be selling its best players to placate the bank manager and to the detriment of team building.

It had been hoped that manager Roughton would be given money to strengthen the side, now here were Saints, letting it be known that there was no capital available for such a positive venture.

Although the team began relatively well and were placed towards the top of the table, attendances dwindled, thus compounding the club's financial problems. With Ted Bates now having ended his playing career, and Judd being forced to quit the game because of a serious injury, Saints' forward line lacked experience. Only Eric Day found Third Division defences more accommodating and he ended the season with 26 goals to become Southampton's top scorer.

One new arrival was Bob McLaughlin, who came from Cardiff City with Saints' Dudley going in the opposite direction. McLaughlin was a tough little half-back and he added some resilience to Saints' performances, particularly at The Dell.

But the depressing fact was that Southampton, a Second Division side for so long, soon began to take on the appearance of a Third Division side.

FA Cup

NOW that Saints were no longer in the Second Division their FA Cup quest began in the first round, and in November — at a stage of the season when Southampton fans hadn't normally given the Cup a second thought — they were drawn against local rivals, Bournemouth, at The Dell.

It was the first time the two clubs had met in the Cup but that did not prevent them from serving up a traditional 'derby' game, full of robust tackling.

After 18 minutes, Hoskins was fouled in the penalty area and Eric Day slammed home the spot kick. It was a lead that Saints held until the very last minute, when Fidler, the Bournemouth centre-forward, turned a cross over the Southampton goal-line.

Four days later, the sides met again at Dean Court where the crowd had to wait until the 63rd minute for a goal. Then Purves put Saints ahead following a Traynor free-kick.

Saints decided to try and sit on that lead instead of extending it and that probably proved their undoing.

Bournemouth hit back, not once, but three times to gain a deserved victory. Saints had been lacking in all departments and only centre-half Clements emerged from the game with any credit.

Round 1
Nov 21 v Bournemouth & BA (h) 1-1
Day
Christie; Gregory, Traynor, Wilkins, Clements, McLaughlin, Flood, Williams, Day, Walker, Hoskins.
Att: 22,102
Replay
Nov 25 v Bournemouth & BA (a) 1-3
Purves
Christie; Gregory, Traynor, Wilkins, Clements, Elliott, Purves, Williams, Day, Walker, Hoskins.
Att: 13,580

Total home attendance: 342,290. Average: 14,882.

Boxing Day 1953 and Eric Day's shot is saved by Bournemouth goalkeeper Godwin as Saints' John Walker closes in. Saints won 2-1 to avenge a Christmas Day defeat at Dean Court.

1953-54
Division 3 (South)

Player columns (left to right): Brown P, Christie J, Clements S, Day E, Digby D, Dudley F, Ellerington W, Elliott B, Flood J, Gaynor L, Gregory J, Horton H, Hoskins J, Kiernan F, McGowan J, McLaughlin R, Oakley R, Parker P, Purves C, Simpson A, Traynor T, Turner F, Walker J, Whittle J, Wilkins L, Williams R

Date		Opponent	Result	Scorers	Att.
Aug 19	(h)	Watford	W 2-0	Dudley, Walker	16,754
22	(a)	Crystal P	L 3-4	Hoskins 2, Day	17,790
24	(a)	Newport C	W 4-0	Day 2, Hoskins, Flood	8,571
29	(a)	Bristol C	W 4-2	Hoskins 2, Walker, Day	17,832
Sep 2	(h)	Newport C	W 4-0	Flood 3, Day	14,454
5	(a)	Aldershot	D 1-1	Horton	13,250
7	(a)	Queen's Park R	W 1-0	Hoskins	12,100
12	(h)	Swindon T	W 3-1	Day 2, Williams	19,302
16	(h)	Queen's Park R	W 3-1	Williams, Day, Horton	16,246
19	(a)	Walsall	L 0-1		9,666
23	(a)	Colchester U	W 2-1	Day, Horton	14,842
26	(h)	Shrewsbury T	W 4-2	Day 2, Horton, Flood	17,273
Oct 1	(a)	Colchester U	W 1-0	Day	6,705
3	(a)	Exeter C	L 0-4		13,691
10	(h)	Gillingham	W 1-0	Walker	17,801
17	(a)	Northampton T	L 0-3		14,403
24	(h)	Torquay U	D 2-2	Wilkins, Flood	15,792
31	(a)	Watford	L 0-2		12,507
Nov 7	(h)	Brighton & HA	W 1-0	Flood	19,579
14	(a)	Southend U	L 1-2	Day	11,000
28	(a)	Leyton O	W 4-1	Day 2, Flood 2	17,000
Dec 5	(h)	Millwall	W 4-2	Flood, Walker, Horton, Digby	15,411
19	(h)	Crystal P	W 3-1	Williams 2, Flood	12,221
25	(a)	Bournemouth	L 1-3	Williams	11,900
26	(h)	Bournemouth	W 2-1	Walker 2	18,493
Jan 2	(a)	Bristol C	L 0-1		21,456
16	(h)	Aldershot	W 2-0	Flood 2	14,320
23	(a)	Swindon T	W 1-0	Walker	12,942
Feb 13	(a)	Shrewsbury T	L 2-3	Walker, Horton	9,872
20	(h)	Exeter C	W 2-0	Day 2	16,327
27	(h)	Gillingham	L 0-2		13,084
Mar 6	(h)	Northampton T	W 1-0	Day	14,195
13	(a)	Reading	L 1-4	Hoskins	14,463
17	(h)	Walsall	D 0-0		8,762
20	(h)	Leyton O	W 4-1	Day 2, Hoskins, Walker	14,516
24	(h)	Norwich C	D 0-0		11,131
27	(a)	Brighton & HA	L 1-2	Day	31,029
Apr 3	(h)	Southend U	L 3-5	Day 2, Hoskins	13,224
7	(a)	Ipswich T	L 1-2	Day	15,051
10	(a)	Millwall	L 1-2	Gaynor	13,007
17	(h)	Ipswich T	D 1-1	Flood	17,562
19	(h)	Coventry C	W 2-1	Hoskins 2	9,664
20	(a)	Coventry C	L 1-2	Day	9,640
24	(a)	Torquay U	D 1-1	Hoskins	7,165
28	(h)	Reading	D 1-1	Day	6,589
30	(a)	Norwich C	L 0-1		11,768

Appearances: Brown P 1, Christie J 43, Clements S 36, Day E 46, Digby D 11, Dudley F 3, Ellerington W 18, Elliott B 31, Flood J 37, Gaynor L 12, Gregory J 42, Horton H 21, Hoskins J 35, Kiernan F 3, McGowan J 1, McLaughlin R 17, Oakley R 3, Parker P 8, Purves C 3, Simpson A 19, Traynor T 21, Turner F 2, Walker J 32, Whittle J 2, Wilkins L 33, Williams R 26

Goals: Day E 26, Digby D 1, Dudley F 1, Flood J 14, Gaynor L 1, Horton H 6, Hoskins J 12, Walker J 9, Wilkins L 1, Williams R 5

Final Table

	P	W	D	L	F	A	Pts
Ipswich T	46	27	10	9	82	51	64
Brighton & HA	46	36	9	11	86	61	61
Bristol C	46	25	6	15	88	66	56
Watford	46	21	10	15	85	69	52
Northampton T	46	20	11	15	82	55	51
Southampton	46	22	7	17	76	63	51
Norwich C	46	20	11	15	73	66	51
Reading	46	20	9	17	86	73	49
Exeter C	46	20	8	18	68	58	48
Gillingham	46	19	10	17	61	66	48
Leyton O	46	18	11	17	79	73	47
Millwall	46	19	9	18	74	77	47
Torquay U	46	17	12	17	81	88	46
Coventry C	46	18	9	19	61	56	45
Newport C	46	19	6	21	61	81	44
Southend U	46	18	7	21	69	71	43
Aldershot	46	17	9	20	74	86	43
Queen's Park R	46	16	10	20	60	68	42
Bournemouth	46	16	8	22	67	70	40
Swindon T	46	15	10	21	67	70	40
Shrewsbury T	46	14	12	20	65	76	40
Crystal P	46	14	12	20	60	86	40
Colchester U	46	10	10	26	50	78	30
Walsall	46	9	8	29	40	87	26

Back row (left to right): E.Day, J.McGowan, J.Flood, J.Walker, B.Hillier, J.Gregory, D.Milward, I.Creed, J.Hoskins, C.Purves, R.Williams. Middle: D.Featherstone (physio), E.Bates (trainer), F.Turner, L.Wilkins, A.Simpson, W.Ellerington, P.Parker, F.Kiernan, J.Christie, R.Oakley, S.Clements, F.Dudley, W.Judd, T.Traynor, J.Gallagher (trainer). Front: Mr G.Roughton (manager), Messrs G.Reader and R.W.Jukes (directors), C.T.Cosgrove, J.R.Sarjantson (chairman), G.E.H.Prince OBE, W.Turner, H.F.Didham (secretary).

125

1954-55

SOUTHAMPTON fans were nothing if not optimistic in the early 1950s and, yet again, the new season was eagerly awaited with Saints confidently expecting a return to Division Two.

During the summer, two new forwards had arrived at The Dell, in the form of Foulkes and Mulgrew, and they were expected to add the missing fire-power which would lift Saints to promotion.

Hopes soared when, in the opening match, Saints beat Brentford 6-4 and Tommy Mulgrew scored after only 15 seconds.

In an effort to improve their away form, the decision was taken that, wherever possible, Saints' team would travel on the Friday before an away match, thus giving them more time to settle. If anything, however, their away form was slightly worse than the previous season and it was their performances on opponents' grounds which eventually cost them dear in the promotion race.

In defence, skipper Len Wilkins was tried at centre-half and

proved a great success. Wilkins was an ever-present and an inspiration to his colleagues.

Most of Saints' problems centred around the forward line, despite those six goals in the opening game, and Welsh international Billy Foulkes suffered a serious back injury which restricted his appearances.

Mulgrew had shown plenty of promise but it was largely unfulfilled and he was not scoring consistently. Walker, the other inside-forward, was immensely frustrating, scoring quite brilliant goals and then missing absolute 'sitters'.

Ever-reliable Eric Day again topped the scoring charts with an impressive 27 goals from 44 games. Saints ended the season in third place and thus missed promotion. Supporters had to be content with the knowledge that the club had some useful reserves and Saints' second string, under the guidance of Ted Bates and Jimmy Gallagher, won the Football Combination Cup.

FA Cup

SAINTS began their 1954-55 Cup campaign against the amateur side, Barnet, from the Athenian League. Fog threatened the game but had cleared by the time Saints kicked off down the slope which then existed on Barnet's ground.

The amateurs were without their best player, Sullivan, and after Day had put Southampton ahead in the eighth minute they never really posed a threat. Saints eventually ran out comfortable winners.

A second round tie at Grimsby was not considered to be a particularly easy draw but, even, so, Saints gave a most lethargic display in the face of a Grimsby team playing some of its best football of the season. The issue was not in doubt for very long and Southampton's interest in the Cup was over for another season.

> **Round 1**
> **Nov 20 v Barnet (a) 4-1**
> *Day 2, Mulgrew 2*
> Kiernan; Turner, Traynor, McLaughlin, Wilkins, Simpson, Flood, Mulgrew, Day, Walker, Hoskins.
> *Att: 5,800*
> **Round 2**
> **Dec 11 v Grimsby Town (a) 1-4**
> *Walker*
> Kiernan; Turner, Traynor, McLaughlin, Wilkins, Simpson, Flood, Mulgrew, Day, Walker, Hoskins.
> *Att: 10,075*

> *At home to Coventry, Tommy Mulgrew became the first Southampton player for 22 years to be sent off.*

> *Total home attendance: 338,391. Average: 14,712.*

On the opening day of the season, John Walker completes his hat-trick as Saints win a ten-goal feast against Brentford.

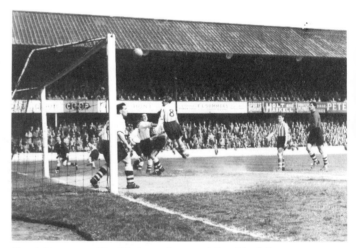

Derek Reeves, making his home League debut, just fails to score with a header against Crystal Palace at The Dell in April 1955. It was the start of a long and distinguished Saints career.

1954-55
Division 3 (South)

Date	V	Opponent	Result	Scorers	Att	Brown P	Christie J	Clements S	Day E	Digby D	Ellerington W	Elliott B	Flood B	Foulkes W	Hoskins J	Kiernan F	McGowan J	McLaughlin R	Mulgrew T	Oakley R	Parker P	Reeves D	Simpson A	Traynor T	Turner F	Walker J	Wilkins L	Williams R
Aug 21	(h)	Brentford	W 6-4	Walker 3, Mulgrew 2, Day	21,453	1			9			4		7	11				8		5	6		3		10	2	
25	(a)	Gillingham	L 0-1		12,034				9			4		7	11	1			8		5	6		3		10	2	
28	(a)	Brighton & HA	W 2-1	Day, Hoskins	22,148				9			4		7	11	1			8		5		6	3		10	2	
Sep 1	(h)	Gillingham	W 3-1	Day 2, Walker	16,690				9			4		7	11	1			8		5		6	3		10	2	
4	(h)	Torquay U	D 0-0		20,138				9			4		7	11	1			8		5		6	3		10	2	
9	(a)	Leyton O	L 1-4	Day	11,188				9			4		7	11	1			8		5		6	3		10	2	
11	(a)	Bristol C	L 0-2		24,550				9			4		7	11	1			8		5		6	3		10	2	
15	(h)	Leyton O	W 1-0	Mulgrew	11,998		5		9					7	11	1		4	8				6	3		10	2	
18	(h)	Walsall	W 2-1	Day, Hoskins	14,533		5		9					7	11	1		4	8				6	3		10	2	
20	(a)	Millwall	L 0-2		11,237		5		9			4		7	11	1			10				6	3		8	2	
25	(a)	Shrewsbury T	L 1-3	Day	8,294		5		9			4		7	11	1			8				6	3		10	2	
29	(a)	Millwall	W 3-0	Day 2, Flood	10,601				9	2			7		11	1		4	8				6	3		10	5	
Oct 2	(h)	Reading	W 3-1	Simpson, Day, Digby	17,172				9	2			7		11	1		4	8				6	3		10	5	
9	(a)	Queen's Park R	D 2-2	Flood, Mulgrew	16,899				9		2		7		11	1		4	8				6	3		10	5	
16	(h)	Newport C	W 2-0	Day, Walker	13,880				9		2		7		11	1		4	8				6	3		10	5	
23	(a)	Exeter C	W 1-0	Day	9,000				9		2		7		11	1		4	8				6	3		10	5	
30	(h)	Northampton T	W 4-0	Walker 2, Day, Hoskins	16,049				9		2		7		11	1		4	8				6	3		10	5	
Nov 6	(a)	Norwich C	L 0-2		17,262				9		2		7		11	1		4	8				6	3		10	5	
13	(h)	Southend U	W 3-0	Walker 2, Day	15,965				9		2		7		11	1		4	8				6	3		10	5	
27	(h)	Swindon T	D 1-1	Hoskins	12,001				9		2		7		11	1		4	8				6	3		10	5	
Dec 4	(a)	Crystal P	W 2-1	Hoskins 2	9,857				9		2		7		11	1		4	8				6	3		10	5	
18	(a)	Brentford	W 3-0	Day 2, Hoskins	9,400				9		2		7		11	1		4	8				6	3		10	5	
25	(a)	Coventry C	D 1-1	Foulkes	23,507			7			2			9	11	1		4	8				6	3		10	5	
27	(h)	Coventry C	W 1-0	Walker	22,528			7			2			9	11	1		4	8				6	3		10	5	
Jan 1	(h)	Brighton & HA	W 3-2	Walker 2, Day	16,164				9		2		7		11	1		4	8				6	3		10	5	
8	(h)	Colchester U	L 0-1		12,449				9		2		7		11	1		4	8				6	3		10	5	
15	(a)	Torquay U	D 2-2	Williams, Day	6,000				9		2		7		11	1		4					6	3		10	5	8
22	(h)	Bristol C	W 2-1	Flood, Day	18,334				9		2		7		11	1		4					6	3		10	5	8
29	(h)	Bournemouth	D 0-0		18,528				9		2		7		11	1		4					6	3		10	5	8
Feb 5	(a)	Walsall	D 0-0		13,292				9		2		7		11	1		4	8				6	3		10	5	
12	(h)	Shrewsbury T	W 2-1	Day, Hoskins	12,224				9		2		7		11	1		4	8				6	3		10	5	
19	(a)	Reading	W 1-0	Hoskins	7,281				9		2		7		11	1		4	8				6	3		10	5	
26	(h)	Queen's Park R	D 2-2	McLaughlin, Hoskins	12,396				9		2		7		11	1		4	8				6	3		10	5	
Mar 5	(a)	Newport C	W 1-0	Walker	7,512				9		2		7		11	1		4	8				6	3		10	5	
12	(h)	Exeter C	W 3-0	Mulgrew 2, Hoskins	12,419				9		2		7		11	1		4	8				6	3		10	5	
19	(a)	Northampton T	L 1-2	Mulgrew	6,855				9		2		7		11	1		4	8				6	3		10	5	
26	(h)	Norwich C	W 3-1	Day 2, Flood	10,780				9		2	6	7		11	1		4	8					3		10	5	
Apr 2	(a)	Southend U	W 1-0	Flood	10,000				9		2	6	7		11	1		4	8					3		10	5	
8	(a)	Watford	L 1-2	Day	12,780				9		2	6	7		11	1		4	8					3		10	5	
9	(h)	Aldershot	D 1-1	Hoskins	13,123				9		2	6	7		11	1		4	8					3		10	5	
11	(h)	Watford	W 2-0	Day, Walker	10,178				9		2	6	7		11	1		4	8					3		10	5	
16	(a)	Swindon T	L 0-1		6,448				9		2	6	7		11	1		4	8					3		10	5	
20	(a)	Bournemouth	D 1-1	Reeves	9,792		1		9		2		7		11			4	8			6		3		10	5	
23	(h)	Crystal P	D 2-2	Day 2	8,788	7	1		9		2	6			11			4	8	10				3			5	
27	(a)	Aldershot	L 0-2		6,333	7	1		9		2	6			11			4	8					3		10	5	
30	(a)	Colchester U	W 5-3	Brown, Mulgrew, Day, Walker, Hoskins	6,386	7	1		9		2	6			11			4	8					3		10	5	
App						3	5	4	44	4	17	19	20	23	44	41	3	34	41	1	7	3	36	46	17	43	46	5
Goals						1			27	1			5	1	13			1	8			1	1			15		1

	P	W	D	L	F	A	Pts
Bristol C	46	30	10	6	101	47	70
Leyton O	46	26	9	11	89	47	61
Southampton	46	24	11	11	75	51	59
Gillingham	46	20	15	11	77	66	55
Millwall	46	20	11	15	72	68	51
Brighton & HA	46	20	10	16	76	63	50
Watford	46	18	14	14	71	62	50
Torquay U	46	18	12	16	82	82	48
Coventry C	46	18	11	17	67	59	47
Southend U	46	17	12	17	83	80	46
Brentford	46	16	14	16	82	82	46
Norwich C	46	18	10	18	60	60	46
Northampton T	46	19	8	19	73	81	46
Aldershot	46	16	13	17	75	71	45
Queen's Park R	46	15	14	17	69	75	44
Shrewsbury T	45	16	10	20	70	78	42
Bournemouth	46	12	18	16	57	65	42
Reading	46	13	15	18	65	73	41
Newport C	46	11	16	19	60	73	38
Crystal P	46	11	16	19	52	80	38
Swindon T	46	11	15	20	46	64	37
Exeter C	46	11	15	20	47	73	37
Walsall	46	10	14	22	75	86	34
Colchester U	46	9	13	24	53	91	31

Back row (left to right): Parker, McGowan, Christie, Traynor, Elliott, Wilkins (captain). Front: Reeves, Walker, Mulgrew, Day, Hoskins.

1955-56

THE ever-hopeful Saints fans trusted that this would be a case of 'third time lucky' in Southampton's quest for the return of Second Division football. However, they had a nasty shock in store. Manager George Roughton, disillusioned with football, announced his resignation following the home defeat by Northampton Town in early September.

The directors were quick to react, appointing reserve-team manager and former Southampton player, Ted Bates. Bates had done a good job with the club's youngsters.

Bates took over a first team which had seen the addition of only one new player in the close season. Brian Bedford, a forward from Reading, had arrived on a free-transfer and it was the tail-end of the season before he made his League debut in Saints' colours.

Southampton had lost £10,000 the previous year and there was no money available for incoming transfers. Saints' chairman was quoted as saying: "In the past nine years, £35,000 more has been spent than received in transfers."

With such financial restrictions, Bates was obviously going to find team-building a difficult task. He relied, not unnaturally, on young players he had known in the reserves to break through into League football. Reeves and Page, in particular, made steady progress.

Eric Day was a model of consistency, missing only one match (and that because of the death of his father). Although Saints form improved after the appointment of Bates, a bad slump towards the end of the season meant that the club finished in their lowest-ever League position.

FA Cup

SAINTS began their 1955-56 FA Cup programme with a hard-fought draw at Selhurst Park. The slippery pitch posed difficulties for both sets of players but Saints played the better football and twice might have scored in the last two minutes, through Hoskins and Elliott.

A replay at The Dell saw Saints carry on where they had left off and it was a surprise to those present that, in the end, they managed to defeat Crystal Palace by only a two-goal margin.

The second round draw paired Southampton with Walsall. It was a blustery day at Fellows Park and Saints started the game kicking into the teeth of a gusting wind. Within four minutes Walsall were 2-0 ahead — one goal coming direct from a corner, largely the result of the wind and Saints faced an immense struggle to get back in the game.

Nevertheless, they managed to pull a goal back in the 24th minute when Flood scored from close-range. That was all they could manage, however, and on the day their forwards somehow lacked the 'killer' approach which might have earned them a reprieve.

> **Round 1**
> **Nov 19 v Crystal Palace (a) 0-0**
> Christie; Wilkins, Traynor, McGowan, Parker, Elliott, Walker, Reeves, Day, Mulgrew, Hoskins.
> *Att: 16,864*
> **Replay**
> **Nov 23 v Crystal Palace (h) 2-0**
> *Reeves, Day*
> Christie; Wilkins, Traynor, McGowan, Parker, Elliott, Walker, Reeves, Day, Mulgrew, Hoskins.
> *Att: 11,883*
> **Round 2**
> **Dec 10 v Walsall (a) 1-2**
> *Flood*
> Kiernan; Wilkins, Traynor, McGowan, Parker, Elliott, Flood, Reeves, Day, Mulgrew, Hoskins.
> *Att: 17,021*

> *Saints continued their policy of playing lucrative floodlit friendly matches and on 13 February 1956, an All Star XI, which inlcuded Stanley Matthews, attracted a crowd of 13,775 to The Dell, despite the fact that the second half was televised live.*

> *Total home attendance: 265,625. Average: 11,548.*

Tommy Mulgrew scores in Saints' 6-2 win over Torquay United at The Dell on 27 December 1955. Traynor, McLaughlin, Hoskins, Walker and Flood scored the others and that is the only time in the club's history that six different Southampton players have found the net in the same match.

1955-56
Division 3 (South)

Date		Opponent	Result		Scorers	Att.	Bedford B	Brown P	Christie J	Day E	Ellerington W	Elliott B	Flood J	Gill M	Gunter D	Hoskins J	Kiernan F	Logan D	McGowan J	McLaughlin R	Mulgrew T	Oakley R	Page J	Parker P	Reeves D	Traynor T	Walker J	Wilkins L
Aug 20	(h)	Swindon	W	2-1	Mulgrew, Walker	17,773		7		9	2	6				11	1		4		8					3	10	5
24	(a)	Ipswich T	L	2-4	Brown, Mulgrew	12,554		7		9	2	6				11	1		4		8					3	10	5
27	(a)	Queen's Park R	L	0-4		10,595		7		10	2	6			3	11	1		4		8						9	5
31	(h)	Ipswich T	D	2-2	Mulgrew, Walker	9,898		7		9	2	6			3	11	1		4		8						10	5
Sep 3	(h)	Northampton T	L	2-3	Day 2	12,263		7		9	2	6			3	11	1		4		8	2					10	5
8	(a)	Newport C	L	0-1		7,048			1	9	2	6	7		3				4		8			11			10	5
10	(a)	Aldershot	L	2-3	Walker 2	6,940			1	9	2	6	7			11			4		8					3	10	5
14	(h)	Newport C	D	3-3	Flood, Day, Hoskins	7,779			1	9	2	6	7			11			4		8					3	10	5
17	(h)	Crystal P	W	3-1	Day 3	11,530			1	9	2	6	7			11			4		8					3	10	5
21	(h)	Walsall	W	4-1	Day 2, McGowan, Walker	7,980			1	9	2	6	7			11			4		8					3	10	5
24	(a)	Brighton & HA	L	0-5		16,366			1	9	2	6	7			11			4		8					3	10	5
26	(a)	Shrewsbury T	L	0-2		7,000			1	9		4	7		3	11			8		6	2					10	5
Oct 1	(a)	Bournemouth	W	3-1	Reeves 2, Mulgrew	10,561			1	9		6	7			11			4		10				5	8	3	2
8	(h)	Millwall	W	3-0	Reeves, Day, Mulgrew	12,461			1	9		6	7						4		10				5	8	3	2
15	(a)	Reading	D	1-1	Mulgrew	11,585			1	9		6	7						4		10				5	8	3	2
22	(h)	Watford	W	2-0	Reeves, Mulgrew	11,305			1	9		6	7						4		10				5	8	3	2
29	(a)	Brentford	L	1-2	Mulgrew	12,300			1	9		6	7						4		10				5	8	3	2
Nov 5	(h)	Coventry C	W	3-0	Day 2, Mulgrew	13,690			1	9		6	7						4		10				5	8	3	2
12	(a)	Southend U	L	1-2	Day	14,000			1	9		6	7						4		10				5	8	3	2
26	(a)	Leyton O	L	0-4		14,760			1	9		6				11			4		10				5	8	3	2
Dec 3	(h)	Colchester U	W	3-0	Reeves, Day, Hoskins	11,072				9		6	7			11	1		4		10				5	8	3	2
17	(a)	Swindon T	D	1-1	Day	7,046				9		6	7			11	1		4		10				5	8	3	2
24	(h)	Queen's Park R	W	4-0	Day 2, Mulgrew 2	9,502				9		6	7			11	1		4		10				5	8	3	2
26	(a)	Torquay U	L	2-3	Day 2	9,585				9		6	7			11	1		4		10				5	8	3	2
27	(h)	Torquay U	W	6-2	Traynor, McLaughlin, Flood, Walker, Mulgrew, Hoskins	17,222				9		6	7			11	1		4	5	10				3	8	2	
31	(a)	Northampton T	L	1-3	Day	11,045				9		6	7		3	11	1		4	5	10					8	2	
Jan 7	(h)	Shrewsbury T	D	1-1	Day	10,218				9		6	7			11	1		4		10				5	8	3	2
14	(h)	Aldershot	W	3-1	Reeves, Day, Hoskins	10,214				9			7			11	1		4	6	10				5	8	3	2
21	(a)	Crystal P	W	2-0	Reeves 2	8,882				9			7			11	1		4	6	10				5	8	3	2
28	(a)	Norwich C	W	4-1	Reeves, Flood, Day, Hoskins	17,034				9			7			11	1		4	6	10				5	8	3	2
Feb 4	(h)	Brighton & HA	L	1-2	Hoskins	14,895				9			7			11	1		4	6	10				5	8	3	2
11	(h)	Bournemouth	W	3-2	Mulgrew 2, Day	9,185				9			7			11	1		4	6	10				5	8	3	2
18	(a)	Millwall	L	2-3	Reeves, Hoskins	6,049				9			7			11	1		4	6	10				5	8	3	2
25	(h)	Reading	W	5-2	Reeves 2, Day 2, Mulgrew	9,013		7		9						11	1		4	6	10		2		5	8	3	
Mar 3	(a)	Watford	L	0-1		4,244				9			7			11	1		4	6	10		2		5	8	3	
10	(h)	Brentford	D	1-1	Page	11,678				9			7			11	1		4	6	10		2		5	8	3	
17	(a)	Coventry C	L	0-2		13,471		7		9		4				11	1			6	10		2		5	8	3	
24	(h)	Southend U	D	0-0		9,329	9			7		4				11	1			6	10		2		5	8	3	
30	(a)	Gillingham	W	2-1	McGowan, Reeves	9,764	9			7		6					1	4					2	5	8	3		11
31	(h)	Exeter C	W	5-0	Day 2, Reeves, Bedford, Walker	9,924	9			7		6				11	1	4					2	5	8	3	10	
Apr 2	(h)	Gillingham	D	1-1	Bedford	11,233	9			7		6					1	4		10			2	5	8	3	11	
7	(h)	Leyton O	L	1-2	McGowan	18,699	9			7	3	6					1	4					2	5	8	11	10	
11	(a)	Exeter C	W	2-1	Brown, Reeves	6,933	8	7		6			3				1	4					2	5	9	11	10	
14	(a)	Colchester U	L	2-3	Mulgrew, Traynor	5,540				7		6					1	4		8			2	5	9	11	10	3
21	(h)	Norwich C	L	2-5	Day, Reeves	9,762				7				6	4					8			2	5	9	11	10	3
28	(a)	Walsall	W	3-1	Reeves 2, Walker	13,469		10				4	11	1					6		8			5	9	2	7	3
App							5	9	15	45	11	36	30	1	7	32	30	1	33	26	39	2	22	25	32	40	29	36
Goals							2	2		28		3				7			3	1	16		1		18		2	8

Back row (left to right): Dibden, Gunter, Page, Kiernan, Christie, Mulholland, Traynor, Hoskins. Middle row: Bates, Mulgrew, Ritchie, Walker, Bedford, Oakley, Parker, Ellerington, L.Wilkins, Brown, Gallagher. Front row: McLaughlin, Reeves, Flood, Roughton (manager), Elliott, McGowan, Logan.

	P	W	D	L	F	A	Pts
Leyton O	46	29	8	9	106	49	66
Brighton & HA	46	29	7	10	112	50	65
Ipswich T	46	25	14	7	106	60	64
Southend U	46	21	11	14	88	80	53
Torquay U	46	20	12	14	86	63	52
Brentford	46	19	14	13	69	66	52
Norwich C	46	19	13	14	86	82	51
Coventry C	46	20	9	17	73	60	49
Bournemouth	46	19	10	17	63	51	48
Gillingham	46	19	10	17	69	71	48
Northampton T	46	20	7	19	67	71	47
Colchester U	46	18	11	17	76	81	47
Shrewsbury T	46	17	12	17	69	66	46
Southampton	46	18	8	20	91	81	44
Aldershot	46	12	16	18	70	90	40
Exeter C	46	15	10	21	58	77	40
Reading	46	15	9	22	70	79	39
Queen's Park R	46	14	11	21	64	86	39
Newport C	46	15	9	22	58	79	39
Walsall	46	15	8	23	68	84	38
Watford	46	13	11	22	52	85	37
Millwall	46	15	6	25	83	00	36
Crystal P	46	12	10	24	54	83	34
Swindon T	46	8	14	24	34	78	30

129

1956-57

THIS was Ted Bates' first full season in charge and during the build-up to the new campaign he concentrated on the players' physical fitness.

One major signing was that of Irishman Jimmy Shields who came from Sunderland for £1,000, although he had yet to make his League debut. Shields was considered to be Eric Day's replacement for, although Saints still held Day's registration, he was prepared to play only on a part-time basis.

Although Shields was the only new signing, it is interesting to note an item in the *Football Echo* in August 1956: "Terry Paine, a Winchester City player in whom Arsenal were interested, has signed pro forms and has been added to Saints' list."

Whether or not it was due to the players' new-found fitness is not clear, but Saints began the season well and by the end of 1956 they were two points clear at the top of the Third Division South, with the defence playing particularly well.

Promotion hopes soared when Bates signed his old Saints team-mate, Don Roper, from Arsenal in the New Year but, inexplicably, Saints' splendid form vanished almost overnight and they slipped down the table.

Lack of 'bite' in the forward line was blamed and it was no surprise when Bates began to look for new blood. On 16 March, the manager introduced 17-year-old Paine to the attack for the visit of Brentford. Despite his tender years, Paine made an immediate impact and although it was now too late to consider promotion, Saints fans were cheered by the prospect of a star in the making.

They were further cheered by the introduction of another young winger when John Sydenham, also 17, began his League career and quickly caught the eye with some electrifying bursts of speed. Saints ended the season in fourth place and with two teenage wingers promising great things for the future. Southampton supporters were already looking eagerly towards the new kick-off.

FA Cup

ERIC Day, recently recalled to Saints' forward line, laid on Reeves' opening goal in the 66th minute when Saints defeated Northampton Town 2-0 in the first round of the FA Cup.

A Mulgrew header, three minutes from time, sealed the result with Saints' defence holding firm despite the fact that Parker had broken his nose in the first half.

Non-League Weymouth were the visitors for the second round and the game aroused much interest along the south coast. The game was a typical cup-tie with Weymouth putting up a gallant fight and Saints struggling, especially after Shields was sent off following an incident involving the Weymouth goalkeeper.

Mulgrew with a header, then a lob, gave Saints a half-time lead and in the second half the game boiled over and the referee saw fit to lecture both teams before Reeves scored a third. Weymouth were not done for, however, and a goal seven minutes from time left Saints with some worrying last moments.

Heavy rain did not spoil the third round tie at Newport where the sides shared six goals in an exciting tussle. Saints were 2-0 down after only 11 minutes before Walker, Shields and Wilkins put them 3-2 ahead on the hour. Nine minutes later Newport equalised and by the time the teams took the field at The Dell they knew that a 'plum' tie with Arsenal awaited the victors.

That pleasure fell to a competent Newport team who thoroughly deserved their 1-0 victory over the Saints.

> Total home attendance: 340,086. Average: 14,786

> Saints had the best defensive record of any League team in 1956-57.

> On 5 September 1956, the floodlights at The Dell were used for the first time in a League game when they were switched on 20 minutes from the end of the match against Colchester United.

Round 1
Nov 17 v Northampton Town (h) 2-0
Reeves, Mulgrew
Christie; Wilkins, Traynor, McLaughlin, Parker, Elliott, Day, Reeves, Shields, Mulgrew, Hoskins.
Att: 16,757
Round 2
Dec 8 v Weymouth (h) 3-2
Mulgrew 2, Reeves
Christie; Wilkins, Traynor, McLaughlin, Parker, Elliott, Dowsett, Reeves, Shields, Mulgrew, Walker.
Att: 21,664
Round 3
Jan 5 v Newport County (a) 3-3
Walker, Shields, Wilkins
Christie; Wilkins, Traynor, McLaughlin, Parker, Elliott, Flood, Reeves, Shields, Mulgrew, Walker.
Att: 19,000
Replay
Jan 9 v Newport County (h) 0-1
Christie; Wilkins, Traynor, McLaughlin, Parker, Elliott, Flood, Reeves, Shields, Mulgrew, Walker.
Att: 22,372

Terry Paine, making his League debut, leaves the Brentford defence flat-footed.

1956-57
Division 3 (South)

Date		Opponent	Res	Scorers	Att	Brown P	Christie J	Day E	Dowsett R	Elliott B	Flood J	Hoskins J	Logan D	McGowan J	McLaughlin R	Mulgrew T	Page J	Paine T	Parker P	Reeves D	Roper D	Shields J	Stevens B	Sydenham J	Traynor T	Walker J	Wilkins L
Aug 18	(h)	Bournemouth	W 3-0	McLaughlin, Reeves, Shields	18,133		1			6	7				4	10			5	8		9			3	11	2
20	(a)	Coventry C	L 1-2	Mulgrew	20,235		1			6	7			4		10			5	8		9			3	11	2
25	(a)	Exeter C	W 4-0	Shields 2, Mulgrew, Walker	9,127		1			6	7			4		10			5	8		9			3	11	2
29	(h)	Coventry C	D 1-1	Flood	15,097		1			6	7			4		10			5	8		9			3	11	2
Sep 1	(h)	Crystal P	W 3-0	Reeves, Shields, Mulgrew	14,118		1			6	7				4	10			5	8		9			3	11	2
5	(h)	Colchester U	W 2-1	Shields, Walker	11,783		1			6	7				4	10			5	8		9			3	11	2
8	(a)	Southend U	W 2-1	Elliott, Shields	12,000	8	1			6	7				4	10			5			9			3	11	2
10	(a)	Colchester U	L 1-3	Mulgrew	7,208	8	1			6	7				4	10			5			9			3	11	2
15	(h)	Northampton T	W 2-0	Mulgrew, Walker	16,018		1			6	7				4	10			5	8		9			3	11	2
22	(a)	Queen's Park R	W 2-1	Shields 2	12,750		1			6	7				4	10			5	8		9			3	11	2
29	(h)	Plymouth A	D 2-2	Shields, Mulgrew	17,192		1			6	7	11			4	10			5	8		9			3		
Oct 3	(h)	Norwich C	W 2-0	Shields 2	18,986		1			6	7				4	10			5	8		9			3	11	2
6	(a)	Millwall	D 0-0		14,272		1			6	7				4	10			5	8		9			3	11	2
13	(h)	Brighton & HA	W 1-0	Reeves	22,103		1			6	7				4	10			5	8		9			3	11	2
20	(a)	Gillingham	D 0-0		10,375		1			6	7				4	10			5	8		9			3	11	2
27	(h)	Swindon T	W 2-1	Reeves	16,739		1			6	7	11			4	10			5	8		9			3		2
Nov 3	(a)	Brentford	L 0-4		14,180		1			6	7	11			4	10			5	8		9			3		2
10	(a)	Aldershot	W 1-0	Reeves	14,852		1	7		6		11			4	10			5	8		9			3		2
24	(h)	Shrewsbury T	W 4-0	Reeves, Shields, Mulgrew, Hoskins	13,195		1	7		6		11			4	10			5	8		9			3		2
28	(a)	Norwich C	W 3-0	Reeves, Mulgrew, Day	8,094		1	7		6		11			4	10			5	8		9			3		2
Dec 1	(a)	Walsall	D 1-1	Reeves	8,571		1	7		6		11			4	10			5	8		9			3		2
15	(a)	Bournemouth	L 0-1		13,646		1		7	6					4	10			5	8		9			3	11	2
22	(h)	Exeter C	D 2-2	Shields, Walker	12,339		1		7	6					4	10			5	8		9			3	11	2
26	(h)	Reading	W 4-1	Reeves 2, Flood, Shields	16,179		1			6	7				4	10			5	8		9			3	11	2
29	(a)	Crystal P	W 2-1	Reeves, Mulgrew	15,805		1			6	7				4	10			5	8		9			3	11	2
Jan 12	(h)	Southend U	L 1-2	Flood	18,121		1			6	7				4	10			5	8	9				3	11	2
19	(a)	Northampton T	L 1-2	Reeves	8,923		1	11		6	7				4	10			5	8	9				3		2
Feb 2	(h)	Queen's Park R	L 1-2	Flood	17,074		1			6	7				4	10			5	8	11	9			3		2
9	(a)	Plymouth A	L 1-2	Mulgrew	14,000		1			6	7	11			4	10			5	8		9			3		2
23	(a)	Brighton & HA	L 0-1		8,102		1	7		6		11			4	8			5	9	10				3		2
25	(h)	Millwall	W 4-0	Reeves 2, Day, Mulgrew	14,034		1	7		6		11			4	10			5	8		9			3		2
Mar 2	(h)	Gillingham	L 0-1		16,559		1	7		6		11			4	10			5	8		9			3		2
9	(a)	Ipswich T	L 0-2		18,831		1	7		6		11			4	10			5		8	9			3		2
16	(h)	Brentford	D 3-3	Reeves, Flood, Traynor	12,166		1			6	7				4			11	5	9	8				3	10	2
23	(a)	Aldershot	D 1-1	Paine	6,473		1			6	7				4		2	11	5	9	8				3	10	
26	(a)	Reading	W 4-2	McLaughlin, Roper, Walker, Paine	8,115		1			6	7				4		2	11	5	9	8				3	10	
30	(h)	Watford	W 3-1	Reeves 2, Roper	11,992		1			6	7				4		2	11	5	9	8				3	10	
Apr 4	(a)	Newport C	W 3-2	Roper 2, Walker	6,990		1			6	7	11			4		2		5	9	8				3	10	
6	(a)	Shrewsbury T	D 0-0		6,590		1			6	7	11			4	10	2		5	9	8				3		
13	(h)	Walsall	W 3-1	Roper, Reeves, Walker	11,499		1			6	7	11			4		2		5	9	8				3	10	
19	(a)	Torquay U	L 0-2		14,223		1			6	7	11			4		2		5	9	8				3	10	
20	(a)	Swindon T	D 0-0		10,515		1	7		6			8	4				11	5			3	9			10	2
22	(h)	Torquay U	W 1-0	Shields	15,240		1	7		6				4				11	5		8	3	9			10	2
27	(a)	Watford	L 2-4	Shields, Day	7,257		1	7		6				4				11	5		8	3	9			10	2
May 1	(h)	Ipswich T	L 0-2		10,946			7		6		11	1	4					5		8	9	1		3	10	2
4	(h)	Newport C	W 3-0	Shields 2, Roper	5,721			7		6			1	4					5		8	9	1	11	3	10	2
App						2	44	13	2	34	31	16	12	7	39	35	7	9	46	41	17	35	2	1	43	31	39
Goals								3		1	5	1			2	11		2		19	6	18			1	7	

Back row: (left to right, players only): McGowan, North, Walker, Dowsett, Gunter, Gill, Christie, Ellerington, Page, Hoskins, Elliott, Clarke. Middle row: Horsfall, Brown, Mulgrew, McLaughlin, Logan, Dibden, Oakley, Parker, Wilkins, Traynor, Reeves, Flood, Gallagher.

	P	W	D	L	F	A	Pts
Ipswich T	46	25	9	12	01	54	59
Torquay U	46	24	11	11	89	64	59
Colchester U	46	22	14	10	84	56	58
Southampton	46	22	10	14	76	52	54
Bournemouth	46	19	14	13	88	62	52
Brighton & HA	46	19	14	13	86	65	52
Southend U	46	18	12	16	73	65	48
Brentford	46	16	16	14	78	76	48
Shrewsbury T	46	15	18	13	72	79	48
Queen's Park R	46	18	11	17	61	60	47
Watford	46	18	10	18	72	75	46
Newport C	46	16	13	17	65	62	45
Reading	46	18	9	19	80	81	45
Northampton T	46	18	9	19	66	73	45
Walsall	46	16	12	18	80	74	44
Coventry C	46	16	12	18	74	84	44
Millwall	46	16	12	18	64	84	44
Plymouth A	46	16	11	19	68	73	43
Aldershot	46	15	12	19	79	92	42
Crystal P	46	11	18	17	62	75	40
Exeter C	46	12	13	21	61	79	37
Gillingham	46	12	13	21	54	85	37
Swindon T	46	15	6	25	66	96	36
Norwich C	46	8	15	23	61	94	31

131

1957-58

THIS season had special importance because the final positions would determine the composition of the new Third and Fourth Divisions, with the regional Third Divisions being swept away. Saints needed to finish in the top half of the table.

Ted Bates kept faith with the squad and the only new arrival was Sam Stevens, a half-back from Airdrie. Yet, while the old guard never looked in danger of finishing below halfway, neither did they appear to be serious contenders for promotion.

Jimmy Shields, who had won a Northern Ireland cap in his first season with Southampton, had the misfortune to break a leg before the new season began and much, therefore, rested on the young shoulders of Terry Paine who responded well and ended the season only missing two games. With John Sydenham also developing well, Ted Bates knew he could build his team around the two youngsters, and Reeves, in particular, was benefiting from their presence.

Saints became the first team this season to score 100 League goals and the fans, if not watching a promotion chase, could at last enjoy some attacking football.

In March, Len Wilkins announced his retirement and Bates was forced to use the transfer market, bringing Birch, a wing-half, from Everton and Davies, a full-back, from Cardiff. These two players settled in well and the patient Saints fans ended yet another season with little to remember, but with high hopes of the next one.

FA Cup

In the Cup, Saints were pitted against the amateurs, Walton & Hersham. The first half of the match on the non-League ground was fairly even with Saints edging into a 2-1 lead through Reeves and Hoskins. In the second half, Saints took complete control and Reeves scored three more. A Mulgrew header completed the rout and Southampton coasted home 6-1.

Their reward was a second-round tie at Selhurst Park and midway into the second half it appeared likely that there would be a repeat of the goalless Cup encounter between the two sides in 1955.

In the 71st minute, however, Christie saved Berry's first shot but could not hold it. The Palace player followed up to smash the ball home and Saints were out of the Cup.

Total home attendance: 341,496. Average: 14,847.

Round 1
Nov 16 v Walton & Hersham (a) 6-1
Reeves 4, Hoskins, Mulgrew
Christie; Page, Traynor, McGowan, Parker, Logan, Paine, Roper, Reeves, Mulgrew, Hoskins.
Att: 6,000
Round 2
Dec 12 v Crystal Palace (a) 0-1
Christie; Page, Traynor, McLaughlin, Parker, Logan, Paine, Roper, Reeves, Mulgrew, Hoskins.
Att: 14,794

Saints scored a record 78 League goals at The Dell in 1957-58. The home and away total of 112 was also a Southampton record, although they came in 46 matches, not the usual 42-match programme of Second Division football. On three occasions, Saints scored seven in a match; six once; and five on no less than five occasions, one of them away to Aldershot.

Goalmouth action as Hoskins and Sheppard challenge for the ball against Coventry City at The Dell in February 1958. Saints won 7-1, one of three occasions on which they shot seven in a match in 1957-8.

1957-58
Division 3 (South)

Date		Opponent	Result	Scorers	Att.	Birch K	Brown P	Christie J	Clarke G	Clifton B	Davies R	Elliott B	Flood J	Hillier B	Hoskins J	Logan D	McGowan J	McLaughlin R	Mulgrew T	Page J	Paine T	Parker P	Reeves D	Roper D	Stevens B	Sydenham J	Traynor T	Walker J	Wilkins L
Aug 24	(a)	Millwall	W 2-1	Reeves 2	16,291			1		6					11			4			7	5	9	8			3	10	2
28	(h)	Walsall	W 4-1	Hoskins 2, Roper, Reeves	17,242			1		6					11			4			7	5	9	8			3	10	2
31	(h)	Gillingham	W 5-1	Hoskins 3, Paine, Roper	18,057			1		6					11			4			7	5	9	8			3	10	2
Sep 5	(a)	Walsall	D 1-1	Paine	12,085			1		6					11			4			7	5	9	8			3	10	2
7	(a)	Exeter C	D 2-2	Roper, Hoskins	9,467			1		6					11			4			7	5	9	8			3	10	2
11	(h)	Port Vale	L 0-3		18,877			1		6					11		4				7	5	9	8			3	10	2
14	(h)	Queen's Park R	W 5-0	Reeves 3, Paine, Walker	15,965			1		6				3	11			4			7	5	9	8				10	2
16	(a)	Port Vale	L 0-4		11,021			1		6					11			4			7	5	9	8			3	10	2
21	(a)	Southend U	L 2-3	McLaughlin, Hoskins	20,000					6					11			4		5	7		9	8	1		3	10	2
25	(h)	Plymouth A	L 0-1		14,251					6					11			4	9	5	7			8	1		3	10	2
28	(h)	Brighton & HA	W 5-0	Roper 2, Clifton 2, Hoskins	18,043					9					11			4		6	7	5		8	1		3	10	2
30	(a)	Plymouth A	L 0-4		25,600					9					11			4		6	7	5		8	1		3	10	2
Oct 5	(h)	Bournemouth	W 7-0	Clifton 2, Walker 2, Hoskins 2, Reeves	22,047					9					11			4		6	7	5	8		1		3	10	2
9	(h)	Swindon T	L 1-3	McGowan	8,829					9					11	4				6	7	5	8	2	1		3	10	
12	(a)	Coventry C	D 0-0		17,227					9						2		6	4		5	7		8		1	11	3	10
19	(a)	Shrewsbury T	D 2-2	Reeves, Paine	13,829	7		2	9							6	4			5	11		8		1		3	10	
26	(a)	Reading	L 0-1		14,409					9					11	6	4		2	7	5	8	5	8	10	1	3		
Nov 2	(h)	Northampton T	W 2-1	McGowan, Mulgrew	13,479							6	4				10	2	7	5		9	1	11	3	8			
9	(a)	Watford	L 0-3		7,890		1						11	6	4		10	2	7	5	9	8			3				
23	(a)	Torquay U	D 1-1	Mulgrew	8,431		1						11	6	4		10	2	7	5	9	8			3				
30	(h)	Brentford	W 4-2	Roper 2, Reeves, Mulgrew	13,690		1						3	11	6		4	10	2	7	5	9	8			3			
Dec 14	(h)	Norwich C	W 7-3	Paine 2, Roper 2, Reeves 2, Hoskins	11,430		1			6				11			4	10	2	7	5	9	8			3			
21	(h)	Millwall	W 3-2	Page, Reeves, Hoskins	11,003		1			6				11			4	10	2	7	5	9	8			3			
25	(a)	Aldershot	W 5-1	Reeves 2, Paine, Roper, Mulgrew	3,803		1			6				11			4	10	2	7	5	9	8			3			
26	(h)	Aldershot	D 2-2	Paine, Page	18,383		1			6				11			4	10	2	7	5	9	8			3			
28	(a)	Gillingham	L 1-2	Paine	10,884		1	8		6				11			4	10	2	7	5	9				3			
Jan 4	(a)	Newport C	D 1-1	Hoskins	5,117		1	8		6				11			4	10	5	7		9			3	2			
11	(h)	Exeter C	W 6-0	Reeves 2, Sydenham 2, Roper, Mulgrew	12,668		1			6							4	10	5	7		9	8		11	3	2		
18	(a)	Queen's Park R	L 2-3	Roper, Sydenham	8,509		1			6							4	10	5	7		9	8		11	3	2		
25	(h)	Crystal P	W 2-1	Paine, Sydenham	13,046		1			6							4	10	5	7		9	8		11	3	2		
Feb 1	(h)	Southend U	D 2-2	Reeves, Opp own goal	15,306		1			6							4	10	5	7		9	8		11	3	2		
8	(a)	Brighton & HA	D 1-1	Opp own goal	17,304		1			6		3					4	10	5	7		9	8		11		2		
15	(a)	Bournemouth	L 2-5	Roper, Reeves	21,752		1			6		3		4				10	5	7		9	8		11		2		
22	(h)	Coventry C	W 7-1	Roper 2, Reeves 2, Hoskins 2, Traynor	11,195		1				7			10			4	6	5			9	8		11	3	2		
Mar 1	(a)	Shrewsbury T	W 3-1	Reeves 3	6,701		1							10			4	6	5	7		9	8		11	3	2		
8	(h)	Reading	L 0-1		22,830		1							10			4	6	5	7		9	8		11	3	2		
15	(a)	Northampton T	W 3-1	Roper, Reeves, Hoskins	9,374	4	1				7			11				6	10	5		9	8			3	2		
22	(h)	Torquay U	W 4-2	Roper, Reeves, Paine, Page	12,728	4	1							11			6	10	5	7		9	8			3	2		
29	(a)	Norwich C	W 2-0	Traynor, Hoskins	21,827	4	1							11			6	10	5	7		9	8			3	2		
Apr 5	(h)	Watford	W 5-0	Reeves 3, Mulgrew 2	11,832	4	1							11			6	10	5	7		9	8			3	2		
7	(a)	Swindon T	L 0-1		15,170	4	1		2					11			6	10	5	7		9	8			3			
12	(a)	Brentford	D 0-0		11,650	4	1		2					11			6	10	5	7		9	8			3			
19	(h)	Colchester U	W 3-2	Reeves, Roper, Page	13,842	4	1		2					11			6	10	5	7		9	8			3			
23	(h)	Newport C	W 2-1	Clifton, Hoskins	12,925	4	1		8	2				11			6	10	5	7		9				3			
26	(a)	Crystal P	W 4-1	Clifton 2, Paine, Reeves	10,480	4	1		8	2				11			6	10	5	7		9				3			
May 1	(a)	Colchester U	L 2-4	Reeves, Mulgrew	8,914	4	1	2	8					11			6	10	5	7						3			
			App			10	1	36	2	12	5	22	2	5	37	8	8	37	30	38	44	22	42	38	10	11	42	17	27
			Goals							7					18		2	1	8	4	12		31	18		4	2	3	

Opp own goal 2

Back row (left to right): Brown, Ellerington, Page, Traynor, Hillier, Logan, McGowan, Elliott. Third row: Clarke, J.Flood, Clifton, B.Flood, B.Stevens, Christie, Parker, Reeves, Simpson, Roper. Second row: Hunt, Paine, Shields, Wilkins, McLaughlin, S.Stevens, Holmes. Front: Maughan, Walker, Sydenham, Hoskins, Mulgrew.

	P	W	D	L	F	A	Pts
Brighton & HA	46	24	12	10	88	64	60
Brentford	46	24	10	12	82	56	58
Plymouth A	46	25	8	13	67	48	58
Swindon T	46	21	15	10	79	50	57
Reading	46	21	13	12	79	51	55
Southampton	46	22	10	14	112	72	54
Southend U	46	21	12	13	90	58	54
Norwich C	46	19	15	12	75	70	53
Bournemouth	46	21	9	16	81	74	51
Queen's Park R	46	18	14	14	64	65	50
Newport C	46	17	14	15	73	67	48
Colchester U	46	17	13	16	77	79	47
Northampton T	46	19	6	21	87	79	44
Crystal P	46	15	13	18	70	72	43
Port Vale	46	16	10	20	67	58	42
Watford	46	13	16	17	59	77	42
Shrewsbury T	46	15	10	21	49	71	40
Aldershot	46	12	16	18	59	89	40
Coventry C	46	13	13	20	61	81	39
Walsall	46	14	9	23	61	75	37
Torquay U	46	12	13	22	49	74	35
Gillingham	46	13	9	24	52	81	35
Millwall	46	11	9	26	63	91	31
Exeter C	46	11	9	26	57	99	31

133

1958-59

SAINTS enjoyed a good start to the new Third Division and moved to the top of the table before injuries to Reeves and Mulgrew blunted their early form.

Reeves scored four goals in the opening match as Saints won 6-1 at Mansfield, then broke a toe; his replacement, Livesey, also scored four goals, at home to Hull — and then he too broke a toe.

Yet these injuries did not seem to affect Saints' overall scoring rate and, again, the fans were treated to plenty of goals, although not as many as the record-breaking previous season.

Generally speaking, however, the season was one of disappointment with the expected boost from the younger players not materialising. Home defeats by Brentford (who won 6-0 at The Dell) and Tranmere particularly depressed supporters who were concerned at unfulfilled potential.

The season which had opened with that six-goal romp on an away ground ended with a 4-0 defeat and an air of despondency settled over The Dell. Ted Bates reacted swiftly, and before the season had even ended he put 14 players on the transfer list.

FA Cup

FA Amateur Cup holders, Woking, were the first-round visitors to The Dell and, although not lacking in enthusiasm, were no match for the Saints who cruised into a three-goal lead after only 25 minutes. Saints then relaxed and their fourth goal did not come until seven minutes from time.

Over 1,000 Saints fans travelled to West London for the second-round tie against Queen's Park Rangers and they saw goalkeeper Tony Godfrey enjoy a fine debut for Southampton.

Godfrey made several fine saves after Reeves had pressurised a QPR defender into conceding an own-goal after only six minutes, and the young 'keeper's vital contribution helped Saints hold out for a fine win.

Blackpool at The Dell was Saints' third-round reward and over 29,000 spectators saw a match marred by a frozen pitch which induced errors on both sides. After only nine minutes Page proved too slow to prevent Blackpool from taking the lead. Page made amends by providing the free-kick which enabled Reeves to head an equaliser shortly afterwards.

Besides being frozen the pitch was also covered in a light dusting of snow which made conditions even worse, yet despite numerous defensive mistakes, neither side seemed capable of getting the winner.

Then, with only two minutes remaining, Stanley Matthews placed over a free-kick of pin-point accuracy and up rose Dave Charnley to head home.

Round 1
Nov 15 v Woking (h) 4-1
Mulgrew 2, Livesey, Paine
Christie; Davies, Traynor, Birch, Parker, Simpson, Paine, Roper, Livesey, Mulgrew, Sydenham.
Att: 18,141
Round 2
Dec v Queen's Park Rangers (a) 1-0
Opp.og
Godfrey; Davies, Traynor, Simpson, Page, Mulgrew, Paine, Roper, Livesey, Reeves, Sydenham.
Att: 13,166
Round 3
Jan 10 v Blackpool (h) 1-2
Reeves
Christie; Davis, Traynor, Birch, Page, Mulgrew, Paine, Roper, Livesey, Reeves, Sydenham.
Att: 29,265

Total home attendance: 314,842. Average: 13,688.

The defeat by Brentford equalled the greatest home reverse suffered by Saints in the Football League. Plymouth Argyle also beat Saints 6-0 at home in season 1931-2.

Woking right-back Ellerby and goalkeeper Burley make a desperate attempt to clear a Livesey header at The Dell. Terry Paine is waiting for a defensive slip. For this FA Cup match, Saints wore unusual crimson and blue quartered shirts, the colours of the Hampshire County FA XI.

Terry Paine (number 7) challenges Bradford City's Lawler and Hudson at The Dell in February 1959, whilst Reeves looks on. Paine scored for Saints but they went down 2-1 to the Yorkshire club.

Division 3

Date		Opponent	Res	Scorers	Att	Birch K	Christie J	Clarke G	Clifton B	Davies R	Godfrey A	Hillier A	Hoskins J	Livesey C	McLoughlin R	Maughan W	Mulgrew T	Page J	Paine T	Parker P	Pring D	Reeves D	Roper D	Shields J	Simpson T	Stevens S	Sydenham J	Traynor T	Vine P
Aug 23	(a)	Mansfield T	W 6-1	Reeves 4, Hoskins, Paine	14,038	4	1			2			11		6		10	5	7			9	8					3	
25	(a)	Chesterfield	D 3-3	Paine, Clifton, Mulgrew	10,387	4	1		8	2			11				10	5	7			9				6		3	
30	(h)	Swindon T	D 1-1	Roper	19,988	4	1		10	2			11	9	6			5	7				8					3	
Sep 1	(h)	Chesterfield	D 0-0		14,903	4	1			2			11	9	6		10	5	7				8					3	
6	(a)	Brentford	L 0-2		12,980	4	1		9	2			11		6		10	5	7				8					3	
8	(a)	Halifax T	L 0-2		6,288	4	1			2			10	9			8	5	7							6	11	3	
13	(h)	Hull C	W 6-1	Livesey 4, Mulgrew, Paine	14,461	4	1			2			10	9			8	5	7							6	11	3	
17	(h)	Halifax T	W 5-0	Livesey 2, Page, Birch, Hoskins	16,493	4	1			2			10	9			8	5	7							6	11	3	
20	(a)	Bradford C	W 3-2	Paine, Roper, Hoskins	15,534	4	1			2			10				8	5	7				9			6	11	3	
25	(a)	Notts C	W 2-1	Reeves, Paine	6,171	4	1			2			11				8	5	7			9	10			6		3	
27	(h)	Wrexham	L 1-2	Reeves	18,048		1		4	2			10				8	5	7			9				6	11	3	
Oct 1	(h)	Notts C	W 3-0	Page, Livesey, Roper	16,548	4	1			2			11	9				5	7			10	8			6		3	
4	(h)	Reading	D 3-3	Reeves, Hoskins, Opp own goal	17,382	4	1			2			11	9	10			5	7				8			6		3	
8	(a)	Accrington S	D 0-0		8,600	4	1			2			11	9	6			5	7			10	8					3	
11	(a)	Bournemouth	L 1-2	Hoskins	18,448	4	1			2			11	9	6		10	5	7				8					3	
18	(h)	Norwich C	D 1-1	Birch	15,744	4	1			2			11	9	6			5	7			10	8					3	
25	(a)	Southend U	D 1-1	Roper	13,300	4	1			2			11		6		10	5	7			9	8					3	
Nov 1	(h)	Bury	W 4-2	Livesey 2, Sydenham, Birch	14,972	4	1			2				9			10	5	7				8			6	11	3	
8	(h)	Queen's Park R	D 2-2	Livesey, Mulgrew	11,158	4	1			2				9			10	5	7				8			6	11	3	
22	(a)	Tranmere R	L 0-2		12,814	4	1			2				9			10	5	7				8			6	11	3	
29	(h)	Plymouth A	W 5-1	Paine 2, Reeves, Roper, Sydenham	21,830		1			2				9			6	5	7			10	8		4		11	3	
Dec 13	(h)	Stockport C	W 2-1	Page, Roper	14,437					2	1		9				6	5	7			10	8		4		11	3	
20	(h)	Mansfield T	W 3-2	Page, Shields, Clifton	17,901				10	2	1						6	5	7				8	9	4		11	3	
25	(a)	Newport C	L 2-4	Shields, Clifton	9,034				10	2	1	3	11				6	5	7				8	9	4				
27	(h)	Newport C	D 3-3	Paine 2, Clifton	21,495				10	2	1	3	11				6	5	7				8	9	4				
Jan 3	(a)	Swindon T	L 1-3	Clifton	12,070				10	2	1	3	11	9			6	5	7				8		4				
24	(a)	Doncaster R	L 2-3	Roper, Reeves	6,251		1			2			11	9			6	5	7			10	8		4			3	
31	(a)	Hull C	L 0-3		14,441					2	1		11		6		10	5	7			9	8		4			3	
Feb 2	(h)	Rochdale	W 6-1	Reeves 2, Mulgrew 2, Hoskins 2	7,193	4			8	2	1		11		6		10	5	7			9						3	
7	(h)	Bradford C	L 1-2	Paine	11,730	4				2	1		11		6		10	5	7	3		9	8						
14	(a)	Wrexham	W 3-1	Livesey 3	9,787				10	2	1		11	9	4		3		7	5			8		6				
21	(h)	Reading	L 1-4	Reeves	10,372				10	2	1		11		4		3		7	5		9	8		6				
28	(h)	Bournemouth	D 0-0		16,896	4				2	1		11	9			10	5	7	3			8		6				
Mar 7	(a)	Norwich C	L 1-3	Paine	23,873					2	1		11	9	4		3	5	7			10	8		6				
9	(h)	Brentford	L 0-6		7,765					2	1		11	9	4		3	5	7			10	8		6				
14	(h)	Southend U	W 3-2	Page, Roper, Reeves	9,251		1		4	2			11				10	5	7			9	8		6			3	
21	(a)	Bury	L 0-1		6,360		1		4	2			11		6		10	5	7			9						3	8
27	(a)	Colchester U	W 3-1	Paine, Reeves, Hoskins	8,943		1		4	2			11	8	6		10	5	7			9						3	
28	(h)	Queen's Park R	W 1-0	Reeves	9,208	4	1			2			11		6		10	5	7			9			8			3	
30	(h)	Colchester U	W 3-0	Reeves, Page, Mulgrew	8,502	4	1			2			10		6		8	5	7			9					11	3	
Apr 4	(a)	Rochdale	L 0-1		3,948		1	2	4				10		6		8	5	7			9					11	3	
11	(h)	Tranmere R	L 2-3	Paine, Opp own goal	7,505		1		4	2							10	5	7			9	8		6		11	3	
18	(a)	Plymouth A	L 0-1		23,775				4	2	1						10	5	7			9	8		6		11	3	
22	(h)	Accrington S	W 3-1	Mulgrew 2, Livesey	6,808				4	2	1			9			10	5	7				8		6		11	3	
25	(h)	Doncaster R	D 1-1	Traynor	5,782				4	2	1			9			10	5	7				8		6		11	3	
27	(a)	Stockport C	L 0-4		4,000				4	2	1	3	11	9			10	5	7				8		6				
App						24	29	1	19	39	17	4	36	25	16	1	42	36	46	23	4	30	25	3	18	14	17	36	1
Goals						3			5				8	14			8	6	13			16	8	2			2	1	

Opp own goal 1

Back row (left to right): Holmes, Davies, Traynor, Godfrey, B.Stevens, Christie, Page, Hillier, Elliott. Third row: Livesey, Clarke, Shields, Maughan, Harley, Simpson, S.Stevens, Hoskins, Clifton, Parker. Second row: Birch, Ellerington, Roper, Bailey, Mulgrew, McLoughlin, Reeves. Front row: Fryer, Paine, Sydenham, Vine, Scurr, Heaney.

	P	W	D	L	F	A	Pts
Plymouth A	46	23	16	7	89	59	62
Hull C	46	26	9	11	90	55	61
Brentford	46	21	15	10	76	49	57
Norwich C	46	22	13	11	89	62	57
Colchester U	46	21	10	15	71	67	52
Reading	46	21	8	17	78	63	50
Tranmere R	46	21	8	17	82	67	50
Southend U	46	21	8	17	85	80	50
Halifax T	46	21	8	17	80	77	50
Bury	46	17	14	15	69	58	48
Bradford C	46	18	11	17	84	76	47
Bournemouth	46	17	12	17	69	69	46
Queen's Park R	46	19	8	19	74	77	46
Southampton	46	17	11	18	88	80	45
Swindon T	46	16	13	17	59	57	45
Chesterfield	46	17	10	19	67	64	44
Newport C	46	17	9	20	69	68	43
Wrexham	46	14	14	18	63	77	42
Accrington S	46	15	12	19	71	87	42
Mansfield T	46	14	13	19	73	98	41
Stockport C	46	13	10	23	65	78	36
Doncaster R	46	14	5	27	50	90	33
Notts C	46	8	13	25	55	96	29
Rochdale	46	8	12	26	37	79	28

1959-60

WITH 14 players leaving the club, and nine new men arriving, Ted Bates had underlined the need for drastic action. Of the new arrivals, Cliff Huxford, a wing-half from Chelsea, was arguably the most important and he soon became Saints' skipper and a tower of strength on and off the pitch.

Another player who fitted in from the outset was George O'Brien, who teamed up with Derek Reeves to form a formidable goalscoring combination. Paine and Sydenham were now more experienced players and seemed to be rounding Third Division full-backs virtually at will.

With the forwards in such fine fettle, Saints ought to have been top of the table in the early stages but the defence was letting in nearly as many goals as the forwards scored. As the season progressed, however, the rearguard, under Huxford, began to settle and Southampton crept up the table.

By February they were four points clear with two games in hand and seemed certain of promotion. But many fans could remember those days of the 1940s when promotion had seemed equally 'certain'. They refused to believe that Saints

would maintain their challenge.

This time, though, their fears were groundless and Saints maintained their form and stormed back to Division Two, playing irrepressible football and finishing the season nine points clear of the third-placed club. Saints clinched their first Championship since 1921-2 by scoring 106 goals.

This time they had steered clear of injuries and were able to field a settled side, this as much as anything helping them maintain the consistency that had been so lacking in previous seasons.

Mention must be made of the signings in March of two experienced players in inside-forward Gordon Brown, from Derby County, and Spurs' reserve goalkeeper Ron Reynolds. They helped steady the team when two heavy defeats, at Newport and Coventry, showed that nerves were beginning to fray. Brown's winning goal at Loftus Road towards the end of March was particularly crucial.

Derek Reeves hit 39 goals, still a League record for Southampton.

FA Cup

TRAILING 1-0 after only 16 minutes of their first-round tie at Coventry, Saints fought back with an equaliser from Reeves after 57 minutes. Four days later, Coventry never adapted to a waterlogged pitch at The Dell and after Reeves had set the scene by hitting the bar in only the second minute, Saints emerged comfortable winners.

Southend played much better than the 3-0 scoreline suggests when they visited The Dell in the second round. The best goal of the game was Saints' third, a full-length diving header by Reeves who was enjoying a fine season.

Southampton's finest hour was yet to come, however. It seemed that, when Manchester City took an 18th-minute lead through Colin Barlow at Maine Road in the third round, Saints' faint hopes against the First Division side were dashed.

But within minutes, Reeves had equalised, then Paine made another goal for the centre-forward, and Saints went to the dressing-room 2-1 ahead.

The second half belonged to Paine. Time after time he rounded his full-back to set up chances and Reeves and

O'Brien both took advantage. For Reeves it was an unforgettable afternoon and a rocket of a shot brought him his fourth goal and Saints' fifth.

The fourth round brought Watford to The Dell and O'Brien twice equalised and then had what he thought was a last-minute winner disallowed. Saints missed him when injury ruled him out of the replay and a 32nd-minute goal at muddy Vicarage Road sent Saints tumbling out.

Jubilant Saints pictured in the Maine Road dressing-room after hammering First Division Manchester City 5-1.

Round 1
Nov 14 v Coventry City (a) 1-1
Reeves
Charles; Davies, Traynor, Connor, Page, Huxford, Paine, O'Brien, Reeves, Mulgrew, Sydenham.
Att: 14,291
Replay
Nov 18 v Coventry City (h) 5-1
Page, Simpson 2, O'Brien, Paine
Charles; Davies, Traynor, Connor, Page, Huxford, Paine, O'Brien, Reeves, Simpson, Sydenham.
Att: 18,650
Round 2
Dec 5 v Southend United (h) 3-0
Paine 2, Reeves
Charles; Davies, Traynor, Conner, Page, Huxford, Paine, O'Brien, Reeves, Mulgrew, Sydenham.
Att: 21,692
Round 3
Jan 9 v Manchester City (a) 5-1
Reeves 4, O'Brien
Charles; Davies, Traynor, Conner, Page, Huxford, Paine, O'Brien, Reeves, Mulgrew, Sydenham.
Att: 42,065
Round 4
Jan 30 v Watford (h) 2-2
O'Brien 2
Charles; Davies, Traynor, Conner, Page, Huxford, Paine, O'Brien, Reeves, Mulgrew, Sydenham.
Att: 28,619
Replay
Feb 2 v Watford (a) 0-1
Charles; Davies, Traynor, Conner, Page, Huxford, Paine, Maughan, Reeves, Mulgrew, Sydenham.
Att: 27,925

Total home attendance: 415,385. Average: 18,060.

1959-60
Division 3

Date	Opponent	Res	Scorers	Att	Brown G	Charles R	Clifton B	Conner R	Davies R	Godfrey A	Harrison B	Holmes C	Huxford C	Kennedy P	Maughan W	Mulgrew T	O'Brien G	Page J	Paine T	Reeves D	Reynolds R	Scurr D	Simpson T	Sydenham J	Traynor T
Aug 22 (h)	Norwich C	D 2-2	Reeves, Sydenham	22,581				4	2	1			6	3		10	8	5	7	9				11	
24 (a)	Chesterfield	L 2-3	Page, O'Brien	8,740				4	2	1			6	3		10	8	5	7	9				11	
29 (a)	Brentford	D 2-2	Paine, Reeves	15,740				4	2	1			6			10	8	5	7	9				11	3
Sep 2 (h)	Chesterfield	W 4-3	O'Brien 2, Conner, Reeves	15,266				4	2	1			6			10	8	5	7	9				11	3
5 (h)	Colchester U	W 4-2	Huxford, Paine, Reeves, Mulgrew	14,704				4	2	1			6			10	8	5	7	9				11	3
7 (a)	Port Vale	D 1-1	O'Brien	13,853				4	2	1			6			10	8	5	7	9				11	3
12 (a)	Southend U	W 4-2	Reeves 3, O'Brien	10,692				4	2	1			6			10	8	5	7	9				11	3
16 (h)	Port Vale	W 3-2	Reeves 2, Huxford	17,009				4	2	1			6			10	8	5	7	9				11	3
19 (h)	Mansfield T	W 5-2	Reeves 3, O'Brien, Mulgrew	15,831				4	2	1			6			10	8	5	7	9				11	3
23 (h)	Shrewsbury T	W 6-3	Reeves 2, Paine, O'Brien, Mulgrew, Sydenham	19,172				4	2	1			6			10	8	5	7	9				11	3
26 (a)	Halifax T	L 1-3	Reeves	12,163				4	2	1			6			10	8	5	7	9				11	3
28 (a)	Shrewsbury T	D 1-1	Paine	8,240		1		4	2				6			10	8	5	7	9				11	3
Oct 3 (h)	Bury	L 0-2		18,160		1		4	2				6			10	8	5	7	9				11	3
7 (a)	Barnsley	L 0-1		4,549		1		6	2		7		4			10	8	5	11	9					3
10 (h)	Swindon T	W 5-1	Reeves 4, Paine	15,647		1		4	2		7		6			10		5	8	9				11	3
14 (h)	Barnsley	W 2-1	Mulgrew 2	16,937		1		4	2		7		6			10		5	8	9				11	3
17 (a)	York C	D 2-2	O'Brien	8,371		1		4	2				6			10	8	5	7	9				11	3
24 (h)	Coventry C	W 5-1	Page 2, Reeves, O'Brien, Mulgrew	16,613		1		4	2				6			10	8	5	7	9				11	3
31 (a)	Accrington S	D 2-2	Page, Reeves	3,300		1		4	2				6			10	8	5	7	9				11	3
Nov 7 (h)	Queen's Park R	W 2-1	Reeves, O'Brien	18,619		1		4	2				6			10	8	5	7	9				11	3
21 (h)	Wrexham	W 3-0	O'Brien 2, Reeves	15,974		1		4	2				6				8	5	7	9		10		11	3
28 (a)	Tranmere R	W 4-2	Mulgrew 2, Paine, Reeves	7,927		1		4	2				6			10	8	5	7	9				11	3
Dec 12 (a)	Bradford C	L 0-2		9,426		1		4	2				6			10	8	5	7	9				11	3
19 (h)	Norwich C	W 2-1	O'Brien, Reeves	13,747		1		4	2				6			10	8	5	7	9				11	3
26 (h)	Newport C	W 2-0	Reeves 2	19,167		1		4	2				6			10	8	5	7	9				11	3
Jan 2 (h)	Brentford	W 2-0	O'Brien 2	16,993		1		4	2				6			10	8	5	7	9				11	3
23 (h)	Southend U	W 3-1	Paine, Mulgrew, Opp own goal	13,535		1		4	2				6			10	8	5	7	9				11	3
Feb 6 (a)	Mansfield T	L 2-4	Paine, Reeves	7,435		1		4	2				6		8	10		5	7	9				11	3
13 (h)	Halifax T	W 3-2	Mulgrew 2, Reeves	11,515		1		4	2				6		8	10		5	7	9				11	3
20 (a)	Bury	W 2-1	Reeves, Conner	14,413		1		4	2				6			10	8	5	7	9				11	3
24 (h)	Bournemouth	W 4-3	Clifton 2, O'Brien, Reeves	20,800		1	10	4	2				6				8	5	7	9				11	3
27 (a)	Swindon T	W 3-0	O'Brien, Reeves, Clifton	16,645		1	10	4	2				6				8	5	7	9				11	3
Mar 5 (h)	York C	W 3-1	O'Brien, Reeves, Clifton	20,844		1	10	4	2				6				8	5	7	9				11	3
7 (a)	Newport C	L 1-5	Page	6,429		1		4	2				6			10	8	5	7	9				11	3
12 (a)	Coventry C	L 1-4	Reeves	17,842		1		4	2				6			10	8	5	7	9			3	11	
19 (h)	Tranmere R	D 1-1	Brown	18,576	10			4	2				6				8	5	7	9	1			11	3
21 (a)	Colchester U	D 1-1	Reeves	10,105	10			4	2				6				8	5	7	9	1			11	3
26 (a)	Queen's Park R	W 1-0	Brown	11,593	10			4	2				6				8	5	7	9	1			11	3
Apr 2 (h)	Grimsby T	D 1-1	O'Brien	20,376	10			4	2				6				8	5	7	9	1			11	3
9 (a)	Wrexham	L 1-2	O'Brien	7,583				4	2			5	6			10	8		7	9	1			11	3
15 (a)	Reading	L 0-2		23,673	10			4	2				6				8	5	7	9	1			11	3
16 (h)	Accrington S	W 5-1	O'Brien 2, Page, Clifton, Reeves	20,356			10	4	2				6				8	5	7	9	1			11	3
18 (h)	Reading	W 1-0	Clifton	25,042			10	4	2				6				8	5	7	9	1			11	3
23 (a)	Bournemouth	W 3-1	Page 2, Clifton	21,657			10	4	2				6				8	5	7	9	1			11	3
26 (a)	Grimsby T	L 2-3	Reeves, Clifton	11,500			10	4	2				6				8	5	7	9	1			11	3
30 (h)	Bradford C	W 2-0	Reeves, O'Brien	21,848				4	2				6			10	8	5	7	9	1			11	3
App					5	24	8	45	46	11	3	1	46	2	2	33	42	45	46	46	11	1	1	45	43
Goals					2		8	2					2			11	23	8	8	39				2	

Opp own goal 1

Back row (left to right): D.Scurr, B.Clifton, C.Holmes, T.Mulgrew, B.Harrison. Middle row: W.Maughan, P.Kennedy, D.Conner, R.Reynolds, J.Page, G.Brown, T.Traynor. Front row: J.Gallagher (trainer), J.Sydenham, T.Paine, C.Huxford, C.O'Brien, D.Reeves, E.Bates (manager).

	P	W	D	L	F	A	Pts
Southampton	46	26	9	11	106	75	61
Norwich C	46	24	11	11	82	54	59
Shrewsbury T	46	18	16	12	97	75	52
Coventry C	46	21	10	15	78	63	52
Grimsby T	46	18	16	12	87	70	52
Brentford	46	21	9	16	78	61	51
Bury	46	21	9	16	64	51	51
Queen's Park R	46	18	13	15	73	54	49
Colchester U	46	18	11	17	83	74	47
Bournemouth	46	17	13	16	72	72	47
Reading	46	18	10	18	84	77	46
Southend U	46	19	8	19	76	74	46
Newport C	46	20	6	20	80	79	46
Port Vale	46	19	8	19	80	79	46
Halifax T	46	18	10	18	70	72	46
Swindon T	46	19	8	19	69	78	46
Barnsley	46	15	14	17	65	66	44
Chesterfield	46	18	7	21	71	84	43
Bradford C	46	15	12	19	66	74	42
Tranmere R	46	14	13	19	72	75	41
York C	46	13	12	21	57	73	38
Mansfield T	46	15	6	25	81	112	36
Wrexham	46	14	8	24	68	101	36
Accrington S	46	11	5	30	57	123	27

1960-61

SOUTHAMPTON were now back in Division Two where they had spent most of their League career. Ted Bates sensibly gave the promotion-winning players a chance to prove themselves still further and confidence soared with two fine home victories over Liverpool and Portsmouth, followed by a win at Anfield within the first month.

This good start was maintained and by Christmas it seemed possible that Saints could astound everyone and go straight into the First Division. But with the New Year came heavier grounds and this seemed to stifle Saints' style of play. They lost touch with the leaders and finished in eighth place.

More sober Saints fans voiced the opinion that promotion would have done more harm than good and that another season or two was needed to improve the squad of players.

FA Cup

GEORGE O'Brien scored a hat-trick when Saints crushed fellow promotion-seekers, Ipswich Town, at The Dell in the third round. It was an amazing performance as O'Brien's three had come by the 28th minute. Indeed, in one spell Saints hit four goals in seven minutes.

In the fourth round it was Saints' turn to be on the receiving end of a shock result when unfancied Leyton Orient beat them 1-0 at The Dell. The pitch was so waterlogged that the game was nearly called off, and Traynor fell ill on the morning of the game. Even so, Saints fans wondered how their side could score seven goals in one tie and then fall to a rank outsider the next.

Round 3
Jan 7 v Ipswich Town (h) 7-1
O'Brien 3, Mulgrew 2, Penk, Paine
Reynolds; Davies, Traynor, Davies, Conner, Page, Huxford, Paine, O'Brien, Reeves, Mulgrew, Penk.
Att: 20,422
Round 4
Jan 28 v Leyton Orient (h) 0-1
Reynolds; Davies, Scurr, Conner, Page, Huxford, Paine, O'Brien, Reeves, Mulgrew, Penk.
Att: 21,392

Total home attendance: 391,969. Average: 18,665.

During this season there was a degree of 'player unrest' throughout the Football League and players at Southampton were asked if they would be prepared to strike. Fifteen voted against strike action with seven in favour. The seven were: Conner, Penk, Davies, Huxford, Mulgrew, Traynor and Paine.

The Portsmouth match in August 1960 was the first local derby for 33 years.

Ipswich centre-half Nelson clears this Saints' attack but the Suffolk club were still hit for seven goals in the FA Cup.

Football League Cup

SOUTHAMPTON were not one of the clubs who ignored the fledgling League Cup and were rewarded by marching to the fifth round before losing 4-2 to Burnley.

One real highlight was a third-round victory at Anfield — Saints beat Liverpool three times in 1960-61 — when two goals from Terry Paine sank the Merseysiders, but the fourth-round game against Leeds was perhaps the most amazing ever witnessed at The Dell.

There was a 29-minute delay when the floodlights failed, and five minutes after Reeves put Saints in front with a header, they lost goalkeeper Reynolds who was injured. As Reynolds was carried off, the lights failed yet again. When illumination was restored it revealed Huxford in the green jersey.

Reeves hit three more goals, then Leeds pulled back four goals — the equaliser coming from a penalty, before ten-man Saints snatched the winner with 30 seconds left. Inevitably, Reeves was the scorer to give him all five goals.

Round 1
Oct 10 v Newport County (a) 2-2
Page, Paine
Reynolds; Davies, Traynor, Conner, Page, Clifton, Paine, O'Brien, Reeves, Mulgrew, Penk.
Att: 6,139
Replay
Oct 17 v Newport County (h) 2-2
O'Brien, Reeves
Reynolds; Davies, Traynor, Conner, Page, Clifton, Paine, O'Brien, Reeves, Mulgrew, Sydenham.
Att: 8,000
Second Replay
Oct 26 v Newport County (h) 5-3
Paine 2, O'Brien, Reeves, Traynor
Reynolds; Davies, Traynor, Conner, Page, Clifton, Paine, O'Brien, Reeves, Mulgrew, Sydenham.
Att: 8,414
Round 2
Oct 31 v Colchester United (a) 2-0
Paine, Sydenham
Reynolds; Davies, Traynor, Huxford, Page, Clifton, Paine, O'Brien, Reeves, Mulgrew, Sydenham.
Att: 6,264
Round 3
Nov 12 v Liverpool (a) 2-1
Paine 2
Reynolds; Davies, Traynor, Huxford, Page, Clifton, Paine, O'Brien, Reeves, Mulgrew, Sydenham.
Att: 14,036
Round 4
Dec 5 v Leeds United (h) 5-4
Reeves 5
Reynolds; Davies, Traynor, Conner, Page, Huxford, Paine, O'Brien, Reeves, Mulgrew, Sydenham.
Att: 13,487
Round 5
Feb 6 v Burnley (h) 2-4
Clifton, Reeves
Reynolds; Davies, Traynor, Conner, Page, Huxford, Paine, Clifton, Reeves, Mulgrew, Penk.
Att: 26,534

1960-61
Division 2

Date		Opponent	Res	Score	Scorers	Att	Brown G	Charles R	Clifton B	Conner R	Davies R	Godfrey A	Heaney A	Huxford C	Lindsay H	Maughan W	Mulgrew T	O'Brien G	Page J	Paine T	Penk H	Reeves D	Reynolds R	Scurr D	Simpson T	Sydenham J	Traynor T
Aug 20	(a)	Rotherham U	L	0-1		10,476				4	2			6			10	8	5	7		9	1			11	3
24	(h)	Liverpool	W	4-1	Paine, Reeves, O'Brien, Sydenham	24,823			4		2			6			10	8	5	7		9	1			11	3
27	(h)	Portsmouth	W	5-1	Paine, O'Brien, Mulgrew, Huxford, Opp own goal	28,845			4		2			6			10	8	5	7		9	1			11	3
31	(a)	Liverpool	W	1-0	O'Brien	37,604			4		2			6			10	8	5	7		9	1			11	3
Sep 3	(h)	Leeds U	L	2-4	Paine, Reeves	21,872			4		2			6			10	8	5	7		9	1			11	3
7	(h)	Derby C	W	5-1	O'Brien 2, Clifton 2, Paine	21,250			10	4	2			6				8	5	7		9	1	3		11	
10	(a)	Middlesbrough	L	0-5		16,526			10	4	2			6				8	5	7	11	9	1				3
14	(a)	Derby C	D	2-2	Clifton, Paine	12,950	9		4		2			6			10	8	5	7			1			11	3
17	(h)	Brighton & HA	W	4-2	O'Brien 4	19,349	9	1	6	4			2				10	8	5	7						11	3
24	(a)	Ipswich T	D	3-3	Paine 2, Mulgrew	15,307	9		6	4	2						10	8	5	7			1			11	3
Oct 1	(h)	Scunthorpe U	W	4-2	Page 2, Paine, Opp own goal	17,464			6	4	2						10	8	5	7		9	1			11	3
8	(a)	Huddersfield T	L	1-3	Penk	11,220			6	4	2						10	8	5	7	11	9	1				3
15	(h)	Sunderland	W	3-2	O'Brien, Reeves, Mulgrew	20,188			6	4	2						10	8	5	7		9	1			11	3
22	(a)	Plymouth A	W	3-1	O'Brien, Paine, Sydenham	23,017			6	4	2						10	8	5	7		9	1			11	3
29	(h)	Norwich C	D	2-2	O'Brien, Reeves	21,979			6	4	2						10	8	5	7		9	1			11	3
Nov 5	(a)	Charlton A	W	3-1	Mulgrew 2, Reeves	15,622			6		2				4		10	8	5	7		9	1			11	3
12	(h)	Sheffield U	L	0-1		27,405			6		2				4		10	8	5	7		9	1			11	3
19	(a)	Stoke C	W	2-1	Page, O'Brien	10,465				4	2			6			10	8	5	7		9	1			11	3
26	(h)	Swansea T	W	5-0	Paine 2, Mulgrew 2, Sydenham	16,077				4	2			6			10	8	5	7		9	1			11	3
Dec 3	(a)	Luton T	L	1-4	O'Brien	12,927				4	2			6			10	8	5	7		9	1			11	3
10	(h)	Lincoln C	L	2-3	Page, Mulgrew	15,159	1			4	2			6			10	8	5	7		9				11	3
17	(h)	Rotherham U	W	3-2	Paine, O'Brien, Mulgrew	13,120				4	2			6			10	8	5	7	11	9	1				3
26	(h)	Bristol R	W	4-2	Reeves 2, Page, O'Brien	21,901				4	2			6			10	8	5	7	11	9	1				3
31	(a)	Portsmouth	D	1-1	Mulgrew	31,509				4	2			6			10	8	5	7	11	9	1				3
Jan 14	(a)	Leeds U	L	0-3		14,039				4	2			6			10	8	5	7	11	9	1				3
21	(h)	Middlesbrough	W	3-2	Paine, Reeves, Penk	18,560				4	2			6			10	8	5	7	11	9	1				3
Feb 4	(a)	Brighton & HA	W	1-0	Mulgrew	20,640				4	2			6			10	8	5	7	11	9	1				3
11	(h)	Ipswich T	D	1-1	O'Brien	19,946				4	2			6			10	8	5	7	11	9	1				3
18	(a)	Scunthorpe U	L	0-2		8,341	9			4	2			6			10	8	5	7	11		1				3
25	(h)	Huddersfield T	W	4-2	O'Brien 2, Paine, Reeves	14,368				4	2	1		6			10	8	5	7	11	9					3
Mar 11	(h)	Plymouth A	D	1-1	Mulgrew	18,949				4	2	1		6			10	8	5	7	11	9					3
18	(a)	Lincoln C	W	3-0	O'Brien 2, Paine	5,082			6	4	2						10	8	5	7	11	9	1				3
20	(a)	Bristol R	L	2-4	O'Brien, Paine	15,699			6	4	2	1					10	8	5	7	11	9					3
25	(h)	Charlton A	L	1-2	Paine	18,527			6	4	2						10	8	5	7		9	1			11	3
29	(a)	Leyton O	D	1-1	Mulgrew	11,247				4	2	1		6			10	8	5	7		9				11	3
Apr 1	(a)	Swansea T	L	1-4	Penk	13,708				4	2	1		6			10	8	5	7	11	9					3
3	(h)	Leyton O	D	1-1	Traynor	12,199				4	2	1		6			10	8	5	7	11	9					3
8	(h)	Stoke C	L	0-1		12,972				4	2	1		6			10	8	5	7	11	9					3
15	(a)	Sheffield U	L	1-2	Maughan	21,225			10	4	2			6		9		8	5	7			1			11	3
17	(a)	Sunderland	L	1-3	Clifton	14,635			10	4	2			6		9		8	5	7	11		1				3
22	(h)	Luton T	W	3-2	Paine, Reeves, Clifton	7,016			10	4	2			6				8		7	11	9	1		5		3
29	(a)	Norwich C	L	0-5		18,756			8	4	2	1		6			10			7	11	9			5		3
App							3	2	26	33	41	8	1	34	2	2	36	41	40	42	20	35	32	1	2	22	39
Goals									5					1		1	13	22	5	18	3	10				3	1

Opp own goal 2

Back row (left to right): Traynor, Charles, Reynolds, Davies. Middle: E.Bates, Scurr, Reeves, Page, Brown, Huxford, Gallagher. Front: Conner, Penk, Paine, O'Brien, Maughan, Clifton, Mulgrew.

	P	W	D	L	F	A	Pts
Ipswich T	42	26	7	9	100	55	59
Sheffield U	42	26	6	10	81	51	58
Liverpool	42	21	10	11	87	58	52
Norwich C	42	20	9	13	70	53	49
Middlesbrough	42	18	12	12	83	74	48
Sunderland	42	17	13	12	75	60	47
Swindon T	42	18	11	13	77	73	47
Southampton	42	18	8	16	84	81	44
Scunthorpe U	42	14	15	13	69	64	43
Charlton A	42	16	11	15	97	91	43
Plymouth A	42	17	8	17	81	82	42
Derby C	42	15	10	17	80	80	40
Luton T	42	15	9	18	71	79	39
Leeds U	42	14	10	18	75	83	38
Rotherham U	42	12	13	17	65	64	37
Brighton & HA	42	14	9	19	61	75	37
Bristol R	42	15	7	20	73	92	37
Stoke C	42	12	12	18	51	59	36
Leyton O	42	14	8	20	55	78	36
Huddersfield T	42	13	9	20	62	71	35
Portsmouth	42	11	11	20	64	91	33
Lincoln C	42	8	8	26	48	95	24

1961-62

THE slump that had occurred towards the end of the previous season was uppermost in the mind of Ted Bates who spent the close season hunting for at least one new player.

Bates knew exactly the sort of man he wanted — someone who could add 'backbone' to a team which was always capable of playing attractive, attacking football but which somehow lacked staying power.

Bates' search ended only hours before the kick-off to the new season when he spent a club record fee of £27,500 to bring Tony Knapp from Leicester City. The size of the fee was spectacular by Saints' standards as their previous record purchase had been that of John Walker who had cost £12,000 when he joined Southampton from Wolves in 1952.

Knapp soon proved his worth and took over the captaincy. With Huxford and Clifton proving reliable partners in the half-back line, and O'Brien maintaining his goalscoring

powers, Saints again started well and looked a good bet for promotion.

Yet some felt that O'Brien still lacked the support of a quality partner and Bates, realising the need for another attacker, finalised a deal which would have brought Arsenal's John Barnwell to The Dell. But the player could not agree terms with Saints who started their now familiar slump.

Barnwell's refusal to move to Southampton was probably the turning point of the Saints' season, for his presence could have made the difference between promotion and their eventual sixth position.

Thus, another season that had started so well had ended in disappointment. Saints' fans could, however, take heart from the fact that at last the policy seemed to be to buy rather than sell quality players. Southampton's management was aware of the weaknesses and was trying to rectify them.

FA Cup

SAINTS' third-round tussle with Sunderland at The Dell was a real 'ding-dong' affair. O'Brien put Southampton ahead from the penalty spot before Sunderland equalised, also from a penalty, and the sides went in level at half-time.

Then it was Sunderland's turn to take the lead and Saints' to fight back. The Wearsiders edged in front after 59 minutes and it was three minutes from time before O'Brien levelled the scores following a defensive mix-up. Saints were perhaps fortunate to survive and they had goalkeeper Tony Godfrey to thank for a string of fine saves.

A massive crowd of more than 58,000 greeted the teams at Roker Park and the replay turned out to be worthy of such a large attendance. It was Sunderland's ability to capitalise on chances which gave them the edge over Saints who spurned three good opportunities in the first 12 minutes. It was left to Sunderland's forwards to show Saints how to score goals.

Round 3
Jan 6 v Sunderland (h) 2-2
O'Brien 2
Godfrey; Patrick, Traynor, Clifton, Knapp, Huxford, Paine, O'Brien, Reeves, Mulgrew, Penk.
Att: 22,248
Replay
Jan 10 v Sunderland (a) 0-3
Godfrey; Patrick, Traynor, Clifton, Knapp, Huxford, Paine, O'Brien, Reeves, Mulgrew, Penk.
Att: 58,527

Football League Cup

SAINTS' League Cup campaign was over almost before it had started. They went out to Fourth Division Rochdale, although the humiliation was later tempered by the fact that Rochdale went all the way to the League Cup Final before losing over two legs to Norwich City.

Round 1
Sep 13 v Rochdale (h) 0-0
Godfrey; Davies, Traynor, Clifton, Knapp, Huxford, Paine, O'Brien, Maughan, Mulgrew, Penk.
Att: 7,783
Replay
Sep 27 v Rochdale (a) 1-2
Reeves
Godfrey; Davies, Traynor, Clifton, Knapp, Huxford, Paine, O'Brien, Reeves, Mulgrew, Penk.
Att: 5,449

Total home attendance: 289,239. Average: 13,773.

George O'Brien topped Saints' scoring charts in 1961-2 with 28 League goals.

Paine (11) and Reeves are involved in an assault on the Scunthorpe goal at The Dell in March 1962. Both men got on the scoresheet in a high-scoring game which Southampton won 6-4.

1961-62
Division 2

Date	V	Opponent	Res	Score	Scorers	Att	Chadwick D	Clifton B	Davies R	Godfrey A	Huxford C	Knapp A	Maughan W	Mulgrew T	O'Brien G	Paine T	Patrick R	Penk H	Reeves D	Reynolds R	Simpson T	Sydenham J	Traynor T	Wimshurst K
Aug 19	(h)	Plymouth A	L	1-2	Clifton	16,505		4	2		6	5		10	8	7	3		9	1		11		
21	(a)	Leyton O	W	3-1	Mulgrew 2, O'Brien	12,479		4	2	1	6	5		10	8	7	3		9			11		
26	(a)	Huddersfield T	L	0-1		13,998		4	2	1	6	5		10	8	7	3		9			11		
30	(h)	Leyton O	L	1-2	O'Brien	14,352		4	2	1	6	5		10	8	7	3		9			11		
Sep 2	(h)	Swansea T	W	5-1	Paine 2, O'Brien 2, Opp own goal	12,003		4	2	1	6	5			8	7		11	9				3	10
6	(h)	Walsall	D	1-1	O'Brien	15,074		4	2	1	6	5			8	7		11	9				3	10
9	(a)	Bury	W	2-0	O'Brien, Mulgrew	12,987		4	2	1	6	5	9	10	8	7		11					3	
16	(a)	Luton T	W	4-1	O'Brien 3, Penk	13,209		4	2	1	6	5		10	8	7		11	9				3	
19	(a)	Walsall	W	2-0	O'Brien, Reeves	18,689		4		1	6	5		10	8	7	2	11	9				3	
23	(h)	Newcastle U	W	1-0	O'Brien	20,064		4	2	1	6	5		10	8	7		11	9				3	
30	(a)	Middlesbrough	D	1-1	O'Brien	13,667		4	2	1	6	5		10	8	7		11	9				3	
Oct 7	(h)	Brighton & HA	W	6-1	Paine 2, O'Brien 2, Clifton, Penk	16,324		4	2	1	6	5		10	8	7		11	9				3	
13	(a)	Scunthorpe U	L	1-5	Paine	10,657		4	2	1	6	5		10	8	7		11	9				3	
18	(h)	Preston NE	D	0-0		14,322		4	2	1	6	5		10	8	7		11	9				3	
21	(h)	Norwich C	D	2-2	Reeves, Mulgrew	15,567		4	2	1	6	5		10	8	7		11	9				3	
28	(a)	Leeds U	D	1-1	O'Brien	10,145		4	2	1	6	5		10	8	7		11	9				3	
Nov 4	(h)	Bristol R	L	0-2		14,840	7	4		1	6	5		10	9	8	2					11	3	
18	(h)	Sunderland	W	2-0	O'Brien, Reeves	16,690	7	4	2	1	6	5		10	8			11	9				3	
25	(a)	Rotherham U	L	2-4	O'Brien, Reeves	9,743		4	2	1	6	5		10	8	7		11	9				3	
Dec 2	(h)	Liverpool	W	2-0	O'Brien, Mulgrew	21,445		4	2	1	6	5		10	8	7		11	9				3	
9	(a)	Stoke C	L	2-3	Reeves, Mulgrew	18,354		4	2	1	6	5		10	8	7		11	9				3	
16	(a)	Plymouth A	L	0-4		13,531		4	2	1	6	5		10	8	7		11	9				3	
23	(h)	Huddersfield T	W	3-1	Clifton 2, Mulgrew	11,262		4		1	6	5		10	8	7	2	11	9				3	
26	(a)	Derby C	D	1-1	Mulgrew	20,196		4		1	6	5		10	8	7	2	11	9				3	
30	(h)	Derby C	W	2-1	Clifton, O'Brien	12,392		4		1	6	5		10	8	7	2	11	9				3	
Jan 13	(a)	Swansea T	W	1-0	Mulgrew	9,709		4		1	6	5		10	8	7	2	11	9				3	
20	(h)	Bury	W	5-3	O'Brien 2, Mulgrew 2, Penk	12,315		4		1	6	5		10	8	7	2	11	9				3	
Feb 3	(h)	Luton T	W	3-0	O'Brien, Mulgrew, Reeves	13,037		4		1	6	5		10	8	7	2	11	9				3	
10	(a)	Newcastle U	L	2-3	O'Brien, Paine	30,564		4		1	6	5		10	8	7	2	11	9				3	
21	(h)	Middlesbrough	L	1-3	O'Brien	13,535	7	4		1	6	5			8	10	2	11	9				3	
24	(a)	Brighton & HA	D	0-0		11,852		4	2	1	6	5		10	8	7			9			11	3	
Mar 3	(h)	Scunthorpe U	W	6-4	Paine 2, Clifton, O'Brien, Reeves, Mulgrew	10,455	7	4	2	1	6	5		10	8	11			9				3	
6	(a)	Charlton A	L	0-1		15,089	7	4	2	1	6	5		10	8	11			9				3	
10	(a)	Norwich C	D	1-1	O'Brien	17,176	7	4		1	6	5		10	8	11	2		9				3	
17	(h)	Leeds U	W	4-1	Mulgrew 2, Reeves, Opp own goal	11,924	7	4		1	6	5		10	8		2	11	9				3	
24	(a)	Bristol R	L	0-1		12,336	7	4		1	6	5		10	8	11	2		9				3	
31	(h)	Charlton A	D	1-1	Simpson	9,446		4		1	6	5		10	8	7	2	11			9		3	
Apr 7	(a)	Sunderland	L	0-3		28,860		8		1	6	5		10		7	2	11	9				3	4
14	(h)	Rotherham U	W	2-1	Clifton 2	8,107		8		1	6	5		10		7	2	11	9				3	4
21	(a)	Liverpool	L	0-2		40,410		8		1	6	5		10		7	2	11	9				3	4
23	(a)	Preston NE	D	1-1	Clifton	13,292	7	10		1	6	5			8	11	2		9				3	4
28	(h)	Stoke C	W	5-1	O'Brien 2, Reeves 2, Clifton	9,558	7	10		1	6	5			8	11	2		9				3	4
App							10	42	23	41	42	42	1	37	38	41	23	30	39	1	1	6	38	7
Goals								10						15	28	8		3	10				1	

Opp own goal 2

Back row (left to right): Page, Reynolds, Godfrey, Wimshurst. Middle: Reeves, Simpson, Traynor, Patrick, Davies, Maughan. Front: E.Bates, Clifton, Mulgrew, Paine, O'Brien, Huxford, Chadwick, Penk, Gallagher.

	P	W	D	L	F	A	Pts
Liverpool	42	27	8	7	99	43	62
Leyton O	42	22	10	10	69	40	54
Sunderland	42	22	9	11	85	50	53
Scunthorpe U	42	21	7	14	86	71	49
Plymouth A	42	19	8	15	75	75	46
Southampton	42	18	9	15	77	62	45
Huddersfield T	42	16	12	14	67	59	44
Stoke C	42	17	8	17	55	57	42
Rotherham U	42	16	9	17	70	76	41
Preston NE	42	15	10	17	55	57	40
Newcastle U	42	15	9	18	64	58	39
Middlesbrough	42	16	7	19	76	72	39
Luton T	42	17	5	20	69	71	39
Walsall	42	14	11	17	70	75	39
Charlton A	42	15	9	18	69	75	39
Derby C	42	14	11	17	68	75	39
Norwich C	42	14	11	17	61	70	39
Bury	42	17	5	20	52	76	39
Leeds U	42	12	12	18	50	61	36
Swansea T	42	12	12	18	61	83	36
Bristol R	42	13	7	22	53	81	33
Brighton & HA	42	10	11	21	42	86	31

1962-63

THE previous season had shown that Saints' board were serious about winning promotion and the fans knew that if the right players could be found, then the directors would make available the money to buy them. Yet, after eight games of this season, Southampton were bottom of the table and Bates' quest for new talent had to be intensified.

Mulgrew had left the club after failing to agree new terms and, despite the progress of 17-year-old reserve striker, Martin Chivers, Saints decided to sign George Kirby from Plymouth, in a bid to give the attack some bite.

West Brom full-back, Stuart Williams, was also signed, and when Albion's ball-juggling inside-forward, Davey Burnside, arrived a few weeks later, it meant that Ted Bates had spent £48,000 in a month, quite a sizeable figure in those days.

The new men helped Saints rally and by Christmas they stood 15th. The New Year of 1963 saw the start of one of the country's worst-ever winters and for some weeks football was virtually wiped out.

When the League programme got underway again in late February, every club had a massive backlog of fixtures and the FA Cup had not passed even the third round stage. Saints enjoyed a good Cup run, but the burden of fitting in their League games, even though the season was extended, proved too great. Despite spending heavily in the transfer market, Saints finished in a lowly position.

FA Cup

THE enforced lay-off did not seem to bother Saints unduly as they romped to an easy 5-0 third round win over York after the tie had been postponed nine times. The goal of the game came in the 50th minute, a perfectly-timed header by Burnside.

Watford and Sheffield United were the next to fall. Strangely, the only previous Cup meetings between the Saints and United were the 1902 Final and the 1925 semi-final. Saints lost them both but this time gained ample revenge in a thriller which was settled by Kirby's 35th-minute header.

Bitterly cold weather did nothing to upset Saints and Nottingham Forest in the quarter-final tie at the City Ground. Both sides gave a superb display of attacking football, although the goals came late in the game. McKinlay headed Forest in front and Paine levelled the scores with a coolly taken lob over Grummitt's head.

The replay was one of the greatest games ever seen at The Dell. With 20 minutes left Forest were 3-0 ahead and apparently coasting towards a semi-final against Manchester United. Such a scoreline would normally have quietened the losing side's fans but on this night the Saints supporters roared their team back into the game.

Two headers by Kirby brought the game to an amazing climax and when Burnside's right-foot shot sent the game into extra-time, The Dell erupted. Inspired by Wimshurst, Saints had fought back from the dead. The emotion-charged atmosphere at The Dell that night has probably never been repeated, although there were no further goals in extra-time.

An estimated 25,000 Saints fans travelled to White Hart Lane for the second replay and they saw Saints pull off another amazing result, putting the issue beyond any doubt with a superb 5-0 victory.

The semi-final at Villa Park was an anti-climax. Saints went out to a scrappy Denis Law goal and although O'Brien came close to an equaliser in the final moments, Southampton's Cup run had run out of steam.

Football League Cup

THREE games against Scunthorpe United was the modest total of Saints' League Cup run in 1962-3. Considering the fixture congestion that was yet to come it was probably as well.

Round 2
Sep 26 v Scunthorpe United (h) 1-1
Paine
Reynolds; Davies, Traynor, Wimshurst, Knapp, Huxford, Chadwick, O'Brien, Reeves, Paine, Sydenham.
Att: 5,905
Replay
Oct 2 v Scunthorpe United (a) 2-2
Paine, O'Brien
Reynolds; Williams, Traynor, Hollywood, Knapp, Huxford, Paine, O'Brien, Kirby, Wimshurst, Sydenham.
Att: 6,506
Second Replay
Oct 9 v Scunthorpe United (at London Road, Peterborough) 0-3
Reynolds; Williams, Traynor, Hollywood, Knapp, Huxford, Paine, O'Brien, Reeves, Wimshurst, Sydenham.
Att: 4,948

Round 3
Feb 13 v York City (h) 5-0
Wimshurst, O'Brien 3, Burnside
Reynolds; Williams, Traynor, Wimshurst, Knapp, Huxford, Paine, O'Brien, Kirby, Burnside, Sydenham.
Att: 11,722
Round 4
Feb 27 v Watford (h) 3-1
O'Brien 2, Kirby
Reynolds; Williams, Traynor, Wimshurst, Knapp, Huxford, Paine, O'Brien, Kirby, Burnside, Sydenham.
Att: 13,336
Round 5
Mar 16 v Sheffield United (h) 1-0
Kirby
Reynolds; Williams, Traynor, Wimshurst, Knapp, Huxford, Paine, O'Brien, Kirby, Burnside, Sydenham.
Att: 20,647
Round 6
Mar 30 v Nottingham Forest (a) 1-1
Paine
Reynolds; Williams, Traynor, Wimshurst, Knapp, Huxford, Paine, O'Brien, Kirby, Burnside, Sydenham.
Att: 28,642
Replay
Apr 3 v Nottingham Forest (h) 3-3
Kirby, Burnside, opp.og
Reynolds; Williams, Traynor, Wimshurst, Knapp, Huxford, Paine, O'Brien, Kirby, Burnside, Sydenham.
Att: 29,479
Second Replay
Apr 8 v Nottingham Forest (at White Hart Lane) 5-0
Burnside 2, O'Brien 2, Wimshurst
Reynolds; Williams, Traynor, Wimshurst, Knapp, Huxford, Paine, O'Brien, Kirby, Burnside, Sydenham.
Att: 42,256
Semi-final
Apr 27 v Manchester United (at Villa Park) 0-1
Reynolds; Williams, Traynor, Wimshurst, Knapp, Huxford, Paine, O'Brien, Kirby, Burnside, Sydenham.
Att: 68,312

Total home attendance: 320,308. Average: 15,252.

Division 2

Date		Opponent	Result	Scorers	Att	Burnside D	Chadwick D	Chivers M	Clifton B	Davies R	Godfrey A	Hollywood D	Huxford C	Kirby G	Knapp A	O'Brien G	Paine T	Patrick R	Penk H	Reeves D	Reynolds R	Sydenham J	Traynor T	White I	Williams S	Wimshurst K
Aug 18	(a)	Scunthorpe U	L 1-2	O'Brien	9,533			10		1			6	5	8	7	2					11	3	4	9	
22	(h)	Luton T	D 2-2	O'Brien, Reeves	14,863			10		1			6	5	8	7	2			9		11	3	4		
25	(h)	Bury	L 0-3		13,107				2	1			6	5	8	7	3			9		11		4		10
29	(a)	Luton T	L 2-3	O'Brien, Paine	7,230			10		1			6	5	8	7	2			9		11	3	4		
Sep 1	(a)	Rotherham U	L 0-2		11,157		7	10		1			6	5	8	11	2			9			3	4		
8	(h)	Charlton A	W 1-0	O'Brien	13,118		7	9		1			6	5	8	10	2					11	3	4		
10	(a)	Chelsea	L 0-2		18,595		7	9					6	5	8	10	2				1	11	3	4		
15	(a)	Stoke C	L 1-3	Chadwick	16,092		7						6	5	8	10	2			9	1	11	3	4		
19	(h)	Chelsea	W 2-1	White, Kirby	18,717		7						6	9	5	8	10				1	11	3	4	2	
22	(h)	Sunderland	L 2-4	Kirby 2	18,535		7						6	9	5	8	10				1	11	3	4	2	
29	(a)	Leeds U	D 1-1	Opp own goal	25,408	10							6	9	5	8	7				1	11	3		2	4
Oct 6	(h)	Preston NE	W 1-0	Kirby	16,853	10					4		6	9	5	8	7				1	11	3		2	
13	(a)	Portsmouth	D 1-1	O'Brien	32,407	10			3				6	9	5	8	7				1	11			2	4
27	(a)	Huddersfield T	W 3-2	Kirby, Burnside, Sydenham	15,586	10			3				6	9	5	8	7				1	11			2	4
31	(h)	Cardiff C	L 3-5	O'Brien 3	16,616	10			3				6	9	5	8	7				1	11			2	4
Nov 3	(h)	Middlesbrough	W 6-0	Kirby 3, O'Brien 2, Paine	14,956	10							6	9	5	8	7				1	11	3		2	4
10	(a)	Derby C	L 1-3	Paine	9,708	10							6	9	5	8	7				1	11	3		2	4
17	(h)	Newcastle U	W 3-0	O'Brien, Burnside, Sydenham	13,581	10							6	9	5	8	7				1	11	3		2	4
24	(a)	Walsall	D 1-1	Kirby	8,005	10							6	9	5	8	7				1	11	3		2	4
Dec 1	(h)	Norwich C	W 3-1	Kirby, O'Brien, Burnside	15,132	10							6	9	5	8	7				1	11	3		2	4
8	(a)	Grimsby T	L 1-4	Kirby	6,966	10							6	9	5	8	7				1	11	3		2	4
15	(h)	Scunthorpe U	D 1-1	Wimshurst	11,113	10							6	9	5	8	7				1	11	3		2	4
26	(a)	Swansea T	D 1-1	Sydenham	8,000	10							6	9	5	8	7				1	11	3		2	4
Feb 23	(a)	Preston NE	L 0-1		10,057	10							6	9	5	8	7				1	11	3		2	4
Mar 2	(h)	Portsmouth	W 4-2	Burnside 2, Williams, Paine	25,463	10							6	9	5	8	7				1	11	3		2	4
9	(a)	Cardiff C	L 1-3	O'Brien	12,246	10			2				6	9	5	8	7				1	11	3			4
20	(a)	Huddersfield T	W 3-1	Burnside 2, O'Brien	11,957	10			2				6	9	5	8	7				1	11	3			4
23	(a)	Middlesbrough	W 2-1	Burnside 2	15,210	10							6	9	5	8	7				1	11	3		2	4
Apr 6	(a)	Newcastle U	L 1-4	Chivers	28,744	10		9							5	8	7		11		1		3	6	2	4
12	(a)	Plymouth A	L 1-2	O'Brien	18,207	10						6		9	5	8	7				1	11	3		2	4
13	(h)	Walsall	W 2-0	O'Brien, Kirby	18,048	10							6	9	5	8	7				1	11	3		2	4
15	(h)	Plymouth A	D 1-1	O'Brien	22,422	10						6		9	5	8	7				1	11	3		2	4
20	(a)	Norwich C	L 0-1		18,628	10							6	9	5	8	7				1	11	3		2	4
22	(h)	Swansea T	W 3-0	Paine 2, Burnside	14,290	10							6	9	5	8	7				1	11	3		2	4
May 1	(h)	Derby C	W 5-0	Burnside 2, O'Brien 2, Kirby	10,756	10							6	9	5	8	7				1	11	3		2	4
4	(a)	Sunderland	L 0-4		34,612	10							6	9	5	8	7				1	11	3		2	4
7	(a)	Bury	D 1-1	Knapp	7,878	10							6	9	5	8	7				1	11	3		2	4
11	(h)	Rotherham U	W 1-0	O'Brien	12,136	10							6	9	5	8	7				1	11	3		2	4
13	(h)	Grimsby T	W 4-1	O'Brien 2, Burnside, Sydenham	8,728	10							6	9	5	8	7				1	11	3		2	4
15	(h)	Leeds U	W 3-1	Wimshurst, Burnside, Paine	11,619	10							6	9	5	8	7				1	11	3		2	4
18	(a)	Charlton A	L 1-2	Paine	11,005	10							6	9	5	8	7				1	11	3		2	4
20	(h)	Stoke C	W 2-0	Paine 2	18,298	10							6	9	5	8	7				1	11	3		2	4
App						32	6	3	4	6	6	2	38	33	42	42	42	8	1	5	36	40	38	11	32	35
Goals						14	1	1						13	1	22	10			1		4		1	1	2

Opp own goal 1

Back row (left to right): S.Williams, T.Traynor, K.Wimshurst, R.Reynolds, T.Knapp, C.Huxford.
Front row: T.Paine, G.O'Brien, G.Kirby, D.Burnside, J.Sydenham.

	P	W	D	L	F	A	Pts
Stoke C	42	20	13	9	73	50	53
Chelsea	42	24	4	14	81	42	52
Sunderland	42	20	12	10	84	55	52
Middlesbrough	42	20	9	13	86	85	49
Leeds U	42	19	10	13	79	53	48
Huddersfield T	42	17	14	11	63	50	48
Newcastle U	42	18	11	13	79	59	47
Bury	42	18	11	13	51	47	47
Scunthorpe U	42	16	12	14	57	59	44
Cardiff C	42	18	7	17	83	73	42
Southampton	42	17	8	17	72	67	42
Plymouth A	42	15	12	15	76	73	42
Norwich C	42	17	8	17	80	79	42
Rotherham U	42	17	6	19	67	74	40
Swansea T	42	15	9	18	51	72	39
Portsmouth	42	13	11	18	63	79	37
Preston NE	42	13	11	18	59	74	37
Derby C	42	12	12	18	61	72	36
Grimsby T	42	11	13	18	55	66	35
Charlton A	42	13	5	24	62	94	31
Walsall	42	11	9	22	53	89	31
Luton T	42	11	7	24	61	84	29

1963-64

THE previous season's exciting Cup run had proved that Saints could, on occasions, hold their own against high-standard opposition. Yet they still found difficulty in finding consistency and were just as likely to fail against weaker opponents.

The feeling in the town was that the new signings of the previous year should now have settled down, and that 1963-4 should see Saints launch a serious promotion challenge.

Hopes rose on the first day of the season when Charlton were beaten 6-1 after George Kirby scored a hat-trick in the first 15 minutes.

Sadly, this great start did not inspire Saints to further significant successes and before long the team had settled into the relative anonymity of a mid-table position. Supporters were understandably disillusioned and frustrated, for they knew that the players were capable of better things.

The fans' humour was not improved by the fact that local rivals, Portsmouth, completed a League double over Southampton. Additionally, the Saints' normally good home record was suffering with defeats by clubs such as Bury, Plymouth, and Middlesbrough.

In March, Kirby was sold to Coventry for £14,000 and with him went any serious hopes of promotion. The season ended as it had started, with a 6-1 home win, but the fact that the attendance was almost 5,000 fewer than the opening day of the season spoke volumes for the frustration which had been felt in between.

One bright spot was the emergence of Martin Chivers who, with Terry Paine, finished as Saints' joint leading League goalscorer. Chivers' 21 goals came from only 28 games and he began to look an international prospect, being capped for England Under-23 during the season.

FA Cup

IN one of those quirks of fate that Cup football sometimes throws up, Saints were drawn to meet Manchester United, the side that had knocked them out of the semi-finals the previous season.

Southampton, wearing gold shirts and black shorts, looked as if they were going to take immediate revenge when they stormed into a two-goal lead by half-time, thanks to goals from Chivers and Paine.

But United gave one of their most spirited performances in the second half and Moore and Herd drew them level. Five minutes from time, with Saints pushing for a winner as the daunting prospect of an Old Trafford replay loomed, Paddy Crerand shot United in front and a famous fightback was complete.

Round 3
Jan 4 v Manchester United (h) 2-3
Chivers, Paine
Godfrey; Davies, Traynor, McGuigan, Knapp, Huxford, Paine, Chivers, Kirby, White, Sydenham.
Att: 29,164

Football League Cup

THE League Cup was still not a glamour competition and Saints found themselves breaking new ground with a visit to Prenton Park where Tranmere Rovers beat them 2-0.

Round 1
Sep 25 v Tranmere Rovers (a) 0-2
Reynolds; Davies, Williams, White, Knapp, Huxford, Paine, Dean, Kirby, McGuigan, Sydenham.
Att: 8,802

When Saints visited Newcastle United for a midweek Second Division match in September 1963, it was the first time that the club had used air travel for an away match.

Total home attendance: 361,552. Average: 17,216.

Terry Paine (left) and Martin Chivers finished the 1963-4 season as Saints' joint-leading League scorers with 21 goals each. Paine missed only one League game but Chivers' goals came from only 28 matches. Chivers and Paine also found the net against Manchester United in the FA Cup but Saints went down at home.

1963-64

Division 2

Date		Opponent	Res	Score	Scorers	Att	Burnside D	Chadwick D	Chivers M	Davies R	Godfrey A	Hennigan M	Hollywood D	Huxford C	Kirby G	Knapp A	McGuigan J	O'Brien G	Paine T	Paton D	Penk H	Reynolds R	Sydenham J	Traynor T	White I	Williams S	Wimshurst K
Aug 24	(h)	Charlton A	W	6-1	Kirby 4, Williams, O'Brien	17,362	10							6	9	5		8	7			1	11	3		2	4
28	(h)	Huddersfield T	D	1-1	Sydenham	21,456	10							6	9	5		8	7			1	11	3		2	4
31	(a)	Grimsby T	D	2-2	Sydenham, O'Brien	11,255	10							6	9	5		8	7			1	11	3		2	4
Sep 3	(a)	Huddersfield T	L	0-4		13,619	10							6	9	5		8	7			1	11	3		2	4
7	(h)	Preston NE	L	4-5	Kirby 2, O'Brien, Burnside	15,925	10							6	9	5		8	7			1	11	3		2	4
11	(a)	Newcastle U	D	2-2	O'Brien 2	42,879	10						5	6	9			8	7			1	11	3		2	4
14	(a)	Leyton O	L	0-1		12,809	10						5	6	9			8	7			1	11	3		2	4
18	(h)	Newcastle U	W	2-0	O'Brien, Kirby	18,540	10							6	9	5		8	7			1	11	3		2	4
21	(h)	Swansea T	W	4-0	McGuigan 2, O'Brien, Paine	15,904								6	9	5	10	8	7			1	11	3		2	4
28	(a)	Portsmouth	L	0-2		29,459								6	9	5	10	8	7			1	11	3		2	4
Oct 1	(a)	Rotherham U	W	3-2	Paine 3	10,496					1			6	9	5	10	8	7				11	3		2	4
5	(a)	Middlesbrough	L	0-1		19,669					1			6	9	5	10	8	7				11	3		2	4
19	(a)	Norwich C	D	1-1	Paine	16,328					1			6	9	5		8	7				11	3	10	2	4
26	(h)	Leeds U	L	1-4	Kirby	18,036	10				1			6	9	5		8	7				11	3		2	4
Nov 2	(a)	Swindon T	W	2-1	Paine, Chivers	21,787			8		1			6	9	5			7				11	3	10	2	4
9	(h)	Manchester C	W	4-2	Chivers 2, Wimshurst, Kirby	17,142			8		1			6	9	5			7				11	3	10	2	4
23	(h)	Northampton T	W	3-1	Paine 2, Wimshurst	18,025			8		1			6	9	5			7				11	3	10	2	4
30	(a)	Sunderland	W	2-1	White, Wimshurst	34,998			8		1			6	9	5			7				11	3	10	2	4
Dec 7	(h)	Cardiff C	W	3-2	Kirby, White	17,861			8		1			6	9	5	4		7				11	3	10	2	
14	(a)	Charlton A	D	2-2	McGuigan, Sydenham	18,477			8		1			6	9	5	4		7				11	3	10	2	
21	(h)	Grimsby T	W	6-0	Chivers 2, Sydenham 2, McGuigan, Kirby	19,242			8		1			6	9	5	4		7				11	3	10	2	
26	(h)	Plymouth A	L	1-2	McGuigan	21,778			8		1			6	9	5	4		7				11	3	10	2	
28	(a)	Plymouth A	D	1-1	Kirby	17,914			8	2	1			6	9	5	4		7				11	3	10		
Jan 11	(a)	Preston NE	L	1-2	Paine	18,465			8		1			6	9	5			7				11	3	10	2	4
18	(h)	Leyton O	W	3-0	Paine, Kirby, White	14,876	10		8		1			6	9	5			7				11	3		2	4
29	(h)	Scunthorpe U	W	7-2	Chivers 2, Wimshurst, Kirby, Burnside, Sydenham, Opp og	14,221	10		8		1			6	9	5			7				11	3		2	4
Feb 8	(h)	Portsmouth	L	2-3	Chivers, Paine	26,171	10		8		1			6	9	5			7				11	3		2	4
15	(h)	Middlesbrough	D	2-2	Kirby, Paine	14,978	10		8		1			6	9	5			7				11	3	4	2	
22	(a)	Scunthorpe U	W	2-1	Chivers, McGuigan	5,587	10		8		1			6		5	9		7				11	3	4	2	
29	(h)	Bury	L	0-1		14,358	10		8		1			6		5	9		7				11	3	4	2	
Mar 3	(a)	Swansea T	L	0-6		15,255			8		1			6	9	5			7				11	3	10	2	4
7	(a)	Leeds U	L	1-3	McGuigan	24,077			8		1		3	6	9	5	10		7				11		4	2	
21	(a)	Manchester C	D	1-1	Chivers	13,481			9		1		3	6		5	10	8	7				11		4	2	
28	(h)	Norwich C	W	3-0	Chivers, O'Brien, Sydenham	13,151			9		1		3	6		5	10	8	7				11		4	2	
30	(a)	Derby C	L	2-3	Chivers, O'Brien	11,296			9		1		3	6		5	10	8	7				11		4	2	
Apr 1	(h)	Derby C	W	6-4	Paine 3, Chivers 2, Sydenham	11,392			9		1	5	3	6			10	8	7				11		4	2	
4	(a)	Northampton T	L	0-2		8,047			9		1		3	6			10	8	7	5			11		4	2	
11	(h)	Sunderland	D	0-0		21,944	7		9		1		3	6			10	8			5		11		4	2	
18	(a)	Cardiff C	W	4-2	Chivers 2, O'Brien, McGuigan	10,966			9		1		3	6		5	10	8	7				11		4	2	
21	(a)	Bury	W	5-1	Paine 2, O'Brien 2, Chivers	7,013			9		1		3	6		5	10	8	7				11		4	2	
25	(h)	Swindon T	W	5-1	Chivers 3, O'Brien, Paine	16,651			9		1		3	6		5	10	8	7				11		4	2	
27	(h)	Rotherham U	W	6-1	O'Brien 3, Paine 2, Burnside	12,539	10		9		1		3	6		5		8	7				11		4	2	
App							16	1	28	1	32	3	11	42	30	37	21	24	41	2	1	10	41	31	23	41	26
Goals							3		21						15		8	16	21				8		2	1	4

Opp own goal 1

Back row (left to right, players only): Paton, Hennigan, Kirby, Reynolds, Godfrey, Chivers, Traynor, Huxford. Third row: Ellerington, Horsfall, White, Williams, Dean, Knapp, Read, Wimshurst, Davies, Burnside, McCann, Gallagher. Second row: McGuigan, Paine, O'Brien, Chadwick, Hare, Hollywood, Wilkinson, Sydenham, Penk.

	P	W	D	L	F	A	Pts
Leeds U	42	24	15	3	71	34	63
Sunderland	42	25	11	6	81	37	61
Preston NE	42	23	10	9	79	54	56
Charlton A	42	19	10	13	76	70	48
Southampton	42	19	9	14	100	73	47
Manchester C	42	18	10	14	84	66	46
Rotherham U	42	19	7	16	90	78	45
Newcastle U	42	20	5	17	74	69	45
Portsmouth	42	16	11	15	79	70	43
Middlesbrough	42	15	11	16	67	52	41
Northampton T	42	16	9	17	58	60	41
Huddersfield T	42	15	10	17	57	64	40
Derby C	42	14	11	17	56	67	39
Swindon T	42	14	10	18	57	69	38
Cardiff C	42	14	10	18	56	81	38
Leyton O	42	13	10	19	54	72	36
Norwich C	42	11	13	18	64	80	35
Bury	42	13	9	20	57	73	35
Swansea T	42	12	9	21	63	74	33
Plymouth A	42	8	16	18	45	67	32
Grimsby T	42	9	14	19	47	75	32
Scunthorpe U	42	10	10	22	52	82	30

145

1964-65

SAINTS kicked off the new season with one addition to the previous year's playing staff. Spurs goalkeeper, John Hollowbread, arrived to follow another former Spurs 'keeper, Ron Reynolds, who had been forced to retire through injury.

A 3-0 opening-day defeat by Middlesbrough at The Dell instantly revived memories of the previous campaign when Saints' shortcomings were all too apparent.

This time, however, Southampton put the setback behind them and settled down to play some constructive football which pushed them towards the top of the table. By the New Year, with Jimmy Melia now at The Dell, there was real hope.

In the end Saints finished fourth, behind Newcastle and, surprisingly, Northampton Town, their old foes from Southern League days. Given the history of both clubs it seemed strange that the Cobblers would reach Division One before Saints. Northampton were in the middle of the extraordinary rise from Fourth to First Division and back again within eight seasons.

Southampton produced some good quality football during the season, as everyone knew they could, but expensive defensive mistakes sometimes cost them dear, especially at home where the loss of points was particularly frustrating.

One man who had cause to remember the season with relish, however, was George O'Brien who finished with 35 League and Cup goals.

FA Cup

LEYTON Orient and Saints served up a typical tough Cup tie with goals from Paine and O'Brien giving Saints a 2-1 half-time lead.

In the second half Orient struggled manfully to get on even terms and it was not until the 82nd-minute that O'Brien made the game safe following good work from Sydenham and Paine.

Another home tie, against Crystal Palace, was Saints' reward and again the match was fiercely contested. Palace went ahead after only 25 seconds and from then on Saints found it difficult to settle into any rhythm.

Tony Knapp sustained a rib injury which considerably reduced his mobility, and there appeared to be little co-ordination between attack and defence. Southampton's goal came, almost inevitably, from O'Brien, in the shape of a 69th-minute penalty. Another home defeat simply underlined Saints' need for greater consistency if they were to get amongst the honours.

> **Round 3**
> **Jan 9 v Leyton Orient (h) 3-1**
> *Chivers, O'Brien 2*
> Hollowbread; Williams, Hollywood, Wimshurst, Knapp, Huxford, Paine, O'Brien, Chivers, Melia, Sydenham.
> *Att: 20,019*
> **Round 4**
> **Jan 30 v Crystal Palace (h) 1-2**
> *O'Brien*
> Hollowbread; Williams, Hollywood, Byrne, Knapp, Huxford, Paine, O'Brien, Chivers, Melia, Sydenham.
> *Att: 26,398*

Football League Cup

GEORGE O'Brien's two goals helped Saints to a 3-2 win over Cardiff in the second round of the League Cup, but Southampton failed to find the net at Selhurst Park in the next round and had so far never managed to repeat their success in the competition's inaugural season.

> **Round 2**
> **Sep 23 v Cardiff City (h) 3-2**
> *O'Brien 2, Paine*
> Hollowbread, Williams, Hollywood, Wimshurst, Knapp, Huxford, Paine, O'Brien, Chivers, Burnside, Sydenham.
> *Att: 13,076*
> **Round 3**
> **Oct 26 v Crystal Palace (a) 0-2**
> Hollowbread; Williams, Traynor, Wimshurst, Paton, Huxford, Paine, O'Brien, Chivers, Burnside, Sydenham.
> *Att: 11,538*

> *When Saints beat Rotherham 6-1 on 21 November 1964 it was the first time that two Saints players had scored hat-tricks in the same match since 1935-6. Chivers and O'Brien were the men on target.*

> *Mike Channon, aged 15 years and 10 months, became the youngest player to appear in Saints reserve team when he played — and scored — in September 1964. A year later that record was broken by Ray Ames.*

> *Total home attendance: 359,565. Average: 17,122*

George O'Brien beats the Plymouth defence on his way to a hat-trick in Saints' 5-0 win at The Dell on Boxing Day 1964.

1964-65
Division 2

Date	Ven	Opponent	Res	Scorers	Att	Burnside D	Chadwick D	Chivers M	Davis R	Godfrey A	Hollowbread J	Hollywood D	Huxford C	Knapp A	McGuigan J	Melia J	O'Brien G	Paine T	Paton D	Sydenham J	Traynor T	White I	Williams S	Wimshurst K
Aug 22	(h)	Middlesbrough	L 0-3		18,848			9			1	3	6	5	10		8	7		11			2	4
26	(h)	Bolton W	W 3-2	O'Brien, Paine, Chivers	17,240			9			1	3	6	5	10		8	7		11			2	4
29	(a)	Newcastle U	L 1-2	O'Brien	24,531			9			1	3	6	5	10		8	7		11			2	4
Sep 2	(a)	Bolton W	L 0-3		10,791	10		9			1	3	6	5			8	7					2	4
5	(h)	Northampton T	W 2-0	Wimshurst, Sydenham	13,989	10		9			1	3	6	5			8	7		11			2	4
12	(a)	Portsmouth	W 3-0	Sydenham, Paine, Chivers	25,024	10		9			1	3	6	5			8	7		11			2	4
16	(h)	Preston NE	W 3-1	Sydenham, O'Brien, Burnside	18,719	10		9			1	3	6	5			8	7		11			2	4
19	(a)	Huddersfield T	W 3-0	O'Brien, Chivers, Opp own goal	6,969	10		9			1	3	6	5			8	7		11			2	4
26	(h)	Coventry C	W 4-1	Paine 2, O'Brien, Burnside	22,276	10		9			1	3	6	5			8	7		11			2	4
Oct 10	(h)	Manchester C	W 1-0	Curtis	18,412	10		9			1	3	6	5			8	7		11			2	4
13	(a)	Swindon T	L 1-2	O'Brien	19,311	10		9			1	3	6	5			8	7		11			2	4
17	(a)	Charlton A	W 5-2	Burnside 2, Paine, O'Brien, Chivers	14,265	10		9			1		6				8	7	5	11	3		2	4
24	(h)	Leyton O	D 2-2	Burnside, O'Brien	17,536	10		9			1		6				8	7	5	11	3		2	4
30	(a)	Bury	D 3-3	Paine, O'Brien, Chivers	6,553	10		9			1	3	6				8	7	5	11			2	4
Nov 2	(a)	Preston NE	D 0-0		15,398	10					1	3	6		9		8	7	5	11			2	4
7	(h)	Crystal P	L 0-1		20,161	10		9			1	3	6	5			8	7		11			2	4
14	(a)	Norwich C	D 2-2	O'Brien 2	18,217			9			1	2	6	5	10		8	7		11	3			4
21	(h)	Rotherham U	W 6-1	O'Brien 3, Chivers 3	17,035			9			1	3	6	5	10		8	7		11			4	2
28	(a)	Swansea T	D 3-3	O'Brien, Paine, Knapp	10,951		11	9			1	3	6	5	10		8	7					4	2
Dec 5	(h)	Derby C	D 3-3	Paine 3	14,401		11	9			1	3	6	5	10		8	7					4	2
12	(a)	Middlesbrough	L 1-4	Paine	12,499		11	9			1	2	6	5			8	7	3	10				4
19	(h)	Newcastle U	L 0-1		22,365			9			1	3	6	5		10	8	7		11			2	4
26	(h)	Plymouth A	W 5-0	O'Brien 3, Wimshurst, Chivers	21,891			9			1	3	6	5		10	8	7		11			2	4
Jan 2	(a)	Northampton T	D 2-2	Chivers, Opp own goal	15,245		11	9			1	3	6	5		10	8	7					2	4
16	(h)	Portsmouth	D 2-2	Melia 2	23,911			9			1	3	6	5		10	8	7		11			2	4
23	(h)	Huddersfield T	D 3-3	O'Brien 2, Paine	17,473			9			1	3	6	5		10	8	7		11			4	2
Feb 6	(a)	Coventry C	D 1-1	O'Brien	25,298			9			1		6			10	8	7	5	11	3		2	4
13	(h)	Cardiff C	D 1-1	O'Brien	14,740			9			1	3	6			10	8	7	5	11			2	4
17	(a)	Plymouth A	L 0-4		14,813				3		1		6		9	10	8	7	5	11			2	4
20	(a)	Manchester C	L 1-3	Melia	10,047						1		6	5	9	10	8	7	2	11	3			4
27	(h)	Charlton A	W 4-0	O'Brien 4	12,310			9		1		3	6	5		10	8	7		11			2	4
Mar 6	(a)	Derby C	L 1-2	Chivers	13,520			9		1		3	6	5		10	8	7		11			2	4
13	(h)	Bury	W 3-1	O'Brien 2, Chivers	11,893			9		1		3	6	5		10	8	7		11			2	4
20	(a)	Crystal P	W 2-0	O'Brien, Chivers	12,737			9		1		3	6	5		10	8	7		11			2	4
24	(a)	Cardiff C	D 2-2	O'Brien, Chivers	9,780			9		1		3	6	5		10	8	7		11			2	4
27	(h)	Norwich C	W 1-0	Opp own goal	14,340			9		1		3	6	5		10	8	7		11			2	4
Apr 3	(a)	Rotherham U	W 3-1	Chivers 2, O'Brien	7,387			9		1		3	6	5		10	8	7		11			2	4
10	(h)	Swansea T	W 3-1	O'Brien, Chivers, Paine	13,317			9		1		3	6	5		10	8	7		11			2	4
17	(a)	Leyton O	D 0-0		8,991			9		1		3	6	5		10	8	7		11			2	4
19	(a)	Ipswich T	L 0-2		15,243			9		1		3		5		10	8	7		11		6	2	4
21	(h)	Ipswich T	D 1-1	White	11,377			9		1		3		5		10	8	7		11		6	2	4
24	(h)	Swindon T	W 2-1	Huxford, Paine	17,331			9		1		3	6	5		10	8	7		11			4	2
App						13	4	39	1	12	30	37	40	35	12	21	41	42	8	37	5	9	40	36
Goals						5		18				1	1			3	32	14		3		1		2

Opp own goal 3

Back row (left to right, players only): Treagust, Channon, Ellard, Chivers, Hollowbread, Gurr, Godfrey, Davies, McCarthy, White, Traynor. Third row: Stansbridge (groundsman) Horsfall, Paine, Williams, Dean, Paton, Knapp, Wimshurst, McGuigan, Norman, Burnside, Huxford, Ellerington. Front: Wilkinson, Sydenham, Hollywood, Chadwick, Moffatt, Judd, Russell, Hare, McCann, O'Brien.

	P	W	D	L	F	A	Pts
Newcastle U	42	24	9	9	81	45	57
Northampton T	42	20	16	6	66	50	56
Bolton W	42	20	10	12	80	58	50
Southampton	42	17	14	11	83	63	48
Ipswich T	42	15	17	10	74	67	47
Norwich C	42	20	7	15	61	57	47
Crystal P	42	16	13	13	55	51	45
Huddersfield T	42	17	10	15	53	51	44
Derby C	42	16	11	15	84	79	43
Coventry C	42	17	9	16	72	70	43
Manchester C	42	16	9	17	63	62	41
Preston NE	42	14	13	15	76	81	41
Cardiff C	42	13	14	15	64	57	40
Rotherham U	42	14	12	16	70	69	40
Plymouth A	42	16	8	18	63	79	40
Bury	42	14	10	18	60	66	38
Middlesbrough	42	13	9	20	70	76	35
Charlton A	42	13	9	20	64	75	35
Leyton O	42	12	11	19	50	72	35
Portsmouth	42	12	10	20	56	77	34
Swindon T	42	14	5	23	63	81	33
Swansea T	42	11	10	21	62	84	32

1965-66

ALTHOUGH Ted Bates had spent a sizeable sum in the transfer market, Saints had yet to taste First Division football. Good teams had been built, hopes had been raised, then something had always gone wrong. Who could blame the fans for being disillusioned?

But Saints, fortified by the arrival of defender David Walker from Burnley, began the season with a 3-0 win at Derby and by the middle of September they were top of the table.

Wolves had just been beaten by the amazing scoreline of 9-3, their heaviest post-war defeat — and that after Knapp had put the Midlanders ahead with an own-goal after only 35 seconds.

Saints' goals had all come in the first 60 minutes but they showed no reservations about the man who let them in when they signed Wolves goalkeeper Dave MacLaren a year later.

With Chivers scoring freely and admirably supported by Paine, Dean and O'Brien, thoughts of promotion occupied the minds of all Saints fans. But with 12 games left, they had fallen to sixth place and it was at that point that Bates signed David Webb from Leyton Orient. Although a full-back, Webb repaid some of his fee immediately with a goal which earned Saints a valuable point against fellow promotion-seekers, Wolves.

Yet still the nerve ends twitched and when Charlton visited The Dell on 30 April, Saints desperately needed both points. It was the 89th-minute before Terry Paine ended the fans' suffering with the only goal of the game.

There was another nail-biting 90 minutes before Saints beat Plymouth 3-2 and that meant that they now needed only one point from their last two games. They earned it in the first of those matches, when the irrepressible Paine took advantage of a 52nd minute defensive error to net the equaliser against Leyton Orient at Brisbane Road.

Only a 6-0 defeat away to Champions-elect, Manchester City, could put Saints below Coventry and a goalless draw at Maine Road ensured Southampton's long-awaited dream. First Division football had arrived at The Dell.

This triumphant season saw the departure of a great favourite, George O'Brien, to Leyton Orient, and the emergence of one who was to achieve even greater popularity, when Mike Channon made his debut against Bristol City on Easter Monday and, portentously, scored.

FA Cup

SAINTS spent most of their third round tie at Boothferry Park fighting a rearguard action on a snow-covered pitch and although chances fell to both Chivers and Wimshurst, Southampton went down to the only goal of the game.

> **Round 3**
> **Jan 22 v Hull City (a) 0-1**
> Forsyth; Hare, Williams, Wimshurst, Knapp, Huxford, Paine, Chivers, Dean, Melia, Sydenham.
> *Att: 28,851*

> *Total home attendance: 397,337. Average: 18,920.*

Saints' programme cover for their promotion-winning season.

Football League Cup

MARTIN Chivers' hat-trick earned Saints ample revenge over Rochdale, the team who had knocked them out of the League Cup in 1961. But First Division Burnley at Turf Moor were a much more difficult proposition and although Saints fought hard, they went down by the odd goal in five.

> **Round 2**
> **Sep 29 v Rochdale (h) 3-0**
> *Chivers 3*
> Godfrey; Jones, Williams, Walker, Knapp, Huxford, Paine, O'Brien, Melia, Chivers, Sydenham.
> *Att: 12,188*
> **Round 3**
> **Oct 13 v Burnley (a) 2-3**
> *Wimshurst, Paine*
> Godfrey; Williams, Huxford, Wimshurst, Knapp, Walker, Paine, O'Brien, Melia, Chivers, Sydenham.
> *Att: 11,036*

Terry Paine heads past Leyton Orient goalkeeper Rouse and Saints seal their promotion to Division One.

> *Substitutes were allowed in League football for the first time, for injured players only in this initial season, and Ken Wimshurst was the first to be used by Saints, at home to Coventry on 8 September.*

1965-66

Division 2

Date		Opponent	Res	Scorers	Att	Chadwick D	Channon M	Chivers M	Dean N	Forsyth C	Godfrey A	Hare T	Hollowbread J	Hollywood D	Huxford C	Jones K	Kemp F	Knapp A	Melia J	O'Brien G	Paine T	Spencer T	Sydenham J	Traynor T	Walker D	Webb D	White I	Williams S	Wimshurst K
Aug 21	(a)	Derby C	W 3-0	O'Brien 2, Chivers	13,359			9					1	3	6			5	10	8	7		11		4			2	
25	(h)	Carlisle U	W 1-0	O'Brien	21,928			9					1	3	6			5	10	8	7		11		4			2	
28	(h)	Portsmouth	D 2-2	Chivers, Melia	26,665			9					1	3	6			5	10	8	7		11		4			2	
31	(a)	Carlisle U	L 0-1		15,260			9					1	3	6			5	10	8	7		11		4			2	
Sep 4	(h)	Bury	W 6-2	O'Brien 4, Chivers, Wimshurst	15,363			9					1	3	6			5		8	7		11		4			2	10
8	(h)	Coventry C	W 1-0	Chivers	19,870			9					1*	3	6			5	10	8	7		11		4			2	12
11	(a)	Norwich C	W 4-3	Chivers, Paine, Dean, Melia	14,523			8	9	1				3	6			5	10		7		11		4			2	
14	(a)	Coventry C	L 1-5	Paine	30,042			8	9	1					6	2		5	10		7		11		4			3	
18	(h)	Wolves	W 9-3	Chivers 4, Paine 2, Sydenham 2, O'Brien	23,226			10		1					6	2		5	9	8	7		11		4			3	
25	(a)	Rotherham U	L 0-1		13,119			10		1				3	6			5	9	8	7		11		4			2	
Oct 2	(h)	Manchester C	L 0-1		21,504	7		10		1					6	2		5	9	8*			11		4			3	12
9	(h)	Bolton W	W 3-2	O'Brien 2, Chivers	12,325			10		1				3				5	9	8	7		11		6			2	4
16	(h)	Ipswich T	L 1-2	Chivers	19,050	7		10		1				3				5		8	9		11		6			2	4
23	(a)	Birmingham C	W 1-0	Chivers	11,687			10		1						2		5	9	8	7		11		6			3	4
30	(h)	Leyton O	W 1-0	O'Brien	15,700	7		10		1						2		5	9	8			11		6			3	4
Nov 6	(a)	Middlesbrough	D 0-0		11,555			10		1					6	2		5	9	8	7		11					3	4
13	(h)	Huddersfield T	L 0-1		21,660			10		1		2			6			5	9	8	7		11					3	4
20	(h)	Crystal P	L 0-1		12,697			10		1		2			6	12		5	9	8	7		11					3*	4
27	(h)	Preston NE	W 5-2	Chivers 2, Dean, Kemp, Sydenham	14,776			8	9	1		2					10	5			7		11		6			3	4
Dec 4	(a)	Charlton A	D 2-2	Chivers 2	10,627			8		1		2			6		10	5			7		11		4			3	9
11	(h)	Plymouth A	W 4-1	Chivers 2, Paine, Sydenham	18,179			8	9	1		2						5	10		7		11		6			3	4
18	(a)	Ipswich T	L 0-3		9,801			8	9	1		2						5	10		7		11		6			3	4
27	(a)	Cardiff C	W 5-3	Chivers 3, Paine 2	14,897			8		1		2			6		10	5			7		11		4			3	9
Jan 1	(h)	Bolton W	W 5-1	Chivers 2, Dean 2, Sydenham	18,807			8	9	1		2			6			5	10		7		11					3	4
8	(h)	Huddersfield T	L 0-2		17,989			8		1		2			6			5	10		7		11	9				3	4
29	(h)	Derby C	W 3-1	Chivers, Dean, Sydenham	16,679			8	9	1		2			6			5	10		7		11					3	4
Feb 5	(a)	Portsmouth	W 5-2	Dean 3, Chivers 2	25,860			8	9	1		2			6			5	10		7		11	12				3	4*
19	(a)	Bury	W 3-1	Chivers 2, Dean	4,725			8	9	1		2			6			5	10		7		11					3	4
26	(h)	Norwich C	D 2-2	Chivers 2	15,864			8	9		1				6	2		5	10		7		11					3	4
Mar 5	(h)	Birmingham C	L 0-1		18,292			8	9		1	2			6			5	10		7		11					3	4
12	(a)	Wolves	D 1-1	Webb	26,876			8	9		1				6			5	10		7		11*		4	2		3	12
19	(a)	Rotherham U	D 1-1	Paine	15,766			8	9		1				6			5	10		7		11		4	2		3	
Apr 2	(h)	Middlesbrough	W 3-1	Paine 2, Williams	13,687		8				1			3	6				10		7	9	11		5	4		2	
8	(a)	Bristol C	W 1-0	Opp own goal	25,106		8*				1			3	6			5	10		7	9	11		2	4	12		
11	(h)	Bristol C	D 2-2	Paine, Channon	23,120		8				1			3	6			5	10		7	9*	11		2	4	12		
16	(h)	Crystal P	W 1-0	Dean	15,780	11		8	9		1			3	6				10		7				5	4		2	
20	(h)	Cardiff C	W 3-2	Paine 2, Dean	18,941			8	9		1			3	6				10		7		11		5	4		2	
23	(a)	Preston NE	D 1-1	White	11,227			8	9		1			3	6				10		7		11		5	4	2		
30	(h)	Charlton A	W 1-0	Paine	22,480			8	9		1			3	6			5	10		7		11			4	2		
May 7	(a)	Plymouth A	W 3-2	Paine, Melia, Hollywood	18,992			8	9		1			3				5	10		7		11		6	4	2		
9	(a)	Leyton O	D 1-1	Paine	19,839			8	9		1			3				5	10		7		11		6	4	2		
16	(a)	Manchester C	D 0-0		34,643			8	9		1			3				5	10		7		11		6	4	2		
App						4	3	39	18	22	14	13	6	18	33	7	4	38	38	16	40	3	41	1	27	12	10	35	20
Sub app																1								1			2		3
Goals							1	30	11					1			1		3	11	16		6			1	1	1	1

On 8 September 1965, when Wimshurst was substituted for Hollowbread, Huxford went in goal.

Opp own goal 1

Back row (left to right): T.Spencer, D.Walker, S.Williams, C.Forsyth, T.Knapp, D.Webb, T.Traynor. Middle row: E.Bates (manager) D.Hollywood, K.Jones, I.White, C.Huxford, K.Wimshurst, J.Gallagher. Front row: J.Sydenham, T.Hare, N.Dean, T.Paine, J.Melia, D.Chadwick, M.Channon, F.Kemp. Inset: M.Chivers.

	P	W	D	L	F	A	Pts
Manchester C	42	22	15	5	76	44	59
Southampton	42	22	10	10	85	56	54
Coventry C	42	20	13	9	73	53	53
Huddersfield T	42	19	13	10	62	36	51
Bristol C	42	17	17	8	63	48	51
Wolves	42	20	10	12	87	61	50
Rotherham U	42	16	14	12	75	74	46
Derby C	42	16	11	15	71	68	43
Bolton W	42	16	9	17	62	59	41
Birmingham C	42	16	9	17	70	75	41
Crystal P	42	14	13	15	47	52	41
Portsmouth	42	16	8	18	74	78	40
Norwich C	42	12	15	15	52	52	39
Carlisle U	42	17	5	20	60	63	39
Ipswich T	42	15	9	18	58	66	39
Charlton A	42	12	14	16	61	70	38
Preston NE	42	11	15	16	62	70	37
Plymouth A	42	12	13	17	54	63	37
Bury	42	14	7	21	62	76	35
Cardiff C	42	12	10	20	71	91	34
Middlesbrough	42	10	13	19	58	86	33
Leyton O	42	5	13	24	38	80	23

149

1966-67

SOUTHAMPTON took their place amongst soccer's elite knowing that staying in Division One would be at least as difficult as getting there in the first place.

George O'Brien's departure the previous March had left a gap in Saints' forward line and in the close season the club paid £55,000, then their record fee, to bring the Norwich and Wales centre-forward, Ron Davies, to The Dell.

At only 23, already a proven goalscorer, and with five Welsh caps to his name, Davies was arguably Ted Bates' best-ever signing for Southampton. Certainly over the next two seasons his goals did as much as anything to keep Southampton in Division One.

Saints were fortunate, too, to have Terry Paine at his best. Paine was a master at the art of crossing the ball and the supply to Ron Davies' head seemed never-ending.

Saints' first game in Division One was against Manchester City, the team they had played right at the end of the previous season. Southampton's first-ever goal in Division One came in the 42nd minute of that game, at the Archers Road End, and the honour of scoring it fell, fittingly, to Terry Paine.

The game ended 1-1 and the following Saturday came Saints' first win in Division One when Davies opened his account at Blackpool.

As the season unfolded, Saints began to struggle and, more often than not, no matter how many goals the attack scored, the defence would let in at least as many and probably more.

Saints were not helped when goalkeeper Campbell Forsyth broke a leg in the home game against Liverpool. They quickly signed Dave MacLaren, the man who had been on the receiving end of nine goals at The Dell the previous year.

The accident to Forsyth unsettled the team and by the time the heavier pitches arrived Saints were staring relegation in the face. In March, Bates signed Eric Martin. a goalkeeper from Dunfermline, and Hugh Fisher, a midfielder from Blackpool. They helped stabilise the team and the immediate effect was a 1-0 win at Everton.

Saints avoided the drop with a 2-1 win over Nottingham Forest in the penultimate match. A tense game was settled by a Terry Paine penalty 14 minutes from time and in their final match a now relaxed Southampton beat Aston Villa 6-2.

Ron Davies, in his first season in the top flight, and playing in a struggling team, had the remarkable record of 37 goals which made him the First Division's leading scorer.

FA Cup

FOURTH Division Barrow caused Saints' hearts to flutter at Holker Street in the third round. Although Chivers gave Southampton the lead in a fast and furious tie, Barrow equalised two minutes later and took the lead in the 65th minute. Davies pulled Saints level five minutes later and three second-half goals — two more from Davies, despite an injury scare — at The Dell ended Barrow's hopes.

The goal which sent Saints out of the FA Cup at Ashton Gate was a scrappy one, when the ball took a rebound off Huxford, and it left Southampton to concentrate on staying in Division One.

> **Round 3**
> **Jan 28 v Barrow (a) 2-2**
> *Chivers, Davies*
> MacLaren; Hollywood, Jones, Webb, Knapp, Walker, Paine, Chivers, Davies(Huxford), Melia, Thompson.
> *Att: 15,002*
> **Replay**
> **Feb 1 v Barrow (h) 3-0**
> *Davies 2, Chivers*
> MacLaren; Webb, Hollywood, Wimshurst, Knapp, Walker, Paine, Chivers, Davies, Melia, Sydenham.
> *Att: 24,697*
> **Round 4**
> **Feb 18 v Bristol City (a) 0-1**
> MacLaren; Webb, Hollywood, Walker, Knapp, Huxford, Paine, Chivers, Davies, Melia, Sydenham.
> *Att: 38,017*

> *Total home attendance: 536,062. Average: 25,526.*

Football League Cup

NEW centre-foward Ron Davies scored a hat-trick to help beat battling Plymouth in the second round of the League Cup at The Dell, but he could not help Saints overcome Carlisle United.

After being held at The Dell, Southampton were always going to find it difficult at Brunton Park, and so it proved.

> **Round 2**
> **Sep 14 v Plymouth Argyle (h) 4-3**
> *Davies 3, Paine*
> Forsyth; Webb, Hollywood, Wimshurst, Knapp, Walker, Paine, Chivers, Davies, Melia, Sydenham.
> *Att: 11,544*
> **Round 3**
> **Oct 5 v Carlisle United (h) 3-3**
> *Chivers, Melia, Sydenham*
> MacLaren; Webb, Hollywood, Wimshurst, Paton, Huxford, Paine, Chivers, Davies, Melia, Sydenham.
> *Att: 13,317*
> **Replay**
> **Oct 12 v Carlisle United (a) 1-2**
> *Chivers*
> MacLaren; Webb, Hollywood, Wimshurst, Knapp, White, Paine, Chivers, Davies, Melia, Sydenham.
> *Att: 13,275*

Terry Paine scores Saints' first-ever goal in Division One, against Manchester City.

1966-67
Division 1

Date		Opponent	Result	Scorers	Att	Byrne A	Channon M	Chivers M	Davies R	Fisher H	Forsyth C	Gurr G	Hollywood D	Huxford C	Jones K	Knapp A	MacLaren D	Martin E	Melia J	Paine T	Paton D	Sydenham J	Thompson D	Walker D	Webb D	White I	Wimshurst K
Aug 20	(h)	Manchester C	D 1-1	Paine	19,900			8	9		1		3			5			10	7		11		6	2		4
24	(a)	Sunderland	L 0-2		27,161			8	9		1		3			5			10	7		11		6	2		4
27	(a)	Blackpool	W 3-2	Chivers 2, Davies	15,258			8	9		1		3		12	5*			10	7		11		6	2		4
31	(h)	Sunderland	W 3-1	Paine, Chivers, Davies	24,288			8	9		1		3			5			10	7		11		6	2		4
Sep 3	(h)	Chelsea	L 0-3		29,479			8	9		1		3			5			10	7		11		6	2		4
5	(a)	Aston Villa	W 1-0	Davies	18,417			8	9		1		3			5			10	7		11		6	2	4	
10	(a)	Leicester C	D 1-1	Davies	23,060			8	9		1		3			5			10	7		11		6	2	4	
17	(h)	Liverpool	L 1-2	Davies	28,287			8	9		1*		3			5			10	7		11		6	2	12	4
24	(a)	West Ham U	D 2-2	Davies, Chivers	32,280			8	9				3			5	1		10	7		11		6	2	4	
Oct 1	(h)	Sheffield W	W 4-2	Davies, Chivers, Melia, Webb	21,595			8	9				3			5	1		10	7		11		6	2	4	
8	(h)	Sheffield U	L 2-3	Davies, opp own goal	23,625			8	9				3			5	1		10	7		11		6	2	4	
15	(a)	Stoke C	L 2-3	Davies 2	25,554			8	9				3			5	1		10	7		11		6	2	4	
25	(h)	Everton	L 1-3	Davies	27,179			8	9				3			5	1		10	7			11	6	2	4	
29	(a)	Leeds U	W 1-0	Davies	32,232			8	9				3			5	1		10	7			11	6	2		4
Nov 5	(h)	Stoke C	W 3-2	Davies 2, Paine	23,227			8	9				3			5	1		10	7			11	6	2		4
12	(a)	Burnley	L 1-4	Paine	16,729			8	9				3			5	1		10	7			11	6	2		4
19	(h)	Manchester U	L 1-2		29,458			8	9				3			5	1		10	7			11	6	2		4
26	(a)	Tottenham H	L 3-5	Davies 2, Paine	35,736			8	9				3			5	1		10	7			11	6	2		4
Dec 3	(h)	Newcastle U	W 2-0	Davies, Melia	21,488			8	9				3			5	1		10	7		11		6	2		4
10	(a)	Fulham	L 1-3	Paine	20,000			8	9				3			5	1		10	7		11		6	2		4
17	(a)	Manchester C	D 1-1	Davies	20,104			8	9				3			5	1		10	7		11		6	2		4
26	(a)	Arsenal	L 1-4	Davies	29,527			8	9				3			5	1		10	7		11	12	6	2*		4
27	(h)	Arsenal	W 2-1	Paine, Melia	27,781			8	9				3			5	1		10	7		11		6	2		4
31	(h)	Blackpool	L 1-5		21,336			8	9				3			5	1		10	7		11		6	2		4
Jan 7	(a)	Chelsea	L 1-4	Hollywood	27,719			8	9				3			5	1		10	7		11		6	2		4
14	(h)	Leicester C	D 4-4	Davies 3, Chivers	25,444			8	9				3			5	1		10	7			11	6	2		4
21	(a)	Liverpool	L 1-2	Davies	47,545			8	9				3			5	1		10	7			11	6	2		4
Feb 4	(h)	West Ham U	W 6-2	Chivers 2, Paine 2, Davies, Hollywood	30,123			8	9				3			5	1		10	7		11		6	2		4
11	(a)	Sheffield W	L 1-4	Chivers	26,199			8	9				3			5	1		10	7		11		6	2		4
25	(a)	Sheffield U	L 0-2		17,648			8	9				3			5	1		10	7		11		6	2		4
Mar 4	(h)	Leeds U	L 0-2		26,150			8	9			1	3			5			10	7		11		6	2		4
18	(a)	Everton	W 1-0	Chivers	44,997			8	9	4			3			5		1	10	7			11	6	2		
25	(h)	Fulham	W 4-2	Chivers, Paine, Davies, opp own goal	27,945			8	9	4			3			5		1	10	7			11	6	2		
27	(a)	West Brom A	L 2-3	Davies 2	20,551			8	9	4			3			5		1	10	7			11	6	2		
29	(h)	West Brom A	D 2-2	Walker, Melia	28,870			8	9	4			3			5		1	10	7			11	6	2		
Apr 1	(a)	Nottingham F	L 1-3	Davies	37,731			8	9	4			2		3	5		1	10	7			11	6			
8	(h)	Burnley	W 4-0	Davies 3, Hollywood	23,442			8	9	4			2		3	5		1	10	7			11	6			
18	(a)	Manchester U	L 0-3		54,921	11		8	9	4			2		3	5		1	10	7				6			
22	(h)	Tottenham H	L 0-1		30,285			8	9	4			2		3			1	10	7	5	11		6			
29	(a)	Newcastle U	L 1-3	Chivers	42,410	11	8*	12	9	4			2		3			1	10	7	5			6			
May 6	(h)	Nottingham F	W 2-1	Chivers, Paine	25,305			8	9	4			3			5		1	10	7		11		6	2		
13	(h)	Aston Villa	W 6-2	Davies 4, Chivers 2	20,855			8	9	4			3			5		1	10	7		11		6	2		
App						2	1	41	41	11	8	1	33	1	19	39	22	11	42	42	2	27	14	39	35	7	24
Sub app							1								1								1			1	
Goals								14	37				3						4	11		1		1	1		

2 own-goals

	P	W	D	L	F	A	Pts
Manchester U	42	24	12	6	84	45	60
Nottingham F	42	23	10	9	64	41	56
Tottenham H	42	24	8	10	71	48	56
Leeds U	42	22	11	9	62	42	55
Liverpool	42	19	13	10	64	47	51
Everton	42	19	10	13	65	46	48
Arsenal	42	16	14	12	58	47	46
Leicester C	42	18	8	16	78	71	44
Chelsea	42	15	14	13	67	62	44
Sheffield U	42	16	10	16	52	59	42
Sheffield W	42	14	13	15	56	47	41
Stoke C	42	17	7	18	63	58	41
West Brom A	42	16	7	19	77	73	39
Burnley	42	15	9	18	66	76	39
Manchester C	42	12	15	15	43	52	39
West Ham U	42	14	8	20	80	84	36
Sunderland	42	14	8	20	58	72	36
Fulham	42	11	12	19	71	83	34
Southampton	42	14	6	22	74	92	34
Newcastle U	42	12	9	21	39	81	33
Aston Villa	42	11	7	24	54	85	29
Blackpool	42	6	9	27	41	76	21

Back row (left to right): David Webb, Ron Davies, Campbell Forsyth, Gerrry Gurr, Martin Chivers, David Walker. Middle row: Cliff Huxford, Norman Dean, David Paton, Ken Jones, Ken Wimshurst, Tony Knapp, Mike Channon, Jimmy Gallagher (trainer). Front row: Tommy Hare, Ian White, David Thompson, Denis Hollywood, Ted Bates (manager), Terry Paine, Jimmy Melia, John Sydenham, Fred Kemp.

1967-68

WHEN Ted Bates signed Fisher and Martin the previous March he was also interested in a third Scotsman but at the time, he and Jimmy Gabriel could not agree terms. In the close season, however, negotiations were reopened and the Everton defender became a Saints player.

The 92 goals conceded the previous season had almost earned Southampton a quick return to Division Two and Gabriel's arrival was an attempt to tighten an over-benevolent defence.

The season began well and a sensational 6-2 win at Chelsea on the third Saturday of the season saw Saints move into the top six. Yet such fine form was not maintained and all the previous season's inadequacies were soon apparent.

In October, Leicester won 5-1 at The Dell and insult was added to injury when Peter Shilton, the Leicester 'keeper, punted the ball into a following wind and scored Leicester's fifth after Forsyth completely misjudged the bounce. That single incident seemed to summarise most of Saints' problems.

Bates began to experiment with Paine in midfield, especially in away games, and whilst this did cut down the number of goals conceded it also meant that the attack suffered.

In late December, Saints suffered a severe blow to their attacking resources when Chivers asked for a move and was sold to Spurs for an English record fee of £125,000. Chivers' departure shocked the fans but Bates knew that Mick Channon was going to be a more than able replacement.

Fortunately, Ron Davies was still in fine form and he again came to the rescue, scoring 28 goals to make him the First Division's joint top-scorer for the second year in succession.

Some of the 'Chivers money' was put to immediate good use when Saints signed Spurs striker, Frank Saul, for £45,000 as part of the deal. And in February they brought the big Newcastle centre-half, John McGrath, to The Dell for £30,000. He was the commanding sort of player that Saints badly needed and from 21st place when he arrived, Saints climbed to finish 16th.

FA Cup

NEW signing Frank Saul made his Saints' debut against Newport in the third round of the FA Cup and made an immediate impact by opening the scoring. But overall Saints played badly and allowed the Welsh side to equalise when Walker gave away a 60th-minute penalty.

At Somerton Park, Southampton were unlucky to lose Gabriel with an injury after only two minutes, but they kept their heads. Webb and Walker played well and Mick Channon, who had come on for Gabriel, had the pleasure of scoring his first FA Cup goal as Saints finished 3-2 winners.

A visit to The Hawthorns in the fourth round looked difficult but Saints surprised almost everybody by taking the lead through Saul. Albion levelled the score early in the second half and threatened to run riot. But, in contrast to what had become expected of them, Saints' defence held firm to take West Brom to The Dell.

Again Saul was on the mark early in the game, putting Saints ahead after only ten minutes, but Albion had some luck when the ball struck some frozen mud in the goalmouth and was deflected past Martin for the equaliser.

With a fifth-round tie against local rivals, Portsmouth, at stake, Saints became increasingly anxious and West Brom, perhaps sensing that this was their day, pushed forward. Indeed, this was to be Albion's year and their eventual 3-2 win at The Dell set them further on a road which would ultimately lead to victory at Wembley.

Round 3
Jan 27 v Newport County (h) 1-1
Saul
Martin; Jones, Hollywood, Gabriel, Webb, Walker, Paine, Saul, Davies, Channon, Sydenham.
Att: 23,789
Replay
Jan 30 v Newport County (a) 3-2
Saul, Sydenham, Channon
Martin; Jones, Hollywood, Gabriel(Channon), Webb, Walker, Paine, Saul, Davies, Fisher, Sydenham.
Att: 17,600
Round 4
Feb 17 v West Bromwich Albion (a) 1-1
Saul
Martin; Webb, Jones, Fisher, Walker, Gabriel, Channon, Saul, Davies, Paine, Sydenham.
Att: 29,922
Replay
Feb 21 v West Bromwich Albion (h) 2-3
Saul, Fisher
Martin; Webb, Jones, Fisher, Walker, Gabriel, Channon(Thompson), Saul, Davies, Paine, Sydenham.
Att: 26,036

In April the ex-Chelsea player and Sunderland coach, John Mortimore, was appointed as Saints' assistant manager.

Total home attendance: 517,970. Average: 24,665.

Football League Cup

THERE was to be an early exit from the League Cup and Saints got no further than Portman Road where Ipswich beat them 2-1. Even Saints' goal was courtesy of an Ipswich defender and although the defeat was followed by a League victory over Liverpool, it heralded the beginning of Saints' slide down the table.

Round 2
Sep 12 v Ipswich Town (a) 2-5
Chivers, opp.og
Forsyth; Webb, Hollywood, Fisher, Gabriel, Walker, Paine, Channon, Chivers, Melia, Sydenham.
Att: 17,251

1967-68

Division 1

Date	Opponent	Result	Scorers	Att	Byrne A	Channon M	Chivers M	Davies R	Fisher H	Forsyth H	Gabriel J	Hollywood D	Jones K	Judd M	Kirkup J	McCarthy R	McGrath J	Martin E	Melia J	Paine T	Paton D	Saul F	Sydenham J	Thompson D	Walker D	Webb D	Wimshurst K
Aug 19	(a) Newcastle U	L 0-3		33,700			8	9	4		5	3						1	10	7			11		6	2	
23	(h) Manchester C	W 3-2	Davies 2, Chivers	23,675			8	9	4	1	5	3							10	7			11		6	2	
26	(h) West Brom A	W 4-0	Davies 2, Paine, Sydenham	22,714			8	9	4	1	5	3							10	7			11		6	2	
30	(a) Manchester C	L 2-4	Davies, Chivers	22,002			8	9	4	1	5	3							10	7			11		6	2	
Sep 2	(a) Chelsea	W 6-2	Davies 4, Chivers 2	31,876			8	9	4	1	5	3							10	7			11		6	2	
5	(a) Coventry C	L 1-2	Chivers	32,986			8	9*	4	1	5	3							10	7			11		6	2	12
9	(h) Leeds U	D 1-1	Gabriel	25,522	12		8	9	4	1	5	3							10	7			11*		6	2	
16	(h) Liverpool	W 1-0	Chivers	29,512			8	9	4	1	5	3							10	7			11		6	2	
23	(a) Stoke C	L 2-3	Chivers 2	18,681			8	9	4	1	5	3							10	7			11		6	2	
30	(h) Nottingham F	W 2-1	Davies, Paine	26,724			8	9	4	1	5	3							10	7			11		6	2	
Oct 7	(a) Everton	L 2-4	Davies, Gabriel	47,896			8	9	4	1	5	3							10	7			11		6	2	
14	(a) Leicester C	L 1-5	Davies	21,719			8	9	4	1	5	3							10	7			11		6	2	
23	(a) West Ham U	W 1-0	Paine	31,500			8	9	6		11	3	2					1	10	7					5	4	
28	(h) Burnley	D 2-2	Channon, Gabriel	22,696		9	8		4		11	3	2					1	10	7					6	5	
Nov 4	(a) Sheffield W	L 0-2		26,941			8	9	4		11	3	2					1	10	7					6	5	
11	(h) Tottenham H	L 1-2	Chivers	29,902			8	9	4		11	3	2					1	10	7					6	5	
18	(a) Manchester U	L 2-3	Chivers, Davies	48,732	3	11	8	9			4		2					1	10	7					6	5	
25	(h) Sunderland	W 3-2	Davies, Paine, Channon	22,344		11	8	9		1	4	3				2			10	7					6	5	
Dec 2	(a) Wolves	L 0-2		29,488		11	8	9		1	4	3				2			10	7					6	5	
16	(h) Newcastle U	D 0-0		19,498		11	8	9		1	4	3	2						10	7					6	5	
23	(a) West Brom A	D 0-0		24,637		11	8	9		1	4	3	2						10	7					6	5	
26	(h) Sheffield U	D 3-3	Chivers 2, Paine	22,816		11	8	9		1	4	3	2						10	7					6	5	
30	(a) Sheffield U	L 1-4	Chivers	20,130		11	8	9		1	4	3	2						10	7					6	5	
Jan 6	(h) Chelsea	L 3-5	Davies 2, Channon	27,132	10*	11	8	9		1	4	3	2	12						7					6	5	
13	(a) Leeds U	L 0-5		31,474	10	8		9			4	3						1		7		5	11		6	2	
20	(a) Liverpool	L 0-2		44,906	10			9	4			3	2					1		7		8	11		6	5	
Feb 3	(h) Stoke C	L 1-2	Davies	20,880		7		9	4			3	2					1	10			8	11		6	5	
10	(a) Nottingham F	D 2-2	Davies, Channon	27,381		7		9	4		6	3						1	10			8	11		5	2	
26	(h) Everton	W 3-2	Davies, Saul, Gabriel	25,860		7		9	4		6	3			2		5	1	10			8	11				
Mar 2	(a) Sunderland	W 3-0	Davies 2, Paine	23,775		7		9	4		6	3			2		5	1	10			8	11				
8	(h) Fulham	W 2-1	Channon 2	29,051		7		9	4*		6	3			2		5	1	10			8	11	12			
16	(h) West Ham U	D 0-0		27,734		7		9			6	3			2		5	1	10			8	11		4		
23	(a) Burnley	L 0-2		9,595		7		9			6	3			2		5	1	10			8	11		4		
30	(h) Sheffield U	W 2-0	Davies, Paine	17,852		7		9	4		6	3			2		5	1	10			8	11				
Apr 6	(a) Tottenham H	L 1-6	Davies	41,834		7		9	4		6	3			2		5	1	10			8	11				
10	(h) Arsenal	W 2-0	Davies 2	23,207		8		9	4		6	3			2		5	1	10	7			11				
13	(h) Manchester U	D 2-2	Davies, Paine	30,079		8		9	4		6*	3			2		5	1	10	7			11	12			
15	(a) Arsenal	W 3-0	Paine, Kirkup, Judd	23,165		8			4			3		9	2		5	1	10	7			11		6		
20	(a) Leicester C	L 1-4	Davies	19,518		8		9	4		6	3			2		5	1	10	7			11				
27	(h) Wolves	D 1-1	Davies	23,436		8		9	4		6	3			2		5	1	10	7			11				
May 4	(a) Fulham	D 2-2	Channon, Fisher	13,451		8		9	4		6	3			2		5	1	10	7			11				
11	(h) Coventry C	D 0-0		25,617		8		9	4		6	3			2		5	1	10				11	7			
App					3	27	24	40	30	18	40	36	18	1	13	2	14	24	30	41	1	16	23	2	31	28	
Sub app					1									1										2			1
Goals						7	13	28	1		4			1	1					9		1	1				

Back row (left to right): David Webb, Eric Martin, Gerry Gurr, Campbell Forsyth, Ron Davies. Middle row: George Horsfall (asst trainer-coach), Ken Wimshurst, David Walker, David Paton, Martin Chivers, Ken Jones, Jimmy Gabriel, Hughie Fisher, James Gallagher, Trainer. Front row: Terry Paine, David Thompson, Dennis Hollywood, Tony Knapp, Ted Bates (manager), Jimmy Melia, Mick Channon, Anthony Byrne, John Sydenham.

	P	W	D	L	F	A	Pts
Manchester C	42	26	6	10	86	43	58
Manchester U	42	24	8	10	89	55	56
Liverpool	42	22	11	9	71	40	55
Leeds U	42	22	9	11	71	41	53
Everton	42	23	6	13	67	40	52
Chelsea	42	18	12	12	62	68	48
Tottenham H	42	19	9	14	70	59	47
West Brom A	42	17	12	13	75	62	46
Arsenal	42	17	10	15	60	56	44
Newcastle U	42	13	15	14	54	67	41
Nottingham F	42	14	11	17	52	64	39
West Ham U	42	14	10	18	73	69	38
Leicester C	42	13	12	17	64	69	38
Burnley	42	14	10	18	64	71	38
Sunderland	42	13	11	18	51	61	37
Southampton	42	13	11	18	66	83	37
Wolves	42	14	8	20	66	75	36
Stoke C	42	14	7	21	50	73	35
Sheffield W	42	11	12	19	51	63	34
Coventry C	42	9	15	18	51	71	33
Sheffield U	42	11	10	21	49	70	32
Fulham	42	10	7	25	56	98	27

153

1968-69

AUSTRALIA'S cricketers delayed the start of the 1968-9 season for Saints when their visit to play Hampshire at the County Ground saw Southampton's first game switched to an evening kick-off to avoid losing spectators to the tour match.

It turned out to be an unhappy day for local sports fans when the Australians gave Hampshire a torrid time and Leeds won 3-1 at The Dell.

Nevertheless, Saints soon shrugged off the disappointment of losing at home on the first day of the season and Channon, in particular, had a good campaign, showing why Bates had been ready to let Chivers go.

Other youngsters, such as Gurr, Judd and Kemp, were beginning to blossom and at last Saints were making a real mark on the First Division, especially when they did the League double over Manchester United.

The New Year heralded a run of good results and on 5 February, Saints moved into fifth position after hammering Chelsea 5-0 at The Dell. European football now beckoned and over Easter, Saints gave a first-team chance to young Bobby Stokes, who responded with two goals on his debut, against Burnley.

Saints 5-1 win was followed by victory in the next home game, against FA Cup Finalists, Manchester City, and again Stokes found the back of the net. Defeat at White Hart Lane in the last match of the season still left Saints in seventh place and a place in the Fairs Cup.

European football after only three years in the top flight was quite an achievement and the combination of experienced men like Paine, McGrath and Gabriel, and youngsters like Channon, Stokes and Kemp, had paid a handsome dividend.

FA Cup

RON Davies' controversial last minute equaliser at Oxford allowed Saints to fight again after they had looked on the way to a shock defeat in the third round of the FA Cup.

It was the first time that Saints and Oxford had met in a competitive match and Oxford showed little respect for their First Division opponents, taking a 25th-minute lead. Saul hit a post but with only seconds remaining, Oxford were already celebrating a famous victory when the referee ruled that Davies' powerful header had crossed the line despite fierce protests from the home side.

At The Dell, Oxford lost their centre-half through injury and their concentration through the fact that they were still seething. Two goals from Paine — he was denied a hat-trick by a last-minute goal-line clearance — gave Saints a fourth-round tie with Aston Villa.

Villa, under new manager Tommy Docherty, were enjoying something of a revival in their fortunes and were 2-0 ahead by half-time at The Dell. In the 62nd minute, McGrath scored his first goal for Saints and 14 minutes later, Davies coolly flicked home the equaliser.

Villa's changing fortunes swelled the crowd to nearly 60,000 for the replay but Channon temporarily silenced them with a goal. The crowd soon found their voices again and Villa levelled the scores. Three minutes into the second half, Kemp had what looked a perectly good goal disallowed and with it went their confidence, allowing Villa to take the tie.

Round 3
Jan 4 v Oxford United (a) 1-1
Davies
Gurr; Kirkup, Hollywood, Gabriel, McGrath, Kemp(Fisher), Paine, Channon, Davies, Walker, Saul.
Att: 15,192
Replay
Jan 8 v Oxford United (h) 2-0
Paine 2
Gurr; Kirkup, Hollywood, Fisher, McGrath, Gabriel, Paine, Saul, Davies, Walker, Sydenham.
Att: 24,470
Round 4
Jan 25 v Aston Villa (h) 2-2
McGrath, Davies
Gurr; Kirkup, Hollywood, Kemp, McGrath, Gabriel, Paine, Saul (Channon), Davies, Walker, Sydenham.
Att: 27,581
Replay
Jan 29 v Aston Villa (a) 1-2
Channon
Gurr; Kirkup, Hollywood, Kemp, McGrath, Gabriel, Paine, Channon, Davies, Walker, Sydenham.
Att: 59,084

Football League Cup

SAINTS equalled their best-ever League Cup placing when they reached the fifth round before losing in front of a 35,000 crowd at White Hart Lane.

Frank Saul found the competition particularly to his liking, with two goals against Crewe (after coming on as a substitute for Melia), and another brace when Saints beat Norwich to go into the quarter-finals.

But on his old hunting ground at Tottenham, even Saul struggled and Saints were left to search for a different avenue to European football.

Round 2
Sep 4 v Crewe Alexandra (h) 3-1
Saul 2, Channon
Martin; Kirkup, Hollywood, Kemp, McGrath, Gabriel, Paine, Channon, Davies, Melia(Saul), Sydenham.
Att: 12,893
Round 3
Sep 25 v Newcastle United (h) 4-1
Channon 2, Davies, opp.og
Gurr; McCarthy, Hollywood, Kemp, McGrath, Gabriel, Paine, Channon(Saul), Davies, Fisher, Sydenham.
Att: 13,840
Round 4
Oct 16 v Norwich City (a) 4-0
Saul 2, Kemp, Davies
Gurr; Kirkup, Jones, Kemp(Fisher), McGrath, Gabriel, Paine, Channon, Davies, Walker, Saul.
Att: 25,309
Round 5
Oct 30 v Tottenham Hotspur (a) 0-1
Gurr; Kirkup, Jones, Kemp, McGrath, Gabriel, Paine, Channon, Davies, Walker, Saul.
Att: 35,199

Total home attendance: 472,596. Average: 22,504.

Fred Kemp shoots past Gordon West to score the Saints' second goal against Everton.

1968-69

Division 1

Date		Opponent	Result	Scorers	Att.	Byrne A	Channon M	Davies R	Fisher H	Gabriel J	Gurr G	Hollywood D	Jones K	Judd M	Kemp F	Kirkup J	McCarthy R	McGrath J	Martin E	Melia J	Paine T	Saul F	Stokes R	Sydenham J	Walker D
Aug 10	(h)	Leeds U	L 1-3	opp own goal	25,749			9	4	6		3				2		5	1	10	7	8		11	
14	(h)	Liverpool	W 2-0	Davies, Paine	24,453			9	4	6		3				2		5	1	10	7	8		11	
17	(a)	Sunderland	L 0-1		30,968			9	4	6		3				2		5	1	10	7	8		11	
20	(a)	Burnley	L 1-3	Melia	12,370		8	9	4	6		3				2		5	1	10	7			11	
24	(h)	Wolves	W 2-1	Kemp, Paine	19,746		8			6		3	11		4	2		5	1	10	7	9			
28	(h)	Stoke C	W 2-0	Paine, Channon	20,712		8			6		3			4	2		5	1	10	7	9		11	
31	(a)	Leicester C	L 1-3	Kemp	21,086	12	8			6		3			4	2		5	1	10	7	9		11*	
Sep 7	(h)	Arsenal	L 1-2	Paine	25,126		8	9		6		3			4	2		5	1		7	10		11	
14	(a)	Manchester C	D 1-1	Davies	29,031		11	9		6	1	3	8			2		5		10	7			4	
21	(h)	Ipswich T	D 2-2	Channon, Sydenham	19,599		8	9		6	1	3	10			2		5			7			11	4
28	(a)	Queen's Park R	D 1-1	Paine	20,765		8	9	10	6	1	3			4	2		5			7	11			
Oct 5	(a)	West Ham U	D 0-0		29,558		8	9	10	6	1	3*			4	2		5			7	12		11	
9	(a)	Stoke C	L 0-1		14,105		8	9	10	6	1		3		4	2		5			7			11	
12	(h)	Everton	L 2-5	Kemp, Gabriel	21,688		8	9	10	6	1		3		4	2		5			7			11	
19	(a)	Manchester U	W 2-1	Davies, Saul	46,026		8	9		6	1		3		4	2		5			7	11			10
26	(h)	Sheffield W	D 1-1	Davies	20,047		8	9		6	1		3		4	2		5			7	11			10
Nov 2	(a)	Coventry C	D 1-1	Paine	24,124	6	8	9			1		3		4	2		5			7	11			10
9	(h)	West Brom A	W 2-0	Davies, Channon	19,885		8	9		6	1		3		4	2		5			7	11			10
16	(a)	Chelsea	W 3-2	Davies, Channon, opp own goal	31,249		8	9		6	1		3		4	2		5			7	11			10
23	(h)	Tottenham H	W 2-1	Davies 2	27,384		8	9		6	1		3		4	2		5			7	11			10
30	(a)	Newcastle U	L 1-4	Paine	20,490		8	9		6	1		3		4	2		5			7	11			10
Dec 3	(a)	Liverpool	L 0-1		45,527		8	9		6	1		3		4	2		5			7	11			10
7	(h)	Nottingham F	D 1-1	Channon	17,957		8	9		6	1		3		4	2		5			7	11			10
14	(a)	Everton	L 0-1		36,299	4	8	9		6	1		3			2		5			7	11			10
21	(h)	Manchester U	W 2-0	Davies, Channon	26,194	6	8	9		4	1	3*	12			2		5			7	11			10
26	(h)	West Ham U	D 2-2	Davies 2	27,465		8	9		4	1	3			6	2		5			7	11			10
28	(a)	Sheffield W	D 0-0		27,398		8	9		4	1	3			6	2		5			7	11			10
Jan 11	(h)	Coventry C	W 1-0	Gabriel	19,616			9		6	1	3			4	2		5			7	8		11	10
18	(a)	West Brom A	W 2-1	Kemp, Davies	22,000			9		6	1	3			4	2		5			7	8		11	10
Feb 1	(h)	Chelsea	W 5-0	Davies 2, Channon, Gabriel, opp own goal	28,147		8	9		6	1	3			4	2		5			7			11	10
15	(h)	Newcastle U	D 0-0		22,213		8	9		6	1	3			4	2		5			7			11	10
Mar 1	(a)	Leeds U	L 2-3	Gabriel, Channon	33,205		8	9		6	1	3			4	2		5			7			11	10
8	(h)	Sunderland	W 1-0	Davies	19,843		8	9		6	1	3	2	11	4			5			7				10
11	(a)	Nottingham F	L 0-1		19,031		8	9		6	1	3	2	11	4			5			7				10
15	(a)	Wolves	D 0-0		24,322		8	9		6	1	3	2	11	4			5			7				10
22	(h)	Leicester C	W 1-0	Davies	18,864		8	9		6	1	3	2	11	4			5			7				10
29	(a)	Arsenal	D 0-0		28,740		8	9		6	1	3	2	11	4			5			7				10
Apr 5	(h)	Queen's Park R	W 3-2	Davies 2, opp own goal	22,103		8	9		6	1	3	2	11	4			5			7				10
7	(h)	Burnley	W 5-1	Stokes 2, Paine, Davies, Judd	19,551			9	12	6	1	3	2	11	4			5			7*		8		10
12	(a)	Ipswich T	D 0-0		19,931					6	1	3	2	11	4			5			7	9	8		10
19	(h)	Manchester C	W 3-0	Stokes, Paine, Judd	26,254			9		6	1	3	2	11	4			5			7		8		10
22	(a)	Tottenham H	L 1-2	Davies	29,201			9		6	1	3	2	11	4			5			7		8		10
App						3	33	38	11	38	34	28	23	11	36	32	1	42	8	8	42	23	4	15	32
Sub app						1			1				1							1					
Goals							8	20		4				2	4					1	9	1	3	1	

4 own-goals

Back row (left to right): J.McGrath, D.Walker, F.Kemp, D.Hollywood, G.Gurr, J.Gabriel. Front row: J.Kirkup, M.Channon, T.Paine, R.Davies, J.Melia.

	P	W	D	L	F	A	Pts
Leeds U	42	27	13	2	66	26	67
Liverpool	42	25	11	6	63	24	61
Everton	42	21	15	6	77	36	57
Arsenal	42	22	12	8	56	27	56
Chelsea	42	20	10	12	73	53	50
Tottenham H	42	14	17	11	61	51	45
Southampton	42	16	13	13	57	48	45
West Ham U	42	13	18	11	66	50	44
Newcastle U	42	15	14	13	61	55	44
West Brom A	42	16	11	15	64	67	43
Manchester U	42	15	12	15	57	53	42
Ipswich T	42	15	11	16	59	60	41
Manchester C	42	15	10	17	64	55	40
Burnley	42	15	9	18	55	82	39
Sheffield U	42	10	16	16	41	54	36
Wolves	42	10	15	17	41	58	35
Sunderland	42	11	12	19	43	67	34
Nottingham F	42	10	13	19	45	57	33
Stoke C	42	9	15	18	40	63	33
Coventry C	42	10	11	21	46	64	31
Leicester C	42	9	12	21	39	68	30
Queen's Park R	42	4	10	28	39	95	18

1969-70

SAINTS fans had an extra dimension to their season with entry into the Fairs Cup, a competition which saw Southampton reach the third round before being knocked out, ironically, by an English club, Newcastle United (see *Saints in Europe*).

In the League there were high hopes after the previous season's highest-ever position, and those hopes were further heightened in only the third match of the season when Saints enjoyed a spectacular 4-1 win at Old Trafford. John Sydenham enjoyed perhaps his best game for Saints that day, supplying a seemingly never-ending succession of crosses for Davies to score all four goals.

Yet the season did not continue in that vein and Saints' form began to return to that of two seasons earlier. The disheartened fans watched as the team slumped alarmingly near the relegation zone. Ted Bates had refrained from any close-season signings, hardly surprising considering the progress being made by the club's youngsters.

Now, however, Bates realised that new blood was needed but a move to bring Blackburn Rovers and England full-back, Keith Newton, to The Dell for £100,000 foundered when the player proved reluctant to move south.

A home defeat by Nottingham Forest in mid-December saw Saints drop to 20th position and injuries to Davies and McGrath made matters worse. The groin injury suffered by Davies was particularly frustrating as it meant that the Welsh international missed a quarter of the season.

For the Forest game, Bates unveiled his first signing for two years, a young winger from Reading, Tom Jenkins. Jenkins looked a skilful and promising player but he lacked experience — and it was the defence which needed strengthening most.

A 3-1 win over weakened Leeds at Elland Road finally staved off relegation and, the drop having been avoided, Saints set about the hard work needed before a new season dawned.

FA Cup

SAINTS began their FA Cup programme with a sparkling home win over Newcastle. Channon put them ahead in the first half and Saul, who had come under mounting criticism from the fans, netted twice in the second period — his first goals since October 1968.

Despite being given a tenth-minute lead by Stokes in their fourth-round game against Leicester, Saints struggled and Leicester soon equalised. Apart from a Davies header which beat Shilton but hit the crossbar, Saints were always second best after that.

On a cloying, sandy Filbert Street pitch four days later, Saints fell two goals behind, yet they stuck manfully to their task and fought back into the game with goals from Paine and Channon. Alas, Leicester were the stronger team in extra-time and a penalty and a deflected shot sent Saints out.

Football League Cup

AFTER their progress to the League Cup quarter-finals in 1968-9, Saints were eliminated at the very first hurdle although it did take Arsenal two attempts to knock them out.

Round 2
Sep 2 v Arsenal (h) 1-1
Channon
Martin; Jones, Hollywood, Kemp, McGrath, Gabriel, Paine, Channon, Saul, Walker, Sydenham.
Att: 21,111
Replay
Sep 4 v Arsenal (a) 0-2
Martin; Jones, Hollywood, Kemp, McGrath, Gabriel, Paine, Channon, Saul, Walker, Sydenham.
Att: 26,356

Round 3
Jan 3 v Newcastle United (h) 3-0
Channon, Saul 2
Martin; Kirkup, Byrne, Fisher, Gabriel, Walker, Thompson, Channon, Saul, Paine, Sydenham.
Att: 19,010
Round 4
Jan 24 v Leicester City (h) 1-1
Stokes
Martin; Jones, Byrne, Fisher, Gabriel, Walker, Paine, Channon, Davies, Stokes, Sydenham.
Att: 26,660
Replay
Jan 28 v Leicester City (a) 2-4
Paine, Channon
Martin; Jones(Kemp), Byrne, Fisher, Gabriel, Walker, Paine, Channon, Davies, Stokes, Thompson.
Att: 33,399

Total home attendance: 480,925. Average: 22,901.

Terry Paine and Saints manager Ted Bates pictured outside the Cavendish Hotel, Lancaster Gate, London, in February 1970, after Paine had appeared before a disciplinary hearing following three cautions.

Division 1

Date		Opponent	Result	Scorers	Att	Byrne A	Channon M	Davies R	Fisher H	Gabriel J	Gurr G	Hollywood D	Jenkins T	Jones K	Judd M	Kemp F	Kirkup J	McCarthy R	McGrath J	Martin E	O'Brien G	Paine T	Saul F	Stokes R	Sydenham J	Thompson D	Walker D
Aug 9	(h)	West Brom A	L 0-2		22,093	10		9	4	6	1	3		2	11				5			7		8*	12		
13	(a)	Wolves	L 1-2	opp own goal	32,485	10		9	4	6	1	3		2	11				5			7		8			
16	(a)	Manchester U	W 4-1	Davies 4	47,436	10		9	4	6	1	3		2					5			7	8		11		
20	(a)	Wolves	L 2-3	Davies, Channon	25,792	10*	12	9	4	6	1	3		2					5			7	8		11		
23	(h)	Chelsea	D 2-2	Kemp, Paine	25,935		8	9		6	1	3		2		4			5			7			11		10
27	(h)	Ipswich T	W 4-2	Kemp, Gabriel, Channon, Sydenham	20,598		9			6	1	3		2		4			5			7		8	11		10
30	(a)	Stoke C	L 1-2	Gabriel	21,000		8	9		6		3		2		4			5	1		7			11		10
Sep 6	(h)	Burnley	D 1-1	Kemp	19,339		8*		6	9		3		2		4			5	1		7		12	11		10
10	(a)	Derby C	L 0-3		35,826		8	9	11	6		3				4	2		5*	1		7			12		10
13	(a)	Nottingham F	L 1-2	Paine	23,220		8	9	6	5		3				4	2			1		7			11		10
20	(h)	Newcastle U	D 1-1	Channon	19,130	10	8		6			3				4	2		5	1		7	9		11		
27	(a)	Everton	L 2-4	Kemp, Stokes	46,942	10	12		11	6*		3				4	2		5	1		7	9	8			
Oct 4	(h)	Tottenham H	D 2-2	Gabriel, Stokes	23,901	10	9			6		3				4	2		5	1		7		8	11		
8	(h)	Manchester U	L 0-3		31,044	10	9		12	6		3	2*			4			5	1		7		8	11		
11	(a)	Sheffield W	D 1-1	Kemp	20,488	10	9		6			3				4	2		5	1		7		8	11		
18	(h)	Coventry C	D 0-0		20,238	10	9			6		3				4	2		5	1		7		8	11		
25	(a)	Liverpool	L 1-4	Channon	41,611	10	9		11	6		3				4	2		5	1		7		8			
Nov 1	(h)	West Ham U	D 1-1	Channon	26,894		8	9		6		3				4	2		5	1		7			11		10
8	(a)	Manchester C	L 0-1		27,069	3	8	9	4	6							2		5	1		7			11		10
15	(h)	Leeds U	D 1-1	Davies	23,963	3	8	9	4	6							2		5	1		7				11	10
22	(a)	Sunderland	D 2-2	Channon 2	15,385	3	8	9	4	6							2		5	1		7				11	10
29	(h)	Crystal P	D 1-1	Gabriel	19,876	3	8	9	4	6							2		5	1		7				11	10
Dec 6	(a)	Arsenal	D 2-2	Gabriel, Davies	24,509	3	8	9	4	6	1						2		5			7				11	10
13	(h)	Nottingham F	L 1-2	Davies	20,153	3	8	9	4	6			11				2		5	1		7					10
26	(a)	Chelsea	L 1-3	Channon	41,489	3	8	9*	4	5			11				12	2		1		7	6				10
27	(h)	Stoke C	D 0-0		23,215	3	8		4*	5			11				12	2		1		7	9	10			6
Jan 17	(h)	Everton	W 2-1	Channon 2	27,156	3	8	9	4	5			11				2			1		7		10			6
31	(a)	Tottenham H	W 1-0	Davies	27,693	3	8	9	4	5			11				2			1		7		10			6
Feb 7	(h)	Sheffield W	W 4-0	Davies 2, Paine, Channon	19,470	3	8	9*	4				11				2		5	1		7		10	12		6
11	(a)	Newcastle U	L 1-2	Channon	28,830	3	8		4	6			11				2		5	1	9	7					10
20	(a)	West Brom A	L 0-1		19,414	3	8		4	6			11				2		5	1		7	9*	12			10
28	(a)	West Ham U	D 0-0		27,088	3	8	9	4	6			11				2		5	1		7					10
Mar 7	(h)	Sunderland	D 1-1	Channon	19,374	3	8	9	4	6			11				2		5	1		7					10
11	(h)	Liverpool	L 0-1		23,239	3	8	9	4	6			11				2		5	1	7						10
14	(a)	Crystal P	L 0-2		20,867	3	8	9	4	6			11				2		5	1	7						10
21	(h)	Arsenal	L 0-2		23,902	3	8	9	6	5			11*			4	2			1	12	7					10
24	(a)	Burnley	D 1-1	Channon	11,166	3	11	9	10	4						6	2		5	1		7		8			
28	(a)	Leeds U	W 3-1	Channon, Davies, opp own goal	38,370	3	11	9	8	6						4*	2		5	1		7		12			10
31	(a)	Coventry C	L 0-4		25,550	3	11	9	8	6						4	2		5	1		7					10
Apr 4	(a)	Ipswich T	L 0-2		21,767	3	8		4	6			11				2		5	1		7	9				10
8	(h)	Manchester C	D 0-0		24,384	3	8	9	4	5			11				2			1		7		10			6
15	(h)	Derby C	D 1-1	Byrne	21,229	3	8	9	4	5			11				2			1		7		10			6
App						35	37	29	35	39	7	16	16	12	2	18	29	3	34	35	5	36	8	16	15	4	31
Sub app						2		1						1		2								2	2	2	1
Goals						1	15	12		5						5						3		2	1		

2 own-goals

Back row (left to right): Gabriel, McCarthy, Walker, McGrath, Paton, Davies, Jones, Saul, Byrne.
Middle row: Stokes, Judd, Kirkup, Martin, Gurr, Channon, Hollywood, Fisher, Horsfall. Front row:
Mortimore, Thompson, Paine, Bates, Sydenham, Kemp, Gallagher.

	P	W	D	L	F	A	Pts
Everton	42	29	8	5	72	34	66
Leeds U	42	21	15	6	84	49	57
Chelsea	42	21	13	8	70	50	55
Derby C	42	22	9	11	64	37	53
Liverpool	42	20	11	11	65	42	51
Coventry C	42	19	11	12	58	48	49
Newcastle U	42	17	13	12	57	35	47
Manchester U	42	14	17	11	66	61	45
Stoke C	42	15	15	12	56	52	45
Manchester C	42	16	11	15	55	48	43
Tottenham H	42	17	9	16	54	55	43
Arsenal	42	12	18	12	51	49	42
Wolves	42	12	16	14	55	57	40
Burnley	42	12	15	15	56	61	39
Nottingham F	42	10	18	14	50	71	38
West Brom A	42	14	9	19	58	66	37
West Ham U	42	12	12	18	51	60	36
Ipswich T	42	10	11	21	40	63	31
Southampton	42	6	17	19	46	67	29
Crystal P	42	6	15	21	34	68	27
Sunderland	42	6	14	22	30	68	26
Sheffield W	42	8	9	25	40	71	25

1970-71

SOUTHAMPTON'S poor showing during the previous season had meant a busy summer for Ted Bates and the search for new players was partly successful when midfielder, Brian O'Neil, signed from Burnley for a Saints record fee of £75,000.

There had also been intense media speculation throughout the summer that Ron Davies had been the subject of a huge bid from Manchester United and it is to their eternal credit that Saints' board resisted the offer.

O'Neil soon settled into the side and Saints enjoyed a comparatively good start, settling into a mid-table position, although at times their football could have been described as 'physical'.

Determined not to be pushed around, they incurred the wrath of several managers, notably Bill Shankly who branded them 'ale-house footballers'.

Certainly Saints had decided that their days as 'pushovers' were over and rightly or wrongly (and they were the subject of national debate) the defence improved its record. Perhaps it was simply that opponents, used to meeting 'gentlemanly' Southampton, did not like the fact that the Saints had introduced some devil into their play.

On Boxing Day, they travelled to Highbury and emphasized their new approach with a fighting display which held the Gunners to a goalless draw on a snow-covered pitch. Goalkeeper Eric Martin had a superb game and Saints entered 1971 in eighth place.

Another fine result in North London, against Spurs, pushed Saints even higher and their final placing of seventh qualified them for the newly-named UEFA Cup which had taken over from the Fairs Cup.

Greater steel in defence, and the additional tenacity of O'Neil in midfield, had gone a long way to helping Saints back into European football. But the attack was still found wanting and Saints were short of the blend which would have made them title contenders.

FA Cup

BRISTOL City, then hovering at the foot of Division Two and despite missing five first-team regulars, held Saints at bay for 70 minutes of the third round FA Cup tie at The Dell before they caved in. Saints gained revenge for their Cup defeat a couple of seasons earlier.

An exciting game at York City's sloping Bootham Crescent ground saw Jimmy Gabriel, pushed up into the attack, head Saints into the lead in the second half. Channon scored a disputed second and it looked as though gallant York were done for.

Yet they pulled back a goal, allowed Ron Davies to restore Saints' two-goal lead with a characteristic header, and then found two goals in the last three minutes for one of the Cup's most dramatic fight-backs.

The replay followed the pattern of the first game and with six minutes left Saints were 3-1 ahead. York's South African forward, Johanneson, scored a second for them but this time there was no reprieve, although it took a flying save by Martin to beat out a 35-yard rocket of a shot from Johanneson in the dying seconds.

A 29th-minute Chris Lawler goal at Anfield, coupled with a superb display of goalkeeping by Ray Clemence, denied Saints in the fifth round, despite a fighting display by the Southampton team.

> **Round 3**
> **Jan 11 v Bristol City (h) 3-0**
> *O'Neil, Davies 2*
> Martin; Kirkup, Hollywood, Fisher, McGrath, Gabriel, Paine, Channon, Davies, O'Neil, Jenkins(Byrne).
> *Att: 24,131*
> **Round 4**
> **Jan 23 v York City (a) 3-3**
> *Gabriel, Channon, Davies*
> Martin; Kirkup, Hollywood, Fisher, McGrath, Gabriel, Paine, Channon, Davies, O'Neil, Walker.
> *Att: 13,775*
> **Replay**
> **Feb 1 v York City (h) 3-2**
> *O'Neil, Kirkup, Davies*
> Martin; Kirkup, Hollywood, Fisher, McGrath, Gabriel, Paine, Channon, Davies, O'Neil, O'Brien.
> *Att: 25,034*
> **Round 5**
> **Feb 13 v Liverpool (a) 0-1**
> Martin; Kirkup, Hollywood, Fisher, McGrath, Gabriel, Paine, Channon, Davies, O'Neil, Walker.
> *Att: 50,226*

> *Total home attendance: 467,761. Average: 22,274.*

Football League Cup

DEFEAT at Filbert Street was all Southampton had to show for their entry into the 1970-71 League Cup. Goals from Channon and a Leicester defender could not turn the tide.

> **Round 2**
> **Sep 9 v Leicester City (a) 2-3**
> *Channon, opp.og*
> Martin; Kirkup, Hollywood, Fisher, McGrath, Walker, Paine, Channon, Davies, O'Neil, Jenkins.
> *Att: 20,728*

Hugh Fisher and John McGrath see the ball into Eric Martin's hands during Saints' goalless draw at Highbury on Boxing Day 1970 when Martin had perhaps his best game for Southampton.

1970-71
Division 1

Date		Opponents	Res	Score	Scorers	Att	Byrne A	Channon M	Davie A	Davies R	Fisher H	Fry R	Gabriel J	Harfield L	Hollywood D	Jenkins T	Kirkup J	McGrath J	Martin E	O'Brien G	O'Neil B	Paine T	Stokes R	Thompson D	Walker D
Aug 15	(h)	Manchester C	D	1-1	Davies	24,699	3	8		9	4		5			11	2		1		10	7			6
18	(a)	Huddersfield T	L	1-3	Davies	24,424	3	8		9	4		5			11	2		1		10	7			6
22	(a)	Coventry C	L	0-1		26,133	3	8		9	4		5			11	2		1		10	7			6
25	(h)	Tottenham H	D	0-0		27,149		8		9	4		5*		3	11	2	12	1		10	7			6
29	(h)	Ipswich T	W	1-0	Davies	18,784		8*		9	4				3	11	2	5	1		10	7	12		6
31	(a)	West Ham U	D	1-1	Jenkins	26,213		8		9	4				3	11	2	5	1		10	7			6
Sep 5	(a)	Blackpool	W	3-0	Davies, Channon, O'Neil	18,035		8		9	4				3	11	2	5	1		10	7			6
12	(h)	Derby C	W	4-0	Davies 2, Channon 2	19,429		8		9	4		6		3	11	2	5	1		10	7			
19	(a)	Leeds U	L	0-1		32,713		8		9	4		6		3	11	2	5	1		10	7			
26	(h)	Liverpool	W	1-0	opp own goal	26,155	12	8		9	4		6		3	11*	2	5	1		10	7			
Oct 3	(a)	Crystal P	L	1-3		26,663		8		9	4		6		3	11	2	5	1		10	7			
10	(h)	Wolves	L	1-2	Channon	21,769		8		9	4		6		3	11	2	5	1		10	7			
17	(a)	Manchester C	D	1-1	Davies	31,998		8		9	4				3	11	2	5	1		10	7			6
24	(h)	Burnley	W	2-0	Channon 2	19,709		8		9	4				3	11	2	5	1		10	7			6
31	(a)	Chelsea	D	2-2	Channon 2	42,325	12	8		9*	4		6		3	11	2	5	1		10	7			
Nov 7	(h)	Newcastle U	W	2-0	Channon, Gabriel	19,250		8			4		6		3		2	5	1	11	10	7	9*		12
14	(a)	West Brom A	L	0-1		17,309		8		9*	4		6		3		2	5	1		10	7			12
21	(h)	Manchester U	W	1-0	Gabriel	30,202	6	8			4		9		3	11	2	5	1		10	7			
28	(a)	Stoke C	D	0-0		16,525		8		9	4		6		3	11	2	5	1		10	7			
Dec 5	(h)	Nottingham F	W	4-1	Davies 2, O'Neil, Jenkins	19,016		8		9	4		6		3	11	2	5	1		10	7			
12	(a)	Everton	L	1-4	Channon	33,125	12	8		9	4		6		3*		2	5	1	11	10	7			
19	(h)	Coventry C	W	3-0	Channon, Davies, O'Neil	17,569	3	8		9	4		6			11	2	5	1		10	7			
26	(a)	Arsenal	D	0-0		34,169		8		9	4		6		3	11	2	5	1		10	7			
Jan 9	(h)	Huddersfield T	W	1-0	Paine	19,422		8		9	4		6		3	11	2	5	1		10	7			
16	(a)	Tottenham H	W	3-1	Channon 2, Fisher	39,486		8		9	4		6		3		2	5	1		10	7			11
30	(h)	Stoke C	W	2-1	Davies, O'Neil	19,500		8		9	4		6		3	11	2	5	1		10	7			
Feb 6	(a)	Nottingham F	L	0-2		18,009		8		9	4		6	11	3		2	5	1		10	7			
16	(h)	Everton	D	2-2	Davies, Gabriel	22,183		8		9	4		6		3		2	5	1		10	7			11
20	(a)	Manchester U	L	1-5	Gabriel	36,060		8	1	9	4		6		3		2	5			10	7			11
27	(h)	Chelsea	D	0-0		29,937		8		9	4		6		3		2	5	1		10	7			
Mar 6	(a)	Burnley	W	1-0	Channon	15,756		8		9	4		6		3	11	2	5	1		10	7			
13	(h)	West Brom A	W	1-0	Paine	19,008		8		9	4		6		3	11	2	5	1		10	7			
20	(a)	Newcastle U	D	2-2	Gabriel, McGrath	15,410	12	8*		9	4		6		3	11	2	5	1		10	7			
27	(h)	Blackpool	D	1-1	Davies	17,833	12	8*		9	4		6		3	11	2	5	1		10	7			
Apr 3	(a)	Ipswich T	W	3-1	Davies, Channon, Gabriel	16,390		8		9	4		6		3	11	2	5	1		10	7			
10	(h)	Arsenal	L	1-2	Paine	30,231		8		9	4		6		3	11	2	5	1		10	7			
12	(a)	Derby C	D	0-0		26,217		8		9	4		6		3	11	2	5	1		10	7			
17	(a)	Wolves	W	1-0	Channon	23,760		8		9	4		6		3	11	2	5	1		10	7			
24	(h)	Leeds U	L	0-3		30,001		8		9	4		6		3	11	2	5	1		10	7			
27	(h)	West Ham U	L	1-2	Davies	19,935		8		9	4		6		3	11	2	5	1		10	7			
May 1	(a)	Liverpool	L	0-1		38,437		8		9	4		6		3	11	2	5	1		10	7			
4	(h)	Crystal P	W	6-0	Channon 2, Gabriel, Davies, O'Neil, Harfield	15,980		8		9	4	3	6	11			2	5	1		10	7			
App							5	42	1	40	42	1	37	2	37	35	42	38	41	2	42	41	1	1	12
Sub app							5																1		2
Goals								18		17	1		7	1		2		1			5	3			

1 own-goal

	P	W	D	L	F	A	Pts
Arsenal	42	29	7	6	71	29	65
Leeds U	42	27	10	5	72	30	64
Tottenham H	42	19	14	9	54	33	52
Wolves	42	22	8	12	64	54	52
Liverpool	42	17	17	8	42	24	51
Chelsea	42	18	15	9	52	42	51
Southampton	42	17	12	13	56	44	46
Manchester U	42	16	11	15	65	66	43
Derby C	42	16	10	16	56	54	42
Coventry C	42	16	10	16	37	38	42
Manchester C	42	12	17	13	47	42	41
Newcastle U	42	14	13	15	44	46	41
Stoke C	42	12	13	17	44	48	37
Everton	42	12	13	17	54	60	37
Huddersfield T	42	11	14	17	40	49	36
Nottingham F	42	14	8	20	42	61	36
West Brom A	42	10	15	17	58	75	35
Crystal P	42	12	11	19	39	57	35
Ipswich T	42	12	10	20	42	48	34
West Ham U	42	10	14	18	47	60	34
Burnley	42	7	13	22	29	63	27
Blackpool	42	4	15	23	34	66	23

Back row (left to right): Tom Jenkins, Bob McCarthy, Ron Davies, Eric Martin, Sandy Davie, David Walker, Ken Jones, Denis Hollywood. Middle row: Brian O'Neil, Hugh Fisher, Jimmy Gabriel, Joe Kirkup, John McGrath, Mike Channon, Roger Fry, Fred Kemp, Tony Byrne. Front row: Jimmy Gallagher (physiotherapist) David Thompson, Terry Paine, Ted Bates (manager), John Mortimore (asst manager), Gerry O'Brien, Bobby Stokes, George Horsfall (trainer).

1971-72

TED Bates' assistant, John Mortimore, left the club during the close season for a job in Greek football, and in late August former Southampton defender, Stuart Williams, returned to The Dell as his replacement.

Only four days before the start of the season, Ron Davies suffered an ankle injury which was to sideline him for eight matches yet, despite this setback, Saints settled into a mid-table position. There was however, a double blow just around the corner.

In a four-day spell Saints were eliminated from the UEFA Cup by Bilbao (see *Saints in Europe*), and then had Hugh Fisher carried off with a broken leg against Arsenal at The Dell. Saints' confidence began to slide and in the weeks up to Christmas they dropped down the table until the nadir of their season was reached with an 8-0 thrashing at Goodison Park to equal their heaviest-ever League defeat.

That dreadful result against Everton was followed immediately by a 5-2 reverse at The Dell by Manchester United. Morale was at an all-time low and there was little comfort when Bates tried to sign Swindon full-back, Rod Thomas, for £90,000, only for the deal to fall through. At last a signing was made and Dundee defender, Jim Steele, added some grit to the rearguard.

Another casualty was Brian O'Neil, out of the side for five weeks with a cartilage injury followed by a nine-week suspension. A 7-0 defeat by Leeds was televised nationwide and Saints were glad to see the back of a season which ended with them in 19th place, six points from relegation. Success followed by failure was becoming a habit.

FA Cup

BOBBY Charlton shot Manchester United into the lead on a heavy pitch at The Dell, despite the fact that Saints had begun their third round FA Cup match with vigour and renewed determination.

It was a fast and thrilling game and Gabriel equalised for Saints to earn them an Old Trafford replay.

Southampton had much the better of the early exchanges in Manchester and Ron Davies hit a post before Channon scored the goal which deservedly separated the teams at the interval.

In the 55th minute Paine, normally so reliable, hit a simple cross behind with Davies unmarked in the middle and United were fortunate to be still in the game.

With that missed chance went Southampton's Cup prospects for the season. Shortly afterwards United equalised and then scored three goals in extra-time. Saints had played so well during normal time and the result was a bitter disappointment, particularly for Gerry O'Brien who had enjoyed probably his best game for the club.

Round 3
Jan 15 v Manchester United (h) 1-1
Channon
Martin; McCarthy, Fry, Stokes, Gabriel, Byrne, Paine, Channon, Davies, O'Brien, Jenkins.
Att: 28,160
Replay
Jan 19 v Manchester United (a) 1-4
Channon
Martin; McCarthy, Fry, Stokes, Gabriel, Byrne, Paine, Channon (Kirkup), Davies, O'Brien, Jenkins.
Att: 50,966

Total home attendance: 445,281. Average: 21,203.

Football League Cup

HAVING disposed of one Merseyside rival in the shape of Everton, Saints were unable to overcome Liverpool at Anfield and were still looking for a really convincing run in the competition which had now assumed great importance.

Round 2
Sep 7 v Everton (h) 2-1
Stokes, Jenkins
Martin; Kirkup, Hollywood, Fisher, McGrath, Gabriel, Paine, Channon, Stokes, O'Neil, Jenkins
Att: 17,833
Round 3
Oct 5 v Liverpool (a) 0-1
Martin; Kirkup, Fry, Stokes, McGrath, Gabriel, Paine, Channon, Davies, O'Neil, Jenkins.
Att: 28,964

Brian O'Neil in action against Coventry at The Dell in September 1971.

Division 1

Date		Opponent	Result	Att.	Bennett P	Byrne A	Channon M	Davies R	Fisher H	Fry R	Gabriel J	Gilchrist P	Hollywood D	Jenkins T	Kirkup J	Lovett G	McCarthy R	McGrath J	Martin E	O'Brien G	O'Neil B	Paine T	Steele J	Stokes R	Talkes W	Walker D
Aug 14	(a)	Sheffield U	L 1-3 O'Neil	25,917			8		4		6		3	11	2			5	1		10	7		9		
17	(h)	Stoke C	W 3-1 Channon, Stokes, opp own goal	18,382			8		4		6		3	11	2			5	1		10	7		9		
21	(h)	Ipswich T	D 0-0	17,931			8		4		6		3	11	2			5	1		10	7		9		
24	(a)	Nottingham F	W 3-2 Fisher, Stokes, Jenkins	14,350			8		4		6		3	11	2			5	1		10	7		9		
28	(a)	Derby C	D 2-2 Gabriel, Stokes	28,498			8		4		6		3	11	2			5	1		10	7		9		
Sep 1	(a)	Leicester C	W 1-0 Channon	22,055			8		4		6		3	11	2			5	1		10	7		9		
4	(h)	Huddersfield T	L 1-2 Gabriel	17,732	12		8		4*	3	6			11	2			5	1		10	7		9		
11	(a)	Liverpool	L 0-1	45,878			8		4		6		3	11	2			5	1		10	7		9		
18	(h)	Coventry C	W 3-1 Fisher, Paine, Channon	17,443			8	9*	4		6		3	11	2			5	1		10	7		12		
25	(a)	Manchester C	L 0-3	27,896		6	8	9*	4				3	11	2			5	1		10	7		12		
Oct 2	(h)	Arsenal	L 0-1	23,738			8	9	4*		6		3		2			5	1		10	7		11	12	
9	(a)	Wolves	L 2-4 Kirkup, Channon	21,418			8			3	6			11	2			5	1		10	7		9	4	
16	(h)	Sheffield U	W 3-2 Channon 2, Jenkins	19,033			8	9		3				11	2			5	1		10	7		4	6	
23	(a)	Chelsea	L 0-3	38,940	12		8			3	6			11	2			5	1	9*	10	7		4		
30	(h)	West Brom A	D 1-1 Channon	16,972			8	9		3				11	2			5	1		10	7		4	6	
Nov 6	(a)	Newcastle U	L 1-3 O'Neil	32,520			8	9		3	6			11	2			5	1		10	7		4	6	
13	(h)	Leeds U	W 2-1 Channon, Davies	25,331			8	9			6			11	2		3	4	5	1	10*	7		12	6	
20	(a)	Everton	L 0-8	29,018			8	9			6			11	2		3	4	5	1		7		10	6	
27	(h)	Manchester U	L 2-5 Gabriel, Davies	30,323			8*	9			6			11	2		3	4	5	1	12	7		10	6	
Dec 4	(a)	Tottenham H	L 0-1	31,351		6	8	9		3				11	2			5	1			7		10	4	
11	(h)	West Ham U	D 3-3 Gabriel, Paine, Channon	20,506		6	8	9		3				11	2			5	1	12		7		10	4*	
18	(a)	Huddersfield T	W 2-0 Davies, Stokes	10,436		6	8	9		3				11		2		5	1		10	7		4		
27	(h)	Crystal P	W 1-0 McCarthy	28,310		6	8	9		3				11		2		5	1		10	7		4		
Jan 1	(a)	Coventry C	L 0-1	17,802		6	8	9		3				11		2		5	1		10	7		4		
8	(h)	Derby C	L 1-2 O'Brien	19,321		6	8	9		3				11		2		5	1		10	7		4		
22	(a)	Stoke C	L 1-3 Byrne	17,480		6	8	9		3				11		2		5	1		10	7		4		
29	(h)	Nottingham F	W 4-1 Channon, Davies, Stokes, opp own goal	17,043		6	8	9		3						2		5	1		10	7	4	11		
Feb 19	(a)	West Brom A	L 2-3 Gabriel, Channon	19,000		6	8	9		3						2		5	1		10	7	4	11		
26	(h)	Newcastle U	L 1-2 opp own goal	18,894		6	8	9		3						2		5	1	10*	12	7	4	11		
Mar 4	(a)	Leeds U	L 0-7	34,275	12		8	9		3				11		2		5	1		10	7*	6	4		
11	(h)	Wolves	L 1-2 Channon	16,958	3*		8	9			5			11	2				1	10	4	7	6	12		
18	(a)	Ipswich T	D 1-1 Stokes	15,524			9			6		3			2		5	1	10	8	11	4	7			
25	(h)	Liverpool	L 0-1	21,680			9			6	12	3			2		5	1	10	8	11*	4	7			
28	(a)	Arsenal	L 0-1	27,172			8			6	9*	3			2		5	1	10	11	12	4	7			
Apr 1	(a)	Crystal P	W 3-2 Channon 2, Stokes	23,776			8	9		6		3			2		5	1	10	11	12	4	7*			
4	(h)	Manchester C	W 2-0 Davies 2	27,374			8	9		6		3			2		5	1	10	11		4	7			
8	(h)	Everton	L 0-1	19,711			8	9		6*		3			2		5	1	10	11	12	4	7			
11	(h)	Leicester C	W 1-0 Davies	18,752			8	9				3			2		5	1	10	6	11	4	7			
15	(a)	Manchester U	L 2-3 Davies 2	48,347			8	9				3		11*	2		5	1	10	6		4	7		12	
18	(h)	Chelsea	D 2-2 Davies 2	24,933			8	9				3			2		5	1	10	6	11	4	7			
22	(h)	Tottenham H	D 0-0	24,914	5		8	9				3			2			1	10	6	11	4	7			
May 1	(a)	West Ham U	L 0-1	18,479	5		8	9			12	3			2			1	10*	11	7	4		6		
App					2	12	42	27	11	22	36	1	16	28	23	3	19	27	42	21	30	37	16	37	1	9
Sub app					3				1	1										2	1	3		4		2
Goals						1	14	11	2		5			2	1		1			1	2	2		7		

3 own-goals

	P	W	D	L	F	A	Pts
Derby C	42	24	10	8	69	33	58
Leeds U	42	24	9	9	73	31	57
Liverpool	42	24	9	9	64	30	57
Manchester C	42	23	11	8	77	45	57
Arsenal	42	22	8	12	58	40	52
Tottenham H	42	19	13	10	63	42	51
Chelsea	42	18	12	12	58	49	48
Manchester U	42	19	10	13	69	61	48
Wolves	42	18	11	13	65	57	47
Sheffield U	42	17	12	13	61	60	46
Newcastle U	42	15	11	16	49	52	41
Leicester C	42	13	13	16	41	46	39
Ipswich T	42	11	16	15	39	53	38
West Ham U	42	12	12	18	47	51	36
Everton	42	9	18	15	37	48	36
West Brom A	42	12	11	19	42	54	35
Stoke C	42	10	15	17	39	56	35
Coventry C	42	9	15	18	44	67	33
Southampton	42	12	7	23	52	80	31
Crystal P	42	8	13	21	39	65	29
Nottingham F	42	8	9	25	47	81	25
Huddersfield T	42	6	13	23	27	59	25

Back row (left to right): Jimmy Gallagher (physio), Hugh Fisher, Roger Fry, Robert McCarthy, Ron Davies, Eric Martin, Alex Davie, John McGrath, Tom Jenkins, Jimmy Gabriel, Joe Kirkup, George Horsfall (trainer). Front row: Tony Byrne, Brian O'Neil, Terry Paine, Bob Stokes, Ted Bates, Denis Hollywood, Gerry O'Brien, Leslie Harfield, Mick Channon.

1972-73

TED Bates was now the League's longest serving manager and yet his enthusiasm for each new season was as fresh as ever. Francis Burns, the Manchester United full-back, had been signed in the close season but he was the only new face and the campaign can be seen as one of consolidation in Division One.

At one stage Saints enjoyed the best defensive record in the First Division, a considerable change from the days, not so far distant, when the Southampton rearguard had the reputation of sometimes being too generous. Defender Jim Steele had adjusted well to English football and his maturity had much too do with Saints' improved defensive record.

There were no relegation worries this season, yet little to cheer either as Saints finished in mid-table. One bright note, of course, was Mick Channon's first full England cap; and Saints' other England international, the seemingly ageless Terry Paine, was playing as well as ever.

But attendances were dwindling and as the season ground to its close, Bates tried to sign new players, without luck. Gabriel and Hollywood had left The Dell before the season had started, and before it ended another old favourite had departed.

Ron Davies had suffered a couple of bad injuries in recent months and was not enjoying his football. He asked for a move and Saints reluctantly let him go to neighbours Portsmouth for a £40,000 fee. Many supporters felt it was the end of an era.

FA Cup

SAINTS were eliminated by Crystal Palace in the third round of the FA Cup. They failed to take their chances and even substitute Ron Davies, when he replaced Gilchrist, failed miserably, although after a six-week lay-off because of injury, it was not surprising that he lacked sharpness.

Palace deserved their success and the key to it was winger, Don Rogers, who ran the Saints defence ragged. Rogers scored one goal, made the other for Cooke and generally made life unpleasant for Southampton.

> **Round 3**
> **Jan 13 v Crystal Palace (a) 0-2**
> Martin; McCarthy, Kirkup, Fisher, Bennett, Steele, Paine, Channon, Gilchrist(Davies), O'Neil, O'Brien.
> *Att: 31,604*

> *On 20 January 1973, only 12,125 spectators watched Ron Davies score his last-ever goal for Saints when Sheffield United were the visitors. It was, at that time, the lowest attendance to watch a First Division match at The Dell, and a long way short of the 21,500 'break-even' figure which Saints needed.*

> Total home attendance: 380,356. Average: 18,120.

John McGrath out-jumps Derek Dougan during the 1-1 draw with Wolves at The Dell in August 1972. Francis Burns is the other Saints player.

Football League Cup

AFTER taking three games to get rid of Fourth Division Chester, Saints were knocked out of the League Cup by Third Division Notts County at The Dell.

Yet again the League Cup had proved an unhappy experience for Saints who, despite having played in the competition every season since its inception in 1960, still had to appear in their first semi-final.

> **Round 2**
> **Sep 5 v Chester (h) 0-0**
> Martin; McCarthy, Burns, Fisher, McGrath, Steele, Paine, Channon, Davies, O'Neil, Jenkins(Stokes).
> *Att: 10,236*
> **Replay**
> **Sep 13 v Chester (a) 2-2**
> *Burns, Channon*
> Martin; McCarthy, Burns, Fisher, McGrath, Steele, Paine, Channon, Davies, Byrne, Stokes.
> *Att: 8,308*
> **Second Replay**
> **Sep 20 v Chester (at The Hawthorns) 2-0**
> *Channon, Davies*
> Martin; McCarthy, Burns(O'Neil), Fisher, McGrath, Steele, Paine, Channon, Davies, Byrne, Stokes.
> *Att: 2,417*
> **Round 3**
> **Oct 3 v Notts County (h) 1-3**
> *Paine*
> Martin; McCarthy, Mills, Fisher, McGrath(Jenkins), Steele, Paine, Channon, Davies, Byrne, O'Neil.
> *Att: 11,095*

Ron Davies, in his last season with Saints, flashes a header towards the Wolves goal at The Dell.

1972-73

Division 1

Date		Opponent	Result	Scorers	Att	Beaney W	Bennett P	Burns F	Byrne A	Channon M	Davies R	Fisher H	Gilchrist P	Jenkins T	Kirkup J	Martin E	McCarthy R	McGrath J	Mills S	O'Brien G	O'Neil B	Paine T	Spinner T	Steele J	Stokes R	Talkes W	Walker D
Aug 12	(h)	Derby C	D 1-1	Channon	20,525			3		8	9	4	11		2	1	5			7	10			6			
15	(h)	Stoke C	W 1-0	Channon	18,292			3		8	9	4	11		2	1	5			7	10			6			
19	(a)	Coventry C	D 1-1	Steele	18,484			3		8	9	4	11*		2	1	5			7	10			6	12		
23	(a)	Norwich C	D 0-0		25,708			3		8	9	4	11		2	1	5				10			6	7		
26	(h)	Wolves	D 1-1	opp own goal	19,456			3		8	9	4	11*		2	1	5				10	7		6	12		
30	(a)	Leeds U	L 0-1		31,401			3		8	9	4			2	1	5				10	11		6	7		
Sep 2	(a)	Sheffield U	L 1-3	Davies	18,758			3		8	9	4			2	1	5			7	10	12		6	11*		
9	(h)	Ipswich T	L 1-2	Channon	13,919			3	10	8	9	4	12		2	1	5			7				6	11*		
16	(a)	Everton	W 1-0	Davies	18,758			3	10	8	9	4	11		2	1	5			7				6			
23	(h)	Crystal P	W 2-0	Davies, O'Neil	15,469				10	8	9	4		3	2	1	5				11	7		6			
30	(a)	Arsenal	L 0-1		34,694				10	8	9	4		3	2*	1	5				11	7		6	12		
Oct 7	(a)	Leicester C	L 0-1		18,092		5		10	8	9	4			2	1	3				11	7		6			
14	(h)	Liverpool	D 1-1	Channon	24,100		5		10	8	9	4			2	1	3				11	7		6			
21	(a)	Birmingham C	D 1-1	Bennett	30,757		5		10	8	9*	4	12		2	1	3				11	7		6			
28	(h)	West Brom A	W 2-1	Davies, Stokes	15,810		5		10*	8	9	4	12		2	1	3					7		6	11		
Nov 4	(h)	Norwich C	W 1-0	McCarthy	17,775		5		12	8*	9	4			2	1	3				10	7		6	11		
11	(a)	Stoke C	D 3-3	Channon, Davies, Stokes	17,772		5			8	9	4			2	1	3				10	7		6	11		
18	(h)	Chelsea	W 3-1	Davies 2, O'Neil	24,164		5			8	9	4			2	1	3				10	7		6	11		
25	(a)	Manchester U	L 1-2	Channon	36,073		5		12	8*	9	4			2	1	3				10	7		6	11		
Dec 2	(h)	Tottenham H	D 1-1	Channon	16,486		5	3		8	9	4			2	1					10	7		6	11		
9	(a)	Newcastle U	D 0-0		23,750		5	3		8	9	4			2	1					10	7		6	11		
16	(a)	Manchester C	L 1-2	opp own goal	24,825		5	3		8	9	4			2	1					10	7		6	11		
23	(h)	West Ham U	D 0-0		19,429		5	3		8	9	4			2	1					10	7		6	11		
26	(a)	Crystal P	L 0-3		30,935		5	3		8	9*	4			2	1				12	10	7		6	11		
30	(h)	Coventry C	W 2-1	Gilchrist, opp own goal	15,261		5			8	9	4			2	1	3			11	10	7		6			
Jan 6	(a)	Wolves	W 1-0	Channon	16,547		5			8	9	4			2	1	3			11	10	7		6			
20	(h)	Sheffield U	D 1-1	Davies	12,125		5			8	9	4			2	1	3			11	10	7			6		
27	(a)	Ipswich T	D 2-2	Channon, Davies	19,628		5			8	9	4			2	1	3			11	10	7			6		
Feb 10	(h)	Everton	D 0-0		16,756		5			8	9	4			2	1	3			11	10	7		6			
17	(a)	Derby C	L 0-4		26,426		5			8	9	4			2	1	3			11	10	7		6			
Mar 3	(h)	Leicester C	D 0-0		14,134		5	3		8	9	4			2	1					10	7		6	11		
6	(h)	Manchester C	D 1-1	O'Neil	16,188		5	3		8	9	4			2	1					10	7		6	11		
10	(a)	Liverpool	L 2-3	Channon, Gilchrist	41,674		5	3		8	9	4			2	1					10	7		6	11		
17	(h)	Birmingham C	W 2-0	Channon 2	14,674		5	3		8	9	4			2	1					10	7		6	11		
24	(a)	West Brom A	D 1-1	Gilchrist	11,711		5	3		8	9	4			2	1					10*	7		6	11	12	
31	(h)	Manchester U	L 0-2		23,161		5	3		8	9	4	12		2	1					10	7		6	11*		
Apr 7	(a)	Tottenham H	W 2-1	Channon 2	23,693		5			8	9	4			2	1					10	7		3	11		6
14	(h)	Newcastle U	D 1-1	Gilchrist	14,785		5			8	9	4			2	1					10	7		3	11		6
20	(a)	West Ham U	L 3-4	Gilchrist 2, Channon	33,039	12	5			8	9	4			2	1					10	7		3*	11		6
21	(a)	Chelsea	L 1-2	Kirkup	19,699	6	5				9	4			2	1			3		10	7	8*	12	11		
23	(h)	Arsenal	D 2-2	Stokes 2	23,919		5				9	4			2	1			3		10	7		6	8		11
28	(h)	Leeds U	W 3-1	Channon, O'Neil, Stokes	24,108		5			8	9		12		2	1			3		10	7		11	4*		6
App						1	31	20	8	40	24	41	19	5	27	42	31	11	3	10	40	36	1	38	23	5	6
Sub app						1		1	1		1	1	3							1		1			4		1
Goals							1			16	9		6		1		1				4	1		1	5		

3 own-goals

Back row (left to right): Paul Bennett, Joe Kirkup, Tony Byrne, Ron Davies, Eric Martin, Jim Steele, David Walker, Paul Gilchrist, Bobby McCarthy. Centre row: Don Taylor (physio), Mike Channon, Wayne Talkes, Roger Fry, John McGrath, Hugh Fisher, Tom Jenkins, George Horsfall (trainer). Front row: Brian O'Neil, Terry Paine, Stuart Williams (asst manager), E.T.Bates (manager), Gerry O'Brien, Bobby Stokes, Francis Burns.

	P	W	D	L	F	A	Pts
Liverpool	42	25	10	7	72	42	60
Arsenal	42	23	11	8	57	43	57
Leeds U	42	21	11	10	71	45	53
Ipswich T	42	17	14	11	55	45	48
Wolves	42	18	11	13	66	54	47
West Ham U	42	17	12	13	67	53	46
Derby C	42	19	8	15	56	54	46
Tottenham H	42	16	13	13	58	48	45
Newcastle U	42	16	13		60	51	45
Birmingham C	42	15	12	15	53	54	42
Manchester C	42	15	11	16	57	60	41
Chelsea	42	13	14	15	49	51	40
Southampton	42	11	18	13	47	52	40
Sheffield U	42	15	10	17	51	59	40
Stoke C	42	14	10	18	61	56	38
Leicester C	42	10	17	15	40	46	37
Everton	42	13	11	18	41	49	37
Manchester U	42	12	13	17	44	60	37
Coventry C	42	13	9	20	40	55	35
Norwich C	42	11	10	21	36	63	32
Crystal P	42	9	12	21	41	58	30
West Brom A	42	9	10	23	38	62	28

1973-74

THE departure of Ron Davies was seen by many as the signal for a shake-up of playing staff at The Dell and, as if to confirm this, in June the club announced that Lawrie McMenemy had been appointed team manager designate.

The plan was that when McMenemy, the former Doncaster and Grimsby manager, had settled in, and when Ted Bates felt the time was right, the new man would assume full control over team affairs.

Almost at once Saints slipped into impressive form and, despite a 6-2 defeat at Derby, entered December in eighth place. A 2-0 win over Ipswich at The Dell on 15 December pushed them into fifth place and McMenemy was given total control. Completing the managerial team were Jim Clunie, also from Grimsby, and John McGrath, who looked after the younger players.

Unfortunately for McMenemy, nothing seemed to go right from that moment. Confidence evaporated as Saints slipped down the table and when McMenemy's first signing, full-back David Peach from Gillingham, made his debut, Saints were thrashed 7-0 at Ipswich.

Then came a signing which amazed many Saints fans. Southampton paid a club record fee of £235,000 to bring Chelsea striker Peter Osgood to The Dell. But Osgood was not the sort of player that Saints needed at that stage and he had not played competitive football for some months. Osgood struggled to find his touch and it seemed that McMenemy's ambition was not going to keep Saints in Division One.

The situation worsened when Saints lost at home to fellow strugglers, Birmingham, and defeat at Burnley on 22 April sealed their fate. After eight years in the First Division they were relegated.

Ironically, in their last game, free from pressure, they waved goodbye to the top flight with a splendid 3-0 win at Everton — and Osgood scored his first goal for the club. Alas, both goal and victory came too late for Saints who were the first victims of the three-up-three-down rule. Twentieth place the previous season would have saved them.

FA Cup

TERRY Paine, whose skills were normally in his feet, headed Saints into a fifth-minute lead over Blackpool in the third round, and although Blackpool equalised and threatened to take the lead, a 30-yarder from Bennett in the 66th minute gave Saints a win they hardly deserved.

Against Bolton, in pouring rain at The Dell, Saints built up a two-goal lead through Fisher and Channon before an injury to O'Neil reduced them to ten men. In the last five minutes Bolton scored twice to revive memories of the epic York City fightback of a few years before.

The replay at Burnden Park, played on a Wednesday afternoon because of the ban on floodlights at the time, was a dour struggle and Martin had a fine game in Saints' goal. It took two extra-time goals from Bobby Stokes, who was celebrating his birthday, to end the deadlock.

There was humiliation to follow, however, and when Wrexham's Smallman headed home a 55th-minute corner at The Dell to prevent Saints progressing to the quarter-finals, it capped one of Southampton's worst-ever home displays in the Cup.

> **Round 3**
> **Jan 5 v Blackpool (h) 2-1**
> *Paine, Bennett*
> Martin; McCarthy, Mills, Fisher, Bennett, Steele, Paine, Channon, Gilchrist, O'Neil, Stokes.
> *Att: 16,212*
> **Round 4**
> **Jan 26 v Bolton Wanderers (h) 3-3**
> *Fisher, Channon, Stokes*
> Martin; McCarthy, Mills, Fisher, Bennett, Walker, Paine, Channon, Gilchrist(O'Brien), O'Neil, Stokes.
> *Att: 20,265*
> **Replay**
> **Jan 30 v Bolton Wanderers (a) 2-0**
> *Stokes 2*
> Martin; McCarthy, Mills, Fisher, Bennett, Walker, Paine, Channon, Stokes, Byrne, O'Brien.
> *Att: 21,788*
> **Round 5**
> **Feb 16 v Wrexham (h) 0-1**
> Martin; McCarthy, Mills, Fisher, Bennett, Steele, Paine, Channon, Gilchrist, Byrne(O'Brien), Stokes.
> *Att: 24,797*

> *Total home attendance: 443,709. Average: 21,129.*

Football League Cup

ALTHOUGH Bobby Stokes' two goals helped Saints on the way to League Cup victory over Third Division Charlton there was, yet again, to be no real run in the competition and after an easy win over Chesterfield, another Third Division team, Saints were beaten at home by Norwich, one of the teams who would accompany them to Division Two at the end of the season.

> **Round 2**
> **Oct 8 v Charlton Athletic (h) 3-0**
> *Stokes 2, Gilchrist*
> Martin; McCarthy, Mills, Fisher, Bennett, Steele, Paine(Talkes), Channon, Gilchrist, O'Neil, Stokes.
> *Att: 10,047*
> **Round 3**
> **Oct 30 v Chesterfield (h) 3-0**
> *Fisher, Channon, Stokes*
> Martin; McCarthy, Mills, Fisher, Bennett, Steele(MacLeod), Paine, Channon, Gilchrist, O'Neil, Stokes.
> *Att: 13,663*
> **Round 4**
> **Nov 2 v Norwich City (h) 0-2**
> Martin; McCarthy, Mills, Fisher, Bennett(O'Brien), Steele, Paine, Channon, Gilchrist, O'Neil, Stokes.
> *Att: 14,415*

> *In their last home game of the season, against fellow relegation strugglers Manchester United, Saints enjoyed a crowd of 30,789, their second biggest-ever 'gate'.*

Peter Osgood celebrates what he thinks is his first goal for Saints but Chelsea defender Ron Harris clears off the line and the game at The Dell in April 1974 ended goalless.

1973-74

Division 1

Date		Opponent	Res	Scorers	Att	Bennett P	Byrne A	Channon M	Chatterley L	Earls M	Fisher H	Gilchrist P	Holmes N	Kirkup J	McCarthy R	McGrath J	MacLeod A	Martin E	Middleton S	Mills S	O'Brien G	O'Neil B	Osgood P	Paine T	Peach D	Spinner T	Steele J	Stokes R	Talkes W	Turner I	Walker D
Aug 25	(a)	Queen's Park R	D 1-1	Channon	18,602	5	12	8			4	9		3	2			1				10		7			6*	11			
29	(a)	Newcastle U	W 1-0	Channon	25,531	5	6	8			4	9		3	2*			1	12			10		7				11			
Sep 1	(h)	Wolves	W 2-1	Channon, Stokes	17,457	5	6	8			4	9			2			1		3*		10		7			12	11			
4	(h)	Norwich C	D 2-2	Gilchrist 2	17,658	5	6	8			4	9			2			1		3		10		7				11			
8	(a)	Coventry C	L 0-2		19,347		3	8			4	9			2	5*		1	12			10		7				11			6
12	(a)	Norwich C	L 0-2		25,023	5	6	8			4	9		3*	2			1	12			10		7				11			
15	(h)	Leeds U	L 1-2	O'Neil	27,770	5	6	8			4	9			2			1		3		10		7				11			8
22	(a)	Derby C	L 2-6	O'Neil 2	25,500	5	6	8			4	9			2			1				10		7				11			3
29	(h)	Sheffield U	W 3-0	Channon, Gilchrist, Stokes	14,572	5	3	8			4	9			2			1				10		7			6	11*			12
Oct 6	(a)	Manchester C	D 1-1	Channon	27,727	5	3	8			4	9			2			1				10		7*			6	11			12
13	(h)	Liverpool	W 1-0	Channon	22,018	5		8			4	9			2			1		3		10		7			6	11			
20	(h)	Stoke C	W 3-0	Stokes 2, Paine	15,521	5		8*			4	9			2			1		3	12	10		7			6	11			
27	(a)	Leicester C	W 1-0	Channon	18,753	5		8			4	9			2			1		3		10		7			6	11			
Nov 3	(h)	Burnley	D 2-2	Channon, Byrne	21,541	5	6	8			4	9			2			1		3		10		7				11			
10	(a)	Birmingham C	D 1-1	Fisher	25,297	5		8			4	9			2			1		3		10		7			6	11			
17	(h)	Tottenham H	D 1-1	Channon	22,887	5		8			4	9			2			1		3		10		7			6	11			
24	(a)	Chelsea	L 0-4		22,596	5		8			4	9			2			1		3		10		7			6	11			
Dec 1	(h)	Everton	W 2-0	Channon, O'Neil	16,992	5		8			4	9			2			1		3	12	10		7*			6	11			
8	(a)	Manchester U	D 0-0		31,648	5		8			4	9			2			1		3		10		7			6	11			
15	(h)	Ipswich T	W 2-0	Channon, Gilchrist	14,663	5		8			4	9			2			1		3	12	10		7*			6	11			
22	(a)	Sheffield U	L 2-4	Channon, Gilchrist	17,173	5	10*	8			4	9			2			1		3	12			7			6	11			
26	(h)	Arsenal	D 1-1	Gilchrist	24,153	5		8			4	9			2			1		3		10		7			6	11			
29	(h)	Coventry C	D 1-1	Channon	18,345	5		8			4	9			2			1		3		10		7			6	11			
Jan 1	(a)	Wolves	L 1-2	Stokes	26,354	5		8			4	9			2			1		3	12	10		7			6	11*			
12	(a)	Leeds U	L 1-2	Channon	35,000	5		8			4	9			2		11*	1		3		10		7			6	12			
19	(h)	Queen's Park R	D 2-2	Channon 2	22,689	5		8			4*	9			2			1		3		10		7	12		6	11			
Feb 2	(a)	Ipswich T	L 0-7		20,053	5	10*	8			4				2			1				11		7	3	12	6	9			
5	(h)	Newcastle U	W 3-1	Channon, Fisher, Peach	16,497	5		8*			4	9			2			1		3	12			7	10		6	11			
23	(h)	Manchester C	L 0-2		19,234	5		8			4	9*			2		12	1		3				7	10		6	11			
26	(a)	Liverpool	L 0-1		27,014			8		5	4	9			2			1		3				7	10		6	11			
Mar 2	(a)	Arsenal	L 0-1		19,210		6	8			4	9	3		2			1		2				7	10		5	11			
5	(h)	Derby C	D 1-1	Channon	17,191	5	12	8			4	9			2			1				10		7*	3		6	11			
16	(a)	Stoke C	L 1-4	opp own goal	20,415	5		8			4	10			2			1					9	7	3		6	11			
18	(h)	Leicester C	W 1-0	Stokes	26,600	5		8			4	10			2			1		3			9	7			6	11			
23	(h)	Birmingham C	L 0-2		23,349	5		8			4	10			2			1		3*			9	7	12		6	11			
Apr 6	(h)	Chelsea	D 0-0		27,268	5		8			4				2			1		3		10	9	7			6	11			
12	(a)	West Ham U	L 1-4	Channon	34,163	5		8			4*	12			2			1		3		10	9	7			6	11			
13	(a)	Tottenham H	L 1-3	opp own goal	21,456	5		8			4	10			2				12				9	7*	3		6	11		1	
15	(h)	West Ham U	D 1-1	Stokes	26,515			8		5	4	10			2								9	7	3		6	11		1	
20	(h)	Manchester U	D 1-1	Channon	30,789			8		5	4	10			2			1					9	7	3		6	11			
22	(a)	Burnley	L 0-3		15,187			8	10	5	4	12			2								9	7*	3		6	11		1	
27	(a)	Everton	W 3-0	Channon, Osgood, O'Neil	30,500	6		8	10	5	4	7			2							11	9		3					1	
App						36	13	41	2	5	42	38	1	3	40	1	2	35	3	27	2	27	10	41	12		34	40	1	4	2
Sub app							2				1	1					1			4	6				2	1	1	1		2	
Goals						1		21			2	6										5	1	1	1			7			

2 own-goals

Back row (left to right): W.Beaney, A.Macleod, J.Kirkup, J.McGrath, P.Bennett, R.McCarthy, W.Talkes, G.O'Brien. Centre row: D.Taylor (physiotherapist), T.Byrne, D.Walker, P.Gilchrist, E.Martin, J.Steele, M.Channon, S.Mills, G.Horsfall (trainer). Front row: T.Spinner, R.Stokes, T.Paine, L.McMenemy (team manager designate), E.T.Bates (team manager), H.Fisher, B.O'Neil, F.Burns.

	P	W	D	L	F	A	Pts
Leeds U	42	24	14	4	66	31	62
Liverpool	42	22	13	7	52	31	57
Derby C	42	17	14	11	52	42	48
Ipswich T	42	18	11	13	67	58	47
Stoke C	42	15	16	11	54	42	46
Burnley	42	16	14	12	56	53	46
Everton	42	16	12	14	50	48	44
Queen's Park R	42	13	17	12	56	52	43
Leicester C	42	13	16	13	51	41	42
Arsenal	42	14	14	14	49	51	42
Tottenham H	42	14	14	14	45	50	42
Wolves	42	13	15	14	49	49	41
Sheffield U	42	14	12	16	44	49	40
Manchester C	42	14	12	16	39	46	40
Newcastle U	42	13	12	17	49	48	38
Coventry C	42	14	10	18	43	54	38
Chelsea	42	12	13	17	56	60	37
West Ham U	42	11	15	16	55	60	37
Birmingham C	42	12	13	17	52	64	37
Southampton	42	11	14	17	47	68	36
Manchester U	42	10	12	20	38	48	32
Norwich C	42	7	15	20	37	62	29

1974-75

WITH the club back in the Second Division where it had spent most of its Football League career, everyone at Southampton began to take stock of the situation. Ted Bates must have been particularly dismayed. After 18 years as manager, carefully nurturing the Saints' playing staff and guiding the club into Division One, he had seen them lose that status within six months of his relinquishing the job.

Terry Paine had ended his long and illustrious Saints career and moved to Hereford, but with experienced players like Channon and Osgood still at The Dell, supporters hoped for a quick return. Norwich and Manchester United, the clubs to come down with Saints, did indeed go straight back up, but there was to be no promotion for Southampton.

Saints stumbled through the start of the season and it was their seventh match — the first local League 'derby' against Pompey for many years — before they scored a win. Mel Blyth came from Crystal Palace to add experience to the defence, but Saints' erratic form continued.

There were good wins at Bristol Rovers and Oxford, and bad home defeats by Sheffield Wednesday and Nottingham Forest. One bright moment was the Boxing Day win at Fratton Park, Saints' first double over Portsmouth since 1920-21. In December 1974 though, exactly one year after standing fifth in Division One, Saints were 17th in Division Two.

In the New Year, Saints rallied a little, boosted by the signing of the experienced Scottish international midfielder, Jim McCalliog, from Manchester United. Indeed, McMenemy was showing a preference for signing older players and he would become well-known for revitalising many an experienced man's flagging career.

Saints ended the season in 13th place with youngsters like Holmes, Andruszewski and Waldron all showing promise. Channon was top scorer with 20 goals and Osgood netted 13, but it was obvious that much had yet to be done before Saints could return to the top flight.

FA Cup

GAMES between Saints and West Ham had always been traditionally open, entertaining affairs and the third-round FA Cup tie between the two in January 1975 was no exception.

Eric Martin had been restored to Saints' goal but after 25 minutes he dropped a long-range shot from Frank Lampard into his own net to give Hammers the lead.

Seven minutes later, Gould scored West Ham's second goal and although Channon pulled a goal back in the second half, from the penalty spot, battling Saints could not find another and West Ham went through on the way to winning the Cup that season. Saints fans would have been less dismayed had they known that it would be Southampton's last FA Cup defeat for over two years.

> **Round 3**
> **Jan 4 v West Ham United (h) 1-2**
> *Channon*
> Martin; Mills, Steele, Holmes, Bennett, Blyth, Stokes(Peach), Channon, Osgood, Crabbe, O'Brien.
> *Att: 24,615*

Football League Cup

IT was one of the ironies of Southampton's season that, after defeating League Champions elect, Derby County, 5-0 in the third round of the League Cup, they should crash to Third Division Colchester in the next round.

Mick Channon's hat-trick destroyed Derby — their goalkeeper, Colin Boulton, would later play a few games on loan to Southampton — but Colchester proved much more difficult opponents.

> **Round 2**
> **Sep 10 v Notts County (h) 1-0**
> *Osgood*
> Turner; Mills, Peach, Fisher, Bennett, Steele, Gilchrist, Channon, Osgood, O'Neil, O'Brien.
> *Att: 10,649*
> **Round 3**
> **Oct 8 v Derby County (h) 5-0**
> *Channon 3, Stokes, Osgood*
> Turner; McCarthy, Peach, Fisher, Bennett, Mills, Stokes, Channon, Osgood, Holmes(Chatterley), Steele.
> *Att: 14,911*
> **Round 4**
> **Nov 13 v Colchester United (a) 0-0**
> Turner; McCarthy, Mills, Fisher, Bennett, Steele, Stokes, Channon, Osgood, Peach, Gilchrist.
> *Att: 9,515*
> **Nov 28 v Colchester United (h) 0-1**
> Turner; McCarthy, Mills, Fisher, Bennett, Steele, Stokes, Channon, MacLeod, Peach, Gilchrist.
> *Att: 11,492*

> *Total home attendance: 333,766. Average: 15,893.*

> *Terry Paine returned to The Dell at the end of 1974-5 to take part in his testimonial game against Ipswich Town.*

Bobby Stokes scores the first of his two goals against York City at The Dell in December 1974.

1974-75

Division 2

Date		Opponent	Res	Scorers	Att	Andruszewski E	Beaney W	Bennett P	Berry M	Blyth M	Channon M	Chatterley L	Crabbe J	Earles P	Earls M	Fisher H	Gilchrist P	Holmes N	McCalliog J	McCarthy R	Martin E	Mills S	Neville S	O'Brien G	O'Neil B	Osgood P	Peach D	Steele J	Stokes R	Turner I	Waldron M
Aug 17	(h)	Hull C	D 3-3	Gilchrist 2, Osgood	16,730	6	5			8	11					4	7				2	1				10	9	3			
21	(a)	Norwich C	L 0-1		21,650		5			8	11					4*	7				2	1				10	9	3	6	12	
24	(a)	Sunderland	L 1-3	Channon	34,021		5			8	11*					4	7				2	1				10	9	3	6	12	1
27	(h)	Norwich C	D 1-1	Fisher	16,367					8					5	4	7					2				10	9	3	6	11	1
31	(h)	Blackpool	D 1-1	Stokes	14,694					8					5	4*	7					2		12		10	9	3	6	11	1
Sep 7	(a)	Notts C	L 2-3	Peach, Osgood	7,830		5			8				11*		4	7					2				10	9	3	6	12	1
14	(h)	Portsmouth	W 2-1	Osgood 2	19,361		5			8						4	7*					2		11		10	9	3	6	12	1
21	(a)	Bristol C	L 0-2		15,708		5		6	8						4	10					2		7*			9	3	11	7	1
25	(a)	Oxford U	W 4-0	Channon 3, Osgood	11,135		5		6	8						4			12		2			10*			9	3	11	7	1
28	(h)	Aston Villa	D 0-0		18,599		5		6	8						4			10		2						9	3	11	7	1
Oct 5	(h)	Nottingham F	L 0-1		15,703		5		6	8						4	12				2			10*			9	3	11	7	1
12	(a)	Millwall	L 0-4		9,306		5		12	8						4			10*		2	6					9	3	11	7	1
19	(h)	Orient	W 4-2	Channon, Osgood, Gilchrist, Peach	14,542				5	8	12					4	11				2	3					9	10	6*	7	1
26	(a)	Manchester C	L 0-1		48,724				5	8						4	11				2	3					9	10	6	7	1
Nov 2	(a)	Bristol R	W 1-0	Channon	15,182		5		6	8						4	11				2	3					9	10		7	1
9	(h)	West Brom A	W 1-0	Channon	15,638		5		6	8						4	11				2	3					9	10		7	1
16	(a)	Bolton W	L 2-3	Channon, Peach	14,348		5*		6	8						4	12				2	3					9	10	11	7	1
29	(a)	Cardiff C	D 2-2	Channon, Stokes	10,654		5		6	8						4					2		11			9	10	3	7	1
Dec 7	(h)	York C	W 2-1	Stokes 2	13,224		5		6	8						4			3		2		11			9	10		7	1
14	(a)	Hull C	D 1-1	Channon	9,004				5	8	12					4					2	3	11			9	10	6	7*	1
21	(h)	Fulham	D 0-0		13,560				5	8			12			4*					2	3	11			9	10	6	7	1
26	(a)	Portsmouth	W 2-1	Osgood, Peach	19,543		5		6		8					4		12			2		11			9*	10	3	7	1
28	(h)	Sheffield W	L 0-1		15,243		5		6		8*					4		12			2		11			9	10	3	7	1
Jan 10	(a)	York C	D 1-1	Osgood	8,245		5		6	8		7						4			1	2	11			9	10	3			
14	(h)	Sunderland	D 1-1	Osgood	16,738		5		6	8		10						4			1	2	11			9		3	7		
25	(h)	Oldham A	W 1-0	Blyth	12,400		5*		6	8		10						12	4		1	2	11			9		3	7		
Feb 1	(a)	West Brom A	W 3-0	Stokes, Channon, Osgood	16,823	5			6	8		10*				4			3		1	2	11			9	12		7		
8	(h)	Bristol R	W 3-0	Channon 3	17,490	5			6	8						4			3		1	2	11			9	10		7		
15	(a)	Oldham A	D 1-1	Gilchrist	12,397	5			6	8						4	9	3	10		1	2	11						7		
22	(h)	Bolton W	L 0-1		18,339	5			6	8						4	12	3	10		1	2	11	9*					7		
Mar 1	(a)	Blackpool	L 0-3		8,831	5			6	8						4	12	3	10	2	1		11		9*				7		
15	(a)	Aston Villa	L 0-3		31,967	2		5	6	8						4		3	10				11	9					7	1	
18	(h)	Oxford U	W 2-1	Channon, Gilchrist	11,491	2		5	6	8		7					11	4	10					9	3					1	
22	(h)	Notts C	W 3-2	Channon 2, Holmes	12,973	2		5	6	8		7					11	4	10					9	3					1	
24	(a)	Fulham	L 2-3	Peach, Holmes	11,939	2		5	6	8		7				11*	4	12						9	3	10				1	
28	(h)	Bristol C	L 0-1		21,019	2		5	6	8		12					4	7*						9	3	10	11	1			
31	(a)	Sheffield W	W 1-0	Osgood	8,505	2		5	6	8						4		7	10					9	3	11*	12	1			
Apr 5	(h)	Manchester U	L 0-1		21,866	2		5*	6	8						4		7	10					9	3	11	12	1			
12	(a)	Nottingham F	D 0-0		11,554	2			6	8						4		7	10					9	11	3			1	5	
18	(h)	Millwall	W 3-2	Osgood 2, Channon	13,516	2			6	8						4		7	10	12				9	3			11	1	5	
22	(h)	Cardiff C	W 2-0	Channon, O'Brien	14,273	5			2	6	8					4		12	10				11	9	3			7*	1		
26	(a)	Orient	L 1-2	Channon	7,580	5			2	6	8			11*		4		10					7	9	3					1	12
App						16	1	27	2	34	40	5	8		3	34	16	20	13	16	10	24	19	9	40	36	27	28	32	2	
Sub app								1			2	1	1				5	4	1					1	1		1		7	1
Goals										1	20					1	5	2						1		13	5		5		

Back row (left to right): Bob McCarthy, Bill Beaney, Nick Holmes, Mike Earls, Alisdair MacLeod, Steve Mills, David Peach. Middle row: Don Taylor (physiotherapist), Paul Gilchrist, Jim Steele, Eric Martin, Ian Turner, Lew Chatterley, Paul Bennett, George Horsfall (trainer). Front row: Gerry O'Brien, Bobby Stokes, Mike Channon, Lawrie McMenemy (manager), Peter Osgood, Hugh Fisher, Brian O'Neil.

	P	W	D	L	F	A	Pts
Manchester U	42	26	9	7	66	30	61
Aston Villa	42	25	8	9	69	32	58
Norwich C	42	20	13	9	58	37	53
Sunderland	42	19	13	10	65	35	51
Bristol C	42	21	8	13	47	33	50
West Brom A	42	18	9	15	54	42	45
Blackpool	42	14	17	11	38	33	45
Hull C	42	15	14	13	40	53	44
Fulham	42	13	16	13	44	39	42
Bolton W	42	15	12	15	45	41	42
Oxford U	42	15	12	15	41	51	42
Orient	42	11	20	11	28	39	42
Southampton	42	15	11	16	53	54	41
Notts C	42	12	16	14	49	59	40
York C	42	14	10	18	51	55	38
Nottingham F	42	12	14	16	43	55	38
Portsmouth	42	12	13	17	44	54	37
Oldham A	42	10	15	17	40	48	35
Bristol R	42	12	11	19	42	64	35
Millwall	42	10	12	20	44	56	32
Cardiff C	42	9	14	19	36	62	32
Sheffield W	42	5	11	26	29	64	21

1975-76

THIS was, of course, the year that Saints won the FA Cup for the first time in their history and yet it came at a time when the club's League form was quite mediocre.

Full-back Peter Rodrigues was the only new face, and he came on a free transfer from Sheffield Wednesday. Yet within eight months he was to find his career transformed as Saints lifted the Cup.

Saints began their Second Division programme well, but with bad results against Charlton, Nottingham Forest and Orient, they were soon settled into their now customary mid-table position.

In December, McMenemy set up an exchange deal which would have taken Stokes to Portsmouth and brought Paul

Went to The Dell. Bobby Stokes refused terms and a few months later, all Saints fans were eternally grateful that he had.

Encouraged by their Cup successes, Saints eventually climbed to fifth place, only four points short of third-placed West Brom who took the last promotion place. Had Saints won their two Easter games at Plymouth and Bristol Rovers, then they would have pipped Albion who they had beaten twice in the League and also knocked out of the Cup.

It was the defence which let Saints down in the League, and yet they conceded only four goals in eight Cup games. That probably showed the real reasons for Saints' contrasting form in the two competitions.

FA Cup

SOUTHAMPTON were only 60 seconds from defeat in their very first match of the 1976 FA Cup campaign. Aston Villa led through an Andy Gray goal, scored when Chris Nicholl — later to become Saints manager — headed against the Southampton crossbar and the Scottish striker hit home the rebound.

It had looked all over for Saints before Hugh Fisher chose that moment to score his first goal of the season.

Few people rated Saints' chances at Villa Park, but right from the kick-off they took the game to their opponents and

were amply rewarded when McCalliog, six yards from goal, headed home Channon's cross in the 32nd minute.

Only the brilliance of Burridge in the Villa goal prevented Saints extending their lead before, right against the run of play, Graydon equalised four minutes before half-time. In the second half it was Turner in the Saints goal who was called upon to perform heroics.

In the 13th minute of extra-time, McCalliog capped a fine individual performance by scoring the winner with a shot which took a deflection on its way past Burridge.

Bobby Stokes hits the most important goal in Saints' history — the one that brought the FA Cup to Southampton for the first time.

1975-76
Division 2

Date		Opponent	Result	Scorers	Att	Andruszewski E	Bennett P	Blyth M	Channon M	Crabbe J	Earles P	Fisher H	Gilchrist P	Holmes N	McCalliog J	Middleton S	Mills S	O'Brien G	Osgood P	Peach D	Rodrigues P	Steele J	Stokes R	Turner I	Waldron M	Williams S
Aug 16	(h)	West Brom A	W 3-0	Channon 2, Holmes	15,246		5	6	8					4	10	1		7		11	2	3	9			
23	(a)	Notts C	D 0-0		8,495		5	6	8					4	10	1		7		11	2	3	9			
26	(h)	Bristol C	W 3-1	Stokes 2, Peach	16,833		5	6	8					4	10	1		7		11	2	3	9			
29	(h)	Plymouth A	W 1-0	Channon	19,000		5	6	8					4	10	1		7*	12	11	2	3	9			
Sep 6	(a)	Bolton W	L 0-3		9,188		5	6	8				12	4	10	1		7	9	11*	2	3				
13	(h)	Blackburn R	W 2-1	Stokes, Peach	13,279		5	6	8					4		1		7	9	11	2	3	10			
20	(a)	Blackpool	L 3-4	Rodrigues, Steele, Holmes	9,564		5	6	8				12	4		1		7*	9	11	2	3	10			
27	(h)	Portsmouth	W 4-0	Channon 3, Peach	17,310		5	6	8			7		4	10	1			9	3	2		11			
Oct 4	(a)	Hull C	D 0-0		6,342		5	6	8			7		4	10	1			9	3	2		11			
11	(h)	Chelsea	W 4-1	Channon 2, Stokes, Holmes	21,227		5	6	8			7		4	10	1			9	3	2		11			
18	(a)	Nottingham F	L 1-3	Osgood	12,677		5	6	8			7*	12	4	10	1			9	3	2		11			
21	(a)	Oldham A	L 2-3	Holmes 2	11,219		5		8	12		7		4	10	1			9	11	2	3*			6	
25	(h)	York C	W 2-0	Channon, McCalliog	13,501		5	6	8			7		4	10	1		12		11	2		9		3*	
31	(a)	Charlton A	L 1-4	Osgood	16,036		5	6	8			7		4	10	1			9	3	2		11			
Nov 8	(h)	Luton T	W 3-1	Stokes, Channon, McCalliog	13,885		5	6	8					4	10	1		12	9	11	2*	3	7			
14	(a)	Orient	L 1-2	McCalliog	6,332		5	6	8					4	10	1			9	11	2	3	7			
22	(h)	Nottingham F	L 0-3		14,245		5	6	8					4	10	1		12	9	11*	2	3	7			
29	(a)	Carlisle	L 0-1		6,977		5*		8			7	11	4	10				9	3	2	6	12	1		
Dec 6	(h)	Sunderland	W 4-0	Osgood 2, Holmes, Blyth	17,598			5	8			7	11	4	10				9	3	2	6		1		
13	(h)	Notts C	W 2-1	Holmes, McCalliog	12,571			5	8			7	11	4	10				9	3	2	6		1		
19	(a)	West Brom A	W 2-0	Peach, Channon	17,071			5	8	12		7	11	4	10					3	2	6*	9	1		
26	(h)	Bristol R	W 3-0	Channon, Stokes, Holmes	19,556			5	8			7*	11	4	10			12		3	2	6	9	1		
27	(a)	Oxford U	W 2-1	Holmes, Stokes	12,004			5	8			7	11	4	10					3	2	6	9	1		
Jan 17	(h)	Bolton W	D 0-0		20,363			5	8			7		4	10				9	3	2	6	11	1		
28	(a)	Blackburn R	D 1-1	Osgood	8,786			5	8			7		4	10				9	3	2	6	11	1		
31	(h)	Oldham A	W 3-2	Osgood, Channon, Stokes	14,294			5	8			7		4	10				9	3	2	6	11	1		
Feb 7	(a)	Bristol C	D 1-1	Holmes	22,316			5	8			7		4	10				9	3	2	6	11	1		
21	(h)	Orient	W 3-0	McCalliog 2, Stokes	17,230			5	8			7	9	4	10					3	2	6	11	1		
24	(h)	Fulham	W 2-1	Blyth, Channon	23,575			5	8			7	9*	4	10			12		3	2	6	11	1		
28	(a)	York C	L 1-2	Channon	3,777			5	8			7	9	4	10					3	2	6	11	1		
Mar 2	(a)	Luton T	L 0-1		13,737	6		5	8			7		4	10				9	3	2		11	1		
9	(a)	Fulham	L 0-1		8,731	6		5	8			7		4	10				9	3	2		11	1		
13	(a)	Chelsea	D 1-1	Channon	29,011			5	8			7		4	10				9	3	2	6	11	1		
20	(h)	Carlisle U	D 1-1	Peach	18,304			5	8			7	12	4	10				9	3	2	6	11*	1		
27	(a)	Sunderland	L 0-3		34,946			5	8			7	12	4	10				9	3	2*	6	11	1		
Apr 6	(a)	Portsmouth	W 1-0	Channon	24,115	6		5	8		9	7		4						3	2		11	1		10
10	(h)	Blackpool	W 3-1	Channon, Holmes, Peach	21,758			5	8			7	12	4	10				9	3	2*	6	11	1		
12	(h)	Charlton A	W 3-2	Channon 2, McCalliog	23,686	2		5	8			7		4	10				9	3		6	11	1		
16	(a)	Plymouth A	L 0-1		25,305			5	8			7		4	10				9	3	2	6	11	1		
17	(a)	Bristol R	L 0-2		11,834	6		5	8		12	7*	10	4						3	2		11	1		
19	(h)	Oxford U	W 2-1	Rodrigues, opp own goal	18,870			5	8		12	7*	10	4					9	3	2	6	11	1		
24	(h)	Hull C	W 1-0	Stokes	18,272			5	8			7		4	10		3		9		2	6	11	1		
App						6	20	37	42		1	27	20	39	37	17	1	7	29	41	41	32	37	25	2	1
Sub app										2	5	2	1					2	4				1			
Goals								2	20					11	7				6	6	2	1	10			

1 own-goal

Back row (left to right): John Crabbe, Pat Earles, Paul Gilchrist, Ian Turner, Forbes Phillipson-Masters, Steve Middleton, Nick Holmes, Mike Berry, David Peach. Middle row: Jim Clunie (trainer), Manny Andruszewski, Mel Blyth, Jim Steele, Malcolm Waldron, Paul Bennett, Don Taylor (physiotherapist), George Horsfall (trainer). Front row: Jim McCalliog, Peter Rodrigues, Peter Osgood, Lawrie McMenemy (manager), Mike Channon, Bobby Stokes, Gerry O'Brien.

	P	W	D	L	F	A	Pts
Sunderland	42	24	8	10	67	36	56
Bristol C	42	19	15	8	59	35	53
West Brom A	42	20	13	9	50	33	53
Bolton W	42	20	12	10	64	38	52
Southampton	42	21	7	14	66	50	49
Luton T	42	19	10	13	61	51	48
Notts C	42	19	11	12	60	41	49
Nottingham F	42	17	12	13	55	40	46
Charlton A	42	15	12	15	61	72	42
Blackpool	42	14	14	14	40	49	42
Chelsea	42	12	16	14	53	54	40
Fulham	42	13	14	15	45	47	40
Orient	42	13	14	15	37	39	40
Hull C	42	14	11	17	45	49	39
Blackburn R	42	14	12	16	45	50	38
Plymouth A	42	13	12	17	48	54	38
Oldham A	42	13	12	17	57	68	38
Bristol R	42	11	16	15	38	50	38
Carlisle U	42	12	13	17	49	59	37
Oxford U	42	11	11	20	39	59	33
York C	42	10	8	24	39	71	28
Portsmouth	42	9	7	26	33	61	25

Blackpool, a club steeped in Cup tradition but now on the decline, fell to a Channon header in only the fifth minute of the fourth-round match at The Dell.

Blackpool did well to keep the score down to that single goal at half-time. Then Stokes increased the lead after Osgood had miskicked, and Channon headed his second and Saints' third. Alcock grabbed a consolation goal for Blackpool near the end.

Channon, Stokes, Holmes and Gilchrist all felt unwell on the morning of the fifth-round clash with West Brom at The Hawthorns but there were no ready replacements and they all played. Albion had a poor record against Saints but Tony Brown gave them a 58th-minute lead. In the 75th minute, Stokes scored a deserved equaliser with a shot from the edge of the penalty area.

The crowd had hardly settled into their places for the replay when Mick Channon scored after only 52 seconds. Within half an hour Saints were three up, thanks to a spectacular goal from Gilchrist and another from Channon who went on to complete his hat-trick with a second-half penalty.

Southampton were now in the quarter-finals for the first time since 1963 and their opponents, Fourth Division Bradford, controversially raised the admission charges to produce the smallest FA Cup sixth-round crowd since the war.

Steele and Holmes reported unfit and Bennett was drafted in, with Gilchrist dropping back to replace Holmes. The game was a hard-fought affair and the only difference between the sides was a little flash of skill from Osgood and McCalliog four minutes before half-time.

Osgood nonchalantly flicked up a free-kick for McCalliog to volley the ball past Downsborough in the Bradford goal. Saints survived some late pressure from a determined Bradford side to go into the semi-finals.

The last time Saints had reached this stage they were the underdogs against Manchester United; this time they were expected to beat their opponents, Third Division Crystal Palace.

As so often happens at this stage of the Cup, the semi-final at Stamford Bridge was a mediocre affair. Saints gave a thoroughly professional display to end Palace's dreams of being the first Third Division side to reach Wembley for an FA Cup Final.

Gilchrist scored Saints' first goal in the 74th minute, playing a one-two with Osgood before crashing home a 25-yarder. Then Channon was fouled in the penalty area and Peach coolly stroked the spot kick home.

There would hardly be anyone alive who could claim to remember the last time Southampton reached an FA Cup Final back in 1902, in the days of C.B.Fry and Edgar Chadwick. Their opponents on this occasion were Manchester United, managed by Tommy Docherty and, in their first season back in Division One, having a splendid year.

The game itself was never a classic and few people expected it would be. Neither did they expect Saints to do particularly well and that probably helped the Southampton players to overcome the tensions. By half-time, with the game still goalless, Saints began to feel that they had a very real chance of springing a surprise.

Round 3
Jan 3 v Aston Villa (h) 1-1
Fisher
Turner; Rodrigues, Peach, Holmes, Blyth, Steele, Fisher, Channon, Stokes, McCalliog, Gilchrist(Earles).
Att: 24,138
Replay
Jan 7 v Aston Villa (a) 2-1
McCalliog 2
Turner; Rodrigues, Peach, Holmes, Blyth, Steele, Fisher, Channon, Osgood, McCalliog, Stokes.
Att: 44,623
Round 4
Jan 24 v Blackpool (h) 3-1
Channon 2, Stokes
Turner; Rodrigues, Peach, Holmes, Blyth, Steele, Fisher, Channon, Osgood, McCalliog(O'Brien), Stokes.
Att: 21,553
Round 5
Feb 14 v West Bromwich Albion (a) 1-1
Stokes
Turner; Rodrigues, Peach, Holmes, Blyth, Steele, Fisher, Channon, Gilchrist, McCalliog, Stokes.
Att: 36,634
Replay
Feb 17 v West Bromwich Albion (h) 4-0
Channon 3, Gilchrist
Turner; Rodrigues, Peach, Holmes, Blyth, Steele, Fisher, Channon, Gilchrist, McCalliog, Stokes(O'Brien).
Att: 27,614
Round 6
Mar 6 v Bradford (a) 1-0
McCalliog
Turner; Rodrigues, Peach, Gilchrist, Blyth, Bennett, Fisher, Channon, Osgood, McCalliog, Stokes.
Att: 14,195
Semi-final
Apr 3 v Crystal Palace (at Stamford Bridge) 2-0
Peach, Gilchrist
Turner; Rodrigues, Peach, Holmes, Blyth, Steele, Gilchrist, Channon, Osgood, McCalliog, Stokes.
Att: 52,810
Final
May 1 v Manchester United (at Wembley) 1-0
Stokes
Turner; Rodrigues, Peach, Holmes, Blyth, Steele, Gilchrist, Channon, Osgood, McCalliog, Stokes.
Att: 100,000

A happy Mel Blyth displays the FA Cup after Saints' great win over Manchester United.

Left: Wembley programme for Saints' first-ever FA Cup Final appearance at the Empire Stadium. Bottom: Southampton's triumphant players show the Cup to their fans.

Opposite (top): An open-top bus ride by the team through Southampton brought out tens of thousands of rapturous supporters. (Bottom): Manager Lawrie McMenemy speaks to the fans alongside Peter Rodrigues, Mick Channon and Peter Osgood.

Thousands of Saints fans greet the team as they ride triumphantly through the town.

Visibly growing in confidence they began to press forward and test Stepney in the United goal. Channon, Osgood and Stokes all got in shots which brought Saints' fans to their toes and then, in the 83rd minute, they were off their feet altogether.

Jim McCalliog guided a perfect through ball and Bobby Stokes ran on to it and slotted the ball left-footed past the diving Stepney.

One end of the great stadium erupted in a crescendo of cheering; the other was deathly silent. The last seven minutes were agonising moments for Saints supporters, yet United already looked a beaten side and threatened little.

There are those who reckon that when the final whistle sounded, the cheer could be heard back on St Mary's Street where it had all begun 91 years before.

Saints skipper, Peter Rodrigues, climbed the steps to the Royal Box to receive the FA Cup from the Queen, and all the trials and tribulations that had dogged Southampton Football Club since 1885 were banished from the mind.

Amidst the euphoria, though, one had to spare a thought for the Saints substitute who did not get a kick that day. Yet had it not been for Hugh Fisher's last-gasp equaliser on a wintry afternoon four months earlier, then none of what we were now witnessing would have been possible.

Football League Cup

BEFORE the FA Cup campaign started, Southampton made their now customary early exit from the League Cup, losing at home to fellow Second Division club, Bristol Rovers.

Round 2
Sep 9 v Bristol Rovers (h) 0-1
Middleton; Rodrigues, Steele, Holmes, Bennett, Blyth, O'Brien, Channon, Osgood, Stokes, Peach.
Att: 10,757

Two days after Saints won the FA Cup at Wembley, Mick Channon had the good fortune to stage his testimonial match against Queen's Park Rangers. A capacity crowd packed The Dell, with thousands more locked outside on one of the most emotional nights that Southampton has ever seen.

Total home attendance: 370,603. Average: 17,647.

173

1976-77

WITH the FA Cup won and the memory safely locked away in the fans' minds, the main priority facing Lawrie McMenemy was to restore Southampton to Division One.

The Cup Final victory over Manchester United had proved that Saints already had the players capable of rising to the big occasion — but could they perform consistently well over 42 League games?

In his heart, McMenemy knew that they could not and once Fisher had replaced Blyth in the Charity Shield match against Liverpool on the eve of the new season, the side that had won the Cup for Southampton never played together again.

As Cup holders, Saints had the added problem of being the Second Division's prize scalp, the team everyone wanted to beat. Carlisle wasted no time in tearing into Saints and winning at The Dell in the first League game of the new season.

After seven games Southampton were bottom of Division Two — hardly the place for a side about embark on the European Cup-winners' Cup trail. Ted MacDougall was signed and once he had found his scoring touch, Saints did at least pull away from anchor position although the side was hardly settled.

In January, McMenemy dug into the coffers again and made one of the club's best-ever signings when he brought Alan Ball, one of the midfield stars of England's World Cup triumph in 1966, to The Dell.

Ball was an integral part of McMenemy's new-look side but he came too late for the team to make any impact on the season's promotion race. Saints eventually finished ninth, a disappointment to everyone, but with the emergence in midfield of Steve Williams, and the proven abilities of players like MacDougall and Ball, there was at least a glimmer of hope for the future.

One sign that Saints were still capable of mixing with the best came in the Cup-winners' Cup in which they went to the quarter-finals before losing to Anderlecht (see *Saints in Europe*).

FA Cup

AFTER being held to a home draw by Chelsea in the third round of the FA Cup, Saints looked on their way to an early exit, yet they took Chelsea to extra-time at Stamford Bridge and then rattled in three goals on a heavy pitch against a side reputed to be one of the fittest in the League.

The crowd who watched the fourth-round tie at the City Ground were treated to six goals and plenty of excitement as Saints and Forest produced a classic Cup tie.

Saints went behind after 34 minutes when Ball conceded a penalty, but the little midfielder made amends in the 51st minute with his first goal for the club. Osgood and Channon were the other Saints scorers and a draw was a fair result. The replay was equally entertaining as both sides threw caution to the wind. It was fitting that Steve Williams, Saints' best player on the day, should score the opening goal.

A re-run of the previous season's Final saw Saints and Manchester United produce some vintage football at The Dell, Macari putting United ahead in the 13th minute and Peach equalisng from the penalty spot. Gordon Hill, who had a poor game at Wembley, put United in front again but Saints drew level once more when Holmes converted Channon's pass.

The Old Trafford replay was another splendid match but Saints at last had to release their hold on the Cup after a marvellous 14-match unbeaten run in the competition.

Round 3
Jan 8 v Chelsea (h) 1-1
Channon
Wells; Andruszewski, Peach, Holmes, Blyth, Steele, Ball, Channon, Osgood, McCalliog, MacDougall.
Att: 26,041
Replay
Jan 12 v Chelsea (a) 3-0
MacDougall, Channon, Peach
Wells; Andruszewski, Peach, Holmes, Blyth, Steele, Ball, Channon, Osgood, McCalliog, MacDougall.
Att: 42,868
Round 4
Jan 29 v Nottingham Forest (a) 3-3
Ball, Channon, Osgood
Wells; Andruszewski, Peach, Holmes, Blyth, Steele, Ball, Channon, Osgood, Williams, MacDougall.
Att: 38,284
Replay
Feb 1 v Nottingham Forest (h) 2-1
Williams, MacDougall
Wells; Andruszewski, Peach(Fisher), Holmes, Blyth, Steele, Ball, Channon, Osgood, Williams, MacDougall.
Att: 29,401
Round 5
Feb 26 v Manchester United (h) 2-2
Peach, Holmes
Wells; Andruszewski, Peach, Holmes, Blyth, Waldron, Ball, Channon, Osgood, Williams, MacDougall.
Att: 29,137
Replay
Mar 8 v Manchester United (a) 1-2
Peach
Wells; Andruszewski, Peach, Holmes, Blyth, Steele, Ball, Channon, Osgood, Williams, MacDougall.
Att: 58,103

Total home attendance: 402,997. Average: 19,190.

Football League Cup

FELLOW Second Division side, Charlton Athletic, knocked Saints out of the League Cup — and then went on to hammer Southampton 6-2 in the League just over a fortnight later.

Round 2
Aug 31 v Charlton Athletic (h) 1-1
Earles
Middleton; Rodrigues, Peach, Holmes, Waldron, Andruszewski, Fisher(Williams), Channon, Osgood, McCalliog, Earles.
Att: 13,371
Replay
Sep 7 v Charlton Athletic (a) 1-2
Channon
Middleton; Rodrigues, Peach(Gilchrist), Holmes, Waldron, Blyth, Fisher, Channon, Osgood, McCalliog, Williams.
Att: 13,198

Division 2

Date		Opponent	Res		Scorers	Att
Aug 21	(h)	Carlisle U	L	1-2	Osgood	18,695
25	(a)	Millwall	D	0-0		13,544
28	(a)	Hull C	L	0-4		7,774
Sep 4	(h)	Sheffield U	D	1-1	Channon	12,809
11	(a)	Burnley	L	0-2		9,116
18	(h)	Nottingham F	D	1-1	Stokes	23,006
24	(a)	Charlton A	L	2-6	Peach, MacDougall	9,662
Oct 2	(h)	Fulham	W	4-1	Blyth 2, MacDougall 2	28,489
5	(a)	Wolves	W	6-2	Holmes 2, Channon 2, Earles, McCalliog	21,286
16	(h)	Hereford U	W	1-0	Holmes	24,910
23	(a)	Luton T	W	4-1	Peach 2, Holmes, MacDougall	12,123
30	(a)	Chelsea	L	1-3	MacDougall	42,654
Nov 6	(h)	Orient	D	2-2	MacDougall, Blyth	16,974
10	(a)	Cardiff C	L	0-1		15,190
20	(h)	Bolton W	L	1-3	MacDougall	17,611
27	(a)	Oldham A	L	1-2	Andruszewski	10,663
Dec 4	(h)	Notts C	W	2-1	Holmes, Channon	14,153
7	(h)	Chelsea	D	1-1	MacDougall	19,909
18	(h)	Blackpool	D	3-3	Channon 3	14,918
27	(a)	Plymouth A	D	1-1	MacDougall	24,787
29	(h)	Bristol R	W	2-1	Channon 2	19,790
Jan 15	(a)	Millwall	L	0-2		20,527
22	(a)	Carlisle U	W	6-0	Holmes 2, Peach, Channon, Osgood, MacDougall	9,617
Feb 5	(h)	Hull C	D	2-2	MacDougall 2	20,353
12	(a)	Sheffield U	D	2-2	Osgood, MacDougall	17,634
19	(h)	Burnley	W	2-0	Peach, MacDougall	17,981
Mar 5	(h)	Charlton A	W	2-1	Andruszewski, MacDougall	8,421
11	(a)	Fulham	D	1-1	Hebberd	13,408
22	(a)	Nottingham F	L	1-2	Rodrigues	12,393
Apr 2	(h)	Luton T	W	1-0	Ball	19,923
8	(h)	Plymouth A	W	4-1	MacDougall 2, Peach, Channon	20,914
9	(a)	Bristol R	W	3-2	Osgood, Hebberd, MacDougall	11,479
11	(h)	Cardiff C	W	3-2	Channon 2, MacDougall	22,674
16	(a)	Bolton W	L	0-3		20,095
20	(a)	Blackburn R	L	0-3		5,923
23	(h)	Oldham A	W	4-0	Channon 2, Osgood, MacDougall	14,586
26	(a)	Orient	W	3-2	MacDougall 2, Channon	5,226
30	(a)	Notts C	L	1-3	MacDougall	10,651
May 3	(h)	Wolves	W	1-0	Holmes	20,216
7	(h)	Blackburn R	W	2-0	Peach, Channon	16,138
11	(a)	Hereford U	L	0-2		6,886
14	(a)	Blackpool	L	0-1		10,768

Appearances and goals (shirt numbers per match)

Player columns: Andruszewski E, Ball A, Blyth M, Boulton C, Channon M, Coak T, Crabbe J, Earles P, Fisher H, Gilchrist P, Hayes A, Hebberd T, Holmes N, MacDougall E, McCalliog J, Middleton S, Mills M, Montgomery J, Osgood P, Peach D, Phillipson-Masters F, Rodrigues P, Sharpe J, Steele J, Stokes R, Turner I, Waldron M, Wells P, Williams S

Date	And	Ball	Bly	Boul	Cha	Coak	Cra	Ear	Fis	Gil	Hay	Heb	Hol	MacD	McC	Mid	Mil	Mon	Osg	Pea	P-M	Rod	Sha	Ste	Sto	Tur	Wal	Wel	Wil
Aug 21					8					7			4	10					9	3		2		6	11	1	5		
25					8				11	7			4	10					9	3		2		6			5		
28	6				8				11	7			4	10*	1				9	3		2					5		12
Sep 4			6		8					7			4	10	1				9	3		2			11		5		7
11			6	1	8					7				10					9			2	3				5		11
18			6	1	8					7*					10		12		9	3		2			4		5		11
24			6	1	8					7	11			9	4					3		2					5		10
Oct 2			6	1	8					11				7	10				9	3		2	4*	12			5		
5			6	1	8			9	11				4	7	10					3		2					5		
16			6	1	8				11				4	7	10	1				3		2					5		
23			6		8				11				4	9	10			1		3		2					5		7
30			6		8				11				4	9	10			1		3		2			12		5		7*
Nov 6			6						7				4	8			2	1	9	3				10			5		11
10			6*		8				12	7			4	9	10		2	1		3							5		11
20	2		6		8				12	7			4	9	10*			1		3							5		11
27	2		6		8								4	9	10					3		2					5		7
Dec 4			6		8								4	9	10					3		2			11	1	5		7
7			6		8								4	9	10					3		2			11	1	5		7
18			5		8								4	11	10				9	3			6			2	1	7	
27	2	7	5		8								4	11	10				9	3			6				1		
29	2	7	5		8	12								11	10*				9	3			6				1	4	
Jan 15	2	7	5		8									11	10*				9	3			6	12			1		
22	2	7	5		8							12	4	11					9*	3			6				1	10	
Feb 5	2	7	5		8							9	4	11						3	6						1	10	
12	2	7	5		8							12	4	11					9	3		6*					1	10	
19	2	7	5		8								4	11					9	3					6	1		10	
Mar 5	2	7	5		8*							12	4	11					9	3					6	1		10	
11	2	7	5									8	4						9	3					6	11	1	10	
22		7	5		8							12	4	11					9*	3		2		6			1	10	
Apr 2		7	5		8								4	11					9	3	2						6	1	10
8		7	5		8							12	4	11					9	3	2*						6	1	10
9		7	5		8							10	4	11					9	3	6		2				1		
11		7	5		8								4	11					9	3	6		2				1	10	
16		7	5		8							12	4	11					9*	3		2					6	1	10
20		7	5*		8				9			12	4	11						3		2					6	1	10
23		7	5*		8							12	4	11					9	3		2					6	1	
26		7			8	3						10	4	11					9		5	2					6	1	
30		7			8								4	11					9	3	5	2					6	1	10
May 3		7			8								4	11					9	3	5	2					6	1	10
7		7			8								4	11					9	3	5	2					6	1	10
11		7			8								4	11					9	3	5	2					6	1	10
14		7			8						12	9*	4	11						3	5						6	1	10
App	12	23	33	5	40	1		3	13	2	1	5	38	36	20	4	2	5	30	39	8	18	11	13	8	4	32	24	32
Sub app		1	2						2		7	1											3						1
Goals	2	1	3		17			1				2	8	23	1				5	7		1			1				

Back row (left to right): Bobby Stokes, Steve Neville, Pat Earles, Jim McCalliog, John Sharpe, Paul Gilchrist, Ian Turner, Steve Middleton, Nick Holmes, David Peach, Mike Berry, Peter Rodrigues, Austin Hayes, Hugh Fisher. Third row: Jim Clunie (trainer), John McGrath (trainer), Tim Coak, Paul Arnold, Malcolm Waldron, Mel Blyth, Mike Channon, Jim Steele, Forbes Phillipson-Masters, Peter Osgood, Trevor Hebberd, Manny Andruszewski, Steve Williams, Don Taylor (physiotherapist), George Horsfall (trainer). Second row: M.Price (commercial manager), B.Truscott (box-office manager), K.F.Honey (secretary), L.McMenemy (team manager), F.G.Askham (director), E.C.Chaplin (vice chairman), G.Reader (chairman), B.G.W.Bowyer (director), A.A.Woodford (director), L.E.T.Bates (chief executive), W.Ellerington (chief scout), D.Rayner (asst secretary). Front row: Kevin Dawtry, Wayne Pratt, Kevin Hart, Tony Sealy, Farzand Ali, Graham Baker, George Shipley, Gary Wheatcroft.

	P	W	D	L	F	A	Pts
Wolves	42	22	13	7	84	45	57
Chelsea	42	21	13	8	73	53	55
Nottingham F	42	21	10	11	77	43	52
Bolton W	42	20	11	11	75	54	51
Blackpool	42	17	17	8	58	42	51
Luton T	42	21	6	15	67	48	48
Charlton A	42	16	16	10	71	58	48
Notts C	42	19	10	13	65	60	48
Southampton	42	17	10	15	72	67	44
Millwall	42	15	13	14	57	53	43
Sheffield U	42	14	12	16	54	63	40
Blackburn R	42	15	9	18	42	54	39
Oldham A	42	14	10	18	52	64	38
Hull C	42	10	17	15	45	53	37
Bristol R	42	12	13	17	53	68	37
Burnley	42	11	14	17	46	64	36
Fulham	42	11	13	18	54	61	35
Cardiff C	42	12	10	20	56	67	34
Orient	42	9	16	17	37	55	34
Carlisle U	42	11	12	19	49	75	34
Plymouth A	42	8	16	18	46	65	32
Hereford U	42	8	15	19	57	78	31

1977-78

DURING the close season Mick Channon had asked for a transfer and moved to Manchester City, perhaps realising that he had achieved all he could as a Southampton player. Supporters viewed his departure with dismay and saw it as a real set-back in the promotion fight.

There were, however, three new faces to start the season. Phil Boyer, a proven goalscorer, was Channon's replacement and he renewed a famous partnership with MacDougall that had started at Bournemouth and carried on to Norwich.

Defender Chris Nicholl's arrival was seen as a good omen, for Nicholl had immediately won promotion every time he signed for a new club. Finally, Barnsley defender Mick Pickering joined Saints and soon slotted in comfortably beside Nicholl in the Saints rearguard.

Saints began well and were soon jostling with Bolton, Spurs, Brighton and Blackburn for the promotion placings. Osgood had returned from a loan spell at Norwich and was playing well until a black day at fellow promotion candidates, Blackburn. Some inconsistent refereeing saw the game boil over and Osgood was ordered off, soon to be followed by Steve Williams. Four other Saints players were booked, making it by far their worst-ever example of indiscipline —and to make matters worse, they lost 2-1. It was Osgood's last game for Saints and shortly afterwards he was transferred to

NASL side, Philadelphia Furies.

On a brighter note, youngsters Graham Baker and Tony Funnell emerged and both made significant contributions as Saints kept up with the leaders. Williams shrugged off the Blackburn incident and, playing alongside Ball, quickly matured into an effective midfielder.

In the last four and a half months of the season Saints lost only twice, at Millwall and Cardiff, and this fine run earned them runners-up spot and First Division soccer once more. In their penultimate game Saints were at Brisbane Road, just as they were at the same stage of the 1965-6 season. Again, a 1-1 draw took them up, and again the goal came from a header, this time from Funnell.

In the last few weeks of the season Funnell had emerged as something of a hero with his knack of scoring important goals and he managed eight in only 11 games, many of them earning Saints priceless points.

In the final game of the season Saints entertained Spurs and needed victory to overhaul Bolton and become Champions. Spurs, meanwhile, needed at least a draw to pip Brighton for the third promotion place. Funnell hit a post for Saints but Spurs got their point and Southampton had to be satisfied with second place. Nevertheless, promotion was secured — and they had done it without Mike Channon.

FA Cup

SAINTS were lucky to survive the first two games against Lawrie McMenemy's old club, Grimsby and goalkeeper Ian Turner saved their blushes at The Dell with a string of fine saves.

At Leicester, however, Saints at last began to look a competent side and Ted MacDougall scored one and had a hand in Saints' other three goals. The best of the four came from Boyer, in the 38th minute, after he had played a neat one-two with MacDougall.

Two goals from 19-year-old Paul Randall, recently signed from non-League football, sank Saints at Eastville where they never looked like piercing a solid Bristol Rovers defence.

Round 3
Jan 7 v Grimsby Town (a) 0-0
Turner; Sharpe, Peach, Williams, Nicholl, Pickering, Ball, Boyer, MacDougall, Holmes, Waldron.
Att: 16,582
Replay
Jan 10 v Grimsby Town (h) 0-0
Turner; Waldron, Holmes, Williams, Nicholl, Pickering, Ball, Boyer, MacDougall, Hebberd(Funnell), Neville.
Att: 22,462
Second Replay
Jan 16 v Grimsby Town (at Filbert Street) 4-1
Peach, Boyer, Holmes, MacDougall
Turner; Waldron, Peach, Williams, Nicholl, Pickering, Ball, Boyer, MacDougall, Holmes, Coak.
Att: 11,356
Round 4
Jan 28 v Bristol Rovers (a) 0-2
Turner; Waldron, Peach, Williams, Nicholl, Pickering, Ball, Boyer, MacDougall, Holmes, Coak(Neville).
Att: 26,574

During the 1978 close season, Alan Woodford became Saints chairman following the death of George Reader who had been connected with the club for well over 50 years.

Total home attendance: 444,205. Average: 21,152.

Football League Cup

AFTER two difficult games against Crystal Palace, Saints' reward was a visit to Arsenal, one of the front-runners in the First Division. A near-41,000 Highbury crowd saw Southampton battle but fall short against powerful opponents.

Round 2
Aug 30 v Crystal Palace (a) 0-0
Turner; Andruszewski, Peach, Williams, Waldron, Pickering, Ball, Boyer, Osgood, Funnell, MacDougall.
Att: 19,565
Replay
Sep 13 v Crystal Palace (h) 2-1
Boyer, Funnell
Turner; Andruszewski, Peach, Williams, Nicholl, Pickering(Funnell), Ball, Waldron, Osgood, Boyer, MacDougall.
Att: 19,836
Round 3
25 Oct v Arsenal (a) 0-2
Wells; Waldron, Peach, Williams, Nicholl, Pickering, Ball, Boyer, Osgood, Holmes, MacDougall.
Att: 40,749

Ted MacDougall gets a telling off from referee Tom Reynolds at home to Blackburn in April 1978.

1977-78

Division 2

Date		Opponent	Result	Scorers	Att.	Andruszewski E	Baker G	Ball A	Boyer P	Coak T	Funnell A	Hayes A	Hebberd T	Holmes N	MacDougall E	Neville S	Nicholl C	Osgood P	Peach D	Phillipson-Masters F	Pickering M	Sealy A	Sharpe J	Turner I	Waldron M	Wells P	Williams S
Aug 20	(h)	Brighton & HA	D 1-1	Ball	24,306	2		7	8			9		10	11		5		3		6			1			4
24	(a)	Stoke C	L 0-1		13,867	2		7	8					10	11		5	9	3		6			1			4
27	(h)	Mansfield T	W 1-0	Peach	15,981	2		7	8				12	10*	11		5	9	3		6			1			4
Sep 3	(a)	Notts C	W 3-2	Peach, Osgood, Funnell	9,088	2		7	10						11		5	9	3		6			1	8		4
10	(h)	Burnley	W 3-0	Boyer 2, Peach	17,412	2		7	10						11		5	9	3		6			1	8		4
17	(a)	Millwall	L 0-3		9,952	2		7	10						11		5	9	3		6			1	8		4
24	(h)	Hull C	W 1-0	MacDougall	18,503			7	8					10	11		5	9	3		6			1	2		4
Oct 1	(a)	Sheffield U	L 2-3	Osgood, MacDougall	13,109			7	8					10	11		5	9	3		6			1	2		4
4	(h)	Orient	W 1-0	Osgood	15,789			7	8					10	11		5	9	3		6				2	1	4
8	(h)	Sunderland	W 4-2	Nicholl, Williams, Boyer, Holmes	17,696			7	8					10	11		5	9	3		6				2	1	4
15	(a)	Crystal P	W 2-1	Boyer, Holmes	22,652			7	8				12	10	11		5	9*	3		6				2	1	4
22	(h)	Bolton W	D 2-2	Boyer, Holmes	27,296			7	8					10	11		5	9	3		6				2	1	4
29	(a)	Bristol R	D 0-0		12,031	7			8					10	11		5	9	3		6				2	1	4
Nov 5	(a)	Blackburn R	L 1-2	Peach	9,930	2		7	8					10	11		5	9	3		6					1	4
12	(h)	Blackpool	W 2-0	Peach, Baker	18,356	2	4	7*	8		12	9		10	11		5		3		6					1	
19	(a)	Oldham A	D 1-1	Hebberd	6,452	2	4	7	8				9	10		11	5				6		3	1			
26	(h)	Fulham	W 2-0	Holmes, Neville	21,085	3	4	7	8				9	10		11	5				6				2	1	
Dec 3	(a)	Tottenham H	D 0-0		37,873			7	8					10	9	11				5	6		3		2	1	4
10	(h)	Luton T	L 0-1		19,907	3		7	8				12	10	9	11*	5				6				2	1	4
17	(a)	Blackpool	W 1-0	MacDougall	8,640			7	8		11			10	9		5		3		6		2			1	4
26	(h)	Cardiff C	W 3-1	MacDougall, Ball, Boyer	21,861			7	8		11			10	9		5		3		6		2			1	4
27	(a)	Charlton A	W 3-1	MacDougall, Ball, Boyer	18,721			7	8					10	9		5		3		6		2		11	1	4
31	(h)	Stoke C	W 1-0	Boyer	23,460			7	8		12			10	9		5		3		6		2		11	1	4*
Jan 2	(a)	Brighton & HA	D 1-1	Williams	33,097			7	8					10	9		5		3		6		2		11	1	4
14	(a)	Mansfield T	W 2-1	Ball, MacDougall	8,673			7	8	3				10	9		5				6		2	1	11		4
21	(h)	Notts C	W 3-1	Boyer 2, Williams	20,174			7	8		11			10	9		5		3		6			1	2		4
Feb 4	(a)	Burnley	D 3-3	Boyer, Peach, MacDougall	10,950	11		7	8		12			10*	9		5		3		6			1	2		4
11	(h)	Millwall	L 2-3	Peach, MacDougall	19,575	11		7	8		12			10	9		5		3		6			1	2*		4
25	(h)	Sheffield U	W 2-1	Boyer, MacDougall	17,679			7	8		12			10	9			3*			6	11	2		5	1	4
Mar 4	(a)	Sunderland	D 0-0		20,975	11		7	8					10	9		5		3		6		2			1	4
11	(h)	Crystal P	W 2-0	Funnell 2	22,480	2		7	8		12			10	9				3		6		11*		5	1	4
18	(a)	Bolton W	D 0-0		23,770	2		7	8		12		11*	10	9		5		3		6				5	1	4
25	(h)	Charlton A	W 4-1	Williams 2, MacDougall, Funnell	22,098	2		7	8		11			10	9		5		3		6					1	4
27	(h)	Bristol R	W 3-1	Boyer 2, MacDougall	24,826	2		7	8		11			10	9		5		3		6					1	4
29	(a)	Cardiff C	L 0-1		11,359	2		7	8	3	11*		12	10	9		5				6					1	4
Apr 1	(h)	Blackburn R	W 5-0	Boyer 2, MacDougall, Holmes, Funnell	21,087	2		7	8		11			10	9		5		3		6					1	4
7	(a)	Fulham	D 1-1	Funnell	16,915	2		7	8		11			10	9		5		3		6					1	4
11	(a)	Hull C	W 3-0	Ball, Boyer, MacDougall	7,299	2		7	8		11			10	9		5		3		6					1	4
15	(h)	Oldham A	D 2-2	Holmes, Funnell	25,788	2		7	8		11			10	9		5		3		6					1	4
22	(a)	Luton T	W 2-1	MacDougall, Peach	14,302	2		7	8		11			10	9		5		3		6					1	4
25	(a)	Orient	D 1-1	Funnell	19,248	2		7	8		11		12	10	9		5		3		6*					1	4
29	(h)	Tottenham H	D 0-0		28,846	2		7	8		11			10	9		5		3		6			1			4
					App	27	3	41	41	3	11	1	5	39	40	5	39	13	34	1	41	2	10	12	25	30	39
					Sub app						4	1	7														
					Goals		1	5	17		8	1		6	14	1	1	3	8								5

	P	W	D	L	F	A	Pts
Bolton W	42	24	10	8	63	33	58
Southampton	42	22	13	7	70	39	57
Tottenham H	42	20	16	6	83	49	56
Brighton & HA	42	22	12	8	63	38	56
Blackburn R	42	16	13	13	56	60	45
Sunderland	42	14	16	12	67	59	44
Stoke C	42	16	10	16	53	49	42
Oldham A	42	13	16	13	54	58	42
Crystal P	42	13	15	14	50	47	41
Fulham	42	14	13	15	49	49	41
Burnley	42	15	10	17	56	64	40
Sheffield U	42	16	8	18	62	73	40
Luton T	42	14	10	18	54	52	38
Orient	42	10	18	14	43	49	38
Notts C	42	11	16	15	54	62	38
Millwall	42	12	14	16	49	57	38
Charlton A	42	13	12	17	55	68	38
Bristol R	42	13	12	17	61	77	38
Cardiff C	42	13	12	17	51	71	38
Blackpool	42	12	13	17	59	60	37
Mansfield T	42	10	11	21	49	69	31
Hull C	42	8	12	22	34	52	28

Back row (left to right): J.McGrath (coach), T.Hebberd, M.Blyth, P.Osgood, F.Phillipson-Masters, I.Turner, P.Wells, C.Nicholl, M.Waldron, M.Pickering, N.Holmes, J.Clunie (Coach). Seated: D.Taylor (physio), J.Sharpe, D.Peach, P.Boyer, A.Ball, L.McMenemy (manager) E.MacDougall, S.Williams, M.Andruszewski, A.Hayes, G.Horsfall (reserve Coach).

1978-79

Saints looked in no difficulty back in Division One and finished the season just below halfway. Terry Curran, a clever if sometimes frustrating, winger signed from Derby and another new arrival, though it took several weeks for his registration papers to be approved, was Yugoslavian international full-back, Ivan Golac, who was to become one of Saints most popular players.

Saints first match was at Norwich and former Southampton striker Martin Chivers, back from a spell in Swiss football, opposed them. When Ted MacDougall went back to Bournemouth,

Saints were short of forwards and McMenemy set up the transfer of Charlie George from Derby for £400,000.

The negotiations dragged through December and when George eventually became a Saints player he was found to have a knee injury. It was March before he made his Saints debut and, incredibly, the following season before he played a match at The Dell. Nevertheless, his arrival showed that Saints' board, led by new chairman Alan Woodford, wanted only the best for the club.

FA Cup

SAINTS reached the FA Cup quarter-finals after two replays. Boyer's two goals and Ball's inspiration swept aside Wimbledon in the third round, and Ball netted the only goal of a potentially difficult tie at Preston to put Saints into the fifth round. Ball was particularly determined to succeed that day at Deepdale, for Preston had, some years earlier, sacked his father from the manager's job.

A rearguard action at The Hawthorns earned Saints a replay against West Brom which came only five days before the team were due to meet Nottingham Forest in the League Cup Final at Wembley. Saints fought back from 1-0 down and in extra-time a magnificent header from Boyer sealed their victory.

Only 48 hours after their Wembley date, Saints took on Arsenal in the FA Cup quarter-finals and after Hayes put them ahead, Arsenal scored a fortunate equaliser when Gennoe mishandled. George made a surprise Saints debut in the replay but there was to be no happy return to Highbury for him and Arsenal were too good for a Southampton team playing their 14th Cup match of the season

---

Total home attendance: 448,483. Average: 21,356.

Round 3
Jan 9 v Wimbledon (a) 2-0
Boyer 2
Gennoe; Golac, Peach, Williams, Nicholl, Waldron, Ball, Boyer, Hebberd, Holmes, Curran.
Att: 9,254
Round 4
Feb 12 v Preston North End (a) 1-0
Ball
Gennoe; Golac, Peach, Williams, Nicholl, Waldron, Ball, Boyer, Hebberd, Holmes, Curran.
Att: 20,727
Round 5
Mar 10 v West Bromwich Albion (a) 1-1
Boyer
Gennoe; Golac, Peach, Williams, Nicholl, Waldron, Ball, Boyer, Hayes (Andruszewski), Holmes, Curran.
Att: 30,712
Replay
Mar 12 v West Bromwich Albion (h) 2-1
Boyer, Peach
Gennoe; Golac, Peach, Williams, Nicholl, Waldron, Ball, Boyer, Hayes, Holmes, Curran.
Att: 25,775
Round 6
Mar 19 v Arsenal (h) 1-1
Hayes
Gennoe; Golac, Peach, Williams, Nicholl, Waldron, Ball, Boyer, Hayes, Holmes, Curran.
Att: 24,536
Replay
Mar 21 v Arsenal (a) 0-2
Wells; Golac, Andruszewski(Baker), Williams, Nicholl, Waldron, Ball, Boyer, Hayes, Holmes, George.
Att: 44,820

Saints' manager Lawrie McMenemy (centre) and trainer Lew Chatterley (left) are surrounded by exultant fans at The Dell after the League Cup semi-final triumph over Leeds in January 1979.

1978-79
Division 1

Date		Opponent	Res	Score	Scorers	Att	Andruszewski E	Baker G	Ball A	Boyer P	Curran T	Dawtry K	Funnell A	Gennoe T	George C	Golac I	Hayes A	Hebberd T	Holmes N	MacDougall E	Nicholl C	Peach D	Pickering M	Sealy A	Waldron M	Wells P	Williams O	Williams S
Aug 19	(a)	Norwich C	L	1-3	MacDougall	21,133		10*	7	8	11									12	9	5	3	6	2	1		4
22	(h)	Bolton W	D	2-2	MacDougall, Boyer	21,059		10	7	8	11*							2		12	9	5	3	6		1		4
26	(h)	Middlesbrough	W	2-1	Nicholl, Ball	20,691		10	7	8	11							2			9	5	3	6		1		4
Sep 2	(a)	Aston Villa	D	1-1	Nicholl	34,067	10*		7	8	11							2		12	9	5	3	6		1		4
9	(h)	Wolves	W	3-2	MacDougall, Waldron, Boyer	22,060			7	8	11							2	12	10*	9	5	3		6	1		4
16	(a)	Bristol C	L	1-3	Holmes	21,420			7	8	11							2	12	10	9*	5	3		6	1		4
23	(a)	Derby C	L	1-2	Peach	21,623			7	9	11				1			2	10*	12		5	3	4	6			8
30	(h)	Ipswich T	L	1-2	MacDougall	21,264			7	8	11				1			2	10	9		5	3		6			4
Oct 7	(a)	Everton	D	0-0		38,769	3		7	8	11				1			2*	12	10	9	5			6			4
14	(h)	Queen's Park R	D	1-1	MacDougall	22,803			7	8	11*				1			2	10	9		5	3	12	6			4
21	(a)	Arsenal	L	0-1		33,074	3		7	8	11				1			2	10	9		5			6			4
28	(h)	Nottingham F	D	0-0		22,530			7	8	11*				1			2	10	9		5	3	12	6			4
Nov 4	(a)	Manchester U	D	1-1	Holmes	46,259			7	8	11				1			2	10	9		5	3		6			4
11	(h)	Norwich C	D	2-2	Nicholl, Holmes	21,183			7	8	11				1			2	10	9		5	3		6			4
18	(a)	Middlesbrough	L	0-2		17,169	3		7	8	11				1			2	10	9*		5		12	6			4
21	(h)	Aston Villa	W	2-0	Holmes, Baker	20,880		11	7	8					1			2	10	9		5	3		6			4
25	(h)	Leeds U	L	0-4		23,592		11	7	8	12				1			2	10	9*		5	3		6			4
Dec 2	(h)	Birmingham C	W	1-0	Boyer	18,957			7	8	11				1			2	10	9		5	3		6			4
9	(a)	Manchester C	W	2-1	Boyer, opp own goal	33,450			7	8	11				1			2	10	9		5	3		6			4
16	(h)	Coventry C	W	4-0	Waldron, Boyer, Hebberd, Baker	19,102		11	7	8					1			2	10	9		5	3	12	6			4*
26	(h)	Chelsea	D	0-0		20,770			7	8	11				1			2	10	9		5	3		6			4
Jan 17	(a)	Wolves	L	0-2		15,104			7	8	11				1			2	10	9		5	3		6			4
Feb 3	(h)	Derby C	L	1-2	Peach	21,109			7	8	11*				1			2	10	9		5	3	12	6			4
10	(a)	Ipswich T	D	0-0		19,520		12	7	8					1			2	10	9		5	3*		6			4
17	(a)	Everton	W	3-0	Peach, Baker, Boyer	20,673		4	7	8	11				1		9	2	10			5	3		6			
20	(h)	Bristol C	W	2-0	Hayes, Holmes	19,845		4	7	8	11				1		9	2	10			5	3		6			
24	(a)	Queen's Park R	W	1-0	Holmes	13,636			7	8	11				1		9	2	10			5	3		6			4
Mar 3	(h)	Arsenal	W	2-0	Waldron, Hayes	25,052	2		7	8					1		9		10			5	3		6		11	4
24	(a)	Bolton W	L	0-2		19,879	3		7	8	11						9	2	10			5			6	1		4
28	(a)	Tottenham H	D	0-0		23,570		11	7	8							9*	2	10	12		5	3		6	1		4
31	(h)	Leeds U	D	2-2	Waldron 2	21,805		11	7	8							9	2	10			5	3		6	1		4
Apr 7	(a)	Birmingham C	D	2-2	Hayes, Baker	12,125	5	11	7	8					1		9	2	10				3		6			4
13	(h)	West Brom A	D	1-1	Waldron	22,063		11	7	8							9	2	10			5	3		6	1		4
14	(a)	Chelsea	W	2-1	Peach, Holmes	18,243		11	7	8							9	2	10			5	3		6	1		4
16	(h)	Tottenham H	D	3-3	Peach, Ball, Boyer	22,096		11	7	8							9	2	10			5	3		6	1		4
21	(a)	Coventry C	L	0-4		17,750		11	7	8							9	2	10			5	3		6	1		4
24	(h)	Liverpool	D	1-1	Holmes	23,181		11	7	8							9*	2	10			5	3		6	1	12	4
28	(a)	Manchester C	W	1-0	Hebberd	19,744		12	7	8							9	2*	10			5	3		6	1	11	4
30	(h)	Manchester U	D	1-1	Boyer	21,616	5	11	7	8							9	2	10				3		6	1		4
May 2	(a)	Nottingham F	L	0-1		20,388	2	5	7	8	12						9		10				3		6	1	11*	4
5	(a)	Liverpool	L	0-2		46,687	2	4	7	8	11						9		10			5	3		6	1		
8	(a)	West Brom A	L	0-1		17,526		11	7	8							9		10	2		5	3		6	1		4
App							10	20	42	42	25			2	23	2	36	13	16	38	10	38	38	3	42	19	4	39
Sub app								2			1	1					2	6						5		1		
Goals								5	2	7							3	2	8	5		3			5			

1 own-goal

	P	W	D	L	F	A	Pts
Liverpool	42	30	8	4	85	16	68
Nottingham F	42	21	18	3	61	26	60
West Brom A	42	24	11	7	72	35	59
Everton	42	17	17	8	52	40	51
Leeds U	42	18	14	10	70	52	50
Ipswich T	42	20	9	13	63	49	49
Arsenal	42	17	14	11	61	48	48
Aston Villa	42	15	16	11	59	49	46
Manchester U	42	15	15	12	60	63	45
Coventry C	42	14	16	12	58	68	44
Tottenham H	42	13	15	14	48	61	41
Middlesbrough	42	15	10	17	57	50	40
Bristol C	42	15	10	17	47	51	40
Southampton	42	12	16	14	47	53	40
Manchester C	42	13	13	16	58	56	39
Norwich C	42	7	23	12	51	57	37
Bolton W	42	12	11	19	54	75	35
Wolves	42	13	8	21	44	68	34
Derby C	42	10	11	21	44	71	31
Queen's Park R	42	6	13	23	45	73	25
Birmingham C	42	6	10	26	37	64	22
Chelsea	42	5	10	27	44	92	20

Back row (left to right): I.Golac, M.Pickering, F.Phillipson-Masters, M.Waldron, P.Wells, T.Gennoe, C.Nicholl, T.Hebberd, N.Holmes, E.Andruszewski. Middle row: W.Pratt, G.Shipley, A.Funnell, P.Arnold, J.Sharpe, S.Neville, A.Sealy, T.Coak, K.Dawtry. Front row: G.Baker, D.Peach, P.Boyer, A.Ball, E.MacDougall, S.Williams, T.Curran, A.Hayes.

Football League Cup

SAINTS began their League Cup campaign in style, hammering Birmingham City 5-2 at St Andrew's, and finished it at Wembley where they came so close to lifting the trophy for the first time.

The Birmingham game was a triumph for Andruszewski who marked the Blues' star striker, Trevor Francis, out of the game. Golac also had a fine game and laid on the first and fifth goals.

Phil Boyer's goal, the only one of the match, beat Derby — the club that had let him go to York on a free transfer some years earlier, and that gave Southampton a fourth-round game against Reading.

The match was something of a local 'derby' and Reading, the only side outside Division One that Saints would encounter on this run to Wembley, offered stout resistance to take Southampton to a replay at The Dell where goals from Nicholl and Hebberd finally overcame them.

Manchester City, with recent signing Mike Channon in their ranks, were beaten on a rainy evening at The Dell and Saints went into the League Cup semi-finals for the first time.

They began the first-leg, against Leeds at Elland Road, badly and were 2-0 down after 47 minutes. Terry Curran then made a good run down the wing before crossing to where Holmes was waiting to head home. In the 64th minute Williams equalised with a tremendous volley and, despite having Boyer sent off in the closing stages, Saints were satisfied with their night's work.

Andruszewski replaced the suspended Boyer in a hard-fought replay at The Dell where he did a good job of marking Tony Currie, Leeds' most dangerous player. Terry Curran never scored a League goal for the Saints but in the 11th minute of this game he lashed the ball high into the roof of the Leeds net. Saints held on and with Waldron having a particularly fine game, went through to their third appearance at Wembley in as many years.

Round 2
Aug 29 v Birmingham City (a) 5-2
Boyer 2, MacDougall 2, Peach
Wells; Golac, Peach, Williams, Nicholl, Waldron, Ball, Boyer, MacDougall, Andruszewski, Curran.
Att: 18,464

Round 3
Oct 3 v Derby County (h) 1-0
Boyer
Gennoe; Golac, Peach(Hebberd), Williams, Nicholl, Waldron, Ball, Boyer, MacDougall, Holmes, Curran.
Att: 19,109

Round 4
Nov 8 v Reading (a) 0-0
Gennoe; Golac, Peach, Williams, Nicholl, Waldron, Ball, Boyer, Hebberd, Holmes, Curran.
Att: 24,046

Replay
Nov 14 v Reading (h) 2-0
Hebberd, Nicholl
Gennoe; Golac, Andruszewski, Williams, Nicholl, Waldron, Ball, Boyer, Hebberd, Holmes, Curran(Hayes).
Att: 22,892

Round 5
Dec 12 v Manchester City (h) 2-1
Boyer, Hebberd
Gennoe; Golac, Peach, Williams, Nicholl, Waldron, Ball, Boyer, Hebberd, Holmes, Curran.
Att: 21,500

Semi-final (1st leg)
Jan 24 v Leeds United (a) 2-2
Holmes, Williams
Gennoe; Golac, Peach, Williams, Nicholl, Waldron, Ball, Boyer, Hebberd, Holmes, Curran.
Att: 33,415

Semi-final (2nd leg)
Jan 30 v Leeds United (h) 1-0 (agg 3-2)
Curran
Gennoe; Golac, Peach, Williams, Nicholl, Waldron, Ball, Andruszewski (Baker), Hebberd, Holmes, Curran.
Att: 23,645

Final
Mar 17 v Nottingham Forest (at Wembley) 2-3
Peach, Holmes
Gennoe; Golac, Peach, Williams, Nicholl, Waldron, Ball, Boyer, Hayes(Sealy), Holmes, Curran.
Att: 100,000

Chris Nicholl gets in a tackle during the 1979 League Cup Final.

Although Wembley suffered a heavy snowfall on the eve of the 1979 League Cup Final, the pitch was in splendid condition and the sun shining when Saints and Forest came out.

The Football League's new red and white football was in use for the first time and Alan Ball seemed to show due repugnance when he made a couple of dreadful passes in the first ten minutes. In the 17th minute, however, he laid on a superb ball for for David Peach to run on to and hit a shot past Shilton to put Saints ahead.

The goal gave Saints confidence and Shilton had to move smartly to deny Boyer and Holmes. Yet as half-time approached Southampton appeared to slacken their grip and they began the second half in much the same manner.

Forest meanwhile — no doubt stirred by a stern half-time lecture from manager Brian Clough — pressed forward eagerly. After 50 minutes a bad back-pass by Holmes put Chris Nicholl under pressure and Birtles quickly seized upon the chance to fire home the equaliser high into Terry Gennoe's net.

Forest, and in particular Birtles, were now in full flow and a second goal was not long in coming. Again, Birtles was the scorer. When Tony Woodcock struck home Forest's third, Saints' fans resigned themselves to the fact that the Nottingham club were the better side on the day.

In the final minute Nick Holmes showed a touch of class by reducing the margin to a single goal with a fine left-foot volley. It was a moment to remember from Southampton's third visit to the Empire Stadium in as many years and Saints could also take pride from the fact that they had contributed to one of the most open Wembley Cup Finals for many years.

Saints' Curran (in background) watches as Peach opens the scoring in the 1979 League Cup Final against Nottingham Forest at Wembley. The stranded goalkeeper is Peter Shilton who later joined Southampton.

1979-80

CHARLIE George made his long-awaited home debut for Saints in the first home game of the season, against Manchester United, as Southampton looked to further establish themselves as one of the First Division's leading teams.

Apart from George there were no other new faces for Saints fans to savour although McMenemy, it was reported, had spent the close season busily searching for new talent.

On 8 September, McMenemy made a signing, although the player could not have been described as a 'new face'. Mick Channon, unsettled at Maine Road, returned to The Dell for £100,000, less than Saints had originally sold him for.

It was a good piece of business with Channon teaming up with Boyer, his replacement when he went to City, and the two of them helped destroy Spurs, 5-2 at The Dell. In the next home match, against Derby, Boyer hit a hat-trick, and followed that with another in the next home match, against Crystal Palace.

McMenemy's involvement in the transfer market was not yet over and he further surprised Saints fans by bringing England centre-half, Dave Watson, back to English soccer from the West German club, Werder Bremen.

The accumulation of such experienced internationals at The Dell showed how ambitious Southampton had become and a draw at Liverpool gave them their first point from Anfield since the old Second Division days. The result underlined Saints' new-found maturity and confidence and it edged them into third place,

their highest-ever position. It was a fine achievement in only their second season back in Division One.

At the end of January, in the home game against Manchester City, McMenemy sent on substitute Steve Moran for his first taste of League football and he had been on the pitch only a couple of minutes when he scored what was to be the first of many opportunist goals.

Saints fans were now getting used to surprise transfer deals and big-name signings, but when, in February, the manager announced that Kevin Keegan would be wearing Southampton colours the following season, it dumbfounded even the most imaginative supporter.

McMenemy had been 'trailing' the England captain for months and yet the announcement surprised everyone in football. Keegan was arguably Europe's top player and in great demand. McMenemy deserved massive credit for pulling off such a coup.

At the end of the season, Alan Ball decided to try his hand at management and left to take over at his old club, Blackpool. Saints were then fifth in the League, considerably higher than when Ball joined them and the fans were sorry to see him depart. They did not know, of course, that, like Channon, he would return to The Dell.

Five defeats in March and April ensured that Saints finished eigth but with the imminent arrival of Keegan the whole town was buzzing and the new season could not arrive quickly enough.

FA Cup

TELEVISION cameras seemed to prove that the first of Birmingham's two goals in their third round tie against Southampton at St Andrew's was offside.

The goal came in the eighth minute and TV pictures appeared to show Frank Worthington (later to join Saints) standing in an offside position and interfering with play. Saints equalised through a 36th-minute Channon penalty but Birmingham, showing unexpected enterprise for a Second Division side, scored the winner 15 minutes from time.

Round 3
Jan 5 v Birmingham City (a) 1-2
Channon
Wells; Golac, Waldron, Williams, Watson, Nicholl, Ball, Boyer, Channon, Holmes, Hebberd.
Att: 24,648

Ivan Golac, Saints' Yugoslav full-back who scored twice during 1979-80.

Football League Cup

SECOND Division Wrexham felt the full blast of Southampton's fire-power in both legs of the Football League Cup first round clash between the two clubs.

Arsenal at Highbury were a much more difficult proposition but Saints fought hard before Liam Brady's late goal eventually eliminated them.

Round 2 (1st leg)
Aug 28 v Wrexham (h) 5-0
Boyer 2, Baker 2, George
Gennoe; Golac, Peach, Williams, Nicholl, Waldron, Baker, Boyer, Hebberd, George, Holmes.
Att: 13,920
Round 2 (2nd leg)
Sep 5 v Wrexham (a) 3-0 (agg 8-0)
Hebberd, Hayes, Holmes
Gennoe; Golac, Peach, Williams, Nicholl, Waldron, Baker, Boyer, Hebberd, Hayes, Holmes.
Att: 13,200
Round 3
Sep 25 v Arsenal (a) 1-2
Williams
Gennoe; Golac, Peach, Williams, Nicholl, Waldron, Ball, Boyer, Hebberd, Baker, Holmes.
Att: 34,145

Starting with Saints' home game against Liverpool on 1 September 1979, Phil Boyer began an amazing scoring sequence in which he scored in every home match up to and including the visit of Bolton on 29 December, a total of ten games and 16 goals. Oddly enough, he did not score his first away League goal until 12 January when he netted against Liverpool.

Total home attendance: 447,892. Average: 21,238.

1979-80

Division 1

Player columns (left to right): Andruszewski E, Baker G, Ball A, Boyer P, Channon M, Gennoe T, George C, Golac I, Hayes A, Hebberd T, Holmes N, Katalinic I, McGrath M, Moran S, Nicholl C, Peach D, Rogers A, Shipley G, Waldron M, Watson D, Wells P, Williams O, Williams S

Date		Opponent	Res	Scorers	Att	And	Bak	Bal	Boy	Cha	Gen	Geo	Gol	Hay	Heb	Hol	Kat	McG	Mor	Nic	Pea	Rog	Shi	Wal	Wat	Wel	WiO	WiS
Aug 18	(h)	Manchester U	D 1-1	Peach	21,768		7		8		1	10	2		9	11				5	3			6				4
21	(a)	Crystal P	D 0-0		31,756		2		8		1	10		7*	9	11				5	3		12	6				4
25	(a)	Bolton W	L 1-2	George	14,714				8		1	10	2*		9	11				5	3		7	6			12	4
Sep 1	(h)	Liverpool	W 3-2	George, Hebberd, Boyer	21,402		7*		8		1	10	2	12	9					5	3		11	6				4
8	(a)	Manchester C	W 1-0	Holmes	34,920		7		8		1		2	10	9	11				5	3			6				4
15	(h)	Tottenham H	W 5-2	Holmes 2, Baker, Channon, Boyer	22,573	10	7		8	9	1				2	11				5	3			6				4
22	(a)	Brighton & HA	D 0-0		26,918	10	7*		8	9	1		12		2	11				5	3			6				4
29	(h)	Derby C	W 4-0	Boyer 3, Channon	22,583		7		8	9	1	10			2	11				5	3			6				4
Oct 6	(a)	Aston Villa	L 0-3		24,377	5	7		8	9	1	10			2	11					3			6				4
9	(h)	Crystal P	W 4-1	Boyer 3, Holmes	23,174	5	7		8	9	1	10			2	11					3			6				4
13	(h)	Coventry C	L 2-3	Boyer, George	22,986	5	7		8	9	1	10			2	11					3			6				4
20	(a)	West Brom A	L 0-4		22,500		7		8	9	1	10			2	11					3			6	5			4
27	(h)	Leeds U	L 1-2	Boyer	23,259		7		8	9	1	10			2	11					3			6	5			4
Nov 3	(a)	Manchester U	L 0-1		50,215	5	7*		8	9		10			12	2	11				3			6	1			4
10	(h)	Nottingham F	W 4-1	Boyer 2, Watson, Channon	22,072	10	7		8	9					2	11	3							6	5	1		4
17	(a)	Norwich C	L 1-2	Andruszewski	18,215	10	7		8	9					2	11	3							6	5	1		4
24	(a)	Ipswich T	L 1-3	Williams	18,685	12	7		8	9					2*	11	3	10						6	5	1		4
Dec 1	(h)	Stoke C	W 3-1	Boyer 2, Channon	20,095		7		8	9					2	11	10				6			3	5	1		4
8	(a)	Middlesbrough	W 1-0	Williams	15,469		7		8	9					2	11	10				6			3	5	1		4
15	(h)	Everton	W 1-0	Boyer	19,850		7		8	9					2	11	10				6			3	5	1		4
21	(a)	Bristol C	W 1-0	Channon	12,489		7		8	9					2	11	10				6			3	5	1		4
26	(a)	Wolves	D 0-0		22,808		7		8	9					2	11	10				6			3	5	1		4
29	(h)	Bolton W	W 2-0	Boyer, Peach	21,407		7		8	9					2	11	10				6			3	5	1		4
Jan 1	(h)	Arsenal	L 0-1		22,473		3		7	8	9				2	11	10				6				5	1		4
12	(a)	Liverpool	D 1-1	Boyer	44,655		4	7	8	9				11	2	10					6		3	5	1			
19	(h)	Manchester C	W 4-1	Watson, Ball, Channon, Moran	21,455		4	7	8	9				2*	11	10			12	6			3	5	1			
Feb 2	(a)	Tottenham H	D 0-0		37,155		4	7	8	9					2	11	10			6			3	5	1			
9	(h)	Brighton & HA	W 5-1	Watson, Boyer, Channon, Holmes, Hebberd	21,856		4	7	8	9					2	11	10			6			3	5	1			
16	(a)	Derby C	D 2-2	Watson, Baker	16,534		4	7	8	9				11	2	10				6			3	5	1			
23	(a)	Coventry C	L 0-3		18,034		4	7	8	9				11	2	10				6		6	3	5	1			
Mar 1	(h)	West Brom A	D 1-1	Baker	22,138		4		8	9				11	2	7	10			6			3	5	1			
8	(a)	Leeds U	L 0-2		21,169		4	7	8	9					2	11*	10	12		6			3	5	1			
15	(h)	Aston Villa	W 2-0	Golac, Channon	20,735		4	7	8	9			11	2			10			6			3	5	1			
22	(a)	Nottingham F	L 0-2		27,625	2	4		8	9			11		12	7	10			6			3*	5	1			
29	(h)	Norwich C	W 2-0	Baker, Nicholl	18,921	3	4		8	9			11	2			10	1		6				5			7	
Apr 5	(a)	Arsenal	D 1-1	Boyer	34,521	3	4*		8	9			11	2		12	10	1		6				5			7	
7	(h)	Wolves	L 0-3		22,307	3	4		8	9			11	2			10	1		6				5			7	
12	(a)	Stoke C	W 2-1	Golac, Boyer	15,030	3			8	9			2	11	7		10			6				5	1			4
19	(h)	Ipswich T	L 0-1		22,053	3			8	9			2	11	7*		10			6			12	5	1			4
26	(a)	Everton	L 0-2		23,549	3			8	9			12	11	7		10	1		6			2	5*				4
29	(h)	Bristol C	W 5-2	Boyer 3, Channon, Hayes	16,309				8	9			2	11*	7		10			6			12	3	5	1		4
May 3	(h)	Middlesbrough	W 4-1	Waldron 2, Channon, Hayes	18,476				8	9			2	11	7		10			6				3	5	1		4
App						11	23	26	42	37	13	20	30	7	35	41	4			33	21	2	30	30	25			32
Sub app						1							1	4	1			1	1				2	1				1	
Goals						1	4	1	23	10		3	2	2	2	5			1	1			2	2	4			2

Back row (left to right): Ivan Golac, Manny Andruszewski, Terry Gennoe, Peter Wells, Chris Nicholl, Malcolm Waldron. Middle row: Lew Chatterley (trainer), Steve Williams, Graham Baker, Nick Holmes, Mike O'Donoghue, George Shipley, Trevor Hebberd, John Mortimore (assistant manager). Front row: Austin Hayes, Mike Channon, Alan Ball, Lawrie McMenemy (manager), Phil Boyer, Charlie George, David Peach.

	P	W	D	L	F	A	Pts
Liverpool	42	25	10	7	81	30	60
Manchester U	42	23	10	8	65	35	58
Ipswich T	42	22	9	11	68	39	53
Arsenal	42	18	16	8	52	36	52
Nottingham F	42	20	8	14	63	43	48
Wolves	42	19	9	14	58	47	47
Aston Villa	42	16	14	12	51	50	46
Southampton	42	18	9	15	65	53	45
Middlesbrough	42	16	12	14	50	44	44
West Brom A	42	11	19	12	54	50	41
Leeds U	42	13	14	15	46	50	40
Norwich C	42	13	14	15	58	66	40
Crystal P	42	12	16	14	41	50	40
Tottenham H	42	15	10	17	52	62	40
Coventry C	42	16	7	19	56	66	39
Brighton & HA	42	11	15	16	47	57	37
Manchester C	42	12	13	17	43	66	37
Stoke C	42	13	10	19	44	58	36
Everton	42	9	17	16	43	51	35
Bristol C	42	9	13	20	37	66	31
Derby C	42	11	8	23	47	67	30
Bolton W	42	5	15	22	38	73	25

1980-81

KEVIN Keegan made his eagerly awaited debut for Saints on 16 August 1981, against Manchester City at The Dell. The England star was applauded on to the pitch and responded with a display which convinced Saints fans that the good times were just around the corner. Southampton won the match 2-0 and Channon scored both the goals.

August went well with two more wins and a creditable draw at Highbury in front of 41,000 specatators, but the arrival of September coincided with an injury to Keegan and Saints started to slide. A home draw with Ipswich on 8 November left them in 15th place, and there was the further humiliation of being hammered by Watford in the League Cup.

Katalinic and Wells were both having uncertain matches and the goalkeeping position was a particular problem. Fortunately, Chris Nicholl held the defence together with help from Watson and Golac and gradually, with Keegan's return, the team began to string together some more convincing performances.

One man who really profited from playing alongside Channon and Keegan was Steve Moran and his 18 goals from 30 games did much to help push Saints back into the top half of Division One.

The side was further reinforced by the return of Alan Ball for the last ten games, and a 3-2 win in the final match of the season saw Saints attain their highest-ever final placing in the First Division. Sixth position qualified them for a place in the UEFA Cup, a satisfactory achievement, particularly considering that Keegan missed 15 games through injury.

FA Cup

CHELSEA, then in the Second Division, had Saints under pressure for long periods of their third round FA Cup clash at The Dell before the classy finishing of Keegan and Moran helped Southampton achieve a rather flattering 3-1 scoreline.

Another Second Division team, Bristol Rovers, visited The Dell in the fourth round and they too fought hard, with vastly experienced players like Terry Cooper and Stuart Barrowclough in their ranks, and with 18-year-old goalkeeper Phil Kite showing the kind of form which later induced McMenemy to sign him for Saints.

Moran opened the scoring in the 17th minute with a glancing header which took a deflection, and with chances going begging at the other end it was with some relief that Williams rifled home Saints' second in the 59th minute following a magnficent crossfield ball from the previously subdued George.

Moran netted Saints' third with a typical piece of opportunist finishing but Rovers still found time to score a consolation goal and a frenzied last ten minutes saw Baker booked. It completed an unhppy afternoon afternoon for the locally-born midfielder who had earlier seen a 25-yarder crash into the Rovers net, only for Keegan to be ruled offside.

A fast and furious fifth round tie against Everton at The Dell saw the middle of the park a minefield of lunging players all desperate not to concede the initiative. McMenemy admitted afterwards that the longer the game went on, the less likely Saints looked like scoring. Pessimism was well-founded the following Tuesday when Everton, in another hard-fought match, edged Saints out by the only goal of the game.

Round 3
Jan 3 v Chelsea (h) 3-1
Baker, Moran, Keegan
Wells; Golac, Holmes, Williams, Watson, Nicholl, Keegan(Hebberd), Channon, George, Moran, Baker.
Att: 23,694
Round 4
Jan 24 v Bristol Rovers (h) 3-1
Moran 2, Williams
Wells; Golac, Nicholl, Watson, Holmes, Baker, Williams, Keegan, Channon, Moran, George.
Att: 23,597
Round 5
Feb 5 v Everton (h) 0-0
Wells; Golac, Waldron, Williams, Watson, Nicholl, Keegan, Channon, George, Moran(Hebberd), Holmes.
Att: 24,152
Replay
Feb 17 v Everton (a) 0-1
Wells; Golac(Hebberd), Waldron, Williams, Watson, Nicholl, Keegan, Channon, George, Holmes, Baker.
Att: 49,192

Football League Cup

AFTER building up a four-goal lead in the first-leg, Saints were confident of passing into the second round of the League Cup when they travelled to Vicarage Road in September 1980.

But Graham Taylor's long-ball specialists demolished that advantage and in extra-time found further goals to take them through in one of the shocks of that season's competition. Six different Watford players found the net in the replay as the Second Division club marched towards the quarter-finals.

Round 2 (1st leg)
Aug 26 v Watford (h) 4-0
George 2, Holmes 2
Katalinic; Golac, McCartney, Williams, Watson, Nicholl, Keegan, Channon, George, Holmes, Baker.
Att: 16,659
Round 2 (2nd leg)
Sep 2 v Watford (a) 1-7 (agg 5-7)
Opp.og
Katalinic; Waldron, McCartney, Williams, Watson, Nicholl, Hebberd, Channon, George(Moran), Holmes, Baker.
Att: 15,992

On 7 March 1981, against Manchester United, Saints fielded four men who had captained England — Channon, Watson, Ball and Keegan. It was certainly a club record and perhaps a record for any League side.

When Saints played at Old Trafford on 29 November 1980, Danny Wallace, at 16 years 314 days, became the youngest Southampton first-teamer since the war.

Total home attendance: 450,929. Average: 21,472.

Lawrie McMenemy now had Kevin Keegan in his team and, despite his worried look here, the Saints' manager must have been pleased at his side's qualification for Europe.

1980-81
Division 1

Date		Opponent	Result	Scorers	Att.	Agboola R	Ball A	Baker G	Baker S	Boyer P	Channon M	George C	Golac I	Hebberd T	Holmes N	Katalinic I	Keegan K	McCartney M	Moran S	Nicholl C	Pratt W	Puckett D	Rogers A	Waldron M	Wallace D	Watson D	Wells P	Williams S
Aug 16	(h)	Manchester C	W 2-0	Channon 2	23,320			11		8	9		2		10	1	7		3	6						5		4
19	(a)	Arsenal	D 1-1	Baker	43,050			11		8	9		2*	12	10	1	7		3	6						5		4
23	(a)	Sunderland	W 2-1	Nicholl, George	41,141			11		8	9		2		10	1	7		3	6						5		4
30	(h)	Birmingham C	W 3-1	Keegan, Channon, Baker	21,683			11		8	9		2*	12	10	1	7		3	6						5		4
Sep 6	(h)	Brighton & HA	W 3-1	Golac, Williams, Baker	22,225			11		8	9		2		10			7	3	6						5	1	4
13	(a)	Norwich C	L 0-1		18,158			11		7	8	9	2	12	10				3*	6						5	1	4
20	(h)	Liverpool	D 2-2	Nicholl, Boyer	24,085			11		9	8		2		10		7		3	6						5	1	4
27	(a)	West Brom A	L 1-2	George	20,845			11		9	8	4	2		10		7		3	6						5	1	
Oct 4	(a)	Everton	L 1-2	Channon	36,544			11		8	9		2	12	10	1	7*		3	6						5		4
7	(h)	Wolves	W 4-2	McCartney, Baker, Nicholl, Moran	21,712			11		9	8*		2	12	10	1		7	3	6						5		4
11	(h)	Stoke C	L 1-2	George	19,473			11		9	8	7	2	12	10	1			3*	6						5		4
18	(a)	Middlesbrough	D 1-1	Watson	15,858			11		9	8		2		10	1	7		3	6						5		4
21	(a)	Crystal P	L 2-3	Moran 2	20,630			11		9	8		2		10	1	7		3	6						5		4
25	(h)	Aston Villa	L 1-2	Moran	21,249					9	8		2		10	1	7		11	6				3		5		4
Nov 1	(a)	Nottingham F	L 1-2	Moran	24,669			7		9	8		2		10	1			11	6				3		5		4
8	(h)	Ipswich T	D 3-3	Moran, Williams, Boyer	21,261			11		9	8		2		10	1	7		3	6						5		4
11	(h)	Arsenal	W 3-1	Moran, Holmes, Watson	21,244			11		9	8		2		10		7		3	6						5	1	4
15	(a)	Manchester C	L 0-3		32,661			11		9	8		2	12	10		7*		3	6						5	1	4
22	(h)	Leeds U	W 2-1	Channon, George	20,278			11		8	9		2		10		7		3	6						5	1	4
29	(a)	Manchester U	D 1-1	Holmes	46,840	4		11		8	9		2		10				3	6				7		5	1	
Dec 6	(h)	Coventry C	W 1-0	Holmes	18,847	4		11		8	9		2		10				3	6				7		5	1	
13	(a)	Wolves	D 1-1	Moran	18,147	4		11		8	9		2		10		7		3	6						5	1	
20	(h)	Crystal P	W 4-2	Moran, Channon, George, opp own goal	19,332			11		8	9		2		10		7		3	6						5	1	4
26	(h)	Tottenham H	D 4-4	Moran 2, George, Baker	28,792			11		8	9		2		10		7			6						5	1	4
27	(h)	Leicester C	W 4-0	Moran, Keegan, George, Baker	21,886	5		11		8	9		2		10		7		3	6							1	4
Jan 10	(a)	Leeds U	W 3-0	Holmes 2, Channon	21,007			11		8	9		2		10		7		3	6						5	1	4
17	(a)	Birmingham C	W 3-0	Keegan, Channon, Moran	16,491	12		11		8	9		2		10		7		3	6						5*	1	4
31	(h)	Sunderland	W 2-1	Keegan 2	21,345					8	9		2		10		7		3	6			11			5	1	4
Feb 7	(h)	Norwich C	W 2-1	Williams, George	20,454			11		8	9		2		10		7		3	6						5	1	4
21	(h)	West Brom A	D 2-2	Golac, Moran	21,910			11		8	9		2	12	10		7*		3	6						5	1	4
24	(a)	Brighton & HA	L 0-2		23,715			11		8	9		2		10		7*		3	6				12		5	1	4
28	(a)	Liverpool	L 0-2		41,575			11		8	9	4	2		10		7		3	6						5	1	
Mar 7	(h)	Manchester U	W 1-0	Keegan	22,698	4		11		8	9		2		10		7		3	6						5	1	
14	(a)	Stoke C	W 2-1	Keegan 2	14,828		11			8	9		2		10		7		3	6						5	1	4
17	(h)	Everton	W 3-0	Williams, Keegan, Baker	20,829		11	9			8*		2		10		7		3	6					12	5	1	4
21	(h)	Middlesbrough	W 1-0	Moran	20,651		11	9*			8		2		10		7		3	6					12	5	1	4
28	(a)	Aston Villa	L 1-2	opp own goal	32,467		11*	9			8		2		10		7		3	6					12	5	1	4
Apr 4	(h)	Nottingham F	W 2-0	Keegan, Channon	22,712		11	9			8*		2		10		7		3	6					12	5	1	4
18	(a)	Leicester C	D 2-2	Moran, Baker	21,349		11	9			8		2		10		7		3	6						5	1	4
20	(h)	Tottenham H	D 1-1	Channon	23,735		11	9			8		2		10		7*	4	3	6					12	5	1	
25	(a)	Coventry C	L 0-1		18,213		11	9			8		2		10			4*	3	6					12	5	1	7
May 13	(a)	Ipswich T	W 3-2	Moran 2, Keegan	19,504		11	9	2		8*				10		7	4	3	6					12	5	1	
App						5	10	39	1	13	42	22	41	4	41	12	27	22	30	42	1			7	2	38	30	33
Sub app						1								7				1				7	1					
Goals								8		2	10	8	2	1	5		11	1	18	3						2		4

2 own-goals

	P	W	D	L	F	A	Pts
Aston Villa	42	26	8	8	72	40	60
Ipswich T	42	23	10	9	77	43	56
Arsenal	42	19	15	8	61	45	53
West Brom A	42	20	12	10	60	42	52
Liverpool	42	17	17	8	62	42	51
Southampton	42	20	10	12	76	56	50
Nottingham F	42	19	12	11	62	44	50
Manchester U	42	15	18	9	51	36	48
Leeds U	42	17	10	15	39	47	44
Tottenham H	42	14	15	13	70	68	43
Stoke C	42	12	18	12	51	60	42
Manchester C	42	14	11	17	56	59	39
Birmingham C	42	13	12	17	50	61	38
Middlesbrough	42	16	5	21	53	61	37
Everton	42	13	10	19	55	58	36
Coventry C	42	13	10	19	48	68	36
Sunderland	42	14	7	21	52	53	35
Wolves	42	13	9	20	43	56	35
Brighton & HA	42	14	7	21	54	67	35
Norwich C	42	13	7	22	49	73	33
Leicester C	42	13	6	23	40	67	32
Crystal P	42	6	7	29	47	83	19

Back row (left to right): Ivan Golac, Chris Nicholl, Peter Wells, Terry Gennoe, Ivan Katalinic, Mike McCartney, Malcolm Waldron. Middle row: Lew Chatterley (trainer), Steve Williams, Graham Baker, Phil Boyer, Trevor Hebberd, John Mortimore (asst manager). Front row: Austin Hayes, Dave Watson, Nick Holmes, Lawrie McMenemy (manager), Kevin Keegan, Mike Channon, Charlie George.

1981-82

WITH Keegan now completely fit Southampton were raring to go as the new season dawned and, despite the disappointment of losing to Nottingham Forest on the opening day, they were soon pushing for a place amongst the leaders.

Keegan scored in his first four matches and was ably supported by record signing, David Armstrong, who had joined Saints from Middlesbrough for £600,000 in the close season. Armstrong ended the season with 15 goals from midfield, an impressive figure in the face of some ultra-defensive football.

Not for Saints, though, the current obsession with defence at all costs. They were not only winning matches, they were doing so in attacking, entertaining style and on 30 January, Keegan's goal at Middlesbrough sent them to the top of Division One for the first time in their 97-year history.

Southampton proved that this was no flash in the pan and even if they did not win the League Championship, they spent more time on top of the table than any other club that season.

Saints' arrival at the top coincided with a severe back injury to young striker, Steve Moran. He needed an operation and losing him at such a vital stage of the season was a cruel blow

to the club and the player, who was out of first-team action for nine months.

Yet Saints' League form was as exciting as any in memory and it eased the disappointment of a disastrous home UEFA Cup game against Sporting Lisbon (see *Saints in Europe*). As the season approached its climax, however, Southampton found the pressure too much for them and they slipped to seventh, which still carried the compensation of UEFA Cup qualification once more.

Keegan ended the season as top marksman in Division One with 26 goals, two of which came in a remarkable 5-5 draw with Coventry City at The Dell.

Towards the end of the season, McMenemy, anxious to replace centre-half Dave Watson who had moved to Stoke City, signed a raw, lanky central defender from Oxford called Mark Wright. The youngster did not have much chance to impress in his three League outings but it would not be long before the fans saw the astuteness of McMenemy's purchase.

Soon after Wright's arrival Saints waved goodbye, a little rashly it turned out later, to Mike Channon, the old favourite who had now become top scorer in Southampton's history.

FA Cup

SAINTS had never found Filbert Street a happy hunting ground in the FA Cup and 1982 proved no exception. Southampton seemed to lack resilience against a Leicester team which went on to reach the semi-finals.

Round 3
Jan 2 v Leicester City (a) 1-3
Keegan
Katalinic; Golac, Holmes, Williams, Nicholl(Wallace), Waldron, Keegan, Channon, Moran, Armstrong, Ball.
Att: 20,589

The 5-5 draw with Coventry City on 4 May 1982 was the first time The Dell had witnessed such a high-scoring draw, apart from a match in 1945-6, the season before League football resumed.

Total home attendance: 458,676. Average: 21,841.

Football League Cup

AFTER being held to a draw at The Dell by Second Division Chelsea, Saints went out of the League Cup after extra-time at Stamford Bridge. Walker and Fillery netted Chelsea's goals and another League Cup campaign was over for Southampton almost before it had started.

Round 2 (1st leg)
Oct 6 v Chelsea (h) 1-1
Keegan
Wells; Golac, Holmes(Lawrence), G.Baker, Watson, Waldron, Keegan, Channon, Moran, Armstrong, Ball.
Att: 16,901
Round 2 (2nd leg)
Oct 28 v Chelsea (a) 1-2 (agg 2-3)
Moran
Katalinic; S.Baker, Holmes, Williams, Nicholl, Waldron(Moran), Keegan, Channon, Lawrence, Agboola, Puckett.
Att: 27,370

David Armstrong

Stephen Baker

David Puckett

1981-82

Division 1

Date		Opponent	Result	Scorers	Att	Agboola R	Armstrong D	Baker G	Baker S	Ball A	Cassells K	Channon M	Golac I	Hebberd T	Holmes N	Katalinic I	Keegan K	Lawrence G	Moran S	Nicholl C	Puckett D	Rogers A	Waldron M	Wallace D	Watson D	Wells P	Whitlock M	Williams S	Wright M
Aug 29	(a)	Nottingham F	L 1-2	Keegan	25,234			10		11		8	2		3		7		9	6*	12		5			1		4	
Sep 1	(h)	Wolves	W 4-1	Channon 2, Keegan, Moran	21,315		10	4		11*		8	2		3		7		9		12		5			1		6	
5	(h)	Everton	W 1-0	Keegan	21,624		10	4		11		8	2		3		7		9	6			5			1			
12	(a)	Manchester C	D 1-1	Keegan	42,003	6	10	4		11		8	2		3		7		9				5			1			
19	(h)	Middlesbrough	W 2-0	Watson, Moran	20,105		10*	4		11		8	2		3		7		9		12		6		5	1			
22	(a)	West Ham U	L 2-4	Waldron, Armstrong	34,263	4	10	8		11			2		3		7		9		12		6		5*	1			
26	(a)	Coventry C	L 2-4	Keegan 2	12,610		10	4*		11		8	2		3		7		9		12		6		5	1			
Oct 3	(h)	Ipswich T	W 4-3	Armstrong 2, Keegan, Moran	22,557		10	4		11		8	2		3		7		9				6		5	1			
10	(a)	Birmingham C	L 0-4		16,938		10	4		11		8	2		3*		7		9		12		6		5	1			
17	(h)	Notts C	W 3-1	Keegan 2, Moran	18,900		10			11			2		3		7	8	9	6			5			1		4	
24	(a)	West Brom A	D 1-1	Channon	15,730		10			11*	2	8			3	1	7		9	6			5	12				4	
31	(h)	Tottenham H	L 1-2	Moran	24,131		10*		2	11		8			3	1	7	12	9	6			5					4	
Nov 7	(a)	Stoke C	W 2-0	Keegan, Armstrong	13,864		10			11		8	2		3	1	7		9	5			6					4	
21	(h)	Leeds U	W 4-0	Keegan, Armstrong, Channon, Moran	21,127		10			11		8	2		3	1	7		9	5			6					4	
24	(a)	Wolves	D 0-0		15,438		10			11		8	2		3	1	7		9	5			6					4	
28	(a)	Liverpool	W 1-0	Moran	35,189		10			11		8	2		3	1	7		9	5			6					4	
Dec 5	(h)	Manchester U	W 3-2	Keegan, Moran, Armstrong	24,404		10			11		8	2		3	1	7		9	5			6					4	
8	(h)	Brighton & HA	L 0-2		22,305		10			11		8	2		3	1	7		9	5			6					4	
28	(h)	Swansea C	W 3-1	Keegan 2, Armstrong	22,703		10			11		8	2		3	1	7		9	5			6					4	
Jan 19	(a)	Everton	D 1-1	Moran	22,855		10	7		11		8	2		3	1			9	5			6					4	
23	(h)	Arsenal	W 3-1	Puckett 2, Armstrong	22,263		10			11		8	2		3	1	7			5	9		6					4	
30	(a)	Middlesbrough	W 1-0	Keegan	12,693		10	4		11		8	2	9	3	1	7			5			6						
Feb 6	(h)	Manchester C	W 2-1	Baker, Armstrong	22,645	3	10	4		11		8	2	9		1	7			5			6						
10	(a)	Aston Villa	D 1-1		24,287		10	4		11		8	2	9	3	1	7			5			6						
13	(a)	Nottingham F	W 2-0	Keegan, Channon	21,350		10	4		11		8	2	9	3	1	7			5			6						
16	(a)	Ipswich T	L 2-5	Keegan, Puckett	20,635		10	4		11		8	2*		3	1	7	12		5	9		6						
20	(h)	West Ham U	W 2-1	Channon, Armstrong	24,026		10	4		11		8	2		3	1	7			5	9		6						
27	(h)	Birmingham C	W 3-1	Baker 2, Keegan	20,620		10	4		11		8	2		3	1	7			5	9		6						
Mar 6	(a)	Notts C	D 1-1	Keegan	12,474		10	4		11		8	2		3	1	7			5	12		6	9*					
10	(a)	Sunderland	L 0-2		15,747		10	4		11		8	2*		3	1	7			5	12		6	9					
13	(h)	West Brom A	D 0-0		21,376		10	4		11		8	2		3	1	7			5	9*		6	12					
20	(a)	Tottenham H	L 2-3	Baker, Armstrong	46,827	2	10	4		11*		8			3	1	7			5	12		6	9					
27	(h)	Stoke C	W 4-3	Whitlock, Waldron, Channon, Armstrong	20,058		10			11		8	2		3	1	7		9	6			5				4		
Apr 3	(a)	Brighton & HA	D 1-1	Keegan	20,977		10			11		8	2		3	1	7			5	9*		6	12			4		
10	(h)	Aston Villa	L 0-3		22,801		10			11		8	2		3	1	7			5			6	9			4		
13	(a)	Swansea C	L 0-1		23,771		10		2	11	9	8			3	1	7			5			6				4		
17	(a)	Leeds U	W 3-1	Keegan 2, Armstrong	21,353		10	4*	2	11		8			3	1	7			5	12		6	9					
24	(h)	Liverpool	L 2-3	Keegan, Channon	24,704		10	4		11	9*	8	2		3	1	7			5	12		6						
May 1	(a)	Manchester U	L 0-1		40,038	3	10	4	2	11	12	8*				1	7		9	5			6						
4	(h)	Coventry C	D 5-5	Keegan 2, Cassells 2, Ball	18,552		10			11	9	8	2		3	1	7			5	12		6*				4		
8	(h)	Sunderland	W 1-0	Armstrong	21,110		10			11	9	8	2		3	1	7			5			6				4		
15	(a)	Arsenal	L 1-4	Armstrong	28,534		10	4		11	12	8	2		3	1	7			5			6*	9					
				App		5	41	26	5	41	4	40	36	4	40	32	41	2	18	34	8		34	3	5	10	9	21	3
				Sub app								2							2		9	2	4						
				Goals			15	4		1	2	8					26		9		3		2		1		1		

Back row (left to right): G.Baker, N.Holmes, C.Nicholl, T.Hebberd, S.Moran. Middle row: L.Chatterley (trainer), D.Armstrong, S.Williams, I.Katalinic, P.Wells, I.Golac, M.Waldron, J.Mortimore (asst manager). Front row: M.Channon, K.Keegan, L.McMenemy (manager), D.Watson, A.Ball.

	P	W	D	L	F	A	Pts
Liverpool	42	26	9	7	80	32	87
Ipswich T	42	26	5	11	75	53	83
Manchester U	42	22	12	8	59	29	78
Tottenham H	42	20	11	11	67	48	71
Arsenal	42	20	11	11	48	37	71
Swansea C	42	21	6	15	58	51	69
Southampton	42	19	9	14	72	67	66
Everton	42	17	13	12	56	50	64
West Ham U	42	14	16	12	66	57	58
Manchester C	42	15	13	14	49	50	58
Aston Villa	42	15	12	15	55	53	57
Nottingham F	42	15	12	15	42	48	57
Brighton & HA	42	13	13	16	43	52	52
Coventry C	42	13	11	18	56	62	50
Notts C	42	13	8	21	61	69	47
Birmingham C	42	10	14	18	53	61	44
West Brom A	42	11	11	20	46	57	44
Stoke C	42	12	8	22	44	63	44
Sunderland	42	11	11	20	38	58	44
Leeds U	42	10	12	20	39	61	42
Wolves	42	10	10	22	32	63	40
Middlesbrough	42	8	15	19	34	52	38

1982-83

THE previous season had ended with the satisfaction of qualification for the UEFA Cup, but during the summer of 1982 there were three dramatic moves involving Saints in the transfer market — and not all of them pleased the fans.

On the positive side, McMenemy at last solved Saints' long-standing goalkeeping problem by signing the man acknowledged by most people as the world number-one, Peter Shilton, who came from Forest for £300,000.

Southampton had to finance Shilton's signing by selling popular Graham Baker to Manchester City for £225,000, but with two of the world's best players in Keegan and Shilton now teamed together at The Dell, Saints fans again relished the arrival of a new season.

Their joy was short-lived, however, when Keegan announced that he would be joining Newcastle United with only days to the kick-off. Saints had agreed that if Keegan wanted to leave them, they would release him immediately, so they had little choice in the matter, although their supporters felt angry at the timing of Keegan's move.

Many fans claimed they had bought season tickets on the strength of Keegan still being a Saints player and there was plenty of ill feeling. Keegan's controversial decampment upset the club, too, for it meant that they were now desperately short of strikers.

McMenemy quickly secured Justin Fashanu on loan from Forest and he helped ease the immediate crisis, although with no cash to spare — Southampton had lost £200,000 on the previous season's workings — Saints could not make Fashanu's move permanent.

This dismal start to the season was compounded by an early exit from the UEFA Cup (see *Saints in Europe*) and the scandal of having two players, Steve Moran and Mark Wright, detained by Swedish police following accusations — which later turned out to be totally false — by a young girl.

Heavy defeats by Liverpool and Spurs anchored Saints to the foot of the table and in mid-season Alan Ball announced his immediate retirement. On 2 October, with Moran still in Swedish police custody, Saints entertained Notts County in front of 16,000 fans who braved driving rain to give the club some of the loudest vocal support in memory.

Saints won and slowly they emerged from their nightmare. In November they signed the former England full-back, Mick Mills. Mills helped stabilize the team and the future brightened with youngsters Wright, Wallace, Agboola and Moran all demonstrating that it is not always neccessary for clubs to buy their way out of trouble.

Moran had recovered from injury and his distressing experience in Sweden and, despite losing his strike partners, Keegan and Channon, he found his goalscoring touch, notably with a hat-trick against Manchester City. Saints' revival threatened to carry them into Europe once more but their form fell away in the last few matches and they finished mid-table.

Having failed to fill Keegan's place with youngsters like Baird and Foyle, McMenemy knew that he would have to resort to the transfer market for an experienced replacement. Saints had, though, satisfactorily negotiated a most difficult season.

FA Cup

DESPITE the fact that Spurs were without six first-teamers for their third-round match with Southampton at White Hart Lane, Saints failed to scrape even a draw. Perhaps remembering a 6-0 defeat at Tottenham earlier in the season, Saints were over cautious and fell to Mick Hazard's goal early in the second half.

> **Round 3**
> **Jan 8 v Tottenham Hotspur (a) 0-1**
> Shilton; Agboola, Mills, Williams, Nicholl, Wright, Holmes, Cassells, Moran, Armstrong, Wallace.
> *Att: 38,040*

Milk Cup

GOALS from Gordon McQueen and Norman Whiteside at Old Trafford sank Southampton in the fourth round of the Football League Cup, now renamed the Milk Cup after sponsorship from the Milk Marketing Board.

Saints had produced a workmanlike performance over the two-legged tie with Fourth Division Colchester United. And they showed equal professionalism in removing Manchester City after a replay.

But Manchester United proved more difficult and Saints became their latest victims as United moved a stage closer to the Milk Cup Final at Wembley where they eventually lost to Liverpool.

> *Mark Hateley's 14-second goal for Coventry on 15 January 1983 was the fastest in a peacetime game at The Dell, beating by one second Tommy Mulgrew's goal against Brentford in 1964.*

> *Total home attendance: 394,069. Average: 18,765.*

> **Round 2 (1st leg)**
> **Oct 6 v Colchester United (a) 0-0**
> Shilton; Baker, Rofe, Williams, Nicholl, Agboola, Ball, Cassells, Wallace, Armstrong, Lawrence.
> *Att: 7,967*
> **Round 2 (2nd leg)**
> **Oct 26 v Colchester United (h) 4-2 (agg 4-2)**
> *Wallace, Cassells, Armstrong, Moran*
> Shilton; Rofe(Puckett), Holmes, Williams, Nicholl, Wright, Ball, Moran, Cassells, Armstrong, Wallace.
> *Att: 9,676*
> **Round 3**
> **Nov 10 v Manchester City (a) 1-1**
> *Wright*
> Shilton; Agboola, Rofe, Williams, Nicholl, Wright, Holmes, Moran, Cassells, Armstrong, Wallace.
> *Att: 17,463*
> **Replay**
> **Nov 24 v Manchester City (h) 4-0**
> *Williams, Moran, Puckett, Holmes*
> Shilton; Agboola, Rofe, Williams, Nicholl, Wright, Holmes, Moran, Cassells(Puckett), Armstrong, Wallace.
> *Att: 13,298*
> **Round 4**
> **Dec 1 v Manchester United (a) 0-2**
> Shilton; Agboola, Rofe(Puckett), Williams, Nicholl, Wright, Holmes, Moran, Cassells, Armstrong, Wallace.
> *Att: 28,378*

1982-83
Division 1

Date		Opponent	Result	Scorers	Att	Agboola R	Armstrong D	Baird I	Baker S	Ball A	Cassells K	Fashanu J	Foyle M	Holmes N	Lawrence G	Mills M	Moran S	Nicholl C	Puckett D	Rofe D	Shilton P	Waldron M	Wallace D	Wells P	Williams S	Wright M
Aug 28	(a)	Coventry C	L 0-1		10,356	4	10		2	7	12	9		8*				5	11	3	1					6
31	(h)	Watford	L 1-4	Lawrence	19,714	6	10			7		9			8			5	11	3	1				4	2
Sep 4	(h)	Aston Villa	W 1-0	Fashanu	17,943		10		2	7		9			8			5	11	3	1				4	6
8	(a)	Tottenham H	L 0-6		26,579	8	10		2	7		9			12			5	11	3*	1				4	6
11	(a)	Norwich C	D 1-1	Armstrong	16,492	8	10		2	7	11	9						5		3	1				4	6
18	(h)	Manchester U	L 0-1		21,700	11	10		2	7	8						9	5		3	1		12		4	6*
25	(a)	Liverpool	L 0-5		32,996	11	10		2	7*	8			3			9	5			1		12		4	6
Oct 2	(h)	Notts C	W 1-0	Fashanu	16,230	6	10			7	8	9		3	11			5	2		1				4	
9	(a)	Sunderland	D 1-1	Williams	15,635	6	10			7		9		3	11*	8		5	2		1		12		4	
16	(h)	West Ham U	W 3-0	Williams, Ball, Moran	19,840		10			7		9		3	11*	8	12	5	2		1				4	6
23	(a)	Swansea C	L 2-3	Fashanu, Wallace	10,694		10			7		9		3		8		5	2				11	1	4	6
30	(h)	Everton	W 3-2	Moran, Cassells, Wallace	18,141		10			7	9			3			8	5	2		1		11		4	6
Nov 6	(a)	Manchester C	L 0-2		25,115		10		2		9			7*			8	5	12	3	1		11		4	6
13	(h)	Nottingham F	D 1-1	Moran	18,178	2	10				9*			7		3	8	5	12		1		11		4	6
20	(h)	Ipswich T	L 0-1		18,449	2	10				9*			7		3	8	5	12		1		11		4	6
27	(a)	Luton T	D 3-3	Cassells, Armstrong, Wallace	11,196	2	10				9					3	8	5		7	1		11		4	6
Dec 4	(h)	Stoke C	W 1-0	Wallace	17,198	2	10							7		3	9	5	8		1		11		4	6
11	(a)	Birmingham C	W 2-0	Moran, Wallace	11,199	2	10							7		3	8	5	9		1		11		4	6
18	(h)	West Brom A	W 4-1	Moran, Puckett, Armstrong, Wallace	16,896	2	10							7		3	8	5	9				11	1	4	6
27	(a)	Brighton & HA	W 1-0	Wallace	21,794	2	10							7			8	5	9	3	1		11		4	6
28	(h)	Arsenal	D 2-2	Holmes, Puckett	22,025	2	10				12			7			9	5	8	3*	1		11		4	6
Jan 1	(a)	Ipswich T	L 1-2	Wright	18,866	2	10							7		3	9	5	8		1		11		4	6
3	(a)	Aston Villa	L 0-2		19,925	2	10				12			7		3	9	5	8*		1		11		4	6
15	(h)	Coventry C	D 1-1	Armstrong	17,145	2	10						8	7		3	9	5			1		11		4	6
22	(a)	Watford	L 0-2		17,189	2	10						8	7		3	9	5			1		11		4	6
Feb 5	(h)	Norwich C	W 4-0	Williams, Holmes, Moran, Wallace	17,244	2	10				12			7		3*	9	5	8		1		11		4	6
15	(a)	Notts C	W 2-1	Puckett, Wallace	5,856	2	10							7		3	9	5	8		1		11		4	6
19	(h)	Sunderland	W 2-0	Mills, Holmes	17,326	2	10	12						7		3	9	5	8*		1		11		4	6
26	(a)	West Ham U	D 1-1	Wallace	19,626	2	10	8						7		3	9	5			1		11		4	6
Mar 5	(h)	Swansea C	W 2-1	Baird, Armstrong	16,842	2	10	8						7		3	9	5			1		11		4	6
15	(a)	Everton	L 0-2		15,002	2	10	8					12	7*		3	9	5	4		1		11			6
19	(h)	Manchester C	W 4-1	Moran 3, Baird	17,201	2	10*	8					12	7		3	9	5			1		11			6
26	(a)	Nottingham F	W 2-1	Armstrong, Wallace	13,461	2	10	8						7		3	9	5			1		11		4	6
Apr 2	(a)	Arsenal	D 0-0		24,911	2	10	8						7		3	9	5			1		11		4	6
5	(h)	Brighton & HA	D 0-0		18,253	2	10	8*						7		3	9	5	12		1		11		4	6
9	(a)	Manchester U	D 1-1	Foyle	37,120	2	10				8		12			3	9	5			1	7*	11		4	6
16	(h)	Liverpool	W 3-2	Holmes 2, Moran	23,578	2	10				8			7		3	9	5			1		11		4	6
23	(a)	Stoke C	D 1-1	Wallace	14,903	2	10				8*			7		3	9	5	12		1	6	11		4	
30	(h)	Luton T	D 2-2	Wright, Armstrong	18,237	2	10	8*						7		3	9	5	12		1		11		4	6
May 3	(h)	Tottenham H	L 1-2	Armstrong	21,602	2	10*						12	7		3	9	5	8		1		11		4	6
7	(a)	West Brom A	L 0-1		11,241	2		10						7		3*	9	5	8	12	1	4	11			6
14	(h)	Birmingham C	L 0-1		20,327	2	10	12						7		3	9	5	8*		1		11		4	6
App						37	41	9	7	12	9	9	5	35	5	27	36	42	17	16	39	3	32	3	39	39
Sub app							2		4		3	1	1						7				3			
Goals							8	2		1	2	3	1	5	1	1	10		3				12		3	2

Back row (left to right): Dennis Rofe, Mark Whitlock, Justin Fashanu, Mark Wright, George Lawrence, Keith Cassells, David Armstrong. Middle row: Lew Chatterley (coach), Steve Baker, Reuben Agboola, Peter Wells, Peter Shilton, David Puckett, Danny Wallace, John Mortimore (asst manager). Front row: Steve Moran, Steve Williams, Alan Ball, Lawrie McMenemy (manager), Nick Holmes, Malcolm Waldron, Chris Nicholl.

	P	W	D	L	F	A	Pts
Liverpool	42	24	10	8	67	37	82
Watford	42	22	5	15	74	57	71
Manchester U	42	19	13	10	56	38	70
Tottenham H	42	20	9	13	65	50	69
Nottingham F	42	20	9	13	62	50	69
Aston Villa	42	21	5	16	62	50	68
Everton	42	18	10	14	66	48	64
West Ham U	42	20	4	18	68	62	64
Ipswich T	42	15	13	14	64	50	58
Arsenal	42	16	10	16	58	56	58
West Brom A	42	15	12	15	51	49	57
Southampton	42	15	12	15	54	58	57
Stoke C	42	16	9	17	53	64	57
Norwich C	42	14	12	16	52	58	54
Notts C	42	15	7	20	55	71	52
Sunderland	42	12	14	16	48	61	50
Birmingham C	42	12	14	16	40	55	50
Luton T	42	12	13	17	65	84	49
Coventry C	42	13	9	20	48	59	48
Manchester C	42	13	8	21	47	70	47
Swansea C	42	10	11	21	51	69	41
Brighton & HA	42	9	13	20	38	68	40

1983-84

LAWRIE McMenemy made two close-season signings, reinforcing the defence with Ken Armstrong, from Kilmarnock for £60,000, and responding to Saints' need for a centre-forward by buying Frank Worthington from Sunderland for £20,000.

Chris Nicholl, who had been an admirable servant, moved to Grimsby, as Dave Booth's assistant; and Ian Branfoot, who had done so much good work with Saints' youngsters, became Reading manager, thus ending a 20-year association with McMenemy.

A fine opening burst to the season saw Arsenal, Manchester United, Sunderland and Forest all beaten without Saints conceding a goal. Worthington's experience was paying dividends and although the lanky striker was not finding the net, he was creating plenty of chances for the others.

Yet just when it seemed that Saints were credible title challengers, they suffered a series of injuries which left Agboola, Mills and Wright all sidelined at the same time. Losing half their defence inevitably caused Saints' charge to falter and only when the trio were restored to the team at the beginning of December did the team's impetus return.

New faces arrived in the shape of Dennis (Birmingham) and Curtis (Swansea) and both men played their part in an exciting second half of the season. At the end of 1983, Saints earned a point at Highbury and moved into fourth place before embarking on an exciting FA Cup run. Throughout, Saints mantained their League form and after the semi-final defeat they stood fifth with nine games to play.

The Cup defeat did not trigger a collapse and Southampton finished the season without losing another game. They hammered Coventry 8-2 and spectacular away wins, at West Brom and Notts County in their last two games, edged Saints into the runners-up spot, just three points adrift of Champions, Liverpool, by far their best-ever League position.

FA Cup

DESPITE being drawn away in every round, and always against in-form teams, Southampton enjoyed their best FA Cup run for seven years.

Two fine goals from Moran late in the game eliminated Forest and set up a mouth-watering fourth-round clash with neighbours Portsmouth. Second Division Pompey were desperate for success and there was a phenomenal demand for tickets in an almost hysterical build-up to the game.

A classic Cup tie which swung from end to end was settled only in the dying seconds when Moran stunned Pompey's fans with a left-foot shot from David Armstrong's cross.

After beating Blackburn, Saints again faced Second Division promotion challengers on their own ground. Had Wallace and Worthington made more of their opportunities against Sheffield Wednesday, then the issue could have been settled there and then.

There was a shock in store when Wednesday took the lead at The Dell, but Saints shrugged off their sluggish start as Wednesday folded.

Revitalised Everton stood between Southampton and Wembley and, in hindsight, it might have been better if Saints had not risked skipper Steve Williams, who was injured in the sixth-round replay.

Adrian Heath's winner three minutes from the end of extra-time was arguably the most devastating goal that Saints had ever conceded.

```
Round 3
Jan 7 Nottingham Forest (a) 2-1
Moran 2
Shilton; Mills, Dennis, Williams, Wright, Agboola, Holmes, Moran,
Worthington, D.Armstrong, Wallace.
Att: 19,271
Round 4
Jan 28 v Portsmouth (a) 1-0
Moran
Shilton; Mills, Dennis, Williams, Wright, Agboola, Holmes, Moran,
Worthington, D.Armstrong, Wallace.
Att: 36,000
Round 5
Feb 18 v Blackburn Rovers (a) 1-0
Armstrong
Shilton; Mills, Dennis, Williams, Wright, Agboola, Holmes, Moran,
Worthington, D.Armstrong, Wallace.
Att: 15,357
Round 6
Mar 11 v Sheffield Wednesday (a) 0-0
Shilton; Mills, Dennis, Williams, Wright, Agboola, Holmes, Moran,
Worthington, D.Armstrong, Wallace.
Att: 40,030
Replay
Mar 20 v Sheffield Wednesday (h) 5-1
Williams, Wright, Armstrong, Moran, opp.og
Shilton; Mills, Dennis, Williams, Wright, Agboola, Holmes, Moran,
Worthington, D.Armstrong, Wallace.
Att: 20,590
Semi-final
Apr 14 v Everton (at Highbury) 0-1
Shilton; Mills, Dennis, Williams, Wright, Agboola, Holmes, Moran,
Worthington, D.Armstrong, Wallace.
Att: 46,587
```

```
Total home attendance: 379,062. Average: 18,050.
```

Milk Cup

SUBSTITUTE Martin Foyle's two goals helped Saints overcome a two-goal first-leg deficit against Carlisle in the first round of the Milk Cup, but when Southampton faced Third Division Rotherham United at Millmoor they were without several key defenders including goalkeeper Peter Shilton.

Rotherham took advantage of Saints' injury problems and goals from Rhodes and Mitchell sent them through.

```
Round 2 (1st leg)
Oct 4 v Carlisle United (a) 0-2
Shilton; Agboola, Mills, Williams, K.Armstrong, Wright, Holmes,
Moran, Worthington, D.Armstrong, Wallace.
Att: 8,570
Round 2 (2nd leg)
Oct 25 v Carlisle United (h) 3-0 (agg 3-2)
Foyle 2, D.Armstrong
Shilton; Agboola, Baker, Williams, K.Armstrong, Wright, Holmes,
Moran, Baird(Foyle), D.Armstrong, Wallace.
Att: 12,483
Round 3
Nov 8 v Rotherham United (a) 1-2
D.Armstrong
Sperring; Agboola, Baker, Rofe, Whitlock, Wright(Foyle), Holmes,
Moran, Worthington, D.Armstrong, Wallace.
Att: 8,821
```

Liverpool's visit on 16 March was the first match to be televised live from The Dell under the new agreement between the League and the TV companies. A nationwide audience saw two remarkable goals from Danny Wallace earn Saints a fine win.

1983-84
Division 1

Date		Opponent	Result	Scorers	Att	Agboola R	Armstrong D	Armstrong K	Baird I	Baker S	Curtis A	Dennis M	Foyle M	Golac I	Holmes N	Juryeff I	Mills M	Moran S	Puckett D	Rofe D	Shilton P	Wallace D	Whitlock M	Williams S	Worthington F	Wright M
Aug 27	(a)	Nottingham F	W 1-0	Wallace	14,626	2	10	5							7		3	8			1	11		4	9	6
29	(h)	Queen's Park R	D 0-0		19,522	2	10	5							7		3	8			1	11		4	9	6
Sep 3	(h)	Arsenal	W 1-0	Baird	19,377	2	10	5	8						7		3				1	11		4	9	6
6	(a)	Liverpool	D 1-1	Mills	26,331	2	10	5	8	4				12	7		3				1	11			9*	6
10	(a)	Sunderland	W 2-0	Moran 2	12,716	2	10	5							7		3	8			1	11		4	9	6
17	(h)	Manchester U	W 3-0	Williams 2, D.Armstrong	20,674	2	10	5							7		3	8			1	11		4	9	6
24	(a)	Aston Villa	L 0-1		21,209	2	10	5							7		3	8			1	11		4	9	6
Oct 1	(h)	Wolves	W 1-0	Worthington	16,589	2	10	5							7		3	8			1	11		4	9	6
22	(a)	Luton T	L 1-3	D.Armstrong	12,389	2	10	5	9	3					7			8			1	11		4		6
29	(h)	Ipswich T	W 3-2	Williams, Holmes, Moran	18,515		10	5		3				8	7			12			1	11	2	4	9	6*
Nov 5	(a)	Norwich C	L 0-1		14,303		10			3				6	7			8		2	1	11	5	4		
12	(h)	West Brom A	W 1-0	Moran	16,450	2	10	5		3					7			8			1	11	6	4	9	
19	(h)	Notts C	L 0-2		15,009	2	10	5		3*				12	7			8			1	11	6	4	9	
26	(a)	Coventry C	D 0-0		11,579		10	5		3					7	12		8		2	1	11	6	4*	9	
30	(a)	Leicester C	L 1-2	Worthington	14,181		10	5	2			3*			7	12		8			1	11	6	4	9	
Dec 3	(h)	Stoke C	W 3-1	Mills, D.Armstrong, Wallace	15,301	6	10	5			8	3			7		2				1	11		4	9	
10	(a)	Tottenham H	D 0-0		29,711	6	10	5			8	3			7		2				1	11		4	9	
17	(h)	Birmingham C	W 2-1	opp own goal 2	15,248	6	10	5			8	3			7		2		12		1	11		4	9*	
26	(a)	West Ham U	W 1-0	Wallace	22,221	6	10	5			8*	3			7		2		12		1	11		4	9	
27	(h)	Watford	W 1-0	D.Armstrong	20,759	6	10	5				3			7		2	8			1	11		4	9	
31	(a)	Arsenal	D 2-2	Moran 2	27,596	6	10					3			7		2*	8	12		1	11		4	9	5
Jan 2	(h)	Aston Villa	D 2-2	Moran, D.Armstrong	18,963	6	10	5				3			7			8	12		1	11		4	9*	2
21	(a)	Manchester U	L 2-3	Moran 2	40,371	4	10	5*				3			7		2	8	12		1	11			9	6
23	(h)	Nottingham F	L 0-1		17,420	4	10	5				3			7		2	8	12		1	11			9*	6
Feb 4	(a)	Wolves	W 1-0	Moran	9,943	6	10					3			7		2	8			1	11		4	9	5
11	(h)	Sunderland	D 1-1	Moran	16,968	5	10					3			7		2	8			1	11		4	9	6
21	(a)	Ipswich T	W 3-0	Moran, Worthington, D.Armstrong	14,934	5	10					3			7		2	8			1	11		4	9	6
25	(h)	Luton T	W 2-1	Wright, D.Armstrong	17,947	5	10					3			7		2	8			1	11		4	9	6
Mar 3	(h)	Norwich C	W 2-1	D.Armstrong, Puckett	17,456	6	10	5			8*	3			7		2		12		1	11		4	9	
16	(h)	Liverpool	W 2-0	Wallace 2	19,698	6	10					3			7		2	8	12		1	11		4	9*	6
24	(a)	Queen's Park R	L 0-4		15,407	5	10					3			7		2	8	4		1	11	12		9	6*
31	(a)	Everton	L 0-1		20,244		10		9			3			7		2*	8	4	12	1	11	5			6
Apr 7	(h)	Leicester C	D 2-2	Moran, Wallace	17,455	5	10					3		4	7		2	8	12		1	11			9*	6
17	(h)	Everton	W 3-1	D.Armstrong 2, Moran	16,978	5	10				12	3		4	7		2*	8			1	11			9	6
21	(h)	West Ham U	W 2-0	Moran, Holmes	20,846		10					3		4	7		2	8			1	11	5		9	6
24	(a)	Watford	D 1-1	D.Armstrong	16,744		10		9			3		4	7		2	8			1	11	5			6
28	(h)	Coventry C	W 8-2	Moran 3, Wallace 3, Worthington, D.Armstrong	16,746		10				4*			3	7		2	8	12		1	11	5		9	6
May 5	(a)	Stoke C	D 1-1	Holmes	12,131	3	10		9					4*	7		2	8	12		1	11	5			6
7	(h)	Tottenham H	W 5-0	D.Armstrong 2, Wallace 2, Puckett	21,141	4	10							3	7		2	8	9		1	11	5			6
12	(a)	Birmingham C	D 0-0		16,445		10	5	11*				12	3	7		2	8	9		1		4			6
14	(a)	West Brom A	W 2-0	Moran, Puckett	10,365	4	10	5						3	7		2	8	9		1	11				6
17	(a)	Notts C	W 3-1	Moran 2, D.Armstrong	6,035	4	10	5						3	7		2	8	9		1	11				6
App						33	42	26	6	8	8	20	2	11	42		34	33	7	2	42	41	15	27	34	29
Sub app									1			3		2		2			1	1			1			1
Goals							15	1	1						3		2	21	3			11		3	4	1

2 own-goals

Back row (left to right): Danny Wallace, Reuben Agboola, Martin Foyle, Dennis Rofe, Steve Baker. Middle row: Lew Chatterley (coach), Mick Mills, Malcolm Waldron, Alistair Sperring, Peter Shilton, Kenneth Armstrong, Ian Baird, John Mortimore (asst manager). Front row: Steve Moran, Frank Worthington, Nick Holmes, Lawrie McMenemy (manager), Steve Williams, Mark Wright, David Armstrong.

	P	W	D	L	F	A	Pts
Liverpool	42	22	14	6	73	32	80
Southampton	42	22	11	9	66	38	77
Nottingham F	42	22	8	12	76	45	74
Manchester U	42	20	14	8	71	41	74
Queen's Park R	42	22	7	13	67	37	73
Arsenal	42	18	9	15	74	60	63
Everton	42	16	14	12	44	42	62
Tottenham H	42	17	10	15	64	65	61
West Ham U	42	17	9	16	60	55	60
Aston Villa	42	17	9	16	59	61	60
Watford	42	16	9	17	68	77	57
Ipswich T	42	15	8	19	55	57	53
Sunderland	42	13	13	16	42	53	52
Norwich C	42	12	15	15	48	49	51
Leicester C	42	13	12	17	65	68	51
Luton T	42	14	9	19	53	66	51
West Brom A	42	14	9	19	48	62	51
Stoke C	42	13	11	18	44	63	50
Coventry C	42	13	11	18	57	77	50
Birmingham C	42	12	12	18	39	50	48
Notts C	42	10	11	21	50	72	41
Wolves	42	6	11	25	27	80	29

1984-85

FRANK Worthington, after a dispute over personal terms, resumed his travelling ways and moved along the South Coast to Brighton. McMenemy, anxious to replace him as soon as possible, signed another veteran striker in Joe Jordan, the former Leeds and Scotland star who had been playing Italian League football with Verona.

Although Jordan was somewhat injury prone, he soon settled at The Dell where his courageous style of play won the fans' admiration. Moran, in particular, took advantage from the fact that Jordan's aerial powers often caused panic amongst defenders and let in other strikers.

Despite Jordan's impact, however, the team could not make the same impact whch had taken Saints to runners-up spot the previous season. Some felt that the 1984 semi-final defeat was having a delayed effect.

Rumours circulated that McMenemy was now unhappy at The Dell and there was a series of undignified public disagreements between the manager and some of his players. Agboola was the first to leave when, after an incident at a night club, he was sold to Sunderland.

Then, after a Milk Cup match against QPR, Wright and Williams spoke to the Press about their disagreements with the manager. The repercussions saw Williams granted a transfer request, and Wright dropped from the England squad.

Saints fans were upset and mystified. The club was enjoying its longest unbeaten League run since 1920-21, and Agboola and Williams had been with Southampton since their schooldays and were regarded as important to the club's future.

The unbeaten run ended at Coventry and there were some bad home results when Watford and Sheffield Wednesday both won at The Dell in the last home games of 1984.

Williams, in particular, was sorely missed and McMenemy hastened to buy Brighton and former Liverpool midfielder, Jimmy Case, for £20,000. It was the manager's last-ever signing for Southampton and proved to be one of his best.

Danny Wallace broke a leg against Leicester but, despite the handicap of losing their best forward, Saints buckled down to produce some good end-of-season results and again qualify for Europe. Unfortunately, the UEFA ban following the Brussels tragedy made that purely academic.

FA Cup

SAINTS resumed their FA Cup challenge against relegation-threatened Sunderland on a difficult frost-bound pitch at The Dell. Moran tapped home the first goal after 32 minutes and ended the scoring in the 86th minute with a first-time shot. In between, a curling shot from Curtis and a drive from Jordan had made light work of playing in such tricky conditions.

Jordan and Moran scored goals either side of half-time to knock-out Orient (third round conquerors of West Brom) but Second Division Barnsley proved a more difficult proposition.

The game had twice been postponed because of bad weather and when it finally got underway, Moran scored first for the Saints. Barnsley, though, showed typical Yorkshire grit and went through with goals from Agnew and Owen (penalty). To emphasize Saints' miserable night, they missed a spot kick.

```
Round 3
Jan 5 v Sunderland (h) 4-0
Moran 2, Curtis, Jordan
Shilton; Mills, Dennis(Lawrence), Curtis, Bond, Wright, Holmes,
Moran, Jordan, Armstrong, Wallace.
Att: 15,535
Round 4
Jan 26 v Orient (a) 2-0
Jordan, Moran
Shilton; Mills, Dennis, Curtis, Bond, Wright, Lawrence, Moran,
Jordan, Armstrong, Wallace.
Att: 17,622
Round 5
Mar 4 v Barnsley (h) 1-2
Moran
Shilton; Mills, Dennis, Curtis, Wright, Bond, Lawrence(Puckett),
Moran, Jordan, Armstrong, Wallace.
Att: 20,971
```

Saints' unbeaten League run encompassed 14 matches, their best since 1920-21.

Total home attendance: 378,802. Average: 18,038.

Milk Cup

STEVE Moran missed the opportunity to put Southampton into the Milk Cup quarter-finals when he failed with a penalty kick, five minutes from the end of the fourth round replay

against Queen's Park Rangers at Loftus Road.

The second replay, also at Rangers' ground, saw Saints go two goals down by half-time and eventually lose 4-0 to goals from Fenwick (2), Waddock and Neill.

Saints played no less than seven Milk Cup ties this season — enough to win the competition under some circumstances, but struggled to get past Wolves before Rangers took them to three games.

```
Round 2 (1st leg)
Sep 26 v Hull City (h) 3-2
Moran 2, Jordan
Shilton; Mills, Dennis, Williams, Bond, Wright(Collins), Holmes,
Curtis, Jordan, Moran, Wallace.
Att: 11,824
Round 2 (2nd leg)
Oct 9 v Hull City (a) 2-2 (agg 5-4)
Wallace, Moran
Shilton; Mills, Dennis, Williams, Wright, Bond, Holmes, Curtis,
Jordan, Moran, Wallace.
Att: 16,393
Round 3
Oct 30 v Wolverhampton Wanderers (h) 2-2
Wright, Wallace
Shilton; Mills, Dennis, Agboola(Baird), Wright, Bond, Holmes,
Curtis, Jordan, Armstrong, Wallace.
Att: 14,164
Replay
Nov 6 v Wolverhampton Wanderers (a) 2-0
Wallace, Jordan
Shilton; Mills, Dennis, Agboola, Wright, Bond, Holmes, Curtis,
Jordan, Moran(Puckett), Wallace.
Att: 13,064
Round 4
Nov 20 v Queen's Park Rangers (h) 1-1
Curtis
Shilton; Mills, Dennis, Williams, Wright, Bond, Holmes, Curtis,
Jordan, Armstrong, Wallace.
Att: 14,830
Replay
Nov 27 v Queen's Park Rangers (a) 0-0
Shilton; Mills, Dennis, Moran, Whitlock, Bond, Holmes, Curtis
(Puckett), Jordan, Armstrong, Wallace.
Att: 13,754
Second replay
Dec 5 v Queen's Park Rangers (a) 0-4
Shilton; Mills, Dennis, Moran(Puckett), Whitlock, Bond, Holmes,
Curtis, Jordan, Armstrong, Wallace.
Att: 12,702
```

1984-85

Division 1

Date	Venue	Opponent	Result	Scorers	Att.	Agboola R	Armstrong D	Baird I	Baker S	Bond K	Case J	Collins E	Curtis A	Dennis M	Golac I	Holmes N	Jordan J	Kite P	Lawrence G	Mills M	Moran S	Puckett D	Shilton P	Townsend A	Wallace D	Whitlock M	Williams S	Wright M
Aug 25	(a)	Sunderland	L 1-3	Armstrong	18,000	5	10						12	3			9			2	8		1		11	7*	4	6
28	(h)	Manchester U	D 0-0		22,183	5	10							3			9			2	8		1		11	7	4	6
Sep 1	(h)	West Ham U	L 2-3	Jordan, Armstrong	18,488	5	10						12		3*		9			2	8		1		11	7	4	6
4	(a)	Sheffield W	L 1-2	Jordan	23,784	5	10							3			9			2	8		1		11	7	4	6
8	(a)	Luton T	D 1-1	Curtis	8,657	5	10						11	3			9			2	8		1			7	4	6
15	(h)	Norwich C	W 2-1	Jordan, opp own goal	16,431	5	10*						8	3		7	9			2		12	1		11		4	6
22	(a)	Everton	D 2-2	Moran 2	22,354								8	3		7	9			2	10		1		11	5	4	6
29	(h)	Queen's Park R	D 1-1	Moran	18,497			9		6		12	8*	3		7				2	10		1		11		4	5
Oct 6	(h)	Tottenham H	W 1-0	Moran	21,827					6			8	3		7	9			2	10		1		11		4	5
13	(a)	Stoke C	W 3-1	Williams, Curtis, opp own goal	9,643					6			8	3		7	9			2	10		1		11		4	5
20	(h)	Chelsea	W 1-0	Moran	20,212			9		6			8	3		7				2	10		1		11		4	5
27	(a)	West Brom A	D 0-0		11,959	4		9	12	6			8	3		7				2	10*		1		11			5
Nov 3	(h)	Nottingham F	W 1-0	Puckett	17,818					6			8	3	4	7	9			2		10	1		11			5
10	(a)	Liverpool	D 1-1	Jordan	36,382		10			6			8	3		7	9			2			1		11		4	5
17	(a)	Aston Villa	D 2-2	Jordan 2	13,937		10		12	6			8*	3		7	9	1		2					11		4	5
24	(h)	Newcastle U	W 1-0	Armstrong	18,895		10			6			8	3		7	9			2	4		1		11			5
Dec 1	(a)	Ipswich T	W 1-0	Armstrong	14,113		10			6			8	3		7	9			2	4	12	1		11*			5
8	(h)	Arsenal	W 1-0	Curtis	20,243		10			6			8	3		7	9			2	4	11	1					5
15	(a)	Coventry C	L 1-2	Jordan	10,369	5	10			6			4	3		7	9			2	8*	12	1		11			
22	(a)	West Ham U	W 3-2	Jordan, Wallace, opp own goal	14,221		10						12	3*		7	9			2	8	4	1		11	5		6
26	(h)	Watford	L 1-2	Curtis	20,759		10						8	3		7				2	9	12	1		11	5*	4	6
29	(h)	Sheffield W	L 0-3		18,922		10						8	3		7				2	9	4	1		11	5		6
Jan 1	(a)	Leicester C	W 2-1	Armstrong, Wallace	15,257	3	10			5			4			7	9			2	8		1		11			6
12	(a)	Norwich C	L 0-1		13,735		10		12	5			4	3		7*	9			2	8		1		11			6
29	(h)	Sunderland	W 1-0	Jordan	15,326		10			5			4	3		7	9			2	8		1		11			6
Feb 2	(a)	Queen's Park R	W 4-0	Jordan, Moran, Armstrong, Wallace	10,664		10	7		5			4	3			9			2	8		1		11			6
23	(a)	Nottingham F	L 0-2		14,752		10	9	7	5			4	3*						2	8	12	1		11			6
Mar 2	(h)	West Brom A	W 4-3	Baird 2, Armstrong, Wallace	15,567		10	9		6			4	3					7	2	8		1		11			5
9	(a)	Chelsea	W 2-0	Armstrong, Wallace	15,202		10	7		6			4*	3			9			2		12	1		11	8		5
16	(h)	Stoke C	D 0-0		14,608		10	7		6		12	4	3*			9			2			1		11	8		5
23	(a)	Tottenham H	L 1-5	Wallace	33,722		10			6		12	4	3			9		7*	2			1		11	8		5
30	(h)	Everton	L 1-2	Jordan	18,754		10			6		12	4*	3			9		7	2			1		11	8		5
Apr 2	(h)	Luton T	W 1-0	Wallace	14,006		10			6			4	3		7	9		8	2*			1		11	12		5
6	(a)	Watford	D 1-1	Holmes	17,689		10			6			4	3		7			8	2	9		1		11	12		5*
9	(h)	Leicester C	W 3-1	Bond, Jordan, Lawrence	15,638		10			6			4	3		7	9		12	2	8		1		11*			5
20	(h)	Aston Villa	W 2-0	Moran, Armstrong	15,736		10			6			4			7	9		11	2	8		1	3				5
24	(a)	Manchester U	D 0-0		31,291		10			6			4	3		7	9		11	2	8		1					5
27	(a)	Newcastle U	L 1-2	Case	20,771		10			6	7		4				9		11	2	8		1	3				5
May 4	(h)	Ipswich T	W 3-0	Moran 3	16,156		10			6	7		4				9		11	2	8		1	3				5
6	(a)	Arsenal	L 0-1		21,214		10			6	7		4				9		11	2	8*	12	1	3				5
11	(h)	Coventry C	W 2-1	Moran, opp own goal	15,735		10			6	7		4	3*			9		11	2	8		1			12		5
14	(h)	Liverpool	D 1-1	Armstrong	23,001		10			6	7		12				9		11	2	8*		1	3			4	5
App						9	35	5	6	32	10	1	25	31	4	29	34	1	12	42	32	6	41	5	33	19	14	36
Sub app								3	1		2	5							1			7			3			
Goals							10	2		1	1		4			1	12		1		11	1			7		1	

4 own-goals

	P	W	D	L	F	A	Pts
Everton	42	28	6	8	88	43	90
Liverpool	42	22	11	9	68	35	77
Tottenham H	42	23	8	11	78	51	77
Manchester U	42	22	10	10	77	47	76
Southampton	42	19	11	12	56	47	68
Chelsea	42	18	12	12	63	48	66
Arsenal	42	19	9	14	61	49	66
Sheffield W	42	17	14	11	58	45	65
Nottingham F	42	19	7	16	56	48	64
Aston Villa	42	15	11	16	60	60	56
Watford	42	14	13	15	81	71	55
West Brom A	42	16	7	19	58	62	55
Luton T	42	15	9	18	57	61	54
Newcastle U	42	13	13	16	55	70	52
Leicester C	42	15	6	21	65	73	51
West Ham U	42	13	12	17	51	68	51
Ipswich T	42	13	11	18	46	57	50
Coventry C	42	15	5	22	47	64	50
Queen's Park R	42	13	11	18	53	72	50
Norwich C	42	13	10	19	46	64	49
Sunderland	42	10	10	22	40	62	40
Stoke C	42	3	8	31	24	91	17

Back row (left to right): Eamonn Collins, Dennis Rofe, Mick Mills, Joe Jordan, Ivan Golac, Alan Curtis, Mark Dennis. Middle row: Lew Chatterley (trainer), Steve Moran, Peter Shilton, Mark Whitlock, Phil Kite, David Puckett, John Mortimore (asst manager). Front row: Danny Wallace, Mark Wright, Steve Williams, Lawrie McMenemy (manager), Nick Holmes, Reuben Agboola, David Armstrong.

1985-86

BANNED from playing in European competition, along with all other League clubs, Saints suffered another blow when manager Lawrie McMenemy moved back to his native North-East to manage Sunderland, with Lew Chatterley as his assistant.

This meant that Southampton approached their centenary season without a manager and after much deliberation the board appointed former Saints defender, Chris Nicholl, who in turn chose Tony Barton, the former Portsmouth player who had managed Villa and Northampton, as his assistant.

Since leaving The Dell, Nicholl had spent two seasons coaching at Grimsby and the early months of the new season were an awkward managerial baptism which culminated in a humiliating 7-0 defeat at Luton, a game in which Nicholl's first signing, Glen Cockerill made his debut.

But Saints, prompted by Cockerill's midfield drive, began a mini-revival in the wake of that shameful defeat and slowly they eased away from the relegation zone.

The New Year arrived with relegation not entirely ruled out, although the side built by McMenemy looked too good to go down. Right-back, though, was a problem position following Mills' departure in the close season and Nicholl signed Forrest from Rotherham, although he was ineligible to play in the FA Cup.

Saints' away form in the League was dreadful, although they achieved some fine away wins in the Cup. The last few months of the season saw injuries to key players allow chances for youngsters like Blake, Tankard, Maskell, and a young goalkeeper called Granger. Granger replaced the injured Shilton and let in 11 goals in the final two games, against Everton and Spurs, but was by no means disgraced.

FA Cup

DANNY Wallace's hat-trick at Middlesbrough, was the first by a Saints player in an away FA Cup tie since Derek Reeves in 1960.

Against Wigan, Saints cantered through to the fifth round where they did well to win at Millwall after being held at home by a very intimidating team.

Cockerill and Moran, with a header which ended a personal goal famine going back to 20 December, earned Saints a somewhat unexpected win at Brighton, and a place in their second semi-final in three years.

Wallace, injured in the quarter-final, was obviously not firing on all cylinders when Saints met Liverpool and when Mark Wright broke a leg in a collison with Shilton and Johnston, it was one of the cruellest blows ever suffered by FA Cup semi-finalists.

Nevertheless, Saints were still very much in the game as it went into extra-time but when Rush netted following a rare mistake from Bond, it was all over.

> **Round 3**
> **Jan 13 v Middlesbrough (a) 3-1**
> *Wallace 3*
> Shilton; Baker, Dennis, Case, Wright, Bond, Holmes, Cockerill, Puckett, Armstrong, Wallace.
> *Att: 12,012*
> **Round 4**
> **Jan 25 v Wigan Athletic (h) 3-0**
> *Armstrong 2, Cockerill*
> Shilton; Baker, Dennis, Case, Wright, Bond, Holmes, Cockerill, Puckett, Armstrong, Wallace.
> *Att: 14,462*
> **Round 5**
> **Feb 15 v Millwall (h) 0-0**
> Shilton; Baker(Lawrence), Dennis, Case, Wright, Bond, Holmes, Cockerill, Moran, Armstrong, Wallace.
> *Att: 6,356*
> **Replay**
> **Mar 3 v Millwall (a) 1-0**
> *Wallace*
> Shilton; Baker, Holmes, Case, Wright(Townsend), Bond, Lawrence, Cockerill, Moran, Armstrong, Wallace.
> *Att: 10,625*
> **Round 6**
> **Mar 8 v Brighton & Hove Albion (a) 2-0**
> *Cockerill, Moran*
> Shilton; Baker, Holmes, Case, Wright, Bond, Lawrence, Cockerill, Moran, Armstrong, Wallace(Townsend).
> *Att: 25,069*
> **Semi-final**
> **Apr 5 v Liverpool (at White Hart Lane) 0-2**
> Shilton; Holmes, Dennis, Case, Wright(Townsend), Bond, Lawrence, Cockerill, Moran, Armstrong, Wallace.
> *Att: 44,605*

Milk Cup

YET again Southampton found their Milk Cup progress dogged by replays. Their two-legged second round match with Millwall ended all-square before Saints won on penalties, and there were two games each against Birmingham and Arsenal before teenager Martin Hayes scored his first senior goal for the Gunners and Saints were on their way out of the competition after doing the difficult bit and drawing at Highbury.

> **Round 2 (1st leg)**
> **Sep 25 v Millwall (a) 0-0**
> Shilton; Baker, Townsend, Case, Wright, Bond, Curtis, Moran, Jordan, Armstrong, Wallace.
> *Att: 7,958*
> **Round 2 (2nd leg)**
> **Oct 7 v Millwall (h) 0-0 (agg 0-0; Saints won on penalties)**
> Shilton; Baker, Dennis, Case, Wright, Bond, Lawrence, Moran, Jordan, Armstrong, Curtis(Puckett).
> *Att: 9,480*
> **Round 3**
> **Oct 29 v Birmingham City (a) 1-1**
> *Puckett*
> Shilton; Baker, Dennis, Case, Wright, Bond, Wallace, Holmes, Puckett, Armstrong, Curtis.
> *Att: 4,832*
> **Replay**
> **Nov 6 v Birmingham City (h) 3-0**
> *Armstrong 2, Wallace*
> Shilton; Dennis, Baker, Case, Wright, Bond, Holmes, Curtis(Moran), Puckett, Armstrong, Wallace.
> *Att: 9,085*
> **Round 4**
> **Nov 19 v Arsenal (a) 0-0**
> Shilton; Baker, Townsend, Case, Wright, Whitlock, Curtis, Collins, Puckett, Armstrong, Wallace.
> *Att: 18,244*
> **Replay**
> **Nov 26 v Arsenal (h) 1-3**
> *Armstrong*
> Shilton; Baker, Townsend, Case, Wright, Whitlock, Holmes, Moran, Puckett, Armstrong, Wallace.
> *Att: 14,010*

> *Total home attendance: 315,724. Average: 15,034.*

> *Tony Barton, Saints newly-appointed assistant manager, was the first League substitute to appear at The Dell when he came on for Portsmouth in August 1960.*

1985-86
Division 1

Date		Opponent	Result	Scorers	Att	Armstrong D	Baker S	Blake M	Bond K	Case J	Cockerill G	Curtis A	Dennis M	Forrest G	Gittens J	Golac I	Granger K	Holmes N	Jordan J	Kite P	Lawrence G	McManus S	Maskell C	Moran S	Puckett D	Shilton P	Tankard A	Townsend A	Wallace D	Whitlock M	Wright M
Aug 17	(h)	Newcastle U	D 1-1	Puckett	16,401	10			6	4						2		7		12				8*	9	1		3	11		5
20	(a)	Arsenal	L 2-3	Armstrong 2	21,623	10			6	4	12					2		7			8				9*	1		3	11		5
24	(a)	Nottingham F	L 1-2	Armstrong	12,643	10			6	4	9					2		7*			8				12	1		3	11		5
27	(a)	Aston Villa	D 0-0		14,220	10*			6	4	9		3			2								12	8	1			11	7	5
31	(a)	Ipswich T	D 1-1	Armstrong	11,588	10			6	4	9		3			2								8		1		7	11		5
Sep 3	(h)	West Ham U	D 1-1	Curtis	14,477	10			6	4	8		3			2			9*		12					1		7	11		5
7	(h)	Manchester C	W 3-0	Case, Lawrence, opp own goal	14,308	10			6	4	8		3			2			9*		12					1		7	11		5
14	(a)	Chelsea	L 0-2		16,711	10	3		6		8					2			9		12	4*				1		7	11		5
21	(h)	Coventry C	D 1-1	Armstrong	12,674	10			6	4			3				2*		9		12			8		1		7	11		5
28	(a)	Manchester U	L 0-1		52,449	3	2		6	4					10*				9		12			8		1		7	11		5
Oct 5	(h)	Watford	W 3-1	Moran 3	14,172	10	2		6	4		11	3						9		12			8		1		7*			5
12	(a)	Liverpool	L 0-1		32,113		2		6	4		11	3						9*		7			8	10	1				12	5
19	(a)	Luton T	L 0-7		8,896	10	2		6	4	9		3								7			8		1			11		5
26	(h)	Queen's Park R	W 3-0	Wallace 2, Cockerill	15,615	10	2		6	4	8		3											9		1			11	7	5
Nov 2	(h)	Tottenham H	W 1-0	Puckett	17,740	10	2		6	4	8		3					7							9	1			11		5
9	(a)	Leicester C	D 2-2	Puckett, Armstrong	8,080	10	2			4	8		3					7							9	1			11	6	5
16	(h)	Birmingham C	W 1-0	Wallace	13,167	10	2			4	8		3					7*			12			9		1			11	6	5
23	(a)	Sheffield W	L 1-2	Wright	18,955	10	2		6	4	8										12			9		1		3*	11	7	5
30	(h)	Everton	L 2-3	Cockerill, Moran	16,917	10	2		6	4	8		3											9		1			11	7	5
Dec 7	(h)	Arsenal	W 3-0	Bond, Armstrong, Moran	15,052	10			6	4	8		3	2				7						9		1			11		5
14	(a)	Newcastle U	L 1-2	Moran	19,229	10			6	4	8		3	2				7						9		1			11		5
20	(h)	Nottingham F	W 3-1	Moran 2, Armstrong	12,500	10			6	4	8			2				7						9		1		3	11		5
26	(a)	Oxford U	L 0-3		11,266	10			6	4*	8			2				7			12			9		1		3	11		5
Jan 1	(h)	West Brom A	W 3-1	Cockerill, Armstrong, Wallace	13,154	10			6		8		3	2				7						9		1		4	11		5
11	(a)	Manchester C	L 0-1		21,674	10			6		8		3	2				7						9		1		4	11		5
18	(h)	Ipswich T	W 1-0	Wallace	13,164	10			6	4	8		3	2				7						9		1			11		5
Feb 1	(a)	Aston Villa	D 0-0		8,456	10			6	4	8		3	2				7						9		1			11		5
8	(h)	Luton T	L 1-2	Armstrong	13,740	10			6	4	8		3	2				7						9		1			11		5
22	(a)	Coventry C	L 2-3	Wright, Cockerill	10,881	10			6	4	8			2				3			7			9		1			11		5
Mar 1	(h)	Manchester C	W 1-0	Cockerill	19,012	10			6	4	8			2				3			7			9		1			11		5
11	(a)	Queen's Park R	W 2-0	Cockerill, McManus	14,521	10			6	4	8			2				3			7*	11		9		1		12			5
15	(h)	Liverpool	L 1-2	Lawrence	19,784	10			6		8		3	2				4			7	11*		9		1		12			5
22	(h)	Chelsea	L 0-1		15,509	10			6		8		3	2				4	9		7*	11				1		12			5
29	(a)	West Brom A	L 0-1		7,324	10			6	4	8			2				3*	9		7	12				1			11		5
Apr 1	(h)	Oxford U	D 1-1	Wright	15,350	10	2		6	4	8		3					7	9						11	1					5
8	(a)	West Ham U	L 0-1		22,531	10			6	4	8		3	2				7	9				11*			1		5	12		
12	(a)	Leicester C	D 0-0		13,403	10				4	8		3	2		5*			9		12					1		7	11		6
19	(a)	Birmingham C	W 2-0	Cockerill, Wallace	5,833	10				4	8		3*	2		5							12	9		1		7	11		6
26	(h)	Sheffield W	L 2-3	Case, Wallace	15,365	10				4	8			2		5								9		1	3	7	11		6
29	(a)	Watford	D 1-1	Townsend	11,868	10				4	8			2		5								9		1	3	7	11		6
May 3	(a)	Everton	L 1-6	Puckett	33,057	10				4	8			2		5*	1							9	12		3	7	11		6
5	(a)	Tottenham H	L 3-5	Wallace, Maskell, opp own goal	13,036	3	2	5		4	8			7			1						12	9				10	11*		6
App						41	13	1	34	36	30	10	24	22	4	9	2	26	12	3	12	2		24	13	37	3	25	34	12	33
Sub app												1									9		2	4	2			2	1	2	
Goals						10			1	2	7	1									2	1	1	8	4			1	8		3

2 own-goals

Back row (left to right): Stuart McManus, Mark Whitlock, Jimmy Case, Andy Townsend, Kevin Bond, Alan Curtis, Kevin Brown. Middle row: Dennis Rofe (reserve-team coach), Dave Merrington (youth coach), Joe Jordan, Peter Shilton, George Lawrence, Phil Kite, Mark Dennis, Don Taylor (physiotherapist), George Horsfall (first-team coach). Front row: Danny Wallace, Steve Moran, Eammon Collins, Mark Wright, Chris Nicholl (manager), Nick Holmes, David Armstrong, David Puckett, Steve Baker.

	P	W	D	L	F	A	Pts
Liverpool	42	26	10	6	89	37	88
Everton	42	26	8	8	87	41	86
West Ham U	42	26	6	10	74	40	84
Manchester U	42	22	10	10	70	36	76
Sheffield W	42	21	10	11	63	54	73
Chelsea	42	20	11	11	57	56	71
Arsenal	42	20	9	13	49	47	69
Nottingham F	42	19	11	12	69	53	68
Luton T	42	18	12	12	61	44	66
Tottenham H	42	19	8	15	74	52	65
Newcastle U	42	17	12	13	67	72	63
Watford	42	16	11	15	69	62	59
Queen's Park R	42	15	7	20	53	64	52
Southampton	42	12	10	20	51	62	46
Manchester C	42	11	12	19	43	57	45
Aston Villa	42	10	14	18	51	67	44
Coventry C	42	11	10	21	48	71	43
Oxford U	42	10	12	20	62	80	42
Leicester C	42	10	12	20	54	76	42
Ipswich T	42	11	8	23	32	55	41
Birmingham C	42	8	5	29	30	73	29
West Brom A	42	4	12	26	35	89	24

1986-87

CHRIS Nicholl had watched Bournemouth's Northern Ireland international striker Colin Clarke several times during 1985-6 and, after Clarke's impressive showing in the World Cup Finals in Mexico, Nicholl paid a fee of £400,000 to bring the player to The Dell. Clarke wasted no time in justifying his price tag — in the opening game of the season he scored a hat-trick as QPR were beaten 5-1.

Despite this heartening start, Saints were soon displaying many of the previous season's shortcomings — notably in away games — and it was mainly thanks to Clarke's consistent goalscoring that the team kept clear of the relegation zone. Many fans had expected Steve Moran to be Clarke's partner up front but he was surprisingly sold to Leicester for £300,000 before he had the chance.

During the autumn Saints suffered several injuries to key players. Holmes, Wallace, Armstrong and new goalkeeper Tim Flowers joined broken-leg victims Mark Wright and Andy Townsend on the sidelines. In particular, the injuries to Armstrong, Holmes and Townsend, all being left-sided players, unbalanced the team. The centre of defence was also a problem where Bond, Blake and Gittens all took turns in partnering Wright who had encouragingly made a complete

recovery from his broken leg.

Sadly, Southampton Football Club seemed to make as many headlines off the field. In December, Dennis and Shilton's names were both coupled with some unhappy newspaper articles and domestic incidents. Mark Wright asked for a transfer and the media was full of stories of players' unrest at The Dell. Results on the pitch confirmed that all was not well and home defeats by Chelsea and Norwich sent Saints sliding down the table.

Amongst all the turmoil Gordon Hobson arrived from Grimsby to play alongside Clarke who almost immediately suffered a thigh injury which saw him miss most of the last third of the season. George Lawrence proved an able deputy for the Irishman whilst Hobson helped Saints score important victories over fellow strugglers Aston Villa and Manchester City.

These results came against a background of continued dressing-room unrest between Nicholl and Dennis which resulted in the player being sensationally dismissed. It was a controversial move and some fans called for the resignation of the manager instead.

FA Cup

Drawn away to Everton in the FA Cup third round, Saints could hardly have fancied their chances, especially since they had recently hit a bad patch whilst Everton were looking for a fourth consecutive appearance at Wembley.

Round 3
Jan 10 v Everton (a) 1-2
Hobson
Shilton; Forrest, Dennis, Bond, Wright, Gittens, Hobson, Cockerill, Clarke, Holmes, Wallace(Le Tissier).
Att: 32,320

Littlewoods Challenge Cup

DESPITE their poor League form, Southampton progressed to the semi-final of the newly-named Littlewoods Challenge Cup before falling to Liverpool at Anfield.

Had Wallace accepted a simple chance at Old Trafford in the third round there would have been no need for a replay. The game at The Dell was notable for substitute Le Tissier's two second-half goals which helped dump United 4-1. The following day Ron Atkinson lost his job at Old Trafford — defeat by Saints had been seen as the final humiliation for an unhappy United team.

Three players — Dennis (Southampton) and Keown and Williams (Aston Villa) — were sent off in a stormy fourth-round match at The Dell which Saints won through goals from Case and Clarke. Second Division strugglers Shrewsbury gave Saints a scare before Clarke's penalty put them into the semi-final.

Liverpool barred Saints' way and even after Paul Walsh had been sent off for clattering Bond soon after the start of the second half, Southampton could make no headway.

At Anfield Saints defended manfully for 70 minutes before caving in to allow Liverpool three late goals. For the second successive season Saints had been denied a Wembley Final by the Merseysiders.

Round 2 (1st leg)
Sep 23 v Swindon Town (h) 3-0
Lawrence 2, Jordan
Shilton; Forrest, Dennis, Case, Gittens, Bond, Lawrence, Cockerill, Clarke, D.Armstrong, Jordan.
Att: 10,458

Round 2 (2nd leg)
Oct 8 v Swindon Town (a) 0-0 (agg 3-0)
Shilton; Forrest, Dennis, Case, Wright, Gittens, Lawrence, Cockerill, Clarke, Baker, Wallace(Le Tissier).
Att: 9,453

Round 3
Oct 29 v Manchester United (a) 0-0
Shilton; Forrest, Dennis, Case, Wright, Gittens, Lawrence, Cockerill, Clarke, Baker, Wallace.
Att: 23,639

Replay
Nov 4 v Manchester United (h) 4-1
Lawrence, Wallace, Le Tissier 2
Shilton; Forrest, Dennis, Case, Wright, Gittens, Lawrence, Cockerill, Clarke, Baker, Wallace(Le Tissier).
Att: 17,915

Round 4
Nov 18 v Aston Villa (h) 2-1
Case, Clarke
Shilton; Forrest, Dennis, Case, Wright, Bond, Lawrence, Cockerill, Clarke, Baker, Wallace.
Att: 13,402

Round 5
Jan 26 v Shrewsbury Town (h) 1-0
Clarke
Shilton; Baker, Holmes, Case, Wright, Bond, Townsend(Le Tissier), Cockerill, Clarke, Armstrong, Wallace.
Att: 12,940

Semi-final (1st leg)
Feb 11 v Liverpool (h) 0-0
Shilton; Forrest, Dennis, Case, Wright, Bond, Holmes(Lawrence), Cockerill, Clarke, Armstrong(Townsend), Wallace.
Att: 22,818

Semi-final (2nd leg)
Feb 25 v Liverpool (a) 0-3 (agg 0-3)
Shilton; Forrest, Armstrong(Baker), Case, Wright, Bond, Wallace, Cockerill, Clarke, Townsend(Le Tissier), Lawrence.
Att: 38,481

Total home attendance: 313,914. Average: 14,948.

1986-87
Division 1

Date		Opponent	Res	Score	Scorers	Att	Armstrong D	Baker S	Blake M	Bond K	Case J	Clarke C	Cockerill G	Dennis M	Flowers T	Forrest G	Gittens J	Hobson G	Holmes N	Jordan J	Lawrence G	Le Tissier M	Maskell C	Nixon E	Shilton P	Tankard A	Townsend A	Wallace D	Wright M
Aug 23	(h)	Queen's Park R	W	5-1	Clarke 3, Holmes, Wallace	14,711			5	6	4	9	8	3		2			10		7				1			11	
26	(a)	Luton T	L	1-2	Clarke	8,777		12	5	6	4	9	8	3		2			10*		7				1			11	
30	(a)	Norwich C	L	3-4	Wallace, Blake, Dennis	15,250			5	6	4	9	8	3		2			10		7*	12			1			11	
Sep 2	(h)	Tottenham H	W	2-0	Wallace, Clarke	17,911			5	6	4	9	8	3		2			10*		7	12			1			11	
6	(h)	Nottingham F	L	1-3	Clarke	14,604		12	5	6	4	9	8	3		2*					7		10		1			11	
13	(a)	Manchester U	L	1-5	Clarke	40,135	7		5	6	4	9	8	3	1	2						12	10*					11	
20	(h)	Liverpool	W	2-1	Armstrong, Cockerill	20,452	10	12		6	4	9	8	3		2		5			7				1			11*	
27	(a)	Wimbledon	D	2-2	Lawrence, Cockerill	7,147	10	12		6	4	9	8	3		2*		5		11	7				1				
Oct 4	(h)	Newcastle U	W	4-1	Clarke 3, Dennis	14,622	10				4	9	8	3		2		6		11*	7	12			1				
11	(a)	Aston Villa	L	1-3	Wallace	16,211		10		6	4	9	8	3		2					7				1			11	5
18	(h)	Everton	L	0-2		18,009	10			6	4	9	8	3		2					7*	12			1			11	5
25	(a)	Leicester C	W	3-2	Lawrence, Clarke, Wallace	9,186		10			4	9	8	3		2		6			7				1			11	5
Nov 1	(h)	Manchester C	D	1-1	Clarke	14,352		10			4	9	8	3		2		6			7*	12			1			11	5
8	(a)	Sheffield W	L	1-3	Le Tissier	20,802	3	10*			4	9	8			2		6			7	12			1			11	5
15	(h)	Arsenal	L	0-4		18,728	3	10			4	9	8		1*	2		6			7	12						11	5
22	(a)	Charlton A	W	3-1	Clarke, Lawrence, Case	5,930		10			4	9	8	3		2					7				1			11	5
29	(h)	Watford	W	3-1	Clarke, Wright, Hobson	14,537				6	4	9	8	3		2		10			7*	12			1			11	5
Dec 6	(a)	West Ham U	L	1-3	Clarke	18,111			5	6	4	9	8			2		10			7				1	3		11	
20	(a)	Nottingham F	D	0-0		15,394		10		6	4	9	8	3		2					7				1			11	5
26	(h)	Chelsea	L	1-2	Clarke	12,709		10		6*	4	9	8	3		2					7	12		1				11	5
27	(a)	Arsenal	L	0-1		38,138		10	3		4	9*	8			2		6			7	12		1				11	5
Jan 1	(a)	Oxford U	L	1-3	Case	9,777		10			4	9	8			2		6			7			1		3		11	5
3	(h)	Manchester U	D	1-1	Holmes	20,409		4*				9	8	3		2		6	10		7	12		1				11	5
24	(a)	Queen's Park R	L	1-2	Case	10,200		2		6	4	9	8					7		10	3*	12			1		11		5
Feb 3	(h)	Coventry C	W	2-0	Cockerill 2	11,508	10			6	4	9	8*	3		2		11			7				1		12		5
7	(h)	Norwich C	L	1-2	Cockerill	12,754	10			6	4	9	8	3	1	2		11			7*						12		5
14	(a)	Tottenham H	L	0-2		22,066	3			6	4		8			2		11		12	9				1	10*	7		5
28	(a)	Liverpool	L	0-1		33,133	3			6			8			2		10			9	7			1	4		11	5
Mar 7	(h)	Leicester C	W	4-0	Le Tissier 3, Hobson	11,611	3			6	4		8			2		10			9	7			1			11	5
14	(a)	Everton	L	0-3		26,564	3			6	4		8			2		10			9	7			1			11	5
21	(h)	Aston Villa	W	5-0	Clarke 2, Hobson, Wallace, Cockerill	13,686	3	12		6	4	9*	8			2		10			7				1			11	5
24	(h)	Luton T	W	3-0	Lawrence 2, Townsend	12,117	3			6	4		8			2					9	7			1		10	11	5
28	(a)	Newcastle U	L	0-2		22,717	3	12		6	4		8			2					9	7*			1		10	11	5
Apr 7	(h)	Wimbledon	D	2-2	Lawrence, opp own goal	12,811	3			6	4		8			2*		10			9	7			1		12	11	5
11	(a)	Manchester C	W	4-2	Hobson 3, Wallace	18,193	3	2		6	4		8					10			9				1		7	11	5
18	(h)	Oxford U	W	3-0	Hobson, Wallace, Cockerill	15,025	3	2		6	4		8		1		5	10			9						7	11	
20	(a)	Chelsea	D	1-1	Clarke	11,512	3	2		6	4	9	8		1		12	5			10						7	11*	
22	(h)	Sheffield W	D	1-1	Le Tissier	13,014	3	2*		6	4	9	8		1		5	10			7	12						11	
25	(h)	Charlton A	D	2-2	Bond, Lawrence	13,534	3			6	4	9	8		1	2		10			7	12					11*		5
May 2	(a)	Watford	D	1-1	Le Tissier	13,067	3			6	4	9	8		1	2		10				7					11		5
4	(h)	West Ham U	W	1-0	Clarke	16,810	3			6	4	9	8		1	2		10			7*	11	12						5
9	(a)	Coventry C	D	1-1	Lawrence	22,619	3	12		6	4*	9	8			2		10			7				1		11		5
App							22	19	8	34	39	33	42	20	9	37	14	20	8	2	34	12	2	4	29	2	11	31	30
Sub app								7												1	2	12	2				3		
Goals							1		1	1	3	20	7	2				7	2		8	6					1	8	1

1 own-goal

Back row (left to right): Steve Baker, Gerry Forrest, Ian Hamilton, Phillip Parkinson, Mark Blake, Colin Clarke, Jon Gittens, Craig Maskell, Kevan Brown. Middle row: Don Taylor (physiotherapist), Dennis Rofe (reserve-team trainer), Joe Jordan, George Lawrence, Tim Flowers, Peter Shilton, Glenn Cockerill, Andy Townsend, George Horsfall (first-team trainer), Dave Merrington (youth-team trainer). Front row: Tony Barton (asst manager), Steve Moran, Danny Wallace, Mark Wright, David Armstrong, Nick Holmes, Jimmy Case, Kevin Bond, Chris Nicholl (manager).

	P	W	D	L	F	A	Pts
Everton	42	26	8	8	76	31	86
Liverpool	42	23	8	11	72	42	77
Tottenham H	42	21	8	13	68	43	71
Arsenal	42	20	10	12	58	35	70
Norwich C	42	17	17	8	53	51	68
Wimbledon	42	19	9	14	57	50	66
Luton T	42	18	12	12	47	45	66
Nottingham F	42	18	11	13	64	51	65
Watford	42	18	9	15	67	54	63
Coventry C	42	17	12	13	50	45	63
Manchester U	42	14	14	14	52	45	56
Southampton	42	14	10	18	69	68	52
Sheffield W	42	13	13	16	58	59	52
Chelsea	42	13	13	16	53	64	52
West Ham U	42	14	10	18	52	67	52
Queen's Park R	42	13	11	18	48	64	50
Newcastle U	42	12	11	19	47	65	47
Oxford U	42	11	13	18	44	69	46
Charlton A	42	11	11	20	45	55	44
Leicester C	42	11	9	22	54	76	42
Manchester C	42	8	15	19	36	57	39
Aston Villa	42	8	12	22	45	79	36

Colin Clarke scores the second goal of his hat-trick on his Saints' debut against Queen's Park Rangers at The Dell in August 1986.

More action from the game against Queen's Park Rangers at the beginning of 1986-7.

Southampton's defensive wall against Newcastle at The Dell. Left to right: Forrest, Armstrong, Cockerill, Lawrence, Case, Clarke, Dennis and Gittens.

Gordon Hobson scores in the 4-0 home win over Leicester City in March 1987.

SOUTHAMPTON HONOURS
All major and minor competitions

Football League Division One
Runners-up 1983-84
Division Two
Runners-up 1965-66, 1977-78
Division Three Champions
1959-60
Runners-up 1920-21
Division Three (South) Champions
1921-22
FA Cup Winners
1975-76
Runners-up 1899-00, 1901-02
Football League Cup
Runners-up 1978-79
Southern League Champions
1896-97, 1897-98, 1898-99, 1900-01, 1902-03, 1903-04
Western League Section A winners
1907-08
Championship runners-up 1907-08
League runners-up 1903-04, 1905-06
United League
Runners-up 1898-99
South Western Combination
Runners-up 1915-16
Southern Charity Cup Winners
1907-08
Runners-up 1906-07, 1913-14
Hampshire Junior Cup Winners
1887-88, 1888-89, 1889-90
Hampshire Senior Cup Winners
1890-91, 1891-92, 1894-95
Runners-up 1892-93, 1893-94
Hampshire Cricket Club Charity Cup Winners
1890-91, 1893-94

Portsmouth & District Cup
Runners-up 1893-94
Hampshire Benevolent Cup Winners
1908-09, 1911-12, 1919-20, 1921-22, 1922-23(joint), 1924-25(joint),
1926-27, 1928-29, 1929-30(joint), 1931-32(joint)
Rowland Hospital Charity Cup Winners
1922-23, 1928-29, 1930-31(joint)
Hampshire Combination Cup Winners
1943-44
Texaco Cup
Runners-up 1974-75
Tennent-Caledonian Cup Winners
1976-77
Charles Guinier Cup (St Malo) Winners
1933-34
Rotterdam Tournament Winners
1980-81
Aberdeen Tournament
Runners-up 1981-82
Celta Vigo Tournament Winners
1983-84
Port Cup Winners
1980-81 v Hamburg
Patrick Cup Winners
1980-81 v Swansea City
Wooldridge Cup Sixes Tournament Winners
1888-89, 1889-90, 1892-93, 1893-94
Runners-up 1887-88, 1891-92
Daily Express Fives Tournament Winners
1971, 1983
Runners-up 1981
Norfolk & Norwich Charity Cup Winners
1959-60(joint)

Southampton players celebrate winning the FA Cup in 1976, the highest peak the club has achieved.

SAINTS AGAINST OTHER LEAGUE CLUBS
1920-1987

Southampton have played 91 clubs in the Football League since 1920. Below is the Saints' record against each club. Some clubs changed their names (eg Small Heath became Birmingham then Birmingham City) and some clubs modified their titles (eg Bournemouth & Boscombe Athletic became AFC Bournemouth). In all cases the last name used by each club covers all games under previous names.

	P	W	D	L	F	A	last home defeat	last away win	last League meeting
Aberdare	2	2	0	0	2	0	NEVER	1921-22	1921-22
Accrington	4	2	0	2	10	4	NEVER	NEVER	1959-60
Aldershot	10	4	2	4	18	12	NEVER	1957-58	1957-58
Arsenal	34	9	15	10	37	43	1986-87	1967-68	1986-87
Aston Villa	26	7	10	9	30	36	1981-82	1966-67	1986-87
Barnsley	44	16	18	10	72	65	1952-53	1952-53	1959-60
Birmingham City	28	13	8	7	33	27	1982-83	1985-86	1985-86
Blackburn Rovers	22	10	8	4	34	30	1938-39	1951-52	1977-78
Blackpool	36	16	15	5	69	68	1966-67	1977-78	1977-78
Bolton Wanderers	20	5	11	4	23	37	1976-77	1965-66	1979-80
AFC Bournemouth	14	7	4	3	30	20	NEVER	1959-60	1959-60
Bradford	30	10	13	7	50	51	1947-48	1947-48	1949-50
Bradford City	30	13	10	7	53	38	1958-59	1958-59	1959-60
Brentford	32	12	11	9	44	51	1958-59	1954-55	1959-60
Brighton & Hove A	28	14	6	8	44	27	1955-56	1982-83	1982-83
Bristol City	26	13	8	5	42	33	1974-75	1979-80	1979-80
Bristol Rovers	16	10	4	2	28	16	1961-62	1976-77	1977-78
Burnley	34	13	13	8	49	46	1946-47	1970-71	1977-78
Bury	52	21	21	10	81	75	1963-64	1965-66	1965-66
Cardiff City	28	10	9	9	50	50	1962-63	1965-66	1977-78
Carlisle United	6	2	3	1	9	5	1976-77	1976-77	1976-77
Charlton Athletic	32	17	12	3	71	53	1961-62	1986-87	1986-87
Chelsea	42	12	18	12	60	66	1986-87	1984-85	1986-87
Chesterfield	24	8	10	6	29	43	1937-38	1950-51	1959-60
Colchester United	14	9	4	1	32	22	1954-55	1958-59	1959-60
Coventry City	72	24	29	19	112	111	1979-80	1949-50	1986-87
Crystal Palace	32	19	8	5	60	34	1964-65	1977-78	1980-81
Darlington	4	3	1	0	10	6	NEVER	1926-27	1926-27
Derby County	34	11	12	11	62	58	1978-79	1965-66	1979-80
Doncaster Rovers	14	6	3	5	20	13	NEVER	1951-52	1958-59
Everton	40	14	19	7	50	72	1986-87	1973-74	1986-87
Exeter City	14	8	3	3	31	11	NEVER	1956-57	1957-58
Fulham	46	20	13	13	77	55	1935-36	1947-48	1977-78
Gillingham	12	5	4	3	17	11	1956-57	1955-56	1957-58
Grimsby Town	24	9	8	7	48	35	1949-50	1948-49	1963-64
Halifax Town	4	2	2	0	9	7	NEVER	NEVER	1959-60
Hereford United	2	1	1	0	1	2	NEVER	NEVER	1976-77
Huddersfield Town	18	7	9	2	26	33	1971-72	1971-72	1971-72
Hull City	40	14	11	15	59	50	1950-51	1977-78	1977-78
Ipswich Town	40	11	16	13	53	69	1982-83	1984-85	1985-86
Leeds United	52	14	27	11	62	93	1979-80	1981-82	1981-82
Leicester City	46	19	10	17	74	60	1967-68	1986-87	1986-87
Lincoln City	8	4	2	2	16	8	1960-61	1960-61	1960-61
Liverpool	38	12	19	7	39	51	1985-86	1981-82	1986-87
Luton Town	44	17	14	13	73	78	1985-86	1977-78	1986-87
Manchester City	46	17	14	15	65	62	1973-74	1986-87	1986-87
Manchester United	54	16	22	16	60	79	1982-83	1969-70	1986-87
Mansfield Town	6	5	1	0	19	10	NEVER	1977-78	1977-78
Middlesbrough	28	13	8	7	41	39	1964-65	1981-82	1981-82
Millwall	38	17	16	6	62	55	1977-78	1957-58	1977-78
Merthyr Town	4	2	0	2	8	2	NEVER	1921-22	1921-22
Nelson	2	1	0	1	3	0	NEVER	NEVER	1923-24
Newcastle United	44	14	20	10	53	66	1971-72	1973-74	1986-87
Newport County	20	12	3	5	44	22	NEVER	1956-57	1959-60
Northampton Town	18	9	7	2	35	23	1955-56	1957-58	1964-65
Norwich City	60	23	21	16	99	95	1986-87	1965-66	1986-87
Notts County	40	24	7	9	80	51	1983-84	1983-84	1983-84
Nottingham Forest	74	29	31	14	111	110	1986-87	1983-84	1986-87
Oldham Athletic	32	12	11	9	48	42	1932-33	1934-35	1977-78
Orient	38	15	14	9	57	45	1961-62	1976-77	1977-78
Oxford United	8	5	2	1	15	10	NEVER	1975-76	1986-87
Plymouth Argyle	54	18	21	15	74	83	1963-64	1965-66	1976-77
Portsmouth	24	12	5	7	45	29	1963-64	1975-76	1975-76
Port Vale	30	8	13	9	36	48	1957-58	1935-36	1959-60
Preston North End	32	11	11	10	48	55	1963-64	1949-50	1965-66
Queen's Park Rangers	40	16	9	15	69	48	1956-57	1985-86	1986-87
Reading	28	11	7	10	44	36	1957-58	1956-57	1959-60
Rochdale	2	1	1	0	6	2	NEVER	NEVER	1958-59
Rotherham United	18	9	6	3	39	29	1952-53	1964-65	1965-66
Scunthorpe United	8	4	3	1	22	19	NEVER	1963-64	1963-64
Sheffield United	34	9	16	9	51	71	1966-67	1950-51	1977-78
Sheffield Wednesday	36	12	16	8	59	55	1985-86	1947-48	1986-87
Shrewsbury Town	10	4	3	3	19	15	NEVER	1957-58	1957-58
Southend United	18	7	6	5	35	24	1956-57	1959-60	1959-60
South Shields	12	3	5	4	16	18	1927-28	1926-27	1927-28
Stockport County	12	7	2	3	18	14	NEVER	1925-26	1958-59
Stoke City	52	22	22	8	78	78	1980-81	1981-82	1983-84
Sunderland	32	15	10	7	46	44	1962-63	1983-84	1984-85
Swansea City	56	27	17	12	100	81	1952-53	1961-62	1982-83
Swindon Town	22	12	6	4	43	26	1957-58	1963-64	1964-65
Torquay United	10	3	2	5	19	15	NEVER	NEVER	1957-58
Tottenham Hotspur	62	18	25	19	76	115	1982-83	1972-73	1986-87
Tranmere Rovers	6	2	2	2	11	10	1958-59	1959-60	1959-60
Walsall	14	7	1	6	24	10	NEVER	1961-62	1962-63
Watford	24	10	9	5	37	30	1984-85	NEVER	1986-87
West Bromwich A	50	18	18	14	65	63	1969-70	1983-84	1985-86
West Ham United	58	16	23	19	80	99	1984-85	1984-85	1986-87
Wimbledon	2	0	2	0	4	4	NEVER	NEVER	1986-87
Wolverhampton W	46	19	16	11	76	69	1979-80	1983-84	1983-84
Wrexham	4	2	2	0	8	5	1958-59	1958-59	1959-60
York City	6	3	1	2	11	1	NEVER	NEVER	1975-76

Saints in Europe

SOUTHAMPTON have qualified for European competition seven times since they were first promoted to Division One in 1966. Their first taste of life in European soccer came after they had finished seventh in Division One in 1968-69 and benefitted from the rule that only one club per city could qualify.

Arsenal, Spurs and Chelsea all finished higher than Southampton but only Arsenal could qualify as London's representative. During the close season, Spurs and Chelsea appealed and Saints had to wait for two anxious weeks before knowing for certain that they would be hosting European football for the first time.

Since then, Saints fans have seen some ups and downs in Europe. One highlight was the comprehensive defeat of Marseilles, 4-0 in the European Cup-winners' Cup in 1976-7 at The Dell. Malcolm Waldron opened the scoring after half an hour, and three minutes later Channon headed home Steele's free-kick.

After only another two minutes Williams, who was enjoying a particularly impressive European debut, centred for Osgood to head Saints' third. Channon got the fourth with a 70th-minute penalty and goalkeeper Turner had also played his part, saving a first-half penalty.

The return leg was a violent affair and when Peach's 67-minute goal cancelled out an earlier Marseilles effort, the Frenchmen lost their composure and kicked almost everything in sight. It was one of the most appalling spectacles ever witnessed in a game involving Southampton. Marseilles scored a second in the 80th minute and seven minutes later, Fisher was sent off.

After disposing of the Irish club, Carrick Rangers, in the next round, Saints came up against the crack Belgian side, Anderlecht, and a glut of good football made up for the Marseilles nightmare.

In Belgium, Saints were unlucky to lose 2-0 and Channon appeared to have scored a legitimate goal that was ruled offside. At The Dell, Peach made it 2-1 on aggregate from the penalty spot, and in the 77th minute Ted MacDougall, playing in his first European tie, levelled the scores after Channon deflected the ball to him. Saints looked to have saved the game but Steele failed to clear a loose ball and Van Der Elst nipped in for the winner.

In the Fairs Cup (later the UEFA Cup) Saints have twice been eliminated on the away-goals rule, in 1970 by Newcastle, and in 1982 by Norköpping. The Newcastle defeat was a particular blow because it came at The Dell after Saints had played well to earn a goalless draw at St James' Park.

A first-half header by Channon put Saints ahead and Ron Davies might have put the result beyond doubt in the 80th minute but instead crashed a header against the bar after apparently being blinded in the glare of the floodlights. Then 'Pop' Robson levelled the scores with six minutes left and Newcastle went through.

Southampton qualified for the 1985-6 UEFA Cup but all Football League clubs were banned because of the tragedy at the previous season's European Cup Final.

1969-70
European Fairs Cup

Round 1 (1st leg)
Sep 17 v Rosenborg (a) 0-1
Martin; Jones, Hollywood, Fisher, Gabriel, Byrne, Paine, Channon, Davies(Saul), Walker, Stokes.
Att: 20,330

Round 1 (2nd leg)
Oct 1 v Rosenborg (h) 2-0 (agg 2-1)
Davies, Paine
Martin; Kirkup, Hollywood, Kemp, McGrath, Gabriel, Paine, Stokes, Davies(Fisher), Byrne, Sydenham.
Att: 22,329

Round 2 (1st leg)
Nov 4 v Vitoria Guimaraes (a) 3-3
Paine, Channon, Davies
Martin; Kirkup, Byrne, Fisher(Hollywood), McGrath, Gabriel, Paine, Channon(Saul), Davies, Walker, Sydenham.
Att: 10,000

Round 2 (2nd leg)
Nov 12 v Vitoria Guimaraes (h) 5-1 (agg 8-4)
Davies 2, Channon, Gabriel, opp.og
Martin; Kirkup, Byrne, Fisher, McGrath, Gabriel, Paine, Channon, Davies, Walker, Sydenham.
Att: 21,414

Round 3 (1st leg)
Dec 17 v Newcastle United (a) 0-0
Martin; Kirkup, Byrne, Fisher, McGrath(Stokes), Gabriel, Paine, Channon, Davies, Walker, Jenkins.
Att: 37,800

Round 3 (2nd leg) 1-1 (agg 1-1; Newcastle won on away-goals rule).
Channon
Martin; Kirkup, Byrne, Fisher, Gabriel, Walker, Jenkins, Channon, Davies, Paine, Sydenham(Stokes).
Att: 25,182

ROSENBORG
SOUTHAMPTON

«EUROPEAN FAIRS CUP»
Pris kr. 1,—

1971-72
UEFA Cup

Round 1 (1st leg)
Sep 15 v Athletic Bilbao (h) 2-1
Channon, Jenkins
Martin; Kirkup, Hollywood, Fisher, McGrath, Gabriel, Paine, Channon, Stokes(Davies), O'Neil, Jenkins.
Att: 21,600
Round 2 (2nd leg)
Sep 29 v Athletic Bilbao (a) 0-2 (agg 2-3)
Martin; Kirkup, Hollywood, Fisher(O'Brien), McGrath, Walker, Paine, Channon, Stokes(Davies), O'Neil, Jenkins.
Att: 22,000

Mick Channon's 16 appearances and nine goals in European football are both Southampton records.

1976-77
European Cup-winners' Cup

Round 1 (1st leg)
Sep 15 Olympique Marseilles (h) 4-0
Channon 2, Osgood, Waldron
Turner; Rodrigues, Steele, Holmes, Waldron, Blyth, Fisher, Channon (Earles), Osgood, Stokes, Williams.
Att: 19,150
Round 1 (2nd leg)
Sep 29 v Olympique Marseilles (a) 1-2 (agg 5-2)
Peach
Turner; Rodrigues, Steele, Williams, Waldron, Blyth, Fisher, Channon, Osgood, Stokes, Peach.
Att: 17,834
Round 2 (1st leg)
Oct 20 v Carrick Rangers (a) 5-2
Channon 2, Osgood, McCalliog, Stokes
Middleton; Rodrigues, Peach, Holmes, Waldron, Blyth, Williams, Channon, Osgood, McCalliog(Earles), Stokes.
Att: 6,500
Round 2 (2nd leg)
Nov 3 v Carrick Rangers (h) 4-1 (agg 9-3)
Hayes 2, Stokes, Williams
Middleton; Mills, Peach, Holmes, Waldron, Blyth, Williams, Hayes, Osgood, McCalliog, Stokes.
Att: 15,130
Round 3 (1st leg)
Mar 2 v Anderlecht (a) 0-2
Wells; Andruszewski, Peach, Holmes, Blyth, Steele, Williams, Channon, Osgood, McCalliog, MacDougall.
Att: 33,500
Round 3 (2nd leg)
Mar 16 v Anderlecht (h) 2-1 (agg 2-3)
MacDougall, Peach
Wells; Andruszewski(Stokes), Peach, Holmes, Blyth, Steele, Williams, Channon, Osgood, McCalliog(Hayes), MacDougall.
Att: 24,337

1981-82
UEFA Cup

Round 1 (1st leg)
Sep 16 v Limerick (a) 3-0
Moran 2, Armstrong
Wells; Golac, Holmes, G.Baker, Watson, Agboola, Keegan, Channon, Moran, Armstrong, Ball.
Att: 8,000
Round 1 (2nd leg)
Sep 29 v Limerick (h) 1-1 (agg 4-1)
Keegan
Katalinic; Golac, Holmes, G.Baker, Watson, Agboola, Keegan, Channon, Moran, Armstrong, Ball.
Att: 12,814
Round 2 (1st leg)
Oct 21 v Sporting Lisbon (h) 2-4
Keegan, Channon
Wells; Golac, Holmes, Williams, Nicholl, Whitlock(Lawrence), Keegan, Channon, Moran, Armstrong, Ball.
Att: 18,573
Round 2 (2nd leg)
Nov 4 v Sporting Lisbon (a) 0-0 (agg 2-4)
Katalinic; S.Baker, Holmes, Williams, Nicholl, Agboola, Keegan, Channon, Moran, Lawrence(Wallace), Ball.
Att: 60,000

1982-83
UEFA Cup

Round 1 (1st leg)
Sep 15 v Norrköping (h) 2-2
Williams, Wright
Shilton; S.Baker, Rofe, Williams, Nicholl, Wright, Ball, Cassells, Moran, Armstrong, Agboola.
Att: 10,155
Round 1 (2nd leg)
Sep 29 v Norrköping (a) 0-0 (agg 2-2; Norrköping won on away-goals rule)
Shilton; S.Baker, Holmes, Williams, Nicholl, Wright, Ball, Cassells, Moran, Armstrong, Agboola.
Att: 10,269

Ted MacDougall's goal in the 1976-76 Cup-winners' Cup game against Anderlecht was not enough to put Saints through.

1984-85
UEFA Cup

Round 1 (1st leg)
Sep 19 v Hamburg (h) 0-0
Shilton; Mills, Dennis, Williams, Whitlock, Wright, Holmes, Curtis (Moran), Jordan, Armstrong, Wallace.
Att: 19,000
Round 1 (2nd leg)
Oct 3 v Hamburg (a) 0-2 (agg 0-2)
Shilton; Mills, Dennis, Williams, Wright, Whitlock, Holmes, S.Baker, Jordan, Moran, Wallace.
Att: 32,000

Peter Shilton and Peter Wells (left) each made four appearances for Southampton.

European Appearances and Goalscorers

Listed in numerical order of appearances with goals scored shown in brackets. Mick Channon made more appearances and scored more goals in European football than any other Saints player.

Channon 16 (9); Williams 12 (2); Holmes 12; Fisher 9; Stokes 8 (2); Paine 8 (2); Martin 8; Kirkup 7; Gabriel 7 (1); Moran 7 (2); McGrath 6; Blyth 6; Byrne 6; Walker 6; Ball 6; Davies 6 (4); Osgood 6 (2); D.Armstrong 6 (1); Peach 5 (2); Agboola 5; Wells 4; Shilton 4; S.Baker 4; Hollywood 4; Steele 4; Waldron 4 (1); Nicholl 4; Wright 4 (1); Jenkins 4(1); Keegan 4 (2); McCalliog 4 (1); Sydenham 4; Rodrigues 3; Golac 3; Whitlock 3; Turner 2; Middleton 2; Katalinic 2; Andruszewski 2; M.Mills 2; Dennis 2; G.Baker 2, Watson 2; Cassells 2; Jordan 2; O'Neil 2; MacDougall 2; Wallace 2; Jones 1; S.Mills 1; Rofe 1; Hayes 1 (2); Curtis 1; Lawrence 1; Kemp 1.
Substitute appearances: Stokes 3; Davies 2; Earles 2; Saul 2; Fisher 1; Hayes 1; Hollywood 1; Lawrence 1; Moran 1; O'Brien 1; Wallace 1.

Charity Shield
1976
Aug 14 v Liverpool (at Wembley) 0-1
Turner; Rodrigues, Peach, Holmes, Blyth(Fisher), Steele, Gilchrist, Channon, Osgood, McCalliog, Stokes.
Att: 76,500

British Tournaments

Texaco Cup

1974
Group Two
Aug 3 v Luton Town (a) 1-1
Chatterley
Aug 6 v Orient (h) 2-1
Channon, Osgood
Aug 10 v West Ham United (h) 2-0
Gilchrist, O'Neil

Quarter-final
Sep 18 v Glasgow Rangers (a) 3-1
Osgood 2, O'Brien
Oct 1 v Glasgow Rangers (h) 2-0 (agg 5-1)
Gilchrist, opp.og

Semi-Final
Oct 22 v Oldham Athletic (a) 3-1
Channon 2, Blyth
Nov 5 v Oldham Athletic (h) 2-1 (agg 5-2)
Channon, Stokes

Final
Nov 27 v Newcastle United (h) 1-0
Channon
Dec 11 v Newcastle United (a) 0-3 (agg 1-3; a.e.t.)

Tennent-Caledonian Cup

(All games played at Ibrox Park, Glasgow)

1976
Aug 2 v Manchester City 1-1*
Earles
(*Score 11-11 after penalties, Saints won on toss of coin)
Aug 3 v Glasgow Rangers 2-1
Channon, Peach

1977
Aug 6 v Glasgow Rangers 1-3
Peach
Aug 7 v St Mirren 2-1
Ball, Osgood
(Third place play-off)

1978
Aug 5 v West Bromwich Albion 1-1*
Boyer
Saints won 4-1 on penalties
Aug 6 v Glasgow Rangers 1-4
MacDougall

Aberdeen Tournament

(all games played at Pittodrie)

1981
Aug 1 v Manchester United 3-1
George, Holmes, Keegan
Aug 2 v Aberdeen 1-5
Moran

Super Cup

1985
Sep 17 v Liverpool (a) 1-2
Wallace
Oct 2 v Tottenham Hotspur (a) 1-2
Moran
Oct 22 v Liverpool (h) 1-1
Armstrong
Dec 17 v Tottenham Hotspur (h) 1-3
Wallace

Full Members Cup

1986
Nov 25 v Hull City (h) 2-1
Le Tissier 2
Dec 9 v Norwich (h) 1-2 (a.e.t.)
Case

Southern Charity Cup

1902-03
Round 1
Oct 27 v West Ham United (h) 1-2
Barlow

1903-04
Round 1
Oct 21 v Portsmouth (a) 5-4
Harrison 2, Bowman, Evans, Fraser
Semi-final
Dec 2 v Millwall (a) 1-3
Hedley

1904-05
Round 1
Oct 26 v Reading (a) 0-1

1905-06
Round 1
Nov 13 v Portsmouth (h) 4-2
Soye 2, Harris, Mouncher
Semi-final
Mar 28 v Reading (a) 0-1

1906-07
Round 1
Nov 14 v Portsmouth (a) 2-0
Harrison, Mouncher
Semi-final
Feb 18 v Millwall (h) 4-1
Harris 2, Glen, Harrison
Final
Apr 30 v Tottenham Hotspur (a) 0-2

1907-08
Round 1
Feb 10 v Reading (h) 4-1
Jefferis 2, Beare, Lewis
Semi-final
Apr 27 v West Ham United (h) 4-2
Costello 2, Bainbridge, Jefferis
Final
Feb 22 1909 v Portsmouth (h) 1-0
Ward

1908-09
Round 1
Mar 15 v Portsmouth (h) 1-2
Bainbridge

1909-10
Round 1
Sep 20 v Portsmouth (h) 3-2
McGibbon 2, Brittleton
Round 2
Nov 24 v Brighton & Hove Albion (a) 0-1

1910-11
Round 1
Sep 14 v Reading (a) 1-3
Buckenham

1911-12
Round 1
Sep 13 v Brighton & Hove Albion (h) 1-1
Small
Replay
Nov 15 v Brighton & Hove Albion (a) 2-6
H.Brown, Wilcox

1912-13
Round 1
Dec 9 v Brighton & Hove Albion (h) 1-1
Small
Replay
Jan 29 v Brighton & Hove Albion (a) 1-4
Penton

1913-14
Round 1
Nov 26 v Reading (h) 3-0
Blake, Dominy, opp.og
Round 2
Feb 18 v Croydon Common (a) 3-0
Andrews 2, Denby
Semi-final
Mar 4 v Merthyr Town (at Cardiff) 3-1
Dominy, Hollins, opp.og
Final
Apr 1 v Coventry City (at Chelsea) 2-2
Hollins 2
Replay
Apr 22 v Coventry City (at Millwall) 0-1

Southern Professional Floodlight Cup

1957-58
Oct 28 v Luton Town (h) 0-2

1958-59
Oct 27 v Watford (h) 0-0
Nov 4 v Watford (a) 3-2
Reeves 2, Shields
Feb 18 v Luton Town (a) 0-4

1959-60
Oct 26 v Aldershot (h) 3-0
Paine 2, O'Brien
Dec 14 v Crystal Palace (a) 2-2
O'Brien, Reeves
Jan 18 v Crystal Palace (h) 2-1
Reeves 2
Mar 28 v Coventry City (a) 1-2
Brown

Hampshire Combination Cup/ Professional Cup

1931-32
Apr 18 v Portsmouth (h) 1-0
Arnold
Apr 27 v Bournemouth & BA (h) 2-3
Drake, opp.og

1932-33
Oct 5 v Portsmouth (a) 0-6

1933-34
Nov 22 v Portsmouth (h) 0-1

1934-35
Apr 3 v Bournemouth & BA (a) 2-4
McIlwane 2

1935-36
Oct 16 v Aldershot (a) 0-4

1940-41
Apr 5 v Bournemouth & BA (a) 1-1
Stroud
May 3 v Bournemouth & BA (a) 3-2
Roper 2, J.Harris
Jun 2 v Portsmouth (a) 1-8
Roper

1943-44
Apr 10 v Army XI (h) 4-2
Dawes 2, Bates, Roper

1944-45
May 21 v Chelsea (h) 4-6
Roper 4

1945-46
May 11 v Bournemouth & BA (h) 3-4
Davies 2, Bates

1946-47
May 21 v Bournemouth & BA (h) 1-1
Bradley

1981-82
Dec 22 v Portsmouth (a) 1-2
Channon

1982-83
Nov 16 v AFC Bournemouth (h) 2-3
Moran 2

1983-84
Apr 30 v AFC Bournemouth (a) 5-3
Moran 2, Baird, Collins, Puckett
May 15 v Aldershot (h) 3-1*
S.Baker, Foyle, Knill
*Reserve team fielded

Hampshire Benevolent Cup
Southampton v Portsmouth Charity Matches

Nov 1 1905 at Portsmouth 0-1
Apr 8 1907 at Southampton 0-1
Mar 10 1909 at Portsmouth 1-1
Foster
Apr 19 1909 at Southampton 4-3
Carter 2, Jefferis, Jordan
Nov 29 1909 at Southampton 2-3
McGibbon 2

Nov 30 1910 at Portsmouth 1-2
H.Brown
Oct 25 1911 at Southampton 5-1
Hamilton 2, H.Brown, D.Slade, Wilcox
Oct 16 1912 at Portsmouth 0-2
Oct 8 1913 at Southampton 0-1
Apr 28 1915 at Portsmouth 0-2
May 15 1920 at Southampton 2-0
Dominy, Foxall
May 11 1921 at Portsmouth 0-1
May 8 1922 at Southampton 3-1
Dominy 2, Rawlings
Apr 24 1923 at Southampton 2-2
Dominy, Johnson
May 7 1924 at Portsmouth 0-2
May 6 1925 at Southampton 1-1
Dominy
May 5 1926 at Portsmouth 1-5
Dominy
May 9 1927 at Southampton 4-1
Rawlings 2, Rowley 2
May 8 1929 at Southampton 3-2
Bradford, Coates, Rowley
May 5 1930 at Portsmouth 0-0
May 4 1931 at Southampton 0-4*
*Due to players refusing terms Southampton were forced to field reserves, ex-players and county players.
May 11 1932 at Portsmouth 1-5
Neal
Apr 27 1936 at Southampton 1-2
Watson

Rowland Hospital Cup
Apr 16 1923 at Portsmouth 2-1
Johnson, Rawlings
May 5 1924 at Southampton 2-3
Rawlings 2
May 4 1925 at Portsmouth 0-2
May 3 1926 at Southampton 2-4
Bullock, Keeping
May 11 1927 at Portsmouth 1-5
Lohse
May 6 1929 at Portsmouth 2-1
Jepson, Rowley
May 7 1930 at Southampton 0-2
May 6 1931 at Portsmouth 2-2*
Allen, Haddleton
*Due to players refusing terms Southampton were forced to field reserves, ex-players and county players.
May 9 1932 at Southampton 2-2
Holt, Neal

Benevolent & Rowland Cups combined
May 7 1928 at Portsmouth 1-6
Petrie
May 3 1933 at Portsmouth 0-5
May 7 1934 at Southampton 1-4
Tully
May 8 1935 at Portsmouth 0-1

Overseas Tournaments

Charles Guinier Cup
St Malo, France

1934
May 20 v Union Sportive Servannaise et Malourne 4-0
Cole 2, Brewis, Tully
May 21 v Stade Reneais Universite Club 5-1
Tully 2, Brewis, Cole, Luckett

Astora Tournament
Alkmaar, Holland
1977
Jul 29 v Haarlem 2-3
S.Williams, Osgood
Jul 31 v Beerschot 3-2
MacDougall 2, Osgood

Rotterdam Tournament
Holland

1980
Aug 8 v Schalke 04 7-2
George 2, Keegan 2, Nicholl, Channon, Holmes
Aug 9 v Bruges 3-1
G.Baker 2, Channon

Trans-Atlantic Trophy
1981
Jul 11 v Seattle Sounders 1-3
Channon
Jul 15 v New York Cosmos 1-2
Blochel
Jul 18 v Glasgow Celtic 1-2
Moran

Seville International Tournament
Spain

1981
Aug 18 v Sevilla 1-3
Holmes
Aug 20 v Real Betis 1-2
Whitlock

Celta Vigo Tournament
Spain

1983
Aug 18 v Dynamo Bucharest 0-0
(Saints won 5-4 on penalties)
Aug 20 v Celta 1-1
Moran

Tom Brewis

Nick Holmes

Steve Moran

Saints' games in other leagues

In 1897 the Saints entered the United League to augment their Southern League matches, which at the time were too infrequent to bring in a regular income at the turnstiles. After two seasons they entered the Southern District Combination and followed this by entering the Western League. All these matches were regarded as first team fixtures and not only provided the club with much needed revenue, but kept the players busy. In 1912, the Saints also entered a midweek league known as the Southern Alliance and this gave the opportunity to people who worked on Saturdays to view matches on a midweek afternoon. A list of these matches follows, with scorers.

UNITED LEAGUE

1897-98
Sep 25 v Wellingborough Town (h) 3-1
Meston, Buchanan, Keay
Oct 6 v Loughborough Town (h) 3-0
Naughton 2, Keay
Oct 25 v Rushden (a) 0-1
Nov 3 v Luton Town (h) 0-2
Dec 20 v Woolwich Arsenal (a) 1-1
J.Turner
Jan 12 v Millwall (h) 4-1
Brown, Farrell, Keay, J.Turner
Jan 19 v Tottenham Hotspur (h) 2-2
Haynes, A.Chadwick
Feb 14 v Luton Town (a) 0-2
Mar 9 v Millwall (a) 0-5
Mar 24 v Tottenham Hotspur (a) 0-7
Mar 30 v Rushden (h) 2-0
Taylor, Buchanan
Apr 2 v Wellingborough Town (a) 2-3
Stevens, Buchanan
Apr 9 v Kettering Town (h) 2-1
Meston, Brown
Apr 13 v Woolwich Arsenal (h) 3-0
A.Chadwick, Meston, J.Turner
Apr 23 v Kettering (a) 1-2
Thomas
Apr 27 v Loughborough Town (a) 0-0

1898-99
Oct 5 v Kettering Town (h) 4-0
Hartley 2, Wood, Stevens
Oct 10 v Tottenham Hotspur (a) 0-4

Oct 17 v Millwall (a) 1-1
Hartley
Oct 29 v Woolwich Arsenal (h) 5-1
Hartley 2, Keay, McKenzie, Robertson
Nov 9 v Brighton United (a) 3-5
Robertson, Hartley, Keay
Nov 14 v Luton Town (a) 0-2
Nov 19 v Woolwich Arsenal (a) 1-2
Hartley
Nov 30 v Wellingborough Town (h) 4-1
Hartley 2, T.Smith, Robertson
Dec 14 v Rushden (h) 3-1
Hartley 2, Robertson
Dec 19 v Wellingborough Town (a) 4-0
Hartley 3, T.Smith
Jan 4 v Bristol City (h) 6-0
Hartley 3, Wood, T.Smith, A.Chadwick
Jan 14 v Reading (a) 0-3
Jan 18 v Brighton United (h) 3-0
Nicol, Wood, Hartley
Feb 15 v Tottenham Hotspur (h) 2-1
Stevens 2
Mar 8 v Luton Town (h) 8-0
T.Smith 2, McLean 2, Hartley 2, Wood, opp.og
Mar 13 v Kettering Town (h) 2-1
McLean, Hartley
Mar 20 v Rushden (a) 0-8
Apr 12 v Millwall (h) 1-0
Wood
Apr 15 v Reading (h) 4-1
Robertson, Nicol, Wood, Englefield
Apr 19 v Bristol City (a) 1-2
Buchanan

1897-98

	P	W	D	L	F	A	Pts
Luton T	16	13	2	1	49	11	28
Tottenham H	16	8	5	3	40	27	21
Arsenal	16	8	5	3	35	24	21
Kettering T	16	9	1	6	28	25	19
Rushden	16	7	1	8	24	26	15
Southampton	16	6	3	7	23	28	13*
Millwall	16	4	4	8	27	27	12
Wellingborough T	16	3	3	10	17	41	9
Loughborough	16	1	2	13	8	42	4

*2 points deducted

1898-99

	P	W	D	L	F	A	Pts
Millwall	20	14	3	3	42	19	31
Southampton	20	12	1	7	53	32	25
Arsenal	20	10	4	6	30	30	24
Tottenham H	20	11	2	7	36	25	24
Bristol C	20	11	0	9	43	31	22
Reading	20	8	5	7	36	25	21
Brighton U	20	10	1	9	41	42	21
Wellingborough T	20	7	1	12	32	40	15
Kettering T	20	8	1	11	25	38	15*
Rushden	20	6	1	13	26	45	13
Luton T	20	2	3	15	24	71	7

*2 points deducted

SOUTHERN DISTRICT COMBINATION

1899-1900
Sep 13 v Queen's Park Rangers (h) 2-1
A.Chadwick, Wood
Oct 11 v Woolwich Arsenal (h) 3-0
A.Turner, McLeod, Milward
Oct 18 v Portsmouth (a) 1-5
Wood
Nov 13 v Queen's Park Rangers (a) 0-2
Nov 22 v Bristol City (h) 5-1
Farrell 2, Wood 2, Milward
Nov 29 v Reading (a) 1-1
Yates
Dec 6 v Millwall (h) 2-2
Yates, Milward

Dec 13 v Chatham (a) 2-0
Wood, opp.og
Jan 8 v Tottenham Hotspur (a) 2-3
Yates, Cavendish
Jan 10 v Reading (h) 3-1
McLeod 2, Meston
Feb 28 v Bristol City (a) 1-4
Yates
Mar 5 v Woolwich Arsenal (a) 0-1
Mar 12 v Millwall (a) 0-3
Apr 2 v Portsmouth (h) 1-0
Milward
Apr 4 v Chatham (h) 0-1
Apr 30 v Tottenham Hotspur (h) 1-4
Cavendish

1899-1900

	P	W	D	L	F	A	Pts
Millwall	16	12	2	2	30	10	26
Tottenham H*	15	10	3	2	40	16	23
Portsmouth	16	9	2	5	30	16	20
Arsenal*	15	7	1	7	25	21	15
Bristol C	16	5	3	8	25	32	13
Southampton	16	5	2	9	23	30	12
Reading	16	4	4	8	16	28	12
Chatham	16	5	2	9	12	35	12
Queen's Park R	16	4	1	11	19	28	9

*Match between Arsenal & Tottenham at Plumstead abandoned after 55 minutes because of crowd trouble, the game was never replayed.

WESTERN LEAGUE

1900-01
Nov 14 v Bristol City (a) 1-4
E.Chadwick
Dec 12 v Reading (a) 1-1
A.Turner
Dec 22 v Tottenham Hotspur (a) 0-2
Dec 25 v Swindon Town (h) 3-0
Killean, Yates, Small
Jan 16 v Millwall (a) 0-1
Jan 30 v Millwall (h) 5-0
A Turner 3, E.Chadwick, Yates
Feb 27 v Bristol Rovers (h) 2-0
Toman, Milward

Mar 6 v Portsmouth (h) 0-4
Mar 11 v Tottenham Hotspur (h) 1-1
E.Chadwick
Mar 20 v Portsmouth (a) 1-2
Wood
Mar 27 v Queen's Park Rangers (h) 1-0
Yates
Apr 1 v Bristol City (h) 2-1
Meston, Toman
Apr 13 v Swindon Town (a) 1-3
Toman
Apr 15 v Bristol Rovers (a) 0-2
Apr 17 v Reading (h) 1-2
Small

Apr 20 v Queen's Park Rangers (a) 1-6
E.Chadwick

1901-02
Sep 4 v Portsmouth (a) 0-1
Sep 11 v Portsmouth (h) 1-3
E.Chadwick
Sep 18 v Reading (h) 1-2
Harrison
Sep 25 v Bristol Rovers (h) 1-4
J.Turner
Sep 28 v Tottenham Hotspur (a) 0-5
Oct 2 v Reading (a) 0-0

Oct 7 v Queen's Park Rangers (a) 3-2
McDonald 2, Harrison
Oct 16 v Queen's Park Rangers (h) 5-1
Brown 4, McDonald
Oct 23 v Swindon Town (h) 3-0
Harrison, Wood, E.Chadwick
Nov 11 v Millwall (a) 0-3
Dec 18 v Swindon Town (h) 4-0
Brown, Small, J.Turner, opp.og
Dec 25 v West Ham United (a) 0-1
Jan 11 v Tottenham Hotspur (h) 5-1
J.Turner 2, A.Turner, Wood, Brown
Feb 12 v Millwall (h) 3-1
Bowman, Small, E.Chadwick
Mar 31 v West Ham United (h) 2-1
Harrison 2
Apr 14 v Bristol Rovers (a) 1-2
Cavendish

1902-03
Sep 1 v Portsmouth (h) 3-1
Evans, Fraser, Barlow
Sep 10 v Portsmouth (a) 1-4
Fraser
Sep 13 v Tottenham Hotspur (h) 1-1
Fraser
Sep 20 v West Ham United (a) 1-1
Fraser
Sep 22 v Brentford (a) 2-0
Fitchett, Lee
Oct 6 v Queen's Park Rangers (a) 2-3
Turner 2
Oct 13 v Reading (h) 5-2*
Wood 2, Meston, Bowman, Barlow
*Played five minutes short. Game completed 31 March 1903)
Oct 20 v Bristol Rovers (a) 0-0
Nov 17 v Millwall (h) 1-1
Barlow
Dec 27 v Tottenham Hotspur (a) 0-0
Jan 3 v West Ham United (h) 4-0
Turner, Fitchett, Harrison, Bell
Jan 16 v Millwall (a) 0-3
Jan 19 v Queen's Park Rangers (h) 6-0
Barlow 2, Harrison, Fitchett, Bell, Turner
Jan 26 v Brentford (h) 2-1
Lee, Wood
Mar 23 v Bristol Rovers (h) 3-2
Wood, Harrison, Fraser
Mar 31 v Reading (a) 1-2
Evans

1903-04
Sep 2 v Portsmouth (a) 2-1
Hedley, Fraser
Sep 7 v Portsmouth (h) 5-2
Harrison 4, J.Turner
Sep 16 v Reading (a) 3-2
Harrison 2, Evans
Sep 28 v Brentford (h) 3-0
Evans, Wood, Harrison
Oct 5 v Bristol Rovers (h) 3-3
Harrison, Fraser, Mouncher
Oct 12 v Brentford (h) 4-0
Hedley 3, Spence
Nov 2 v Queen's Park Rangers (h) 5-1
Harrison 2, Fraser 2, Hedley
Nov 18 v Plymouth Argyle (a) 0-2
Dec 14 v Reading (h) 1-0
J.Turner
Dec 19 v West Ham United (h) 3-0
Spence, Hedley, Harrison
Dec 28 v Tottenham Hotspur (a) 0-1
Jan 4 v Plymouth Argyle (h) 1-2
Harrison
Jan 18 v Queen's Park Rangers (a) 0-0
Apr 16 v West Ham United (a) 0-0
Apr 18 v Bristol Rovers (a) 0-5
Apr 23 v Tottenham Hotspur (h) 1-0
Mouncher

1904-05
Sep 1 v Portsmouth (h) 2-2
Harrison 2
Sep 7 v Portsmouth (a) 2-0
Lee, Harrison
Sep 12 v Queen's Park Rangers (a) 4-1
Harrison 3, Hedley

Sep 19 v Plymouth Argyle (h) 1-2
Mouncher
Sep 28 v Plymouth Argyle (a) 1-4
Lee
Oct 3 v West Ham United (a) 0-1
Oct 10 v Fulham (h) 2-1
Houlker, A.Turner
Nov 7 v Queen's Park Rangers (h) 5-0
Hedley 3, Bluff, Dainty
Nov 14 v Reading (h) 0-1
Nov 21 v West Ham United (h) 8-0
Hedley 4, A.Turner 3, H.Turner
Dec 5 v Brentford (h) 5-1
Dainty 2, Harrison 2, Bluff
Dec 10 v Bristol Rovers (h) 5-1
Harrison 4, Webb
Dec 27 v Bristol Rovers (a) 2-3
Bluff, Mouncher
Jan 9 v Brentford (a) 0-1
Jan 23 v Millwall (h) 2-0
Meston, A.Turner
Feb 6 v Millwall (a) 0-1
Mar 15 v Reading (a) 3-2
Harrison 2, Yates
Mar 20 v Fulham (a) 1-0
Harrison
Mar 29 v Tottenham Hotspur (a) 1-1
Harrison
Apr 22 v Tottenham Hotspur (h) 1-0
Mouncher

1905-06
Sep 6 v Portsmouth (a) 2-0
Harrison 2
Sep 11 v Portsmouth (h) 5-2
Harrison 2, Brown, Soye, Metcalf
Sep 16 v Plymouth Argyle (h) 1-1
Brown
Sep 18 v Bristol Rovers (h) 3-2
Tomlinson 2, Harris
Oct 2 v Millwall (a) 1-1
Soye
Oct 9 v Brentford (a) 3-1
Hedley, Soye, Brown
Oct 16 v Brentford (h) 4-1
Harrison 3, Brown
Oct 23 v Reading (h) 1-1
Soye
Oct 30 v Queen's Park Rangers (a) 1-5
Soye
Nov 6 v Millwall (h) 3-1
Hogg, Tomlinson, Brown
Nov 27 v Queen's Park Rangers (h) 2-3
Hedley, Harris
Dec 4 v Fulham (a) 3-2
Soye, Hedley, Harris
Dec 23 v Tottenham Hotspur (a) 0-5
Dec 27 v Bristol Rovers (a) 0-3
Jan 15 v Fulham (h) 2-0
Soye, Harrison
Jan 20 v Plymouth Argyle (a) 1-2
Opp.og
Feb 14 v Reading (a) 2-2
Jefferis, Brown
Mar 19 v West Ham United (a) 1-1
Jefferis
Apr 2 v West Ham United (h) 5-2
Harrison 3, Brown 2
Apr 25 v Tottenham Hotspur (h) 1-0
Richman

1906-07
Sep 10 v Tottenham Hotspur (a) 3-2
Radford 2, Harrison
Sep 19 v Portsmouth (h) 2-3
Glen, G.Harris
Sep 26 v Portsmouth (a) 2-3
Harrison 2
Oct 3 v Tottenham Hotspur (h) 2-0
Harrison 2
Oct 10 v Plymouth Argyle (a) 0-1
Oct 22 v Millwall (a) 1-0
Hoskins
Oct 30 v West Ham United (a) 0-3
Nov 5 v West Ham United (h) 0-1
Nov 26 v Millwall (h) 3-1
Glen 2, G.Harris
Dec 3 v Plymouth Argyle (h) 1-2
Jefferis

1907-08
Sep 16 v Plymouth Argyle (h) 2-1
Glover, Bainbridge
Oct 2 v Plymouth Argyle (a) 0-1
Oct 7 v Brentford (a) 3-3
Harrison, Jefferis, Hodgkinson
Oct 14 v Leyton (h) 6-0
Harrison 4, Jefferis, Lewis
Oct 21 v Queen's Park Rangers (h) 4-0
Harrison 2, Bell, Hodgkinson
Oct 28 v Brighton & Hove Albion (h) 2-1
Glover, Costello
Nov 4 v Queen's Park Rangers (a) 4-2
Harrison 3, Jefferis
Nov 11 v Brentford (h) 3-0
Hoskins, Harrison, Hodgkinson
Nov 27 v Brighton & Hove Albion (a) 0-3
Dec 4 v Portsmouth (a) 2-0
Glover, G.Smith
Dec 16 v Portsmouth (h) 0-1
Dec 30 v Leyton (a) 4-0
G.Smith 2, Jefferis, Lewis
Western League championship
(played at Tottenham)
Apr 13 v Millwall (n) 0-1

1908-09
Sep 30 v Portsmouth (a) 2-4
McPherson, Hughes
Oct 3 v Bristol Rovers (h) 1-3
Hughes
Oct 19 v Brentford (h) 2-0
S.Smith, Jordan
Oct 28 v Portsmouth (h) 4-1
McGhee 2, Jordan 2
Nov 4 v Plymouth Argyle (a) 1-0
Hughes
Nov 9 v West Ham United (h) 2-1
Trueman, Costello
Nov 16 v Plymouth Argyle (h) 1-0
Costello
Nov 23 v Millwall (a) 1-3
Hodgkinson
Nov 30 v Millwall (h) 2-1
Jepp, Costello
Dec 7 v West Ham United (h) 4-3
Jefferis 2, Costello, Hodgkinson
Jan 4 v Brentford (a) 0-3

1900-01

	P	W	D	L	F	A	Pts
Portsmouth	16	11	2	3	36	23	24
Millwall	16	9	5	2	33	14	23
Tottenham H	16	8	5	3	37	19	21
Queen's Park R	16	7	4	5	39	24	18
Bristol C	16	6	4	6	27	24	16
Reading	16	5	5	6	23	31	15
Southampton	16	5	2	9	19	29	12
Bristol R	16	4	1	11	18	42	9
Swindon T	16	2	2	12	9	35	6

1901-02

	P	W	D	L	F	A	Pts
Portsmouth	16	13	1	2	53	16	27
Tottenham H	16	11	3	2	42	17	25
Reading	16	7	3	6	29	22	17
Millwall	16	8	1	7	25	29	17
Bristol R	16	8	0	8	25	31	16
Southampton	16	7	1	8	30	28	15
West Ham U	16	6	2	8	30	24	14
Queen's Park R	16	5	1	10	17	43	11
Swindon T	16	0	2	14	8	53	2

1902-03

	P	W	D	L	F	A	Pts
Portsmouth	16	10	4	2	34	14	24
Bristol R	16	9	2	5	36	22	20
Southampton	16	7	6	3	32	20	20
Tottenham H	16	6	7	3	20	14	19
Millwall	16	6	3	7	23	29	15
Reading	16	7	0	9	20	21	14
Queen's Park R	16	6	2	8	18	31	14
Brentford	16	3	4	9	16	34	10
West Ham U	16	2	4	10	15	29	8

1903-04

	P	W	D	L	F	A	Pts
Tottenham	16	11	3	2	32	12	25
Southampton	16	9	3	4	30	18	21
Plymouth A	16	8	4	4	22	18	20
Portsmouth	16	7	2	7	24	23	16
Brentford	16	6	4	6	19	22	16
Queen's Park R	16	5	5	6	15	21	15
Reading	16	4	4	8	16	26	12
Bristol R	16	4	3	9	29	29	11
West Ham U	16	2	4	10	13	31	8

1904-05

	P	W	D	L	F	A	Pts
Plymouth A	20	13	4	3	52	18	30
Brentford	20	11	6	3	30	23	28
Southampton	20	11	2	7	45	22	24
Portsmouth	20	10	3	7	29	30	23
West Ham U	20	8	4	8	37	43	20
Fulham	20	7	3	10	29	32	17
Millwall	20	7	3	10	32	39	17
Tottenham H	20	5	6	9	20	28	16
Reading	20	6	3	11	28	37	15
Queen's Park R	20	6	3	11	27	45	15
Bristol R	20	7	1	12	32	44	15

1905-06

	P	W	D	L	F	A	Pts
Queen's Park R	20	11	4	5	33	27	26
Southampton	20	10	5	5	41	35	25
Plymouth A	20	8	8	4	34	23	24
Tottenham H	20	7	7	6	28	17	21
Bristol R	20	8	3	9	34	34	19
Millwall	20	7	5	8	28	29	19
Portsmouth	20	6	7	7	26	29	19
West Ham U	20	7	5	8	32	35	19
Reading	20	6	6	8	28	35	18
Fulham	20	5	5	10	23	32	15
Brentford	20	6	3	11	25	36	15

1906-07 (Section B)

	P	W	D	L	F	A	Pts
West Ham U	10	7	1	2	25	14	15
Plymouth A	10	5	3	2	16	10	13
Portsmouth	10	4	2	4	16	19	10
Tottenham H	10	3	3	4	13	15	9
Southampton	10	4	0	6	14	16	8
Millwall	10	1	3	6	5	15	5

1907-08 (Section A)

	P	W	D	L	F	A	Pts
Southampton	12	8	1	3	30	12	17
Portsmouth	12	7	1	4	25	18	15
Brighton & HA	12	6	2	4	19	19	14
Plymouth A	12	5	2	5	14	12	12
Queen's Park R	12	5	1	6	20	23	11
Brentford	12	2	5	5	13	21	9
Leyton	12	2	2	8	11	27	6

1908-09

	P	W	D	L	F	A	Pts
Millwall	12	8	2	2	24	11	18
Southampton	12	7	0	5	20	20	14
Plymouth A	12	6	1	5	12	13	13
Portsmouth	12	5	2	5	21	21	12
West Ham U	12	5	0	7	21	23	10
Bristol R	12	4	1	7	16	23	9
Brentford	12	3	2	7	10	13	8

Queen's Park Rangers players protest but this goal scored by Southampton's George Hedley in 1905 was allowed to stand.

SOUTHERN ALLIANCE LEAGUE

1912-13
Sep 18 v Luton Town (h) 2-2
Small 2
Sep 25 v Luton Town (a) 0-2
Oct 2 v Brighton & Hove Albion (h) 3-1
Taylor, Kimpton, Prince
Oct 9 v Southend United (a) 2-0
Taylor, Prince
Oct 23 v Croydon Common (a) 0-1
Oct 30 v Southend United (h) 1-1
Andrews
Nov 6 v Portsmouth (h) 0-3
Nov 13 v Cardiff City (a) 2-1
Kimpton, Blake
Nov 20 v Portsmouth (a) 0-2
Nov 27 v Brighton & Hove Albion (a) 1-1
Andrews
Dec 4 v Millwall (h) 1-3
Andrews
Dec 11 v Cardiff City (h) 3-1
Kimpton, Turnbull, Penton
Jan 1 v Brentford (h) 5-3
Ireland 2, Taylor, Turnbull, opp.og
Jan 22 v Croydon Common (h) 1-2
Prince
Feb 1 v Millwall (a) 0-4
Feb 5 v Brentford (a) 2-3
Taylor, Salway

1913-14
Sep 17 v Portsmouth (a) 1-3
Andrews
Sep 24 v Portsmouth (h) 1-0
Prince
Oct 1 v Croydon Common (a) 0-1
Oct 13 v Brentford (a) 0-2
Oct 29 v Brentford (h) 5-0
Andrews 3, Denby, Small
Nov 5 v Brighton & Hove Albion (a) 1-2
Andrews
Nov 12 v Brighton & Hove Albion (h) 2-2
Bradley 2
Nov 19 v Luton Town (a) 1-3
Kimpton
Dec 3 v Luton Town (h) 2-4
Small, Bradley
Dec 10 v Newport County (h) 4-2
Hinton 3, Andrews
Jan 29 v Newport County (a) 1-2
W.Smith
Feb 4 v Croydon Common (h) 1-3
Andrews
Feb 11 v Cardiff City (h) 2-0
Binder, W.Smith
Feb 25 v Southend United (h) 4-1
Small, Dominy, W.Smith, Andrews
Mar 18 v Cardiff City (a) 1-6
Denby
Mar 25 v Southend United (a) 1-1
McAlpine

1912-13

	P	W	D	L	F	A	Pts
Croydon Common	16	9	6	1	31	16	24
Brighton & HA	16	8	5	3	28	19	21
Luton T	16	7	5	4	30	29	18
Millwall	16	7	3	6	36	26	17
Portsmouth	16	7	2	7	24	20	16
Southend U	16	5	4	7	31	29	14
Southampton	16	5	3	8	23	30	13
Brentford	16	5	1	10	30	39	11
Cardiff C	16	4	2	10	24	35	10

1913-14

	P	W	D	L	F	A	Pts
Brighton & HA	16	11	2	3	39	15	24
Luton T	16	11	1	4	36	20	23
Croydon Common	16	10	2	4	24	16	22
Cardiff C	16	5	4	7	26	25	14
Newport C	16	6	2	8	20	23	14
Portsmouth	16	6	0	10	22	28	12
Southampton	16	5	2	9	27	32	12
Brentford	16	4	4	8	18	33	12
Southend U	16	4	3	9	15	35	11

Friendly Matches 1885 to 1987

1885-86
Nov 21 v Freemantle (h) 5-1
A.A.Fry 2, C.Bromley 3
Jan 9 v Southampton Harriers (h) 0-0
Jan 23 v Freemantle (a) 1-0
Deacon
Feb 13 v Totton (a) 3-0
McIvor, Abbott, A.A.Fry
Mar 13 v Southampton Harriers (h) 2-0
C.Bromley 2

1886-87
Oct 16 v Southampton Harriers (h) 1-1
Muir
Nov 20 v Freemantle (h) 2-0
Sommerville, McIvor
Nov 27 v Bannister Court (a) 1-2
Sommerville
Dec 4 v Handel College (a) 4-0
Sommerville, C.Bromley 2, Hitchcock
Dec 15 v Caledonians (h) 3-0
Deacon, C.Bromley 2
Dec 18 v Southampton Harriers (h) 0-0
Jan 22 v Freemantle (h) 1-0
Varley
Jan 29 v Greenhill Rovers (h) 2-0
McDonald, Sommerville
Feb 12 v Freemantle (a) 3-0
C.Bromley, Noble 2
Feb 16 v Handel College (h) 5-1
Deacon, Sommerville, C.Bromley, Hickman 2
Feb 26 v Cowes (h) 1-0
G.Muir
Mar 12 v Southampton Harriers (h) 0-2
Mar 19 v Greenhill Rovers (a) 2-0
Steele, Warn

1887-88
Oct 19 v Handel College (a) 3-2
Warn 2, C.Bromley
Oct 29 v Southampton Harriers (h) 1-0
C.Bromley
Nov 12 v Freemantle (h) 1-0
C.Bromley
Feb 4 v Freemantle (a) 0-3
Feb 11 v Totton (a) 4-1
Carter, A.A.Fry, C.Bromley 2

1888-89
Oct 6 v Woolston Works (h) 1-2
Delamotte
Nov 3 v Winchester Rovers (a) 1-2
Varley
Dec 1 v Christchurch (at County Ground) 2-2
C.Bromley, Farwell
Dec 29 v Freemantle (a) 1-1
Warn
Feb 2 v Cowes (a) 0-1
Feb 9 v Bannister Court (h) 2-1
Warn, Delamotte
Feb 16 v Fremantle (h) 2-3
Deacon, F.Bromley
Feb 19 v Winchester (h) 1-0
A.A.Fry

1889-90
Oct 12 v Winchester City (h) 4-0
Scorers unknown
Oct 19 v Portsmouth Grammar (h) 5-0
Verney, Deacon, Delamotte 2, Kiddle
Oct 26 v Cowes (h) 6-1
Warn, Farwell 2, Kiddle 3
Nov 16 v Bournemouth (h) 2-1
Farwell, Kiddle
Nov 23 v Geneva Cross (a) 2-0
Farwell, Kiddle
Nov 30 v London Incogniti (h) 5-0
Scorers unknown
Dec 14 v Poole Harriers (h) 7-0
Deacon 2, Warn, Farwell, Kiddle, Bromley, Delamotte
Dec 21 v Geneva Cross (h) 3-0
Scorers unknown
Dec 28 v South Saxon Swallows (h) 3-1
Scorers unknown
Jan 1 v South Saxon Swallows (at County Ground) 2-0
Scorers unknown
Jan 4 v Geneva Cross (h) 1-0
Scorer unknown
Jan 18 v Medical Staff Corps (h) 3-0
Warn 2, Bromley
Feb 8 v Bannister Court (h) 1-1
Scorers unknown
Feb 22 v London Caledonians (h) 2-0
Farwell 2
Mar 8 v Christchurch (h) 2-0
Carter 2

Apr 12 v Royal Engineers (at County Ground) 2-1
Delamotte, Warn
Apr 19 v Freemantle (at County Ground) 4-0
Bromley, Delamotte, Farwell. opp.og

G.W.Verney

1890-91
Sep 20 v London Caledonians (h) 1-3
Farwell
Oct 4 v Freemantle (h) 4-0
Bromley, Deacon, Delamotte, Farwell
Oct 11 v Bournemouth (a) 1-0
Verney
Oct 18 v Geneva Cross (a) 3-3
Bromley 2, Farwell
Oct 23 v Winchester City (a) 6-0
Nicholls 3, Delamotte 2, Sims
Oct 25 v Cowes (a) 3-1
Bromley, Delamotte, Kiddle
Nov 1 v 93rd Highland Regiment (h) 0-4
Nov 8 v Swindon Town (h) 2-3
Stride, Wilkins
Nov 15 v Weymouth College (h) 2-0
Carter, Farwell
Sep 22 v Royal Engineers (h) 4-3
Nicholls 3, Kiddle
Dec 13 v Bournemouth (h) 5-0
Farwell 2, Nicholls 2, Kiddle
Feb 7 v Reading (h) 1-3
Stride
Feb 14 v Royal Engineers (a) 1-5
Nicholls
Feb 28 v 93rd Highland Regiment (a) 0-4
Mar 7 v Cowes (h) 2-0
Bromley, Reid
Mar 28 v Mr Gray's Cambridge XI (h) 2-0
Delamotte, Farwell
Mar 30 v London Caledonians (at County Ground) 2-0
Bromley, Richardson
Apr 8 v Freemantle (at County Ground) 3-1
Bromley, Farwell, Warn

1891-92
Sep 26 (h) Reading (h) 2-2
Delamotte 2
Oct 10 v 93rd Highland Regiment (at County Ground) 0-2
Oct 31 v Swindon Town (a) 1-5
Mulford
Nov 6 v Royal Engineers (h) 0-0
Dec 5 v Medical Staff (h) 1-0
Delamotte
Dec 10 v Canadians (h) 2-2
Delamotte, Evans
Dec 19 v Bournemouth (a) 3-3
Fleming, Kiddle, Nicholls
Dec 26 v South Staffordshire Regiment (h) 1-6
Kiddle
Jan 2 v Old Weymouthians (h) 1-1
Stride
Jan 9 v Swindon Town (h) 3-1
Carter, Cruickshank, Farwell
Jan 23 v Reading (a) 0-3

Jan 30 v Bournemouth (h) 4-0
Carter, Delamotte, Farwell, Nicholls
Feb 6 v South Staffordshire Regiment (h) 0-2
Feb 13 v Weymouth College (a) 3-0
Carter, Kiddle, Ruffell
Feb 27 v Woolwich Arsenal (h) 2-6
Delamotte, Mulford
Mar 5 v Newbury (h) 2-2
Delamotte, Kiddle
Mar 26 v Lincolnshire Regiment (h) 0-3
Apr 16 v Great Marlow (at County Ground) 0-1
Apr 18 v Aldershot Division (at County Ground) 3-1
Miller, Nicholls, Ridges

1892-93
Sep 17 v South Staffs Regiment (at County Ground) 0-4
Sep 24 v Reading (h) 0-1
Oct 1 v Newbury (a) 2-3
Dollin, Mulford
Oct 8 v Highland Light Infantry (h) 2-3
Peck, Verney
Oct 22 v Royal Engineers (h) 2-2
Bailey, Deacon
Nov 5 v Swindon Town (h) 0-5
Nov 12 v King's Own Lancasters (h) 3-1
Delamotte, Kiddle, Verney
Nov 26 v Freemantle (h) 1-1
Dollin
Dec 3 v Maidenhead (h) 0-2
Dec 10 v Woolwich Arsenal (h) 2-0
Dollin, Mulford
Dec 26 v North Staffordshire Regiment (h) 2-2
Delamotte, Nineham
Dec 31 v Freemantle (h) 3-3
Nicholls 3
Jan 14 v Bournemouth (h) 4-0
Dorkin 2, Delmotte, Dollin
Jan 18 v 15th Company Royal Artillery (h) 1-2
Dorkin
Jan 21 v Newbury (h) 5-0
Nicholls 3, Dorkin, G.Marshall
Jan 28 v Reading (a) 1-0
Delamotte
Feb 1 v King's Own Rifles (h) 2-0
Dollin 2
Feb 11 v Bournemouth (a) 1-2
Dollin
Feb 18 v Royal Artillery (h) 7-0
Delamotte 2, Dorkin 2, Nicholls, Nineham, Verney
Feb 25 v Highland Light Infantry (h) 1-0
Dorkin
Mar 4 v Woolwich Arsenal (a) 0-0
Mar 18 v King's Own Rifles (h) 7-1
Dollin 2, Dorkin 2, Kiddle, Nineham, Verney
Mar 22 v Portsmouth (h) 3-0
Dorkin 2, Dollin
Mar 25 v Hampshire Regiment (h) 5-0
Dorkin, Kiddle, G.Marshall, Nicholl, Nineham
Apr 3 v Windsor & Eton (h) 3-1
Dorkin 2, Nicholls
Apr 26 v Stoke (at County Ground) 0-8
Apr 29 v Crouch End (at County Ground) 4-3
Dollin, Nineham, Stride, Verney

1893-94
Sep 22 v Christchurch (h) 9-2
Angus 4, Dorkin 3, Nineham, Taylor
Sep 30 v Trowbridge (h) 4-1
Dorkin 4
Oct 7 v Royal Engineers (h) 7-0
Angus 3, Nicholls 2, Dorkin, Nineham
Oct 14 v 15th Company Royal Artillery (h) 3-1
Angus, Dorkin, Nicholls
Oct 21 v Cowes (a) 1-1
Dorkin
Oct 28 v Bournemouth (h) 4-0
Angus 2, Taylor, Verney
Nov 11 v Newbury (h) 1-1
Nineham
Nov 23 v Bolton Wanderers (h) 0-5
Dec 2 v Cameronians (h) 6-1
Dorkin 2, Angus, Nicholls, Offer, Taylor
Dec 16 v Lancaster Regiment (h) 2-2
Angus, Nicholls
Dec 26 v Tottenham Hotspur (h) 1-0
Nicholls
Dec 27 v United Services (h) 1-2
E.Kiddle
Dec 30 v Surrey Wanderers (h) 4-1
Offer 2, R.Kiddle, Nineham
Jan 13 v Woolwich Arsenal (h) 4-2
Angus 2, Nineham 2
Jan 20 v Cowes (h) 5-0
Angus 3, Miller, Taylor
Jan 27 v 15th Company, Royal Artillery (h) 1-3
Dorkin

Mar 3 v Lancaster Regiment (h) 2-3
Angus 2
Mar 24 v Clapton (h) 2-0
Dorkin, Offer
Mar 26 v 2nd Scots Guards (at County Ground) 4-1
H.Ward 3, Offer
Mar 27 v Poole (h) 1-1
Offer
Apr 11 v Worcester Regiment (at County Ground) 3-2
Offer 2, H.Ward
Apr 14 v Old St Stephen's (at County Ground) 2-4
R.Kiddle, Offer
Apr 25 v Stoke (at County Ground) 2-3
Angus, G.Marshall

1894-95
Sep 8 v Connaught Rangers (h) 13-0
Offer 5, Baker 3, Angus 3, Dorkin 2
Sep 15 v Royal Engineers (h) 6-0
Angus, Hollands, Baker, Offer, Dorkin, Littlehales
Sep 22 v Lancaster Regiment (h) 5-4
Offer 3, Baker, Angus
Sep 29 v Weymouth (h) 6-0
Littlehales 2, Nineham, Offer, Angus, Taylor
Nov 8 v Bolton Wanderers (h) 5-2
Dorkin 2, Offer, Hollands, Angus
Nov 28 v Stoke (h) 1-3
Littlehales
Dec 26 v Freemantle (h) 9-0
Ward 5, Nineham 2, Offer, Thomson
Jan 1 v Dresden United (h) 1-2
Offer
Jan 14 v New Brompton (a) 7-5
Angus 2, Offer 2, Rogers 2, Baker
Jan 15 v Sheppey United (a) 1-1
Angus
Jan 16 v Folkestone (a) 1-0
Rogers
Jan 19 v Wiltshire Regiment (h) 13-0
Rogers 10, Littlehales 2, Baker
Jan 26 v Royal Ordnance (h) 2-2
Rogers 2
Feb 9 v 15th Company Royal Artillery (h) 3-1
Angus, Hollands, Rogers
Feb 13 v New Brompton (h) 2-0
Rogers 2
Feb 16 v Lancaster Regiment (h) 0-3
Mar 2 v Vampires (h) 3-2
Angus, Baker, Hollands
Mar 4 v Freemantle (h) 2-2
Rogers 2
Mar 16 v Worcester Regiment (h) 2-0
Angus, Baker
Mar 20 v Bartholomew's (h) 9-0
Angus 4, Nineham 3, Ward 2
Mar 27 v Freemantle (h) 8-0
Dorkin 4, Angus 2, Ward, opp.og
Apr 15 v Tottenham Hotspur (h) 0-0
Apr 20 v Corinthians (h) 2-0
Baker, Dorkin
Apr 27 v Eastbourne (a) 6-1
Dorkin 3, Hollands 2, Angus
Apr 29 v Royal Artillery (Portsmouth) (h) 5-1
Dorkin 2, Taylor 2, Hollands

1895-86
Sep 4 v Pickfords XI (h) 1-0
Naughton
Sep 7 v Vampires (h) 3-0
Farrell, Littlehales, Rogers
Sep 9 v Glossop (h) 3-1
Baker, Farrell, Keay
Sep 25 v Bourkes XI (h) 6-1
Farrell 3, Baker 2, Naughton
Oct 3 v Dublin Fusiliers (h) 9-0
Farrell 5, Turner 3, Naughton
Oct 9 v Casuals (h) 5-0
Baker 2, Littlehales, Naughton, Turner
Oct 16 v Argyle & Sutherland Highlanders (h) 2-2
Meston 2
Oct 23 v Weymouth Athletic (a) 6-0
Baker 2, Angus, Farrell, Naughton, Turner
Nov 9 v Wolverton (h) 8-0
Taylor 3, Baker 2, Keay 2, Turner
Nov 11 v Leicester Regiment (h) 7-0
Rogers 3, Taylor 2, Kiddle 2
Dec 26 v Aldershot Association (h) 7-0
Naughton 2, Taylor 2, Keay, Rogers, Turner
Dec 27 v Cliftonville (h) 1-1
Farrell
Dec 28 v Royal Artillery (Portsmouth) (h) 6-2
Farrell 3, Keay 2, Rogers
Jan 4 v Ealing (h) 2-0
Hodgkinson, Keay
Jan 8 v 3rd Grenadier Guards (h) 1-1
Rogers
Jan 11 v London Civil Service (h) 9-1
Farrell 3, Turner 3, Keay, Naughton, Rogers
Feb 8 v Grantham Rovers (h) 4-0
Farrell 2, Baker, Naughton

Feb 22 v Royal Ordnance (h) 4-1
Naughton 2, Farrell, Turner
Mar 1 v Newark (h) 6-0
Farrell 3, Turner 3
Mar 11 v City Ramblers (h) 13-0
Farrell 5, Rogers 3, Turner 3, Baker, Hodgkinson
Mar 14 v Manchester Regiment (h) 9-1
Farrell 5, Taylor 2, Baker, Hodgkinson
Mar 24 v Sheffield United (h) 0-3
Apr 6 v Argyle & Sutherland Highlanders (h) 3-2
Baker, Farrell, Keay
Apr 8 v Dundee (h) 2-0
Keay, Naughton
Apr 11 v Kettering (h) 1-0
Farrell
Apr 15 v Royal Artillery (Portsmouth) (h) 1-1
Baker
Apr 18 v Tottenham Hotspur (h) 4-1
Baker, Farrell, Meston, Naughton
Apr 22 v Luton Town (h) 0-0
Apr 25 v Reading (h) 1-1
Farrell
Apr 29 v Freemantle (h) 1-0
Hayter

1896-97
Sep 2 v Kettering (h) 4-0
Farrell 2, Buchanan, Turner
Sep 5 v Aldershot Garrison (h) 9-0
Farrell 3, Buchanan 2, Shenton 2, Reay, Keay
Sep 7 v Lincoln City (h) 0-1
Sep 12 v RE Training Battalion (Chatham) (h) 2-0
Buchanan, McMillan
Sep 14 v Burslem Port Vale (h) 2-1
Farrell, Littlehales
Sep 21 v 1st Scots Guards (h) 2-0
Buchanan, Keay
Sep 23 v Cowes (a) 0-0
Sep 28 v Burton Wanderers (h) 3-0
Littlehales 2, Turner
Oct 5 v Casuals (h) 1-0
Keay
Oct 10 v Blackpool (h) 0-1
Oct 12 v 3rd Grenadier Guards (h) 5-0
Buchanan, Hayter, Shenton, Spellacy, Turner
Oct 19 v Middlesbrough (h) 2-1
Farrell, McMillan
Oct 26 v Gordon Highlanders (h) 2-0
Keay 2
Oct 31 v Lincoln City (h) 1-1
Littlehales
Nov 2 v Casuals (a) 3-0
Buchanan, Keay, Turner
Dec 2 v Gravesend (h) 1-1
Seeley
Dec 26 v White Star Wanderers (h) 4-0
Turner 3, Keay
Dec 28 v Guildford (h) 8-0
Farrell 3, Turner 3, Shenton 2
Jan 4 v Guildford (a) 3-1
Buchanan, Farrell, Turner
Jan 23 v Millwall (h) 0-0
Feb 20 v Cowes (h) 1-1
Lea
Mar 10 v Gravesend (a) 0-3
Mar 15 v Woolwich Arsenal (a) 1-2
Buchanan
Mar 20 v Lancashire Regiment (h) 8-0
Buchanan 3, Farrell 2, Turner 2, Naughton
Mar 22 v Sheffield Wednesday (h) 4-1
Buchanan, Farrell, Littlehales, Turner
Mar 27 v Clapton (a) 3-0
Farrell 2, Buchanan
Apr 3 v Dartford (h) 1-1
Keay
Apr 16 v Clapton (h) 3-0
Buchanan 3
Apr 17 v Darwen (h) 2-0
Haynes, Shenton
Apr 19 v Blackburn Rovers (h) 4-1
Farrell 2, Buchanan, Haynes
Apr 20 v Vampires (h) 0-2
Farrell Benefit game
Apr 24 v Derby County (h) 7-3
Turner 3, Farrell 2, Keay, Naughton
Apr 28 v Woolwich Arsenal (h) 1-5
Turner

1897-98
Sep 1 v Bristol City (a) 1-3
Farrell
Sep 2 v Swindon Town (a) 0-0
Sep 4 v Glossop (h) 2-2
Farrell, Turner
Sep 8 v Burton Swifts (h) 6-1
Farrell 3, Turner 2, Keay
Sep 11 v Pickford XI (h) 7-2
Farrell 3, Turner 2, Brown, Keay
Sep 15 v 3rd Grenadier Guards (h) 1-0
Naughton

Sep 29 v Cowes (a) 5-2
Buchanan, A.Chadwick, Farrell, Meston, Turner
Oct 13 v 2nd Gordon Highlanders (h) 2-1
Keay, Yates
Nov 20 v Sussex (at Littlehampton) 3-1
Keay 2, Turner
Dec 4 v Millwall (h) 1-1
Naughton
Dec 15 v Reading (h) 0-0
Dec 18 v Gravesend (h) 6-0
Buchanan 2, Meston 2, Farrell, Turner
Dec 25 v Hereford Thistle (h) 2-1
Buchanan, Farrell
Dec 27 v Darlington (h) 5-2
A.Chadwick 2, McLean 2, Farrell
Jan 5 v Eastleigh (h) 6-2
Farrell 4, McLean, opp.og.
Littlehales Benefit game
Apr 24 v Middlesbrough (h) 3-1
Scorers unknown
Apr 25 v Derby County (h) 1-4
Turner

1898-99
Sep 1 v Bedminster (a) 2-1
Hartley, Nicol
Sep 2 v West Norwood (a) 5-3
Stevens 2, Buchanan, Englefield, Fairgrave
Sep 5 v Leicester Fosse (a) 0-1
Sep 7 v Richmond Association (h) 1-1
Fairgrave
Sep 10 v Clapton (h) 3-1
A.Chadwick, Englefield, Robertson
Sep 14 v Leicester Fosse (h) 1-0
Fairgrave
Oct 12 v Richmond Association (a) 2-2
Seeley, Wood
Oct 26 v Bournemouth (a) 6-0
Seeley 2, Buchanan, Fairgrave, Keay, T.Smith
Dec 10 v Queen's Park Rangers (a) 3-2
T.Smith 2, Wood
Dec 27 v Darwen (h) 1-0
A.Chadwick
Jan 21 v New Brompton (a) 2-0
Keay, Nicol
Jan 30 v New Brompton (h) 4-1
Seeley 2, Keay, Wood
Keay Benefit game
Feb 4 v Corinthians (a) 0-0
Mar 4 v Casuals (a) 2-2
Nicol, Wood
Mar 16 v Brentford (a) 2-2
Hartley 2
Mar 25 v Corinthians (a) 2-2
Stevens, Wood
Apr 1 v Corinthians (h) 1-2
Wood
Apr 3 v Glasgow Rangers (h) 0-1
Apr 8 v Sheppey United (h) 5-0
Cavendish, Keay, Seeley, T.Smith, Stevens
Apr 19 v Guildford (h) 4-1
Cavendish 2, T.Smith, Yates

1899-1900
Sep 6 v Portsmouth (a) 0-2
Sep 30 v Tottenham Hotspur (h) 2-1
A.Turner, Wood
Oct 2 v Wolverhampton Wanderers (a) 0-1
Oct 4 v Richmond Association (h) 3-0
Cavendish, Keay, opp.og
Oct 7 v Corinthians (a) 1-1
Milward
Oct 23 v Wolverhampton Wanderers (h) 2-5
Yates 2
Haynes Benefit game
Oct 25 v Bournemouth & District (a) 3-0
Farrell 2, Yates
Oct 28 v Tottenham Hotspur (a) 3-4
Milward, A.Turner, Yates
Nov 1 v Richmond Association (a) 5-3
McLeod 2, Cavendish, Meston, Wood
Nov 8 v Cambridge University (h) 5-2
McLeod 2, Farrell, Milward, Yates
Nov 20 v Oxford University (h) 2-4
Cavendish, Haynes
Dec 9 v Woolwich Arsenal (a) 1-1
Yates
Dec 23 v Casuals (a) 1-0
Milward
Jan 1 v Stockton (a) 4-2
Cavendish, Greenless, Meston, opp.og
Jan 3 v Aston Villa (a) 2-4
Farrell, Milward
Jan 29 v Cambridge University (a) 1-2
Milward
Mar 14 v Swindon Town (h) 1-0
McLeod
Meston Benefit game

1900-01
Sep 5 v Reading (h) 6-1
E.Chadwick 2, Toman 2, Milward, A.Chadwick
Sep 8 v Tottenham Hotspur (a) 1-3
A.Turner
Sep 12 v Reading (a) 0-3
Sep 17 v Bristol Rovers (a) 0-2
Oct 1 v Queen's Park Rangers (a) 0-1
Oct 10 v Bournemouth Wanderers (a) 4-1
Wood 3, Milward
Oct 22 v Millwall (a) 0-3
Oct 31 v Bristol City (a) 0-0
Nov 17 v Corinthians (a) 1-3
Wood
Nov 12 v Oxford University (a) 0-0
Nov 21 v Woolwich Arsenal (h) 4-1
Milward 2, E.Chadwick, A.Turner.
A.Chadwick Benefit game
Jan 5 v Berlin (h) 5-1
Milward 2, Toman 2, A.Chadwick
Mar 9 v Corinthians (a) 3-2
Toman 2, Wood
European Tour
Scorers not reported
Apr 21 v the Hague (a) 6-2
Apr 23 v Slavia (a) 5-1
Apr 24 v Prague & Vienna XI (a) 3-0
Apr 27 v Vienna C & FC (a) 7-0
Apr 28 v Vienna Combined (a) 8-0
Apr 29 v Toma Club, Budapest (a) 8-0
Apr 30 v Hungarian Combined XI (a) 13-0

1901-02
Oct 5 v Corinthians (a) 1-0
A.Brown
Nov 19 v Woolwich Arsenal (a) 1-0
McDonald
Apr 22 v Aston Villa (h) 1-4
Small

1902-03
Mar 4 v Eastbourne (a) 5-0
Harrison 2, Barlow, Fraser, J.Turner.
Mar 17 v Cornwall County (at St Austell) 9-1
Harrison 3, Barlow 2, Fraser 2
Mar 18 v Crownhill (at Plymouth) 4-3
Harrison 2, Evans 2
Apr 11 v Corinthians (h) 0-2
European tour
Scorers not reported
Apr 15 v The Hague (a) 4-1
Apr 19 v Toma Club Budapest (a) 14-0
Apr 20 v Budapest Combined XI (a) 15-0
Apr 22 v SK Slavia (a) 4-2
Apr 25 v Prague Combined XI (a) 15-0
Apr 26 v SK Slavia (a) 4-1
Apr 29 v Copenhagen BC 93 (a) 4-0
Apr 30 v Copenhagen Combined XI (a) 3-0

1903-04
Nov 5 v Aston Villa (h) 1-1
Hedley
Jan 16 v Corinthians (a) 1-4
Fraser
Mar 13 v French XI (at Parc de Princes, Paris) 6-1
Scorers not reported
14 v French XI (at Parc de Princes, Paris) 11-0
Scorers not reported
Apr 13 v Portsmouth (a) 2-4
Spence, Wood
Apr 25 v Aston Villa (a) 3-2
Houlker, J.Turner, Wood
Apr 26 v Clapton Orient (a) 2-0
Meston, H.Turner.
Danish Tour
Scorers not reported
May 5 v Copenhagen Combined XI (a) 3-1
May 10 v Newcastle United (a) 0-4

1904-05
South American tour
Scorers not reported
Jul 2 v Alumni (a) 3-0
Jul 3 v Britanico (a) 10-0
Jul 4 v Belgrano (a) 6-1
Jul 9 v Buenos Aires (a) 8-0
Jul 10 v Buenos Aires (a) 5-3
Jul 12 v Montevideo (a) 8-1
Oct 17 v Swindon Town (h) 6-0
Hedley 3, Fraser, H.Turner, Webb
Dawson Benefit game
Apr 26 v Corinthians (h) 3-1
Jefferis 3

1905-06
Sep 4 v Northampton Town (a) 2-2
H.Brown, Soye
Nov 20 v Chelsea (h) 5-2
Soye 3, H.Brown, Harris
Lee Benefit game

Dec 10 v Bristol City (h) 2-1
Harrison 2
Harrison Benefit game

1906-07
Feb 25 v Bristol City (a) 4-2
Glen 2, Harrison, Mouncher
Dec 7 v Royal Navy 5-0
Jefferis 3, Costello, G.Smith

1907-08
European Tour
Scorers not always reported
May 22 v The Hague (a) 4-2
Hughes 3, Ward
May 24 v Madgeburg (a) 9-1
May 26 v Dresden Sporting (a) 5-2
May 28 v Union Club Berlin (a) 5-0
May 31 v Leipzig (a)
Score not reported

1908-09
Feb 15 v Fulham (a) 0-3
Mar 21 v Bristol Rovers (Exhibition match in Paris) 5-5
Scorers not reported
Apr 26 v Fulham (h) 1-0
Jordan

1909-10
Scandinavian tour during this season but no results recorded
Oct 10 v Merthyr (a) 2-4
Brittleton, Jordan

1910-11
Oct 31 v Manchester City (h) 3-3
Jefferis 2, Dunne
Jefferis Benefit game

1911-12
Sep 18 v Portsmouth (h) 2-1
Hamilton, McAlpine
Eastham Benefit game
Sep 27 v Portsmouth (a) 1-1
H.Brown
Feb 3 v Aldershot FA (h) 6-1
Hamilton 5, Gibson
Feb 24 v Portsmouth (a) 0-2

1912-13
May 3 v Birmingham Works XI (h) 4-1
Prince 3, Dominy

1913-14
Nov 29 v Boscombe (a) 3-0
Andrews, Dominy, Prince
Apr 30 v Weymouth (a) 2-0
Andrews, Denby

1914-15
Apr 15 v Swansea Town (a) 2-2
Lee 2
May 1 v Boscombe (a) 1-2
Kimpton

1919-20
Dec 10 v West Ham (h) 3-1
Barratt 2, Hudson
Dec 20 v Millwall (a) 2-2
Boyes, Parker
Feb 23 v Ebbw Vale (a) 4-0
Barratt 3, Dominy

1920-21
Oct 18 v Bridgend (a) 3-1
Dominy, Foxall, Moore
Mar 14 v Aberdare (a) 0-1
May 14 v Reading (a) 1-1
Dominy
(Berkshire charity cup)

Fred Foxall

1921-22
Oct 10 v Portsmouth (h) 4-0
Horton 2, Dominy, Foxall
Arnfield Benefit game
Nov 16 v Portsmouth (a) 0-1
Dec 5 v Preston North End (h) 3-1
Rawlings 2, Foxall
Dominy Benefit game
Feb 18 v Corinthians (h) 1-0
Meston

1922-23
Oct 16 v Woolwich Arsenal (h) 3-5
Rawlings 2, Dominy
Campbell Benefit game
Dec 4 v Portsmouth (h) 1-3
Meston
May 3 v Northampton (a) 2-2
Johnson 2

1923-24
Nov 14 v Portsmouth (h) 0-2
Lee Benefit game
Dec 1 v Corinthians (a) 0-1
Dec 26 v Corinthians (h) 1-2
Price

1924-25
Nov 24 v Plymouth (h) 1-1
Rawlings
Parker Benefit game
Mar 16 v Plymouth (a) 1-1
C.Price

1925-26
Sep 23 v Portsmouth (a) 3-0
Bullock 3
Jan 28 v Corinthians (h) 3-3
Rawlings 2, Henderson
Mar 15 v Leicester City (h) 2-0
Matthews 2
Allen & Shelley Benefit game
Apr 14 v Guildford (a) 1-1
Dominy
Apr 28 v Bournemouth (a) 0-1

1926-27
Sep 22 v Guildford (a) 2-3
Murphy, Rawlings
Nov 3 v Aldershot Command (a) 4-0
Rowley 2, Rawlings, Croom
Apr 25 v Bournemouth (a) 1-0
Rawlings
May 4 v Exeter (a) 1-1
Rawlings

1927-28
Sep 28 v Bournemouth (a) 1-3
Rawlings
Jan 28 v Corinthians (a) 0-5
Apr 23 v Guildford (a) 3-3
Wilson 2, Shelley
Apr 30 v Wimbourne (a) 2-2
Lohse, Shelley
May 2 v Millwall (h) 1-2
Swinden
Keeping & Hough Benefit game

1928-29
Apr 17 v Guildford (a) 2-1
Haines, Arnold
Apr 22 v Warminster (a) 6-1
Haines 3, Bradford, Cribb, Woodhouse
Apr 29 v Wimbourne (a) 6-2
Haines 2, Rowley 2, Arnold, Weale

1929-30
Sep 25 v Aldershot (a) 3-3
Rowley 2, Arnold
Feb 15 v Corinthians (h) 2-0
Haines 2
Apr 9 v Salisbury District XI (a) 2-2
Fraser, Mackie
Apr 16 v Andover (a) 6-1
Haines 3, Fraser 2, Arnold
Apr 28 v Royal Air Force (a) 0-1
Danish Tour
Scorers not always reported
May 25 v Odense (a) 3-0
May 29 v Aarhus (a) 4-0
Jun 1 v Aalborg (a) 3-1
Jun 5 v Horsens (a) 3-4
Fraser, Dougal, Jepson

1930-31
Mar 25 v Boscombe (a) 3-3
Haines 3

1931-32
Nov 18 v Royal Air Force (h) 4-0
Matson 2, Dougal, Holt
Jan 23 v Exeter City (a) 0-2
Mar 9 v Dutch FA (in Rotterdam) 1-6
Wilson
Apr 13 v Southern Command (a) 3-1
Arnold, Brewis, Drake

1932-33
Feb 18 v Gillingham (a) 1-3
Holt
Mar 15 v Tidworth Garrison (a) 3-1
Hunt 2, Clarke

Ted Drake

1933-34
Jan 27 v Fulham (h) 2-1
Drake, Holt

1934-35
Mar 5 v Harve Athletic (a) 2-2
Holt, Tully

1935-36
Jan 25 v Wolverhampton Wanderers (h) 2-3
Fishlock, Watson

1936-37
Feb 20 v Gillingham (a) 0-2
Apr 28 v Brighton (a) 1-1
Holt

1937-38
Feb 9 v Army FA (a) 7-2
Kelly 4, Parkin 3
Apr 27 v North Dorset (a) 8-0
Lock 5, Holt, Kelly, Wall
May 2 v Arsenal (h) 1-2
Osman

1938-39
Aug 20 v Portsmouth (a) 2-4
Bevis, Tomlinson
(Football League Jubilee match)

1939-40
Aug 19 v Portsmouth (h) 0-3
(Football League Jubilee match

1946-47
Aug 14 v Bohemians (a) 4-1
Lewis 2, Roper 2
Aug 23 v Le Havre (h) 7-0
Roper 3, McGibbon 2, Bradley, Veck
May 14 v Guernsey (a) 2-1
Bradley, Lewis
Jun 11 v BAOR XI (a*) 1-4
(*Liberation day match in Germany)

1947-48
Brazilian Tour
May 16 v Fluminense (a) 0-4
May 20 v Botafogo (a) 1-3
Ellerington

May 25 v São Paulo (a) 2-4
Rochford, Wayman
May 29 v Portuguesa (a) 2-1
Grant, Curtis
Jun 2 v Corinthians (a) 1-2
Wayman
Jun 6 v Flamengo (a) 3-1
Wayman 2, Scott
Jun 10 v Vasco da Gama (a) 1-2
Wayman
13 v Minos Gerais (a) 1-1
Wayman

1948-49
Jan 15 v Plymouth (a) 1-0
Gallego

1949-50
Jan 28 v Torquay United (h) 1-0
Dare
Scandinavian Tour
May 25 v Aalborg (a) 6-2
Wayman 4, Bates, Day
May 29 v Hälsingborg (a) 1-2
Bates
Jun 1 v Copenhagen (a) 1-1
Scorer not reported
5 v Aarhus (a) 1-0
Bates
8 v Esbjerg (a) 2-2
Wayman 2

1950-51
Oct 31 v Bournemouth (h) 0-0
Feb 10 v Middlesbrough (h) 1-1
Dudley
Feb 24 v Bournemouth (a) 3-2
Dudley 3
Apr 23 v Boston United (a) 0-1
May 9 v Jersey XI (a) 2-0
E Brown, Edwards
May 14 v Servette (h) 3-0
E.Brown, Curtis, Day
(Festival of Britain game)
May 19 v KB (Copenhagen) (h) 3-3
E.Brown 3
(Festival of Britain game)

1951-52
Aug 4 v Ayr United (a) 4-1
E.Brown 2, Dudley, Edwards
(Festival of Britain game)
Oct 22 v Portsmouth (h) 2-2
Dudley, Edwards
Dec 17 v Middlesbrough (h) 3-2
Bogan, Curtis, Day
Feb 2 v Plymouth (a) 1-5
Lowder
Mar 17 v Dundee (h) 2-3
Bates, Lowder
Apr 2 v Exeter City (a) 2-3
Bates, Dudley

1952-53
Nov 3 v Weymouth (a) 2-1
Dudley, Page
Dec 1 v Sunderland (h) 2-3
Day, Dudley
Mar 2 v Portsmouth (a) 1-1
Williams

1953-54
Oct 7 v Hereford United (a) 1-1
Williams
Nov 11 v South Africa (h) 6-2
Day 3, Flood 2, Walker
Nov 30 v Cardiff City (h) 2-0
Day, Flood
Dec 12 v Watford (a) 1-1
Horton
Mar 1 v Pegasus (h) 3-0
Traynor, Walker, Whittle

1954-55
Nov 8 v Pegasus (h) 3-3
Day 2, Traynor
Jan 31 v Linz (Austria) (h) 3-0
Mulgrew 2, Day
Feb 9 v Grazer Sporting Club (Austria) (h) 2-1
Hoskins, Ritchie
Mar 7 v Portsmouth (h) 1-3
Day

1955-56
Jan 18 v Poole Town (a) 0-1
Feb 1 v San Lorenzo (h) 1-2
Bedford
Feb 13 v Ex International XI (h) 5-1
Mulgrew 3, Day, Walker

Feb 27 v Yeovil Town (a) 2-2
G.Brown, Reeves
May 5 v Burnley (h) 2-2
Day 2
Apr 16 v Luton Town (h) 5-1
Mulgrew 2, Reeves, Traynor, Walker
Apr 25 v Rampla (h) 1-0
Mulgrew
Apr 30 v Ex Saints (h) 1-0
McGowan
May 9 v Guernsey XI (a) 3-1
Mulgrew 2, Walker

John Walker

1956-57
Oct 22 v All Star Managers XI (h) 3-0
Day, Flood, Reeves
Feb 16 v Portsmouth (h) 3-1
Reeves 2, Day
Apr 8 v Kilmarnock (h) 2-1
Reeves, Roper

1958-59
Nov 3 v South Africa (h) 2-2
Hoskins, Roper
Nov 10 v Arsenal (h) 1-1
Mulgrew

1959-60
May 2 v Norwich (a) 0-0
(Norfolk & Norwich Charity Cup)
May 5 v Cambridge City (a) 2-2
O'Brien 2
May 9 v Norwich City (h) 1-1
Traynor
(World Refugee charity match)

1960-61
Mar 1 v Margate (a) 6-2
Reeves 4, Mulgrew, Paine
Apr 10 v Hereford United (a) 3-2
Clifton 2, opp.og

1961-62
Aug 12 v Portsmouth (h) 0-2
Nov 1 v La Paz (Bolivia) (h) 4-0
Paine 3, Chadwick
Jan 26 v West Ham United (h) 2-6
O'Brien, Penk
Jan 31 v Poole Town (a) 4-0
Mulgrew 2, Huxford, Reeves

1962-63
Nov 13 v Bordeaux (France) (h) 2-1
Chadwick, O'Brien
(Friendship Cup)
May 1 v Bordeaux (France) (a) 0-2
(Friendship Cup)

1963-64
Aug 17 v Sheffield Wednesday (h) 3-3
Burnside 2, Kirby
Apr 29 v Chelsea (h) 3-2
Burnside, O'Brien, Wimshurst
Reynolds testimonial game
Denmark & Germany Tour
May 5 v Vejle (a) 2-3
Burnside, Sydenham

May 7 v Nykøbing (a) 4-2
Dean 2, O'Brien 2
May 12 v Aalborg (a) 4-2
Burnside, Chadwick, Dean, O'Brien
May 14 v Svendborg (a) 2-1
Burnside, Sydenham
May 15 v Holstein Kiel (a) 1-3
Dean

1964-65
Aug 15 v Aston Villa (h) 3-2
Burnside, Chivers, Paine
Oct 19 v Vejle (Denmark) (h) 1-0
McGuigan
Mar 16 v Nykøbing (Denmark) (h) 9-1
Chivers 5, Melia 2, Sydenham, Wimshurst
Apr 29 v Oxford United (a) 0-2

1965-66
Aug 7 v Guildford City (a) 3-1
Melia, opp.og 2
Aug 14 v Bournemouth (a) 3-2
O'Brien 2, Paine
Feb 12 v Arsenal (h) 1-3
Chivers
May 10 v Portsmouth (h) 6-1
Chivers 2, Dean 2, Melia, Walker
Hollowbread testimonial game

1966-67
Aug 13 v Bristol City (a) 1-1
Sydenham
Oct 31 v Twente Enschede (Holland) (h) 3-3
Chivers 3
Mar 11 v Portsmouth (a) 2-2
Davies, Judd
Far East Tour
May 20 v Leicester City (In Kuala Lumpur) 1-3
Scorer not reported
May 26 v Malaysian XI (in Alor Star) 7-1
Davies 3, Channon, Chivers, Paine, Sydenham
May 28 v Asian All Stars (in Ipoh) 3-0
Davies 3
Jun 1 v Singapore (in Jalan Besar Stadium) 9-1
Chivers 4, Sydenham 3, Davies, Melia
Jun 5 v Leicester City (in Jalan Besar Stadium) 2-2
Davies 2

1967-68
Aug 5 v Bristol Rovers (a) 7-1
Chivers 3, Davies 3, Paine
Aug 9 v Italian Olympic XI (h) 2-2
Chivers, Davies
Aug 12 v Brighton & Hove Albion (a) 2-0
Chivers, Davies

Ron Davies

1968-69
Jul 27 v Bristol City (a) 3-5
Davies, McGrath, Saul
Aug 20 v Swindon Town (a) 1-3
Hollywood

Aug 3 v Oxford United (a) 3-0
Saul 2, Paine
Bermuda Tour
May 28 v Bermuda XI (in Hamilton) 8-1
Davies 5, Channon, Gabriel, Kemp
Jun 1 v West Ham United (in Hamilton) 4-2
Judd 3, Paine

1969-70
Dutch Tour
Jul 24 v Cloppenburg (a) 10-0
Davies 7, Gabriel 2, Davies
Jul 26 v Holland Sport (a) 2-0
Davies 2
Jul 29 v Schalke 04 (a) 0-2
Aug 2 v Dundee (h) 5-1
Davies 2, Judd 2, Stokes
Dec 3 v St Ouens (a) 15-3
Davies 5, Thompson 3, Channon 2, Stokes 2, Gabriel, Sydenham, opp.og
Apr 20 v Portsmouth (h) 2-4
Channon, Gabriel
Sydenham testimonial game
Far East Tour
May 21 v Ceylon XI (in Colombo) 6-0
Davies 2, Channon, O'Brien, Paine, Walker
May 23 v Ceylon XI (in Colombo) 2-1
Gabriel, Jenkins
May 26 v Bangkok Combined (in Bangkok) 4-2
Paine 2, Davies, opp.og
May 28 v Japan XI (in Tokyo) 3-1
Davies 2, Channon
Jun 2 v Japan XI (in Tokyo) 3-3
Davies, Jenkins, Paine
Jun 4 v Japan XI (in Kobe) 2-1
Kemp 2
Jun 7 v Japan XI (in Fukuoka) 2-0
Gabriel, Stokes

1970-71
Aug 1 v Brighton & Hove Albion (a) 1-0
O'Neil
Aug 4 v Swindon Town (a) 2-2
Channon, Davies
Aug 8 v Queen's Park Rangers (h) 3-0
Paine 2, Channon
Nov 3 v St Ouens (a) 6-1
Channon 2, Paine 2, Gabriel, O'Neil
Feb 22 v British Olympic XI (h) 0-4
Mar 7 v Guernsey (a) 3-0
Davies 2, Fisher
West Indies & El Salvador Tour
May 28 v El Salvador (in San Salvador) 2-1
Channon 2
May 30 v Chelsea (in San Salvador) 3-8
Gabriel 2, Paine
Jun 6 v Chelsea (in Trinidad) 2-6
Gabriel, Paine
Jun 8 v Trinadad (in Trinidad) 1-0
Scorer not reported

1971-72
Jul 31 v Brentford (a) 3-1
Channon, Fisher, O'Neil
Aug 4 v AFC Bournemouth (a) 2-3
Channon, Gabriel
Aug 7 v Japan XI (h) 6-2
Channon 3, Davies, Gabriel, opp.og
May 5 v Portsmouth (a) 7-0
Davies 2, Gabriel 2, O'Neil 2, McGrath

1972-73
Jul 29 v Swindon Town (a) 2-2
Channon, Davies
Aug 1 v Brighton & Hove Albion (a) 0-0
Aug 5 v Partick Thistle (h) 2-0
Davies, Jenkins
Feb 24 v Dundee United (h) 1-1
Gilchrist
Mauritius Tour
Jun 3 v Mauritius National XI (a) 0-0
Jun 10 v Mauritius National XI (a) 5-0
Steele 2, Gilchrist, O'Neil, Stokes

1973-74
Aug 11 v Reading (a) 1-2
Stokes
Aug 14 v Oxford United (a) 0-2
Aug 18 v Crystal Palace (h) 2-1
Channon, Stokes
Mar 9 v Aston Villa (a) 0-3
May 3 v Portsmouth (a) 0-0
May 7 v AFC Bournemouth (at Victoria Park) 2-1
Chatterley, Stokes

1974-75
Aug 13 v Leeds United (h) 1-1
O'Neil
Bates testimonial game

Apr 29 v Ipswich Town (h) 1-1
Channon
Paine testimonial game
May 6 v Portsmouth (a) 1-2
Stokes

1975-76
Norwegian Tour
July 29 v SK Brann (a) 2-1
Channon, Holmes
Aug 5 v Bodo Glimt (a) 2-0
Channon 2
7 v Mjolner Narvik (a) 4-0
Stokes 2, Channon, Gilchrist
Aug 9 v Grimsby Town (a) 2-2
Channon, Holmes
Sep 30 v Swaythling (a) 7-0
Gilchrist 2, Channon, Crabbe, Holmes, Peach, Stokes
Oct 14 v Gillingham (a) 4-3
Stokes 2, Channon, Holmes
Nov 3 v SK Brann (Norway) (h) 2-2
Stokes 2
Feb 3 v Red Star Belgrade (Yugoslavia) (h) 2-0
Channon, McCalliog
May 3 v Queen's Park Rangers (h) 2-2
Stokes 2
Channon testimonial game
May 8 v Heart of Midlothian (h) 2-3
Earles 2
May 11 v Swansea City (a) 4-1
Osgood 2, Earles, Stokes
May 14 v Yeovil Town (a) 4-0
Holmes 2, Stokes 2

1976-77
Barbados Tour
Jun v Presidents XI (a) 2-0
Peach, Stokes
Jun v Combined Clubs XI (a) 0-0
Jul 27 v Girondins de Bordeaux (a) 2-1
Channon, Peach
Icelandic Tour
Jul 29 v Icelandic FA XI (a) 2-0
Earles, Osgood
Jul 30 v Icelandic FA XI (a) 1-1
Channon
Aug 5 v Heart of Midlothian (a) 0-3
Aug 9 v Doncaster Rovers (a) 2-1
Earles, Stokes
Oct 4 v Newport (Isle of Wight) (a) 4-1
MacDougall 2, Earles, Fisher
Norwegian tour
May 16 v Viking Stavanger (in Stavanger) 3-0
MacDougall 2, Williams
May 17 v Vardö (in Haugesund) 3-0
MacDougall 2, Dawtry
May 23 v Bradford City (a) 4-2
MacDougall, Phillipson-Masters, Osgood, opp.og

1977-78
Jul 27 v Gothenburg (a) 3-0
Hayes 2, MacDougall
Aug 8 v Gateshead (a) 1-0
Ball
Aug 13 v Wolverhampton Wanderers (h) 0-0
Mar 7 v Gothenburg (Sweden) (h) 2-1
Funnell, MacDougall
West Indies Tour, May 1978
v Antigua National XI (a) 2-0
MacDougall 2
v Antigua National XI (a) 1-0
Funnell
v Barbados National XI (a) 5-0
Funnell 2, MacDougall 2, Boyer
v Barbados National XI (a) 4-1
Funnell, Holmes, Neville, Williams

1978-79
Jul 29 v Sunderland (a) 1-0
MacDougall
Aug 1 v St Mirren (a) 0-1
Aug 9 v Oxford United (a) 1-0
MacDougall
Aug 13 v Marlines (Belguim) (a) 2-1
Boyer 2
May 11 v Nottingham Forest (h) 0-4
McMenemy testimonial game
Middle East Tour, May 1979
Full details not reported
v Egyptian National XI (a) 0-4
v El Zamalek (a) 1-0
v El Nassar (a)

1979-80
Jul 28 v Linfield (a) 0-1
Jul 30 v Cliftonville (a) 3-1
Holmes, Nicholl, Waldron
Aug 1 v Ballymena (a) 4-0
G.Baker, Holmes, S.Williams 2

Norwegian Tour
Aug 4 v IK Start (a) 4-0
Boyer 2, Puckett, S.Williams
Aug 7 v Hamarkameratene (a) 2-1
Hebberd, opp.og
Aug 9 v Brann Bergen (a) 5-1
Boyer 2, George, Holmes, Jancovic
Aug 11 v Skied Oslo (a) 2-2
Hebberd, S.Williams
Oct 31 v Bristol Rovers (a) 3-4
Boyer 2, Hayes
Dec 5 v Tunisia (a) 1-0
Scorer not reported
Jan 15 v Torquay United (a) 2-0
opp.og 2
25 v Luton Town (h) 1-0
Hebberd
(Abandoned after 65 minutes)
Feb 12 v AFC Bournemouth (a) 3-2
Holmes 2, George
Feb 19 v Poole Town (a) 2-1
Holmes, George
Feb 26 v Benfica (Portugal) (a) 0-4
Mar 11 v Vancouver Whitecaps (h) 3-1
G.Baker, Boyer, Greaves
Apr 22 v Brighton & Hove Albion (a) 3-1
Boyer 2, Andrusewski
May 16 v Portsmouth (a) 4-2
Channon 2, Waldron, Williams
May v Mexico (in Los Angeles) 0-1

1980-81
Jul 23 v Shamrock Rovers (a) 3-1
Channon, Keegan, Watson
Jul 26 v Linfield (a) 4-2
Hebberd 2, Holmes, Nicholl
Jul 29 v Djurgaarden (a) 1-1
opp.og
Aug 1 v Hamburg (West Germany) (a) 0-0 (Saints won 4-2 on penalties)
(Port Cup)
Aug 4 v Servette (Switzerland) (a) 0-1
Sep 23 v Swansea City (a) 5-0
Moran 2, Boyer, Hebberd, Williams
(Patrick Cup)
Oct 28 v Israel National XI (a) 1-0
Moran
Nov 26 v Raja (Morocco) (a) 1-1
George
Middle East Tour
Apr 6 v Al-Qadsia (a) 4-1
Moran 2, G.Baker, Holmes
Apr 8 v Al-Ittihad (a) 0-0
Apr 13 v West Ham United (a) 3-4
Keegan 2, Williams
May 6 v Kuala Lumpur (a) 4-0
Moran 2, Holmes, Keegan

1981-82
Aug 5 v Plymouth (a) 1-0
Puckett
Norwegian tour
Aug 11 v SK Brann (a) 5-3
Keegan 2, Channon, Moran, Williams
Aug 13 v Rosenborg (a) 0-1
Jan 16 v AFC Bournemouth (a) 1-1
Channon
Feb 2 v Fulham (a) 3-0
G.Baker, Hebberd, Lawrence
Feb 22 v Gothenburg (Sweden) (h) 4-4
Armstrong 2, La Ling 2
United Arab Emirates Tour
Mar 16 v Al Nasr (in Dubai) 6-1
G.Baker 2, Puckett 2, Keegan, Wallace
Mar 17 v Emirates Club (in Dubai) 6-0
Keegan 3, Puckett 2, Armstrong
Mar 24 v Ipswich Town (at Ashton Gate) 2-1
Puckett 2

Apr 18 v Darlington (a) 2-5
Channon, Puckett
May 9 v Glasgow Rangers (a) 0-1
May 16 v Glasgow Rangers (h) 4-2
Cassells, Armstrong, Keegan, Puckett
Horsfall testimonial game

1982-83
Aug 3 v Ballymena United (a) 4-2
Keegan 2, G.Baker, Williams
Aug 5 v Linfield (a) 3-0
Cassells 3
Aug 11 v Dundee United (a) 0-2
Aug 14 v Arminia Bielefeld (West Germany) (a) 2-1
Keegan 2
Aug 18 v Utrecht (Holland) (a) 0-0
Aug 20 v Plymouth (a) 4-1
Armstrong, Cassells, Lawrence, Wright
Jan 31 v Queen's Park Rangers (a) 5-2
Moran 2, Futcher, Puckett, Williams
Mar 8 v Aldershot (a) 0-0
May 10 v Brentford (a) 2-0
Holmes, Puckett
May 23 v Cardiff City (a) 3-1
Armstrong, Foyle, Moran

1983-84
Aug 1 v Drogheda United (Republic of Ireland) (a) 3-2
Moran 2, Wallace
Aug 3 v Cobh Ramblers (Republic of Ireland) (a) 4-0
Williams 2, Moran, Worthington
Aug 8 v Oxford United (a) 5-4
K.Armstrong, Moran 2, Worthington, Wright
Aug 10 v AFC Bournemouth (a) 1-1
Waldron
Aug 13 v Crystal Palace (a) 1-1
Wright
Middle East Tour
Oct 8 v Kuwait National XI (a) 1-2
Holmes
Oct 9 v Ramtha (Jordan) (a) 0-0

1984-85
Jul 29 v Galway United (Republic of Ireland) (a) 2-0
D.Armstrong, Moran
Aug 1 v Finn Harps (Republic of Ireland) (a) 1-0
Moran
Aug 2 v Waterford United (Republic of Ireland) (a) 5-0
D.Armstrong 3, Dennis, Puckett
Aug 6 v Oxford United (a) 3-0
D.Armstrong, K.Armstrong, Curtis
Aug 9 v Orient (a) 1-2
Baird
Aug 13 v Reading (a) 1-0
K.Armstrong
Spanish Tour
Aug 16 v Atletico Bilbao (a) 1-2
Moran
Aug 18 v Osasuna (a) 2-2
D.Armstrong, Wright
Sep 11 v Swindon Town (a) 1-0
Puckett
Middle East Tour
Dec 3 v Al-Hilal (a) 2-2
Jordan 2
Dec 5 v Al-Ittihad (a) 3-1
Moran 2, S.Baker
Apr 16 v Grimsby Town (a) 1-1
Moran

1985-86
Jul 27 v Weymouth (a) 6-0
Puckett 2, Wallace 2, Case, opp.og
Jul 31 v Bristol Rovers (a) 2-0
Armstrong, Moran
Aug 7 v Brentford (a) 0-1
Aug 12 v Plymouth Argyle (a) 0-0

1986-87
Aug 2 v Weymouth (a) 3-1
Clarke, Cockerill, Maskell
Aug 5 v Benfica (Portugal) (a) 0-2
Aug 9 v Exeter City (a) 1-1
Armstrong
Aug 11 v Torquay United (a) 2-1
Blake 2

Mark Blake

Aug 13 v Wolverhampton Wanderers (a) 1-1
Maskell
Aug 16 v Benfica (Portugal) (h) 4-1
Case, Clarke, Holmes, Wallace
Holmes testimonial game
Oct 14 v Road Sea (a) 3-1
Sylvanus 2, Mann
Oct 21 v Salisbury (a) 7-1
Maskell 2, Baker, Case, Cockerill, Gittens, Lawrence.
Nov 10 v Melksham Town (a) 3-0
Lawrence 2, Jordan
Apr 28 v Taunton Town (a) 2-2
Maskell, Lawrence

Venues of Southampton Football Club

ALTHOUGH Southampton St Mary's kicked off their original game on the present site of the County Bowls Club, it was to be a piece of land some several hundred yards away that was to become the club's first 'home'.

A pitch was marked out on the Avenue side of the Cowherd's Pond and although some Cup ties were played elsewhere, the majority of the club's home games took place on this first permanent venue.

The position of the pitch was to cause problems, however, and matches sometimes had to be held up to allow pedestrians to cross the playing area.

Club officials tried to find an enclosed pitch and eventually came upon, in the St Mary's area of town, a ground known as the Antelope which was situated on the corner of Brintons Terrace and St Mary's Road.

Although a sub committee was set up to achieve this, no agreement could be reached and the ownership of the Antelope fell into the hands of land developers.

St Mary's now had no home but, thanks to the efforts of Dr Bencraft, the use of the Hampshire CCC ground was secured at an annual rent of £200. During their stay at the County Ground, St Mary's gained the first of many Southern League Championships and decided that a ground of their own was of vital importance.

There was a plan to move to Freemantle's ground but negotiations with the Freemantle committee fell through, leaving the Saints desperately seeking a permanent home.

In 1898, Mr George Thomas was a partner in a well-known local fish merchant business called Thomas & Mowat and it was due to his enterprise and foresight that the Saints were to

Scene inside the Antelope Ground (left) with the 'All England Eleven' public house in the background. Below, the main entrance of the Antelope Ground.

The Antelope had been in existence for some years and at one time had been used by Hampshire County Cricket Club until their move to the County Ground in 1885.

Southampton enjoyed several successful years as leaseholders of the Antelope, averaging 500 spectators per match and moving up from being a junior to a senior club before joining the Southern League in 1894.

As a result of the club's progress, attendances grew. Some 4,000 spectators watched an FA Cup tie against Newbury, whilst Football League side, Nottingham Forest, attracted 7,000 spectators.

During 1895-6, a record gathering of some 12,000 saw the Saints narrowly beaten by Sheffield Wednesday and, with support still increasing, the committee considered purchasing the ground outright.

have their problem solved.

Mr Thomas purchased some land near the lower, or town end, of Hill Lane, only a few hundred yards from the County Ground. This land included a lake, flanked by two wooded banks and Mr Thomas immediately set to work on having the lake filled in so that a pitch could be laid.

An additional problem was that the pitch covered a spring which in medieval times had been directed off the Common to

Rarely seen picture of Mr George Thomas, the man whose foresight in 1898 led to The Dell becoming Saints' home.

continued to nosedive and Southampton struggled to meet the payments each year.

Entry into the Football League in 1920, however, heralded better times and between 1921 and 1923, some £8,000 was spent on ground improvements including increasing the size of the East Stand and installing 3,000 seats.

In 1926, the club approached Mrs Carvolth (formerly Mrs George Thomas) with a view to purchasing the ground and on 26 April that year, Southampton Football Club became the new owners of The Dell, buying it for £26,000.

It was immediately decided to make improvements and in 1927, Mr Archibald Leitch was employed to design a new West Stand. The old stand, together with the secretary's house which stood at the Archers Road end of The Dell, were demolished and in their place a new 400-foot long stand was erected. This new stand was to take 200 tons of steel girders in its construction and included a new boardroom and changing rooms.

It also provided seating for 4,000 people, whilst a further 8,500 could stand underneath. Opened on 7 January 1928, and despite some damage due to bombing in 1941, it remains virtually unchanged to this day.

In the late 1920s, the club could not afford to build a new East Stand, but their plans were dramatically altered in May 1929 when fire destroyed the entire structure.

The directors authorized the building of a new steel stand and this was constructed in Liverpool by Messrs Meston & Co. On 18 July 1929, the stand was moved to Southampton and reassembled over the next two weeks, using 160 tons of steel. Although not completed in time for the new season, some parts were ready for the opening game against Hull on 2 September 1929, with the remainder being finished soon afterwards.

The Dell was now the possessor of two almost identical stands that were to give a total of 6,600 seats and an overall capacity of 35,000, although this figure was never to be realised. Over the next ten years the club settled into Second Division football and with little success in the FA Cup they found it difficult to pay the mortgage on the ground.

During World War Two, with Southampton being a prime target for enemy bombers, The Dell suffered many hits and one bomb, which landed in the Milton Road end of the ground, caused the pitch to be flooded and unplayable.

serve the town. (Water has continued to run under the pitch ever since and once or twice over the next 90 years was to cause problems).

Eventually the arena, that because of its origins became known as The Dell, was finished at a cost of £10,000 and Southampton became the £250 per annum tenants.

The Dell was officially opened on 3 September 1898 and by Victorian standards was regarded as one of the best in the country.

In 1906, the lease came up for renewal and Mr Thomas proposed a new 21-year agreement, asking the Saints for £500 per annum. The club's fortunes were now in decline and the board rejected Mr Thomas's offer. For a period Saints seemed destined to leave The Dell.

However, after lengthy meetings Mr Thomas dropped his rent demand to £400 and on 1 August 1906, a new agreement was signed. Over the next decade or so the club's fortunes

The Dell on 3 September 1898, when Brighton United were the first visitors to the newly-opened ground.

The Dell in 1912-13.

The Milton Road End penalty-area after a German bomb had caused an culvert to burst during an air-raid in November 1940. The bomb left an 18ft crater.

Various venues were substituted including Fratton Park, Portsmouth, for a Cup match against Brentford. In April 1941, the West Stand caught fire and although the damage was not severe, Southampton were forced to open their 1941-2 season at Pirelli General's Dew Lane ground at Eastleigh.

The war's conclusion saw crowds flock back to football and with the attendances nudging capacity limits on several occasions, the Southampton directors considered ideas for enlarging The Dell.

Due to surrounding buildings and roads, increasing the capacity was an awkward problem that was only partially

demolished and replaced by a two-tier terracing, with the upper tier being of a triangular shape. The new upper tier has since been exclusively used for the club's successful family centre.

The cost of this rebuilding was half a million pounds and the club submitted plans to the council for a similar venture at the Archers Road end. The Council refused permission, due to the closeness of the busy Archers Road itself, so the club contented itself with lowering the terracing to give an improved view.

With its present-day capacity of 24,000, The Dell is

Aerial view of The Dell (left) in the 1950s, facing west and showing the unique 'chocolate boxes' behind the Milton Road goal while, pictured below, a BBC cameraman perches precariously over the 'boxes' in February 1981 prior to their demolition the following summer.

solved when three platforms were raised above Milton Road. These unique platforms became affectionately known as 'the chocolate boxes' and were patronized by the younger supporters of the club.

A few years later, in 1951, the Saints became one of the pioneers of floodlit football when, at a cost of £600, Simplex floodlights were installed. These lights were mounted along both East and West Stands, 16 in all, with 1,500-watt lamps initially used for training purposes and friendly matches.

On 1 October 1951, however, The Dell staged one of the first competitive football matches played under floodlights in Britain, when a crowd of 13,654 saw the visit of Tottenham Reserves for a Combination fixture.

Over the next 27 years, The Dell remained basically the same, although there was much talk of selling the ground and having a large all-purpose stadium built elsewhere in Southampton.

At one stage the plans came close to fruition but eventually it was decided to stay put and improve the existing facilities.

In the summer of 1978, 1,300 bench seats were installed under the East Stand and a new television gantry was built on top of the West Stand.

The following year, £35,000 was spent placing a further 1,500 bench seats under the West Stand whilst the pitch, which had suffered from drainage problems, was re-laid at a cost of £17,500.

In the summer of 1981, a major rebuilding scheme was undertaken, when the whole of the Milton Road terracing was

Crowd's-eye view (left) of the elevated family centre at the Milton Road end and the aerial view (below), photographed from the east, shows The Dell in the mid-1980s, with the newly-built centre and bench seating.

obviously not one of Division One's biggest stadiums, but it is a compact venue that, because of its size, produces plenty of atmosphere in comparison with many other larger grounds.

The pitch is also often regarded as being on the small side, but the closeness of the terracing can deceive and at 110yds x 72yds it is bigger than the pitch at Highbury. With the attendances in England on the decline, the feeling is that a costly move has been averted and, for the main part, the fans have been happy to keep The Dell as their home.

In 1986 the total capacity of The Dell is, in theory, 24,800, but for safety reasons, however, actual capacity is limited to 24,000. Today's capacity is not far removed from the turn-out pictured opposite for the FA Cup fourth-round replay at The Dell 80 years ago, when Saints beat Everton 3-2 in front of 21,690 spectators.
The breakdown for each section of The Dell in 1986 was as follows:

Milton Road
Family centre: **3,000**
Terracing: **4,500**

East Stand
Upper seating: **2,500**
Seating under (benches): **1,350**
Terrace: **2,200**

Archers Road
Terraces: **4,000**

West Stand
Upper seating: **3,650**
Seating under (benches): **1,500**
Terrace: **2,100**

J. LAURIE, VICE-CHAIRMAN

"To help — not to hinder"

SAINTS' SUPPORTERS' CLUB

Founded - 1926

Headquarters :
Bedford Hotel, Southampton

PRESIDENT : J. ANGUS HARMAN, ESQ.

J. W. GRANT, HON. GEN. SECY.

Help yourself by helping us. When you visit the Dell, don't forget to subscribe to the BALL and SEASON TICKET. Either may be yours for the modest subscription of one penny

CHAS. F. HOSKINS, CHAIRMAN

Enjoy yourself by patronising our DANCES at the Royal Pier during the Winter. Held on the first Friday in each month. Everything of the very best at the popular price of 1/6

This is the Saints' Jubilee Year.   Let it be yours

2/- Life Membership   **JOIN AT ONCE**   Life Membership 2/-

Ladies may join   This will entitle you to a Club Badge and Book of Rules.   **Ladies may join**

YOU have undoubtedly read all about the Saints' wonderful achievements during their fifty years' existence. Now, turn to the opposite page and read about a few of the Saints' Supporters' Club's modest achievements during its nine years' existence. We are still anxious to do more. We cannot do this without your help. Will you help us ? You can do this by subscribing to all our efforts. Don't be too harsh in your criticism—a kind word goes a long way. We want you to realise our efforts are entirely a labour of love, imbued with the sole desire that the Saints shall be successful in their efforts. This entails real hard work and sacrifice of a certain amount of leisure. This is why we require your help.

The following will be pleased to enrol you as a member or give information :—
Messrs. W. W. Wood (Hon. Treas.), B. Paget (Hon. Social Sec.), T. Perree (Hon. Registration Sec.), 50 Newcombe Road, Southampton.
Committee :—Mrs. F. Baker, Mrs. F. Perree, Mrs. Walker, Messrs. M. Baker, W. Bray, H. S. Bunce, F. Hill, H. A. Havill, E. J. Meacher, F. Poole, F. Parker and A. Ward.

Issued by the Southampton F. & A.C. Supporters' Club.

Advertisement for Southampton's Supporters' Club which was published in the club's Golden Jubilee history souvenir in 1935.

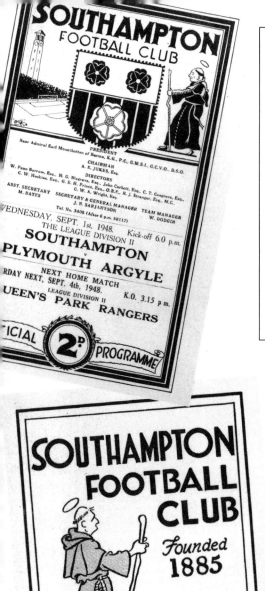

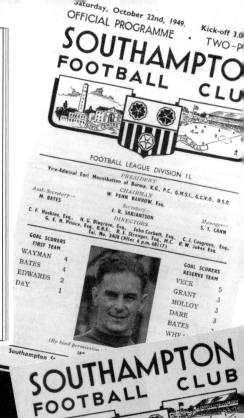

SAINTS
PROGRAMME
PARADE

□□□□□

SOME CHANGES IN POST-WAR DESIGN OF THE CLUB'S OFFICIAL MATCH-DAY PROGRAMME

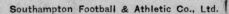
Top and middle: Saints programme, shown actual size, for the home Southern League 'derby' game against Pompey in 1908-09. Bottom: Newspaper cartoon shows Saints showing a clean pair of heels to Plymouth at the end of the race for promotion from Division Three South in 1921-2.

224

Saints Managers

GEORGE SWIFT
April 1911 — April 1912

GEORGE Swift was Southampton's first-ever secretary-manager, appointed by the Saints in April 1911. He had a distinguished playing career, starting at Crewe then moving to Wolverhampton Wanderers with whom he won an FA Cup winners' medal in 1893. Subsequently he transferred to Leicester Fosse and, finally, Notts County where he retired in 1906.

Swift became Leeds City's trainer soon after hanging up his boots and spent two seasons there before taking up his first managerial position with Chesterfield in 1908. After three years at Chesterfield, Swift became secretary-manager at The Dell. He spent the first six weeks after his appointment searching for recruits and spent £1,200 on ten new players for the club. It was these players who were his downfall. None of them proved his worth, resulting in Swift's resignation in April 1912.

JAMES McINTYRE
August 1919 — December 1924

A PLAYER of some repute, Jim McIntyre had a career which took in Walsall, Notts County, Reading and Coventry. After his playing days were over he worked at the Humber car factory in Coventry and spent one season refereeing in the Coventry and North Warwickshire League before joining Coventry as an assistant trainer.

Within one season he was promoted to chief trainer and his

association with Coventry lasted seven years, during which time he produced a number of young players for their Southern League team. It was his success at Coventry that impressed the Southampton directors and they secured his services in April 1912.

Engaged as trainer, McIntyre faced the difficult task of putting Saints back on the football map, a task which would take plenty of endeavour. Saints gradually began to improve their League position but with the outbreak of war in 1914 and the abandonment of League football in April 1915, all progress came to a halt. Jim McIntyre returned to Coventry for the duration, working in a munitions factory. With the resumption of League football in 1919 he returned to The Dell, this time as team manager and, with practically a new squad, he set about building a team for the future.

After Saints' entry into the Football League in 1920, he saw his team just miss out on promotion in their first season, but within another 12 months he had successfully guided Southampton into Division Two. After spending two more enjoyable seasons at The Dell, McIntyre retired in December 1924 and moved to Scotland to run an Edinburgh hotel.

His love of the game soon coaxed him back into management, however, firstly with his old club, Coventry, and later with Fulham, helping them return to Division Two. It was while he was at Fulham that he secured Arnold and Keeping from the Saints, along with a number of promising Southampton youngsters. When he finally retired from management he decided to make Southampton his home and found employment at Follands.

ARTHUR CHADWICK
October 1925 — May 1931

ARTHUR Chadwick was the first ex-player to become team manager, having played for the club at the turn of the century. His managerial career started at Exeter in 1910 where he had been a player since 1908. He guided Exeter through their Southern League period and was in charge when they entered the Football League in 1920. He left Exeter to manage Reading in 1923 but when the Southampton position became vacant he resigned, and in October 1925 became the Saints new team manager.

With the club having to sell its best players at the time, he found it difficult to keep Southampton on an even keel. He gained some success however, and guided Saints to an FA Cup semi-final place only one season after taking charge. Shrewdly he bought several new players and by the end of 1928-9 season had brought Southampton to their best-ever position in Division Two. Two uneventful seasons were to follow and, as he was approaching 60, he decided to call it a day after 23 years in management. He left the area to live in Exeter and it was whilst he was watching a match at Exeter's ground that he collapsed and died in 1936. (See also *Players Biographies*).

GEORGE KAY
May 1931 — May 1936

AFTER spending the initial seasons of his career with Bolton Wanderers, George Kay played for Belfast Distillery. He captained the Irish League XI and became the only Englishman to lead an Irish representative team.

After World War One, during which he served in the Royal Garrison Artillery, Kay moved back to England and joined West Ham United. He was to spend the next seven seasons at Upton Park and captained Hammers to the FA Cup Final in 1923, the first to be held at Wembley. His health was never good, however, and during a tour of Spain with Hammers in 1926, he fell ill. Charlie Paynter stayed with him for the three weeks before he was well enough to travel home.

In 1927 Kay became coach at Luton and then manager, spending two seasons in charge of the Hatters before accepting the challenge to run the Southampton side in May 1931. Kay introduced a new era to the club by creating Saints' first nursery side and, in a short time, a remarkable number of young players came into the League side. Drake, Sillett and Light, to name but three, all came through the nursery ranks.

Kay was tremendously enthusiastic and he worked hard throughout his stay at The Dell, using up a considerable amount of nervous energy at every match. He 'played' every kick and his body would visibly vibrate to the stresses and strains on the playing field.

He resigned as manager in May 1936 to take over at Liverpool. Kay spent 15 seasons at Anfield, guiding them to the first post-war League Championship and to the 1950 FA Cup Final. The stress of football management took its toll on his never-robust health and he had to retire in 1951. George Kay died in April 1954.

GEORGE GOSS
May 1936 — March 1937

LOCAL man George Goss served in the Royal Navy and played for the naval side between 1916 and 1921. On leaving the services he joined The Dell staff as assistant secretary, working closely with long-serving secretary, Ernest Arnfield. On Mr Arnfield's retirement it was George Goss who succeeded him.

In what was to be a long period of service, spanning 13 years, he served under three managers, McIntyre, Chadwick and Kay. With Kay's resignation at the end of the 1935-6 season, the jobs of secretary and manager were combined and Mr Goss, assisted by club captain, John McIlwane, took over at the helm.

His appointment, though, was only temporary until the club found a suitable successor to Kay, but it stretched over the greater part of the 1936-7 season until the arrival of Tom Parker in March 1937.

Mr Goss remained at The Dell until the end of the season and then left to run the Railway Hotel in St Denys. With the outbreak of war in 1939 he returned to sea and took command of a minesweeper. He later emigrated to Australia.

TOM PARKER
March 1937 — June 1943

TOM Parker, then manager of Norwich City, was chosen from 120 applicants in March 1937, coming back to Southampton after having begun his distinguished playing career in the town some 17 years earlier.

Parker had gone straight into the manager's job at Norwich when his playing days at Arsenal finished. On his arrival at The Dell, with money now available for players, Parker set about building a side to push for promotion. Altogether, £9,000 was spent over two seasons, bringing to the club a number of skilful young players including Ted Bates, Billy Bevis, Sam Warhurst and Bill Dodgin.

By 1939, Parker had built a settled side but with the outbreak of war in September that year, all this planning was wasted. Parker continued as secretary-manager through the difficult initial years of the war, fielding sides containing many of the club's pre-war nursery team together with guest players.

In June 1943, he resigned his position to take up employment outside football, as a surveyor with Lloyds registry. He was out of the game for a long period before returning to manage Norwich. Later he returned to The Dell and was the club's chief scout for many years. (See also *Players Biographies*).

J.R.SARJANTSON
June 1943 — June 1947

MR J.R. Sarjantson had a long and varied career with Southampton and was first elected to the board of directors in the 1914-15 season. In 1936 he became chairman, a position he held until June 1943 when he voluntarily resigned to act as secretary-manager during the wartime period.

He held this post until the end of the 1946-7 season, with Arthur Dominy and then Bill Dodgin acting as team managers during this time, leaving Mr Sarjantson to run the club from his desk.

In 1947 he dropped the title of manager and continued as secretary until 1950 when he was co-opted back on to the board. In 1951 he was re-elected to the chairmanship, a position he held until October 1955. After 40 years with the club he retired and was made vice-president soon after.

ARTHUR DOMINY
June 1943 — January 1946

WITH the appointment of Mr Sarjantson as the club's secretary-manager in June 1943, it was Arthur Dominy, a local publican and former captain of the club, who was given the responsibilities of team manager.

With no training facilities at The Dell during the hostilities, the only time Dominy saw the side was on match days. He remained team manager until January 1946 when he handed over to Bill Dodgin ready for the resumption of peace-time soccer. (See also *Players Biographies*).

BILL DODGIN
January 1946 — August 1949

BILL Dodgin had a long playing career, starting with Huddersfield Town in 1929. He subsequently played for Lincoln City, Charlton, Bristol Rovers and Clapton Orient before arriving at The Dell in the close season of 1939. With the 1939-40 League season abandoned after only three games, due to the outbreak of war, he was never to play in the Football League again.

Dodgin continued to turn out for Saints throughout the war and was team captain from 1943 to 1945. With his playing career at an end, he became team coach briefly during the 1945-6 season and, that January, was appointed team manager with the job of rebuilding a team ready for the resumption of League soccer in 1946.

Under his guidance Saints made steady progress and with the appearance of several new faces, including Curtis, Black, Wayman and Mallett, a strong push was made for promotion to Division One. After Southampton finished third in 1947-8, Dodgin knew he had a team worthy of the top flight and they led the Second Division by eight points in April 1949, but an injury to Wayman, amongst other misfortunes, cost Saints promotion.

Dodgin's success at The Dell did not go unnoticed by other clubs and Fulham made him an attractive offer. Southampton matched this offer but Dodgin had made up his mind and left The Dell in August 1949. He spent five years at Craven Cottage, resigning in 1953 with Fulham at the bottom of the First Division. He subsequently managed Brentford, Yiewsley and Bristol Rovers.

SYDNEY CANN
August 1949 — December 1951

FORMER England Schoolboy international, Syd Cann started his football career in his native town, signing for Torquay United at the age of 17. He spent five seasons with Manchester City after leaving Torquay, and played in the 1933 FA Cup Final for the Maine Road club.

In 1935, Cann signed for Charlton Athletic and on the outbreak of war he joined the Army Physical Training Corps reaching the rank of warrant officer during six years in that service. Cann qualified as a masseur at the British College of Physiotherapy and it was in this capacity that he joined the Southampton staff in 1946.

He combined his duties as a masseur with that of trainer for three years and, when Bill Dodgin moved to Fulham, he was promoted to the vacant team manager's position in August 1949. In Cann's first season in charge, he took the club to within a whisker of promotion. Saints finished second equal on 52 points but with a goal average of 1.333 as against Sheffield Wednesday's 1.395.

The year 1950 was the beginning of a gradual decline for Saints with the club losing the services of Black and top scorer Wayman. Although several new players were signed, Cann became frustrated and in December 1951 'as a result of differences of opinion upon matters of club policy' between the manager and the board, he stood down, although he remained as secretary for a short time. He later took an FA coaching job and then joined Wycombe Wanderers as manager.

GEORGE ROUGHTON
March 1952 — September 1955

AFTER being selected for Lancashire Schools, George Roughton played for amateur side, Droylsden, in the Manchester League. He joined Huddersfield Town in 1927-8 and remained there until 1936, when he returned to his native city to sign for Manchester United. He had a successful playing career, earning Football League representative honours and playing in two international trials.

In 1945, Roughton left Manchester United and entered the managerial side of the game with Exeter City. In March 1952 he was appointed manager of Southampton in a move which saw Norman Kirkman go to Exeter as their player-manager. Roughton's appointment proved to be not as fruitful as was expected and in the first full season under his leadership Southampton suffered relegation for the first time. The Saints automatically assumed that Roughton would lead them straight back to the Second Division but this was not to be and, partly for health reasons, he resigned not long after the start of the 1955-6 campaign.

TED BATES
September 1955 — December 1973

AFTER a distinguished playing career with the club, Ted Bates was doing so well as coach to Southampton Reserves that he was the logical choice to succeed George Roughton when Roughton resigned at the onset of the 1955-6 campaign.

Over the next four years, Bates built a side — a blend of youth and experience — that eventually barnstormed to promotion in 1959-60. And, once back in the familiar surroundings of the Second Division, Bates set to work once more, this time to achieve something that had eluded him as a player — First Division football.

Fittingly, it was perhaps Bates' finest 'discovery', winger Terry Paine, who headed the goal which brought First Division soccer to The Dell in 1966. But that was only the start, for like most of the other smaller provincial clubs, Southampton found that the task of remaining in the top flight was much harder than getting there in the first place.

It took all Bates' guile and knowledge, and some astute work in the transfer market, to consolidate the club's position. Even before Saints' first season in Division One had begun, Bates made a major signing when he brought big centre-forward, Ron Davies, from Norwich City for a club record £55,000.

Bates' judgement was sound and over the next few seasons Davies, aided by Terry Paine, scored plenty of goals to ensure that Southampton avoided a quick return to Division Two.

Other sensible, sometimes inspired, signings followed and Saints established themselves as one of the country's leading sides, qualifying for Europe for the first time, in 1969.

By 1973, Ted Bates was the League's longest-serving manager and in December that year he decided to bow out. Lawrie McMenemy took over the managerial reigns, although Bates was still available to be consulted from a position on the board. (See also *Players Biographies*).

LAWRIE McMENEMY
December 1973 — June 1985

LAWRIE McMenemy came to The Dell having earned a reputation training and managing in the lower divisions with clubs such as Doncaster and Grimsby. He was already experienced in the pitfalls of soccer management, having once won promotion with Doncaster, only to be sacked later when the team failed to prosper.

McMenemy was a rarity in management circles in that he had never played League football, but he more than made up for his lack of playing experience with a strong personality and an ability to communicate with players and fans alike.

A former Guardsman who stands 6ft 4in tall, McMenemy cuts an imposing figure and the Southampton board, acting on a recommendation from Don Revie, offered him the position of team manager designate in the summer of 1973.

Ted Bates was still in charge overall and had the task of easing McMenemy into the manager's position. In December 1973, the time was considered right for the new man to assume total control. Five months later, however, Saints had been relegated and McMenemy faced a stern test of his ability and character.

It was indicative of the man that he took the mounting criticism squarely on the jaw and steadfastly refused to be diverted from his task of re-establishing Southampton's position in Division One. Promotion was to take longer than expected but Saints fans were more than compensated for the wait when Southampton won the FA Cup for the first time, in 1976.

One of McMenemy's trademarks had been the revitalisation of senior players' careers and with the help of experienced professionals such as Blyth, Rodrigues and McCalliog, the Saints defeated the much-fancied Manchester United at Wembley. With Southampton's success, McMenemy became a charismatic media personality, with his Geordie wit appealing not only to the footballing public.

In 1978, Saints won promotion back to the First Division and the following season appeared at Wembley in the League Cup Final. Southampton, despite being in the unfashionable provinces, was now regarded as a 'big' club and McMenemy deservedly took most of the credit. He was, by this time, much sought after by clubs such as Manchester United, Leeds and Newcastle, not to mention being shortlisted for the England manager's job.

Loyally, McMenemy resisted all overtures and surprised everyone in football by announcing the signing of, arguably, Europe's best player, Kevin Keegan, in 1980. Keegan's arrival confirmed Southampton's status as one of the country's leading clubs and McMenemy repeated his predecessor Ted Bates' proud record of being the country's longest serving manager. With the Saints marching on, the position looked rosy but, as often happens in football, the situation changed unexpectedly and McMenemy became unsettled.

The seeds had been sown by Saints' last-gasp defeat in the 1984 FA Cup semi-final at the hands of Everton and, although the team then achieved Southampton's best-ever position in the First Division, finishing second, McMenemy was bitterly disappointed, having built what he believed to be his finest side.

The following season, 1984-5, Saints again qualified for Europe but somehow there was less sparkle, not only in the team but in McMenemy's usually ebullient personality. For reasons best known to himself, he had finally decided to leave the Saints, returning 'home' to manage Sunderland.

Southampton directors and supporters were keen to hold on to the manager who had fulfilled their wildest dreams, but he was famed for his determination, and stubbornness, and his mind was made up.

Life at Roker Park was not smooth and just before Easter 1987, McMenemy resigned. Just as his 12 years at The Dell were Saints' golden era, so they might also prove McMenemy's greatest days.

CHRIS NICHOLL
August 1985 —

AFTER ending his career as a Southampton player in 1983, Chris Nicholl became assistant manager at Grimsby, continuing to turn out in League football. When Lawrie McMenemy resigned from The Dell in 1985, it was Nicholl who was asked to take over by the Saints board and he returned to the club where he had enjoyed a six-year career as a defender.

His first season in charge was full of pitfalls, and one particularly humiliating blow was a 7-0 defeat at the hands of Luton Town. Nicholl overcame that and it appeared that he was destined to become a popular successor to McMenemy. But in 1986-7, other problems began to dog Saints' progress and there were rumours of dressing-room unrest. As the season unfolded, Nicholl's task seemed to become increasingly more difficult.

There was a much-publicised row involving defender Mark Dennis which resulted in Dennis being 'sacked', only to be reinstated after he appealed.

Meanwhile, Nicholl's team kept their heads above water and avoided the relegation play-offs. (See also *Players' Biographies*).

Chris Nicholl (third from left) is congratulated by his team-mates, Golac, Williams and Boyer, after scoring a goal for Saints against Middlesbrough in August 1978.

Blyth and Bennett in action against Nottingham Forest in October 1974.

Cliff Huxford, in goal for the injured Reynolds, watches as Traynor clears off the line during an exciting Football League Cup match against Leeds United in December 1960. Saints won 5-4.

Date and place of birth and death are given when known. Figures refer to games and goals in Southern League and Football League respectively (ie. 105-32, means 105 appearances and 32 goals).

ANDREWS. A.
10-0, Half-back, 1919-20.
During World War One, Andrews worked for Harland and Wolf shipyard, and turned out regularly for their works team in the South Hants War League. He joined the Saints in July 1919 and played one season in the Southern League before returning to local football.

ANDREWS. L.
Born: Reading, 9.12.1888. Died: 21.1.1969.
105-32: 59-3, Left-wing, 1912-24.
Len Andrews was one of McIntyre's first signings in 1912, coming from Reading. He soon made his name as a goal scoring left-winger, who could also take penalties — he scored nine out of nine in his first season, and missed only two up to 1915. He played for Saints during World War One and stayed until July 1919 when he returned to his native Reading. Two seasons later he returned again to Southampton and played his part in helping the Saints win the Division Three Championship in 1922. He left Southampton in 1924 to join Watford.

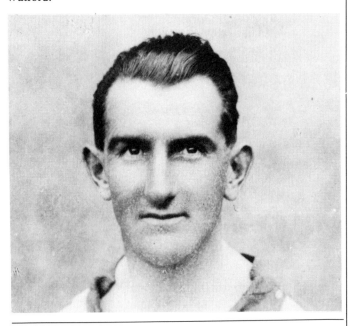

ANGELL J.W.
Born: Woolston, 1883. Died: Romsey, 5 January 1960.
3-0, Half-back, 1906-07.
A regular in the reserves since 1904, John Angell played three games in the first team during the 1906-07 season, deputising for the injured Hogg. Later played for Bitterne Guild and Eastleigh Athletic. Managed Southampton 'A' before the war and manager of Romsey 1945-54. Later chairman and president of that club. The building firm he founded in Southampton is still active.

ANGUS. J.
16-7, Forward, 1894-96.
Jack Angus joined the Saints in 1893 from Ardwick, having started his career at Everton. He was a regular member of the initial Southern League eleven in 1894, and scored four goals on his debut. A more dubious distinction was that he was the first recorded Saints player to be sent off during a match, this coming in a Hants Senior Cup match against Freemantle.

BAINBRIDGE. J.
Born: Seaham, 1880.
84-20, Forward, 1907-10.
Bainbridge came to Southampton at the twilight of his career in 1907, having previously turned out for Silksworth, Sunderland Royal Rovers, Glossop, Reading and Portsmouth. During the Saints' FA Cup run in 1908, he scored the greatest number of goals. He drifted out of professional football in 1910.

BAKER. C.
Born: Stafford, 1871.
33-11, Forward, 1894-96.
Charlie Baker made his name at Stafford Rangers, and from there he joined Stoke were he stayed for two seasons. He then joined Wolves, and again stayed two seasons before rejoining Stoke. In 1894 he joined the Saints and became a firm favourite with the Antelope crowd who appreciated his neat dribbling skills. After two years he retired from first class football.

BAMFORD. W.
7-0, Half-back, 1908-11.
Although Bamford spent three seasons at The Dell, his League appearances amounted to only seven, due to the presence of Trueman and Robertson in the first team.

BARLOW. T.
Born: Bolton, 1873.
22-6, Forward, 1902-03.
Tom Barlow was signed from Bolton in 1902 and found his form straight away, to such extent he was selected to play in the South v North international trial at Tottenham in 1903. Although he enjoyed a fine year at The Dell, Barlow became homesick and he returned to Bolton at the end of the season.

BARRETT. H.
7-0, Goalkeeper, 1894-96.
Barrett first appeared in the first eleven in 1893-94 when he succeeded Ruffell, the very first Saints goalkeeper. He kept goal in the initial Southern League game, but lost his position to Williamson, only to regain his place for the start of the 1895-96 season. When Cain was signed from Everton, Barrett lost his place and he left the club.

BARRATT. J.
Born: Bolkington.
41-5: 52-2, Forward, 1919-22.
A wartime signing during 1918, Josiah Barratt started his career with Leicester before signing for Birmingham and then Southampton. He spent four years with the Saints, helping them make the transition from Southern League to Football League. Along with Foxall he was transferred back to Birmingham in an exchange deal that brought Elkes and Getgood to The Dell. Barratt had the unusual habit of playing with a piece of straw in his mouth. After World War Two he helped run the youth teams at Coventry.

BEARE. G.
Born: Southampton.
1-0, Forward, 1906-07.
Signed from local side, Shirley Warren, Beare impressed in the reserves and was rewarded by selection in the final game of 1906-07 season. Blackpool signed him in the close season of 1907, and he later moved to Everton where he found some success.

BEAUMONT. W.
Born: Ashton, 1883. Died: November, 1911.
27-0, Centre-half, 1910-11.
William Beaumont commenced his football career at Swindon in 1905 and moved to Portsmouth in 1907. The Saints signed him in October 1910 for £75 but he was to catch pneumonia and died within a year.

BELL. E.
Born: Gibraltar, 1887.
4-0, Forward, 1906-08.
Bell joined the Saints in 1906 from Arthur Turner's old club, South Farnborough, although he did have a spell at Crystal Palace on trial. Unlike Turner, he never made the grade and he returned to local football in 1908.

BELL. M.
Born: Edinburgh, 1882.
9-6, Forward, 1902-03.
Mark Bell joined Saints in April 1902, having spent all his footballing career until then in Scotland, playing for Hibernian and Hearts and being awarded a Scottish cap in 1901 against Wales. Although scoring six goals in nine matches he was plagued by injury and he returned to Hearts after only one season. In 1904 he returned south to play for Fulham and Clapton Orient. He ended his career at Gillingham where he played as a half-back.

BENNETT. R.
1-0, Full-back, 1912-13.
This young full-back played only one League game, at Norwich during 1912-13.

BENSON. R.
Born: Saltwell, 1882. Died: February, 1916.
19-0, Full-back, 1904-05.
Robert Benson was a young miner who, although on Newcastle's books, could not break into the first team. The Saints, searching for a full-back at the time, sent an official from the club to the North East specifically to look for a defender and Benson was duly signed. His form was immediately impressive, and Sheffield United signed him after only one season at The Dell. He remained for eight years at Sheffield during which time he won an England cap in 1913. He also developed a famous method of taking penalties by running the full length of the pitch from his full-back position before kicking the ball. He joined Arsenal in 1913 and retired from football upon the outbreak of war. Engaged in wartime munitions work, he was asked, in 1916, to turn out for Arsenal as a late substitute. He had not played for over a year, and he collapsed during the game and died in the dressing room at Highbury.

BINDER. T.
10-1, Forward, 1912-14.
Binder was an amateur with the Saints during the 1912-13 season before signing professional forms in June 1913. He was originally with Kettering and he returned there after finding it impossible to establish himself at The Dell.

BIRD
1-0, Half-back, 1907-08
A reserve half-back who played one League match during 1907-08 and left in the close season of 1908.

BLACKBURN. A.
Born: Blackburn.
9-0, Full-back, 1900-01.
Arthur Blackburn was discovered by Saints representatives whilst living in Blackburn, renovating churches and playing local football. He had played twice for Blackburn Rovers and was thought to be a good find. Unlike his brother, who made a name for himself at West Ham, he never really settled in the South and he was transferred back to Blackburn in the close season of 1901.

BLACKMORE. W.
7-0, Forward, 1912-13.
A local player signed in 1912, Blackmore was on the books of Southampton for one season, although during World War One he guested for the Saints on numerous occasions. In 1919 he was a regular member of the reserve team.

BLAKE. J.
Born: Belsham Walter, 1883. Died: Southampton, 23 February 1931.
148-13, Forward, 1906-20.
Joe Blake came to Southampton in 1905, originally to play in the reserves, but by 1909 he had forced his way into the first eleven. He was at the time an amateur, and was engaged in the shipbuilding trade at Cowes. Blake had previously turned out for Ilford, Tottenham and Cowes, and he remained at The Dell until 1915 when he took up full-time employment at Thorneycrofts as a draughtsman. He turned out for both Thorneycrofts and the Saints during World War One, although Southampton held his registration. After the war he played for the Saints during 1919-20 before being released in March 1920 to play for Thorneycrofts again.

BLUFF. E.
27-10, Forward, 1904-06.
In 1904 Bluff was a soldier in the 1st Army Corps and the Saints were so keen to acquire his full-time services that they bought him out of his army contract. At first it seemed money well spent, as he played so well that he was given an international call up and was first reserve against Ireland in 1905. His rapid rise to prominence was unfortunately followed by an even more rapid decline in fortune. His form deserted him and the Saints sold him to Sheffield United, although he was reluctant to go. Bluff's stay at Sheffield lasted just over a year before he moved on to Birmingham — his last club.

BOWDEN. T.
Born: Manchester, 1880. Died: May, 1951.
29-0, Half-back, 1906-07.
Bowden was signed by West Bromwich in 1904 from local football and in the two years spent at the Black Country club he made nine appearances. The Saints signed him in 1906 and he went straight into the first team in the position of centre-half. For a short while his neat style of play impressed the fans but for reasons unknown he left the area at the end of the 1906-07 season to join Grimsby.

BOWMAN. T.
88-2, Half-back, 1901-04.
Thomas Bowman's League career started at Blackpool before joining Aston Villa in 1898. He was a first-team regular in the three seasons he spent at Villa making 86 appearances. In 1901, the Saints, anxious to replace Chadwick, signed him, and in his first season he helped Saints reach the FA Cup Final. In 1904 he followed Chadwick to Portsmouth and spent six seasons with them until 1910 when he played out his footballing days with Eastleigh Athletic.

BOYES. K.
Born: Southampton, 1896. Died: Eastleigh, October 1963.
4-1:4-0, Forward, 1919-22.
Although a reserve-team player in 1914-15, Ken Boyes had to wait until 1919 before he played in the first team, in their final season as members of the Southern League. He then had to wait until October 1921 to make his baptism in League football. In 1922 he left Southampton to play briefly with Bristol Rovers and Weymouth before returning to play locally for the Civil Service, later becoming the groundsman at Pirelli General's ground.

BRADBURN. G.
Born: Walsall.
28-0:6-0, Centre-half, 1919-22.
George Bradburn was a wartime signing in 1917 from Walsall, and in 1919-20 he became a regular for a short time. Campbell's re-emergence however, meant that he spent long spells in the reserves, and in 1922 he returned to Walsall and featured regularly in their first team during 1922-23.

BRADLEY. W.
3-1, Forward, 1912-13.
Bradley was an amateur centre-forward who came to The Dell from Tidworth, where he served in the Army. He became the reserve centre-forward in 1913-14 but never really pushed for a place in the first eleven and he left the club at the outbreak of World War One. He did play for Saints in three of the wartime seasons.

BRITTLETON. S.
Born: Winsford, 1887.
17-3, Forward, 1909-10.
Sam Brittleton was the brother of the renowned Jas Brittleton, the England forward, and he was snapped up from under the noses of numerous League clubs whilst at Chorley. His first club was Stockport, but, unable to command a regular first-team place, he moved to Chorley. At the Lancashire club his form improved dramatically and the Saints were pleased to acquire his talents in the summer of 1909. He did not live up to expectations, however, and after one season returned to minor league football in the North of England.

BROOKS. R.
Born: Reading.
19-0, Full-back, 1912-14.
Brooks played his early football for the Army and when he left the forces he found employment at Eastleigh Railway works and turned out for Eastleigh Athletic in the Hampshire League. During 1911-12 he played for Reading and attracted the attention of Saints, who signed him prior to to the 1912-13 season. He remained at The Dell until the outbreak of World War One, returning from the hostilities to play for the reserves in 1919-20.

BROWN. A.
Born: Tamworth.
26-25, Forward, 1901-03.
Brown was nicknamed the 'Tamworth Sprinter' because of his impressive speed and being capable of a very hard shot. He scored seven times during an 11-0 victory over Northampton in 1901 — a record that stands today for a Southampton player in a League match. He had arrived from Aston Villa in 1901, and his spell at The Dell encompassed two seasons, in which time he helped the Saints reach the FA Cup Final in 1902, scoring in the replay. An injury early in the 1902-03 season meant that he lost his place and, not content with reserve-team football, he moved to Queen's Park Rangers and then Preston North End.

BROWN. A.C.
Born: Cowes, 1888.
39-0, Goalkeeper, 1910-12.
Arthur Brown was an amateur goalkeeper who originally signed for Saints in 1906, whilst studying at college in the town. In 1907 he moved to Portsmouth where he spent two seasons. In 1909 he returned to play for Cowes and again came to the notice of Southampton who signed him as an amateur. He quickly made the first-team spot his own, until November 1911 when Knight took over in goal. He emigrated to Canada soon after.

C. BROWN

BROWN. C.
Born: Stakeford.
3-0:80-6, Forward, 1919-24.
Charles Brown signed for Saints late in the 1919-20 season and partnered Dominy and Moore for the final three games in the Southern League. He competed with Barratt for the wing position until Barratt left the club to join Birmingham. He seemed to play his best football away from home and for this reason The Dell fans never really appreciated him and he failed to settle at the club. He moved to Queen's Park Rangers in the close season of 1924.

BROWN. G.
2-0, Full-back, 1909-10.
George Brown signed from Longfleet St Mary's in March 1910, playing two matches before returning to Longfleet in the close season.

BROWN. H.
Born: Northampton, 1884. Died: February 1934.
72-26, Forward, 1905-13.
Harry Brown started his career in 1902 with Northampton before signing for West Brom prior to the 1904-05 season. After 14 appearances and five goals, he signed for the Saints and spent a fine season at The Dell. Anxious to move back into the Football League, Brown signed for Newcastle in 1906, and Bradford in 1908. He eventually returned to Southampton in September 1910, but not before spending a short while at Fulham. After two seasons at The Dell, he retired in the summer of 1912, taking a public house, the Kingsland Tavern, purchased from an ex-Saint, Tom Nicol.

BROWN. R.
12-2, Forward, 1897-98.
Brown joined the Saints at the same time as Arthur Chadwick, having previously played with Burton Wanderers in the Football League in 1896-97. He was at The Dell one season, playing in the FA Cup semi-final against Nottingham Forest, replacing the injured Farrell. He moved to Queen's Park Rangers before the start of the new season.

BROWNING. R.
6-0, Forward, 1912-13.
Signing from Queen's Park Rangers in February 1913, Browning was immediately thrust into the first team but did not live up to expectations and after six games was dropped. He left The Dell soon afterwards.

BUCHANAN. R.
41-21, Forward, 1896-99.
Bob Buchanan spent two years at Woolwich Arsenal before moving to Southampton in 1896. He had a curious nickname, earned whilst a Saint — 'Death or Glory Bob' — adopted because of his style of play. He would never give up a seemingly lost cause and his determined manner enabled him to score some unlikely goals, including the ones that knocked out Leicester Fosse and Newcastle in the 1898 FA Cup run. He remained at The Dell until 1899 and then joined Sheppey United for a short while. On retiring from the game he moved back to Woolwich to live, but died prematurely in 1910.

BUCKENHAM. W.
6-2, Forward, 1909-11.
Signed from Woolwich Arsenal in December 1909, he scored on his debut in a 3-1 victory over Norwich. Despite this promising start, his form faltered and he left the club for pastures unknown.

BUCKLEY A.
1-0, Forward, 1913-14.
Buckley was signed in January 1914 from Bath City, but joined up at the outbreak of the war to fight on the front and was not heard of again.

BUNDAY A.
Born: Eastleigh.
1-1, Forward, 1902-03.
A reserve centre-forward during the 1902-03 season, he scored on his first-team debut versus Reading, but was never rewarded with another senior outing.

BURROWS T.
84-0, Goalkeeper, 1904-11.
Thomas Burrows was signed from local side, St Mary's Swifts, in 1904, as a third-choice goalkeeper behind Clawley and Byrne, but managed to make only one appearance in the last League game of the 1904-05 season. For the next seven years he was in and out of the team, competing with Lock and Brown for the goalkeeper's position. In the close season of 1911 he left to join Merthyr Town.

BYRNE M.
5-0, Goalkeeper, 1903-05.
Byrne was from the Bristol area, and in 1903 he signed for Saints to provide cover for Clawley. During his short stay he made five appearances before moving to London to sign for Chelsea as cover for an equally famous 'keeper, 'Fatty' Foulkes. In 1907 he moved north to play for Glossop.

CAIN T.
Born: Sunderland, 1872. Died: 1952.
10-0, Goalkeeper, 1895-96.
Cain started his career at Stoke before moving on to play for Everton. In October 1895 he signed for the Saints and played ten games in the remainder of the season before returning north to play for Grimsby for a fee of £20.

CAMPBELL A.K.
Born: Southampton 1894. Died: June 1943.
19-2: 157-13, Centre-half, 1908-26.
Alec Campbell, 'tall with telescopic legs', was a local man, although

his parents were Scottish. He was educated at King Edward's where he excelled at both football and cricket. Whilst still at school he played for England (at amateur level) in an international versus Holland, the only known occasion a schoolboy has represented his country at that level. He made his debut for the Saints' Southern League side during the 1908-09 season and immediately he aroused the interest of the big clubs, resulting in him joining Glossop until 1913 when he had a brief spell at West Ham before returning to Southampton in 1914. Upon the outbreak of the war, he joined up, but still donned the red and white jersey on frequent occasions during wartime matches. By the time normal football resumed, he had become the Saints' captain, and he remained so for another six years, during which time he led the team to many fine performances. In 1926, he signed for Poole Town, so ending an 18-year association with the Saints. He also represented Hampshire at cricket as early as 1908, proving his prowess as a fine all-round sportsman. When World War Two broke out, he joined the Army and was killed in action in June 1943.

CARTER R.
Born: Sunderland. Died: Sunderland, 1927.
41-12, Forward, 1908-10.
Robert Carter became a Southampton player in March 1909, having previously played for Stockport, Port Vale and Fulham. He took a while to settle but soon his ability to play in any of the five attacking positions became a useful asset. He was the father of the famous England international, Raich Carter, of the 1930s and '40s and because of his small stature was nicknamed 'Toddler'.

CAVENDISH S.
9-2, Forward, 1899-1902.
Syd Cavendish signed for the Saints together with Joyce from Overseal in 1898, but lack of first-team opportunity caused him to move to Freemantle in 1902. He stayed two seasons with the Saints' rivals and then moved to Clapton Orient whom he helped to gain League status in 1905.

CHADWICK A.
Born: Church. Died: March 1936.
81-6, Centre-half, 1897-1901.
Arthur Chadwick gave sterling service to Southampton in two capacities, as player and manager. Starting his footballing career with his local side Church, he moved to Accrington and then Burton Swifts. Upon joining Saints in 1897 he was initially a half-back but

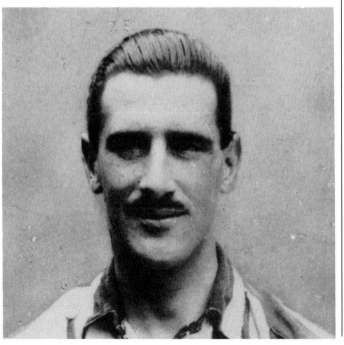

after a few games he successfully converted to the centre-half position to such an extent, that he won two England caps in 1900. Chadwick signed for Portsmouth in May 1901, and three years later signed for Northampton. In 1910 he became manager at Exeter, a position he held for 12 years. January 1923, saw him at the helm for Reading, but with the Southampton job vacant, in October 1925, he resigned from Reading to take charge at The Dell. The highlight of his six seasons in control of the Saints was the guiding of the team to the FA Cup semi-final in 1927. After a long career in football it was perhaps fitting that he should die, in 1936. whilst watching Exeter play, from the stands.

CHADWICK E.
Born: Blackburn, 1869. Died: Blackburn, February 1942.
52-18, Forward, 1900-02.
Edgar Chadwick had a long and distinguished career that spanned 20 years. Commencing with Blackburn Rovers, he signed for Everton in 1888. He was an ever-present in Everton's first two years as a League team. Whilst at Everton he won seven England caps, a Football League Championship medal and an FA Cup runners-up medal. He moved to Burnley in 1899 and a year later decided to move to Southampton in the Southern League, although Burnley held on to his registration as a Football League player. In the two seasons he spent at The Dell, he helped the Saints to the FA Cup Final in 1902. Chadwick bought out his contract with Burnley and signed for Liverpool. Before retiring in 1908 he also turned out for Blackpool, Glossop and Darwen. After 1908 he moved to the Continent where he coached in Germany and Holland. Eventually tiring of football, Chadwick reverted to his trade of baker, back in his native Blackburn.

CHRISTMAS E.
2-0, Forward, 1911-12.
When Christmas made his first-team debut in March 1912 he had been at The Dell for four years, all spent playing in the reserves. At the end of the season he gave up trying to make the grade in professional football and left.

CLARK T.
Born: Tilbury, June 1887.
5-1, Forward, 1909-11.
Discovered by the Saints playing in a trial match in August 1909 having played for local side, Shirley Warren, the previous year. He had the good fortune to score on his debut but failed to make the grade.

CLARKE W.
Born: Northampton, 1880.
51-0, Full-back, 1905-07.
Clarke signed for Northampton in 1903 and when the Saints acquired his signature in 1905, they considered him to be quite a capture. Unfortunately his health deteriorated and he never reproduced his Northampton form for the Saints. He was released at the end of the 1906-07 season, never to play League football again.

CLAWLEY G.
Born: Scholar Green, 1876. Died: July 1920.
163-0, Goalkeeper, 1895-98; 1903-1907.
George Clawley began his career with Stoke but his appearances were limited due to the presence of Rowley, the England international. For this reason he signed for Saints in 1896 and was ever-present for two seasons, and captain for the 1897-98 season. In 1898 he re-signed for Stoke and spent another year at the Potteries club before trying his luck at Tottenham. In the four years he spent with Spurs he won an FA Cup winners' medal. He returned to Saints in 1903 and completed his career, winning one Southern League Championship medal. In 1907 he retired and became the landlord of the Wareham Arms.

COATES A.
Born: Yorkshire.
21-0, Full-back, 1912-13.
Coates played his early football for local sides, Salford United and Heywood United, before signing for Exeter in 1910. He moved to Southampton in 1912 and spent one season at The Dell.

COHAM J.
Born: Southampton, 1892.
6-0, Forward, 1910-11.
John Coham played for local sides, St. Paul's and Eastleigh Athletic, before joining the Saints in 1910 as an understudy to Joe Blake. He returned to local football in 1911.

COSTELLO F.
Born: Birmingham, 1884. Died: December 1914.
41-10, Forward, 1907-09.
Costello came to The Dell via a host of non-League sides from the Birmingham area, in 1907. He had an excellent first season by finishing joint top-scorer in the League for the Saints. He maintained his place for the 1908-09 season but left for West Ham in March 1909. Upon the outbreak of war he signed up for the Army and was killed in action in December 1914.

COX W.
Born: Southampton.
3-0, Goalkeeper, 1894-96.
Cox played his first game for the Saints as an outfield player in 1893 but graduated into being the reserve goalkeeper. He kept goal in the FA Cup matches against Reading and Marlow in 1894-95, although it was not until the following season that he made his Southern League debut. Strangely, after making only two further League outings, he featured in all five Cup matches that season. Clawley's arrival at The Dell forced Cox to seek fresh pastures and he moved to Millwall and then Manchester City.

CRABBE W.
1-0, Full-back, 1899-1900.
Played his only first-team game versus Swindon in January 1900. Released soon afterwards.

CRICK G.
Born: Market Harborough, 1891.
8-0, Half-back, 1914-15.
Crick was signed in 1914, having previously played for his home town club in Leicestershire. He came into the side when Hadley sustained an injury. When the Southern League programme was suspended for the duration of the war, he was released.

CUNNINGHAM C.
1-0, Forward, 1912-13.
Cunningham came to Southampton as a trialist from the London Civil Service in December 1912. After one game he returned to London.

CURRY J.
Born: Newcastle.
7-0, Half-back, 1911-12.
Curry started his career at Scotswood in the North-East, before moving to play for Manchester United. Chances were limited at United and he signed for the Saints in 1911. Injury problems hampered his opportunities and he returned to the North-East.

CURTIN C.
Born: Sunderland, 1891.
29-5, Forward, 1913-15.
Curtin was signed from Norwich in April 1913 and during the 1914-15 season he had some outstanding games on the right wing. When League football was suspended in 1915, due to the war, he was released.

DAINTY H.
Born: Kettering, 1876.
31-1, Centre-half, 1904-05.
Herbert Dainty was something of a nomad and had played for a

variety of clubs before signing for the Saints in 1904. He started with Kettering in 1898, joined Leicester Fosse in 1899 and a year later was at New Brighton Tower before returning to Leicester in 1901. He seemed to favour a move every year because in 1902 he signed for Northampton and in 1903 for Notts County. Any hopes the Saints were to have of keeping this fine player more than the customary season were dashed when Dainty moved to Scotland to play for Dundee. He actually stayed north of the border for six years until he joined Bradford (Park Avenue) and retired there in 1914. Although restless, Herbert Dainty was a cultured centre-half and served all his clubs with distinction.

DALE J.
3-0, Half-back, 1895-96.
Dale played for Stoke in 1895 but followed the trail of Potters' players who were to join Southampton in the Stoke 'invasion' incident. Unlike many of the others he was to make only three appearances before moving back to the Midlands.

DAVIDSON A.
Born: Ayr 1878.
5-0, Centre-half, 1909-10.
Previously with Middlesbrough and Grimsby, Davidson was signed in July 1909 but had a poor five games in the position of centre-half and was transferred back to Grimsby three months later.

DAVIES T.
8-1, Forward, 1909-10.
Davies was a trialist from Salisbury FC who impressed enough in a friendly in April 1909 to be given eight Southern League outings the following season.

DAWE L.
11-3, Forward, 1911-13.
Dawe was an amateur with Dulwich Hamlet before joining the Saints in March 1912. He held on to his amateur status while he remained at The Dell. His studies finally took him away from the Southampton area in January 1913 and he became a teacher, although he still played some football for Ilford.

DENBY J.
127-8, Half-back, 1911-15.
Denby followed manager, Swift, from Chesterfield in the close season of 1911 and helped to solve the Southampton centre-half problem, although he was equally at home in the wing-half position. He continued to give the club sterling service right up to the outbreak of war when he retired from competitive football.

DEWAR G.
Born: Dumbarton, 1870.
4-0, Half-back, 1898-99.
Dewar was an apprentice ship's upholsterer before taking up football, signing for Dumbarton Athletic, with whom he gained county representative honours. He moved south to join Blackburn Rovers and won two FA Cup winners' medals with them. Originally approached by Southampton in 1898, he decided to join New Brighton instead, but soon regretted this decision and quickly organised a move to the Saints a few months later. He did not stay long at The Dell and returned to his native Scotland.

DIAPER A.
1-0, Half-back 1912-13.
Arthur Daiper was a local player who arrived at The Dell in the close season of 1912 from Hampshire League side, Woolston. He stayed with the Saints until 1914.

DOMINY A.
Born: Southampton, February 1894. Died: September, 1974.
112-65 : 222-68, Forward, 1913-26.
Arthur Dominy was born in Woolston and played his early football for Peartree Green, then Bitterne Guild for whom he scored 50 goals in 1911-12. The Saints could not ignore such form and signed him in March 1913. He made his debut a month later and it was not long before he became an integral part of the Southampton forward line. During the war, Dominy was employed at Harland and Wolf and played for them against the Saints in the war league. With the ending of hostilities, and the Saints election to the Football League, Dominy continued to be the mainstay of the Southampton attack, combining with centre-forward, Rawlings, to great effect. Although he took part in many England trial matches, he was never capped, to many people's surprise because he was not only a player of outstanding ability, but an inspirational captain. The Saints' management received many offers for Dominy's services, but resisted them until 1926 when they reluctantly transferred him to Everton. In his first season at Goodison Park he partnered the legendary Dixie Dean and won a League Championship medal. Age was not on his side, however, and he moved to Gillingham and then Clapton Orient. After retiring from League football, he became a licensee in Southampton, although in 1932 he was turning out for Newport (Isle of Wight), partnering none other than Bill Rawlings. Arthur Dominy had a strong feeling for football. His first love was always the Saints and during the difficult World War Two years he was pleased to help manage the team up to when Bill Dodgin took over. After the war he became landlord of the Southampton supporters club and maintained a strong interest in the Saints' fortunes right up to his death.

DONNELLY A.
1-0, Full-back, 1919-20.
Donnelly was a trialist who was given one outing during the 1919-20 season.

DORKIN J.
Born: At sea aboard the SS Tamer, July 1866.
3-3, Forward, 1894-95.
Jack Dorkin's first taste of football was with Ipswich Rangers with whom he gained a county cap in 1883. He went north soon afterwards to join Edinburgh St Bernard's but then enlisted in the Army and moved to Hampshire to sign up with the Royal Engineers at Aldershot. In 1892 he became one of Southampton's first professionals, although by the time the Saints joined the Southern League, two years later, he was past his best. He played three games at the end of 1894-95 and acquitted himself well with three goals but gave up football at the conclusion of that campaign. Two years later he was persuaded to play in a 'sixes' tournament but broke his leg and thus finished his career for good. He later became a sports outfitter in Southampton, along with Victor Barton.

DUNNE M.
Born: Padiham, 1887.
30-9, Forward, 1910-11.
Martin Dunne started his career in Lancashire with Oswaldtwistle Rovers, moving to Accrington soon afterwards. The Saints obtained his signature in the 1910 close season and he was their top scorer for the following season. Unfortunately for everyone concerned, he grew homesick at The Dell and returned to his native Lancashire.

DURBER P.
Born: Stoke, 1874.
43-0, Full-back, 1898-1900.
Peter Durber signed for Stoke in 1896 and joined Southampton two years later. He soon distinguished himself as a polished full-back and was given an England trial in February 1900. He was disappointed not to be chosen for the full England side and moved back to Stoke in the close season of 1900. Two years later he moved to Northampton and remained there until retiring in 1906,

DYER A.E.
1-0, Forward, 1906-07.
Dyer was signed from local football in 1906 but as understudy to Jefferis he found chances limited and he returned to local football to assist Southampton Cambridge.

EASTHAM J.
Born: Blackburn.
161-4, Full-back, 1906-12.
Eastham made his League debut with his home-town club, Blackburn, in 1901-02 and for two years was a first-team regular for the famous Lancashire club. He then spent two years in the reserves and moved to Southampton in 1906. After a dubious start he soon grew in confidence and developed into a fearless, robust full-back, later to become the team's captain. In 1912 he was rewarded with a benefit match against Portsmouth and soon afterwards retired to live in Blackburn.

EDMONDS T.
Born: Edinburgh.
9-0, Centre-half, 1905-06.
Although Scottish-born, Edmonds began playing football in the Preston area, before returning briefly to Scotland to play for Dundee. Returning to Preston, he signed for North End and then transferred to Southport. In 1905 he joined the Saints and despite an excellent game against Reading early in the season, he failed to impress the management and he left in the close season of 1906.

EKE H.
1-0, Forward, 1913-14.
Eke was signed from St Mary's Cray in 1913 but made only one appearance, at Queen's Park Rangers, before returning to local soccer.

ENGLEFIELD F.
Born: Southampton.
1-0, Forward, 1899-1900.
Englefield joined the Saints from Freemantle and although an outside-left, played his only game for the club at left-half.

EVANS R.
Born: Smallthorne, 1875.
41-16, Forward, 1902-04.
During 1898-99, Dick Evans became a member of Burslem Port Vale's Division Two side and quickly developed into a speedy and clever right winger. At the season's conclusion he moved to Reading and gave them three valuable seasons service before moving to Southampton and helping them win the Southern League in 1902-03. Unfortunately, within the year his form left him due to poor health and he was compelled to retire from competitive football.

EVERIST F.
Born: 1884.
8-2, Forward, 1906-07.
Everist was previously with minor sides Grasmead United, Cray Wanderers and Orpington, before joining Saints in 1906. Although he looked good in the reserves he failed to maintain a first-team place and left for Croydon Common in 1907.

FAIRGRAVE W.
Born: Edinburgh, 1876.
1-0, Forward, 1898-99.
Walter Fairgrave came south after playing local football in Scotland for Dairy Primrose and Glasgow Perthshire. He returned to Scotland in the close season of 1899.

FARRELL J.
Born: Tunstall. Died: February 1947.
73-40, Forward, 1895-1900.
Joe Farrell was considered to be one of the best of the Stoke 'imports' and joined Southampton in 1895. He started his career at Dresden United and joined Stoke in 1894, moved south and in three years with the Saints developed a reputation as a goalscorer. He became the captain in 1896 and remained so until he moved to Stoke in 1898. He was back after a year but was forced to compete with McLeod for the centre-forward position. Many fans were surprised when he was selected to play in the 1900 FA Cup Final, in place of McLeod who was definitely the man in form. The controversy caused Farrell to move to New Brighton Tower soon afterwards and from there he subsequently joined Northampton and West Ham United before retiring in 1903.

FENWICK H.
Born: Newcastle.
11-0, Half-back, 1919-20.
Fenwick moved to Southampton during the war years and was employed at the Harland and Wolf shipyards. Whilst turning out for the shipyard team he was spotted by Saints and upon the war's end, was persuaded to sign professional forms. He made 11 appearances during 1919-20 but left the club in the close season.

FITCHETT J.
Born: Manchester.
8-0, Full-back, 1902-02.
Fitchett started his career with local side, Talbot, before moving to Bolton Wanderers in 1897, where he was considered to be one of the best juvenile footballers around. In 1902 he arrived at The Dell but never lived up to his youthful promise and was transferred to Fulham. He went on to play for Plymouth and Manchester United before retiring in 1905. He later became manager of the Vaudeville Theatre, Exeter.

FOSTER J.
Born: Yorkshire.
6-1, Forward, 1908-09.
Although Foster was born in Yorkshire, his first club was Watford, with whom he made his debut in 1906. In 1907 he signed for Sunderland but did not stay long and returned south to play for West Ham, where he became a regular. On 3 March he signed for the Saints in an exchange deal which took Costello to the Hammers. His stay at The Dell was brief and he was released after only six games.

FOXALL F.
Born: Blackheath.
38-5:67-7, Forward, 1919-22.
Fred Foxall started his professional career at Aston Villa but due to the outbreak of war, he drifted out of League football to play for Blackheath Town. The Saints, noticing his potential, signed him in 1918 and he soon forced his way into the first team, where he was appreciated for his quick, accurate crosses. In May 1921 he got involved in a controversy by signing for Aston Villa, without Southampton's permission. The Saints reported him to the FA and he was ordered to re-sign for the Saints. Foxall continued to give Saints good service and when he transferred to Birmingham in March 1922, the fans were sorry to see him go.

FRASER J.
Born: Dumbarton, 1876. Died: October 1952.
73-25, Forward, 1902-05.
Jack Fraser played his initial football for Dumbarton but, like many of his countrymen, he moved south of the border and signed for Notts County in 1897. Two years later he moved to Newcastle and after 30 appearances for the Tynesiders, he returned to Scotland to play for St.Mirren. When he came to The Dell in 1902 he was originally given the number-nine shirt but he was happier at inside-left and it was in the latter position where he had his best games. firm favourite of the crowd, Fraser was to remain in the area for two years and it would have been longer, as his intention was to purchase a tobacconist's business in Southampton. Unfortunately the purchase fell through and he accepted excellent terms by Dundee and so returned to Scotland. The move back to Dundee paid dividends as he

was to gain an international cap in 1907, and a Scottish Cup winners' medal. He later became the manager at Dundee before returning to England in 1919 as Chelsea's assistant manager, a position he was to hold for over 16 years.

FRENCH J.
Born: Southampton.
6-0, Centre-half, 1899-01
Joe French was a local player who started playing football in the junior leagues with Southampton Oxford. In 1899 he joined the Saints to provide regular cover for Chadwick. In 1901 he joined New Brompton but, after only 14 appearances, returned to the Southampton area and turned out for Freemantle.

FRY C.B.
Born: Croydon, April 1872. Died: September 1956.
16-0, Full-back, 1900-03.
Charles Burgess Fry was famous for more reasons than simply his prowess as a Southampton footballer. Athletically and academically gifted, he not only equalled the world long-jump record, but was one of England's best cricketers for many years. He learned his football at Repton School and upon reaching Oxford University he perfected his skills, obtaining his Blue as a matter of course. In 1894 he joined the famous amateur club, The Corinthians, and six years later signed for the Saints, still an amateur. Due to his many other pursuits, he was often unavailable but played his part in several important matches, such as the 1902 FA Cup run. During his spell at Southampton he struck up a telepathic understanding with Robinson, the Saints' goalkeeper, and the pair were selected to play for England against Ireland in March 1901. At the time, it was said that CB, as he was known, 'struck his back passes to Robinson with such ferocity that opposing forwards would have been content to have claimed them as shots'. Whilst playing for the Saints, Fry still turned out for the Corinthians and showed his old allegiances to the amateur side by donning their striped socks even while playing for the Saints. In 1902-03 Fry turned out for the Saints as a forward and failed to show any form in this new position. Reluctant to revert to the full-back position, he decided to try his luck at Portsmouth, but was not there

long before an injury sustained in a Cup match against Everton, virtually ended his footballing career. CB continued to play cricket for Sussex, Hampshire and England right up to 1921 and when he finally retired from competitive sport, he spent his time running a training ship for young sea cadets on the Hamble, whilst dabbling in journalism and politics. His achievements in the cricket, rugby, football and athletic fields won him undying public popularity and respect — he was once offered the kingdom of Albania — and when he died at the grand age of 84, he had already become a legend to the country's sports fans. CB is buried in Repton, Derbyshire, in the shadow of his old school.

FURBY W.
Born: 1871.
5-0, Half-back, 1893-95.
Furby made his initial appearance in a Saints shirt during 1893-94 as a centre-half, but the arrival of Littlehales forced him to try his luck as a wing-half. His first-team chances were limited due to the form of Taylor and Thomson and he left the club in 1895. He was still alive in 1969 aged 98.

GEORGE
1-0, Forward, 1901-02.
George was a reserve player who, like many other reserves, found it very hard to break in the first team due to the wealth of talent at Southampton in 1901. His only appearance came when he replaced the injured Arthur Turner against Reading at Elm Park in March 1902.

GIBSON A.
18-4, Forward, 1911-12.
Gibson was signed 'under the nose of the two Glasgow giants, Rangers and Celtic' in 1911 and arrived at the same time as McAlpine. At the annual general meeting in June 1911, the players were described as 'two great captures' but unlike McAlpine, Gibson never lived up to expectations and was released after only one season to join Leeds City.

GILL
1-0, Full-back, 1899-1900.
Gill arrived at The Dell in 1899 from Poole Town and made his only appearance for the first team against Sheppey United in March 1900.

GLEN A.
Born: Kilsyth, 1879.
29-10, Forward, 1906-07.
Glen was a tall forward who started his professional career at Grimsby in 1901, before moving to Tottenham in 1904. Arriving at The Dell two years later, he was appreciated as an elegant dribbler but his form tailed off towards the end of the season and he was transferred to Portsmouth. His spell at Pompey was brief and he soon moved to Brentford. Before embarking on his footballing career, Glen had been in the Army and fought in the Boer War.

GLOVER H.
Born: Ashford, 1883.
160-4, Full-back. 1906-11.
Glover was introduced to the Saints by their ex-player, Jimmy Yates, who scouted for the club in the Kent area. Spotted playing for Hastings and St.Leonard's in 1906, he was signed under the noses of many of the London clubs. Glover developed into a strong and reliable full-back serving the Saints loyally for five seasons. He completed his League career at West Ham United where he made 29 League appearances.

GOODCHILD A.
Born: Southampton, 1892. Died: Eastleigh, October 1950.
5-0, Goalkeeper, 1909-11.
Goodchild came to The Dell in 1909 after a junior trial match having previously turned out for St.Paul's Athletic the previous season. Became the regular reserve goalkeeper during the 1909-10 season as Burrow's understudy. In 1911 he was released by the Saints and obtained a job in the docks. Manchester City rescued his career by giving him contract and he had a distinguished time at Maine Road that encompassed 16 seasons and an FA Cup runners-up medal in 1926. After retiring from football he became landlord of the Cricketers pub in Eastleigh, and played part-time for Guildford City.

GORDON D.
Born: Edinburgh, 1883.
18-0, Full-back, 1904-05, 1911-12.
Although Daniel Gordon was born in Scotland, his first football club was Everton although he never made their first team. He joined Southampton in 1904 and became the understudy to Molyneux. After one year and six appearances he retured to Scotland to play for St Mirren although his stay north of the border was soon to end and

he later played for Middlesbrough, Bradford and Hull. In 1911 he returned to Southampton and his experience helped the Saints through a difficult season. At the season's end, Gordon retired from competitive football.

GRAY W.
28-0, Half-back, 1906-07.
Gray was signed from Partick Thistle in 1906 and became the regular left-half, missing only six League games during the 1906-07 season. Unfortunately he could not settle in England and returned to Scotland at the season's conclusion.

GRAYER F.
Born: Brighton, February 1890. Died: January 1961.
6-0, Full-back, 1910-12.
Frank Grayer played for St Mary's Athletic before signing for Saints in 1908. He waited patiently in the reserves for three seasons before making his debut in the first eleven. In 1912 he was transferred to Liverpool for £100 and stayed at Anfield for two years before joining up in 1914. Grayer was badly injured at Ypres and never played professional football again. In 1919 he found employment at Shepherd and Hedges and remained there until his retirement in 1955.

GREEN G.
21-0, Full-back, 1913-15.
Green was signed from Northfleet in April 1914 and was a hardworking, reliable full-back throughout the 1914-15 campaign. During the war period he dropped out of football, although the Saints held on to his registration. At the war's end he asked to be released and this the Saints did in July 1919, enabling him to rejoin his first club, Northfleet.

GREENLESS D.
Born: Glasgow, 1876.
8-0, Half-back, 1899-00.
Greenless was previously at St Mirren before joining Southampton in the summer of 1899 and his versatility made him perfect cover for regular half-backs, Meston and Petrie. Tired of being an understudy, he moved back to his native Scotland.

GRUMLEY A.
1-0, Half-back, 1919-20.
Grumley made his one and only appearance in February 1920, against Brighton, replacing the injured Hackett.

HACKETT R.
Born: Cradley Heath.
31-0, Half-back, 1919-20.
Reg Hackett played his early football for Cradley Heath and St Luke's from where he progressed to Blackheath during the war. He gained two wartime junior international caps against Scotland and Ireland during the 1918-19 season and was signed by Southampton in May 1919. Hackett played consistently in Saints' last season in the Southern League but for reasons unknown decided to move back to play in the Birmingham District League.

HADLEY G.

57-4, Half-back, 1913-15.
Prior to joining the Saints. Hadley was a Scottish junior international and Southampton obtained him from local side, Wellinghall Swifts. After taking some time to break into the first team, he never looked back and held his place right up to the suspension of League football in 1915. The Saints retained his registration throughout the war but sold him to Aston Villa in May 1919.

HADLEY H.
Born: Barrow, 1877.
29-0, Half-back, 1907-08.
Hadley started his career as an 18-year-old amateur at Halesowen but was snapped up halfway through his first season by West Bromwich Albion. Turning professional, he remained with Albion

for six seasons and gained an England cap in 1903. In February 1905 he moved to Aston Villa and then to Nottingham Forest in April 1906. A year later he was at Southampton and although he remained only one season, he added a touch of determination to the half-back line. Hadley retired from football after leaving the Saints but in 1919 he returned to become manager of Merthyr Town. In 1922 he moved on to become Chesterfield's manager before having two more spells in charge of Merthyr. In 1927 he took charge at Aberdare before his final managerial post, in charge at Bangor between 1928 and 1929.

HALL H.
1-0, Forward, 1914-15.
Hall arrived at The Dell in May 1914, together with fellow Market Harborough player, Crick, and made his only League appearance in March 1915 against Bristol Rovers. He remained in the Southampton area during the war years assisting, the Saints during the 1917-18 season.

HAMER D.
Born: India 1869.
8-0, Full-back, 1894-97.
Hamer was a soldier who began his footballing career with the Royal Engineers, winning Hampshire Senior Cup medals in 1889 and 1890. He left the Aldershot club for Southampton in 1891 but had a disappointing season and moved to the Isle of Wight to play for Cowes. When Saints joined the Southern League in 1894, he returned to add his experience to the team. After two years he went back to Cowes although in 1898 he returned to Southampton for a third time in the role of assistant first-team trainer.

HAMILTON H.
Born: South Shields.
23-9, Forward, 1911-12.
Hamilton's League career started at Sheffield Wednesday in 1909 but finding first-team opportunities limited, he joined Huddersfield Town who were enjoying their first season as a League team. Whilst at Huddersfield he scored ten goals in 16 games before joining the Saints in 1911. At Southampton he enjoyed the occasional good game at centre-forward, but often seemed to lack a yard in pace. When he left Souhampton before the season ended, he moved to Ireland and played for Belfast Celtic.

HANDLEY G.
Born: Totley.
24-2, Forward, 1911-12.
Handley was a left winger in the Chesterfield side of 1904-05 and was guided by the Chesterfield trainer, George Swift. In 1907 he moved to Bradford, enjoying a successful four seasons, although failure to gain a place in their 1911 FA Cup winning side caused him to join Southampton, who were being managed by George Swift. When Swift resigned from the club in 1912, Handley decided to leave and signed for Goole Town.

HARDY G.
1-0, Forward, 1912-13.
Hardy came to Southampton via Leytonstone although he never signed professional forms for the club. After only one senior outing he returned to minor league footbal.

HARRIS G.
Born: Rochester.
48-9, Forward, 1905-07.
Harris joined Stoke from Uttoxeter in 1902 but in three seasons made only ten first-team appearances. Late in 1904 he moved to Reading and made an impact by scoring 11 times in 28 games. The

Saints quickly signed him and he went straight into the first team at inside-left. He remained at The Dell for two seasons before leaving in the close season of 1907.

HARRIS J.
3-0, Half-back, 1906-07.
Harris was secured from the Royal Engineers in 1906 and was the regular reserve left-half during the 1906-07 campaign.

HARRISON F.
Born: Winchester, August 1880. Died: Southampton, November 1969.
153-83, Forward, 1901-08.
Fred Harrison was discovered playing in the local parks for Fitzhugh Rovers in the Southampton Junior League and he developed into one of the best centre-forwards the club had ever produced. 'Buzzy', as he was nicknamed, was introduced into the League side during the 1901-02 season, although it was not until the following season that he started hitting the headlines for his goalscoring abilities. He was not only fast, but possessed a deadly shot and was clever enough to learn from other more experienced members of the side. With his reputation growing all the time, he was the subject of many large offers from big clubs and in 1904 he was given an England trial. Unfortunately, in the trial match he played in an unfamiliar position and failed to gain the international recognition he richly deserved. Eventually, in November 1907, the Saints reluctantly transferred him for £1,000 to Fulham, much to the sorrow of the Southampton public. Although the Saints had seen the best of Harrison, he went on to give sterling service not only to Fulham but also West Ham and Bristol City. He was gassed in World War One. Harrison started a master plasterers business in Southampton after the war.

HARTLEY A.
Born: Dumbarton. Died: October 1909.
21-14, Forward, 1898-99
Abe Hartley started his footballing days playing for Dumbarton as a full-back. When Everton signed him in 1892 he successfully converted to the forward line and remained at Everton for five and a half years, winning a FA Cup runners-up medal in 1897. Soon after the Cup Final he moved to Liverpool but his stay was brief and the Saints acquired his services in 1898. At Southampton, Hartley developed the curious habit of rolling a cigarette before the match and placing it behind one of his ears for the duration of the first half. In the interval he would smoke the cigarette before taking the field. After only one season at The Dell he moved on to play for Arsenal.

HARTSHORNE A.
Born: Darlaston, 1881.
25-0, Full-back, 1905-06.
By the time Hartshorne arrived at The Dell in 1905 he was already a much-travelled player, starting his career with Moxley White Star before having brief spells at Wolves, Port Vale, Stoke and Aston Villa. His time at Southampton was equally brief and he moved to Northampton in 1906.

HAXTON F.
3-0, Half-back, 1904-06.
Haxton played mainly reserve matches and Western League matches during his two seasons at The Dell, winning a Hampshire Senior Cup winners' medal in 1905.

HAYNES H.
Born: Walsall, 1873. Died: March 1902.
63-4, Full-back, 1896-1900.
Harry Haynes started his working life as a stable fitter in Walsall and it was for Walsall he played his early football. Wolverhampton signed him and he won a regular place in their League eleven in 1894. The following year he moved to Small Heath where he remained for one season before moving to Southampton, much against the wishes of Small Heath who retained his Football League registration. Haynes remained with the Saints for the remainder of his career, eventually retiring to become a landlord in the city in 1900. Whilst in charge of the Edinburgh Castle public house he died suddenly at the age of 29 in 1902.

HAYTER.F.
2-0, Forward, 1896-97.
A young reserve player who provided cover for Keay during the 1896-97 campaign.

HEDLEY G.
Born: Southbank, 1876. Died: August 1942.
70-30, Forward, 1904-06.
George Hedley started his long and successful career as an amateur for Southbank in the Northern League, before joining Sheffield United in 1897. Turning professional in May 1898, Hedley won a FA Cup winners' medal in 1899 followed by another medal in 1902. In 1901 he won an England cap, against Ireland. In 1903, fearing that he might be forced to quit football, because of torn heart muscles, he accepted an invitation to play for Southampton. Once at The Dell he moved from his usual centre-forward position to inside-right and quickly formed a partnership with Harrison. In May 1906 he moved to Wolverhampton where he won his third Cup winners' medal. Although now regarded as a veteran, he remained at Molyneux for six years before retiring in 1912. Hedley became manager of Bristol City in April 1913, a position he held until 1915. He later became a publican in Bristol before moving back to Wolverhampton to run a boarding house.

HENDERSON W.
Born: Reading, 1878.
21-0, Full-back, 1901-02.
Henderson, although born in Reading, started his footballing career with Scottish side, Broxburn Athletic, before signing for Everton. Unable to gain a first-eleven place with Everton, he joined his home-town club, Reading, in 1897 and enjoyed three successful seasons with the Berkshire club. Joining Southampton in 1901, he found first-team chances restricted due to the simultaneous arrival of CB Fry at the club. Henderson was determined to find regular first-team football and tried his luck at Everton, where at last he enjoyed a spell in their League team during the 1902-03 season. In the close season of 1903 he joined Reading yet again and went on to New Brompton in 1906.

HINTON J.
Born: Southampton.
2-0, Forward, 1914-15.
Hinton was a young local-inside forward whose career was cut short by the outbreak of the war.

HOARE J.
Born: Southampton.
8-0, Full-back, 1902-03; 1904-05.
Hoare was Molyneux's understudy during the 1902-03 season and was spotted by Liverpool who acquired his services for the 1903-04 campaign. He played seven League games for them during the season and re-signed for the Saints in 1904, staying at The Dell for another season before going to local football with Bitterne Guild.

HODGKINSON A.
Born: Pembroke Dock, August 1885. Died: November 1959.
57-18, Forward, 1907-09.
When Bert Hodgkinson arrived at The Dell in 1907, he had already played for five other clubs — Old Normanton followed by Grimsby in 1903; he joined Plymouth in 1904 and Leicester in 1905. He seemed to prefer to remain at a club for only one year, and in 1906 he was playing for Bury. With the Saints, he gained a reputation for being a fast, skilful left winger and in April 1908 he won his only Welsh cap, against Ireland. He left Southampton for Croydon Common in 1909 and later moved yet again, to Southend.

HODGKINSON J.
Born: Tunstall.
20-3, Half-back, 1895-97.
Hodgkinson was a reliable half-back who arrived at Southampton in January 1896 and succeeded George Marshall in the team. He left the area later in 1896 and his talents were lost to the Saints.

HOGG J.
Born: Sunderland, May 1881.
43-1, Half-back, 1905-07.
Hogg came from a famous family of footballers in the North-East and joined Sunderland in his youth, but failed to make the League side. His next club was Morpeth Harriers, although it was not long before Sheffield United signed him in time for the 1902-03 season. Hogg spent two years at Sheffield, making only three appearances in two seasons before joining the Saints in 1905. He made steady progress in the 1905-06 season, playing at both centre-half and half-back. Hogg could always be relied upon to give his best, although he had a tendency to be overawed by important matches. He left the club at the culmination of the 1906-07 season.

HOLLANDS F.
15-3, Forward, 1894-95.
Fred Hollands was signed from Millwall in 1894 and was the regular outside-left through the first Southern League season of 1894-95. Quick and nimble, he won a Hampshire Senior Cup winners' medal with the Saints before moving back to London.

HOLLINS A.
Born: Wolverhampton.
18-10, Forward, 1913-15.
Hollins began his football career with his local side, Wolverhampton Early Closers, and subsequently played for Walsall and Wellington. In February 1914 he joined the Saints and found instant success playing centre-forward, although he failed to maintain his form the following season. With the suspension of League football in 1915, he left the club.

HOSKINS A.
Born: Southampton, 1886.
21-0, Forward, 1906-08.
Bert Hoskins was signed from local side, Freemantle, in 1906 and was at home playing at either outside or inside-right. Hoskins was

one of those players who was always on the brink of establishing a first team place but never seemed to quite manage it. In 1908 he moved to Wolves and made 13 appearances over two seasons before joining Dudley in 1911. He later returned to Wolves to become their manager and later Gillingham manager. Hoskins also played for Shrewsbury.

HOULKER A.
Born: Blackburn, April 1892. Died: April 1962.
59-3, Half-back, 1903-06.
A small, enthusiastic half-back, Bert Houlker started his long career at Blackburn Hornets, progressing through a variety of local sides before arriving at Blackburn Rovers in 1894. 'Kelly' as he was nicknamed, remained with Rovers for eight seasons before joining Portsmouth in May 1902. Whilst at Pompey he gained the first of his five England caps and then moved to Southampton in May 1903. Houlker became very popular with the Southampton public and whilst with the Saints he won two England caps and a Southern League Championship medal. In 1906 he intended to retire from professional football but was persuaded to return to Blackburn where he turned out regularly until the end of 1907-08. Again he wanted to retire but was tempted to sign for Colne in 1909. Incredibly, in 1918, at the age of 46, he turned out for Blackburn Rovers in a wartime match. He later became an overseer at a mill before running a coal and haulage business in Blackburn after World War Two. He retired from this trade in 1947.

HOWLAND C.
1-0, Full-back, 1901-02.
Howland was a young trialist full-back who made his only League appearance in March 1902, replacing the injured Molyneux.

HUGHES A.
Born: Birkenhead, 1886.
21-15, Forward, 1908-09.
Hughes arrived at The Dell from Bolton in 1908 and despite a nasty leg injury sustained two months after his arrival, he still managed to be the club's top scorer for the 1908-09 season. At the season's end he signed for Manchester City.

INGLIS.
1-0, Half-back, 1895-96.
Inglis appeared in the last League match of the 1895-96 season, replacing Hodgkinson, but failed to impress and soon returned to his regiment, the Argyle and Sutherland Highlanders.

IRELAND S.

IRELAND S.
Born: Tamworth, 1889.
120-0, Full-back, 1911-15.
Ireland was signed during the close season of 1911 from Kingsbury Colliery and although he initially took time to settle, he won a regular first-team place in late March 1912. Remaining a regular until League football was suspended in 1915, he continued to play for the Saints throughout the war before becoming a PoW in Germany during the later stages of the hostilities. When peace arrived, Ireland returned to Southampton and in June 1919 was transferred to Merthyr Town where he remained for one season before retiring.

JACQUES.
1-0, Forward, 1907-08.
Jacques was at The Dell for one season and played at Plymouth in December, his only Southern League game for the Saints.

JEFFERIS F.
Born: Fordingbridge, July 1884. Died: May 1938.
170-48, Forward, 1905-11.
Jefferis was playing for Fordingbridge Turks when he was invited to The Dell in March 1905 and scored three goals in a reserve match.

The following month he played for the Saints against The Corinthians and capped a clever display by netting another hat-trick. Southampton were immediately impressed and persuaded Jefferis to sign professional, paying Fordingbridge Turks the princely sum of £5.00 for his transfer. Before long Jefferis had won a regular position in the Saints' forward line by his graceful and neat ball play and and his ability to bring the best out of his fellow forwards. In the six seasons he spent at The Dell he was a firm favourite and it was a nasty shock to all the fans when he was transferred to Everton on 16 March 1911. Within a year he had won two England caps and he later assisted Everton in winning the League Championship in 1915. In 1919 he signed for Preston where he won a runners-up medal in the 1922 FA Cup Final. During 1922-23 he was player-coach at Preston before moving to become trainer-coach at Southport. In 1936 he joined Millwall as their trainer and remained there until his death two years later.

JEFFERY J.
13-0, Full-back, 1894-95.
Jeffery signed for St Mary's just after the start of the initial Southern League season of 1894-95 and had previously been on the books of Woolwich Arsenal. He remained in Southampton only the one season, playing some good games at left-back, before moving on.

JEPP S.
Born: Aldershot, February 1887.
70-2, Half-back, 1907-09.
Sam Jepp was a versatile player who came to The Dell from Aldershot Athletic in 1906. At home in many positions, he suffered from being 'jack of all trades but master of none', yet made up for any failings by an unswerving loyalty to Southampton Football Club and stayed at The Dell until retiring in 1911.

JOHNSTON J.
Born: Lennoxtown, 1880.
110-2, Half-back, 1907-11.
Johnston, although born in Scotland, started his football with Stalybridge Rovers from where he joined Bury in 1901. He served Bury loyally for six seasons, appearing in 180 League games and collected an FA Cup winners' medal in 1903. Arriving at The Dell in 1907, along with teammate, Hodgkinson, he served the Saints well over a period of four seasons before joining Stourbridge in 1911.

JONES F.
31-13, Forward, 1914-15.
Jones commenced his professional career at Notts County in 1912 but found his chances in their First Division side somewhat limited, so he joined Coventry City in 1913. The following April saw him join the Saints and he forged a useful partnership with Dominy and Kimpton in the forward line. His career was unfortunately curtailed by the suspension of League football in 1915.

JONES G.
7-5, Forward, 1919-20.
Jones started his career at Elston Rovers in 1912, moving on to play for Crewe Alexandra. Before the start of World War Two he had signed for Bury, although he failed to make their first team and was released. In May 1919 he signed for the Saints and, towards the end of the 1919-20 campaign, showed enough scoring form to be picked to play for the South-East Counties against London Combination, scoring two goals. Despite this impressive scoring rate, he was allowed to leave Southampton and joined Goole Town in 1920.

JORDAN F.
Born: Southampton, 1883. Died: 28 March 1938.
42-5, Forward, 1908-10.
Frank Jordan was a reserve player during the 1907-08 season and moved to South Africa in the close season. He returned to Southampton in time for the beginning of the 1908-09 campaign and was soon a regular member of the Southern League side. Never very skilful, he did at least possess a powerful style although during the 1909-10 season his form deserted him and he went to Stoke, followed by a move to Merthyr Town in 1912.

JOYCE J.
Born: Burton-upon-Trent, 1876.
7-0, Goalkeeper, 1899-00.
Joyce came to Southampton via Burton Pioneers, Woodville and Overseal and made his initial debut against Warmley in December 1898. Warmley, however, later withdrew from the League and the game became void, meaning that the unfortunate Joyce had to wait until October 1899 for his official League debut versus Queen's Park Rangers. He was nicknamed 'Tiny' by the tongue-in-cheek Saints fans as he was well built and rather plump. In 1900, with Robinson playing well in the first team, Joyce moved to Millwall where he became their regular goalkeeper for ten years before joining Blackburn Rovers for a brief spell.

KEAY W.
Born: Whiteinch, 1871. Died: Winchester, January 1943.
60-22, Forward, 1895-1900.
Watty Keay's first club was Partick Thistle, but like so many of his countrymen, he decided to seek fame and fortune south of the border and joined Darlington. In 1893 he signed for Derby, spending two

years with the Midlands side before being tempted to sign for the Saints by Mr McMinn, the Southampton official. In the next four seasons Keay featured regularly and became such a popular inside-forward that he was presented with an inscribed pocket-watch by the fans. Another reason to remember Watty Keay was that he scored the Saints' first-ever goal at The Dell in 1898. Upon his retirement, Keay remained in the area, keenly following local football, and became a shipwright at Camper Nicholsons.

KIDDLE R.
1-0, Forward, 1895-96.
Kiddle had been a regular with Southampton since 1889 and distinguished himself in those pre-League days by winning two Hampshire Senior Cup medals and one Junior medal. He was also in the first team ever to represent the Saints in the FA Cup in 1891. By the time the club had entered the Southern League in 1894, Kiddle was past his best but he did at least have the satisfaction of making the one League appearance in 1895-96.

KILLEAN E.
Born: Blackburn, 1874.
2-0, Half-back, 1900-01.
Edward Killean signed for Blackburn in 1894 and for four seasons was a regular in their first team before losing his place. After two years in Blackburn reserves, he joined the Saints in 1900 as cover for Arthur Chadwick, but in his two League appearances of 1900-01 he failed to impress. In the close season of 1901 he moved on to New Brompton where he was more successful.

KIMPTON G.
Born: Leaverden, 1888.
141-27, Forward, 1910-20.
George Kimpton signed from Leaverden in 1910 and quickly established himself in the first eleven right up to the outbreak of the World War One. During the war years he assisted the Saints and returned to make two further League appearances in the 1919-20

season. He signed for Thorneycrofts and then went to France to play and coach. From there, Kimpton became a coach in Czechoslovakia before returning to France to manage Le Havre in 1945.

KITCHEN G.
Born: Buxton.
37-0, Goalkeeper, 1912-14.
By the time George Kitchen arrived at The Dell he was a veteran, having previously been on the books of Buxton, Stockport, Everton and West Ham. Whilst at Everton he had been selected for an England trial match but was never fortunate enough to win a full cap. In 1905 he had left Goodison for West Ham and spent seven years with the London club before signing for the Saints in 1912. As well as becoming the Saints' goalkeeper, he acquired the position of golf professional at Bournemouth, a career he was to follow after his retirement from football. In 1914 he joined Bournemouth, which meant he was able to combine his two favourite sports with less travelling involved. In 1969, Kitchen was still working, in London as a doorman.

KNIGHT W.
Born: Toogates.
38-0, Goalkeeper, 1911-13.
Knight began his career at Walsall before being spotted by Aston Villa in 1910. He spent 1910-11 playing for Stourbridge, Villa's nursery team. Much against the wishes of Villa he joined the Saints in 1911 and when he replaced Brown in November of the same year, he looked to be an admirable deputy. Unfortunately, the 1912-13 season did not work quite as well and Kitchen took over between the posts, causing Knight to leave Southampton at the season's conclusion.

LEE A.
Born: Bridport, 1879. Died: January 1958.
251-13, Half-back, 1900-06; 1911-15.
Bert Lee came to The Dell in April 1900 as a trialist playing for Poole

Town. He obviously impressed, as he was engaged prior to the start of the 1900-01 season and quickly developed into a fine right-half. He was a member of the Saints' 1902 Cup Final team and in 1904 won an England cap against Wales. In May 1906, Lee signed for Dundee and spent five seasons with the Scottish club, captaining them to a Scottish Cup Final win in 1910, one of the few occasions that an Englishman has captained a Scottish Cup-winning side. Lee returned to The Dell in the close season of 1911 and became player-trainer during 1914-15. During the war he served at the front, before being appointed first-team trainer in 1919, when League football recommenced. Lee was to hold this position for 16 years and when he retired in 1935 he ended a partnership that both parties had enjoyed since the beginning of the century. He later became a salesman in his son's radio business.

LEWIS J.
Born: Aberystwyth, 1882.
24-10, Forward, 1907-08.
Lewis, although born in Wales, started his League career at

Portsmouth in 1900, before moving north to play Second Division football for Burton United. After three seasons he returned to Southern League football with Bristol Rovers and won a Welsh cap, against England in 1906. Lewis then had a spell at Brighton before arriving at Southampton, his third south coast club. Initially his move to the Saints paid dividends and a flourishing partnership with Harrison developed, but after this good start the partnership, along with Lewis's form, declined and he gave up first-class football.

LIDDELL E.
Born: Sunderland.
1-0, Centre-half, 1905-06.
Liddell graduated through local Wearside leagues before signing for Sunderland. He never made Sunderland's first team and in 1905 moved to Southampton. He made one League appearance but was generally lacking in speed and in the close season of 1906, moved to Clapton Orient.

LITTLEHALES A.
51-9, Centre-half, 1894-1898.
Alf Littlehales had played for both Wolves and Stoke before joining Southampton in time for their debut in the Southern League. He was a quality centre-half with considerable skill and a good shot. Age caught up with him in 1898 and he retired from the game but continued to live locally.

LOASBY F.
1-0, Full-back, 1914-15.
Loasby joined the Saints from Desborough and spent the whole season in the reserve eleven, apart from the very last League game before the suspension of football in 1915.

LOCK H.
Born: Southampton, January 1887. Died: 18 March 1957.
55-0: 11-0, Goalkeeper, 1907-09; 1922-23.
Lock was signed by the Saints in 1907 from local side, St Mary's Guild and imediately forced his way into the first team by his brave goalkeeping. In March 1908 his bravery caused him a serious injury at Watford and, strangely, in the next season, again at Watford, he sustained another bad injury. Lock vowed never to play at Watford again and at the end of the season transferred to Glasgow Rangers. His departure was a blow to the Saints as Lock continued to keep goal for Rangers for many years. After the war he signed for the other Rangers — Queen's Park, and stayed there for three seasons before re-signing for Southampton as cover for Tommy Allen in September 1922. He played in the first team following an injury to Allen in March 1923 and then moved on to Bournemouth in the close season. Lock later became a joiner and carpenter with the railway.

McALPINE J.
Born: Motherwell.
132-2, Half-back, 1911-15.
McAlpine was considered to be one of the best captures of the 1911-12 season, when the Saints obtained his signature from Strathclyde. A regular in the first team right up to the suspension of League football, he remained on Saints' books throughout the war and was then sold to Millwall in May 1919.

McDONALD A.
5-5, Forward, 1901-02.
McDonald arrived at The Dell in 1901 and had previously played for Jarrow and Everton. Although he made a sensational start to the

1901-02 season by scoring five goals in three matches, he moved to West Ham in December, due to the fact that Saints already had a wealth of good forwards on their books. He did not remain long at West Ham, joining Pompey in March 1902 and this move was followed by subsequent moves to Wellingborough, Luton and Croydon Common.

McGHEE G.
2-0, Forward, 1908-09.
McGhee was at The Dell only one season, during which time he made two appearances.

McGIBBON C.
Born: Portsmouth, 1880. Died: Hamble, May 1954.
28-19, Forward, 1909-10.
Charlie McGibbon was a soldier throughout his football career which started with Crystal Palace in 1907-08. While at Palace he earned a reputation as a deadly marksman and the Saints were pleased to acquire his signature in the summer of 1908. In the 28 games he played for Southampton, his powerful shot earned him 19 goals, although it could have been more as his finishing was erratic at times. Unfortunately for the Saints, his army career with the Royal Artillery took him to Woolwich before the end of the season and he played four games for Arsenal before moving on to Clapton Orient for the 1909-10 season. Sergeant McGibbon survived the war and in 1919 was employed as chief clerk of the statistical offices at Netley Hospital, where he was the secretary of the local football and cricket teams. Before his death he had witnessed his son, Doug, also play for the Saints.

McKAY.
8-0, Full-back, 1896-97.
McKay was a member of the Woolston Works team before joining Southampton in 1896. He played in the first eight games of the season before losing his place, when Meston was switched to right-back. McKay left Southampton in the close season of 1897, his destination unknown.

McKEER W.
4-0, Half-back, 1909-11.
McKeer was a soldier who had turned out for the RAMC before joining the Saints during the 1909-10 season. After providing cover for Trueman for two season, he left in 1911.

McKENZIE J.
Born: Glasgow, 1877.
6-3, Forward, 1898-99.
Jim McKenzie was an upholsterer by trade and played amateur football for Gatmore, Possel Park, East Stirling and Cowlairs, before signing professional forms with Burton Swifts in 1897. He was at Burton less than a year before returning to Scotland and Clyde, but his stay there was also brief and he moved to Saints in 1898. McKenzie was a nippy outside-left but failed to settle in the Southampton area and moved back to Scotland after only six appearances.

McKIE J.
6-0, Full-back, 1896-97.
McKie joined the Saints from local rivals, Freemantle, in 1896 and played six times before returning on to Chatham in the close season of 1898.

McLEAN D.
Born: Goran, January 1874.
8-3, Forward, 1898-99.
Duncan McLean played for Partick Thistle before joining Cowes, on the Isle of Wight, in 1897. Spotted playing for Cowes by director George Thomas, he signed for the Saints during the 1898-99 campaign but ended his association with the club when he left the area during the summer.

McLEAN R.
Born: Egypt, 1883.
4-0, Half-back, 1906-07.
McLean arrived from Newcastle United in 1906, where he spent several seasons assisting their reserve eleven. In the one year he spent at The Dell, his first-team outings were confined to four appearances and he move back to the north in the summer.

McLEOD R.
Born: Kilsyth, Stirlingshire, February 1872. Died: December 1931.
20-6, Forward, 1898-1900.
Roddy McLeod had a spell with Partick Thistle before joining West Bromwich in 1895. Two years later he moved to Leicester Fosse, becoming their top scorer in 1897-98. A tempting offer from Brighton United lured him into Southern League football and he became their leading scorer for 1898-99. Brighton United were at the time experiencing financial troubles and McLeod was released in April 1899 to join the Saints, playing in the last three matches of the season. The following year he competed with Farrell for the centre-forward position and when Farrell, somewhat undeservedly, was chosen for the FA Cup Final team, the disappointment McLeod felt at being left out caused him to sign for Brentford at the end of the season.

McMILLAN J.
31-3, Half-back, 1895-98.
McMillan joined the Saints in March 1896, having previously played for Hearts in the Scottish League. Due to the manner in which he kicked the ball, he was nicknamed 'Punt' and for a while he held a first-team place. With the squad growing stronger during the 1897-98 season, McMillan's services were not needed and he departed in 1898.

MARSHALL G.
Born: Southampton.
22-0, Half-back, 1894-96.
George Marshall was a convert from the rugby football code and first appeared in a St Mary's shirt during the 1887-88 season. He won two Hampshire Senior Cup medals before Saints entered the Southern League in 1894. Marshall retired in 1896 after playing at both full-back and half-back for the Saints.

MEAD P.
Born: Battersea, March 1887. Died: Bournemouth, 1958.
1-0, Goalkeeper, 1907-08.
Philip Mead was destined to make a name for himself, not on the football field but on the cricket pitches, and was one of Hampshire's greatest batsmen. Although his only appearance for the Saints was as a goalkeeper, in December 1907, he played several games for the reserves as a forward. Mead's first love, however, was always cricket, and despite becoming almost blind later in life, he could still be found at the County Ground supporting Hampshire.

MEEHAN P.
Born: Broxburn, 1874.
36-1, Full-back, 1898-00.
Meehan was a miner before turning to League football as a career, starting with Hibernian and then moving south to join Sunderland. He returned to Scotland in the summer of 1894 to sign for Celtic and whilst with the Glasgow club he gained a Scottish cap, against Ireland in 1896. In 1897 he transferred to Everton for £150 and spent a successful season in Liverpool before joining the Saints for a fee of £200. After helping Southampton retain the Southern League Championship and reach the FA Cup Final, Meehan returned to his local side, Broxburn, and played for them until his retirement.

MESTON S.
Born: Arbroath, January 1871. Died: Ashurst, August 1948.
246-18, Half-back, 1895-1906.
Sam Meston played his early football for local side, Arbroath Victoria, until 1893 when he joined Stoke. He joined Southampton as part of the 'Stoke invasion' and soon proved to be one of the most valuable of all the players signed during those Southern League days. His hard shot earned him the nickname of 'Long Tom' after a cannon that was in regular use in those days. He played over 200 games for the Saints in a variety of positions. Right-half was his favourite and whilst at Southampton he won a record six Southern League Championship medals, as well as two FA Cup runners-up awards. After 11 seasons with the Saints he moved to play for Croydon Common and finally Salisbury City. Twenty years later, his son was to play for the Saints although injury was to prevent him from emulating his father's proud record.

METCALF T.
Born: 1879. Died: May 1938.
1-0, Half-back, 1905-06.
Tom Metcalf spent three seasons at The Dell but made only one League appearance, in September 1905. He moved to Wolves in 1906 and was later employed by brewers Ind Coope and Alsopps Limited.

MILWARD A.
Born: Marlow, 1870. Died: June 1941.
56-36, Forward, 1899-1901.
Alf Milward was a quick left-winger of medium build who forged an exciting partnership with Edgar Chadwick and scored goals with impressive regularity. He played his early football for his local side, Marlow, and signed for Everton in 1888, where he first teamed up with Chadwick. At Everton he won two FA Cup winners' medals, a League Championship medal and four England caps. In 1897 he moved to New Brighton Tower and two years later signed for the Saints. Milward was at The Dell for two years and never missed a League match, helping the team to the Southern League title in 1901 and winning an FA Cup runners-up medal the same year. In the close season of 1901 he signed for New Brompton and spent two years playing for them before he returned to Southampton to turn out for Southampton Cambridge. He settled in the area after his playing days were over.

MOGER H.
Born: Southampton, 1879.
14-0, Goalkeeper, 1900-03.
Henry Moger joined Southampton in 1900 from local rivals, Freemantle, and was unlucky that Jack Robinson was also at The Dell at that time. Moger spent three years playing under Robinson's shadow before Manchester United spotted his undoubted potential and quickly signed him in 1903. Moger spent nine years with United and was their goalkeeper during their first great era when they won two League Championships and the FA Cup.

MOLYNEUX G.
Born: Liverpool, 1875.
142-0, Full-back, 1900-05.
George Molyneux was a fine, quick-tackling full-back, who was to acquire three England caps during his stay at The Dell. Originally a soldier, he played his early football with the Third Grenadiers before moving on to South Shore and Wigan County. In 1898 he signed for Everton and a year later Southampton, where he enjoyed five good seasons. In 1905 he joined Portsmouth and subsequently played for Southend and Colchester Town.

MONK F.
Born: Salisbury, 1887.
20-0, Centre-half, 1910-12.
An amateur throughout his career, Frank Monk played his early soccer at St Mark's College, Chelsea and then his home-town club, Salisbury City. Whilst at Salisbury he won an England amateur cap and came to the attention of the Saints, for whom he signed during the 1910-11 season. Monk never really made the centre-half spot his own, competing with Jepp and Beaumont for the position. In 1911-12 he played for Fulham before returning briefly to help the Saints out during an injury crisis.

MOON C.
1-0, Forward, 1909-10.
Moon was a reserve centre-forward who made his one League appearance against Swindon in April 1910.

MOORE J.
Born: Felling-on-Tyne.
41-10: 42-12, Forward, 1919-21.
Jimmy Moore joined Southampton from Barnsley officially in May 1919, although he first appeared in a Saints' shirt during the 1916-17 wartime season, when employed in Cowes. He was often described as the 'man who never smiled' and had the unhappy distinction of the being the first-ever Saints' player to be sent off in a Football League game, during the 1920-21 campaign. Despite his unsmiling exterior, Moore was a popular player who was particularly clever with his heading and when 'for family reasons' he was transferred to Leeds, in the close season of 1921, the fans were sorry to see him go. After later playing for Halifax, he retired to become a licensee in Barnsley, and after the World War Two he was elected to Barnsley FC's board.

MOUNCHER F.
Born: Southampton.
99-14, Forward, 1903-08.
Fred Mouncher played in the same Fitzhugh Rovers side as Fred Harrison, before moving to play for another local side, Southampton Cambridge. The Saints signed him in 1903, to replace Joe Turner on the left wing, and he played many excellent games before being sold to Fulham in November 1907, for £800, along with fellow forward Fred Harrison. Mouncher, who won a Southern League Championship medal in  his first season at The Dell, was a fast, direct forward. He played in an international trial match at Manchester in January 1908 and towards the end of his career converted to left-half. Ill health dogged his later years and in 1911 he retired because of consumption.

MOUNSEY F.
Born: 1890. Died: November 1914.
1-0, Centre-half, 1914-15.
Mounsey signed from Wellington Athletic in May 1914 and made his debut the following October against Crystal Palace. In November, whilst playing for the reserves at Watford, he was struck by the ball and collapsed. Although he recovered to finish the game and return to Southampton with the rest of the team, two days later he died of heart failure at the tragically early age of 24.

NAUGHTON W.
36-15, Forward, 1895-98.
Naughton signed for Stoke in 1891 and remained there until 1895. when he signed for the Saints along with several other Stoke team members. Nicknamed 'Chippy', he was an inside-forward in his first season, but was moved to the wing with success for the 1896-97 season, supplying many crosses for Farrell and Buchanan. After he left the area in 1898, the Saints missed his talents.

NICOL T.
Born: Broxburn.
25-1, Full-back, 1897-99.
Tom Nicol signed for Burnley in 1890 after playing local football in his native Scotland and he quickly developed into a fine right-winger. In 1896, a £105 transfer took him to Blackburn Rovers, where he remained just one season before joining the Saints. Soon after arriving in Southampton he was converted into a dashing, fearless, right-back and enjoyed two years at the club before retiring and taking over as landlord of the Kingsland Tavern.

NIHAN M.
2-0, Forward, 1911-12.
Nihan was a soldier who came to The Dell in January 1912 for a brief spell, before rejoining his regiment, the 4th Royal Fusiliers, at the end of the season.

NINEHAM G.
7-4, Forward, 1894-95.
Nineham played his first game for St Mary's during the 1892-93 season and became a regular until the introduction of many professionals in 1895. He then stood down from League football and went back to local soccer.

NORBURY V.
Born: Bartley, August 1887. Died: October 1972.
3-0, Full-back, 1906-07.
Victor Norbury arrived at The Dell during the 1905-06 season, fresh from playing local football in the New Forest for Bartley and Brockenhurst. He made three League appearances the following season but gave the game up to concentrate on a promising cricketing career with Hampshire.

NORTHEY G.
Born: Devon.
1-0, Forward, 1901-02.
Northey came to The Dell in April 1902 as a trialist, making one appearance at inside-right before being released.

OFFER H.
Born: Swindon.
13-4, Forward, 1894-95.
Harry Offer had played for Swindon and Arsenal by the time he came to Southampton, and whilst at Arsenal he had played in the their first-ever FA Cup tie. After two years with the Saints, he retired from the game in 1895.

PADDINGTON A.
Born: Bishopstoke, June 1881.
12-0, Half-back, 1900-03.
Paddington appeared for local sides, Bishopstoke, Chandlers Ford and Eastleigh Athletic, before being signed for Southampton in 1900. Searching for regular first-team football, he moved to Brighton and Hove Albion in 1903.

PARKER T.
Born: Woolston, November 1897.
40-4: 206-7, Full-back, 1919-26.
Tom Parker was one of the finest full-backs ever to play for the Saints. His early football was with local sides such as Sholing Rangers, Sholing Athletic and St Mark's in the war league. He first appeared in a Saints' shirt in 1918 and in the next season became Southampton's second-highest scorer, by netting ten penalties. Parker signed professional forms in May 1919 and by then had

already showed his prowess as a quality full-back, developing a splendid partnership with Fred Titmuss, the other Saints back at the time. Gaining his first England cap in 1925, against France, Parker was the subject of many big offers from the top glamour clubs but the Saints resisted all approaches until March 1926 when he was sold to Arsenal for £3,250. Parker graced Highbury for several years, with Arsenal winning both the FA Cup and League title under his captaincy. When Parker retired from playing, he became manager at Norwich from where he joined the managerless Saints in February 1937. An important side effect of Parker rejoining the Saints was the fact that he brought several Norwich players with him, including the young Ted Bates, who of course was to have an even more important role in the history of the Saints. When Tom Parker returned to The Dell, the Saints had endured several gloomy seasons and his task was an arduous one. He stayed to manage Southampton throughout the difficult war years, but after a disagreement with the club, left in 1943. Twenty years later, this time serving under Ted Bates' managership, Parker returned to the Southampton payroll as chief scout in 1963 and he gave the club ten years loyal service in this capacity. Although now almost 90, Tom Parker is still living in the area and maintains more than a casual interest in the fortunes of the Saints. With the exception of Ted Bates, no ex-player has contributed so much to help the club in its struggles over the last century; first signing on as a player in 1919 and eventually retiring from scouting in the mid-1970s.

PATTEN J.
4-2, Forward, 1906-07.
Patten came to The Dell in March 1907 from Shrewsbury and played in four games before leaving at the end of the season.

PENTON B.
Born: Bournemouth, 1890.
14-3, Forward, 1910-13.
Bevan Penton signed from Bournemouth in February 1911, having previously played for Pokesdown in the Bournemouth area. He made his debut two days after arriving at The Dell and played regularly until the end of the season. In the 1911-12 season, he made only one first-team appearance, despite scoring 19 goals for the reserves. He rejoined Bournemouth in 1913.

PETRIE R.
Born: Dundee, 1872.
50-6, Half-back, 1897-1900.
Bob Petrie's English League club was Sheffield Wednesday, whom he joined in 1894 but prior to then, he had turned out for Arbroath, Dundee East End and Dundee. He was a member of the 1895-96 Wednesday FA Cup side that beat the Saints at the Antelope and then went on to win the trophy. Petrie was a determined tackler, who enjoyed a challenge and helped the Saints reach the 1900 FA Cup Final, leaving the club soon afterwards.

PHILLIPS (GUNNER).
1-0, Full-back, 1895-96.
Made his one appearance at the Antelope Ground in April 1896 against Clapton, replacing Hamer. He was on loan from the Royal Artillery.

PIKE E.
1-0, Full-back, 1902-03.
Pike was a reserve full-back, who came into the side when there were a lot of injuries sustained in the 1902-03 season. He replaced Meston (who, in turn, had replaced Molyneux) against Reading in February.

PONTING W.
Born: Andover, 1872. Died: London, March 1952.
5-0, Half-back, 1896-97.
Billy Ponting made a name for himself playing in the Hampshire League, firstly with Andover and later with Ryde, before signing for the Saints in March 1897. His stay with the club was brief and after giving up the game he became an influential insurance broker in London, although his original profession had been a schoolteacher.

PRINCE P.
Born: Liverpool, August 1887. Died: December 1973.
83-25, Forward, 1912-20.
Although Percy Prince was born in Liverpool, he was brought up in Southampton where he played for local youth teams, Cranbury Avenue and Southampton Oxford, before signing as an amateur for Saints in 1907. He waited patiently until December 1912 to make his debut and marked it by scoring. In 1914, still an amateur, he moved to Bournemouth to play for the Saints during the late war seasons and in 1919 he re-signed for the team to play four Southern League games. He retired from football in 1920 and was later employed by Cunard.

RADFORD I.
9-2, Forward, 1906-07.
Radford was a forward who was signed from Wolves in 1906 but failed to make an impression and rejoined the Molineux club in the close season of 1907. He became a League referee after the war.

RAWLINGS W.
Born: Andover, January 1896. Died: Chandlers Ford, September 1972.
33-19: 294-156, Forward, 1919-28.
Bill Rawlings joined the Army in 1914 and served in France with the Wessex Field Ambulance before joining the Saints in 1918, originally as an amateur. Top scorer in 1918-19, he was persuaded to sign professional forms in May 1919 and he quickly developed into a lively, prolific goalscorer, who forged an understanding with Dominy

to great effect. He was a big man but was good on the ground as well as in the air and he was to hold the Saints' goalscoring record for many years. His talents were recognised in 1922 when, despite playing in the Second Division, he became the second Hampshire man to represent England, in the internationals versus Scotland and Wales. In March 1928, he joined Manchester United for a fee of £3,860, a considerable sum considering he was in his 32nd-year. He did not stay long at Old Trafford and he joined Port Vale in November 1929, only to suffer a bad injury that effectively ended his League career. In 1930 he joined New Milton and two years later teamed up with his old hunting partner, Arthur Dominy, to help Newport (Isle of Wight) win the Hampshire Senior Cup. After his playing days were over he became landlord of a Southampton pub before working for the Admiralty at Portland during World War Two. He retired to live in Chandlers Ford but would never be far from the older fans' memories. In the early 1960s he recalled his best-ever goal, scored on 7 March 1925, when he shot home a fierce free-kick from an oblique angle.

REILLY. M.
Born: Donneybrook, Ireland, 1874.
2-0, Goalkeeper, 1895-96.
Matt Reilly was a goalkeeper of considerable ability, who had two games for the Saints whilst on loan — he regularly represented the Royal Artillery in the Southern League. With the RA's demise as a football team he signed for Portsmouth, where he remained four seasons and gained two Irish caps before finishing his career at Dundee.

REYNOLDS J.
Born: Blackburn. Died: March 1917.
2-0, Half-back, 1897-98.
John Reynolds' first-ever League club was Blackburn Rovers but in 1890, he tried his luck in Ireland, playing for Distillery. Whilst in Ireland he won five Irish caps before his English birthright was discovered. In May 1891, he joined West Bromwich Albion, gaining an FA Cup runners-up medal and incredibly, considering his 'Irish past' an England cap. In May 1893, Reynolds moved to Aston Villa with great success, winning three Championship medals, one FA Cup winners' medal and a further seven England caps. Before joining Southampton in January 1898, he had a brief spell in Scotland with Celtic, although there are no records of any Scottish caps won. His stay with Southampton was brief as he moved to Bristol St George in the summer of 1898 and from there he made the unlikely move of going to New Zealand to coach in 1902. His exploits in New Zealand are unknown, but soon this colourful half-back was back helping Stockport County in 1903. When he eventually gave up football and travelling, he settled in Sheffield to become a collier.

RICHARDS L.
Born: Devon.
1-0, Forward, 1912-13.
Richards was a trialist who played only the one game for the Saints before being allowed to return to Devon.

ROBERTSON J.N.
Born: Coilton, 1884.
153-1 Half-back, 1906-12.
Robertson played for Scottish teams, Drogan and Glasgow Rangers, before moving south to join Bolton Wanderers in 1903. Making only 15 appearances in three seasons, he decided to join the Saints in 1906 and rendered six very reliable years service to the team, becoming captain in 1910. In 1911 he represented the Southern League against

both the Irish League and the English Football League before retiring from the game in the close season of 1912.

ROBERTSON J.T.
Born: Dumbarton, February 1877. Died: January 1935.
19-0, Half-back, 1898-99.
Jack Robertson was previously with Greenock Morton before joining Everton in 1897. In 1898 he won his first cap and soon after that the Saints were lucky to acquire his signature during the close season of the same year. During the 1898-99 season he helped the Saints retain the Southern League Championship and despite being a half-back, played the last game of the season on the left wing. Whilst at Southampton he won another cap, captaining Scotland versus England, but decided to move back to his homeland in 1899 — a move that met with further success as a Rangers player. He gained another 14 caps and became one of the finest half-backs ever to have played for Scotland. In 1905 he transferred to the newly-formed Chelsea and was there just over a season before becoming player-manager of Glossop. a position he held for three seasons.

ROBERTSON T.
Born: Newton, Scotland.
45-1, Full-back, 1902-04.
Robertson's early footballing days were spent playing for Newton Thistle and Hibernian before moving south of the border to turn out for Stoke in 1894. He spent six successful seasons in the Potteries and then signed for Liverpool in 1900. When the Saints signed him two years later, Liverpool were upset at his departure, especially as he gave Southampton two excellent seasons of full-back play. In 1904 he moved to Brighton where he spent a season before retiring to become a publican in Hove.

ROBINSON J.W.
Born: Derby 1866. Died: October 1931.
116-0, Goalkeeper, 1898-1903.
Jack Robinson was a spectacular goalkeeper of unquestionable brilliance who was considered to have the safest pair of hands in England at the turn of the century. He began his distinguished career at Derby Midland and then Lincoln City before signing on for Derby  County during the 1890-91 season. Whilst at Derby, he made steady progress and won his first international cap in 1897. In May of the same year he joined New Brighton Tower, gaining three more England caps in the process. Arriving at The Dell in 1898, he soon showed his bravery when, in an important deciding match against Bristol, he badly sprained his hand but refused to leave the field. In his five-year stay at Southampton he won four Southern League Championship medals and represented his country another five times. In May 1903 he moved to Plymouth and followed this by playing for Millwall, Exeter, Plymouth (second spell), Exeter (second spell), and finally Stoke City in 1909. Robinson emigrated to America in 1912 but returned within a few years. In 1922 he was an insurance agent.

ROGERS J.
Born: Macclesfield, November 1874.
15-2 Full-back/Forward, 1894-96.
Joe Rogers arrived at Southampton from his native Macclesfield in 1894 and early in 1895 caused a sensation by scoring ten goals in a friendly against the Wiltshire Regiment. Despite the feat, Rogers was not considered to be a forward, but a full-back, and in 1895-96 he started the season in his regular position. Never really settling in Southampton, he left the area in the summer of 1896 and joined Grimsby. Two years later he moved to Newcastle and was a member of the first England team to tour Germany in 1899. In 1901 he signed for Preston, although he was soon to return to Germany for a spell. In 1906 he returned to live in Grimsby.

SALWAY E.
Born: Nursling, Southampton, July 1891.
10-0, Half-back, 1912-13.
Salway was first seen at The Dell in 1909, in a trial match, but it was not until 1911 that he was taken on to the groundstaff, after previously playing for Nursling United. In March 1912 he represented Hampshire against Somerset and the following year began to establish himself in the Saints' first eleven. A reserve for much of the 1913-14 season, the outbreak of the war saw him serving at the front. In 1915-16 he played for the Saints whilst on leave, but in 1918 he was seriously wounded, losing an eye and a leg. He survived his injuries and returned to Southampton where he was awarded a benefit match.

SANDERS W.
2-0, Forward, 1912-13.
Sanders arrived at Southampton in March 1913 for a brief spell as a trialist, having previously played for RGA Portsmouth as a centre-forward. In his two games, against Brentford and Plymouth, he failed to impress and was released soon after.

SCOTT.
1-0, Forward, 1899-1900.
His only game for the Saints was in April 1900, against Millwall.

SEELEY G.
Born: Southampton, 1879.
9-1, Forward, 1896-97: 1898-99.
George Seeley played for local side, Gordon Avenue, before joining the Saints in 1896. He made one appearance in the Southern League before moving to Bristol and playing for Eastville Rovers. He returned to the Saints during the 1898-1899 season and played a further eight games before moving to Queen's Park Rangers and completed his career at Clapton Orient.

SELSTONE S.
Born: Portsmouth.
4-0, Forward, 1912-13.
Selstone had represented the Army against the Navy in 1911 whilst attatched to the RGA at Sheerness before a brief spell on loan with the Saints during 1912-13 season.

SHAND H.
1-0, Forward, 1904-05.
The Southampton directors went a long way to sign Shand, who was playing in Inverness in 1904. However, after only one game for the Saints he left the area and was next heard of playing for Millwall in 1907.

SHARP A.
Born: Hereford, January 1876.
22-1, Full/Half-back, 1900-01.
Bert Sharp had assisted Hereford Thistle, Hereford Town, Aston Villa and Everton before arriving at The Dell in 1900. He was the brother of the more famous Jack Sharp who played for England. Never really settling down in the area, he returned to Everton at the end of the season.

SHEARER S.
Born: Scotland.
17-0, Forward, 1908-10.
Shearer was a Scot who arrived at The Dell in 1908 and being a skilful player, forced his way into the first team. His lack of experience hampered his progress and he failed to score a goal in 17 outings with the club.

SHEERAN C.
2-0, Forward, 1911-12.
Sheeran was originally an Army recruit playing for the 4th Royal Fusiliers and gaining county honours. He spent the 1911-12 season on Saints' books before dropping into local football with Woolston.

SHELLEY F.A.
Born: Romsey, 11 August 1899. Died: December 1971.
18-1: 392-8, Half-back, 1919-32.
Albert Shelley played for local sides Romsey Comrades and Eastleigh Athletic in the Hampshire League before signing for Southampton during the  1919-20 season. He was in the reserves when Andrews was injured in an FA Cup match at West Ham and Bert Lee persuaded the directors to give Shelley a chance before spending money on a replacement. Shelley repaid Lee's faith by notching up over 400 League appearances to easily claim the Saints' appearance record at that time. An absolute stalwart in the 1920s, Shelley was unlucky not to be capped for England — he did, however, tour South Africa with the FA XI. When his playing days were over in 1932 he became youth-team trainer and three years later, first-team trainer under George Kay, then the Saints' manager. Kay moved to Liverpool in 1936 as their manager and Shelley joined him. In 1963 he was still loyally working behind the scenes at Anfield, although when Paisley took over he retired.

SHENTON.
1-1, Forward, 1896-97.
Shenton was a local player who, despite scoring on his debut, failed to make the grade and dropped into local football in 1897.

SLADE D.
3-0, Forward, 1910-12.
Slade arrived at The Dell during the 1910-11 season but despite scoring plenty of goals in the reserves, found it hard to break into the first eleven. In the summer of 1912 he moved to Lincoln where he spent two seasons before joining Fulham in 1914. During the war he returned to assist Southampton.

SLADE R.
3-0, Full-back, 1914-15.
Slade was signed in 1912 from junior side, Malmesbury United, but had to wait until Januay 1915 before making his first-team bow. He was not rewarded for his patience and the Saints released him in 1915.

SMALL A.
20-3, Forward, 1911-13.
Archie Small joined the Saints as an amateur in 1911 and for the best part of the 1911-12 season became Saints regular inside-right. He left The Dell in 1913.

SMALL H.
4-0, Forward, 1901-02.
Small was signed in 1900 from local rivals, Freemantle, to provide cover for Edgar Chadwick and was allowed to leave in 1902 to join Manchester City.

SMALL J.
Born: Southbank, 1893.
47-2, Half-back, 1913-15.
Small had made only one appearance for Sunderland when he signed

for the Saints, prior to the beginning of the 1913-14 season. In the two seasons of League football left, before the suspension of soccer, he played some fine games either at half-back or full-back. Small

played some football for the Saints during the war but peacetime found him turning out for local side, Thorneycrofts.

SMITH F.
Born: Buxton.
16-0, Full-back, 1913-14.
F.Smith played for his local club, Buxton, before joining Stockport County in 1906. Three years later he joined Derby, where he spent an unsuccessful season before joining non-League Macclesfield. In 1913 he signed for the Saints but could not settle and returned to his home area in 1914.

SMITH G.
Born: Preston. Died: July 1908.
21-5, Forward, 1907-08.
George Smith played for local side, Leyland, before joining Preston North End in 1900, and subsequently moved to Aston Villa in 1901. A move to Blackburn Rovers followed in 1903 and another to Plymouth Argyle in 1906 before he signed for the Saints in 1907. He looked a promising acquistion in his early days at The Dell and everyone was shocked at his tragically sudden death in the close season of 1908.

SMITH S.
Born: Southampton, 1887.
9-0, Forward, 1908-11.
Stan Smith came to the Saints in 1908, having previously turned out for local teams such as Southampton Cambridge, Ryde and Bitterne Guild. He made his debut on Christmas Day 1908 but in three seasons at The Dell, never managed to break into the first team on a regular basis. In 1914 he joined the 14th Hussars and saw action in France.

SMITH T.
Born: Ashton, 1876.
14-1, Forward, 1898-99.
Tom Smith played for local clubs, Ashton Athletic and Aston Town, before signing for Preston North End. At the time there were two Tom Smiths playing for Preston, one being a 'star', the other being an average player and when the Saints and Tottenham signed a T.Smith, both clubs were under the impression that they had acquired the 'star'. As it turned out, Southampton's Smith was the one of average merit and after 14 games for the Saints he was transferred to Queen's Park Rangers.

SMITH V.
4-0, Half-back, 1899-1902.
Victor Smith was at The Dell for three seasons, but managed only four League appearances.

SMITH W.
Born: Denby.
20-4, Forward, 1913-14.
Bill Smith was a former Yorkshire youth player who joined Brentford in 1912 and scored ten goals for them during the 1912-13 season. In the close season of 1913 he joined the Saints and had a rather inconsistent time before leaving the area in 1914.

SMITH W.G.
Born: Southampton.
13-0, Half-back, 1907-11.
W.G.Smith was a local player who was signed from Peartree Green in 1907. He served the Saints loyally for the best part of five seasons making an occasional outing in the first eleven. He remained at The Dell until November 1912 when he emigrated to Australia.

SMOKER.
2-0, Forward, 1903-04.
Smoker spent only the one season at The Dell, making two appearances before being released.

SOUTHERN A.
3-1, Forward, 1910-11.
Southern, a soldier based at Tidworth with the North Lancashire Regiment, was given three trial matches in April 1911. Despite managing a goal, he was not signed on a permanent basis and he returned to his regiment.

SOYE J.
Born: Glasgow, 1884.
18-5, Forward, 1905-06.
James Soye played local football in the Glasgow area before moving over the water to play Irish League football for Belfast Distillery. After several seasons in Belfast, Soye joined the Saints in 1905 and played well during the 1905-06 campaign. For unknown reasons the Saints directors released him at the end of the season, a move they were to regret, as he had two useful seasons at Newcastle and then joined Aberdeen where he became a prolific scorer.

SPENCE G.
Born: Rothsay, 1876.
14-3, Half-back, 1903-04.
George Spence started his career with St Mirren before moving, like so many of his countrymen, south to English football, joining Derby and then Reading. From Reading, Spence went to Preston North End, from where he joined the Saints in 1903. A reliable utility player who performed well when called upon. Spence left the area at the end of the season to join Hull City and later in 1906 signed for Clyde in his native Scotland.

STEAD.
Born: Salisbury.
2-0, Goalkeeper, 1905-06.
Stead was the third-choice goalkeeper at The Dell in 1905, but injuries to Burrows and Clawley gave him the chance to make two League appearances.

STEVENS D.
Born: Dundee, 1878. Died: 1903.
17-6, Forward, 1897-99.
David Stevens played in his native Scotland with Dundee before joining First Division side, Bury, in 1906. After a year Stevens wanted a move, but Bury refused to release his registration to another Football League club, so he decided to play in the Southern League with the Saints. After two seasons at Southampton, during which time he enjoyed his football despite not gaining a regular first team place, he returned to Dundee.

STEVENTON E.
Born: Walsall.
44-0, Goalkeeper, 1913-15.
Steventon, previously with Walsall and Wednesday Old Athletic, was considered to be one of the best junior goalkeepers in the Black Country when he signed for the Saints in 1913 and it was a great pity that the outbreak of World War One brought an abrupt end to a promising career.

TAYLOR E.J.
Born: Liverpool, 1869. Died: Southampton, November 1944.
19-1, Half-back, 1894-96.
Ernest Taylor was employed by the American Line in Liverpool and

played his early football with St Cuthbert's and later Stanley on Merseyside. He moved with his job to Southampton in March 1893 and was an unexpected but welcome addition to the St Mary's squad. He remained an amateur throughout his career and his versatility in the half-back line helped the Saints in the first two season in the Southern League. In 1896 he left to play for Freemantle.

TAYLOR F.
Born: Halesowen.
13-2, Forward, 1912-13.
Fred Taylor started his football career playing for the Aston Villa nursery side, Stourbridge, but was allowed to join Hull City in 1910. The following year he joined Wellington Town and a year later signed for Southampton in 1912. He remained at The Dell for one year and in that time made 13 appearances.

THOMSON W.J.G.
27-1, Half-back, 1894-96.
Thomson joined Southampton from Stoke in 1893 and despite being a full-back when he arrived, he soon developed into a strong and plucky half-back. A regular for two seasons, he joined Cowes in 1896.

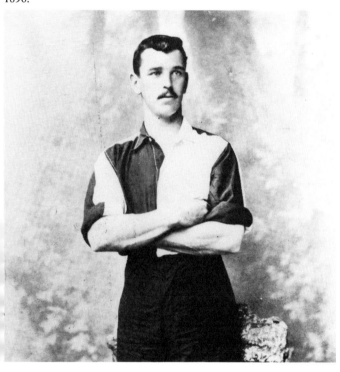

THORPE F.
Born: Glossop, 1880.
65-5, Centre-half, 1906-09.
Frank Thorpe played for Newton Heath amongst other local sides before joining Bury in 1901. He was a regular in the first team throughout his five seasons at Gigg Lane, winning an FA Cup winners' medal in 1903, when Bury beat Derby 6-0. Before joining the Saints in April 1907 he had a brief spell with Plymouth but with Southampton he blossomed into a quick, capable centre-half who had a powerful shot and who captained the team on many occasions. He returned to Bury in 1909.

TITMUSS F.
Born: Hitchin, February 1898. Died: October 1966.
22-0: 188-0, Full-back, 1919-26.
Fred Titmuss had played for his local side, Hitchin, before joining the Army. Whilst playing in various army teams, Titmuss was spotted by Bert Lee, the Saints trainer, and was persuaded to sign forms. Titmuss and Tom Parker, the Saints' other full-back, became arguably the best pair of backs in the country. Titmuss was a connoisseur of the sliding tackle and in 1922 he won his first England cap when he played against Wales. In February 1926, the directors reluctantly sold him to Plymouth for £1,750 and he spent six successful seasons helping the Devon side. He retired in 1932 and for a while played part-time for St Austell, although he soon hung up his boots permanently to become a landlord in Plymouth, the town he lived in until his death.

TOMAN W.
Born: Bishop Auckland.
19-7, Forward, 1900-01.
Toman began his career in Scotland with Victoria Athletic and Dundee, before joining Burnley in 1896. In 1898 he joined Everton and after another two years, Southampton. Toman was a clever centre-forward who was to return to Everton within a year, only to meet with a serious accident that ended his career.

TOMLINSON J.
Born: Chesterfield, 1881.
29-8, Forward, 1905-06.
Tomlinson started out with North Wingfield before joining Chesterfield in 1904 and attracted the attention of Southampton directors when he excelled in an FA Cup tie at Portsmouth. Arsenal pipped the Saints for his signature, but his stay at Plumstead was brief and he moved to Southampton in 1905. Tomlinson was very fast, but suffered terribly from nerves and often before big matches he would be found walking around the ground rather than sitting in the dressing room. After one season with the Saints he moved to Portsmouth.

TOOMER W.
Born: Southampton, February 1883. Died: Southampton, December 1962.
10-0, Half-back, 1906-13.
Although locally born, Toomer spent time with Fulham and Chelsea before arriving at The Dell in 1906. An all-round sportsman, he played cricket and golf well. Toomer spent most of his seven years at Southampton, captaining the reserves. After World War One, he became a teacher and then opened a sports shop which carries his name to this day. In December 1949 he became a director of the club.

TRIGGS W.
2-0, Full-back, 1901-02.
Triggs arrived from Freemantle in 1900 and made two appearances in his two-year stay at The Dell.

TRUEMAN A.
Born: Leicester.
87-4, Half-back, 1908-11.
Trueman played for local sides, Coalville and Hinckley before joining Leicester Fosse in 1906. When he moved to the Saints in 1908 he quickly settled into the half-back line and was equally at home in any of the three positions. A strong and determined player, he gained Southern League honours in 1909 and 1910 and had an international trial during the 1910-11 season. Unfortunately he became unsettled at The Dell and was granted a transfer in March 1911 to Sheffield United. After two seasons at Sheffield he moved to Darlington.

TURNBULL F.
Born: Wallsend, 1888.
23-2, Forward, 1912-13.
Turnbull followed the Saints' trainer, McIntyre, from Coventry in October 1912, to give the forward line some experience which the side lacked at that time. Turnbull had previously spent several years in Newcastle's reserves and by the time he played for the Saints, was past his best.

TURNER A.
Born: Farnborough, 1877. Died: April 1925.
78-24, Forward, 1899-02; 1904-05.
Arthur Turner began his footballing career with Aldershot North End, South Farnborough and Camberley St Michael's, where he came to the attention of Southampton who promptly signed him in 1899. Within two years he had won international honours with England, and in doing so became the first Hampshire-born man to represent his country. Turner was also the only Hampshire-born player in the Saints' FA Cup Final eleven in 1900. In 1902 he moved to Derby and then to Newcastle and Tottenham, before returning to the Saints in 1904. He retired in 1905 and returned to Farnborough to join his father's business.

TURNER H.
Born: Farnborough.
15-6, Forward, 1903-05.
Harry Turner was the younger brother of Arthur, but despite being a reliable player, he did not possess as much skill as Arthur. Graduating through the same South Farnborough team, Harry Turner arrived at The Dell in 1900 and made his debut three years later, in December 1903. He left the club in 1905.

TURNER J.
Born: Burslem. Died: Southampton, November 1950.
124-56, Forward, 1895-98; 1901-04
Joe Turner was signed from Dresden United in 1895 by Mr Robson, the Southampton secretary. He spent three seasons with Southampton as the regular outside-left and as well as scoring freely, was regarded as a very skilful member of the side. In 1898, Turner moved to Stoke and a year later to Everton, before returning to Southampton for a second spell in 1901. He appeared in the Saints' 1902 FA Cup Final team and made his last move in 1904 when he signed for New Brompton.

TURNER W.
Born: Durham, 1896.
27-0: 149-1, Half-back, 1919-24.

Bill Turner played his youth football for local Tyneside teams such as Ripton United, Scotswood and Leadgate Park. It was from Leadgate in 1919 that he joined Southampton for a fee of £200 and when the Saints gained promotion from the newly-formed Third Division South into Division Two, Turner was the only member of the side who had cost a fee. He served the Saints loyally until 1924, when he transferred to Bury in a deal that brought Woodhouse and Callagher to The Dell.

TYSON C.
14-0, Half-back, 1912-13.
Tyson was an amateur on Southampton's books during the 1912-13 season and when not required by the Saints, would turn out for London side, Dulwich Hamlet.

WALLER W.H.
2-0, Goalkeeper, 1900-01.
An amateur who also played for Tottenham Hotspur, Waller emigrated to South Africa in 1906.

WARD A.
1-0, Forward, 1894-95.
Ward made only one Southern League appearance, in March 1895.

WARD H.
Born: London, March 1873. Died: May 1897.
9-6, Forward, 1894-95.
Herbert Ward was a keen cricketer, athlete and footballer who moved from his native London to Hampshire in 1892 and joined St Mary's soon after. He gained Hampshire honours and captained the county twice. He was a hard-working centre-forward and remained with the Saints until 1895. He died two years later, supposedly from sunstroke whilst playing for Hampshire in a county cricket match, although a later verdict diagnosed typhoid fever.

WARD R.
Born: Eastwood, 1885.
4-2, Forward, 1908-09.
Ward arrived at Southampton during the 1908-09 season and the Saints were his sixth club. He had already played for Clowne White Star, Notts County, Brighton, Aberdeen and Bradford (Park Avenue). His wanderlust was not cured at The Dell and he left at the end of the season.

WARNER J.
Born: Preston, 1883. Died: May 1948.
17-0, Full-back, 1905-06.
Warner signed for Preston in 1902, from local side, St Michael's, and gradually gained a place in the League side during the 1903-04 season. In the later stages of 1904, however, he found himself back in the reserves and consequently moved to Southampton in 1905. Although he played well in his 16 games, the directors considered him suspect, due to a nagging knee injury, and he moved to Portsmouth. Proving the Saints' directors wrong, Warner remained at Pompey as a player until 1915 and later became their trainer.

WEBB C.
Born: Higham, March 1880.
16-5, Forward, 1904-05.
Webb joined Southern League team, Kettering, in 1900 and moved Leicester for the 1901-02 season. A move to Wellingborough followed in 1902-03 before he returned to Kettering for a second spell in 1903-04. The Saints acquired his signature in 1904 and at the time, his brilliant wing play convinced the Saints fans that he was the club's best signing for some time. Unfortunately, Webb did not like staying with any club too long, and he moved to Blackpool in 1905.

WHEELER F.
3-0, Forward, 1910-11.
Whilst playing for Colne in the Lancashire League, Wheeler was invited to The Dell in August 1910 for a trial and was duly signed. He spent most of the season in the reserves and departed at the end of the campaign.

WHEELER L.
1-0, Forward, 1914-15.
Wheeler arrived at The Dell during the 1914-15 season and although he played in only one Southern League match before the suspension of League football, he did feature for the Saints during wartime.

WHITING R.
4-0, Half-back, 1901-05.
Whiting was at The Dell for four seasons between 1901 and 1905 and in that time made only three League appearances. He moved to Chelsea in 1905 and stayed there until 1908.

WILCOCK G.
Born: Edinburgh, 1893.
20-0, Goalkeeper, 1919-20.
Wilcock played for Barnsley reserves during 1911-12 and then dropped into non-League football with Goole Town. He served in World War One and was wounded at Loos before being signed for Brighton in 1918. He moved to Southampton in 1919 and for the ensuing season shared the goalkeeping responsibilities with Wood. Wilcock moved to Preston North End in 1920 and played in seven First Division games before dropping out of League football.

WILCOX J.
Born: Stourbridge.
27-5, Forward, 1911-12.
Wilcox played for Dudley before signing for Aston Villa in 1907 but made little headway and moved to Birmingham during 1908-09. Arriving at The Dell in 1911, he became the regular right-winger but found his form erratic, mainly because the whole Saints side were having a poor season. In 1912 he dropped into non-League football with Wellington.

WILLIAMS E.
Born: Ryde.
1-0, Forward, 1912-13.
Williams played for Ryde before joining Portsmouth in December 1906. An amateur throughout his career, he played over 30 Southern League matches. In five seasons at Fratton Park he won two England amateur caps, in 1910-11. In December 1911 he moved to Chelsea but failed to make their first team. He joined the Saints in 1912 but made only one appearance before giving up football to concentrate on a cricketing career.

WILLIAMSON H.
12-0, Goalkeeper, 1894-95.
Williamson made his debut for St Mary's in November 1894 but moved to London six months later and turned out for the Royal Ordnance Factories.

WILSON G.
Born: February 1878. Died: July 1934.
3-0, Forward, 1902-03.
Between 1898 and 1902, George Wilson played for the famous Corinthians and won two England caps in 1900. He was an amateur who had qualified as a physician and surgeon in 1902 and in the following year played three times for the Saints. He was a neat dribbler and when he moved to London to find employment in 1903 his departure disappointed the Saints fans.

WOOD A.
Born: Walsall. Died: April 1941.
41-0: 2-0, Goalkeeper, 1914-21.
Arthur Wood was the son of Harry Wood, the famous Saints' captain, and arrived at The Dell in August 1913. Originally a full-back in his schooldays, he soon graduated into a capable goalkeeper and during the 1914-15 season competed with Stevenson for the first-team place. When war broke out he joined the Army, yet he still managed to feature regularly for the Saints during their wartime matches. With the return of peacetime football, Wood became the regular Saints goalkeeper for the 1919-20 season before losing his place when Tommy Allen arrived at The Dell in 1920. Not content with playing in the reserves, he moved to Clapton Orient in 1921 and spent ten years as first-team goalkeeper there.

WOOD H.
Born: Walsall, 1868. Died: Portsmouth, July 1951.
158-62, Forward, 1898-05.
Harry Wood started his long career with Walsall Town Swifts before

signing for Wolves in 1887. He soon gained two England caps and went on to win an FA Cup winners' medal in 1893 and a losers' medal in 1896. In 1898, Dawson, the Southampton trainer, was holidaying in Birmingham and upon hearing that Wood was unsettled at Wolves, decided to investigate the matter further. Upon making inquiries at a local pub, Wood was contacted and signed for Saints in the same pub. His impact on Southampton was huge and he was quickly made captain, a position he held until 1905. Nicknamed 'the wolf' by his teammates, he was immensely popular, not only for his excellent forward play but for his ability to lead other players and for his influence over younger players. His time at The Dell was one of the most successful periods in the Saints' history and when he retired in 1905, at the remarkable age of 37, his presence was sorely missed. Soon after hanging up his boots he became Portsmouth's trainer, a position he held until 1912 when he became landlord at the Milton Arms, just down the road from Fratton Park.

YATES J.
Born: Sheffield. Died: September 1922.
63-16, Forward, 1897-1901; 1904-05.
Jimmy Yates signed for Sheffield United in 1893 and made 80 appearances for the Blades before joining Southampton in 1897. His experience and tenacity on the ball was of great value to the Saints, especially in their forays in the FA Cup. In 1901 he dropped out of League football to play for Hastings and St Leonard's in Sussex, and in 1903 went to coach in Copenhagen. In 1904-05 he played one more League game before moving to Gravesend. Whilst at Gravesend, Yates scouted for Saints and later returned to live in Southampton. He met a tragic end, committing suicide on the Common in September 1922.

Southampton officials and players pose for the camera during 1905-06 season. Top row (left to right): J.Warner, W.H.Clarke, G.Clawley, T.Burrows, Hartshorne. Second row: A.Lee, S.Meston, T.Edmonds, G.A.Hedley, A.E.Houlker. Third row: Dawson (trainer), J.Tomlinson, F.Jefferis, J.Soye, H.M.Ashton (director), F.Harrison, Sir G.A.E.Hussey (director), H.Brown, G.Harris, F.W.Mouncher. Front: E.Arnfield (secretary), G.Payne, W.Bulpitt, Dr E.Stancome, A.A.Wood, C.Robson, W.Jarvis (all directors).

Date and place of birth and death are given where known. Figures refer to games and goals in Football League only. Substitute appearances are shown in brackets (ie. 105(1)-32 means 105 games, plus one as a substitute, and 32 goals). For players whose careers spanned both Southern League and Football League, see previous biographical section.

ADAMS.W.
Born: Newcastle-upon-Tyne, November 1903. Died: Southampton, 14 March 1963.
196-3, Half-back, 1927-36.
Although Bill Adams arrived at The Dell during the 1925-6 season, from Guildford, it was not until the 1930s that he became a prominent member of the half-back line. He captained the side with distinction during the 1931-2 season and after joining West Ham in 1936 he had a remarkable debut for the Hammers, scoring in his first game — against Southampton. His stay at Upton Park was short and in January 1937, now aged 33, he moved to Southend United. Adams later became a publican.

AFFLECK.D.
Born: Coylton, Ayrshire, 1913.
51-0, Centre-half, 1937-9.
Dave Affleck graduated from Scottish junior football to Notts County and then Bristol City. Before joining Southampton in 1937, he had a spell with Clapton Orient and in his brief time at The Dell he impressed so much that both Chelsea and Spurs made big bids for his services. He made sporadic appearances for the Saints during the

war, but did not appear in League football again. He became a policeman when his footballing days ended.

AGBOOLA.R.
Born: London, 30 May 1962.
89(1)-0, Defender, 1980-85.
Reuben Agboola was a product of the successful Southampton youth policy and made his debut at Manchester United during the 1980-81 season. He looked to have a promising future at The Dell but during 1984-5 he was transferred to Sunderland and has since found it difficult to command a first-team place at Roker Park.

ALLEN.T.
Born: Moxley, May 1897.
291-0, Goalkeeper, 1920-28.
Due to an oversight by Sunderland, Tommy Allen was given a free transfer in May 1920 and he joined Southampton. Tall but slight, Allen gave Saints eight seasons of top quality goalkeeping and notched up a record 291 League appearances for a Southampton goalkeeper. In the close season of 1928 he joined Coventry and then went to Accrington Stanley and Northampton.

ANDERSON.A.
Born: Monifieth, 15 November 1921.
20-0, Full-back, 1949-52.

Alex Anderson joined the Saints from Forfar Athletic on a free transfer in November 1949, spending three seasons as full-back cover before joining Exeter in the close season of 1952.

ARMSTRONG.D.
Born: Durham, 26 December 1954.
243-69, Midfield, 1981-7.
David Armstrong joined Southampton in the close season of 1981 for a record fee of £600,000. His previous club had been Middlesbrough and he had served them admirably, at one stage going seven seasons without missing a single game. A natural left-sided player, Armstrong wasted no time in repaying the Saints some of the huge fee by quickly fitting into midfield and scoring some memorable goals in the process. His talents have earned him England recognition, both at Middlesbrough and Southampton and his reading of the game has meant that he can play in virtually any position, as was proved in the tail-end of the 1985-6 season, when he slotted comfortably into the sweeper role. He was an obvious choice for the role of captain, although during 1986-7 a series of injuries and contractural disputes made his future with Saints look unsettled.

ARMSTRONG.K.
Born: Bridgnorth, 31 January 1959.
26-0, Defender, 1983-4.
Ken Armstrong, although born in Shropshire, grew up in Scotland and made his debut in Kilmarnock's first eleven during the 1978-9 season. He joined the Saints in 1983, for £25,000, and initially impressed with his strength and size. However, before the season ended he had a loan spell with Notts County before joining Birmingham in the close season of 1984. The fee of £100,000 gave Saints a tidy profit in the transfer market. After a year at Birmingham, he moved to Walsall for £125,000 where his career was ended by injury.

ARNOLD.J.
Born: 30 November 1907. Died April 1984.
106-46, Forward, 1928-33.
Johnny Arnold arrived at The Dell via Oxford City in the 1928-9 season. He was at the time qualifying as a professional cricketer for Hampshire. As soon as Chadwick, the Southampton manager, saw

him play, he was reputed to have said, "I have a star here", and his words proved prophetic as Arnold quickly established himself as a skilful winger with an eye for goal. During the 1931-2 campaign, he scored 21 goals, a record from the left-wing for Southampton. In 1933 he joined Fulham, along with Mike Keeping, and within a month had won an England cap, against Scotland. Arnold played for Fulham until the war broke out, at the same time enjoying a second career as a successful cricketer. He was one of the few men to have represented his country at both football and cricket and opened the batting for Hampshire between 1929 and 1950. After his retirement from active sport he became a first-class cricket umpire and enjoyed 20 seasons in that capacity. He died, aged 76, in April 1984.

ANDRUSZEWSKI.E.
Born: Eastleigh, 4 October 1955.
82(1)-3, Defender, 1974-80.
Manny Andruszewski was a tough tackling defender who graduated through the reserves to make his debut during the 1974-5 season. Often brought into the side to do a specific marking job on an individual opponent, he consequently suffered from never having a prolonged run in the first team. During the 1979-80 season he moved to the American club, Tampa Bay Rowdies, for a fee of £150,000, but his stay there was not happy and he soon returned to England. For a brief spell he was re-engaged by Saints as cover, but never played for the first team again. He later signed for non-League Waterlooville.

BAIRD.I.
Born: Southampton, 1 April 1964.
20(2)-5, Forward, 1982-5.
Ian Baird was an England Schoolboy international before signing professional forms for Southampton. A strong, bustling centre-forward, he found it difficult to break into the first team and joined Leeds for £50,000 in 1985.

BAKER.G.
Born: Southampton, 3 December 1958.
111(2)-22, Midfield, 1977-82.
Graham Baker was a local player who had the good fortune to score in the first minute of his debut, against Blackpool, with the game being televised. A hard working player, Baker had pushed his way into a regular position when he was suddenly sold to Manchester

City in 1982. He has played well for Manchester but has suffered from two serious injuries that have sidelined him for lengthy spells during his Maine Road career.

BAKER.S.
Born: Newcastle, 16 June 1962.
59(10)-0, Defender, 1980-87.
Steve Baker made his debut for Saints in the last match of the season, at Ipswich, and in the following five seasons has been in and out of the first team, mainly as cover for Mick Mills. A dedicated full-back who has uncomplainingly spent long spells waiting on the sidelines. Also spent a period on loan to Burnley.

BALL.A.
Born: Farnworth, 12 May 1945.
195-11, Midfield, 1976-83.
Alan Ball started his long career with Blackpool during the 1962-3 season and, despite his small stature, soon made a name for himself as a tenacious competitor who hated to lose. Energetic, he quickly gained international honours and was a member of England's World Cup winning team in 1966. That success coincided with his move to Everton for a fee of £115,000. Ball won a League Championship medal at Goodison Park before joining Arsenal for a record £220,000 in December 1971. Five years later, McMenemy signed him for £50,000 and Ball, more than any other player, pushed the Saints back into Division One with his never-say-die attitude that greatly influenced other Saints players such as the youthful Steve Williams. Winner of 72 England caps, Ball loved nothing more than to be playing and in his mid-30s he spent the summer months turning out, with great success, for Vancouver Whitecaps in the North American Soccer League. In 1980, he became player-manager of Blackpool, his first club. His return to Bloomfield Road was not a happy one and McMenemy — with whom Ball had enjoyed a special rapport — offered him a return to The Dell. Ball accepted, no doubt due to the fact that Kevin Keegan was now on the Saints' books. During 1981-2, Ball, Keegan and Channon inspired Saints to some of their best-ever football and for a long period they led Division One. By the start of the following season, however, Keegan had departed, and Ball, with age not on his side, tried his luck in Hong Kong. Before long, the lure of English football brought him back and he finished 1982-3 playing for Bristol Rovers. Finally hanging up his boots, Ball joined Portsmouth for the 1983-4 season in a coaching capacity, and in June 1984 took over as manager. His two seasons in charge have seen Pompey narrowly miss promotion twice.

BALLARD.E.
Born: Brentford, 16 June 1920.
45-0, Full-back, 1947-51.
Ted Ballard joined the Saints in June 1947 from Leyton Orient and spent four seasons at The Dell, largely in the role of reserve full-back. He re-signed for Orient in August 1952, but did not play in their first team. He later played non-League football for Snowdown Colliery and Hastings before becoming player-manager of Ashford Town. He later became a publican in Hastings.

BARRETT.A.F.
Born: West Ham, 11 November 1903.
1-0, Half-back, 1924-5.
Barrett was an England Amateur international who signed from Leytonstone in March 1925, played one game and then joined Fulham a few months later.

BATES.E.
Born: Thetford, 3 May 1918.
202-64, Inside-forward, 1936-53.
Ted Bates' contribution towards the success of Southampton FC cannot be over-emphasized. Tom Parker brought the 18-year-old

Bates with him from Norwich in 1937, when Saints had just celebrated their golden jubilee. Now the Saints have celebrated their centenary, with Bates still having an active role as one of the club's directors. Bates came from a sporting family, (his father, Billy, played cricket for Yorkshire and football for Leeds and Bolton, whilst his grandfather, Willie, played cricket and rugby for England) and soon forced his way into the Saints' first team, only to have a promising career interrupted by the outbreak of World War Two. Serving in the army, he still managed to turn out for Saints and upon being demobbed, he returned full-time to The Dell to help spearhead the Saints' attack, as they pushed hard for promotion in those heady post-war seasons. Bates was particularly good in the air and together with Wayman, terrorised Second Division defences between 1947 and 1951, although Saints did not gain promotion to the First Division. By the time the Saints were relegated to Division Three South, Bates had retired to become a coach, under George Roughton. (See also *Saints Managers*).

BEANEY.W.
Born: Southampton, 29 May 1954.
2(1)-0, Defender, 1972-5.
Bill Beaney was a local product who showed early promise but failed to make the grade and dropped into non-League football.

BEATTIE.G.
Born: Aberdeen, 16 June 1925.
1-0, Forward, 1947-8.
George Beattie arrived at The Dell in August 1947 and played only one game before signing for Gloucester City. In September 1950 he re-emerged into League football with Newport and then Bradford.

BEDFORD.B.
Born: Ferndale, 24 December 1933.
5-2, Forward, 1955-6.
Brian Bedford had played only three League games for Reading before signing for Southampton in July 1955. After one season at The Dell he moved to Bournemouth and after 75 games there, he joined Queen's Park Rangers. At Loftus Road he met with considerable success, scoring 163 goals in 258 games. He finished his League career with Scunthorpe and Brentford.

BENNETT.P.
Born: Southampton, 4 February 1952.
116-1, Defender, 1971-6.
Paul Bennett was a local product, educated at Tauntons, before joining the Saints in November 1969. A dedicated player, he enjoyed a fair amount of success with the Saints before moving to Reading in July 1976. He played over 100 games for Reading before finishing his League career with Aldershot. He later joined RS Southampton, playing as keenly as ever.

BERNARD.E.
Born: Southampton. Died: Southampton, August 1973.
2-0, Goalkeeper, 1936-7.
Bernard was an amateur goalkeeper who spent the 1936-7 season on Southampton's books. An injured hand ended his career prematurely but during the war he assisted the club and later coached the youngsters. He later found employment in the insurance business.

BERRY.M.
Born: Newbury, 14 February 1955.
2-0, Full-back, 1974-5.
Mike Berry played twice for the League team after graduating from the reserves, but was released in 1975 and later emigrated to Australia where he played semi-professional football.

BEVIS.W.
Born: Southampton, 29 September 1918.
82-16, Forward, 1937-47.
Although Billy Bevis was locally born, he was discovered by Tom Parker when Parker was Norwich manager. Bevis joined Portsmouth at the same time as Parker moved to The Dell and when the player was released by Portsmouth a few months later, Parker was quick to invite him to join Southampton. In the two seasons remaining before the outbreak of war, Bevis developed into a promising outside-right and attracted interest from many top clubs. During the war he served

in the navy and was torpedoed three times, mined once and once spent seven days adrift. Surviving all these calamities, Bevis returned to The Dell and played 14 games in the first proper season after the war, before deciding to retire from League football.

BIRCH.K.
Born: Liverpool, 31 December 1933.
34-3, Half-back, 1957-9.
Ken Birch was a product of Everton juniors and he played 43 League games for the Goodison Park club before joining Saints in March 1958 for a fee of £6,000. His stay at The Dell lasted little more than a year, and he dropped out of League football to play for Chelmsford and Bangor.

BISHOP.A.
Born: Birmingham.
7-0, Forward, 1926-7.
Bishop was an amateur player who spent a year at The Dell whilst serving in the RAF.

BLACK.I.
Born: Aberdeen, 27 March 1924.
97-0, Goalkeeper, 1947-50.
Ian Black had his first taste of professional football during the later stages of World War Two, playing for Aberdeen in 1944 and Chelsea in 1945. When he was demobbed he asked Aberdeen to release him to Southampton, where he had found employment as a mechanic. The Scottish club, realising Black's talents, were reluctant to let him go and Bill Dodgin was lucky to be able to recruit an excellent goalkeeper. Within a few months of arriving at The Dell, Black had won a Scottish cap against England and, strangely, that was the last time to date that a Saints player has appeared for Scotland. In August 1950, Black followed Dodgin to Fulham where he continued to give many impressive performances for several seasons, although he never played for Scotland again. Retiring from football in 1957, after 263 League games, he later ran a sports shop in London.

BLAKE.M.
Born: Portsmouth, 19 December 1967.
9-1, Defender, 1985-7.
Blake was an England Youth international who came into the Saints side in the tail-end of the 1985-6 season due to an injury crisis that had deprived Southampton of their whole defence.

BLYTH.M.
Born: Norwich, 28 July 1944.
104(1)-6, Defender, 1974-7.
Mel Blyth started his football career with non-League Great Yarmouth, before signing for Scunthorpe in November 1967. In the following close season he moved to Crystal Palace for whom he made over 200 League appearances before joining the Saints in August 1974 for a fee of £60,000. Blyth's impact in his first season at The Dell was such that he was voted the supporters' Player of the Year. In the following season he played a dominant part in the Saints winning the FA Cup, having a particularly good game in the Final against Manchester United. In November 1977 he returned to Palace for a brief spell before signing for Millwall.

BLYTH.R.
Born: Muirkirk, Scotland.
8-0, Forward, 1922-3.
Blyth was an outside-right who arrived at The Dell in May 1922 after spending a season on the books of Portsmouth. His stay with the Saints was to last just one year.

BOGAN.T.
Born: Glasgow, 18 May 1920
8-2 Inside-forward, 1951-3.
Tom Bogan was a Scottish wartime international who became Syd Cann's last signing when he came from Aberdeen in December 1951. Originally with Celtic, Bogan had spent a year at Preston and another season at Manchester United. After 18 months at The Dell, he moved on to Blackburn in August 1953.

BOND.K.
Born: London, 22 June 1957.
100(1)-3, Defender, 1984-7.
Kevin Bond made his debut for Norwich during the 1975-6 season, when his father, John, was the Canaries' manager. He followed his father to Manchester City in 1981, after playing in the NASL with Seattle Sounders. McMenemy signed Bond in the autumn of 1984 as a replacement for Agboola for £70,000. In 1986-7 he was appointed Saints' captain.

BOULTON.C.
Born: Cheltenham, 12 September 1945.
5-0, Goalkeeper, 1976-7.
Colin Boulton spent a brief period at The Dell on loan from Derby County. Boulton played more games for Derby than any other

goalkeeper and won two League Championship medals with the Rams. His career also took in Tulsa Roughnecks and Los Angeles Aztecs in the NASL and his playing days were ended by a leg injury sustained whilst with Lincoln City.

BOWDEN.O.
Born: Newcastle.
2-0, Forward, 1938-9.
Bowden came to the Saints from Brighton. He began his career with Newcastle United, although he never played in their League side, and was at Derby and Nottingham Forest before Brighton.

BOWEN.L.
Born: Southampton, 1915.
2-0, Full-back 1936-7.
Bowen was signed from Crystal Palace in October 1934 as an amateur and waited two seasons to play his only League games for the Saints. He retired in 1937 to become a policeman, although he sometimes turned out for Winchester City.

BOYD.W.
Born: Cambuslang.
19-7, Forward, 1936-7.
Willie Boyd joined Southampton in the close season of 1936 from Luton. He burst into prominence whilst working as a tube fitter in a Clyde shipyard, scoring 200 goals in three seasons for local side, Larkhall Thistle. Clyde signed him in 1931 and within months he was on the fringe of Scotland's international side. Sheffield United signed Boyd during 1933-4 and he finished that season as their top scorer. Subsequent moves took him to Workington and Manchester United before returning to Luton. Despite scoring goals at a prolific rate, Boyd rarely stayed long at any club and he soon left The Dell to sign for Weymouth.

BOYER.P.
Born: Nottingham, 25 January 1949.
138-49 Forward, 1977-81.
Phil Boyer was an apprentice at Derby before signing on for York in July 1968. Whilst at York he found himself playing alongside Ted MacDougall and coincidentally this partnership was to blossom and continue whilst playing for three other clubs, Bournemouth, Norwich and Southampton. At Norwich, Boyer won an England cap and arriving in Southampton in August 1977, he capably filled the gap left by the recently departed Channon. Boyer was Saints' top scorer in 1979-80, teaming up with Channon who had returned. The arrival of Keegan meant that Boyer was forced to seek fresh pastures and he joined Manchester City, again stepping into Channon's boots. Unfortunately his stay at City was cut short by an injury. He went to play in Hong Kong, then returned to England to become Grantham Town player-manager, a position he resigned from in February 1987.

BRADFORD.J.A.
Born: Walsall, 1905. Died: Southampton, 13 April 1944.
305-6, Half-back, 1923-36.
Arthur Bradford was one of those unsung players who became an indispensable part of the club over a period of time. He signed in 1923-4, from a Walsall works team, and went on to appear in over 300 League matches, captaining Saints in 1932-3. Bradford's versatility — he even played in goal — was an important factor in his period at The Dell, and when he left to become a pub landlord in 1936, his abilities were sorely missed. He continued to play football and during 1936-7 turned out for Cowes on the Isle of Wight.

BRADLEY.J.
Born: Hemsworth, 27 November 1916.
49-22, Forward, 1946-8.
Bradley joined Saints in 1939 and played periodically during the war. His previous clubs included Huddersfield, Swindon and Chelsea and he had built up a fine reputation mainly due to possessing a particularly good left foot. Bradley left the Saints for Bolton in October 1947 and finished his League career at Norwich.

BREWIS.J.
Born: Newcastle, March 1907.
118-18, Forward, 1931-7.
George Kay signed 23-year old Tom Brewis in March 1932, from York, and during his five seasons at The Dell he was in and out of the side. He had the knack of 'hanging' in the air to score improbable goals with his head, and in 1932-3 he notched a hat-trick at home to Manchester United. In 1936 he left for Newport (IOW) and later became an hotelier before joining the navy on the outbreak of war.

BRIGGS.F.T.
Born: Rotherham.
36-14, Forward, 1938-9.
Briggs, who came to The Dell in the summer of 1938 on a free transfer from Reading, was Southampton's top goalscorer in the last season before World War Two. He also played for Saints during the early war years.

BROAD.T.
9-0, Forward, 1924-5.
Outside-right Broad joined Saints from Stoke in the close season of 1924, having turned out for Manchester City in 1919-20. He moved into non-League football in the summer of 1925.

BROPHY.H.
Born: Highbury, 22 October 1916.
37-5, Forward or Half-back, 1938-9.
Harry Brophy was given a free transfer by Brighton in 1938 and Saints soon found his versatility a great asset in the last pre-war season. After playing for Southampton in the early war years, he turned out for local side, Follands.

BROWN.E.
Born: Preston, 28 February 1926.
57-32. Centre-forward, 1950-52.
Eddie Brown arrived at The Dell with possibly the greatest handicap of all, that being, Charlie Wayman's replacement. Happily, Brown was one of the game's great characters and his sense of fun soon meant that Saints fans were to accept him for his own talents. His career started with Preston, but not before he had flirted with the idea of becoming a priest. Arriving at The Dell in September 1950, his stocky build and bursts of speed meant that he was soon scoring goals with almost the same frequency as Wayman. Unfortunately Brown could not settle at The Dell and after 57 games he asked for a transfer and moved to Coventry. He later played for Birmingham and Leyton Orient and altogether scored 189 goals in 399 games.

BROWN.G.
Born: Ellesmere Port, 30 June 1933.
8-2, Forward, 1959-61.
Originally with Scunthorpe, Gordon Brown joined Southampton in March 1960, from Derby County, to bolster Saints' promotion push. In July 1961 he moved to Barrow and finally Southport.

BROWN.P.
Born: Andover, 13 July 1934.
16-3, Forward, 1954-8.
Peter Brown, product of the Saints' junior sides, spent five years at The Dell playing mainly for the reserves. In July 1958 he transferred to Wrexham.

BROWNING.D.
Born: New Milton, 1916.
26-0, Full-back, 1936-8.
Don Browning joined Saints in 1936 from New Milton FC and remained on the books for two years. He then gave up football to become a farmer.

BRUTON.L.
Born: Coventry.
7-0, Forward, 1923-6.
Bruton arrived at The Dell during the close season of 1923 from Peterborough and his stay lasted three years, before rejoining the

Posh. He later played for Raith Rovers, then had a spell at Blackburn before becoming a trainer at Coventry.

BULLOCK.J.
32-13, Forward, 1924-8.
Bullock spent five seasons at The Dell, mainly as a deputy centre-forward, and never let Saints down when he was asked to play for the first team. He arrived in 1924 from Crewe Alexandra and departed in the close season of 1929.

BURLEY B.
Born: Sheffield, 2 November 1907.
2-0, Forward, 1933-4.
Burley was signed from Sheffield United in the close season of 1933 and left a year later for Grimsby. He later turned out for Norwich, Darlington and Chelmsford. During the war he guested for Southend, Millwall, Brighton, QPR and Crystal Palace. He later coached in Holland before going to live in Norfolk.

BURNS.F.
Born: Glenboig, nr Coatbridge, 17 October 1948.
20(1)-0, Full-back, 1972-3.
Scotland international Francis Burns joined Saints in the close season of 1972, having spent six years with Manchester United. He never enjoyed life in the south and gratefully took the opportunity of a move to Preston in August 1973.

BURNSIDE.D.
Born: Bristol, 10 December 1939.
61-22, Forward, 1962-5.
David Burnside's first League club was West Bromwich Albion, whom he joined whilst a brilliant schoolboy footballer. His skill at juggling a football became famous when, as a youngster, he displayed his talents to the crowds at The Hawthorns before kick-off. An England Youth Under-23 international, Burnside signed for Saints in October 1962 and he settled in well, playing his part in Saints' fine Cup run that season. He sometimes found it difficult, though, to put his incredible skills to good use and Saints reluctantly sold him to Crystal Palace in December 1964 for £12,000. Burnside later played for Wolves, Plymouth, Bristol City and Colchester, before becoming manager of Bath City in 1972. He also played for non-League clubs, Minehead and Bridgewater Town and more recently became involved in running FA coaching courses.

BUSHBY.T.
Born: Shildon, 21 August 1914.
2-0, Half-back, 1946-7.
Tom Bushby had been on Southend's books before World War Two, and had played for Portsmouth during the war, although he did turn out once for Saints in 1942-3. Southampton signed him for the resumption of League football proper in 1946, but his stay at The Dell was brief and he left for Cowes (IOW).

BUTT.L.
Born: Southampton.
17-0, Half-back, 1920-2.
Butt was signed from local side, Thorneycrofts, during the 1920-21 season but due to stiff competition for places, joined Bournemouth in the close season of 1922. He later became a publican in Southampton and played for Cowes (IOW).

BYRNE.A.
Born: Rathdawny, 2 February 1946.
81(12)-3, Defender, 1966-74.
Tony Byrne had made only one League appearance for Millwall when he moved to Southampton in August 1964. He made his debut for Saints in April 1967 at Old Trafford and over the next seven years was in and out of the team, despite winning 14 caps for the Republic of Ireland. He was a quick and enthusiastic defender who found his slight build a handicap in Saints' rugged defensive system of their early First Division days. Having served them loyally, he joined Terry Paine at Hereford and finished his playing days at Newport.

CALLAGHER.J.
1-0, Centre-half, 1924-5.
Callagher arrived from Bury in 1924 and left for Wigan Borough after one season at The Dell. He later became a fireman and was awarded a medal for bravery in 1938.

CAMPBELL.F.
Born: Glasgow.
86-5, Half-back, 1931-5.
Frank Campbell arrived at The Dell from Scottish non-League club, Irvine Meadow, and had a steady first season until the last match when he fractured a thigh. He courageously fought his way back from this serious injury to play a couple more seasons before finally dropping out of League football to play for Newport (IOW) after doctors diagnosed chronic arthritis of the knee.

CARNABY.T.
Born: Ishabelle.
14-0, Centre-half, 1938-9.
Carnaby was signed from Blyth Spartans in time for the last season of pre-war football. During the war years he became a policeman and gave up professional soccer.

CARR.J.
Born: Twickenham.
86-10, Forward, 1923-6.
Jimmy Carr was introduced to League football by Watford at the age of 16 and played for Portsmouth during the 1916-17 war-time season whilst he was an army private. At the resumption of League soccer, Carr burst into prominence at Reading where he formed a promising partnership with Len Andrews. In 1923 both players resumed their partnership at The Dell and Carr gave Saints three good seasons service playing on the left wing. Dogged by injuries he took the unusual step of placing an advertisement in the *Athletic News* in 1926, stating that he wanted to 'assist a club outside the League in exchange for a business'. He eventually moved to Swansea.

CASE.J.
Born: Liverpool, 18 May 1954.
85-6, Midfield, 1984-7.
Jimmy Case was on the books of South Liverpool before making his Liverpool FC debut during 1974-5. He settled into a strong Liverpool side and soon earned a reputation for being a determined tackler and the owner of a fierce shot. After several successful seasons at Anfield, where he was unlucky not to gain a full England cap to add to his Under-23 appearances, he joined Brighton and played over 100 League games for them. Coming to The Dell in the tail-end of 1984-5, as a replacement for Steve Williams, Case soon showed that he had lost none of his tenacity and in 1985-6 was an inspiration during a difficult time for the club. In 1986-7 his impressive form was maintained and he scored some spectacular goals.

CASSELLS.K.
Born: London, 10 July 1957.
13(6)-4, Forward, 1981-3.
Keith Cassells played for Watford, Peterborough (loan) and Oxford before joining Southampton at the same time as Mark Wright. His awkward style confused defenders but at the same time frustrated the fans and he was transferred to Brentford midway through 1982-3. In 1986-7 he was playing for Mansfield.

CATLIN.N.
Born: Liverpool, 1918. Died: May 1941.
6-0, Forward, 1935-7.
As a schoolboy, playing in Southampton, Catlin made national headlines when he scored 17 goals in an English Shield game, and eight more in the following match. He duly represented England Schoolboys and soon afterwards signed amateur forms for Arsenal. On his 17th birthday he signed for Saints, but never found his schoolboy form and played only six games, failing to score a goal. He died when HMS Gloucester was sunk off Crete during World War Two.

CHADWICK.D.
Born: India, 19 August 1943.
25-1, Forward, 1961-6.
David Chadwick graduated through Saints' junior sides and in October 1959, aged 16 years 2 months, he became the youngest player ever to turn out for the reserves. His early promise did not develop as hoped and over the next six seasons he struggled to gain a first team place. Saints sold him to Middlesbrough for £10,000 in July 1966 and he made 100 League appearances for them before signing for Halifax in January 1970. Two years later he joined Bournemouth and finished his League career with spells at Torquay and Gillingham.

CHALK.N.
Born: Bitterne, 28 October 1916.
5-0, Centre-half, 1937-9.
A local man, Chalk graduated through the youth and reserve teams to play five first-team games before deciding to give up football and become a policeman. After 30 years with the force he is now office manager with a firm of solicitors.

CHANNON M.
Born: Orcheston, 28 November 1948.
507(3)-185, Forward, 1965-77; 1979-82.
Michael Channon was probably the greatest forward ever to play for Saints, winning 45 England caps whilst at The Dell (46 altogether)

and scoring more goals than any other Southampton forward. Spotted by Bill Ellerington whilst playing in his native Wiltshire, Channon nearly joined Swindon but with Ted Bates' persuasion and the fact that he had always supported the Saints, he decided to join the Hampshire side. In September 1964, aged 15 years and 10 months he played and scored for the reserves to beat Chadwick's record of being the youngest ever reserve player. He made his League debut in Saints' promotion season of 1965-6, at home to Bristol City, and scored the first of many fine goals. With Saints in the First Division by 1966-7, and Martin Chivers playing so well, Channon only had one League outing, but the following year Ted Bates, realising Channon's potential, decided to sell Chivers to Spurs and from then on Channon's path to success was clear and rapid. His speed and strong running gave him the chance to attack defences, and his ability to get the ball to the by-line caught the eye. He was capped nine times at Under-23 level and in October 1972 he deservedly won his first full England cap, against Yugoslavia. Always a committed player, Channon enjoyed every game and gave Saints fans endless pleasure with his natural flair for entertainment. With Saints being relegated in 1974, Channon remained loyal, despite being at his peak, and was rewarded by being a member of the FA Cup winning side of 1976. In the summer of 1977 Saints and Channon reluctantly parted company. He joined Manchester City for £300,000 and spent two 'up and down' years at Maine Road before McMenemy re-signed him in September 1979. His fee was £200,000 and he quickly established a partnership, first with Boyer and then with Keegan. Channon's return to Southampton enabled him to pass Paine's goalscoring record and he ended his days at The Dell with a record 185 League goals. In the close season of 1982, McMenemy gave him a free transfer, and he moved to Hong Kong. Channon was not, however, someone who could remain out of the British game for long and he returned to have brief spells at Newcastle and Bristol Rovers before signing for Norwich midway through 1982-3. Many in the game thought that Channon's playing days were over, but he proved them wrong, giving Norwich three excellent years' service that culminated in him helping them win the Milk Cup in 1985. Norwich released him in the close season, and at the age of 37 he signed for Portsmouth to play under his old Southampton colleague, Alan Ball. During 1985-6 he played

his part in pushing Portsmouth close to promotion. His enthusiasm for football remains undimmed and there will be a generation of fans who will never forget the memorable sight of Channon in full flight, and the infectious enjoyment he put into playing and scoring goals.

CHARLES.A.
Born: West Indies.
1-0, Forward, 1936-7.
Alf Charles signed in January 1937, from Stalybridge Celtic where he had built up an impressive goalscoring record. Charles was also a professional magician but he could not conjure up the goals for Southampton and returned to Stalybridge exactly a year later. Charles was the first coloured player to represent Saints.

CHARLES.R.
Born: Southampton, 26 December 1941.
26-0, Goalkeeper, 1959-61.
Bob Charles was a local man who in his formative years promised to be an outstanding goalkeeper, representing England at Schoolboy and Youth levels. He unfortunately ran into problems with his fitness and was forced to retire from League football prematurely in 1961. He later had a spell with Weymouth.

CHARLTON.W.
Born: Eastleigh, 1912.
2-1, Forward, 1931-2.
Charlton was an Oxford University soccer Blue, who signed for Saints as an amateur in 1931. In 1934 he signed for Hull City and the following season turned out for Wimbledon, then a non-League club, as well as winning the first of four England Amateur caps. He scored a hat-trick against Ireland in one of these internationals and decided to turn professional with QPR, in time for the 1936-7 season. He finished his career with non-League Barnet.

CHATTERLEY.L.
Born: Birmingham, 15 February 1945.
7(2)-0, Defender, 1973-5.
Lew Chatterley made his name at Aston Villa for whom he signed as an apprentice in 1962. A spell at Doncaster followed and it was here he first met McMenemy, a manager who was to have much influence on his future career. In 1972, after a short period at Northampton, Chatterley rejoined McMenemy at Grimsby and when the manager moved to Southampton, the player soon followed. An England Youth International, Chatterley's stay at The Dell, as a player, encompassed only seven games and early in 1975 he transferred to Torquay. It was not long, however, before McMenemy appointed Chatterley to be his assistant at The Dell and when McMenemy decided to join Sunderland in the close season of 1985, Chatterley followed him to Roker Park.

CHIVERS.M.
Born: Southampton, 27 April 1945.
174-97, Forward, 1962-8.
Martin Chivers was a local man who signed professional forms for Saints in August 1962 and quickly developed into a big, strong forward of immense promise. He made his debut aged 17 years, at home to Charlton, and soon became one of the most feared forwards in the Second Division, winning 12 England Under-23 caps. In the promotion season of 1965-6 he scored 30 goals in his first 29 matches and although he failed to score in his last ten outings, played a huge part in Saints' climb into the First Division. In 1966-7 he

partnered Ron Davies, giving the Welshman splendid support, and the couple scored over 50 League goals between them. Still only 22, Chivers was the envy of other top clubs and he became restless at The Dell. In the autumn of 1967 the Southampton board agreed to his transfer request, bearing in mind that Channon was already showing signs of being a more than adequate replacement. In January 1968, Tottenham paid a fee of £125,000 to make Chivers the most expensive player in Britain at that time. Southampton immediately spent £45,000 on Frank Saul, from Spurs, and the other £80,000 was carefully used to strengthen Saints' squad over the ensuing two seasons. Whilst at Spurs, Chivers blossomed, playing alongside such accomplished stars such as Gilzean and Greaves and soon he became the first Southampton-born man to play in England's forward line. At Tottenham, Chivers was plagued by a series of injuries but still scored over 100 goals and won 24 England caps. In 1975 he moved to Switzerland, spending three years playing for Servette before finishing his League career with brief spells at Norwich and Brighton. He is now a publican in the Brighton area.

CHRISTIE.A.
Born: Glasgow, 27 June 1896. Died: Reading, 22 May 1981.
5-0, Half-back, 1922-3.
Christie was signed from Walsall in 1922 and left for Norwich in 1923. He later played for Rochdale and Exeter.

CHRISTIE.J.
Born: Fraserburgh, 26 September 1929.
192-0, Goalkeeper, 1950-59.
When Syd Cann secured the transfer of John Christie in January 1951 from Ayr United, the player was serving with the RASC in Farnborough. Despite his youth he had already built a reputation in Scottish football and he stayed with Saints throughout the 1950s, giving them loyal service. In June 1959 he moved to Walsall and played over 100 League games for the West Midlands club. In 1977 he was managing a local side, Winchester Castle.

CLARKE.C.
Born: Newry, 30 October 1962.
33-20, Forward, 1986-7.
Colin Clarke's family moved from Newry to Lowestoft when he was 12 and he consequently joined Ipswich as an apprentice, only to break an ankle in his first season. A year later Bobby Robson,

Ipswich's manager, released the Irishman on a free transfer to Peterborough, where he was to spend the next three years. A two-month loan spell at Gillingham was followed by another free-transfer from Peterborough and Clarke's fortunes were rescued by Tranmere Rovers. Tranmere were pushing for promotion into Division Three and although their bid was unsuccessful, Clarke repaid their faith by scoring 29 goals in 1984-85. That summer, Third Division Bournemouth payed £22,500 for him, his goal-scoring feats at Dean Court not only winning him international caps for Northern Ireland, but also the attention of many foreign clubs including Torino of Italy. Whilst appearing for his country in the 1986 World Cup in Mexico, Clarke finally convinced Chris Nicholl of his ability in the top flight and the Saints' manager persuaded Bournemouth to sell their star forward for £400,000. Clarke made immediate history by becoming the only Saints player to score a hat-trick on his debut and followed this with a second three-goal haul, in October against Newcastle. Up until Christmas 1986, Clarke found the net with impressive regularity but a couple of niggling injuries, as well as a slump in Saints' form, saw the genial Irishman's scoring rate fall away. He had, however, already shown to the fans his natural goalscoring talents and with the right support, could join a long line of famous and successful Southampton forwards.

CLARKE.G.
Born: Nottingham, 11 August 1935.
3-0, Full-back, 1957-9.
Clarke signed for Saints in June 1953 and played only three League games before being given a free transfer into non-League football in the close season of 1959.

CLARKE.J.
Born: Newcastle.
20-0, Forward, 1922-3.
Twenty-six year old Clarke impressed Southampton officials when he played against Saints, for Cardiff, in an FA Cup tie in 1921 and he was duly signed that summer. His form during the following season was variable and he was given a free transfer in May 1923.

CLARKE.W.
Born: Leicester.
2-0, Forward, 1938-9.
Clarke played for his home club, Leicester City, during 1936-7 and had a spell at Exeter before arriving at The Dell in the close season of 1938.

CLEMENTS.S.
Born: Portsmouth, 25 June 1923.
116-1, Centre-half, 1946-55.
Stan Clements joined Saints from Gosport Borough in 1944 and spent many patient years as an understudy to Webber, only emerging as a first-team player with Webber's departure. He left Southampton in 1955 to sign for Basingstoke.

CLIFTON.B.
Born: Whitchurch, 15 March 1934.
111-35, Forward, 1957-63.
Southampton was Brian Clifton's first League club. He was spotted by ex-Saints' player, Stan Woodhouse. His versatility in the forward line, coupled with good heading ability, enabled him to score many opportunist goals. In October 1962 he moved to Grimsby for £8,000 and upon retiring from professional football, became a draughtsman in Grimsby whilst turning out for Boston FC.

COAK.T.
Born: Southampton, 16 January 1958.
4-0, Full-back, 1976-8.
Tim Coak was an apprentice full-back who was released in 1978 and went to play in local football.

COATES.H.
Born: London, 1905. Died: Havant, 27 October 1965.
99-26, Forward, 1928-34.
In 1928, Saints were fortunate to secure the signature of 'Rigger' Coates, a sailor and England Amateur international. Serving on the King's yacht, the *Victoria and Albert*, Coates was happy to remain in

the Royal Navy and play for Saints whenever he could. He captained the Royal Navy XI and won seven Amateur caps. Coates had a 'neat and clever' style and had he dedicated his career to the professional game, he could perhaps have reached the top. In 1934 he left the Saints for Leyton. Remained in the Navy until 1945 and settled in Havant.

COCKERILL.G.
Born: Grimsby, 25 August 1959.
72-14, Midfield, 1985-7.
Glenn Cockerill was Chris Nicholl's first signing as Southampton manager, having previously played for Lincoln, Swindon and Sheffield United. A skilful midfield player with an eye for goal, he soon settled in and played a significant part in Southampton reaching the semi-finals of the FA Cup in 1986. In 1986-7 he was probably Saints' most consistent player, striking up a special rapport with Jimmy Case.

COLE.N.
Born: Woolston, 7 November 1913. Died: Southampton, 29 November 1976.
34-13, Forward, 1933-5.
Cole had played local football for Thorneycrofts and Newport (IOW) before joining Saints and when Ted Drake left for Arsenal he was given his chance in the Southampton forward line. Initially he did well, scoring a hat-trick against West Ham, but could not sustain his form and joined Norwich in the close season of 1935.

COLLINS.E.
Born: Dublin, 22 October 1965.
1(2)-0, Midfield 1984-6.
Collins made national news when he appeared in a Texaco Cup game for Blackpool at the age of 14, whilst Alan Ball was the manager. When Ball returned to Southampton, Collins came with him but failed to establish himself and rejoined Ball at Portsmouth in the close season of 1986.

CONNOR.R.
Born: Jarrow, 13 August 1931.
78-2, Half-back, 1959-61.
Dick Connor originally signed for Newcastle in 1950, but failed to make their first team and went to non-League South Shields. Grimsby rescued him from relative obscurity and he spent seven successful seasons with the Humberside club. Ted Bates signed him in the close season of 1959 and Connor, as much as anyone, played a significant part in Saints winning promotion to Division Two that season. His form during the following season was good and it was a surprise when he was allowed to join Tranmere in the summer of

1961. In one season at Prenton Park he only played four games before an equally short career at Aldershot. In 1970 Connor became Rochdale's manager and three years later joined Darlington where he remained in charge until May 1974.

COOPER.J.
Born: Wednesbury.
5-0, Forward, 1921-3.
Cooper arrived at The Dell in April 1921 from Darlaston in the West Midlands and spent two years mainly in the reserves before moving to Notts County.

COUNDON.C.
Born: Sunderland, 1905. Died: Sutton, December 1978.
26-3, Forward, 1925-8.
Coundon joined Saints in 1925 from Jarrow and was a useful reserve forward until 1928 when he transferred to Wolves.

COWPER.P.
Born: Tyldesley, September 1902. Died: September 1962.
5-0, Forward, 1930-32.
Cowper started at Rossendale, moving to West Ham, Grimsby and New Brighton before joining Saints in the summer of 1930. His two seasons at The Dell were spent mainly in the reserves and in 1932 he signed for Southport and later had spells at Carlisle and Wigan.

CRABBE.J.
Born: Weymouth, 20 October 1954.
8(4)-0, Midfield, 1974-6.
John Crabbe was a Southampton apprentice who made his debut in the 1974-5 season but could not find a regular first-team place and left for Gillingham during the 1976-7 campaign. Successive clubs included Carlisle, Hereford, Crewe Alexandra and Torquay.

CRIBB.S.
Born: Gosport.
70-22, Forward, 1924-30.
Stan Cribb came from Gosport in 1924, staying six seasons and earning amongst other things a reputation for being a reliable penalty-taker. He left Saints for West Ham and later had spells at QPR and Cardiff. After retiring from playing, Cribb continued to scout for Saints whilst living in his native Gosport and was present at Southampton's centenary dinner in February 1986.

CUMMING.L.
Born: Londonderry.
20-4, Forward, 1930-31.
Cumming, an Irish international, was signed from Oldham but never reproduced his international form at The Dell and asked for a transfer. In 1931 he moved to Scotland to play for Queen of the South and simultaneously found a job working in advertising with a Scottish newspaper.

CUMMINGS.J.
Born: Plymouth.
1-0, Full-back, 1933-4.
Although signed as a full-back, Cummings made his one appearance at inside-right in the 1-0 defeat at Millwall in April 1934.

CURRAN.T.
Born: Kinsley, 20 March 1953.
25(1)-0, Forward, 1978-9.
Terry Curran was signed by McMenemy from Derby County in the close season of 1978, having started his career with Doncaster, then Nottingham Forest, Bury on loan, and Derby. He was tricky but temperamental and did not impress the Southampton management. He will be best remembered for scoring the winning goal in the semi-final of the League Cup in 1979 against Leeds. Soon after the Final he was allowed to join Sheffield Wednesday for £100,000. He enjoyed an excellent 1979-80 at Wednesday, scoring 22 goals and there was even talk, albeit briefly, of him winning an England cap. In 1982 he moved to Sheffield United and then had spells at Everton, Huddersfield and Sunderland.

CURTIS.A.
Born: Rhondda, 16 April 1954.
43(7)-5, Forward, 1983-6.
Alan Curtis burst into prominence with Swansea and took part in their steady climb from the Fourth Division to the First, winning many Welsh caps on the way. An expensive transfer to Leeds did not work out and he returned to Swansea. McMenemy spent £80,000 to bring him to The Dell, late in 1983, but despite continuing to win Welsh caps, he failed to reproduce his early Swansea form and during 1985-6 he was loaned to Stoke before being released in the close season of 1986, to Cardiff.

CURTIS G.
Born: Orsett, 3 December 1919.
174-11, Inside-forward, 1947-51.
George Curtis was discovered by Arsenal before the war and

graduated through their youth teams before playing 11 League games in 1946-7. When Don Roper was sold to Arsenal in the close season of 1947 Curtis and Rudkin moved to Southampton, with Curtis valued at £10,000. Bill Dodgin had watched him 15 times before signing him and knew that he was a player full of elegant skills. Before long The Dell crowd were to appreciate his commanding style, full of tricks and feints. One of his favourites was to indicate a pass in one direction, and then, without moving his head, send the ball accurately to a team-mate in another position. Curtis was an integral part of the fine Saints sides of 1947-51 and when he hung up his boots, he moved into management. In 1968 he was managing the Norwegian club, Rosenborg, who coincidentally met Southampton that year in Saints' first venture into European football. Later he managed Hitchin Town.

CUTTING.S.
Born: Salhouse, 21 September 1914.
3-0, Half-back, 1938-9.
Cutting joined Saints from Norwich and played only three games before joining Exeter to whom he returned after the war.

DAVIE.A.
Born: Dundee, 10 June 1945.
1-0, Goalkeeper, 1970-71.
Sandy Davie started with his native Dundee before signing for Luton in 1968 and playing 58 games for the Hatters. Saints signed him in May 1970 but he made only one appearance before leaving for Dundee in 1971. In 1977 he was playing in New Zealand.

DAVIES.R.T.
Born: Merthyr Tydfil, 21 September 1932.
162-0, Full-back, 1957-64.
Ron Davies was signed in March 1958 from Cardiff, his first club, to replace the recently departed Len Wilkins and the £7,000 transfer fee was well spent. With his lithe style of play he played his part in Saints' rise from the Third Division to becoming a top Second Division outfit. In August 1964 he moved to Aldershot and retired in 1966, although for many years he continued to turn out for the ex-Saints XI.

DAVIES.R.T.
Born: Holywell, 25 May 1942.
239(1)-134 Centre-forward, 1966-73.
No forward has scored more First Division goals for Saints than Ron Davies and for a spell, whilst he was at The Dell he was justly regarded as the finest centre-forward in Europe. His career started at Chester in 1959, and it was there that Davies was made to hurdle wearing army boots, training he later claimed gave him extra power when jumping for crosses. His travels took him to Luton and Norwich before Saints signed him in August 1966, for a record £55,000. He was already an established Welsh international but most Saints fans did not expect Davies to make such a sudden impact. Saints were about to embark on their first season in Division One and Davies scored 37 goals in 41 games to top the goalscoring charts. With crosses from Paine and Sydenham floating in, Davies continued to dominate the aerial battles and he again headed (along with George Best) the scoring charts for 1967-8. His  heading powers were awesome and when in August 1969 he scored four goals at Old Trafford, Matt Busby said that Davies had no peer in Europe. United headed a whole host of top clubs who were willing to pay a small fortune for Davies' services, but Southampton were determined to hold on to their prize asset. A big but amiable giant, Davies was useful on the ground, but it was in the air where he inflicted most damage, although in Terry Paine he was lucky to have

such a fine crosser of the ball. As the Saints progressed into the 1970s many top clubs learned how to cope with Davies' aerial power and his scoring was reduced somewhat, although he never gave less than his best. By 1973 he was suffering from a series of injuries sustained from too many robust tackles and could no longer command a regular first-team place. Portsmouth signed him that April and in 59 games for Saints' close rivals, he scored 18 goals. Manchester United had not forgotten Davies and they surprised the footballing world by signing him in November 1974. He never began a game in United's first team but made eight substitute appearances before joining Millwall for three League games in November 1975. Davies returned to Southampton to live and for a while continued to play for local sides but more recently moved to California to coach. A talented artist, he often drew caricatures of his colleagues. It will always be his incredible ability to seemingly defy gravity and head home yet another Paine centre, that will linger in the memories of those who saw him play.

DAVIS.R.
Born: Plymouth, 14 November 1943.
1-0, Full-back, 1964-5.
Davis was signed from Plymouth in July 1964 and left for Bristol City exactly a year later.

DAWTRY.K.
Born: Hythe, 15 June 1958.
(1)-0, Forward, 1978-9.
Kevin Dawtry made one appearance as a substitute in the 1978-9 season before joining Crystal Palace and then Bournemouth.

DAY.A.
Born: Ebbw Vale.
22-0, Half-back, 1937-8.
Day came to The Dell in 1937 from Millwall on a free transfer and moved to Tranmere Rovers in the close season of 1938.

DAY.E.
Born: Dartford, 6 November 1921.
398-145, Forward, 1946-57.
Eric Day was a small but tough outside-right who was originally spotted by Arthur Dominy. A commando during the war, Day

played two wartime games for Saints in 1945-6 and stayed to serve the club loyally until 1957. Despite his size he was aggressive, very fast and defenders did not relish playing against him. His fitness enabled him to play well into his 30s and when he retired from League football in 1957 he signed for Dartford FC.

DEAN.N.
Born: Corby, 13 September 1944.
18-11, Forward, 1965-6.
Norman Dean joined Southampton in April 1963 but it was not until 1965-6 that he made an impact, scoring 11 vital goals in Saints' promotion to Division One. He moved to Cardiff in March 1967 and played 20 games for them before joining Barnsley, his last League club, in September 1968.

DENNIS.M.
Born: Streatham, 2 May 1961.
95-2, Defender, 1983-7.
Mark Dennis broke into the Birmingham City side in 1978-9 and made an immediate impact, not only for his immense talent as a fast left-back, but for having a fiery temperament. His five seasons at St Andrew's were consequently stormy and McMenemy paid £30,000 for his services in the autumn of 1983. The fee was small for a man who had been recognised at England Youth and Under-23 levels, but Saints fans were soon to see the two sides of Dennis. At his skilful best he is undoubtedly one of the finest left-backs Saints have ever fielded and were it not for his temper, he would surely be challenging for a full England cap. In 1987 a series of clashes with Nicholl saw Dennis move to Queen's Park Rangers.

DIGBY.D.
Born: Teignmouth, 14 May 1931.
15-2, Forward, 1953-5.
Derek Digby started his footballing career with Dawlish, before moving into League football with Exeter. In September 1953 he joined Saints and stayed for nearly two seasons followed by a move to Weymouth in the close season of 1955.

DOUGAL.P.
Born: Denny.
29-5, Forward, 1929-32.
Dougal was one of two forwards Saints signed from Clyde in September 1929, with the transfer fee being met by the Supporters Club. On form he was described as 'in the Alex James class'. Extremely skilful he possessed a good shot as well, but never knew

when 'to cut the frills or when to release the ball', according to one critic. He left Saints in 1932 to try his luck on the Continent and later returned to play for Arsenal.

DRAKE.E.
Born: Southampton, 16 August 1912.
71-47, Centre-forward, 1931-4.
Although it is true to say that Ted Drake really made his name after leaving The Dell, it is also true that it was Southampton who launched Drake on a hugely successful career in League and international football. He nearly signed for Tottenham as a schoolboy, but due to injury missed the trial match and was soon spotted by George Kay, then Saints' manager, playing for Winchester City. Drake, who was working as a gas-meter inspector at the time, signed for Saints as an amateur in November 1931, aged 19, but soon showed that he had the necessary skills and bravery to reach the very top. After only one season at The Dell, Drake travelled to Arsenal for talks but refused to sign and returned to Southampton to play another season. Described as 'deadly and dynamic' it was a huge blow to Saints fans when he eventually moved to Highbury in March 1934 for a record £6,000. At Arsenal, Drake found immediate and spectacular success, winning England caps and breaking many of the Gunners' goal-scoring records, including netting all seven goals in a 7-1 defeat of Aston Villa in December 1935. The war interrupted a splendid career and Drake served with the RAF, unfortunately damaging his spine in a fall that ended his playing career. He became a manager and guided Chelsea to the League Championship in 1954-5. A fine sportsman, he also represented Hampshire at cricket between 1931-6.

DOWSETT.G.
Born: Chelmsford, 3 July 1931.
2-0 Forward, 1956-7.
Dickie Dowsett was signed by Tottenham from Sudbury in May 1952, He played one game for Spurs, and scored, then joined Saints in July 1956 after spending a season at Southend. He moved to Bournemouth in June 1957 and found success by scoring 79 goals in 169 games for the Cherries. He finished his League career at Crystal Palace, playing for them between 1962-4.

DUDLEY.F.
Born: Southend, 9 May 1925.
67-32, Inside-forward, 1950-54.

Frank Dudley was a tall and fast inside-forward who started his career with Southend in 1946. He spent two seasons at Leeds before joining Saints in February 1951 as part of the deal that sent Stevenson in the opposite direction. Dudley stayed for three seasons and scored many useful goals at a consistent rate. He moved to Cardiff in September 1953 but stayed only three months before moving to Bradford.

DUNMORE.F.
Born: South Shields.
1-0, Forward, 1932-3.
Dunmore came to Saints from Derby County in 1932-3. He never played in Derby's League side and made only one appearance for Southampton before leaving for Mansfield Town in the close season of 1933.

DUNN.W.
Born: Glasgow.
14-3, Forward, 1937-8.
Billy Dunn joined Celtic in 1933 from junior football, moving to Brentford in June 1935. Two years later he joined Saints but did not find form.

DUNNE.J.
Born: Dublin. Died: 1949.
36-14, Forward, 1936-7.
Jimmy Dunne started his professional career with New Brighton in 1925-6 and was transferred to Sheffield United the following year. In 1930-31 he was top scorer in Division One. In 1935, Arsenal reputedly paid £8,000 for his services and three years later he moved to Southampton for £1,000. He captained the Irish Free State but played only one season for Saints before deciding to return to his native Ireland to play for Shamrock Rovers.

EARLES.P.
Born: Titchfield, 22 March 1955.
9(8)-1, Forward, 1973-7.
Pat Earles was a small, nippy forward, who represented England Schoolboys but could not quite make the grade in the top flight. Moving to Reading in January 1977, he found success and scored over 50 goals for the Berkshire side. More recently he has played for RS Southampton.

EARLS.M.
Born: Limerick, 25 March 1954.
3-0, Defender, 1974-5.
Mick Earls was a Southampton apprentice who moved to Aldershot in June 1975 after breaking a leg during his stay at The Dell.

EDWARDS.J.
Born: Manchester, 23 February 1924. Died: 1978.
82-16, Forward, 1949-52.
Jack Edwards, a product of Manchester junior football, slipped the Manchester club's net and signed for Nottingham Forest upon leaving the Royal Navy at the end of the war. He soon earned a reputation as a skilful player with a good left foot and Bill Dodgin paid nearly £10,000 to acquire his talents. In the three seasons he spent at The Dell he had some fine games on the left-hand side of the attack before joining Notts County in November 1952. After only 25 games he retired from League football at the premature age of 29.

ELKES.J.
Born: Wellington, 31 December 1894. Died: 22 January 1972.
33-7, Forward, 1921-3.
Jack Elkes moved to Southampton when Foxall and Barratt joined Birmingham and he made a dream debut, scoring two goals. A tall, clever inside-left, he then had the misfortune to suffer a broken collar-bone in only his second game. Tottenham paid over £1,000 for him in 1923 and he later played for Middlesbrough and Watford.

ELLERINGTON.W.
Born: Southampton, 30 June 1923.
227-10, Full-back, 1946-56.
Arguably the most cultured and elegant right-back ever to be on the Saints' books, Ellerington came from a footballing family with his father playing for Saints during World War One before signing for

Middlesbrough and then Sunderland during the 1920s. Like his father, Bill Ellerington started his football career with Saints during a war and in the years immediately after the conflict, competed with Alf Ramsey for the right-back position. Ellerington was originally first-choice, but his career suffered a big setback when he caught pneumonia during a trip to Newcastle in the 1946-7 season and spent nearly a year out of the game. Ramsey stepped into his boots to such good effect that he was capped for England, and when Ellerington eventually recovered, the Southampton management had an embarrassment of riches in the number-2 position. Ramsey moved to Spurs in 1949 and Ellerington himself won two England caps the same year. He played many fine games for Southampton right up to 1956 and then joined Ted Bates' coaching staff. He later provided assistance to the club as scout and is credited with being the man who spotted Mick Channon. To this day he attends Saints matches, maintaining an interest in the club to whom he gave loyal service.

ELLIOTT.B.
Born: Beeston, 3 May 1925.
235-1, Half-back, 1949-58.
Bernard, or Bryn as he preferred to be known, arrived at The Dell in October 1949 from Nottingham Forest for whom he made ten appearances in 1947-8. Never a powerful player, he more than made up for his size with a terrier-like style, and 100 per cent commitment. He was a neat player who served Saints admirably through to the Third Division days, remaining at The Dell for the remainder of his career. In 1958 he retired, having a brief spell at Poole Town before managing an off-licence in Southampton.

ELLISON.J.
Born: Wales.
1-0, Full-back, 1927-8.
Ellison signed in 1927 from Welsh non-League side, Rhyl Town, and played one game before joining Rochdale on a free transfer.

EMANUEL.T.
Born: Treboreth, Wales.
33-0, Full-back, 1938-9.
Tom Parker paid £2,200 to Swansea Town for their Welsh Schoolboy international, Emanuel, in September 1938. He looked set to have a long future at The Dell but the war intervened.

EPHGRAVE.G.
Born: Swindon, 29 April 1918.
36-0, Goalkeeper, 1946-8.
George Ephgrave, who stood 6ft 4in, played for Aston Villa and Swindon during the war when he also spent some time as a PoW. Upon his release he signed for Saints but in July 1948 moved to Norwich and then Watford. His enormous height enabled him to deal easily with crosses but he was suspect against low shots. His

hand-span was prodigious, enabling him to pick up an old-style leather football with one hand. After leaving League football he spent a year assisting Deal Town before taking a market garden in Guernsey.

EVANS.H.
Born: Lambeth, 17 April 1919. Died: 1962.
1-0, Forward, 1946-7.
Harry Evans played for Saints and Fulham during the war before leaving the RAF to sign professional terms at The Dell in early 1946. In June of the same year he joined Exeter and followed this with a move to Aldershot in March 1949, later becoming manager at the Recreation Ground. He moved to Spurs in the 1950s to become assistant manager.

FASHANU.J.
Born: Kensington, 18 September 1962.
9-3, Forward, 1982-3.
When Southampton were left unprepared for Keegan's sudden departure, McMenemy borrowed Fashanu from Nottingham Forest and the big, tough forward helped Saints through an awkward start to the 1982-3 season. The only 'on loan' player to score for the Saints, he returned to Forest and later played for Notts County and Brighton. A bad injury later forced him to retire permanently.

FISHER.H.
Born: Glasgow, 9 January 1944.
297(5)-7, Midfield, 1966-77.
Hugh Fisher played his early football alongside Alan Ball at Blackpool and was signed by Saints in March 1967, for £35,000 as Ted Bates tried to add some fight to the midfield. Fisher stayed at The Dell for ten seasons and was a dedicated professional. He broke a leg against Arsenal in 1971-2 and that ended a sequence of 50 consecutive appearances. Fisher fought back and no one at The Dell will ever forget his last-gasp equaliser against Aston Villa in the 1976 FA Cup. It was a priceless goal although, overall, he had a poor scoring record. He was unlucky to be substitute for the Final but, typically, did not complain. Fisher left to become player-manager of Southport in March 1977 but returned to Southampton to become a sales representative.

FISHLOCK.L.
Born: Battersea, 2 January 1907. Died: 24 June 1986.
69-14, Forward, 1934-6.
Laurie Fishlock signed from Millwall in 1934 having previously been with Crystal Palace. His initial function was to fill the gap left by the recently departed Arnold — no easy task. An England Amateur

international, he did well for Saints and helped soften the blow of Arnold's transfer. An excellent cricketer for Surrey and England, Fishlock left Saints for Aldershot in 1936 and ended his League days with Gillingham. He later became a cricket coach.

FLOOD.J.
Born: Southampton, 21 October 1932.
122-28, Forward, 1952-8.
An England Schoolboy international, John Flood came from a footballing family, and his brother was an aspiring goalkeeper on Saints' books. Flood promised much in his early days and should probably have achieved more in the game, but after moving to Bournemouth in June 1958 he played only 17 games before dropping out of League football.

FLOWERS.T.
Born: Kenilworth, 3 February 1967.
9-0, Goalkeeper, 1986-7.
Tim Flowers was signed in June 1986 from Wolves. He did not have to wait long for his First Division baptism, making his debut at Old Trafford in September and conceding five goals. After suffering a severe facial injury against Arsenal he joined Swindon on loan in March 1987.

FORREST.G.
Born: Stockton, 21 January 1957.
59(1)-0, Full-back, 1985-7.
Gerry Forrest made his debut in Rotherham's first team in 1977-8 and became a regular for the next seven seasons. He was Chris Nicholl's second signing, in December 1985 for £100,000, and immediately tightened the right-back position that had been suspect since the departure of Mick Mills. A no-nonsense, player, it was a shame he was Cup-tied when Saints' went to the FA Cup semi-finals in 1986.

FORSYTH.C.
Born: Plean, 5 May 1939.
48-0, Goalkeeper, 1965-8.
Campbell Forsyth made his mark playing in goal for Kilmarnock and winning four Scottish caps before Bates signed him in December 1965 for £10,000. He played his part in the 1965-6 promotion push and then had the cruel misfortune to break a leg against Liverpool, after only eight First Division matches. Although playing another 26 games, he never properly recovered from that injury. For many years has served Saints as a scout in Scotland and he recommended Jim Steele, amongst others, to the club.

FOSTER.R.
Born: Bolton.
1-0, Goalkeeper, 1932-3.
Foster was signed from Accrington Stanley and spent a year at The Dell as Scriven's understudy.

FOULKES.W.
Born: Merthyr Tydfil, 29 May 1926.
23-1, Forward, 1954-5.
Billy Foulkes was a Welsh international who arrived from Newcastle United with Mulgrew for a combined fee of £12,000, having previously played for Chester. In his first season for the Saints he suffered a back injury that threatened to end his career and Southampton were angry, believing that he was carrying the injury when he arrived from Newcastle. Saints appealed to the Football League over the £5,000 fee and asked for their money back. In the meantime, Foulkes left the area and played for Winsford United, a non-League side. The League ruled that Saints had no case and in July 1956, Foulkes signed for Chester and went on to play over 170 games for them.

FOYLE.M.
Born: Salisbury, 2 May 1963.
7(6)-1, Forward, 1982-4.
Martin Foyle made his debut in 1982-3 and played a handful of games before joining Aldershot in 1985. A bad injury sidelined him for most of 1985-6. Returned for the 1986-7 season before joining Oxford United for £140,000 in March 1987.

FRASER.W.
Born: Newcastle.
56-11, Forward, 1929-32.
Fraser came to Saints via army football and Aldershot and had three seasons at The Dell during which time he was first reserve for the forward line. In 1932 he moved to Northampton and then Fulham. During 1935-6 he became player-coach of Salisbury FC.

FREEMAN.G.
Born: Bethnal Green, 21 February 1920.
7-2, Forward, 1946-7.
Alf Freeman joined Saints during the war and played in the first peacetime League season. He moved to Crystal Palace in August 1948 but played only one League game for them before dropping out of League football.

FRY.R.
Born: Southampton, 18 August 1948.
23-0, Full-back, 1970-2.
Roger Fry was a local man, who failed to gain a regular first-team place and joined Walsall in July 1973. In 1978 he was playing for Salisbury.

FUNNELL.A.
Born: Eastbourne, 20 August 1957.
13(4)-8, Forward, 1977-9.
Tony Funnell joined Southampton from non-League Eastbourne in January 1977 and proved something of an enigma to supporters because he appeared to have a eye for goal yet did not seem to impress the management. He scored some priceless goals in the promotion campaign of 1977-8, only to be sold to Gillingham in March 1979. Many Saints fans thought the club had been wrong to sell a forward who could score goals but Funnell failed to show any form at Gillingham or Brentford and Saints' decision appeared justified. He later signed for non-League Poole Town.

GABRIEL.J.
Born: Dundee, 16 October 1940.
190(1)-25, Defender, 1967-72.
When Jimmy Gabriel joined Saints in July 1967 from Everton he was already an established First Division player and Scottish international. He was ostensibly a half-back but often played in the forward line. His stay at Everton had been memorable, winning two Scottish caps plus an FA Cup winners' medal in 1966, and he was just the sort of player that the Saints needed at that time. In five seasons at The Dell, Gabriel notched up nearly 200 appearances and when he left for Bournemouth in July 1972 his presence was sorely missed. After some 50 games for the Cherries he had brief spells at Swindon and Brentford. In 1987 he returned from managing a club in the United States to join Bournemouth's coaching staff.

GALLEGO.J.
Born: Spain, 8 April 1923.
1-0, Forward, 1948-9.
Jose Gallego was on the books of Brentford for the 1946-7 season before joining Saints in May 1948. He left Southampton for Colchester in 1950.

GAUGHRAN.B.
Born: Dublin.
7-4, Forward, 1937-8.
Tom Parker spotted Benny Gaughran playing in Ireland but lost out to Celtic in the chase for the Irishman's signature. Gaughran's stay at Parkhead was unproductive, however, and he was given a free transfer to Southampton. After playing only seven games he attracted the attention of the Sunderland manager who offered £1,000 for him. Realising the profitability of such a transfer deal, Gaughran was allowed to move to Roker Park.

GAYNOR.L.
Born: Ollerton, 22 September 1925.
12-1, Forward, 1953-4.
Len Gaynor played two League games for Hull in 1950 before signing

for Bournemouth the following year. In March 1954 he moved to The Dell, but his stay lasted less than a year before he joined his third Hampshire club, Aldershot, in February 1955. He finished his career at Oldham.

GENNOE.T.
Born: Shrewsbury, 16 March 1953.
36-0, Goalkeeper, 1978-80.
Terry Gennoe is one of the game's great travellers, having been with Bury, Blackburn (loan), Leeds (loan), and Halifax before joining Saints in February 1978. In 1978-9 he became Saints' first choice goalkeeper and played in the League Cup Final, although he did not enjoy a good game. His confidence duly suffered and following further loans to Everton and Crystal Palace he joined Blackburn in 1981 and became their regular 'keeper.

GEORGE.C.
Born: Islington, 10 October1950.
44-11, Forward, 1978-81.
Charlie George made his name with Arsenal's 'double' side in the early 1970s, gaining five England Under-23 caps. He moved to Derby in 1975 and continued to impress with his ball control and shooting

abilities, winning a full England cap during his stay at the Baseball Ground. When he signed for Saints for £400,000 in December 1978, the transfer took about a month to negotiate and soon after he signed it was revealed that he had a knee injury and would be sidelined for some months. Saints' fans queried spending so much money on a player who appeared to be carrying an injury and as he did not play his first match at The Dell until the beginning of the following season, their disquiet could be understood. Although George showed flashes of brilliance he never reproduced his old form and, with Keegan, Channon and Moran knitting so well together up front, he had a spell at Nottingham Forest on loan, before going to play in Hong Kong. He later returned for a second spell at Derby but Saints' supporters never saw the best of George due to his injury. The wisdom of spending a then Southampton record fee of over £400,000 must, in hindsight, be questioned. He now runs a pub in Winchester.

GETGOOD.G.
Born: Ayr.
35-1, Half-back, 1921-3.
George Getgood was an accomplished and versatile player equally at home at half-back or forward, who came to Southampton from Birmingham as part of the Foxall and Barrett deal. He returned to the Midlands to play for Wolves in 1923 and later had a spell at Aberdare.

GIBBINS.V.
Born: Forest Gate, 7 January 1901: Died: Herne Bay, November 1979.
2-0, Forward, 1933-4.
Viv Gibbins was an amateur who was on the books for one season after playing for Clapton, West Ham and Brentford. Capped at both Amateur and full England levels (he won two full caps as a Clapton player) he left The Dell in 1934 to join Leyton. A schoolteacher by profession he later became a headmaster in London.

GILCHRIST.P.
Born: Dartford, 5 January 1951.
96(11)-17, Forward, 1971-77.
Paul Gilchrist was a Charlton apprentice and played five League games before joining Doncaster in the close season of 1971. He joined

Saints for £30,000 in March 1972 and over the next five years found himself in and out of the first team. Tall and skilful, he lacked pace but scored the important first goal in the FA Cup semi-final against Palace in 1976. He kept his place for the Final and thus collected a winners' medal, an achievement that must have seemed most unlikely at one stage of his career. He moved to Portsmouth in March 1977 and then had brief stays at Swindon and Hereford before a serious injury ended his career.

GILL.M.
Born: Exeter, 13 April 1931.
1-0, Goalkeeper, 1955-6.
Mervyn Gill was an amateur goalkeeper who had the distinction of being Ted Bates' first signing, having previously played for Woking and Portsmouth. He made his one appearance in the last match of the 1955-6 season and joined Torquay a few months later, enjoying five seasons with the Devon club.

GITTENS.J.
Born: Moseley, 22 January 1964.
18-0, Centre-half, 1985-7.
Jon Gittens was signed from local Birmingham side, Paget Rangers, early in the 1985-6 season and had the experience of making his debut at Birmingham the same season. He covered ably for both Bond and Wright in 1986-7.

GODFREY.A.
Born: Newbury, 30 April 1939.
141-0, Goalkeeper, 1958-66.
Tony Godfrey was an amateur on the books of Norwich before joining Saints in April 1958. His arrival coincided with an upsurge in Saints' fortunes and he competed with Hollowbread, Charles and Reynolds over the next six seasons for the first-team goalkeeping position. When Forsyth arrived at The Dell, Godfrey moved to Aldershot in December 1965 and enjoyed four seasons as their regular goalkeeper before having two further seasons at Rochdale. In July 1972 he returned to Aldershot to finish his League career and later turned out for Basingstoke.

GOLAC.I.
Born: Yugoslavia, 15 June 1950.
167(1)-4, Full-back, 1978-86.
Ivan Golac was a £50,000 signing from Partizan Belgrade in 1978 and he became one of the most successful of all foreign 'imports'. Under

Yugoslavian law a professional footballer, upon reaching the age of 28, is free to negotiate his own transfer and McMenemy was quick to offer the hard-tackling, attacking Golac, a contract at The Dell. There were initial problems with the Home Office over a work permit but, once these snags were ironed out, Golac became the 'darling' of The Dell crowd with his swashbuckling style. A Yugoslav international, he realised an ambition when he played at Wembley in the 1979 League Cup Final and went on to have another three enjoyable seasons at The Dell. A disagreement over terms caused him to move to Bournemouth for the 1982-3 season and, after a brief spell with Manchester City, he returned to Yugoslavia to play for the Second Division club, Bjelasica. Strangely, Golac grew 'homesick' for Hampshire and offered his services to McMenemy late in 1983-4. Golac stayed long enough to play several games in 1985-6, leaving in the autumn.

GRANGER.K.
Born: Southampton, 5 October 1968.
Goalkeeper, 1985-.
Keith Granger was an unknown 'A' team goalkeeper late in 1985-6 when an injury to Shilton, and the recent transfer of Kite, caused Nicholl to throw this young 'keeper in at the deep end. He made his debut against Everton and despite conceding six goals he showed that he had the right attitude and revealed potential for the future. He was the first Southampton schoolboy to make the first team since Bob Charles in 1959.

GRANT.W.
Born: Ashington, 3 August 1920.
61-12, Forward, 1946-50.
Wilf Grant started as an amateur with Newcastle United before signing professional forms with Manchester City in 1943. Having guested for Saints during the war, he moved to The Dell on a permanent basis in October 1946 and enjoyed some success as a clever winger. Moving to Cardiff in 1950, the little forward found success with 65 goals in 155 games. He later had a spell at Ipswich before returning to Cardiff to coach.

GREGORY.J.
Born: Southampton, 25 January 1925.
66-0, Full-back, 1946-54.
A local lad, Jack Gregory signed professional forms in 1943, but despite being at The Dell for ten years, never really established

himself in the first team and moved to Leyton Orient in July 1955. He finished his career at Bournemouth in 1959.

GRIGGS.P.
Born: Southampton, June 1918, Died: Southampton, June 1980.
1-0, Forward, 1938-9.
Griggs was a Southampton schoolboy player who graduated through the 'A' team and represented the FA Amateur XI during the 1938-9 season. Although he decided to turn professional he failed to make any further headway in the game.

GUERAN.S.
Born: Grays, Middlesex.
3-0, Forward, 1936-8.
One of Tom Parker's first signings, Gueran came from Margate on a free transfer in March 1937. He left The Dell, also on a free transfer, in the close season of 1938 for Exeter.

GUNTER.D.
Born: Portsmouth, 4 March 1933.
7-0, Full-back, 1955-6.
David Gunter joined Saints in May 1955, played seven games during the following season, and then joined non-League Sittingbourne.

GURR.G.
Born: Brighton, 20 October 1946.
42-0, Goalkeeper, 1966-70.
Gerry Gurr joined Saints in March 1964 from Guildford City and for a while looked to have a promising future before a particularly bad shoulder injury limited his chances and after 55 games with Aldershot between 1970 and 1972 he ended his League career.

GURRY.J.
Born: London.
9-0, Half-back, 1935-6.
Gurry was signed from Leicester City in the close season of 1935 and moved to Chester after one season at The Dell.

HADDLETON.A.
Born: Newcastle-upon-Tyne, 1911. Died: Eastleigh, January 1971.
17-10, Forward, 1930-32.
Haddleton was signed from non-League Horden Athletic and looked to be a 'find' when, in 1931-2, he scored in eight successive games. Losing form he moved on to Fulham in 1932 and later played for Swindon and Walsall before returning to Hampshire to play for local side Pirelli General.

HAINES.W.
Born: Warminster, 1900. Died: Frome, October 1974.
70-47, Forward, 1928-32.
Willie Haines, known as the 'Farmers Boy' or 'Farmer Haines', came to Southampton from Portsmouth in May 1928. At Pompey he had scored a highly creditable 119 goals in 165 games. He earned his nickname due to being a well-built 'country' boy and he became as popular at The Dell as he had been at Fratton Park. Despite his build and power, Haines based his game and his shooting on placement rather than force and would often take penalties without a run-up. He left League football in 1932 but continued to play for non-League Weymouth with enthusiasm. In 1960 he was president of the Portsmouth Supporters Club.

HARE.T.
Born: Motherwell, 1 April 1944.
13-0, Full-back, 1965-6.
Tommy Hare joined Southampton, his first League club, in April 1963 and played during Saints' promotion season of 1965-6. He joined Luton in July 1967 and played 12 games before signing for Workington a year later.

HARFIELD.L.
Born: Southampton, 22 November 1952.
2-1, Forward, 1970-71.
Les Harfield showed early promise as an England Schoolboy and Youth international but despite scoring in his second game for Saints — the last game of 1970-71 — he was released soon after to join

Luton. He appeared once as a substitute before dropping out of League football.

HARKUS.G. MBE
Born: Newcastle, 25 September 1898. Died: 1950.
220-3, Half-back, 1923-32.

George Harkus had signed from Aston Villa in May 1921 but did not make his debut until January 1923. A man of dynamic personality, he quickly established himself and became captain in 1926-7. Throughout his meritorious stay at The Dell, Harkus never gave less than 100 per cent and was often an inspiration to other players. In 1930 Harkus retired to become a publican although he continued to remain fit, playing for New Milton FC and in February 1932 he returned to The Dell to play two matches to help Saints during an injury crisis. Harkus then went to the Continent to continue playing the game for which he had so much enthusiasm. He was unlucky not to win international honours but did tour Canada in 1926 with the FA. During the war he was a flight lieutenant and was awarded the MBE.

HARRIS.J.
Born: Tunbridge Wells.
2-0, Forward, 1932-3.
Jimmy Harris, a former Folkestone player, was signed in the close season of 1932 from West Ham United and played on the left wing in the first two games of 1932-3. He was released in the close season of 1933.

HARRISON.B.
Born: Worcester, 28 September 1934.
3-0, Forward, 1959-60.
Bernard Harrison was originally on the books of Portsmouth as an amateur and joined Crystal Palace in October 1955. A cricketer for Hampshire he joined Saints in August 1959, but was only at The Dell for a year when he moved to his final League club, Exeter City. In 1967-8 he was playing for Winchester City.

HAYES.A.
Born: London, 15 July 1958. Died: London, 3 December 1986.
22(10)-5, Forward, 1976-80.

Austin Hayes was a diminutive, nippy forward who never quite broke into the first team on a regular basis, spending many games as substitute. As a Londoner, he was shocked to find himself selected to play for the Republic of Ireland, through an ancestral qualification, and so became an international footballer whilst in Saints' reserves. He made his debut for Saints in a European Cup-winners' Cup match, replacing Channon, and scored twice against Carrick Rangers. In March 1980 he transferred to Millwall for £50,000 and in 1983-4 moved to Northampton Town. In 1986 moved to play in Sweden but his life was tragically cut short by cancer in December of that year.

HEANY.A.
Born: Plymouth, 9 May 1940.
1-0, Full-back, 1960-61.
England Youth international, Heaney played only one League game, in 1960-61. He later played for Poole and Netley Sports.

HEATON.W.
Born: Leeds, 26 August 1918.
15-0, Forward, 1948-9.
William Heaton joined Saints for £7,000 from Leeds in February 1949 and despite having a stocky build, played on the wing. He joined Rochdale in November 1950 after asking for a transfer.

HEBBERD.T.
Born: Winchester, 19 June 1958.
69(27)-8, Midfield, 1976-82.
Trevor Hebberd, a Southampton apprentice, made his debut in 1976-7 and a languid style concealed a keen footballing brain and plenty of dribbling skills. Despite this he found himself spending his Saturdays on the substitute's bench and had spells at both Bolton and Leicester on loan. He moved to Oxford in March 1982, when Mark Wright made the opposite move, and has been a prominent member of a fine Oxford side that climbed into Division One in 1985. He played and scored in Oxford's 1986 Milk Cup Final victory.

HENDERSON.D.
Born: Southampton, 1913.
22-0, Full-back, 1935-9.
Henderson was spotted by Albert Shelley, then Saints' trainer, whilst playing on the Common and signed in 1935. For the aborted 1939-40 season he had signed for Bristol City although he returned to Southampton after the war to become a policeman.

HENDERSON.W.
Born: Carlisle, 1900.
152-10, Forward, 1923-8.
Henderson came to Saints from Luton in November 1923, for a fee of £500 having started his career with his hometown club, Carlisle, before joining Arsenal for £1,000. As a winger his footwork was intricate, if unorthodox and he was nicknamed 'Tishy' by the crowd, after a famous racehorse of the day that appeared to cross its legs as it ran. One moment 'Tishy' could be dazzling to watch, the next he could be 'sheer vaudeville'. He left to join Coventry in 1928 and later moved back to Carlisle to become a tobacconist.

HENNIGAN.M.
Born: Thryburgh, 20 December 1942.
3-0, Forward, 1963-4.
Mike Hennigan was an amateur with Rotherham before joining Sheffield Wednesday, but he did not make the first team and joined Saints in June 1962. His stay at The Dell lasted two years and he joined Brighton in July 1964.

HILL.F.
Born: Forfar, 21 May 1906. Died: Luton, June 1970.
51-3, Half-back, 1937-9.
Frank Hill started his professional career with Forfar followed by a spell at Aberdeen. Capped for Scotland, he moved to Arsenal in 1932 and won a League Championship medal in 1933 before signing for Blackpool and becoming their captain. Saints signed him in September 1937, for £2,200 when he was 29, and his versatility made him a useful acquisition. A strong character, he was the automatic choice as

Saints' captain but during the 1938-9 season, after an injury and falling out with sections of The Dell crowd, he left Southampton. Hill became Preston coach and after the war managed Crewe Alexandra and Burnley. His experiences at The Dell did not daunt him from applying for Saints' manager's job in 1952.

HILL.L.
Born: Islington.
10-0, Goalkeeper, 1925-6.
Hill was signed from Queen's Park Rangers as understudy for Tommy Allen and was used ten times in 1925-6. Before QPR he had been with Southend and after leaving Saints he played for Rochdale.

HILLIER.B.
Born: Redcar, 8 April 1936.
9-0, Full-back, 1957-9.
Barry Hillier graduated through Saints' junior sides but had a spell at Chester before making his Southampton debut in the 1957-8 season. He joined Poole Town in 1959. His father had been a professional in the 1930s.

HOBSON.G.
Born: Sheffield, 27 November 1957.
20-7, Forward, 1986-7.
Gordon Hobson's first League club was Lincoln City, for whom he scored 73 goals in 272 League games before transferring to Grimsby Town in 1984-5. He impressed the Mariners' assistant manager, Chris Nicholl, who returned to Blundell Park as Saints boss in December 1986 to pay £120,000 for the nippy inside-forward. Extremely quick on the turn, Hobson scored on his debut, against Watford (he also scored on his debuts for Lincoln and Grimsby). He took a month or two to adjust to the pace of the First Division but has since become a valuable addition and in April 1987 scored three goals at Maine Road, the first hat-trick by a Saints player away from home since Channon's three at Oxford in September 1974.

HOLLOWBREAD.J.
Born: Enfield, 2 January 1934.
36-0, Goalkeeper, 1964-6.
John Hollowbread joined Tottenham from Enfield Town in January 1952 and in 12 seasons spent at White Hart Lane, made 67 appearances. Saints paid £3,000 for 30-year-old Hollowbread's services in May 1964 and, like Tony Godfrey, he left The Dell upon Forsyth's arrival. He continued to play local football in Southampton for many years.

HOLLYWOOD.D.
Born: Govan, 3 November 1944.
234-4, Full-back, 1962-72.
Dennis Hollywood was a Southampton apprentice who showed early promise and was capped for Scotland at Under-23 level.

Although he progressed no further on the international stage, he made his mark at The Dell over a period of ten years. An immensely tough, combative full-back, Hollywood was one of the most feared defenders in the League and he served Saints well during a period when they were struggling to find a footing in the top division. In July 1972, he moved to Blackpool but did not figure in their first team and later returned to Southampton to work in the docks.

HOLMES.C.
Born: Winchester, 28 March 1939.
1-0, Half-back, 1959-60.
Colin Holmes was a promising young half-back who graduated through the same youth teams as Paine and Sydenham. An England Youth international, he failed to improve on early form and played only one League game. After leaving The Dell he played for Winchester City and took up a job with the Post Office.

HOLMES.N.
Born: Southampton, 11 November 1954.
437(7)-56, Midfield, 1973-87.

Nick Holmes was educated at St Mary's College, Southampton, and was an apprentice at The Dell in the early 1970s. A natural left-sided player, he made his debut during 1973-4 and has been equally at home at full-back, midfield, centre-half and, more lately, sweeper. The model of a good professional, he has an eye for goal and over the years has quietly notched up more appearances than anyone else except for Paine and Channon. A member of the 1976 FA Cup winning side, he also played and scored in the 1979 League Cup Final. Selected for England Under-23s, he was unfortunate to miss the game owing to an injury. In 1986 Saints recognised his loyalty by awarding him a testimonial against John Mortimore's Benfica. In May 1987 he was given a free-transfer after suffering a serious pelvic injury.

HOLT.A.
Born: Southampton, 8 April 1911.
206-46, Forward, 1932-9.
Arthur Holt represented Southampton Schoolboys before turning out for Bitterne Congregationals in the Church League. Moving to Totton, in the Hampshire League, he came to the attention of the Saints and signed forms in 1932. He made his debut away to Manchester United in January 1933 and it soon became obvious to George Kay, that along with Ted Drake, Saints possessed two extremely promising young forwards. Holt stayed with Saints throughout the 1930s, playing some outstanding games as a thrustful inside-forward. He played cricket for Hampshire between 1935-48 and later became their coach. Holt opened a sports shop in the city and continues to take a healthy interest in the local sports scene.

HOOPER.H.
Born: Brierly Hill.
19-0, Full-back, 1921-4.
Hooper was signed from non-League football in 1921 and over the next two seasons was an able deputy for either Parker or Titmuss.

HORSFALL.G.
Born: Australia, 19 September 1924.
2-0, Half-back, 1946-7.
George Horsfall's family returned to the North East from Australia when he was two. He signed for Saints towards the end of the war and was transferred to Southend for £1,000 in July 1949. He returned to The Dell in 1955 and has served Saints in a coaching capacity ever since.

HORTON.H.
Born: Malvern, 18 April 1924.
75-12, Wing-half, 1951-4.
A hard, fearless half-back, Henry Horton arrived at The Dell in June 1951 from Blackburn with whom he had started his League career in 1947. He moved to Bradford in May 1954. Horton also played cricket for both Worcestershire and Hampshire.

HORTON.J.
Born: Thurnscoe.
1-0, Forward, 1921-2.
John Horton joined Saints from Midland League football. He left The Dell in the close season of 1922, destination unknown.

HORTON.J.
Born: Thurnscoe.
4-1, Forward, 1934-5.
Horton was a relation of John Horton (1921-2) and joined Saints from Millwall at the same time as Fishlock. He left for Aldershot in 1935.

HOSKINS.J.
Born: Southampton, 10 May 1931.
220-64, Forward, 1952-9.
John Hoskins came to The Dell via Winchester City, where he had caught the eye as a tall, languid left-winger. His uncle Bert played for Saints in 1906-08 and John soon emulated his relation by reproducing his Winchester City form on the left wing. In July 1959 he joined Swindon, but played only ten League games for them before dropping out of League football to play for Cambridge United, then in the Southern League.

HOUGH.E.
Born: Walsall, December 1899. Died: Birmingham, 1978.
175-0, Full-back, 1921-31.
Ted Hough joined Saints from Walsall in 1921, for the unusual transfer fee of 52 pints of beer. Apparently that was the size of the round that a Southampton director had to stand the Walsall management before they would permit Hough to sign for the Saints. The money was well spent, however, because Hough, although never holding down a permanent position, gave the club ten years dependable service. In May 1931 he signed for Portsmouth, played only one game and then joined Bristol Rovers. Retiring from football he became a fitter's mate at Portsmouth Power Station.

HUXFORD.C.
Born: Stroud, 8 June 1937.
276(2)-4, Wing-half, 1959-66.
Cliff Huxford was an uncompromising wing half, who came to Southampton from Chelsea in May 1959 and stayed to help Saints gain promotion to Division One. Huxford was a solid, dependable wing-half who helped provide the backbone of the team. He played

only one game for Saints in the First Division before joining Exeter in the close season of 1967. He still lives locally and turns out for the ex-Saints XI.

JENKINS.T.
Born: London, 2 December 1947.
84-4, Forward, 1969-73.
Tommy Jenkins had one game for Orient before signing for West Ham in December 1967. West Ham released him to non-League Margate and Reading to resurrect his League career when they signed him in July 1969. Enjoying a bright start to the 1969-70 season, he attracted the attention of Southampton who paid £60,000 for his services. At his best Jenkins was a high-class winger with the full repertoire of necessary skills and yet, like so many other wingers, he sometimes exasperated the fans by dribbling himself into trouble. Saints sold Jenkins to Swindon in November 1972 and he remained there for three seasons before dropping out of League football prematurely.

JEPSON.A.
Born: Castleford.
92-18, Forward, 1928-32.
Bert Jepson signed from Huddersfield in 1928 and played some fine games on the right wing in his four seasons at The Dell. He joined the exodus to Fulham in 1932 and later played for Brighton.

JOHNSON.H.
Born: Birmingham.
38-8, Forward, 1921-4.
Harry Johnson joined Saints in April 1921 from Darlaston on a free transfer and over the next three years he played 38 games, mainly as

an inside-left, but failed to hold down a regular place. He left in 1924 to join Sheffield United.

JONES.D.
Born: Shirebrook, Derbyshire.
7-0, Half-back, 1924-5.
Jones arrived from Leicester City in the close season of 1924 and spent one season at The Dell.

JONES E.
Born: Wales, 1922.
44-4, Forward, 1949-52.
Ernie Jones started out as an amateur with Swansea Town, but at the age of 17 signed professional forms for Bolton and made his debut in their first team before the war. He returned to Swansea as a wartime

guest and later re-signed for them on a permanent basis. Spurs signed him in 1947 and whilst at White Hart Lane he won four Welsh caps. Jones came to The Dell as part of the transfer deal that took Ramsey to Tottenham in May 1949, with the Saints also receiving a sizeable sum of money. His stay at The Dell lasted until November 1951 when he moved to Bristol City where he finished his League career. He managed Rhyl Town before returning to Southampton in January 1956 to help out with some training for the youngsters.

JONES.K.
Born: Havercroft, 26 June 1944.
79-0, Full-back, 1965-70.
Ken Jones joined Bradford from Monkton Colliery in September 1961 and in his 100 games for the Park Avenue club gained a reputation as the best full-back in Division Four. Saints paid £15,000 for him in June 1965 but he found the transition to the First Division difficult and in five years at The Dell he never established a regular place. He joined Cardiff in July 1971 but made only six appearances for them before dropping out of League football.

JORDAN.J.
Born: Carluke, 15 December 1951.
48-12, Forward, 1984-7.
Joe Jordan joined Leeds from Morton late in 1970 and his 'battering-ram' style of forward play was an important part of Leeds' success in the early 1970s. Few centre-halves relished playing against the powerful Jordan who also took his share of knocks. In January 1978 he moved to Manchester United and continued to cause problems for First Division defences. He was regular choice as Scotland's centre-

KEEGAN.K.
Born: Armthorpe, 14 February 1951.
68-37, Forward, 1980-2.
Kevin Keegan made his League debut for Scunthorpe in 1968-9 and joined Liverpool in 1971 to become one of the most famous and admired footballers of the 1970s. Many club honours and 63 England caps, including the captaincy of his country, were the rewards for a player who, whilst not being the most naturally gifted footballer, worked hard to become arguably the most complete forward of recent decades. In 1977, Keegan moved to SV Hamburg and enjoyed three seasons there, winning the European Footballer of the Year award in 1978 and 1979, before McMenemy surprised the whole footballing world by tempting him to join Saints. Keegan's arrival set the town alight and although his first season was something of an anti-climax due to injuries, his second season at The Dell saw Saints head Division One for a long period. Voted PFA Player of the Season, Keegan then shocked Saints when he announced just a few days before the start of the 1982-3 season that he was to join Newcastle. Keegan became a folk hero at St James' Park, helping the club back to Division One. Before the new season began, however, Keegan decided to retire from football and he has since spent much of his time living in Spain.

forward and is the only Scot to have scored in three World Cup Finals. In 1980 he moved to AC Milan and then Verona, from where he joined Saints for £150,000 in the 1984 close season. His first season at The Dell was successful and the fans immediately appreciated Jordan's aggression and bravery. During 1985-6, however, he suffered a series of injuries and was transfer-listed in the 1986 close season. In February 1987 he signed for Bristol City, on a free-transfer, as player-coach under his old Leeds colleague Terry Cooper.

JUDD.M.
Born: Southampton, 18 June 1948.
14(1)-3, Forward, 1967-70.
Mike Judd was a promising forward who had the misfortune to suffer from a serious injury that prematurely ended his career. He still lives locally and works as a brewery representative.

JUDD.W.
Born: Salisbury, 25 October 1926.
34-13, Forward, 1950-53.
Walter Judd was a 'Bevin Boy' in a South Wales mine before signing for Saints in August 1949. After two seasons he snapped a leg ligament and the injury virtually ended the career of a forward who was showing great promise. Saints tried to claim insurance but due to the fact that Judd had bravely attempted a comeback in the reserves, the claim was rejected to leave both player and club reflecting on what might have been.

JURYEFF.I.
Born: Gosport, 24 November 1962.
0(2)-0, Forward, 1983-4.
Graduating through the youth and reserve teams, Ian Juryeff spent the summer of 1983 on loan to Swedish club, Munkters, before returning to The Dell to make two substitute appearances the following season. Loan spells at Mansfield and Reading were followed by a permanent transfer to Orient in February 1985.

KATALINIC.I.
Born: Yugoslavia, 17 May 1951.
48-0, Goalkeeper, 1979-82.
Yugoslavian international Ivan Katalinic joined Saints in February 1980 from Hajduk Split but never lived up to the high expectations of Southampton supporters. He could not settle in the English game and returned home in August 1983 to become player-coach with Hajduk Split.

KEEPING.A.
Born: Milford, 23 August 1902. Died: 1984.
265-10, Full-back, 1924-33.
Mike Keeping joined Saints in December 1920 when he was signed from Milford-on-Sea for £25. His initial contract promised him ten shillings a week to cover his travelling expenses. Keeping developed into a 'classic' left-back, being particularly skilful with left foot and very fast. He became Saints' captain and in 1926 toured Canada with the FA. In 1931 he represented the Football League and was expected to play for England that year, but appendicitis ruled him out for the rest of the 1931-2 season. His transfer to Fulham in 1933 was a massive disappointment to the fans. In 1949 he was coaching Real Madrid in Spain and he later managed sides in Denmark, Holland, France and North Africa. He returned to England and in 1959 managed Poole Town in the Southern League.

KELLY.G.
Born: Sunderland.
19-2, Forward, 1937-9.
Gerard Kelly came to The Dell via Huddersfield, Nelson, Charlton and Chester, impressing as a particularly fast right-winger. His career was terminated by the war.

KELLY.H.
Born: Belfast, 17 August 1919.
28-0, Goalkeeper, 1950-51.
Hugh Kelly's early sports days were spent in his native Ireland playing handball and Gaelic football. In 1939 he signed for Irish League club, Glenavon, as an inside-left but during the war converted to goalkeeper, playing for Belfast Celtic. In March 1949 he joined Fulham and when Ian Black left Saints for Fulham, Kelly made the reverse journey. Despite representing Northern Ireland twice whilst on Saints' books, Kelly was not an ideal replacement for Black and he moved to Exeter in June 1952, where he spent three seasons before signing for Weymouth in 1956.

KEMP.F.
Born: Italy, 27 February 1946.
58(3)-10, Midfield, 1965-70.
Fred Kemp had three games for Wolves before signing for Saints in June 1965. Short but powerfully built, Kemp had an exciting style that was typical of players from the land of his birth. Kemp's explosiveness, whilst appreciated by the supporters, did not endear him to the Southampton management and he was sold to Blackpool for £35,000 in November 1970. He joined Halifax a year later, played over 100 games for them and then finished his League career at Hereford in July 1974. In 1976 he was captaining Telford in non-League football.

KENNEDY.P.
Born: Dublin, 9 October 1934.
2-0, Full-back, 1959-60.
Pat Kennedy was one of the original 'Busby Babes' at Manchester United and played one League game before joining Blackburn in August 1956. A reserve at Ewood Park for three seasons, he signed for Saints in July 1959 but after only one season he was given a free transfer to Oldham.

KENNEDY.W.
Born: Ayr.
43-0, Centre-half, 1936-8.
Kennedy arrived from Crewe in the close season of 1936 to stay two seasons before moving to Colchester. In 1939 he moved back to his native Scotland to play for Hamilton Academical.

KIERNAN.F.
Born: Dublin, 7 July 1919.
132-0, Goalkeeper, 1951-6.
Fred Kiernan joined Saints in October 1951 from Shamrock Rovers and for the next four years competed with Christie for the right to be Southampton's first-choice goalkeeper. He won three international caps for the Republic of Ireland whilst on Saints' books.

KING.C.
Born: Plymouth, 1916.
93-2, Half-back, 1934-9.
Cyril King was capped at county level for Devon at the age of 15 and was in Saints' first team by the time he was 19. Appearing at either right-half or centre-half over five seasons, he had a spell at Darlington before returning to Plymouth at the outbreak of the war.

KING.E.S.
2-0, Full-back, 1925-7.
An *Evening Echo* employee before signing for Saints in 1924, King was a mainstay for the reserves over the next three years making over 100 appearances. Despite his obvious dedication he found it hard to break into the first team.

KINGDON.W.
Born: Worcester.
48-1, Half-back, 1936-8.
Kingdon signed for Aston Villa in 1926 as a junior and joined

Southampton ten years later. He was Saints captain for a brief period, leaving to become player-manager of Yeovil and then manager of Weymouth after the war.

KIRBY.G.
Born: Liverpool, 20 December 1933.
63-28, Forward, 1962-4.
Burly George Kirby was already a well-travelled player by the time he arrived at Southampton. Starting with Everton, he moved to  Sheffield Wednesday and then Plymouth. Arriving at The Dell in September 1962 he immediately formed a partnership with O'Brien that thrived on Kirby taking the knocks and O'Brien scoring the goals, although Kirby's goal-scoring record was itself by no means negligible. No centre-half could relax while Kirby was on the field and although he was at The Dell for only 18 months, his robust play left a host of memories. Joining Coventry in March 1964 for £12,000, he went on to play for Swansea, Walsall, New York Cosmos and finally Brentford late in 1968. He moved into management with Halifax and then took charge of Watford in 1972. He later returned to Halifax and also had a spell managing in Iceland.

KIRKMAN.N.
Born: Bolton, 6 June 1920.
20-0, Full-back, 1950-51.
As a schoolboy growing up in Bolton, Norman Kirkman played in the same side as Tommy Lawton. During the war he joined the RAF as a navigator and when in England he would guest for Burnley. After the war he had periods at Rochdale, Chesterfield and Leicester before signing for Saints in July 1950. In March 1952, with George Roughton leaving Exeter to be the Saints new manager, Kirkman moved to Devon to become Exeter's player-manager. He later managed Bradford.

KIRKUP.J.
Born: Sunderland, 17 December 1939.
169-3, Full-back, 1967-74.
England Youth international and capped at Under-23 level, Joe Kirkup found early success at West Ham, winning a European Cup-winners' Cup medal. He joined Chelsea in March 1966 and in February 1968 came to The Dell as part of the transfer deal that sent David Webb in the opposite direction. Dapper and the master of positional play, Kirkup's arrival had a considerable influence on Saints' defensive play and he is remembered as being the most 'gentlemanly' of all Southampton full-backs. In 1974 he left The Dell to try his luck playing in South Africa.

KITE.P.
Born: Bristol, 26 October 1962.
4-0, Goalkeeper, 1984-6.
England Youth international Phil Kite was signed from Bristol Rovers in the close season of 1984 for £50,000 as Shilton's understudy. He failed to impress and was loaned to Gillingham in January 1987 until the end of the season.

KNAPP.A.
Born: Newstead, 13 October 1936.
233-2, Centre-half, 1961-7.
Tony Knapp arrived at The Dell in August 1961 for a then Southampton record fee of £25,000, having had plenty of First Division experience with Leicester. He was a cool, commanding centre-half and he led Saints through the early 1960s to promotion in 1966. He came close to winning England honours and toured Hungary in 1960 but did not play. He left Saints for Coventry in 1967 and moved again in 1969-70 to play for Tranmere. He had a brief spell playing in Los Angeles before returning to England to become Poole Town's player-manager. A short spell as reserve manager at Norwich was followed by a move to Iceland in 1974, and he became

full-time manager of the Icelandic national team in 1976. In 1978 he was appointed manager of Norwegian side, Viking Stavanger, followed by stints at fellow Norwegian clubs, Fredrikstad and Vidar Stavanger. He has remained as part-time manager of Iceland's international side and more recently has taken charge of his fourth Norwegian club, Brann Bergen. Knapp still visits Southampton regularly and watches matches at The Dell whenever he can.

LAWRENCE.G.
Born: London, 14, September 1962.
65(15)-12, Forward, 1981-7.
George Lawrence was spotted by Saints' London scouting network and signed as an apprentice. Once described by McMenemy as 'Slinky', he joined Oxford United during 1982-3 after spending part of the previous season there on loan. He played a significant part in Oxford's success but was surprised when McMenemy bought him back to Southampton in December 1984. A strong runner, he looks awkward but sometimes uses this to his own advantage to baffle opposing defenders. In 1986-7 he gave some spectacular displays but failed to find consistency.

LE TISSIER.M.
Born: St Peter Port, Guernsey, 14 October 1968.
12(12)-6, Forward, 1986-7.
Matt Le Tissier was spotted by Southampton whilst on tour of Hampshire with the Guernsey Under-15 XI and quickly impressed by scoring 56 goals for Saints' youth team in 1985-6. He signed professional forms in the autumn of 1986 and came on as substitute at Norwich on 30 August, making his first full appearance at home to Spurs a few days later. Although only 18, Le Tissier's natural ball-skills and his ability to beat his man make him a delight to watch and in March 1987 he became the youngest hat-trick scorer in Saints' history with three goals against Leicester City.

LEWIS.T.
Born: Merthyr Tydfil, 20 October 1913.
43-12, Forward, 1946-8.
Tom Lewis joined Saints in July 1946 for a 'four-figure fee' from

Watford and had a reasonably successful first season that included a hat-trick against Bury in the third round of the FA Cup. After losing his goalscoring touch, during the 1947-8 season, he transferred to Brighton in the close season of 1948.

LIGHT.W.
Born: Southampton, 1913.
45-0, Goalkeeper, 1933-6.
Bill Light was a local amateur goalkeeper of great promise who joined Saints from local side, Harland and Wolf, in September 1933. Unfortunately he displaced a knee-cap at Hull after only a few appearances but this simply delayed a rise to being one of the country's top goalkeepers. In 1936, with the club experiencing financial problems, he was sold to West Bromwich for £2,000, a transfer that did not impress the fans. On retiring he became trainer to Colchester.

LINDSAY.H.
Born: Ickenham, 23 August 1938.
2-0, Forward, 1960-61.
Hugh Lindsay was an England Amateur international who played for the Saints in the 1960-61 season, his previous club being Kingstonian.

LITTLER.O.
Born: Manchester, 1909.
12-3, Forward, 1929-30.
Littler came to Saints from Rochdale where he had combined his football with working as a wages clerk at a colliery. He never settled in the South and transferred to Southport after a year, finishing his career at Barrow.

LIVESEY.C.
Born: London, 6 February 1938.
25-14, Forward, 1958-9.
Charles Livesey was on the books of Wolves as an amateur before he joined Saints in March 1956. When Derek Reeves broke a toe early on in 1958-59, Livesey was given a chance and responded by scoring six goals in two games before, strangely, he too broke a toe. When fit he continued to score goals and in February, Birmingham reputedly

offered £15,000 for him, only to be turned down by the player himself. The supporters wanted Livesey to stay but Ted Bates had other ideas and in May sold him to Chelsea, receiving Huxford in his place. Two seasons at Chelsea were followed by moves to Gillingham, Watford, Northampton and Brighton.

LOGAN.D.
Born: Aberdeen, 30 August 1933.
21-0, Half-back, 1955-8.
Doug Logan signed for Saints in January 1954 and left in 1958 to join Weymouth.

LONG.H.
Born: Southampton, 1914.
5-0, Forward, 1936-8.
Henry Long was a product of local junior football and played on the left wing.

LOVETT.G.
Born: Sheldon, 5 August 1947.
3-0, Midfield, 1971-2.
Graham Lovett was on the books of West Brom when he suffered a broken neck, the result of a motor accident. He came to Southampton on loan, in an effort to rebuild his career but the idea did not work out and his League career ended at The Dell.

LOWDER.T.
Born: Worksop, 17 October 1924.
39-2, Forward, 1949-53.
Tom Lowder began his career as an amateur with Crystal Palace before signing professional forms with Rotherham in the close season of 1947. After only eight games he dropped out of League football to play for Boston. Saints signed the 'tall and fast' Lowder in October 1949 for £1500 and for three seasons he competed with Ernie Jones for the left wing position. In May 1953 he finished his League career at Southend.

LUCKETT.W.
Born: St.Helens, 1908.
211-10, Half-back, 1927-37.

Luckett was signed from Skelmersdale in the close season of 1927, aged 19, and scored two goals on his debut against Nott County. Although he made the left-half position his speciality, he could play on the left wing when required. Upon retiring from League football he turned out for Cowes (IOW) and after the war returned to The Dell to help run the nursury teams as well as keeping a public house in the town.

McCALL.W.
Born: Scotland, 1900.
8-2, Forward, 1922-3.
McCall was signed from Wolves in February 1923 and featured on the wing eight times during 1922-3.

McCALLIOG.J.
Born: Glasgow, 23 September 1946.
70(2)-8, Midfield, 1974-7.
By the time Jim McCalliog arrived at The Dell in February 1975 he had already played for Chelsea, Sheffield Wednesday, Wolves and Manchester United, earning five Scottish caps along the way. He was a gifted ball-player who will be forever remembered as the architect of the winning goal in the 1976 FA Cup Final. He left Saints in September 1978 for Lincoln and had a spell playing in the United States for Chicago.

McCARTHY.R.
Born: Overton, 2 November 1948.
112-2, Full-back, 1967-75.

Bob McCarthy broke into the first team as a youngster who had worked his way through the apprentice ranks but he experienced a very up-and-down career with the club. Saints never had a settled defence in that period and McCarthy was often picked from the reserves in an effort to solve the defensive problems of the day. A dedicated player, he did his job uncomplainingly and provided useful cover over the eight years he spent at The Dell. In 1975 he drifted out of League football and joined Andover in 1977.

McCARTNEY.M.
Born: Edinburgh, 28 September 1954.
22-1, Defender, 1980-1.
Mike McCartney was a Scottish Schoolboy international who was signed from Carlisle in July 1980 for £50,000 and stayed a year before joining Plymouth for a similar amount. He rejoined Carlisle during 1982-3.

MacDONALD.E.
Born: Derby.
18-0, Forward, 1923-4.
MacDonald signed from non-League Burton Town in the close season of 1923 but disappointed and left to join Southend after only one season.

McDONALD.J.
Born: Maltby, 27 August 1921.
16-4, Forward, 1952-3.
Jock McDonald played for Wolves during the war, signing for Bournemouth in 1946. In 1948 he joined Fulham where he spent four seasons. A move to Saints in August 1952 did not really work out and nine months later he moved to Southend. In 1956 he was with Weymouth and played against Saints in the 1956-7 FA Cup.

MacDOUGALL.E.
Born: Inverness, 8 January 1947.
86-42, Forward, 1976-9.
Ted MacDougall was much travelled by the time he joined Saints in September 1976, having originally been on the books of Liverpool before playing with York, Bournemouth, Manchester United, West Ham and Norwich. He had won seven Scottish caps and at York, Bournemouth and Norwich had forged a great partnership with Boyer, which was renewed at The Dell. MacDougall's strength was inside the penalty area, whilst Boyer would be the one to make all the running. By the time The Dell fans saw him, MacDougall was in the 'autumn' of his career, yet he still scored goals at a rate of one every two games and played a significant part in Saints fighting their way back to Division One. In November 1978 he returned to Bournemouth and ended a long and successful League career at Blackpool. MacDougall has since given his services to a host of non-League clubs including Salisbury, Poole Town and Gosport Borough.

McGARRITY.T.W.
Born: Scotstoun, 24 November 1922.
5-1, Forward, 1952-3.
Tom McGarrity was signed from Morton in October 1952 and scored on his debut, against Hull. He was past his prime by the time he moved to The Dell and played only five games before retiring from League football.

McGIBBON.D.
Born: Southampton, 24 February 1919.
13-9, Forward, 1938-47.
The son of Charles McGibbon (1909-10), Doug McGibbon made his debut in the last League game of the 1938-9 season. Although he returned after the war to score nine goals in only 13 games, he will be best remembered for events that took place at The Dell on 29 December 1945, when Saints beat Chelsea 7-0. Not only did he score a goal, allegedly only 4.6 seconds after the start of the second half, but went on to score five more to give him a double hat-trick. In January 1947 he left for Fulham and played 43 times for them before having a couple of successful seasons with Bournemouth. A serious head injury cut short a career already disrupted by war.

McGOWAN.J.
Born: Cambuslang, 12 January 1924. Died: 1984.
78-9, Half-back, 1949-58.
Jimmy McGowan won Schoolboy international honours for Scotland in 1938 and signed on for his local side, Armadale Thistle, whilst continuing in his chosen trade of coach builder. He duly caught the eye of Celtic and spent two years with the club before moving to Dumbarton. He moved to Grimsby in July 1947 and experienced First Division football with them, before they were relegated. Sid Cann spent £8,000 to acquire his talents and McGowan spent nine seasons at The Dell without truly establishing himself in the first team. Scoring on his debut, he lacked nothing in the way of skill but suffered from a lung infection which sidelined him

for a whole season. In 1958 he moved on to play for Salisbury, before taking a pub in Southampton.

McGRATH J.
Born: Manchester, 23 August 1938.
167(1)-1, Centre-half, 1967-74.

John McGrath was an amateur with Bolton before making his League bow with Bury in 1956. Moving to Newcastle in February 1961 he gave the Tyneside club eight seasons' loyal service before Ted Bates paid £30,000 for him in February 1968. A tough, muscular centre-half, McGrath considerably strengthened Saints' defence and went on to represent the Football League whilst on Saints' books. Never one to shirk a tackle, McGrath cut an awesome sight for opposing centre-forwards, but whilst he was a fierce tackler on the pitch, he was a 'gentle giant' off it. He had three games for Brighton on loan before hanging up his boots to concentrate on coaching The Dell youngsters — a job he did very well. Inevitably he moved into management, first with Port Vale and then Chester and in the summer of 1986 he took charge at Preston North End who subsequently improved considerably under his leadership.

McGRATH.M.
Born: London, 15 October 1960.
0(1)-0, Midfield, 1979-80.
Although capped seven times for England Schoolboys, Martin McGrath failed to establish himself in Division One and moved to Bournemouth before dropping out of League football to play for Oxford City.

McGUIGAN.J.
Born: Motherwell, 29 October 1932.
33-8, Forward, 1963-5.
Jimmy McGuigan was signed from Scunthorpe in August 1963 for £10,000, having previously played for Southend and Newcastle. Scoring on his debut he was, however, into his 30s when he came to The Dell and Saints sold him for £6,000 to Swansea in March 1965.

McILWANE.J.
Born: Falkirk.
117-18, Centre-half, 1930-7.
Johnny McIlwane won distinction as a strong commanding centre-half, playing in Scotland for Falkirk before transferring to Portsmouth and playing in their 1929 FA Cup Final team against Bolton. He joined Saints in 1930 for the club record transfer fee of £2,650 — a record that was to last until after the war. Unfortunately his first season was marred by injury and when eventually he commanded a place in the team it was at centre-forward. In 1932, after a disagreement with Southampton, he was transfer listed at £2,500 but as there were no offers, he chose to move to Llanelli. After

helping Llanelli to win the Welsh League, McIlwane returned to The Dell with good relations being restored and became Saints' captain during the 1935-6 Golden Jubilee celebrations. During the disruptions at the club in 1936-7 he became assistant manager for a brief while and then left for Grimsby upon Tom Parker's appointment. He later became Grimsby's masseur and assistant manager.

MACKIE.J.
Born: Motherwell, 1 January 1894. Died: Chichester, 5 January 1959.
81-24, Forward, 1927-31.
Jerry Mackie joined Portsmouth from Blantyre Celtic in 1920 and became a popular player throughout the eight seasons he spent at Fratton. He transferred to Southampton in March 1928 as a replacement for the recently departed Rawlings and had the satisfaction of scoring a hat-trick on his home debut against Barnsley. He was regarded as a 'shrewd Scottish schemer' and together with another ex-Pompey star, Haines, forged a successful partnership. Retiring from football in 1931, Mackie became a local publican and died in 1959.

MACLAREN.D.
Born: Auchterader, 12 June 1934.
22-0, Goalkeeper, 1966-7.

Dave Maclaren will be remembered as the goalkeeper who conceded nine goals when playing for Wolves against Saints. Bates had obviously not been deterred by Maclaren's performance when Saints beat Wolves 9-3 and, when Forsyth broke his leg early in 1966-7, it was Maclaren who was bought as a replacement. His previous clubs had been Dundee, Leicester and Plymouth before joining Wolves in January 1965. Southampton was Maclaren's last League club. In 1970 he coached in Malaysia, after a spell at Worcester City.

McLAUGHLIN R.
Born: Belfast, 6 December 1925.
169-5, Half-back, 1953-9.
Bob McLaughlin played his early football for Northern Ireland side, Distillery, and then moved to Wales to play for Wrexham and Cardiff. Short but very tough, he joined Southampton in October 1953 as part of the deal that sent Dudley to Cardiff. He gave Saints six seasons of dedicated service. In the close season of 1959 he was given a free transfer and signed for non-League side, Headington, later turning out for Salisbury.

MacLEOD.A.
Born: Glasgow, 1 January 1951.
2(1)-0, Forward, 1973-4.
Ally MacLeod was signed from St Mirren in May 1973 to play two League matches before having a loan period at Huddersfield. He later returned to Scotland to enjoy a more successful career at Hibernian.

McMANUS.S.
Born: Falkirk, 19 March 1965.
2-1, Forward, 1985-6.
Signing for Saints in July 1984, Stuart McManus scored on his debut, at Loftus Road in 1986, but was given a free transfer in the close season.

MALLETT.J.
Born: Gateshead, 8 January 1916.
215-3, Half-back, 1946-53.

Joe Mallett signed for Charlton in 1935 and then QPR in 1939. In February 1947, Saints paid £5,000 for his services and the dependable, thoughtful Mallett, although aged 31 when he arrived, settled down to give Saints sterling service over the next six seasons. He became captain and when he made his last appearance in a red and white shirt on 29 April 1953, he was aged 37 years and 3 months. In July of 1953 he moved to Leyton Orient and later became a coach at Nottingham Forest. He maintains his links with Saints by acting as a scout in the Midlands.

MARTIN.E.
Born: Perth, 31 March 1946.
248-0, Goalkeeper, 1966-75.
Eric Martin was signed for £25,000 from Dunfermline in March 1967 by an anxious Ted Bates, who was seeking to put an end to Saints' goalkeeping problem that had started when Forsyth broke a leg. Martin made his debut away to Everton and the Saints won 1-0, a happy start to this popular goalkeeper's career with Southampton. There were to be times over the next nine years when he was dropped, but Martin always fought his way back into the first team and only Tommy Allen made more appearances as a Saints goalkeeper. At one stage his form between the posts nearly gained him Scottish international honours. In 1975 he moved to the United States to try his luck with Washington Diplomats.

MASKELL.C.
Born: Aldershot, 10 April 1968.
2(4)-1, Forward, 1985-7.
Craig Maskell had scored a lot of goals for the youth team and reserves when Chris Nicholl used him twice as a substitute in the tail end of 1985-6. He scored against Spurs when he came on in his second appearance. Joined Swindon Town on loan in March 1987.

MATSON.F.
Born: Reading.
2-0, Forward, 1931-2.
Outside-right Matson played only two games for Saints before leaving in 1932.

MATTHEWS.F.
Born: Barnsley.
19-6, Forward, 1925-7.
Matthews signed from Barnsley in 1925, spending two years at The Dell and leaving in 1927.

MAUGHAN.W.
Born: Southampton, 17 February 1939.
6-1, Forward, 1958-62.
Wesley Maughan was signed from Cowes (IOW) in May 1957 and spent five seasons at The Dell mainly in the reserves. He joined Reading in March 1962.

MAYER.W.
Born: Stoke.
14-0, Forward, 1936-8.
Wilf Mayer was signed by Tom Parker from Stoke City in March 1937 and spent most of the time up to the war playing in the reserves.

MELIA.J.
Born: Liverpool, 1 November 1937.
139-11, Midfield, 1964-9.

Jimmy Melia won fame and England international honours playing for Liverpool between 1955 and 1963. He had a brief spell at Wolves before Ted Bates splashed out £30,000, a club record at the time, to sign him in November 1964. He was an instigator of shrewd moves and a lovely passer of the ball, although in his later years at The Dell the crowd would barrack him for his lack of pace. He played a significant part in the Saints' promotion season of 1965-6 and in the First Division his vast experience helped Saints avoid relegation. Four years after arriving at The Dell, he moved to Aldershot and finished his League career at Crewe. In later years Melia became a rather flamboyant manager at Brighton, taking them to the 1983 FA Cup Final. Losing his job at Brighton he took up a manager's post in Portugal. Was briefly Stockport's manager at the start of the 1986-7 season.

MESTON.S.
Born: Southampton, 1902. Died: Woolston, October 1953.
10-2, Forward, 1921-6.
Meston was the son of S.Meston (1895-1906), the famous Saints half-back, and was an immensely promising player who looked to have a fine career in front of him until he was cruelly struck by two serious injuries. Having recovered from a broken leg, Meston broke the same leg again in October 1926. After this latest blow he struggled to regain fitness and joined Gillingham. He moved to Everton in 1927 but played only one League game for them before ending his career at Tranmere.

MIDDLETON.S.
Born: Portsmouth, 28 August 1953.
24-0, Goalkeeper, 1973-77.
Steve Middleton signed for Saints in July 1970 as an aspiring young goalkeeper but never managed to win a permanent first-team place. After playing ten games on loan to Torquay he signed for Portsmouth and played 26 games for them before leaving League football.

MILLS.M.
Born: Godalming, 4 January 1949.
103-3, Full-back, 1982-5.
Mick Mills was a young Portsmouth apprentice who was released in 1965 when Pompey abandoned their reserve team. Ipswich snapped up the young Mills and Portsmouth lost a player who went on to win over 40 England caps. Mills stayed at Ipswich for 17 years, winning many of the game's top honours, until McMenemy bought him for £50,000 during 1982-3. A classy full-back, Mills quickly fitted into his new club and the fans were quick to praise his flair and

enthusiasm. Mills was a fine example both on and off the pitch and when he moved to Stoke as player-manager in the close season of 1985, he left a huge gap in Saints' defence.

MILLS.S.
Born: Portsmouth, 9 December 1953.
57(4)-0, Full-back, 1972-7.
Steve Mills was an extremely talented full-back who, having won an England Under-23 cap, looked to have a long and distinguished career in the game. Then a bad car accident ended all hopes of further League football and although Mills tried a comeback, the injury sustained in the accident was serious enough to force his premature retirement. He found employment firstly as a bookmaker and later a a newsagent.

MITCHELL.J.D.
Born: Titchfield, 19 January 1928.
7-0, Forward, 1950-51
John Mitchell was discovered playing junior football in Gosport and, despite a promising home debut against Blackburn, failed to make the grade in League football. He turned down a move to Barnsley and left the game to pursue a career in accountancy.

MITTON.J.
8-0, Half-back, 1927-8.
Mitton was signed from Wolves in 1927 having previously played for Sunderland, and was released in the close season of 1927-8.

MOLLOY.W.
Born: Coventry, 28 August 1929.
1-0, Half-back, 1949-50.
Bill Molloy signed for Saints in October 1949 upon leaving the army, but was released to non-League side, Lockheed, in the close season of 1950. In November of the same year Newport County signed him and he played three games for the Welsh side.

MONTGOMERY.J.
Born: Sunderland, 9 October 1943.
5-0, Goalkeeper, 1976-7.
Jim Montgomery, the noted Sunderland goalkeeper and one of the stars of the 1973 FA Cup Final, spent a brief period at The Dell on loan, playing five games before eventually signing for Birmingham on a permanent basis.

MOORHEAD.G.
Born: Lurgan, Northern Ireland.
9-0, Centre-half, 1920-21.
George Moorhead joined Saints in 1920 from the Army, but due to a technical infringement when he was signed, he had his registration cancelled by the FA and he disappeared from League football. Later had a successful career in Northern Ireland football.

MORAN.S.
Born: Croydon, 10 January 1961.
173(7)-78, Forward, 1979-86.

Steve Moran was spotted by McMenemy whilst the manager was watching local junior football one Sunday morning. He offered the schoolboy a new pair of boots if he scored a hat-trick in the second half — and Moran duly obliged. He signed professional forms with Saints in August 1979, after finishing his schooling, and that season made one appearance as substitute against Manchester City and scored. From then, Moran's career really took off as he showed an uncanny knack of being in the right place to score some priceless opportunist goals. He was fortunate to have Keegan and Channon to play alongside but when they left The Dell, Moran found scoring goals more difficult. A bad back injury suffered during 1981-2 also hampered him. Moran, an England Under-21 player, might have been called up for the full England side but a run of injuries during 1985-6 caused him to lose form. He was transferred, rather suddenly, to Leicester for £300,000 in September 1986 and found himself in a side struggling to avoid relegation and was again troubled by injury.

MULGREW.T.
Born: Motherwell, 13 April 1929.
293-90, Forward, 1954-62.

Tommy Mulgrew started his League career in Scotland with Morton before travelling south to join Northampton in July 1949. He moved to Newcastle in October 1952 but failed to impress and joined Saints at the same time as Foulkes in July 1954. It took him only 15 seconds to repay some of his £7,000 fee by scoring at home to Brentford in his first game. Later in the season he became the first Southampton player for 22 years to be sent off, at home to Coventry. Mulgrew's career at The Dell spanned eight seasons and his goalscoring exploits made him popular with The Dell crowd. In August 1962, Mulgrew, after a disagreement over terms, signed for Aldershot and played over 100 League games for them. He later had a spell at Andover FC before retiring from football to live in Northampton.

MURPHY.W.
Born: St.Helens.
74-9, Forward, 1926-9.
'Spud' Murphy signed for Manchester City during World War One and after scoring 30 goals in 209 League appearances for City he joined Southampton in the close season of 1926. Described at the time as 'cute, quick and clever', he gave the Saints three high-class seasons of fine left-wing play. In 1929 Murphy joined Oldham.

NEAL.R.
Born: Fence, 14 January 1908.
170-17, Forward, 1931-7.
Dick Neal was signed from Derby County in February 1932. He had previously played on the right wing for Blackpool and it was in that position that he had some of his finest games for the Saints. He left during the 1936-7 season to play for Bristol City. In 1987 he was living in Yorkshire.

NEVILLE.S.
Born: London, 18 September 1957.
5(1)-1, Forward, 1977-8.
Steve Neville was discovered by the Saints' London scouting network and played five games during 1977-8. Fast and direct, he did not quite have the talent for the top division but since joining Exeter in 1978 he has fared well, having two seasons at Sheffield United and joining Bristol City in 1985.

NICHOLL.C.
Born: Wilmslow, 12 October 1946.
228-8, Half-back, 1977-83.
Chris Nicholl was originally on the books of Burnley between 1964 and 1966 but did not make their first team and drifted into non-League football with Witton Albion. Halifax rescued his League

career in 1968-9 and from there the tall, commanding centre-half joined Luton where his career began to blossom. In the spring of 1972 he joined Aston Villa and was soon Northern Ireland's regular centre-half, eventually winning 51 caps. Whilst at Villa he had the remarkable distinction of scoring all four goals in a 2-2 draw with Arsenal — a feat never performed before or since. Despite being a big man he was surprisingly agile and possessed an assured air that gave a cultured look about his play. When McMenemy signed him in the summer of 1977 for £80,000, he arrived at The Dell with the proud boast that every side he had joined had won immediate promotion and sure enough, Nicholl helped Saints regain their First Division place that very season. During the next six seasons Nicholl gave Saints reliable defensive experience and there were many who were sorry to see him leave for Grimsby in the close season of 1983. (See also *Saints Managers*).

NIXON.E.
Born: Manchester, 4 October 1962.
4-0, Goalkeeper, 1986-7.
When Shilton and Flowers both suffered injuries in December 1986, Chris Nicholl was fortunate to secure the loan of Manchester City's Eric Nixon who performed admirably in his four games for Saints.

OAKLEY.R.
Born: Tipton, 5 January 1928.
6-0, Full-back, 1953-6.
Roy Oakley spent six years at The Dell, playing mainly in the reserves after being signed from Guernsey in May 1950 as a part-time professional. He signed full-time forms in August 1951 and left in 1956 for Bath City.

O'BRIEN.G.
Born: Dunfermline, 22 November 1935.
244-154, Forward, 1959-66.
George O'Brien started his League career at Leeds in March 1957 before signing for Saints in July 1959 for a fee of £10,000. He became a lethal finisher and in his first season Saints won the Division Three South Championship, with O'Brien and Reeves notching up 62 goals between them. On song, he had a spark of genius about him that set him apart from other forwards. If he had a fault it would be a lack of consistency but he more than made up for this with his shooting powers, and, playing alongside Paine, Sydenham,

Reeves, Mulgrew, Kirby, and later Chivers, he was the perfect inside-right. His scoring rate is second only to Wayman's, and only Paine, Channon and Rawlings have scored more League goals for the club. It was a shame that age was against him when Saints finally gained promotion to Division One. He moved to Orient in March 1966, as Webb came to The Dell, and later the same year he finished his career at Aldershot. He is now a publican in Southampton.

O'BRIEN.G.
Born: Glasgow, 10 November 1949.
66-2(12), Midfield, 1969-76.
When Ted Bates signed Gerry O'Brien from Clydebank in February 1969, the £22,000 fee was a record for a player from the Scottish Second Division. The little Scotsman was a clever, skilful player who at times looked capable of turning a game completely, although his slight build appeared to handicap him. O'Brien remained at the club for seven years, having a brief spell in 1974 on loan to Bristol Rovers. In March 1976 he signed for Swindon and later returned to his first club, Clydebank, only to have his career ended by a hip injury.

O'GRADY.H.
Born: Tunstall, 16 March 1907.
7-2, Forward, 1931-2.
Harry O'Grady was signed in the close season of 1931 from Port Vale and played seven games before moving to Leeds United in August 1932. In May 1933 he signed for Burnley and later played for Bury, Millwall, Carlisle, Accrington Stanley and, finally, non-League Tunbridge Wells Rangers.

O'NEIL.B.
Born: Bedlington, 4 January 1944.
148(1)-16, Midfield, 1970-75.

Brian O'Neil came from a long line of talented Burnley players in the 1960s and Saints splashed out a record £75,000 for his signature in the close season of 1970. Tigerish in his tackling, he was an inspiration in midfield and only a bad disciplinary record stood between him and full England honours. At one stage he was suspended for nine weeks and Saints could ill afford to lose a man of his driving enthusiasm. In October 1974 he left to spend two seasons on the books of Huddersfield and the fans were sorry to see the player who always seemed to have his socks rolled down and his shirt hanging out, leave The Dell.

OSBORNE.F.
Born: Wynberg, South Africa, 14 October 1896.
17-0, Forward, 1931-3.
Frank Osborne, originally played for Bromley, a Kent amateur side, before signing professional forms at Fulham. Tottenham paid a big fee for his services and whilst at Spurs he was capped for England. Arriving at The Dell in the twilight of his career, in 1931, he played 17 games before retiring in 1933. After the war he became involved with Fulham, both as a manager and director.

OSGOOD.P.
Born: Windsor, 20 February 1947.
122(4)-28, Forward, 1973-8.
Peter Osgood signed for Chelsea in September 1964 and his tremendous skills soon made him the idol of Stamford Bridge. Capped four times for England, Osgood played his part in an exciting Chelsea side that made almost as many headlines off the pitch as they did on it. Eventually, after a series of disagreements with the management, he was transfer-listed but Southampton, who were fighting an increasingly desperate battle against relegation, were one of the last clubs thought to be interested. Yet Saints shocked the fans by paying a club record of £275,000 for Osgood, who was to be the first of a long line of 'super stars' brought to The Dell by the ambitious McMenemy. Whilst initially adding thousands to the

home 'gates', Osgood could not prevent Saints' slide into the Second Division and, despite Osgood displaying his vast array of talents in the unfamiliar surrounds of Division Two, Saints made no real impression on the promotion race. Always a delight to watch, Osgood's unconventional approach perhaps cost him further successes, although his time with Saints did earn him his second FA Cup winners' medal. He had a loan spell at Norwich before Saints sold him to Philadelphia Fury in 1977-8 for £50,000. He returned to Chelsea in December 1978 to finish his League career and played ten games. Osgood later played for several non-League clubs and more recently has been coaching in the Far East and in Gambia. In June 1986 he became Portsmouth's youth team coach.

OSMAN.H.J.
Born: Alton, 1911.
70-31, Forward, 1937-9.
Harry Osman was playing for non-League Poole when he was signed by Plymouth, but he struggled to find form with the Devon club and Saints signed him on a free transfer in 1937. Playing on the left wing during 1937-8, he was an immediate success, scoring 22 goals, a record for a Saints' left-winger. His impact was such that Birmingham reputedly offered £7,000 for him. The 1938-9 season was not so successful and Saints eventually sold him to Millwall for £2,000. After the war he played for Bristol City and in the 1950s became manager of Winchester, signing the young Terry Paine and recommending him to Southampton for which the club will be forever grateful.

PAGE.J.
Born: Frimley, 21 October 1934.
190-24, Half-back, 1952-61.
John Page graduated through the junior teams and became known as a solid effective centre-half. Along with Connor and Huxford he formed part of the reliable half-back line which performed consistently in the season that Saints won the Third Division title. As well as being a dependable half-back, Page was a reliable penalty taker. His career at The Dell ended with the arrival of Tony Knapp and it was strange that a man of his abilities could not find himself another League club.

PAINE.T. MBE
Born: Winchester, 23 March 1939.
709(4)-160, Forward, 1956-74.
Terry Paine played his early football for his local club, Winchester, whose manager was former Saints player, Harry Osman. He alerted

Ted Bates to Paine's potential and in August 1956, the *Football Echo* reported: 'Terry Paine, a Winchester City forward, in whom Arsenal were interested, has been added to the playing staff list.' Paine had recently scored twice in a trial match for Arsenal but it was Southampton who snapped him up. In February 1957, Saints signed Paine as a full-timer and the player appeared in a reserve game against Bristol Rovers. The following month he made his League debut at home to Brentford, just week a before his 18th birthday. Paine did not score in the 3-3 draw but the crowd were impressed by his ball-juggling skills, pace and ability to use either foot. The *Echo* commented: 'Generally he looks as if he is going to make the grade.' The writer's reticence was understandable, for Saints had been languishing in the Third Division for some seasons and the game was full of players who had promised much but delivered little. Paine, though, was not to disappoint and scored in his next game, against Aldershot on his 18th birthday. By the end of the season he had become a virtual regular, switching from left wing to right wing. Saints' fortunes took an upward swing and Paine played a significant part with his dashing style. Over the next decade and a half, a host of forwards were to benefit from his skills, particularly his crossing and passing ability. Saints marched back to Division Two in 1960 and Paine was recognised at England Under-23 level. In 1963 he won his first full cap and later that year scored a hat-trick at Wembley against Northern Ireland to become the first outside-right to score three goals for England since Stanley Matthews in 1937. Furthermore, no forward wearing the no.7 shirt had ever scored a hat-trick at Wembley. Paine featured in England manager Alf Ramsey's plans and he was one of the 22-man squad for the 1966 World Cup. He played in only one match, though, against Mexico and was injured in his 19th and, as it turned out, last international. Ramsey, of course, had now found little use for 'old-fashioned' wingers. Saints prepared to face the challenge of First Division football and it was ironic that all Paine's England caps were to be won whilst he was a Second Division player. Ted Bates had just brought Ron Davies to The Dell and over the next few seasons, Paine and the big Welshman were a deadly combination with Paine providing an endless stream of pin-point crosses for the tall striker. As age crept up on him, Paine began

to play in midfield, using his passing skills to crack opposing defences, and he was so successful in his new role that there was a campaign to have him recalled to the England team. Over a long career Paine remained remarkably free from injury and eventually broke both club appearances and goalscoring records for Saints. An era ended when Bates retired from management in 1973 and Paine moved to Hereford in the summer of 1974 to make a further 106 appearances and so play more League games than any other player. He was awarded the MBE for his services to football and when he hung up his boots, he moved into management with non-League club, Cheltenham Town. Recently has been living and coaching in Johannesburg. He made a special trip to Southampton in November 1985 to take part in Saints' Centenary celebrations, making a sentimental appearance on the pitch prior to the game against Everton.

PARKER.P.
Born: Bow, Devon, 15 July 1929.
132-0, Centre-half, 1951-9.
Sid Cann discovered Pat Parker when his local club Newton Abbot played Saints in a friendly in August 1951. He was a useful acquisition for Saints' squad and although he had the misfortune to break a leg in April 1952, he gave Southampton sterling service. Saints were Parker's only League club and when he left The Dell in 1959 he signed for Poole, later becoming player-manager of Cowes.

PARKIN.R.
Born: Crook, County Durham.
57-10, Forward, 1937-9.
Ray Parkin played for Arsenal as a 17-year-old but never quite made it at Highbury and had a spell at Middlesbrough before joining Saints in September 1937 for £1,500. He scored on his debut, against West Ham, which happened to be Saints' first goal in 524 minutes of football. Like so many other players of his generation, his career was swallowed up by the outbreak of war.

PATON.D.
Born: Saltcoats, 13 December 1943.
13-0 Centre-half, 1963-8.
Dave Paton was a tall, commanding centre-half who was signed as cover for Tony Knapp in July 1963 from St Mirren. He spent five seasons at The Dell, playing mainly in the reserves before transferring to Aldershot, and regular first-team football, in November 1969.

PATRICK.R.
Born: Overseal, Burton-upon-Trent, 4 December 1935.
31-0, Full-back, 1961-3.
Roy Patrick made his League debut for Derby County when he was only 16. He moved to Nottingham Forest in May 1959 and was recommended to Saints by Joe Mallett. Patrick joined Southampton in June 1961 but failed to make a lasting impression and signed for Exeter in March 1963. In 1987 he was working for Rolls-Royce in Derby.

PEACH.D.
Born: Bedford, 21 January 1951.
221(3)-34, Full-back, 1973-80.

David Peach had spent five years on the books of Gillingham, by the time he became McMenemy's first signing in January 1974. He started his career at The Dell in midfield but quickly switched to left-back where he was both imaginative and quick when moving up into attack. He became Saints' regular penalty-taker and had a high success rate, notably the second goal against Crystal Palace in the FA Cup semi-final. An FA Cup winners' medal in 1976 was followed by international recognition at England Under-21 and 'B' levels and he also toured South America as Trevor Cherry's deputy with the full England squad in June 1977. He left Saints in March 1980 to join Swindon for £150,000, and later had a spell at Orient where he became the only player in the Football League to have played on every League ground. In 1987 he was living in the New Forest, running his own building and decorating business and was player-manager of Wellworthy, a local Hampshire side.

PEARSON.H.
Born: Brierley Hill.
8-4, Forward, 1923-4.
Centre-forward Harold Pearson joined Saints in the close season of 1923 and played eight games before moving to Coventry.

PENK.H.
Born: Wigan, 19 July 1934.
52-6, Forward, 1960-64.
Harry Penk had played for non-League Wigan when he joined Portsmouth in September 1955. After only one season at Fratton, he moved to Plymouth and from there joined Saints in July 1960 for £1,500. In 1964 he dropped out of League football and signed for Basingstoke.

PERFECT.F.
Born: Gorleston, 9 March 1915. Died: 17 July 1977.
15-0, Full-back, 1938-9.
Frank Perfect came to Saints from Tranmere Rovers aged 23, having previously played for Mansfield and Wolves. As he signed early in 1939 he was given little chance to impress before the outbreak of war and the suspension of League football.

PETRIE.C.
24-7, Forward, 1927-9.
Petrie joined Saints from Swindon in 1927, having previously been on the books of Stalybridge Celtic. He lacked consistency and returned to Stalybridge in the close season of 1929.

PHILLIPSON-MASTERS.F.
Born: Bournemouth, 14 November 1955.
9-0, Half-back, 1976-8.
Phillipson-Masters had an unusual start to his footballing career, as he was originally an apprentice goalkeeper who was given a free transfer from The Dell only to be taken on again as a centre-half. He made nine first-team appearances in his new outfield role, but was loaned to Exeter, Bournemouth and Luton before finally transferring to Plymouth in the close season of 1979. A regular at Plymouth for three years, he moved to Bristol City in 1982-3. More recently he has played for Yeovil Town.

PICKERING.M.
Born: Huddersfield, 29 September 1956.
44-0, Defender, 1977-9.
Mike Pickering had played exactly 100 League games for Barnsley when he was transferred to Saints for £35,000 in the summer of 1977. Missing only one game in the subsequent season, in which Saints regained First Division status, Pickering looked to have a rosy future at The Dell, but McMenemy had other ideas and after only three games in the top flight he sold the surprised Pickering to Sheffield Wednesday. Pickering later had loan spells at Norwich, Bradford City and his old club, Barnsley, before joining Rotherham in 1983-4.

POLLARD.W.
Born: Burnley, 26 September 1906. Died: 1945.
23-3, Forward, 1934-6.
Walter Pollard joined Saints during 1934-5, listing Burnley and West Ham amongst his previous League clubs. Having also spent a year playing for Soucaux in France, he added a touch of experience to Saints' forward line, before moving to Brighton in the close season of 1935.

PRATT.W.
Born: Southampton, 1 March 1960.
1-0, Midfield, 1980-81.
Wayne Pratt was a young midfield player who, after one appearance for the Saints, had spells on the books of Waterlooville, Reading and Gosport.

PRICE.C.
59-16, Forward, 1923-6.
Cliff Price arrived from Halifax Town in December 1923 and was

described as 'a studious inside-left'. For a short period he struck up a promising partnership with Carr on the left-hand side but after three seasons moved to Nottingham Forest.

PRICE.F.T.
Born: Ibstock.
9-0, Forward, 1924-5.
Price was signed in the close season of 1924 from Leicester City and featured nine times on the left wing before moving to Wolves in the summer of 1925.

PRING.D.
Born: Newport, 8 November 1940.
4-0, Forward, 1958-9.
Dennis Pring was a young forward who played only four games before dropping out of League football. He had a more successful brother, Keith, who played for Rotherham, Newport, Notts County and Southport.

PUCKETT.D.
Born: Southampton, 29 October 1961.
51(43)-14, Forward, 1981-6.
Dave Puckett signed professional forms for Saints in October 1978 but spent a lot of his career sitting on the substitute's bench. Indeed, no other player has made more substitute appearances for Southampton. A forward with pace, he sometimes lacked the confidence to take on defenders and never had a prolonged run in the first team. He joined Bournemouth in the close season of 1986 but sustained a bad ligament injury that sidelined him for the second half of the season.

PURVES.C.
Born: High Spen, 17 February 1921.
30-2, Forward, 1951-4.
Charles Purves started his League career with Charlton at the relatively late age of 25, moving to Southampton in June 1951. He spent three years at The Dell before moving into non-League football with Sittingbourne, Margate, Basingstoke and Dorchester.

RAMSEY.Sir A.
Born: Dagenham, 22 January 1920.
90-8, Full-back, 1946-8.

Alf Ramsey had been invited to sign amateur forms for Portsmouth before the war, but had then been overlooked by the Fratton Park club and was therefore free to sign for Saints during 1943-4. He was stationed with the army near Southampton and had impressed Mr Sarjantson, Saints' secretary, when he played in a trial game. Originally a centre-half and even an occasional centre-forward, Ramsey burst into prominence when Bill Ellerington went down with pneumonia in January 1948. Ramsey filled the right-back position so effectively that he went on to be capped by England. A great strategist and reader of the game, Ramsey was injured in a friendly at Plymouth in 1949 and, when fit, found it hard to oust Ellerington from the team. He asked for a transfer and joined Spurs in the close season of 1949, with Ernie Jones making the opposite journey. Ramsey had a successful First Division career with Tottenham but he will be best remembered as the manager who guided England to World Cup success in 1966, an achievement which earned him a knighthood. In the mid-1970s, however, Ramsey was sacked following England's failure to qualify for the 1974 World Cup.

READER.G.
Born: Nuneaton, November 1896. Died: Southampton, July 1978.
3-0, Full-back, 1920-21.
George Reader did not make his mark as a player with Saints but returned to The Dell to become their much-respected chairman. He had arrived from Exeter in 1920 but moved to Cowes in 1921 and later became a top-class referee, officiating in over 20 internationals, (the first in February 1943) and the 1950 World Cup Final. He returned to Southampton to take up a teaching appointment and became the club's chairman in November 1963. He lived long enough to see Saints win the FA Cup for the first time, in 1976 and regain their First Division status in 1978.

REEVES.D.
Born: Bournemouth, 27 August 1934.
273-145, Forward, 1954-63.
Derek Reeves was discovered playing for Bournemouth Gasworks and signed for Saints in December 1954, to become one of their greatest post war centre-forwards. He was a quick, 'tearaway' player and an effective header of the ball who had an eye for the half chance. Whilst it was George Roughton who signed Reeves, it was Bates who nurtured the young Bournemouth man into a deadly scorer. In 1959-60, Reeves scored 39 League goals, a Saints' record that still stands. Later, in a memorable League Cup tie against Leeds, he scored all Saints' goals

in a 5-4 victory. In November 1962 he joined Bournemouth for £8,000 and remained there for the rest of his League career. He later found employment in the building trade.

REYNOLDS.R.
Born: Haslemere, 2 June 1928.
90-0, Goalkeeper, 1959-64.
Ron Reynolds was on Aldershot's books at the end of the war and in July 1950 signed for Spurs. He joined Saints in March 1960, for £10,000, and his experience was to come to the rescue over the next four seasons. During 1963-4 he sustained a bad injury and was forced to retire from the game. Reynolds was one of the few professional footballers known to wear contact lenses.

ROBERTS.A.
Born: Darfield, Yorks, January 1904.
156-0, Full-back, 1930-38.
Roberts came to Saints in 1930 from non-League Ardsley, but spent his first few seasons acting as Keeping's understudy. When Keeping left the club, Roberts enjoyed a consistent run in the first team but left in 1938 to join Swansea.

ROBINSON.E.
Born: Hindley.
1-0, Full-back, 1927-8.
A reserve full-back, Robinson signed from Chorley and made one

appearance in three years at The Dell before moving to Southport in the close season of 1930.

ROCHFORD.W.
Born: Newhouse, 23 May 1913, Died: March 1984.
128-8, Full-back, 1946-50.

Bill Rochford emerged from the North East to spend 14 years at Portsmouth, leading them to victory in the 1939 FA Cup Final. Burly and hard-tackling, Rochford moved to The Dell in July 1946 for £550 and slotted into the Southampton success story of the immediate post-war years. An automatic choice for captain, Rochford was a driving influence on the less experienced players, notably a young Alf Ramsey who later acknowledged the influence of Rochford. In 1949 he became Saints' player-coach and, the following year, the club's full-time coach for a brief period. In July 1950 Rochford signed for Colchester and later retired to the Gateshead area to take up farming.

RODRIGUES.P.
Born: Cardiff, 21 January 1944.
59-3, Full-back, 1975-7.
When Welsh international Peter Rodrigues was given a free transfer to Southampton in the close season of 1975, from Sheffield Wednesday, he probably felt that he had achieved all he could in the game. Yet just nine months later he captained Saints to an FA Cup Final victory. A fast, attacking full-back, he started his career with his native Cardiff City in 1961 and enjoyed a spell at Leicester, playing for them in the 1969 FA Cup Final before moving to Wednesday in October 1970. Along the way he had won 40 caps and yet his proudest moment was

probably when he collected the FA Cup, a feat that had eluded so many famous Southampton captains of earlier days. Retiring from the game in 1977, he took ownership of a pub just outside Southampton.

ROFE.D.
Born: Fulham, 1 June 1950.
18(2)-0, Full-back, 1982-4.
England Under-23 international Dennis Rofe signed on a free transfer from Chelsea, having enjoyed lengthy spells at Leicester and Orient. Bought mainly as cover, he stayed at The Dell upon retiring and spent two years doing invaluable work with the reserves before being appointed first-team trainer in February 1987.

ROGERS.A.
Born: Chatteris, 1 December 1956.
0(5)-0, Forward, 1979-82.
Andy Rogers had a brief spell with Peterborough before dropping out of League football to play for Hampton. Southampton gave him another chance of making the grade but, although he showed some initial promise, he found stiff competition for forward places at The Dell and moved to Plymouth for £50,000. He helped Plymouth to the FA Cup semi-finals in 1983 before joining Reading and then Southend.

ROLES.A.
Born: Southampton, 29 September 1921.
1-0, Full-back, 1948-9.
Although Albie Roles played only one League match for Saints, he was a stalwart for them in the war years. Rochford's arrival limited his chances and he later became player-manager of Cowes.

ROPER.D.
Born: Botley, 14 December 1922.
120-40, Forward, 1946-7, 1956-8.
Don Roper was spotted by Toby Keleher during the early days of the war and by the resumption of normal League football had earned such a reputation as a dashing, two-footed winger that virtually all the big clubs were chasing his services. Saints gave up trying to hold on to him and in July 1947 he moved to Arsenal in an exchange deal which brought George Curtis and Tom Rudkin to The Dell. Roper was valued at £17,000 and after a memorable career at Arsenal spanning nearly 300 League games, he re-signed for Southampton in 1956. The fans welcomed 'the Don' back and he repaid them with two good seasons. A fine sportsman, Roper played cricket for Hampshire and when he gave up League football he turned out for Weymouth.

ROWE.D.
Born: Nottingham.
2-1, Forward, 1934-5.
Rowe was a left winger who was signed during 1934-5 from Lincoln City.

ROWLEY.R.
Born: Enniskillen, 14 January 1904. Died: Southampton, April 1984.
104-52, Forward, 1926-30.

Dick Rowley arrived at The Dell as an amateur and was described at the time as 'tall and bony'. He had previously played for Andover, Swindon and Corinthian Casuals. An excellent all-round sportsman, he quickly rose to prominence at The Dell, scoring five goals in the 1926-7 FA Cup run. Such goal-scoring attracted the attention of the glamour clubs and during the 1929-30 season he scored an impressive 25 goals in only 25 games to tempt Tottenham to step in with an irresistible offer of £3,750 for his services. Rowley won six caps for Northern Ireland, four of them whilst a Saints' player, and eventually wound up his career with Preston. He maintained his sporting links by becoming secretary to the Hampshire CCC Supporters Club.

RUDDY.T.
Born: Stockton.
24-3, Forward, 1932-4.
Tom Ruddy joined Derby County from Darlington in May 1928 and scored nine goals in 22 League games for the Rams before moving to Chesterfield in December 1931. Southampton signed him in 1932 but he failed to establish himself in the first team and left in 1934.

RUDKIN T.
Born: Peterborough, 17 June 1919.
9-0, Forward, 1947-9.
Tom Rudkin moved to Southampton from Arsenal with George Curtis as part of deal which took Don Roper to Highbury. Rudkin was a valued at £3,000 and, not meeting with the same success as Curtis, he signed for Bristol City in May 1949.

SALTER J.M.
Born: Southampton, 1898. Died: Southampton, June 1982.
1-0, Forward, 1923-4.
Salter was spotted playing for his local side, Bitterne Sports, and signed for Saints in 1923. After only one outing he returned to the local scene to play for the Southampton Civil Service.

SAUL.F.
Born: Canvey Island, 23 August 1943.
49(3)-2, Forward, 1967-70.
Frank Saul had spent six seasons at Spurs and scored in their 1967 FA Cup Final win against Chelsea. An England Youth international, he was a capable forward and joined Southampton as part of the Martin Chivers transfer in January 1968. He struggled to settle with Saints and the crowd were slow to realise that it was unfair to expect him to replace Chivers. In May 1970 he moved to QPR and in March 1972 joined Millwall.

SCOTT.A.
Born: Sunderland, 19 February 1921.
45-9, Forward, 1947-50.
Auggie Scott was discovered by a Luton Town scout whilst playing for Hylton Colliery. He moved to The Dell in July 1947 without having played in Luton's first team. He never found the necessary consistency and moved to Colchester in August 1951 where he spent the next three seasons.

SCOTT.J.
Born: Barnsley, 4 December 1905. Died: 9 March 1976.
1-0, Forward, 1937-8.
When Tom Parker left Norwich City to take over managerless Southampton in 1937, Scott came with him to run Saints 'A' team. An injury crisis saw him play one game in the first team. One of the fittest players of his day, he originally played Rugby League for Featherstone Rovers, joining Norwich as a centre-half in 1931 and rendering the Canaries five years' solid service.

SCRIVEN.H.
Born: Andover, February 1908.
225-0, Goalkeeper, 1930-7.
Bert Scriven joined Saints in 1930 after attracting attention with his performances for local side, Totton. Over the next seven years he notched up an impressive 225 appearances which was beaten between the wars, only by Allen. Scriven added much-needed stability to the Southampton defence. In 1937 he retired from League football but continued to turn out for Salisbury.

SCURR.D.
Born: Netley, 25 September 1939.
2-0, Full-back, 1959-61.
David Scurr was a young local full-back who was released into non-League football after two seasons at The Dell.

SEALY.A.
Born: London, 7 May 1959.
2(5)-0, Forward, 1977-9.
Tony Sealy was a small, fast, promising forward who, despite coming on as a substutute for Saints in the League Cup Final, never developed as much as was hoped. After moving to Crystal Palace in March 1979 he found later success in 1982-3 with Queen's Park Rangers. After spells at Fulham and Port Vale (loan) he joined Leicester during 1985-6 and started to score goals regularly. In March 1987 he went to Bournemouth on loan.

SHARP.A.
1-0, Centre-half, 1929-30.
Sharp was a trialist from Ayr United.

SHARPE.J.
Born: Portsmouth, 9 October 1957.
21-0, Full-back, 1976-78.
John Sharpe was a quick-tackling full-back who at one time looked to have a future at The Dell until he was sold for £50,000 to Gillingham in 1978. He enjoyed five seasons with the Kent side before being given a free transfer and re-engaged on a non-contract basis by McMenemy towards the end of 1984-5. He did not reappear for the first team, however, and was released in the close season of 1985 and played briefly for Swansea City during 1985-6.

SHIELDS.J.
Born: Londonderry, 26 September 1931.
38-20, Forward, 1956-8.
Jimmy Shields played his early football for the Crusaders in his native Northern Ireland before Sunderland signed him in March 1954. He never played in their first team and became Ted Bates' first 'money-signing' when he joined Saints in July 1956 for £1,000. In his first season he won a Northern Ireland cap, got sent off in the FA Cup match against Weymouth and scored 18 League goals. At the beginning of 1957-8 he broke a leg and, never fully recovering, was released into non-League football in the 1958 close season.

SHILTON.P.
Born: Leicester, 18 September 1949.
188-0, Goalkeeper, 1982-7.

Peter Shilton made his debut as a youngster for Leicester in 1965-6, having been an understudy to the England goalkeeper, Gordon Banks. Quick to learn and showing a dedication that has since been a hallmark of his game, Shilton followed Banks into the England side. Saints fans have particular cause to remember his early days — in a match at The Dell in 1967-8 he scored from a drop kick. In 1974, Shilton signed for Stoke and in 1977 moved to Nottingham Forest. With Forest he emerged as arguably the world's best 'keeper, and played his part in Forest's League and European Cup successes. McMenemy, like every other First Division manager, had long cast covetous eyes over Shilton's goalkeeping and with Saints' persistent goalkeeper problems, agreed Forest's asking price of £300,000 in the summer of 1982. Shilton was now 33 but, always a strict trainer, was still at peak condition and has since continued to display his unique goalkeeping talents as well as showing tremendous dedication. The pinnacle of his international career came in the summer of 1986 when, in Bryan Robson's absence, he captained the England side in the World Cup Finals. No aspiring young goalkeeper could do better than to watch Shilton perform week in week out.

SHIPLEY.G.
Born: Newcastle, 7 March 1959.
2(1)-0, Midfield, 1978-80.
George Shipley, although on Saints' books as an apprentice, made his League debut for Reading whilst on loan. He signed for Lincoln in January 1980 for £45,000 and won a regular place in their first team. He later signed for Charlton and helped them win promotion to the First Division.

SILLETT.C.
Born: London, 1907. Died: March 1945.
175-9, Full-back, 1931-8.
Charlie Sillett arrived at The Dell in November 1931 from Tidworth, where he had been stationed as an army PT instructor. Within a couple of months he had made his debut as a centre-forward and scored two goals. Although he also played inside-forward, it was at full-back where he played his best games for Saints. A whole-hearted player, Sillett was made captain in 1937 and attracted a lot of attention from the scouts of the top League clubs. In 1938 he left Saints to play for non-League Guildford City. He was killed during World War Two.

SILLETT.P.
Born: Southampton, 1 February 1933.
59-4, Full-back, 1951-3.
Peter Sillett was the son of Charlie Sillett (1931-8) and inherited his father's skills and more besides. A bulky full-back with a strong kick, he played two seasons before being sold to Chelsea for 'financial reasons'. His brother, John, who was on amateur forms for Saints in 1954, followed him to London and is currently team coach at Coventry City. Peter enjoyed a successful time at Stamford Bridge and when he was later capped for England, Saints were paid a further £2,500 by Chelsea as part of the transfer deal. Sillett won three England caps altogether.

SIMPSON.A.
Born: Glasgow, 24 November 1924.
68-1, Half-back, 1952-5.
Alex Simpson arrived at The Dell via Wolves and Notts County in November 1952. He broke a leg that season, in which Saints were relegated, but recovered to play for Southampton for two more seasons before joining Shrewsbury in July 1955.

SIMPSON.T.
Born: Southampton, 8 October 1938.
22-1, Half-back, 1958-62.
Terry Simpson was a local product who failed to hold down a regular position in Saints' defence and was sold to Peterborough in June 1962 for £5,000. A year later he moved to West Brom and later had spells at Walsall and Gillingham.

SLOAN.T.
Born: Craghead.
1-0, Forward, 1928-9.
Sloan played one match for Saints before joining Cardiff in 1929.

SMALLWOOD.F.
Born: Wrexham.
48-10, Forward, 1936-8.
Fred Smallwood was signed from Macclesfield in the close season of 1936 and enjoyed a successful first season playing in a red and white shirt. He always carried a rabbit's foot in his shorts for luck but must have forgotten it when he sustained a bad injury in a pre-season practice match. Harry Osman's subsequent arrival meant that he found it hard to regain his place and he joined Reading in 1938.

SMITH.G.
Born: Portsmouth, 24 March 1919.
95-1, Half-back, 1938-49.
George Smith made his debut before the war and after serving in the RAF he returned to play for Saints at the end of hostilities. Short and stocky, Smith moved to Crystal Palace in May 1950 and later emigrated to Australia.

SPENCER.T.
Born: Glasgow, 28 November 1945.
3-0, Forward, 1965-6.
Tommy Spencer joined Saints in the summer of 1965 from Celtic, but played only three games. He moved to York in June 1966 and later to Workington, Lincoln and Rotherham.

SPINNER.T.
Born: Woking, 6 November 1953.
1(1)-0, Forward, 1972-3.
Terry Spinner was a Southampton apprentice who joined Walsall in July 1974.

STANSBRIDGE.L.
Born: Southampton, 19 February 1919. Died: Southampton, May 1986.
48-0, Goalkeeper, 1937-52.

Len Stansbridge progressed through the junior ranks to make his debut at Plymouth in May 1938. After spending much of the war as a PoW he returned to The Dell to become the deputy goalkeeper for a further six seasons. He had a spell at Basingstoke before returning to The Dell as groundsman in 1962. Stansbridge cared for the playing surface until May 1984 when he retired and it could safely be said that he knew The Dell pitch better than any other Saints' player.

STEELE.J.
Born: Edinburgh, 11 March 1950.
160(1)-2, Defender, 1971-7.
Jim Steele arrived from Dundee, with a £65,000 price tag around his

neck, but had a reputation as a hard defender who had a bad disciplinary record. He maintained his stern reputation at The Dell, although he also displayed an array of subtle skills which were unusual for a large defender. Predominantly a 'left-sided' footballer, he could play full-back, but was happier in the middle and it was in the number six shirt that he had his best games for the club. The pinnacle of his career came when he was voted Man of the Match in the 1976 FA Cup Final, but a man of his talents should have perhaps gone much further in the game. Steele left League football prematurely in 1977 to play in the NASL for Washington Diplomats.

STEVENS.B.
Born: Andover, 13 November 1933. Died: 10 May 1980.
12-0, Goalkeeper, 1956-8.
Brian Stevens was signed from Andover in September 1956 and was the reserve goalkeeper over the following two seasons before being released in February 1959 to Southport, later signing for Salisbury.

STEVENS.S.
Born: Scotland.
14-0, Half-back, 1958-9.
Sam Stevens was a 21-year-old half-back who signed for Saints from Airdrie in 1958. His stay at The Dell lasted only one year before he was released on a free transfer to Poole.

STEVENSON.E.
Born: Rotherham, 28 December 1923.
24-8, Forward, 1949-51.
Ernie Stevenson played his early football for Wolves before signing for Cardiff in October 1948. He moved to Southampton as part of the deal that took Grant to Cardiff, with Saints also presenting the Welsh club with a 'sizeable cheque'. Whilst Grant enjoyed success at Cardiff, Stevenson failed to find any sort of form for his new club and moved to Leeds in February 1951. His stay at Leeds was equally unspectacular and he dropped out of League football and signed for Wisbech.

STODDART.W.
Born: Leadgate.
12-0, Centre-half, 1928-30.
Stoddart joined Saints from Coventry City and provided cover in the centre-half position for two seasons before moving to Bristol Rovers.

STOKES.R.
Born: Portsmouth, 30 January 1951.
194(22)-40, Forward, 1968-77.
Bobby Stokes came to The Dell as a youngster and made an early impression by scoring two goals on his League debut at home to Burnley, at Easter 1969. A tireless worker, he was small for a forward but lacked nothing in the way of bravery or guile. He was sometimes short of confidence in front of goal, but on 1 May 1976 he shot home the most important goal in the club's history. Scoring the winner at Wembley is every footballer's dream and as one of the most modest and likeable of all Saints players, Stokes' name will always be recalled with affection. He left Saints in 1977 to play for his home-town team, Portsmouth, as well as linking up with Steele and Eric Martin with Washington Diplomats in the NASL. Upon returning from America, he signed for Cheltenham who were then managed by Terry Paine, and in 1987 was a publican in Portsmouth. Stokes was another Saints player who dropped out of League football prematurely but always jokingly blamed this on Terry Paine, claiming that he "used to do all Paine's running for him" and consequently ran out of steam.

STROUD.W.
Born: London, 7 July 1919.
29-4, Half-back, 1946-7.
Bill Stroud was spotted by Toby Keleher, Tom Parker's assistant, and graduated through The Dell youth system. He played consistently during 1946-7 before joining Leyton Orient in the close season. In 1950 he moved to Newport and later played for Hastings United before his playing career was ended by tuberculosis. In 1963 he returned to The Dell to work with the junior teams, retiring in 1986-7 after many years' happy service.

SUMMERS.J.
Born: Manchester.
31-7, Forward, 1936-8.
Derby County signed Summers from Leicester City in May 1935 and he made two appearances for them before moving to Southampton in October 1936 when part of his transfer fee was met by the Southampton Supporters club. He retired from football in 1938 and after the war became a policeman.

SWINDEN.J.
Born: London 1905. Died: Eastleigh, March 1971.
3-0, Forward, 1926-8.
Swinden was a local man who, after featuring mainly in Southampton's reserves, joined local side Pirelli General and later played for Newport(IOW). He had begun his career with Salisbury City.

SYDENHAM.J.
Born: Southampton, 15 September 1939.
341(2)-36, Forward, 1956-70.

John Sydenham was a product of the Southampton youth system and broke into the first team at the same time as Terry Paine, to give Southampton the most exciting pair of wingers that the Third Division had seen in a long time. Educated at St Mary's, he became their first pupil to play for Southampton Schools. In 1955 he joined CPC Sports who at the time doubled as a Saints' nursery side. Sydenham was soon selected for the Saints side which enjoyed an excellent run in the 1956-7 FA Youth Cup. He was now well on his way to a successful career in football and having been selected for England Youth five times, he joined Southampton as a professional in April 1957. He became famous for having an incredible burst of speed and would simply knock the ball past a full-back and then outsprint him to reach it first. Paine and Sydenham tore Third and Second Division defences apart with their wing play and both were selected for England Under-23s. In 1960, Sydenham was called up for National Service which interrupted his progress and for a while he became unsettled at The Dell, only to later rekindle his form and help Saints win promotion to Division One. Slight but lithe, Sydenham was never a prolific goalscorer but was content to make the chances for others and in August 1969 he enjoyed one of his finest games when he laid on all four goals for Ron Davies at Old Trafford. He left Saints for Aldershot in March 1970 and later became involved in management on the Isle of Wight. Later still he has made a home in Perth, Australia where he still spends his time coaching a prominent local side. Sydenham and Paine are two names that will always go together when Southampton football is discussed, which is hardly surprising considering the pair played well over 1,000 League games between them for the club.

TALKES.W.
Born: London, 2 June 1952.
7(2)-0, Midfield, 1971-4.
Wayne Talkes was yet another Southampton discovery from London and for a while looked set to have a future at the club. Not developing as much as hoped, however, he moved to Doncaster in December 1973 and eight months later signed for Bournemouth. Shortly afterwards he moved into non-League football. In 1984 he was managing Brockenhurst.

TANKARD.A.
Born: Fleet, 21 May 1969.
5-0, Full-back, 1985-7.
Allen Tankard, a tall left-back, replaced the injured Dennis towards the end of the 1985-6 season and despite being only 16, impressed many fans with his mature play.

TAYLOR.S.
Born: Sheffield, September 1893, Died: Sheffield 1973.
69-17, Forward, 1926-8.

Sam Taylor was signed from Mansfield for 'less than £1,000', originally as a replacement for Arthur Dominy. Although starting at inside-right he quickly went on to become the established inside-left for two seasons. He was an experienced player, having appeared in Huddersfield's FA Cup team of 1920 before signing for Sheffield Wednesday. As a result of a disagreement with Huddersfield he had been playing with Mansfield, then a non-League club. Renowned as an intelligent, thoughtful player, Taylor was good at billiards and, more unusually, was an accomplished pianist. After two seasons at The Dell he left for Halifax and, later, played for Chesterfield.

TAYLOR.T.
8-4, Forward, 1927-9.
Tom Taylor joined Saints from Manchester City in 1927 and spent the next two years playing mainly in the reserves before departing in the close season of 1929.

THOMAS.E.
Born: Swindon, 9 November 1932.
8-0, Goalkeeper, 1950-51.
Edwin Thomas was an amateur goalkeeper on the books of Saints over the 1950-51 season. He made his debut for Saints whilst still only 17 and won England Youth caps before dropping out of League football to play for Salisbury.

THOMAS.R.
Born: Weymouth.
8-0, Full-back, 1931-2.
Thomas was a signing from non-League Weymouth who provided full-back cover for the 1931-2 season.

THOMPSON.D.
Born: Scotton, 12 March 1945.
21(2)-0, Forward, 1966-71.
Dave Thompson was a young Wolverhampton outside-right for whom Ted Bates paid £7,500 in the close season of 1966. With Terry Paine's presence, Thompson's opportunities were limited and in October 1970 he joined Mansfield. He finished his career at Chesterfield.

THOMPSON.G.
Born: Treeton.
14-0, Goalkeeper, 1927-30.
Thompson was signed as a reserve goalkeeper from York in 1927 and his appearances between the posts were limited due to the good form of first Tommy Allen and then Willie White.

TILFORD.A.
Born: Ilkeston, 14 May 1903.
10-0, Full-back, 1932-3.
Tilford joined Saints from Fulham in February 1933 which was the same time that Keeping and Arnold made the reverse journey. Although the 'loan' system had yet to be conceived, the agreement was that Tilford would stay at The Dell only until the season's end and then rejoin Fulham. Tilford, then 27, thus became Saints' first 'loan' player, at least within the Football League. After returning to Craven Cottage, Tilford later transferred on a permanent basis to Walsall.

TOMLINSON.R.
Born: Sleaford, July 1914, Died: Southampton, May 1971.
36-12, Forward, 1938-9.
Reg Tomlinson joined Grimsby while still in his teens but found breaking into the first team a difficult task and after three years joined Saints. In his first season at The Dell, the last before the outbreak of war, he found a degree of success but lost the rest of his career to the war period. He later became a policeman although he continued to turn out for Saints in the war leagues as a guest.

TOWNSEND.A.
Born: London, 23 July 1963.
41(5)-2, Midfield, 1984-7.
Andy Townsend was a £30,000 signing from Weymouth in January 1985 — the largest fee Saints have ever paid to a non-League team. He possesses deceptive skills and an adaptability to play anywhere on the left-hand side, which Saints have found to be very useful. A broken leg sustained in a pre-season friendly in August 1986, against his old club Weymouth, delayed his progress but he returned to the League side later that season and showed his flair.

TRAYNOR.T.
Born: Dundalk, 22 July 1933.
433-7, Full-back, 1952-66.
Tommy Traynor arrived at The Dell in June 1952 from Dundalk and, as an 18-year-old, had already represented the Republic of Ireland at Amateur level. He soon gained a regular place in Saints' defence and earned a reputation as a merciless tackler who was feared by the opposition. He had a distinguished career at The Dell, winning five full caps and during 1963-4, passing Shelley's League appearances record for Saints. By the time Southampton had won promotion to Division One , Traynor had virtually retired, but his influence and presence at the club was an inspiration in itself, and his contribution to Saints' re-emergence as one of the quality sides of the 1960s was considerable.

TULLY.F.
Born: London.
97-9, Forward, 1933-7.
Fred Tully came from Aston Villa and was originally signed as a possible replacement for Arnold, but found more success on the right wing. He returned to his native London with Clapton Orient during the 1936-7 season.

TURNER.F.
Born: Southampton, 28 Februry 1930. Died: Southampton, 1955.
19-0, Full-back, 1953-5.
Fred Turner was a product of Saints' junior sides, who signed professional forms in February 1950. In August 1951, having failed to reach Saints' first team, he signed for Torquay, but had only one League outing in 19 months before re-signing for Southampton. Just when he appeared to be establishing himself, he died after an illness. He was only 25.

TURNER.I.
Born: Middlesbrough, 17 January 1953.
77-0, Goalkeeper, 1973-8.
Ian Turner followed McMenemy to The Dell from Grimsby in March 1974 and for a period looked to be an answer to the Saints' goalkeeping problems. Playing his part in the 1976 FA Cup victory, he, like many other members of the Cup Final side, struggled to maintain form. Turner left the club for Walsall in January 1979. After dropping out of League football he turned out for a succession of local sides including Salisbury, Waterlooville, RS Southampton and, more recently, Romsey Town.

VECK.R.
Born: Southampton, 1 April 1920.
23-2, Forward, 1946-50.
Bob Veck was a locally produced player who signed for Saints just before the outbreak of war. Originally a left-winger, he became Wayman's understudy in the immediate post-war years and understandably received little chance to stake a consistent first-team place. He moved to Gillingham in July 1950.

VERNON.D.
5-0 Forward, 1928-9.
Vernon was an amateur on the books of Saints for the 1928-9 season, whilst serving in the RAF. He had five consecutive games at centre-forward but failed to score in any of them.

VINE.P.
Born: Southampton, 11 December 1940.
1-0, Forward, 1958-9.
England Youth international, Peter Vine, signed professional forms for Saints in December 1958. He received a free transfer to Poole Town in the close season of 1959.

WALDRON.M.
Born: Emsworth, 6 September 1956.
177(1)-10, Defender, 1974-83.
Malcolm Waldron was a tall, locally produced defender, who promised much in his early days at The Dell, only to later suffer from a loss of form. His nine seasons at Southampton were erratic and one good year would be followed by a bad one. He was sold to Burnley for £90,000 after a miserable 1982-3 campaign. Waldron had the ability to shine in the lower divisions but failed to get on with John Bond, the Burnley manager, and subsequently joined Portsmouth late in 1983-4. After retiring from League football in December 1986, due to a serious injury, Waldron signed for Road Sea, Southampton, in February 1987.

WALKER.D.
Born: Colne, 15 October 1941.
189(8)-1, Defender, 1965-74.

David Walker signed for Burnley in April 1959 and over the next six years made 38 League appearances in a Burnley shirt. Joining Saints in May 1965, for a fee of £20,000, he played his part in the 1965-6 promotion season. An uncompromising defender who showed little emotion on the field, Walker averaged about 30 games a year for Saints in their early First Division days and fitted in well with McGrath, Hollywood, Gabriel and Webb in a Saints defence which gained a reputation as being the 'unholiest' in the League. He retired from League football in 1974 and went to play in South Africa.

WALKER.J.
Born: Glasgow, 17 December 1928.
172-48, Forward, 1952-8.
John Walker signed for Saints from Wolves in October 1952 for a fee reputed to be £12,000 and scored within eight minutes of his debut, at home to Luton. A neat inside-forward, he served Saints well before joining Reading in December 1957. His career at Elm Park was an enjoyable one and he played over 200 games before retiring in 1964.

WALLACE.D.
Born: London, 21 January 1964.
174(8)-50, Forward, 1980-87.
Danny Wallace made his debut for Saints at Old Trafford in November 1980 and, still two months short of his 17th birthday, became their youngest first-teamer since the war. The fans quickly warmed to the little winger, who possessed not only speed but skills which could slice through the sternest defences. Like most wingers,

Wallace can sometimes frustrate, especially with his crossing, and yet he is the sort of player that crowds will always come to see. The scorer of some spectacular goals, Wallace obliged with a typical example when he was awarded his first full England cap, against Egypt in 1986 when he appeared to have a distinguished career ahead of him. However, 1986-7 was not a good season for Wallace as he suffered a leg injury and subsequently lost form in a struggling Saints team.

WALLACE.L.
Born: Isle of Wight.
1-0, Forward, 1938-9.
Wallace was discovered playing for his local Isle of Wight college football team and when he made his debut for Saints in 1938-9 he was still a student.

WARD.F.
Born: Bury.
27-0, Full-back, 1933-5.
Frank Ward joined Saints from Preston in 1933 and stayed two seasons before joining non-League Worcester City in the close season of 1935.

WARHURST.S.
Born: Nelson, 1908. Died: Southampton, February 1981.
78-0, Goalkeeper, 1937-9.
Sam Warhurst joined Saints in 1937 fom Bradford and in the two remaining seasons before the outbreak of war, became the regular Southampton goalkeeper. After the war he returned to The Dell in a coaching capacity.

WARREN.E.
Born: Sunderland.
1-0, Half-back, 1929-30.
Ernest Warren came to Saints from Usworth Colliery to play one League game, and then joined Northampton followed by Hartlepool.

WATERSTON.A.
Born: Musselburgh, 1903. Died: May 1982.
6-1, Forward, 1928-9.
Waterston played his early football for Cowdenbeath and Leicester before arriving in Wales to play for Newport. During 1927-8 he scored 27 goals in 30 games and Saints snapped him up, hoping he could maintain such scoring form in the Second Division.

Unfortunately, Waterston's scoring touch deserted him for the 1928-9 season and in the summer he moved to Tranmere and later Southport.

WATSON.D.
Born: Stapleford, 5 October 1946.
73-8, Centre-half, 1979-82.

Dave Watson started his career at Notts County and then Rotherham before joining Sunderland in 1970-71. Although initially a centre-forward, he converted into a powerful centre-half and soon won the first of 65 England caps. In 1975-6 he joined Manchester City and then had a brief spell playing in West Germany for Werder Bremen. Joining Saints in October 1979 for a fee of £200,000, Watson immediately fitted in well, bringing authority and experience to the Southampton defence. He was to stay for two and a half seasons and played a significant part in Saints' rise to being a First Division force. A very fit and dedicated player, Watson left Saints in 1981-2 and despite being 35 years old, continued to play well, firstly with Stoke and later for Derby. He returned to Notts County as a player-coach before retiring from League football when he signed for Kettering and continued his successful business career outside the game. Watson was capped whilst with five different clubs.

WATSON.R.
Born: Thewell, 26 August 1900.
19-5, Forward, 1929-31.
Watson was secured from Oldham as part of the transfer deal that sent Murphy in the opposite direction. He was a great 'trier' but failed to fill the gap left by Murphy's departure.

WATSON.V.
Born: Girton, Cambridgeshire, 10 November 1897.
36-14, Forward, 1935-6.
Vic Watson was signed from West Ham in the close season of 1935 and arrived at The Dell with a vastly successful career behind him. An England international and the scorer of over 300 League goals, Watson had played for West Ham in the 1923 FA Cup Final. In his only season at The Dell he became the top scorer and it was a pity that youth was no longer on his side. Upon retiring he became a market gardener at Girton.

WAYMAN.C.
Born: Bishop Auckland, 16 May 1921.
100-73, Forward, 1947-50.

Still a legend to those who saw him play, Charlie Wayman was possibly the most popular of all Southampton centre-forwards and his name still haunts present-day strikers at The Dell when a half-chance is wasted. Wayman was originally a miner before playing for Portsmouth during the war. Newcastle signed him for the first season of post-war football and he immediately started to score goals with impressive regularity, including a hat-trick against Saints in the FA Cup. Bill Dodgin, the Southampton manager, signed him in October 1947 for £10,000 and although only 5ft 5in tall, his impact in the number nine shirt was truly amazing. Quick to seize a chance, extremely agile and the owner of a lethal left foot, Wayman led Saints' attack for a memorable three seasons. Unfortunately, Wayman's wife never settled in the area and he joined Preston in September 1950. Wayman continued his spectacular scoring and got one of Preston's goals in the 1954 FA Cup Final. In September 1954

he moved to Middlesbrough and in December 1956 to Darlington where he wound up his professional career. A glance at his League statistics reveals a playing record of 254 goals in 382 games, which confirms his great goalscoring ability. Charlie Wayman later became a brewery representative and in 1987 was living in his native Bishop Auckland.

WEALE.R.
Born: Troed-y-rhiw.
45-10, Forward, 1928-30.
Weale came to The Dell from Swindon for a fee of £1,000, having previously played for West Ham. He showed initial promise by scoring five goals in three games on the right wing. The goals, however, dried up and in 1930 he signed for non-League Guildford, although he later returned to League football with Cardiff, Wrexham and Newport.

WEBB.D.
Born: East Ham, 9 April 1946.
75-2, Full-back, 1965-8.

David Webb joined Saints from Orient in March 1966, with George O'Brien moving to the London side. A very able full-back, Webb was an instant success with his quick tackling and robust, adventurous style. Before long the big London clubs showed interest and in February 1968 he joined Chelsea, with Kirkup moving to Saints. At Chelsea, Webb blossomed into one of the country's top full-backs and could count himself unlucky not to win England recognition. After helping Chelsea win the FA Cup in 1970, he moved across West London to join QPR in 1974 and finished his playing career with spells at Leicester, Derby and Bournemouth. Upon retiring he had managerial spells at Bournemouth and Torquay before taking over from Bobby Moore at Southend in June 1986, a position he held for only nine months.

WEBBER.E.
Born: Portslade, 22 December 1919.
182-0, Centre-half, 1938-51.
Eric Webber graduated through the Southampton junior ranks and made his debut before the outbreak of hostilities in 1939. Guesting for Mansfield during the war, he returned to Saints in 1946 and became a highly effective centre-half in the 'stopper' mould. In October 1951, with age catching up on him, he moved to Torquay where he later became their manager. He became a publican in Southampton before retiring in 1986.

WELLS.P.
Born: Nottingham, 13 August 1956.
141-0, Goalkeeper, 1976-83.
Peter Wells was signed from Nottingham Forest in December 1976 for the modest fee of £8,000 and for a while won a regular place as Saints' goalkeeper. With the arrival of Shilton, Wells joined Millwall in 1983 and later moved to Orient.

WHEATLEY.R.
Born: Nottingham, 20 June 1924.
10-1, Forward, 1948-51.
Roland Wheatley started his League career with Nottingham Forest before joining Southampton in January 1949. He had suffered injuries in the war and at one stage a weak heart, coupled with arthritis, caused him to retire from playing to coach the 'A' team. He courageously overcame these disabilities to return to playing, and joined Grimsby in 1951. In 1955 he was appointed a Saints' scout covering the Midlands, a position he held for 18 years.

WHEELER.A.
Born: Bilston.
11-6, Forward, 1934-5.
Wheeler joined Southampton from Brentford and had initial success, scoring a hat-trick against Bradford. In the close season of 1935 he moved to Northampton.

WHITE.I.
Born: Glasgow, 20 December 1935.
60(1)-5, Half-back, 1962-7.

Ian White played his early football in Scotland before joining Leicester from Celtic in May 1958. After 47 League outings at Filbert Street he signed for Saints in June 1962 for £15,000. He never won a regular place in the first team but provided reliable cover over the next four seasons. He later signed for non-League side, Hillingdon, but sustained a severe ankle injury that forced him to retire from the game. In 1987 he was running a sports shop in Southampton.

WHITE.W.
Born: Kerry Cowdie.
101-0, Goalkeeper, 1928-32.

Willy White was signed from Hearts in 1928 and his acquisition was unusual in that the fee of £800 was lent to Southampton by the recently-formed Supporters Club. White came south with good credentials, having kept goal for Scotland on four occasions, and he certainly did much to improve Saints' defence over the next four seasons. He joined Aldershot in 1932 and later became a publican in Southampton, although he eventually returned to his native Scotland.

WHITELAW.R.
20-1, Half-back, 1936-7.
Bobby Whitelaw signed for Saints from Celtic in the close season of 1936.

WHITLOCK.M.
Born: Portsmouth, 14 March 1961.
55(6)-1, Half-back, 1981-6.
Mark Whitlock was a Southampton apprentice who spent loan periods at Grimsby and Aldershot. He returned to The Dell and stepped into the first team with quiet efficiency whenever required. He was transferred to Bournemouth during the close season in 1986.

WHITTLE.J.
2-0, Forward, 1953-4.
Whittle arrived at The Dell during the 1953-4 season 'on loan' from Hearts and as he was a chartered accountant with the Army in Scotland, his transfer was never made permanent.

WILKINS.K.
Born: Salford, 24 October 1928.
3-0, Forward, 1950-53.
Ken Wilkins was a young forward who started with Saints in October 1949. After two games he transferred to Exeter and played three times before returning to Southampton in July 1952. After a further League outing he transferred to Fulham but failed to make their first team.

WILKINS.L.
Born: Southampton, 20 September 1925.
260-2, Half-back, 1948-58.
A one-club man, Len Wilkins was virtually an institution by the time he left the area to emigrate to Canada. Discovered by Saints whilst

playing football on the Common, he started his life as a half-back but later converted into a reliable full-back. He was at The Dell for a decade and was one of the great 'unsung' players who always gave whole-hearted effort and commitment. Team captain in his last season, he was very popular with the crowd and was given a great ovation when he left the pitch for the last time.

WILKINSON.C.
Born: Durham.
3-0, Full-back, 1938-9.
Charles Wilkinson started his career with Consett in 1928 before joining Leeds soon afterwards. He was at Elland Road until October 1933 when he signed for Sheffield United. After five years at Bramall Lane, Wilkinson moved to Southampton but sustained an injury after only three games, forcing Tom Parker to replace him by signing Emanuel, and with Emanuel apparently established, Wilkinson moved to Bournemouth for 1939-40.

WILLIAMS.F.
22-0, Full-back, 1938-9.
Williams graduated through local Hampshire League football and made his debut for Saints during the 1938-9 season.

WILLIAMS.G.
Born: Netley.
2-0, Forward, 1920-21.
Williams was a local discovery who played twice in the Saints attack before joining Exeter in June 1921.

WILLIAMS.O.
Born: Stockton, 21 April 1958.
4(2)-0, Forward, 1978-9.
Osher Williams was originally on the books of Manchester United before coming to The Dell via non-League Gateshead United. Well-built for a winger, he had a loan spell at Exeter before moving to Stockport in 1979-80 and became a regular in Stockport's first team. In 1986-7 he played for Preston North End.

WILLIAMS.R.
Born: Hereford, 3 March 1932.
41-7, Forward, 1952-3.
Roy Williams originally played for Hereford United in their non-League days before moving to Southampton in November 1952 for £4,000. After two seasons at The Dell he rejoined Hereford and in 1961, was awarded a testimonial against Saints.

WILLIAMS.S.
Born: London, 12 July 1958.
277(2)-18, Midfield, 1975-85.
Steve Williams, undoubtedly one of the best midfield players Southampton ever produced, stepped straight from youth football

into Saints' first team without first appearing in the reserves. Fast, skilful and fierce in the tackle, Williams was a natural midfield player who would have won more than his five England caps had it not been for his sometimes petulant manner towards officials. McMenemy managed to curb most of Williams' aggression and made him team captain until he joined Arsenal in December 1984. At Highbury, Williams continued to cause problems for himself with his temperamental approach and in 1986-7 had still to fully justify his £550,000 transfer fee.

WILLIAMS.S.
Born: Wrexham, 9 July 1930.
148(2)-3, Full-back, 1962-6.
Stuart Williams started his footballing career as an amateur with Wrexham before joining West Brom in February 1951. His stay at The Hawthorns encompassed 226 League games and 34 Welsh caps. In September 1962 he signed for Saints and despite being 32 he played nearly 150 League games for the club and won a further ten caps. Williams was released in the summer of 1966 to return to West Bromwich as a coach. In September 1971 he went back to The Dell as Ted Bates' assistant manager.

WILSON.A.
Born: Newcastle, October 1908.
62-12, Half-back, 1929-32.
Arthur Wilson came to Saints as a half-back from non-League Scotswood but developed the knack of scoring goals and often deputised as an inside-forward. He joined West Ham in 1932 and later played for Chester.

WIMSHURST.K.
Born: South Shields, 23 March 1938.
148(4)-9, Half-back, 1961-7.
Ken Wimshurst was a classy half-back who started his career with Newcastle before having seven League outings with Gateshead. Wolves signed him but he did not play in their first team and joined Southampton in July 1961 for £1,500. He had been recommended to Saints by Bill Rochford and the club soon had cause to thank their old scout as Wimshurst settled in well at The Dell. He had some fine games during the 1963 FA Cup run, with clever passing a particular feature of his play. He left Saints in October 1967 to join Bristol City for £12,000 and gave them equally good service. He later moved behind the scenes at Ashton Gate and more recently has been coaching in Egypt.

WITHERS.E.
Born: Ower.
6-0, Forward, 1936-7.
Withers was a local product who signed professional forms in October 1934 but did not impress The Dell management and signed for Bristol Rovers in 1937. He later returned to Southampton to play for Bramtoco and by the outbreak of the war he was working as a masseur in London.

WOODFORD.G.
Born: Lymington, 22 April 1915. Died: Lymington, April 1966.
6-0, Full-back, 1937-8.
Woodford joined Saints from Norwich where he had started his League career under Tom Parker's guidance. He was given a free transfer in 1939 and went to play for his home-town club, Lymington.

WOODHOUSE.S.
Born: Warrington. Died: Southampton, 13 March 1977.
351-5, Half-back, 1924-36.
Woodhouse signed from Bury in the close season of 1924 as an inside-forward but went on to establish himself as a half-back of some standing. Quietly and efficiently, the stalwart Woodhouse spent 12 loyal seasons at The Dell, making 351 appearances, a figure that put him second only to Shelley at the time. Leaving The Dell in 1936 to play non-League football for Basingstoke, he later became a publican.

WOOLF.L.
Born: Johannesburg.
1-0, Forward, 1937-8.
Woolf was a South African trialist who failed to impress in his one League game.

WORTHINGTON.F.
Born: Halifax, 23 November 1948.
34-4, Forward, 1983-4.
Frank Worthington arrived at The Dell having been a footballing nomad. His previous sides included Huddersfield, Leicester, Bolton, Birmingham, Leeds and Sunderland and along the way he had won eight full England caps as well as a host of appreciative fans. A natural entertainer, Worthington possessed delightful close ball-control and was no mean goalscorer in his early days. McMenemy paid Sunderland £20,000 for his talents and, although he did not score many goals, the cavalier Worthington was part of the 1983-4 success story. In the close season, unable to agree terms, he moved to Brighton and then departed north again as player-manager of Tranmere. Sacked from that position in February 1987, Worthington joined his tenth club when he became player-coach at Preston whose manager was the former Southampton defender, John McGrath.

WRIGGLESWORTH.W.
Born: South Elmshall, 12 December 1912.
12-4, Forward, 1947-8.
Billy Wrigglesworth really made his name before the war, when he was a big star with Manchester United and Bolton. He joined Saints in October 1947 and although scoring on his debut, was well past his prime. One little trick that always pleased the fans was the habit he had of 'trapping' the ball with his backside. He moved to Reading in the close season of 1948.

WRIGHT.F.
Born: Birmingham, 1898.
1-0, Forward, 1920-21.
Wright was signed from a local Birmingham side, Hampstead Colliery, in October 1920.

WRIGHT.M.
Born: Dorchester, 1 August 1963.
170-7, Centre-half, 1981-7.
Mark Wright had played only ten games for Oxford when he signed for Saints but McMenemy had seen enough to realise his full potential. Arriving at The Dell late in 1981-2 as part of the deal that sent Hebberd to Oxford, Wright initially had a few games at full-back but soon became far more at home playing in the middle of the defence. Elegant and skilful, Wright quickly looked to be an international in the making and won his first England cap in 1984. He has had his fair share of injuries and disagreements at Southampton but has emerged as one of the finest defenders the club have ever had on their books. When he broke a leg in the FA Cup semi-final against Liverpool in 1986, the injury deprived him of a trip to Mexico with England. It was a cruel blow to the player and a jolt to England's plans although the player showed the determination and talents necessary to be part of the future international scene. In April 1987, Saints agreed to the unsettled Wright's transfer request.

YEOMANS.H.
Born: Farnborough, April 1901. Died: Bucks, February 1965.
12-0, Goalkeeper, 1924-6.
'Tiny' Yeomans, who stood 6ft 4in tall, was at The Dell for two seasons as understudy to Tommy Allen before leaving in 1926 to join the Southampton police force.

Kevin Keegan comes to town. Top: Keegan, on his Saints' debut against Manchester City in August 1980, leaps for the ball along with Charlie George. Bottom: Keegan scores for Saints in their 3-0 win at Birmingham in January 1981.

Major Transfers

The Southampton transfer trail started in earnest with their admittance into the Football League in 1920 and it is interesting to note that, in the early days, it was Saints who did the 'selling' whilst in modern times they have become one of the 'buying' clubs.

Incoming Transfers

('R' denotes club record)

1898 P.MEEHAN from Everton, £200
1898 J.ROBINSON from Derby County, £400 (R)
1919 W.TURNER from Leadgate, £200
1926 S.TAYLOR from Mansfield Town, £950 (R)
1928 W.WHITE from Heart of Midlothian, £800
1928 W.WEALE from Swindon Town, £1000 (R)
1929 P.DOUGAL from Clyde, (R)   ] £1,650 Combined fee
1929 W.HOOD from Clyde, (R)
1930 J.McILWANE from Portsmouth, £2,650 (R)
1936 J.DUNNE from Arsenal, £1,000
1937 R.PARKIN from Middlesbrough, £1,500
1937 F.HILL from Blackpool, £2,200
1938 T.EMANUEL from Swansea Town, £2,200
1946 J.MALLETT from Queen's Park Rangers, £5,000 (R)
1947 G.CURTIS from Arsenal, £10,000 (R)
1947 C.WAYMAN from Newcastle United, £10,000
1949 E.JONES from Tottenham Hotspur, £15,000 (R)
1952 J.WALKER from Wolverhampton Wanderers, £12,000
1961 A.KNAPP from Leicester City, £25,000 (R)
1964 J.MELIA from Wolverhampton Wanderers, £30,000 (R)
1966 D.WEBB from Orient, £30,000
1966 R.DAVIES from Norwich City, £55,000 (R)
1967 H.FISHER from Blackpool, £35,000
1967 E.MARTIN from Dunfermline Athletic, £25,000
1969 T.JENKINS from Reading, £60,000 (R)
1970 B.O'NEIL from Burnley, £75,000 (R)
1972 J.STEELE from Dundee, £65,000
1974 P.OSGOOD from Chelsea, £275,000 (R)
1977 C.NICHOLL from Aston Villa, £80,000
1977 P.BOYER from Norwich City, £100,000
1978 C.GEORGE from Derby County, £400,000 (R)
1979 D.WATSON from Werder Bremen, £200,000
1979 M.CHANNON from Manchester City, £200,000
1980 K.KEEGAN from SV Hamburg, £400,000
1981 D.ARMSTRONG from Middlesbrough, £600,000 (R)
1982 P.SHILTON from Nottingham Forest, £300,000
1985 G.COCKERILL Sheffield United, £275,000
1986 C.CLARKE from AFC Bournemouth, £400,000

Colin Clarke

Outgoing Transfers

1896 T.CAIN to Grimsby Town, £20 (R)
1907 F.MOUNCHER to Fulham, £700
1907 F.HARRISON to Fulham, £1000 (R)
1911 F.JEFFERIS to Everton, £1000(approx)
1912 F.GRAYER to Liverpool, £100
1923 J.ELKES to Tottenham Hotspur, £1,050 (R)
1926 F.TITMUSS to Plymouth Argyle, £1,750 (R)
1926 T.PARKER to Arsenal, £3,250 (R)
1928 W.RAWLINGS to Manchester United, £3,860 (R)
1930 R.ROWLEY to Tottenham Hotspur, £3,750
1933 A.KEEPING to Fulham,   ] £5,000 Combined Fee
1933 J.ARNOLD to Fulham,
1934 E.DRAKE to Arsenal, £6,000 (R)
1936 W.LIGHT to West Bromwich Albion, £2,000
1939 H.OSMAN to Millwall, £2,000
1947 D.McGIBBON to Fulham, £4,000
1947 D.ROPER to Arsenal, £17,000 (R)
1949 A.RAMSEY to Tottenham Hotspur, £21,000 (R)
1953 P.SILLETT to Chelsea, £15,000
1967 M.CHIVERS to Tottenham Hotspur, £125,000 (R)
1968 D.WEBB to Chelsea, £40,000
1978 M.CHANNON to Manchester City, £300,000 (R)
1978 M.ANDRUSZEWSKI to Tampa Bay Rowdies, £150,000
1979 T.CURRAN to Sheffield Wednesday, £100,000
1980 D.PEACH to Swindon Town, £150,000
1982 G.BAKER to Manchester City, £225,000
1982 K.KEEGAN to Newcastle United, £100,000
1984 K.ARMSTRONG to Birmingham City, £100,000
1984 R.AGBOOLA to Sunderland, £100,000
1984 S.WILLIAMS to Arsenal, £550,000 (R)
1986 S.MORAN to Leicester City, £300,000

Fred Mouncher

Brian O'Neil, seen here in action against Hull City, was Saints' record signing from Burnley in 1970 for £75,000. Unfortunately a bad disciplinary record marred his career but he proved a popular player at The Dell.

League Hat-Tricks

A.DOMINY (2)
3 (h) v Watford 21.1.21
3 (h) v Coventry City 2.5.25

W.RAWLINGS (10)
3 (h) v Charlton Athletic 19.11.21
4 (h) v Northampton Town 24.12.21
4 (h) v Millwall 21.1.22
3 (h) v Rotherham United 31.3.23
3 (h) v Barnsley 19.1.24
3 (h) v Clapton Orient 5.4.24
3 (a) v Oldham Athletic 26.4.24
3 (a) v Chelsea 11.9.26
3 (h) v Fulham 6.11.26
3 (h) v Blackpool 20.11.26

J.MACKIE (1)
3 (h) v Barnsley 24.3.28

W.HAINES (1)
4 (h) v Blackpool 3.11.28

R.WEALE (1)
3 (h) Notts County 26.12.28

R.ROWLEY (3)
3 (h) v Chelsea 21.9.29
3 (a) v Nottingham Forest 28.9.29
4 (a) v Bradford City 2.11.29

J.BREWIS (1)
3 (h) Manchester United 3.9.32

J.ARNOLD (1)
3 (h) West Ham United 24.9.32

E.DRAKE (2)
3 v Grimsby Town (h) 29.10.32
3 v Bradford City (h) 26.8.33

N.COLE (1)
3 v West Ham United (h) 7.4.34

A.WHEELER (1)
3 v Bradford (h) 10.11.34

A.HOLT (1)
3 v Nottingham Forest (h) 15.2.36

V.WATSON (1)
3 v Nottingham Forest (h) 15.2.36

H.OSMAN (1)
3 v Luton Town (h) 30.10.37

F.BRIGGS (1)
3 v Swansea Town (h) 26.11.38

D.McGIBBON (1)
3 v Swansea Town (h) 4.9.46

E.DAY (3)
3 v Chesterfield (h) 20.9.47
3 v Blackburn Rovers(h) 25.4.53
3 v Crystal Palace (h) 17.9.55

C.WAYMAN (2)
5 v Leicester City (h) 23.10.48
3 v Hull City (h) 5.11.49

E.BROWN (1)
3 v Nottingham Forest (h) 29.8.51

E.BATES (1)
3 v Bury (h) 29.3.52

F.DUDLEY (2)
3 v Doncaster Rovers (h) 18.10.52
3 v Fulham (h) 27.12.52

J.FLOOD (1)
3 v Newport County (h) 2.9.53

J.WALKER (1)
3 v Brentford (h) 21.8.54

J.HOSKINS (1)
3 v Gillingham (h) 31.8.57

D.REEVES (7)
3 v Queen's Park Rangers (h) 14.9.57
3 v Shrewsbury Town (a) 1.3.58
3 v Watford (h) 5.4.58
4 v Mansfield Town (a) 23.8.58
3 v Southend United (a) 12.9.59
3 v Mansfield Town (h) 19.9.59
4 v Swindon Town (h) 10.10.59

C.LIVESEY (2)
4 v Hull City (h) 13.9.58
3 v Wrexham (a) 14.2.59

G.O'BRIEN (8)
4 v Brighton & Hove Albion (h) 17.9.60
3 v Luton Town (a) 16.9.61
3 v Cardiff City (h) 31.10.62
3 v Rotherham United (h) 27.4.64
3 v Rotherham United (h) 21.11.64
3 v Plymouth Argyle (h) 26.12.64
4 v Charlton Athletic (h) 27.2.65
4 v Bury (h) 4.9.65

G.KIRBY (2)
3 v Middlesbrough (h) 3.11.62
4 v Charlton Athletic (h) 24.8.63

T.PAINE (3)
3 v Rotherham United (a) 1.10.63
3 v Derby County (h) 1.4.64
3 v Derby County (h) 5.12.64

M.CHIVERS (4)
3 v Swindon Town (h) 25.4.64
3 v Rotherham United (h) 21.11.64
4 v Wolverhampton Wanderers (h) 18.9.65
3 v Cardiff City (a) 27.12.65

N.DEAN (1)
3 v Portsmouth (a) 5.2.66

R.DAVIES (5)
3 v Leicester City (h) 14.1.67
3 v Burnley (h) 8.4.67
4 v Aston Villa (h) 13.5.67
4 v Chelsea (a) 2.9.67
4 v Manchester United (a) 16.8.69

M.CHANNON (4)
3 v Oxford United (a) 25.9.74
3 v Bristol Rovers (h) 8.2.75
3 v Portsmouth (h) 27.9.75
3 v Blackpool (h) 18.12.76

P.BOYER (3)
3 v Derby County (h) 29.9.79
3 v Crystal Palace (h) 9.10.79
3 v Bristol City (h) 29.4.80

S.MORAN (4)
3 v Manchester City (h) 19.3.83
3 v Coventry City (h) 28.4.84
3 v Ipswich Town (h) 4.5.85
3 v Watford (h) 5.10.85

D.WALLACE (1)
3 v Coventry City (h) 28.4.84

C.CLARKE (2)
3 v Queen's Park Rangers (h) 23.9.86 (D)
3 v Newcastle United (h) 4.10.86

M.Le TISSIER (1)
3 v Leicester City (h) 7.3.87

G.HOBSON (1)
3 v Manchester City (a) 11.4.87

'D' denotes debut

Bill Rawlings

Derek Reeves

Terry Paine

Matt Le Tissier completes his hat-trick against Leicester City at The Dell in March 1987.

International and Representative Honours

Many Saints players have won international honours whilst with other clubs. The appearances and totals here are solely for international appearances made while with Southampton. In 1924 the Republic of Ireland began seperate international matches; before then there was just one 'Ireland' team and that position is reflected here.

England

Armstrong D. 1982 West Germany; 1984 Wales (2)
Chadwick A. 1900 v Wales, Scotland (2)
Channon M. 1972 v Yugoslavia; 1973 v Scotland, N.Ireland, Wales, Scotland, Czechoslovakia, USSR, Italy, Austria, Poland, Italy; 1974 v Portugal, Wales, Northern Ireland, Scotland, Argentina, East Germany, Bulgaria, Yugoslavia, Czechoslovakia, Portugal; 1975 v West Germany, Cyprus(twice), Northern Ireland, Wales, Scotland, Switzerland, Czechoslovakia, Portugal; 1976 v Wales, Northern Ireland, Scotland, Brazil, Italy, Finland(twice), Italy; 1977 v Luxembourg, Northern Ireland, Wales, Scotland, Brazil, Argentina, Uruguay (45)
Ellerington W. 1949 v Norway, France (2)
Fry C.B. 1901 v Ireland (1)
Houlker A.E. 1906 v Ireland, Wales (2)
Keegan K. 1981 v Spain, Switzerland, Hungary, Norway, Hungary; 1982 v Northern Ireland, Scotland, Finland, Spain (9)
Lee A.E. 1904 v Wales (1)
Molyneux G. 1902 v Scotland; 1903 v Ireland, Wales, Scotland (4)
Paine T. 1963 v Czechoslovakia, East Germany, Wales, Rest of the World, Northern Ireland; 1964 v Scotland, Uruguay, USA, Portugal, Northern Ireland; 1965 v Hungary, Yugoslavia, West Germany, Sweden, Wales, Austria; 1966 v Yugoslavia, Norway, Mexico (19)

TERRY PAINE

Parker T.R. 1925 v France (1)
Ramsey A. 1948 v Switzerland (1)
Rawlings W. 1922 v Wales; 1923 v Wales (2)
Robinson J.W. 1899 v Wales, Scotland; 1900 v Ireland, Wales, Scotland; 1901 v Ireland (6)

Shilton P. 1982 v Denmark, West Germany, Greece; 1983 v Wales, Greece, Hungary, Northern Ireland, Scotland, Australia(thrice), Denmark, Hungary; 1984 France, Northern Ireland, Wales, Scotland, USSR, Brazil, Uruguay, Chile, East Germany, Finland, Turkey; 1985 v Northern Ireland, Rumania, Finland, Scotland, Italy, West Germany, Rumania, Turkey, Northern Ireland; 1986 v Egypt, Israel, USSR, Scotland, Mexico, Canada, Portugal, Morocco, Poland, Paraguay, Argentina, Sweden, Northern Ireland; 1987 v Spain, Northern Ireland, Brazil (49)
Titmuss F. 1922 v Wales; 1923 v Wales (2)

FREDDIE TITMUSS

Turner A. 1900 Ireland; 1901 Ireland (2)
Wallace D. 1986 v Egypt (1)
Watson D. 1979 v Northern Ireland, Bulgaria; 1980 v Republic of Ireland, Spain, Argentina, Northern Ireland, Scotland, Belgium, Italy, Spain, Norway, Rumania, Switzerland; 1981 v Rumania, Wales, Scotland, Switzerland, Hungary (18)
Williams S. 1983 v Australia(twice); 1984 v France, East Germany, Finland, Turkey (6)
Wright M. 1984 v Wales, East Germany, Finland, Turkey; 1985 v Republic of Ireland, Rumania, Italy, West Germany, Rumania, Turkey, Northern Ireland; 1986 v Egypt, USSR, Yugoslavia; 1987 v Scotland (15)

England 'B'

Ellerington W. 1949 v Finland (1)
Peach D. 1979 v New Zealand (1)
Waldron M. 1979 v New Zealand (1)
Williams S. 1979 Austria; 1980 USA, Australia; 1981 Spain (4)

England Under-23

Channon M. 1970 v Sweden, Wales; 1971 v Scotland, Switzerland; 1972 v Wales, Scotland, East Germany(twice), USSR (9)
Chivers M. 1964 v France, Hungary, Wales, Rumania; 1965 v Scotland, Czechoslovakia, West Germany, Czechoslovakia, Austria, France, Yugoslavia; 1967 v Italy (12)
Mills S. 1974 v Wales (1)
Paine T. 1960 v Holland, East Germany; 1961 v West Germany; 1962 v Turkey (4)
Sydenham J. 1959 v France; 1960 v Scotland (2)

England Under-21

Baker G. 1980 v Norway, Rumania (2)
Moran S. 1981 v Norway; 1984 v France (2)
Peach D. 1977 v Scotland, Finland, Norway(2); 1978 v Italy(twice), Yugoslavia(twice) (8)
Wallace D. 1983 v Greece, Hungary, Denmark, Hungary; 1984 v France(twice), Italy, Spain, Finland, Turkey; 1985 v Israel, Rumania; 1986 v Denmark, Italy (14)
Williams S. 1977 v Scotland, Finland, Norway(twice); 1978 v Italy(twice), Yugoslavia(twice), Denmark; 1979 v Bulgaria, Sweden, Denmark; 1980 v East Germany(twice) (14)

MARK WRIGHT

Wright M. 1983 v Greece, Hungary, Denmark, Hungary (4)

England Amateur Internationals

Campbell A. 1909 v Belgium (1)
Coates H. 1928 v Northern Ireland; 1930 v Northern Ireland, Scotland, Wales; 1931 v Wales, Northern Ireland, Scotland (7)

Scotland

Black I. 1948 v England (1)
Robertson J. 1899 v England (1)

Scotland Under-23

Hollywood D. 1965 v England (1)

Wales

Curtis A. 1984 v Scotland, Spain; 1985 v Norway(twice); 1986 v Hungary (5)
Davies.R. 1966 v Scotland, England; 1967 v Northern Ireland, Scotland; 1968 v Scotland, West Germany, Italy; 1969 v West Germany, Scotland, England, Northern Ireland, Rest of UK; 1970 V England, Scotland, Northern Ireland; 1971 v Czechoslovakia, Scotland, England, Northern Ireland, Rumania; 1972 v England, Scotland, Northern Ireland (23)
Hodgkinson A. 1908 v Ireland (1)
Williams S.G. 1962 v Scotland, Hungary, England; 1963 v Hungary, England, Scotland; 1964 v Scotland, Denmark, England; 1964 v Denmark (10)

Northern Ireland

Clarke C. 1986 v England, Turkey. 1987 v Yugoslavia (3).
Kelly H. 1950 v England, Scotland (2)
Nicholl C. 1977 v Belgium; 1978 v Scotland, England, Wales, Republic of Ireland; 1979 v Bulgaria, England, Bulgaria, England, Wales, Republic of Ireland; 1980 v Israel, Scotland, England, Wales, Australia(thrice), Sweden, Portugal; 1981 v Scotland, Portugal, Scotland, Sweden, Scotland, Israel; 1982 v England, France, Wales, Yugoslavia, Honduras, Spain, Austria, France; 1983 v Scotland, England, Wales (37)
Rowley R. 1929 v Wales, Scotland, England; 1930 v Wales (4)
Shields J. 1956 v Scotland (1)

Republic of Ireland

Byrne A. 1969 v Denmark; 1970 v Poland, West Germany, Poland, Sweden(twice), Italy; 1971 v Italy, Austria, 1972 v France; 1973 v USSR, France, Norway, Poland (14)
Dunne J. 1937 v Switzerland, France (2)
Hayes A. 1979 v Denmark (1)
Kiernan F. 1951 v West Germany; 1952 v West Germany, Austria (3)
Traynor T. 1954 v Luxembourg; 1962 v Austria, Iceland(twice); 1963 v Scotland, Austria(twice); 1964 v Spain (8)

Republic of Ireland Under 21

Collins E. 1985 v England (1)

Representative Matches

Southern League

Chadwick A. 1900 v Amateurs of South
Clawley G. 1897 v London FA
Dominy A. 1921 v Irish League
Durber P. 1900 v Amateurs of South
Ireland S. 1913 v Irish League, Scottish League
Keay W. 1896 v London FA
Milward A. 1900 v Amateurs of South
Robertson J. 1911 v Football League, Irish League
Robinson J. 1900 v Amateurs of South
Trueman A. 1910 v Football League(twice), Irish League, Scottish League
Turner A. 1900 v Amateurs of South
Turner J. 1896 v London FA

United League

Haynes H. 1899 v Thames & Medway Combination (at Millwall)
Robertson J.W. 1899 v Thames & Medway Combination (at Tottenham)
Wood H. 1899 v Thames & Medway Combination (at Tottenham)

Football League

Channon M. 1973 v Scottish League; 1976 v Scottish League
Chivers M. 1967 v League of Ireland
Ellerington W. 1949 v League of Ireland
Keeping A. 1931 v Irish League
McGrath J. 1969 v Scottish League
O'Neill B. 1971 v Scottish League
Paine T. 1964 v Irish League, Italian League, Scottish League; 1965 v Scottish League; 1966 v Irish League
Ramsey A. 1948 v Irish League

England International Trial Matches

For South v North

Barlow T. 1903
Chadwick A. 1900
Durber P. 1900
Fry C.B. 1901
Harrison F. 1904
Houlker A. 1906
Lee A. 1902, 1094
Lock H. 1909
Molyneux G. 1904
Parker T. 1924, 1925
Robinson J.W. 1899, 1900, 1901, 1902
Turner A. 1900

For South v England

Campbell A. 1922
Dominy A. 1921
Rawlings W. 1922
Titmuss F. 1922, 1923

For The Rest v England

Parker T. 1926

For England v The Rest

Keeping A. 1926

For Professionals v Amateurs

Harkus G. 1926 (Charity Shield)
Keeping A. 1926, 1929 (Charity Shield matches)
Lee A. 1905
Molyneux G. 1905
Rawlings W. 1926 (Charity Shield)

For Professionals of South v Amateurs of South

Harrison F. 1906

For Whites v Stripes

Trueman A. 1911

Scottish International Trials

For Anglo Scots v Home Scots

Bowman T. 1902
Robertson J.T. 1899

Additional Representative Honours

Unoffical international

England

Molyneux G. 1902 v Scotland. (Declared unoffical because of disaster)

England XI

Chadwick A. 1899 v Scotland XI. (Players' Union international)
Wood H. 1899 v Scotland XI. (Players' Union international)

FA Tour XI

Harkus G. Canada 1927
Keeping A. Canada 1927; South Africa 1929(3)
Rawlings W. Canada 1927
Shelley A. South Africa 1929(3)

Peter Shilton has won over 90 full caps for England, more than half of them as a Southampton player. His first appearance was in 1970, against East Germany when he was with Leicester City. Shilton emulated the late Frank Swift by captaining England from goal when he led the side in Bryan Robson's absence.

UMMARY

closer study of Saints' record reveals some interesting facts. In thirteen visits, the Saints have never won at Watford, whilst the same team rovide the Saints with their highest success rate of 83% or ten wins out of twelve games at The Dell. Fulham is another ground where Saints have red badly, with only two wins in 23 visits (success rate 8.6%), whereas at The Dell, Saints have secured 18 victories in 23 matches (success rate of 3%). Southampton's consistently 'worst' away ground is Coventry with only two wins in 36 visits (success rate 5.5%) and although Saints' home cord over Coventry is not outstanding, Coventry have only won once at The Dell since the war. Chelsea are the most troublesome visitors at The ell, and in 21 meetings Saints have only won six matches (success rate of 28.5%) and strangely, Port Vale have the next best record, being efeated only five times in 15 matches, (Saints success rate of 33%). Away from home the Saints have won nine matches at Notts County, but the est average is, interestingly, at Portsmouth, where Saints have notched up seven wins in 12 matches. To be fair to Pompey, their record at The ell is good but does not match up to the Saints record at Fratton Park. Finally, as Crystal Palace figure in both our best home and best away sults, they could possibly be regarded as the Saints' favourite team.

EST HOME RECORD
) wins out of 12 v Watford 83%
3 wins out of 23 v Fulham 78%
| wins out of 28 v Swansea 75%
2 wins out of 16 v Palace 75%
| wins out of 16 v Charlton 69%

WORST HOME RECORD
6 wins out of 21 v Chelsea 28.5%
5 wins out of 15 v Port Vale 33%
7 wins out of 20 v Ipswich 35%
4 wins out of 10 v Bolton 40%
13 wins out of 31 v Tottenham 42%

EST AWAY RECORD
wins out of 12 v Portsmouth 58%
wins out of 10 v Newport 50%
wins out of 20 v Notts County 45%
wins out of 16 v Palace 44%
wins out of 20 v Queens Park R 35%

WORST AWAY RECORD
0 wins out of 13 v Watford 0%
2 wins out of 36 v Coventry 5.5%
1 win out of 18 v Sheffield W 5.5%
1 win out of 17 v Arsenal 5.8%
2 wins out of 23 v Fulham 8.6%

Miscellaneous. Saints have played most League games against Nottingham Forest, scored most goals (112) against Coventry City, and ottenham have scored the most goals (115) against Southampton.

MOST CAPPED PLAYER FOR:
ngland: P.Shilton (49)
cotland: J.Robertson (1), I.Black (1)
ales: R.Davies (23)
.Ireland: C.Nicholl (37)
epublic of Ireland: A.Byrne (14)

ver Presents
.Foxall 1920-21, J.Moore 1920-21, W.Turner 1920-21, T.Allen 1921-22, 1923-24, 1926-27, A.Shelley 1921-22, 1922-23, 1923-24, F.Titmuss 1921-22, A.Keeping 1926-27, W.Adams 1931-32, W.Luckett 1932-33, C.Sillett 1935-36, A.Ramsey 1947-48, E.Webber 1948-49, 1949-50, G.Curtis 1949-50, J.Mallett 1950-51, E.Day 1951-52, 1952-53, 1953-54, T.Traynor 1954-55, L.Wilkins 1954-55, T.Paine 1958-59, 1959-60, 1961-62, 1962-63, 1964-65, 1966-67, 1968-69, C.Huxford 1959-60, 1963-64, D.Reeves 1959-60, R.Davies 1959-60, T.Mulgrew 1961-62, B.Clifton 1961-62, T.Knapp 1961-62, 1962-63, G.O'Brien 1962-63, J.Melia 1966-67, J.McGrath 1968-69, B.O'Neil 1970-71, M.Channon 1970-71, 1971-72, 1975-76, 1980-81, .Fisher 1970-71, 1973-74, J.Kirkup 1970-71, E.Martin 1971-72, 1972-73, A.Ball 1978-79, P.Boyer 1978-79, 1979-80, M.Waldron 1978-79, .Nicholl 1980-81, 1982-83, N.Holmes 1983-84, P.Shilton 1983-84, D.Armstrong 1983-84, M.Mills 1984-85, G.Cockerill 1986-87.

HIGHEST NO. OF GOALS SCORED
iv 1 74 1966-67
iv 2 100 1963-64
iv 3 112 1957-58

HIGHEST NO. OF GOALS CONCEDED
Div 1 92 1966-67
Div 2 85 1952-53
Div 3 81 1955-56

LOWEST NO. OF GOALS SCORED
iv 1 46 1969-70
iv 2 40 1922-23, 1924-25
iv 3 64 1920-21

LOWEST NO. OF GOALS CONCEDED
Div 1 38 1983-84
Div 2 31 1923-24
Div 3 21 1921-22

HIGHEST AGGREGATE GOALS SCORED (FOR AND AGAINST) IN A SEASON
iv 1 166 in 42 games 1966-67 3.95 a game
iv 2 173 in 42 games 1963-64 4.12 a game
iv 3 184 in 46 games 1957-58 4.00 a game

OP GOALSCORERS
iv 1 R.Davies 37 1966-67
iv 2 C.Wayman 32 1948-49 G.O'Brien 32 1964-65
iv 3 D.Reeves 39 1959-60

nly player to score 5 in one game: C.Wayman, 1948-49 v Leicester City.
nly player to score three on his debut: C.Clarke, 1986-87 v Queens Park Rangers.
astest goal at The Dell by a Saint: T.Mulgrew, 15 secs v Brentford 1954-55.
astest goal at The Dell by an opponent: M.Hateley, 14 secs for Coventry 1982-83.
ongest unbeaten run: 14 games 1984-85 (Div 1).
3 games 1949-50 (Div 2).
9 games 1921-22 (Div 3).

Charlie Wayman

Highest position in Football League: 2nd in Div 1, 1983-84.
Lowest position in Football League: 14th in Div 3 South, 1955-56.
Longest unbeaten home run: 31 games, 1 January 1921 to 29 August 1922.
Longest unbeaten away run: 9 games, 1949-50 & 1977-78.
Most players used in a season: 31 in 1976-77.
Fewest players used in a season: 17 in 1961-62.
Highest number of consecutive appearances:
159 by T.Paine, 22 March 1958 — 4 November 1961.
153 by M.Channon, 4 October 1969 — 20 April 1973.
Individual scoring in successive games: 10 matches — R.Davies, 1966-67;
9 — G.O'Brien, 1961-62; 8 — A.Haddleton, 1931-32; 7 — W.Rawlings,
1921-22; 5 — J.Bradley, last 2 1946-47, first 3 1947-48.
Youngest player: D.Wallace, 16 years 314 days.
Second youngest player: A.Tankard, 16 years 340 days.
Most appearances: T.Paine, 709.
Most goals: M.Channon, 185.

Bill Rawlings

TOP 25 APPEARANCES & GOALS

APPEARANCES		GOALS	
1. T.Paine	709	M.Channon	185
2. M.Channon	507	T.Paine	160
3. N.Holmes	437	W.Rawlings	156
4. T.Traynor	433	G.O'Brien	154
5. E.Day	398	E.Day	145
6. A.Shelley	392	D.Reeves	145
7. S.Woodhouse	351	R.T.Davies	134
8. J.Sydenham	341	M.Chivers	97
9. A.Bradford	305	T.Mulgrew	90
10. H.Fisher	297	S.Moran	78
11. W.Rawlings	294	C.Wayman	73
12. T.Mulgrew	293	D.Armstrong	69
13. T.Allen	291	A.Dominy	68
14. S.Williams	277	E.Bates	64
15. D.Reeves	273	J.Hoskins	64
16. A.Keeping	265	N.Holmes	56
17. L.Wilkins	260	R.Rowley	52
18. E.Martin	248	D.Wallace	50
19. G.O'Brien	244	P.Boyer	49
20. D.Armstrong	243	J.Walker	48
21. R.T.Davies	239	E.Drake	47
22. B.Elliott	235	W.Haines	47
23. D.Hollywood	234	J.Arnold	46
24. A.Knapp	233	A.Holt	46
25. C.Nicholl	228	E.MacDougall	42

Mick Channon

Largest Home Victory
Div 1	8-2 v Coventry City	1983-84
Div 2	9-3 v Wolverhampton Wanderers	1965-66
Div 3	8-0 v Northampton Town	1921-22

Largest Home Defeat
Div 1	5-1 v Blackpool	1966-67
	5-1 v Leicester City	1967-68
Div 2	6-0 v Plymouth Argyle	1931-32
Div 3	6-0 v Brentford	1958-59

Largest Away Victory
Div 1	6-2 v Chelsea	1967-68
Div 2	6-0 v Carlisle United	1976-77
Div 3	6-1 v Mansfield Town	1958-59

Largest Away Defeat
Div 1	8-0 v Everton	1971-72
Div 2	8-0 v Tottenham Hotspur	1935-36
Div 3	5-0 v Brighton & Hove Albion	1955-56

Highest Scoring Game
9-3 v Wolverhampton Wanderers, 1965-66 (12 goals)

Highest Scoring Draw
5-5 v Coventry City, 1981-82 (10 goals)

Longest period without conceding a goal
845 minutes (15 April 1922 to 28 August 1922)

Longest period without scoring a goal
500 minutes (6 May 1922 to 16 September 1922)

Largest Home Attendance
Div 1	31,044 v Manchester United	1969-70
Div 2	30,586 v West Bromwich Albion	1948-49
Div 3	25,042 v Reading	1959-60

Smallest Home Attendance
Div 1	11,508 v Coventry City	1986-87
Div 2	1,875 v Port Vale	1935-36
Div 3	5,721 v Newport County	1956-57

Lowest Post-War Attendance
Div 2	4,289 v Coventry City	1946-47

Largest Away Attendance
Div 1	54,921 v Manchester United	1966-67
Div 2	70,302 v Tottenham Hotspur	1948-49
Div 3	31,029 v Brighton & Hove Albion	1953-54

Best Average Attendance
Div 1	25,526	1966-67
Div 2	25,465	1948-49
Div 3	18,060	1959-60

Best start to a season
Seven games without losing	1950-51

Worst start to a season
Seven games without a win	1937-38
	& 1976-77

Mick Channon (far left) scores his first goal for Saints, against Bristol City in April 1966, although this picture appears to show Melia rising to head home.

Terry Paine is applauded on to the pitch by his former Saints team-mates. Now playing for Hereford, Paine was making his 806th League appearance.

CARTOON TIME AT THE DELL

Welsh international centre-forward, Ron Davies, had another talent apart from scoring goals. Davies was also an accomplished artist and took his pencil and sketch pad into The Dell dressing-room, where he produced these caricatures. They were published in the Southern Evening Echo.

JOHN McGRATH

JOE KIRKUP

"IT'S NOT ME!"

DENNIS HOLLYWOOD

314

FRANK SAUL

TERRY PAINE

TONY BYRNE

MIKE CHANNON

Cartoonist Frank Gillett sketched this series of
cameos of the 1902 FA Cup Final.

Ron Davies climbs high over a Chester player in the 1972-3 League Cup.

Paul Gilchrist watches as Hugh Fisher (out of picture) scores against Norwich City in August 1974.

Subscribers

4	Gary Chalk	62	David Peter Bassil	120	David Keats	178	Peter J East
5	Duncan Holley	63	June Crabb	121	Rob Turbitt	179	R J A Walker
6	R C Humphries MBE	64	Iain Ranson	122	George Ernest Wiles	180	Hans Peters
7	M S Murray	65	D E Miller	123	B H Standish	181	Gordon Small
8	Colin A Young	66	Nigel John Harding	124	Christopher M Payne	182	Jack Mills
9	Martyn Hagger	67	A H Stemp	125	Wayne Anton Hyde	183	Roger Hudson
10	R F Harris	68	Mrs A M Sims	126	J Wilson	184	F J Lee
11	Nigel I McAllen	69	Mark James Clifford	127	N Graffy	185	Malcolm Hartley
12	Moira & Frederick Furness	70	David Howard	128	I Cruickshank	186	Brian H Hobbs
13	Anthony Kerley	71	T W Hope	129	Mark Sills	187	Guy H C Hill
14	M J Bennett	72	Simon Robert Randell	130	Paul Raymond Went	188	Nigel Cole
15	David S James	73	D J Dominy	131	J M Felstead	189	Michael Frederick Young
16	Andrew Tappern	74	M J Hewson	132	E C Soffe	190	Geoffrey R Peach
17	Derrick S Leach	75	Eric E Craft	133	Alan Martin Stone	191	C W G Sweetman
18	John Sheppard	76	Michael E Craft	134	I A Jenkins	192	Chris Arundale
19	Paul Philip Wilkinson	77	Kevin Hill	135	C L Hawkins	193	John A Harris
20	Richard G Peacock	78	Tim Hill	136	Miss D M A Joslin	194	A & J A Waterman
21	Richard Garstang	79	Andrew John Nunn	137	Charles D G Ducellier	195	Dave Hillam
22	Geoffrey Ian Ford	80	Brigadier A F R Evans	138	A Riste	196	Geoffrey P Smith
23	D W Ashley	81	Paul John Hart	139	E J Houghton	197	James Browning
24	Robert Wright	82	John Badwin	140	S F Sedunary	198	M E Walden
25	Ian David Whitworth	83	Rod Dathan	141	Terry Frost LCIOB	199	Bob Beggs
26	William Edward Noss	84	K Baker	142	Ralph Mortimer	200	David Snow
27	Paul B Symes	85	John W Hibberd	143	John Byrne	201	Rev Canon T M F Biles
28	Steven Churcher	86	Tom Kelly	144	Robert Jex	202	Mark B Neville
29	Stephen Axton	87	Kevin David Harman	145	Lambert Goober	203	David L Wheeler
30	C D Leach	88	B P A Andrews	146	J Ringrose	204	Desmond Elcock
31	Ross Taylor	89	Barrie J Bedford	147	Duncan Watt	205	David Strover
32	Kevin Harding	90	John Graham Parsons	148	Derek T Bryant	206	David John Lock
33	P Snarr	91	Timothy C Green	149	D A R Wicks	207	David R Todd
34	R J Gaiger	92	R D Spanner	150	T C E Marshall	208	Torvid Høiland
35	Alan E Barton	93	Chris Domoney	151	Jon Robinson	209	Chris Bratcher
36	R Mursell	94	Coral Wightman	152	R A Broadway	210	John Warren BEM
37	Lee Wiffen	95	Andrew Soffe	153	Frederick Charles Sibley	211	W Shattock
38	Derek Roy Baker	96	Steven Saunders	154	Malcolm Chamberlain	212	Bill Soffe
39	S E Pannell	97	John Rowlinson	155	Ian McWilliam	213	Neale Adams
40	Eric Tuckwell	98	Gordon Fowkes	156	Glenn Barker	214	Martin Ridges
41	Stephen Hunt	99	Douglas V Fenner	157	Paul Cheffy	215	Roger Porter
42	Neil D Skilton	100	J Motson	158	M J Rogers	216	James G Flux
43	N W Smith	101	Peter Brian Harding	159	Martin Ellwood	217	M R Griffiths
44	James O'Donnell	102	William Henry Bundy	160	K J Quick	218	Percy Alfred Austin
45	David Arthur Clifton	103	John Meatyard	161	Harry Thompson	219	L Herbert
46	Charlie Cooper	104	Brian A Smith	162	P L M Lunn	220	Raymond Viney
47	M A Jeffery	105	Gavin & Robert Naish	163	Richard Wells	221	Richard Burrell
48	Dawn Adams	106	Derek Hyde	164	A P Wheatley	222	Desmond Martin
49	Mr & Mrs T S Bruty	107	Stephen Laski	165	Philip Soar	223	D W Young
50	Mr & Mrs R M Ferguson	108	Dennis Arthur Bulpitt	166	N J Collins	224	Eric Skutt
51	Trevor Lowe	109	Mrs C A Sorrell	167	L J Simmonds	225	J F Vere
52	Gary J Wilkins	110	Mark Smith	168	David L Witt	226	Richard O'Brien
53	J K Hughes	111	Allen Weynberg	169	Paul R C Luscombe	227	Robert Cox
54	R Buckingham-Smith	112	David L Young	170	Johnathan Riley	228	W V Hancock
55	Alan J Pottinger	113	Charles Robert Case	171	Denise Shergold	229	Peter Baxter
56	J W Lawrence	114	W L Quinn	172	David J Misselbrook	230	Jim Wattam
57	Miss Lesley Gatesman	115	Erik Sadler	173	Robert J Surridge	231	A A Dunmore
58	Malcolm Higgins	116	Miss Jennifer Mary Teague	174	Ray Goddard	232	Carsten Grønning
59	Gareth Wayne Strickland	117	R W Middleton	175	Frank White	233	Søren Skafte Jensen
60	Alan Richard Scarff	118	G F Watford	176	Brian Davis	234	R D King
61	Barry G Roberts	119	David Downs	177	H F Saint	235	Keith Coburn

236 Brian Hawkes	303 Mrs A Richards	370 John Budd	436 D J Harrison
237 Willy Hauge	304 R K Cooper	371 Peter Doyle	437 R W Pegg
238 Bo Brown	305 A P Grassick	372 Frank Grande	438 W B Kilmurray
239 Dorothy Sillence	306 B H Hunt	373 John Shippey	439 Ian Price
240 D A G Hindle	307 Dave Bishop	374 B S Tratt	440 T A Beauchamp
241 Simon James Stirrett	308 K Lambert	375 John Ricky Smith	441 Maurice O'Connor
242 Trevor Thornton	309 Michael Hall	376 Miss T G Dune	442 Richard Barrington Clarke
243 Colin Pitcher	310 K J Rideway	377 Mark Cleminson	443 Irene Mitchell
244 Brian F Dawkins	311 Hayden Alexander Hopkins	378 Peter White	444 Simon J Ward
245 Gordon Sloan	312 Russell Smith	379 Matthew Howard Stone	445 T Scott
246 Reginald W Williams	313 Phil Sugden	380 C Alcock	446 Derek Murray
247 Rex Leahy	314 John Linsell	381 Stuart Kirk	447 C T Webber
248 Mr & Mrs J W Granger	315 Keith Hurst	382 Richard Yeates	448 D Ricketts
249 M C Thear	316 John Woodhouse	383 David Adlem	449 R Allison
250 Miss Lisa Holley	317 Jarl Midtun	384 T R Trevis	450 D Hutchinson
251 S A Dibden	318 Christer Svensson	385 N I McAllen	451 Keith Alan Churcher
252 Alison Maxwell	319 T W Graham	386 Edward Williams	452 Alfred Ernest J Churcher
253 A England	320 Jeremy D Fox	387 Norman Green	453 Neil P Roche
254 Stanley C Edwardson	321 Clive Gordon Hevicon	388 J H Dunford	454 Keith Lowe
255 Michael G Gould	322 H Douglas Simmins	389 D G R Holley	455 Roderick J Dean
256 William Muammar	323 Jeannie Spencer	390 G A Dexter	456 B Hourston
257 Miss K Ford	324 Ian Harden	391 David Arthurs	457 Mark Thompson
258 Kenneth M Cole	325 Derek Obee	392 J J J White	458 Patrick Roberts
259 Nigel K Cole	326 Alan Gothard	393 Keith Richard Piant	459 Stephen T Coton
260 Paul A Cole	327 M A O'Connor	394 C J Relleen	460 J Gardiner
261 Angus W Rodger	328 M Taplin	395 Paul Martin	461 Simon John Found
262 M Swart	329 G T J Taplin	396 David Hinton	462 Neil Peter Marriott
263 Domenico Polimeno	330 Clifford J Bannell	397 D Wheatley	463 L A Zammit
264 Mr & Mrs R C Granger	331 Alan T Jones	398 Lt D B Holley RA	464 John D Lambert
265 K M Torgrimsen	332 Dave Juson	399 J Wyatt	465 Nigel Cook
266 Sidney George Davis	333 Jimmy Callinan	400 Michael J Fryer	466 John G Stranger
267 H W Munckton	334 Rita Callinan	401 William Needs	467 Harry R Stranger
268 Malcolm H Lovejoy	335 Raymond Pearce	402 L Bone	468 David Michael Woods
269 Robin Woolman	336 Michael Sharpe	403 Dr D G House	469 John Martin
270 Gary E Gibbens	337 W K Oxford	404 Jonathan Tubb	470 Harald Lohr
271 Terry Knappett	338 Lars-Olof Wendler	405 Martin Bowley	471 John Qvarnberg
272 C J Dyer	339 D A Bevan	406 R H White	472 A K Ambrosen
273 Stuart J Roberts	340 David Bryett	407 D R M Holley	473 Richard Stocken
274 A Prater	341 Steve & Julie Lacey	408 R W Pellan	474 Christian Bastianelli
275 Les Laney	342 Stephen Doyle	409 Miss Heather Marks	475 Peter Pickup
276 Hayley Ginnette Jones	343 Dave Baier	410 R H Crease	476 D G Holmes
277 G W Marshfield	344 D Chapman	411 St Mary's Church of	477 Ruth Martin
278 Brian Field	345 David P Croucher	England, F & M School 478	Andrew P Gosney
279 David Frank Stansbridge	346 Robert Briggs	412 Michael Baker	479 K P Wood
280 Colin Cameron	347 David Barton	413 F A Bellinger	480 Steven Connor
281 David Sullivan	348 Southern Newspapers plc	414 M J Kelsey	481 Keith Robert Pollard
282 Geir Juva	349 Southern Newspapers plc	415 Rick Gulvin	482 Martin McCarthy
283 Robert K Petch	350 Mathew Paul Vickery	416 John Gulvin	483 Stewart Fell
284 Bryan Weller	351 R J O Bean	417 E A Tarbart	484 Ian Harraden
285 John Newman	352 Julian R H Croker	418 P Welch	485 Richard Pickett
286 Nicholas David Mouland	353 Bernard Frowd	419 Martin Vowles	486 Richard Anning
287 Adrian K Poole	354 John Wilde	420 G Adlem	487 David Carroll
288 L W Rice	355 A H Jackson	421 Jayne Beck	488 Brian Tabner
289 Ian Bullivant	356 Denys Todd	422 Jonathan M Bushrod	489 Tom Austin
290 S G Beale	357 Roy Blake	423 James E Hawkins	490 Mike Purkiss
291 Bryan Leonard Croft	358 Maurice Golesworthy	424 Paul Foster	491 Peter Conway
292 Trevor Green	359 Geoffrey Wright	425 M J O'Connor	492 Raymond Leslie Till
293 Paul Behan	360 J M Turner	426 Michael Estall	493 Timothy M Evans
294 M Flew	361 Bryan Dawkins	427 John Taylor	494 A P Chalk
295 Jeremy S Anson	362 Patrick Longworth Bryant	428 F D Harvey	495 Terry Edwards
296 Matthew Aaron Pullinger	363 Peter D P Jobson	429 Andrew J Kershaw	496 Trevor Defferd
297 Nicholas Gilbert	364 Terence Peter Henry	430 Michael H Lawson	497 Mick Spencer
298 Nigel Anthony Wheeler	365 Malcolm Peter Lewis	431 David Edwin Robey	498 David Cross
299 G R Batchelor	366 Brian Tubbs	432 David John Parkin	499 Jonathan Ware
300 Douglas Lamming	367 Stewart Gale	433 James L Browning	500 John Ward
301 Paul Baker	368 Ian Gaywood	434 Robert Lilliman	501 David Iddiols
302 Adrian Curtis	369 Paul Henry Armstrong	435 J M Caddy	502 Ian Griffiths

503 G Protheroe	570 John Fulford	637 K G Guyll	704 Mike Shelton
504 Michael John Mapes	571 A H Leadbetter	638 Peter Miles	705 Michael Loosemore
505 Patricia Arthur	572 P Moody	639 Allen Miles	706 Brian Butler
506 John Williams	573 James A Anscombe	640 Roger J Brenton	707 Brendan O'Sullivan
507 Jonathan Mark Rudd	574 E A Bone	641 Kathryn Bowden	708 Adrian Herbert
508 Ray Atkins	575 D J Dewing	642 Adrian Smith	709 Paul Ronald Atkins
509 M G Strickland	576 Darren Stevens	643 P Kinchington	710 Ronald F W Atkins
510 Mike Gould	577 Anthony G Ware	644 Victor Sammit	711 R B Mason
511 C C Dabinett	578 Martin Bond	645 G T Allman	712 Paul D Chalk
512 Andrew J Beach	579 Andrew Butler	646 J Musgrove	713 Martin Simons
513 Michael John Sheppard	580 Simon Butler	647 Donald Noble	714 P S Thorpe
514 Robert Thomas Clements	581 Fiona M Harding	648 C J Wright	715 Lars-Ake Nilsson
515 P S Chahal	582 James Edwin Holton	649 J A Wise	716 David Trill
516 I Robins	583 E F Hunt	650 Juri Pawlovich Lukosiak	717 K C Weaver
517 D A Tribbick	584 Jarmo Maatta	651 Colin Jose	718 Philip Baulch
518 Lee Curtis	585 Philip Orr	652 Stephen Napier	719 Anthony Bacon
519 David John Gray	586 Brian Mundy	653 R J Lefley	720 George M Shipley
520 Robert Painter	587 J M Burridge	654 Daniel S M Savill	721 David C Smith
521 Barry Hallett	588 Martin R Dean	655 Ian Wheeler	722 S Taylor
522 Pete Spacagna	589 Robert Weekes	656 David Hole	723 G N Painter
523 S Goulding	590 David Smith	657 David J W Pitts	724 E Paul Frost BSc(Hons)
524 John H Fhithyan	591 Clive Piggott	658 Colin Palacio	725 Mrs B J Bennett
525 Julie Aldridge	592 Darren B Gray	659 Ian R K Cunningham	726 Anthony Celleja Sullivan
526 A Carlyle	593 Andrew David Watson	660 Peter Marks	727 P J Young
527 Kevin Stevens	594 Chris Bromage	661 J M Croft	728 Donald Plane
528 E Shadick	595 Mark Adams	662 John Slade	729 Ian Oliver
529 A E M E Fields	596 Joanne Haynes	663 S R Quigley	730 Martyn Wartski
530 E F Rickman	597 Edward Doyle	664 A M Quigley	731 Malcolm Price
531 S J Pearce	598 I D Samways	665 John R Wingfield	732 Miss J E Moody
532 Steven Connell	599 J Samways	666 Russell J Poiner	733 A P W Pepper
533 Louise Kristina Tilley	600 D W Stanley	667 N J Offord	734 R A D Foyle
534 Lee Wright	601 Robert Bailey	668 L L Chalk	735 Mark Davies
535 Malcolm Wing	602 H G Angel	669 W T Prosser	736 Timothy J Barnes
536 K M Oliver	603 Ronald H Beadle	670 Alan Davies	737 Graham Maynard
537 J D Chase	604 A D Marles	671 Alan Denis King	738 Michael Murphy
538 Jonathan Carter	605 Brian T Elsworth	672 Peter S W Horne	739 N E Williamson
539 Jason Craig Harkness	606 E A Jones	673 Trevor Lawrence Clarke	740 John Miller
540 Peter M Sanger	607 David Scammell	674 Benoit Audibert	741 Brian Lamerton
541 Ian Ralph Willis	608 James Neal	675 Keith Price	742 Andrew Bartlett
542 J E Matthews	609 Harvey Anderson	676 J Harrison	743 Joanna Holley
543 N R Morris	610 Michael Conroy	677 Gary Barrett	744 R J Axford
544 Glenn David Carr	611 Dr Gerald T Dunger	678 Tim Newman	745 Walter A Geer
545 Gordon Hiscocks	612 C R Gaiger	679 Oliver Thomas	746 David Stelling
546 David Brindley	613 Tom Blaha	680 Geoffrey Martin	747 Simon Roy Patterson
547 Antony W Brown	614 Martin D House	681 Lorraine Martin	748 J R O'Donnell
548 Miss Helen C Holdaway	615 A Gosling	682 A R Carey	749 T Powell
549 Mrs V I Smith MBE	616 Anthony Webb	683 Terry John Manning	750 P D Fooks
550 Paul Miles	617 Jeremy Hughes	684 Grahame K Bell	751 Russell Wood
551 Chris W J Crouch	618 Mrs Jill Edwards	685 Miss J A Heaton	752 Bernard Fairfax
552 B M Brown	619 Ron Davies	686 Bjørn Langerud	753 Rachel E Littlehales
553 D M Young	620 C O'Bee	687 Arve Stubberud	754 Derek Jones
554 Godfrey C Collyer	621 C J O'Bee	688 Thomas Charles Gradidge	755 Mick Channon
555 P J Hayes	622 B Collier	689 John Etherington	756 Ronald Goodwin
556 Simon Peter Phillips	623 John Treleven	690 Darren Bowman	757 M Pulling
557 L A Fry	624 A E Widger	691 Tony Edward Hansford	758 Ian Scorgie
558 Steve Langdown	625 James Hanrahan	692 I M Cass	759 Simon Keith Proddow
559 Robert Michael Wilson	626 Kevin & Anita Hanrahan	693 A Chalk	760 Ivan Mackrill
560 David Scott Middleton	627 F C Salter	694 R J Miell	761 M Cornelius
561 Tim Brine	628 R P Widger	695 Michael Meredith	762 Jody Wateridge
562 L E Baker	629 P F Simms	696 Paul Steven Dyke	763 John Field
563 David F Young	630 Neil Goulding	697 Peter John Cheeseman	764 William George Lever
564 J R Standfield	631 Alan David Luker	698 M R Steens	765 Barry Philpott
565 Jeremy Bullen	632 B Clayton	699 Karen E Savage	766 Philip Mantell
566 S G Brambley	633 K J Griffin	700 Kevin J Winter	767 Philip Pearson
567 Robert Vernon	634 John Northcutt	701 T W Strudwick	768 Peter J Hole
568 Keith Galliford	635 A L Le Carpentier	702 Mark Shortland	769 Ray C Williams
569 R P Whitlock	636 Marc A Bradley	703 Miss K A Hammond	770 M J Smith